THE TURKISH EXPERIMENT IN DEMOCRACY
1950–1975

THE
TURKISH
EXPERIMENT
IN
DEMOCRACY
1950 – 1975

FEROZ AHMAD

WESTVIEW PRESS · BOULDER · COLORADO
for
THE ROYAL INSTITUTE OF INTERNATIONAL AFFAIRS, LONDON
1977

Published in the United States of America by
WESTVIEW PRESS,
1898 Flatiron Court, Boulder, Colorado 80301
Frederick A. Praeger, President and Editorial Director

Printed in Great Britain

Library of Congress Cataloging in Publication Data

Ahmad, Feroz.
  The Turkish experiment in democracy, 1950-1975.

  Bibliography: p.
  Includes index.
    1. Turkey--Politics and government--1918-1960.
2. Turkey--Politics and government--1960-
3. Political parties--Turkey. I. Royal Institute
of International Affairs. II. Title.
DR590.A694   320.9'561'03   76-25499
ISBN 0-89158-629-6

To the memory of my father
NURUDDIN AHMAD
1904–1974

Contents

CONTENTS

NOTE ON PRONUNCIATION

IT is hoped that the following guidance may be useful to readers unacquainted with Turkish.

    c—*j* as in *jam*
    ç—*ch* as in *church*
b, d—as in English, but at the end of a syllable they are usually pronounced and sometimes written *p*, *t* (e.g. Recep, Rağıp, Ahmet, Cihat for Receb, Rağıb, Ahmed, Cihad). In each case both versions are correct and the reader may come across both in the text.
    ğ—soft *g* lengthens the preceding vowel
    ı—something like *u* in *radium*
    ö—French *eu* as in *deux* or *seul*
    ş—*sh* as in *shut*
    ü—French *u* as in *lumière*

PREFACE AND ACKNOWLEDGEMENTS

THE theme of this book is the experiment in multi-party politics and parliamentary rule instituted in 1945, the future of which, after a full generation, is still in the balance. The first chapter examines the transitional five years (1945–50) which culminated in the electoral defeat of the Republican People's Party, in power since 1923. The two decades that followed, each ending in a military intervention, are discussed thematically. The principal chapter on each decade (chapters II and VII) takes an overview of the period. The chapters that follow (III to VI, and VIII to X) discuss some of the major themes—the political parties, the economy, the role of the army— in this experiment. Chapter XI is concerned with the process of political demilitarization after the intervention of 1971, and chapter XII the new phase marked by the emergence of Bülent Ecevit, who promised to give this experiment a new direction by taking it towards social democracy. The last two chapters, on the role of religion in Turkey's changing political culture and on foreign policy, are intended to provide continuity for the entire period under study.

I am particularly grateful to the Readers, Professor J. C. Hurewitz and Professor Dankwart A. Rustow, who, in accordance with Chatham House practice, undertook a critical examination of the manuscript of this book and gave me the benefit of their comments, thus helping me to revise the text significantly. The manuscript was also read by Dr Kerim Key, Hüseyin Ramazanoğlu, and Tosun Arıcanlı who made valuable suggestions for which I offer them my sincere thanks. I, of course, remain solely responsible for any sub-sisting errors of fact and interpretation.

A book such as this is bound to rely on information, impressions, and interpretations derived from conversations and correspondence with friends, acquaintances, and even strangers, in Turkey, all of whom were always very patient, and generous with their time and knowledge of their country and its politics. Much of what I learned from them has found its way into these pages, transmitted through my own understanding, and they are in no way responsible for the way in which I have used and interpreted what they said. It is not possible for me to acknowledge my debt to all of them individually —in many cases I was asked specifically not to do so—therefore I should like to thank them collectively.

xi The Turkish Experiment in Democracy

Among those with whom I had useful conversations and correspondence, and whom I am able to thank by name are: Mr Samet Ağaoğlu, Mr Basri Aktaş, Professor Sadun Aren, Mr Mehmet Ali Aybar, Mr Celâl Bayar, Professor Hikmet Bayur, Professor Rıfkı Salim Burçak, Mr Süleyman Demirel, Mr Bülent Ecevit, His Excellency Mr Seyfullah Esin, Professor Turhan Feyzioğlu, Mr Kasım Gülek, Professor Turan Güneş, Professor Mübeccel Kıray, Mr Feridun Köymen, Mr Seyfi Kurtbek, Dr Mükerrem Sarol, Professor Mehmet Selik, the late Mr Dündar Taşer, Mr Fethi Tevetoğlu, Mr İhsan Hamid Tigrel, Professor Tarık Zafer Tunaya, Mr Alparslan Türkeş, Professor Aydın Yalçın, the late Mr Ahmed Emin Yalman, Mr Celâl Yardımcı, and Mr Sıtkı Yırcalı.

My grateful thanks are due to Miss Rena Fenteman of Chatham House for her painstaking and invaluable help in the editing of this book. But for her wise counsel, I confess there were times when I would have fallen into serious error.

It is now almost a convention of authorship for authors to thank their wives. My thanks go beyond convention, and I do not exaggerate when I say that this work would not have been written except for the active participation of my wife in all the various stages a book has to pass through. F. A.

Boston, Massachusetts
25 January 1976

CHAPTER I

INTRODUCTION: POLITICAL LIBERALIZATION AND THE DEFEAT OF THE REPUBLICAN PEOPLE'S PARTY 1945-1950

Just as democracy has principles which are common to every nation, there are also characteristics which are peculiar to the character and culture of each nation. The Turkish nation is obliged to find for itself those characteristics of democracy which suit its own structure and character.

İsmet İnönü, Presidential speech inaugurating the new session of the Grand National Assembly, 1 November 1945

The Monoparty System*

IN 1945, at the end of the Second World War, Turkey was still a closed society. The Republican People's Party (RPP), founded in 1923 by Mustafa Kemal, later Atatürk, was in power unopposed in a monoparty system. In this system it was not only the existence of a single party that was significant. More important was the absence of separation between party and government: in fact, the party was the government. Thus in many cases leaders of the provincial party were also governors of provinces, and almost all state officials became members of the RPP.

The Turkish political system of the 1940s was rooted in the period of national struggle of the early 1920s. It was the result of a tacit alliance between the urban middle class and the intelligentsia,†

---

* I am indebted to the late Professor Laski for the term 'monoparty', which I have used in preference to 'one party' or 'single party' in order to emphasize the coalescing of party and state in Turkey during the years 1925-45. See Harold Laski, *Reflections on the Revolution of Our Time* (New York, 1943), 91.

† I have used this word for the Turkish *münevverler—aydınlar* in its most recent usage—to refer to the small, cosmopolitan and educated segment of the population which aspires to independent political thinking and professes a rather exclusive radicalism.

army officers and state officials, and the landowners and notables of Anatolia. This alliance successfully saved Anatolia from being partitioned by the victorious Western powers, and then it laid the foundations of a new régime. Even during the national struggle (*milli mücadele*), the nationalists began to give a new form and structure to the Turkish state. Sovereignty was taken away from the Sultan-Caliph and invested unconditionally in the nation; all powers were invested in the Grand National Assembly, which administered the newly emerging Turkish state.[1]

The Turkish political system was modified over the years in order to meet the needs of changing circumstances. The Association for the Defence of the Rights of Anatolia and Rumelia, founded by the Sivas Congress in September 1919, was transformed in October 1923 into the People's Party, which was renamed the Republican People's Party in November 1924. The various measures which were passed during the national struggle to define the form and structure of the emerging Kemalist state were incorporated into the constitution of 20 April 1924.[2]

The discredited institutions of the Sultanate and the Caliphate were abolished and the Turkish state was declared a Republic (Art. 1). Initially, Islam was retained as the state religion; then, on 10 April 1928, the retaining clause was deleted; and later, on 5 February 1937, Article 2 was amended to describe the Turkish state as secular. Sovereignty was given unconditionally to the nation (Art. 3), and the Grand National Assembly of Turkey became the sole rightful representative of the nation, exercising sovereignty in its name (Art. 4). 'Legislative authority and executive power [were] manifested and concentrated in the Assembly' (Art. 5), which exercised its 'legislative authority directly' (Art. 6), and 'its executive authority through the person of the President of the Republic elected by it, and through a Council of Ministers chosen by the President' (Art. 7).

The Assembly was to be 'composed of representatives[*]elected by the Nation' (Art. 9) and 'Every Turk, woman or man, who has completed his twenty-second year, is entitled to vote in the election of representatives' (Art. 10). But the electoral system was not as

* The 1924 constitution used the word '*mebus*', which may be translated as 'deputy'. But in January 1945 the language of the constitution was 'turkified' and '*mebus*' was replaced by '*milletvekili*', which means 'representative of the nation'. But even in 1924 the deputy was designated a representative of the entire nation and not only of his own constituency. In 1945 this was made even more explicit. I have therefore used 'Representative' in preference to 'Deputy'.

democratic as Articles 9 and 10 seemed to suggest. It was, in fact, a relic of the First and Second Constitutional Periods of 1876-8 and 1908-18 respectively, and it was an indirect system in which the voters elected a college of electors who then elected their representatives to the Assembly. This system, in use until 1946, enabled the local élites to maintain their power and influence in the Assembly throughout the monoparty period. It was one of the obstacles which prevented the radical wing of the RPP, when in power, from implementing policies that would change the social structure in rural areas and erode the dominant position of these local élites. The electoral law became one of the foundation stones of the informal alliance which sprang up during the national struggle between the Republican government and such forces. The representatives of these élites supported modernist reforms of state institutions so long as they did not threaten the existing social and economic structure. Thus, in such a situation, it was possible for the government to introduce a constitution and a modern legal code but not for it to pass and implement a land reform law.

Initially it may not have been the intention of the Kemalists to establish a monoparty state. However, the fear of counter-revolutionary forces, manifested in such movements as the Kurdish rebellion of 1925, led to the outlawing of the Progressive Republican Party; and the Free Republican Party, formed in August 1930, dissolved itself on 17 November 1930. The appearance of an opposition party had encouraged reactionary violence against the régime, demonstrating the danger of such experiments. For the next fifteen years the RPP remained the sole political party in Turkey.

The economic crisis of the thirties in the capitalist world, ushered in by the Great Crash of 1929, gave a sharp impetus to state intervention in Turkey, and this led to the strengthening and development of the monoparty system. The effect of the depression on the Turkish economy was serious enough to force the government to take counter-measures. The crisis came to be seen as a failure of free enterprise, identified with Western capitalism. The Soviet Union, with its system of state control, seemed to have escaped the crisis, and the Kemalists saw it as a model that might usefully be copied in certain areas of the economy.

The Six Principles of Kemalism

In 1930 the Turkish government began to stress the need for greater economic activity by the state. The following year étatism (*devletçilik*) was made one of the six 'fundamental and unchanging principles' which were adopted by the RPP, and incorporated into the constitution on 5 February 1937. Thus Article 2 of the constitution was amended to read: 'The Turkish State is Republican, (*Cumhuriyetçi*), Nationalist (*Milliyetçi*), Populist (*Halkçi*), Étatist (*Devletçi*), Secularist (*Lâik*), and Revolutionary (*İnkilâpçı*).' The constitution did not either define or clarify the meaning of these terms. But the Fourth Great Congress of the RPP (1935) had already done so. In the minutes of the congress the six principles were explained as follows:[3]

(a) The Party is convinced that the Republic is the form of government which represents and realizes most safely the ideal of national sovereignty. With this unshakable conviction, the Party defends, with all its means, the Republic against all danger.

(b) The Party considers it essential to preserve the special character and the entirely independent identity of the Turkish social community in the sense explained in Art. 2. The Party follows, in the meantime, a way parallel to and in harmony with all the modern nations in the way of progress and development, and in international contacts and relations.

(c) The source of Will and Sovereignty is the Nation. The Party considers it an important principle that this Will and Sovereignty be used to regulate the proper fulfillment of the mutual duties of the citizen to the State and of the State to the citizen.

We consider the individuals who accept an absolute equality before the Law, and who recognize no privileges for any individual, family, class or community, to be of the people and for the people (populist).

It is one of our main principles to consider the people of the Turkish Republic, not as composed of different classes, but as a community divided into various professions according to the requirements of the division of labor for the individual and social life of the Turkish people.

The farmers, handicraftsmen, laborers and workmen, people exercising free professions, industrialists, merchants, and public servants are the main groups of work constituting the Turkish community. The functioning of each of these groups is essential to the life and happiness of the others and of the community.

The aims of our Party, with this principle, are to secure social order and solidarity instead of class conflict, and to establish harmony of interests. The benefits are to be proportionate to the aptitude to the amount of work.

(d) Although considering private work and activity a basic idea, it is one of our main principles to interest the State actively in matters where the general and vital interests of the nation are in question, especially in the economic field, in order to lead the nation and the country to prosperity in as short a time as possible.

The interest of the State in economic matters is to be an actual builder, as well as to encourage private enterprises, and also to regulate and control the work that is being done.

The determination of the economic matters to be undertaken by the State depends upon the requirements of the greatest public interest of the nation. If the enterprise, which the State itself decides to undertake actively as a result of this necessity, is in the hands of private entrepreneurs, its appropriation shall, each time, depend upon the enactment of a law, which will indicate the way in which the State shall indemnify the loss sustained by the private enterprise as a result of this appropriation. In the estimation of the loss the possibility of future earnings shall not be taken into consideration.

(e) The Party considers it a principle to have the laws, regulations, and methods in the administration of the State prepared and applied in conformity with the needs of the world and on the basis of the fundamentals and methods provided for modern civilization by Science and Technique.

As the conception of religion is a matter of conscience, the Party considers it to be one of the chief factors of the success of our nation in contemporary progress, to separate ideas of religion from politics, and from the affairs of the world and of the State.

(f) The Party does not consider itself bound by progressive and evolutionary principles in finding measures in the State administration.[2] The Party holds it essential to remain faithful to the principles born of revolutions which our nation has made with great sacrifices, and to defend these principles which have since been elaborated.

[2] More idiomatic translation: The Party does not consider itself and the conduct of the State to be limited to gradual, evolutionary steps of development.

Of these principles, the two that were the most controversial were étatism and revolutionism-reformism. Republicanism and nationalism were acceptable to all the groups who allied together to form the new régime. Populism was also acceptable to them because it legitimized their rule by making them the trustees for 'the people'; at the same time it neutralized the concept of class conflict and class struggle. Secularism was acceptable in principle since religion became a matter for individual conscience and was freed, in theory at least, from the grasp of the conservatives. But secularism aroused controversy when militant secularists in the RPP became dominant and began to view practising Muslims as clericalists and counter-revolutionaries.

Étatism, on the other hand, aroused immediate controversy, for neither the RPP nor the government was able to define the limits of state intervention to the satisfaction of the private sector and its supporters. But the party did specify that agriculture would not be affected at all by étatism. By the end of the Second World War, however, a substantial state sector had come into being, and the appetite of state officials who controlled it had been sharpened. They saw the private sector as being subordinate to the state sector and the future of economic development in the expansion of the latter. The members of the private sector resented this attitude, and, as we shall see, étatism became one of the key subjects of political debate in the multi-party period.

The controversy over the definition and clarification of *inkilâpçılık,* and its most recent form *devrimcilik,* has also been difficult to resolve. Definition of the term has depended on the political position of the person using it. Those on the right wing of the RPP understood it to mean 'reformism'; those on the left defined it as 'revolutionism', implying the party's commitment to an ongoing revolution set in motion by Atatürk. The meaning given to this term was therefore a barometer indicating which faction of the RPP was dominant. For example, until the beginning of the multi-party period in 1945, the connotations of *inkilâpçılık* were invariably revolutionary, or at least radical. Thereafter, as the RPP was forced to tone down its policies in the competition for votes, the meaning came to depend on the political context in which it was used, and that is how the meaning of *devrimcilik* is reflected in the text.

Formalization of the Monoparty State

A tendency towards a monoparty state had been strong ever since the republic was established, and during the RPP congress of 1935 the marriage between party and state was formalized. During the congress the party's Secretary-General, Recep Peker, announced that 'the fundamental principles of the party will become the principles of the new Turkish state after the new party programme has been ratified.'[4] The party provided the ideology for the state, and its Secretary-General assumed the position of Minister of the Interior in the cabinet, while the chairmen of the provincial party organizations became the governors of their provinces.[5] During these years the activities of the Republican People's Party conformed 'fairly closely, in form perhaps more than in content, to what became the pattern of the role of the party in the one-party state in Europe at that time—the Fascist Party in Italy, the Communist Party in Russia, the Nazi Party in Germany.'[6]

Atatürk died on 10 November 1938. Next day the Assembly elected İsmet İnönü, his comrade in arms and political collaborator, President of the Republic. At the Extraordinary Congress of the party, held on 26 December 1938, the party regulations were amended so that İnönü could be elected as the party's Permanent Chairman (clause 3), and Atatürk was declared its founder and eternal chairman (clause 2).[7] At the same congress, İnönü adopted the title 'National Leader' (*Milli Şef*) and soon acquired the status of an institution. Thereafter the 'monolithic form taken by the party was best expressed by the famous slogan "one party, one nation, one leader".'[8]

The Kemalist régime had originated as an alliance of forces to resist the partition of Anatolia by the European powers. Beyond the struggle for independence there was not much agreement among these forces on the character of the new régime. The coalition was composed of army officers, state officials, members of the new professions—lawyers, journalists, and teachers—who composed an intelligentsia, and merchants and businessmen, and the landowners and magnates in the countryside. Initially workers had enjoyed the status and prestige of a group in this coalition, but after 1923 the Kemalist régime became less tolerant of them. This informal alliance founded the new state and the RPP, and the stability of the new régime depended on its continuation.[9]

The members of the armed forces were an important component in this alliance. The army had played a vital role in the founding of the republic. It continued to do so, even though Mustafa Kemal and many of his comrades abandoned their military uniform for civilian attire in order to symbolize the supremacy of the civilian over the soldier in the new régime. There was no conflict between the two, and soldiers enjoyed a privileged position in the party, the government, and the Assembly. So long as Marshal Fevzi Çakmak was Chief of the General Staff there was hardly any question of bringing the army under civilian control. The defence budget was prepared at the General Staff Headquarters, and the Ministry of National Defence and its Minister played only a subordinate role. On Atatürk's death, Marshal Çakmak is said to have been the key figure in deciding that İsmet İnönü should succeed. And when İnönü announced the retirement of the Marshal on 12 January 1944, he explained that this measure was necessary in order to establish civilian control over the army (*Vatan*, 13 January 1944).

There were certain tensions within this alliance but they were resolved by compromise. The officers, the officials, and members of the intelligentsia tended to be radical in their demand for change and wanted the state to be active in implementing a radical programme. The merchants and businessmen, the landowners and the magnates, on the other hand, distrusted state intervention in so far as it threatened their interests by holding out the possibility of land reform and of state monopolies in trade. This alliance was maintained on the basis of an unwritten agreement which enabled the radicals to modernize the structure of the state but without substantially altering the existing social and economic structure. Thus the Kemalist régime introduced a constitution, an assembly, a modern legal code and secularized the state, but no serious attempt was made to alter the structure of rural Turkey, where 80 per cent of the population lived and worked.

The tensions in this alliance were expressed in the politics of the period and usually found a place in the debate on the limits of state intervention. In the thirties, the étatists became dominant to the extent that they succeeded in uniting party and state, and in 1937 there was even talk of implementing land reform. But the threat of war in Europe forced the étatists to compromise in the interest of national solidarity. At the Fifth Great Congress (29 May–3 June 1939), the bonds between state and party were again loosened, and an Independent Group (*Müstakil Grup*) was permitted within the Assembly to play the role of a loyal opposition and critic of the government.[10] But the exigencies of wartime neutrality forced the state to intervene in almost every aspect of Turkish life. The National Defence Law (*Milli Korunma Kanunu*) of 18 January 1940 gave the government extensive emergency powers to control prices and the supply of goods in the market, and to use forced labour to maintain production, especially in the mines. The capital levy (*Varlık Vergisi*) of November 1942 was designed to tax those who had accumulated wealth during the war, namely businessmen—especially the non-Muslims—and owners of large farms. In 1943 the tithe which had been abolished in 1925 was restored in the form of a 'payment-in-kind tax' (*ayniyat vergisi*) on agricultural produce.[11]

The arbitrary character of these laws and the way in which they were implemented undermined the citizen's confidence in the state and in the party. This was particularly true of the businessmen and big farmers, who, though they had accumulated considerable wealth during the war years, could no longer feel secure in the monoparty state because of the government's recent practices, symbolized by the capital levy. By 1945 the political alliance which had provided stability since 1923 had broken down and a new political balance needed to be established once the war was over.

Founding of the Democrat Party, January 1946

In his presidential speech of 1 November 1945 İsmet İnönü hinted that he was prepared to make major political adjustments in the monoparty system in order to bring it into line with the changed circumstances of the time. The bulk of his speech was an apology for the generation of rule by the Republican People's Party, of which he was the chairman. He agreed that the main deficiency in the system was the lack of an opposition party and he declared that 'in keeping with the needs of the country and in the proper functioning of the atmosphere of freedom and democracy, it would be possible to form another political party.'[12] This was the sentence which opened the pandora's box of competitive multi-party politics in Turkey.

This concession came as a result of persistent criticism from within the Republican Party. The party leadership claimed that internal self-criticism had always been encouraged and that the so-called Independent Group had been set up for that purpose. But the Group provided only token opposition and criticism; what the party leadership found more embarrassing was the barbed criticism of individual Republicans like Hikmet Bayur, who took the government to task on a number of occasions during the war.[13]

The RPP had imposed revolutionary changes from the top during the two decades since 1923.[14] These changes had been considered essential for transforming a dead empire into a living nation state, but they brought no substantial improvement to the lives of ordinary people and alienated them from the Kemalist régime. The alienation, serious enough before the six years of mobilized neutrality, with all the material and physical hardships it entailed, was by this time stretched to breaking point. The growing and now vocal opposition was a manifestation of this.

In post-war Turkey the principal issue of the day was the government's economic policy, which had led to great hardship in almost all quarters. It was marked by spiraling inflation and shortages in the urban areas, and controlled prices for a percentage of the produce of the countryside. To enforce this policy heavy bureaucratic controls were established, including the National Defence Law, which gave broad emergency powers to the government. The political consequence of this interventionist policy was to destroy the political alliance which had provided stability and stagnation during the first twenty years of the Republican régime.

There were other factors which encouraged the trend towards political and economic liberalization after World War II. The defeat of the totalitarian régimes of Germany, Italy, and Japan and the triumph of the Western democracies was bound to have an effect on Turkey, which had always reacted to the political climate of the West; furthermore, Turkey's isolation in the post-war world, accentuated by Stalin's hostility, forced the government to lean towards the Western powers. In such a situation it would have been difficult to veto dissension and criticism at home: the critics, realizing this, exploited their advantage.

The climate in post-war Turkey was ripe for change and almost all politicians, even the hard-liners in the ruling party, recognized this. The debate raged on the character of the régime that should carry out the measures necessary to bring Turkey into line with the rapidly changing world. The old guard, described as the hard-line Kemalists, wanted to retain the monoparty state structure and to implement reforms from the top, as the original reforms had been inaugurated. It was argued that those reforms would have been impossible had they been attempted democratically. Under a competitive multi-party system of parliamentary democracy, there would have been pressure groups demanding the retention of the traditional order and the reforms would have been jeopardized. The old guard claimed that the same was true of the new situation as well—that the implementation of measures to eradicate the great socio-economic injustices which existed in Turkish society would still require a consensus within the party and the imposition of reforms from the top. Competitive party politics could act only as a brake on the programme of reform.

The fears of the old guard were soon confirmed. When in January 1945 the government's land reform Bill was placed before the Assembly it immediately ran into criticism and obstruction in the party. In the words of Bernard Lewis, the goals of this Bill

were to provide land and means for peasants with none or too little, and to ensure the full and effective use of the arable lands of the country. The method was to grant land to such peasants, together with twenty-year, interest-free loans for development, and other material help. The land was to come from unused state lands and pious endowments, municipal and other publicly owned land, reclaimed land, land of unknown ownership, and land expropriated from private individuals. For the last-named category, all landed property in excess of 500 *dönüm* (123·5 acres) would be nationalized. Compensation would be paid on a sliding scale; the greater the area held, the lower the rate. It would be paid in instalments, over twenty years, in 4 per cent treasury bonds. The law also laid down that new holdings acquired under its provisions must not be split among heirs. It was estimated that about a third of the rural population, some 5 million persons, would benefit under the law, which, if fully applied, would effect a major revolution, transforming Turkey into a country of independent peasant smallholders.[15]

The Bill was passed on 11 June. Given the long and bitter debates, it seems fair to conclude that the Assembly would not have passed it had an opposition party or parties and competitive politics been in existence. There were powerful forces in the countryside ranged against the Bill and only the discipline within the Republican Party was able to overcome them and to have the Bill passed *unanimously*. It is worth noting, however, that the law was never fully implemented and that, under the pressure of multi-party politics, it was amended by the Republican Party early in 1950, before the general election, as a concession to the landowners who controlled the rural votes.

Perhaps the immediate consequence of the introduction of the land reform Bill was the crystallization of opposition within the RPP. It was noted earlier that the monoparty state was based on an alliance between the military-civilian bureaucracy, the intelligentsia, the urban middle class, and the landholders in Anatolia. This alliance had already been weakened by extensive intervention by the state during the war. The land reform bill was a measure that would weaken the political and economic power of the landlords and strengthen the hand of the state. This was the real issue and Necmettin Sadak, an articulate spokesman for the RPP, expressed it very well:

There is a relationship between the régime of landownership and the structure of property it gives birth to and the internal politics of a country. Just as the structure of landed property brings about discord in the relations of individuals, it also paves the way to disagreements between individuals and the State. It has often been seen that local forces which depend on big landed property cause the authority of the State to weaken. Thus from this point of view every country is obliged to create a system of landed property which suits the mentality of the established State....[16]

Thus if the state was to retain its 'single-party mentality' it must also change the structure of land ownership, since the landowners were one of the main threats to its authority.

Initially the dissidents within the party criticized the government's policy on economic grounds. Land reform as proposed, they said, did not meet the needs of the country and would lead to a decline in production. By breaking up the big estates, the old, pre-capitalist household economy would be restored. By nationalizing farms over 500 *dönüms*, land reform would create insecurity amongst farmers and violate the right to property which was a fundamental principle.[17] In the debate on the economy similar criticisms were made about the deficit in the budget which led to increasing state loans, the unrestricted issue of money which created inflation, the high cost of living, the critical situation of the low-income groups—especially the petty bureaucrats—profiteering, black-marketeering, and the unproductivity and injustices of the taxation system.[18]

However, on 7 June 1945 the critics within the party came out into the open and raised for the first time the question of power. The four founders of the future Democrat Party (DP) (Celâl Bayar, Refik Koraltan, Fuad Köprülü, and Adnan Menderes) presented a proposal to the party's Assembly Group asking that the principle of national sovereignty as stated in the constitution be implemented fully, and that party business be carried out according to the fundamentals of democracy. It is not clear what the four expected the outcome of their initiative to be. It is doubtful whether they wanted to break away and form a new party. They probably wanted the party to relax political controls instead of pursuing a policy of greater centralization. The Assembly Group discussed the proposal on 12 June but rejected it on the grounds that it was outside the competence of the Group, since its aim was the amendment of certain laws and regulations. The competent authority to approach, said the Group, was the National Assembly.[19]

The party organization reacted mildly and there was not even a proposal to expel the four from the RPP. On the contrary, there was even a group in the party which felt that critics should leave the RPP and form a party of their own and İnönü is said to have encouraged this view.[20] However, the initiative to form a new political party came not from one of the Republican dissidents but from an Istanbul industrialist named Nuri Demirağ. On 7 July 1945 he applied to the government to form the *Milli Kalkınma Partisi* (National Development Party) and permission was granted in August.[21]

The dissidents within the RPP kept up their opposition and Menderes and Köprülü soon began to write critical articles in newspapers like *Tan*, run by the socialists Zekeriya and Sabiha Sertel, and Ahmed Emin Yalman's *Vatan*. This was considered a breach of party discipline and both men were expelled on 21 September. Refik Koraltan denounced these expulsions as a violation of party regulations and was in turn expelled. Celâl Bayar resigned his seat in the Assembly and on 1 December left the party. During these months there were constant rumours that Bayar was about to form a new party and the news that he would do so was well received in the RPP.[22] It was noted in the press that Bayar was a product of the RPP and that his new party would be on the same ideological plane as the one he was leaving. In his speech of 1 November İnönü alluded to the lack of an opposition party, even though the National Development Party was already in existence. The Republican leadership was willing to concede that there was a need for a new party which should emerge from the existing party, express the same philosophy, and behave more or less as the old Independent Group had done. Such a party was described by Republicans as a *'Kontrol Partisi'* and Hüseyin Cahit Yalçın wrote that he could not imagine any fundamental difference in the programmes of two such parties.[23] On 7 January 1946 the formation of the Democrat Party was officially announced and Turkey began its new experiment with democracy.

As predicted by political analysts, the programme of the new party hardly differed from that of the old. The Democrats adopted the six principles of Kemalism: republicanism, nationalism, populism, étatism, secularism, and reformism—though they placed a different emphasis and interpretation on each of them. They were virtually compelled to adopt these principles: not to have done so would have been a technical violation of the constitution and would certainly have provided Republican extremists with the pretext to close down the new party. Apart from these six basic guidelines, the Democrats dedicated themselves to their party's task of 'advancing democracy'. That would involve curbing government activity and increasing individual freedom, while also ensuring that political power emanated from below—from the people—rather than from above. These two aspects of the Democrat programme became the main line of attack against the ruling party. Since there could be no precise definition of government activity there was an unlimited possibility of exploiting this issue. This point was also very popular with the mass of the people, whose main grievance was against the tyranny of the bureaucracy intimately identified with the RPP. Finally the Democrats emphasized their reliance on the private sector for the purpose of achieving economic development, and it was this point which received the most attention, especially among Western observers.

Almost all those with Republican sympathies were pleasantly surprised to note that the Democrat Party had adopted the same fundamental principles as those of the RPP. The reformist wing in the RPP was even conciliatory to the different emphasis that was given, for example, to étatism and populism, because it also was looking in a similar direction. In short, the new party was almost an exact replica of the old—no accident, since its founders had spent their entire political lives in the RPP. The Democrats formed their party in order to compete for power with the Republicans, because they believed that they could implement the programme necessary for Turkey's progress better than their rivals. Given the narrow socio-economic basis of Turkish politics, there could be no real differences between the parties.

To the great embarassment and annoyance of the DP leaders, this became one of the principal propaganda claims of their Republican rivals. It was also true that the leaders of the central organization were former Republicans who had paid all their political dues. However, these claims were valid only while the party was new and virtually confined in membership to a limited group. As the DP organization began to grow and to spread into the provinces, the party began to change its character. It was joined by people for whom the only *raison d'être* of the party was hostility to the monoparty state. Such members, unlike the Democrat leaders, wanted power in order to carry out a substantial programme of reform which would require, as its very minimum, the replacement of the bureaucratic state identified with the Republicans. Their principal concern was to end Republican rule and take revenge on their tormentors. Amongst them, hatred of the Republican state, epitomized for the individual by the gendarme and the official, knew no bounds.

Republican propaganda that the Democrat Party was the junior partner, the younger brother with no independent position of its own, began to damage the new party's reputation. Those looking for an alternative to the RPP hardly considered it worth while to join the Democrats, and those hostile to the RPP became almost as hostile to the DP. Many began to see the Democrat Party as a work of collusion (*muvazaa eseri*), like the Free Party (*Serbest Fırka*) of 1930. Bayar complained to the press that some people regarded his party as being in collusion with the ruling party, and stated that they were absolutely wrong to do so. The Democrat Party, he declared, was an independent political body. Turning to the interference of the state bureaucracy in politics, he claimed that the growth of his party in the provinces was being obstructed by pressure and intimidation from that source.[24]

Relations between the RPP and the DP

Soon after the establishment of the Democrat Party rumours began to circulate about a possibility that the general election, not due until September 1947, might be held earlier. In order to discuss electoral matters and to liberalize the internal working of the ruling party, İnönü, in his capacity as party leader, called an extraordinary congress for 10 May 1946. On 29 April, in the Assembly, the Democrats opposed an early election, Menderes arguing that they could see no reason for advancing the date unless it were an attempt to stop their party from gaining strength. Before all else, the Democrats demanded measures to guarantee the integrity of elections, including the amendment of anti-democratic laws, especially an end to martial law, and the impartiality of the bureaucracy. The Republicans, however, argued that an early election was necessary in order to gauge whether the party in power would retain the confidence of the voters in an election held under the direct system in place of the old indirect system.[25]

The Extraordinary Congress met on 10 May and the Republican Party proceeded to democratize itself. The title *Milli Şef* (National Leader) which İnönü had bestowed upon himself soon after he became president in 1938 was abolished. So was the title 'Permanent Chairman' of the party (*Değişmez Başkan*); in future, the chairman would be elected by the Congress every four years. The Independent Group, which had served as a loyal opposition during the monoparty period, was dissolved, having become an anachronism with the creation of the Democrat Party. The Congress also decided to hold the general election in 1946 instead of 1947. Perhaps the decision which aroused the most political controversy was the abolition of Article 22 of the Republican Party's regulations, which had forbidden the founding of 'associations with the purpose of propagating ideas of class distinction, class interest and regionalism. ...' When it lifted this prohibition the RPP emphasized that it would remain a party which sought a balance between class interests and therefore opposed class struggle.[26]

The implications of such a declaration were clear. If the Republican Party was an 'above-class' party, what was the position of the Democrats? This was a delicate question for the Democrats to answer in a society conditioned to believe that, though there were classes in Turkish society, they lived in harmony and that Atatürk's party resolved all tensions and conflicts that arose from time to time, acting as the safeguard against the exploitation of one class by another. The fiction of class harmony had been considered necessary in a new nation in the throes of development. The maintenance of social peace had benefited both private enterprise and the state sector but the interests of labour had been neglected, as the labour legislation of the Republican period amply demonstrates. Except for one problem, it would have been in the interests of the business and industrial groups to back this policy unconditionally; the problem was that, although labour had been kept under control by legislation, the private sector had also been placed under great legal and bureaucratic restraints which prevented its development. The Democrats wanted to remove this bureaucratic interference and their concern was not primarily with the establishment of a class party supported by the private sector. Such a party was not necessary in the political climate which existed in Turkey. With the introduction of multi-party politics, some Republicans wanted to introduce the issue of class into Turkish politics in order to force their own party to reconsider its ideological basis. During the monoparty period they could claim to represent all classes in the name of populism; but, faced with the challenge of a party which was said to appeal to certain specific interests, some Republicans felt that they also ought to appeal to definite groups. They felt that their party ought to seek the support of groups such as the peasants, workers, small farmers, and small businessmen. This became a serious issue after the victory of the Democrats in 1950; for the time being it was put on the shelf and no decision was taken. But the emphasis on the peasant in the 1946 election campaign was a manifestation of this trend.[27]

The idea that the Democrat Party was the party of big business and of the up-and-coming business groups which had grown rich during the war gained wide currency. It was particularly popular in the West, where the Democrats were described as the 'Turkish liberals'. An article on this theme, published in the *Daily Mail* and reproduced in the Turkish press, brought a response from Adnan Menderes, one of the principal spokesmen for the DP. Menderes denied that his party was the party of businessmen and merchants and claimed that the proportion of these groups in both parties was probably about the same. The Democrats, he said, were not representatives of groups striving for their selfish interests: they represented all those who wanted to put an end to the one-party system.[28]

Certainly businessmen were also to be found in the RPP. If Üzeyir Avunduk and Kâzım Taşkent were politically active in the Democrat Party, Vehbi Koç provided the balance in the RPP. But the issue was one of emphasis. The Democrats stressed free enterprise as the major element in their programme and this, with all its implications, seemed to attract businessmen. Not that the Republicans shunned free enterprise. On the contrary, after 1945 they began to emphasize it almost as much as the Democrats; but the commercial class, some of whose members joined the RPP, viewed the party—with its long experiment in étatism—with suspicion. However, before the Republicans lost power in May 1950 they had set Turkey on the road to free enterprise. In fairness to the Democrats, it must be said that after 1945 and until at least 1955 almost all groups (intelligentsia, workers, businessmen, and even the military) supported them enthusiastically. It was, as

Menderes claimed, the party of all those who wanted to end one-party rule.[29]

As explained above, the Democrats were anxious to avoid being categorized as a class party; but, without a positive position, they left themselves open to the charge that there was no difference between the parties. While they constantly denied this claim they were never able to put forward convincing differences.[30] This forced the Democrats into the negative policy of complaining and criticizing and demanding one concession after another from the ruling party. The Republicans claimed that the opposition raised no issues and criticized the government only for the sake of criticizing. It was this negative policy which embittered relations between the parties and gave the experiment in democracy a bad start.

The first manifestation of this negative policy was the Democrats' refusal to participate in either the municipal elections or the general election if they were held in 1946. The boycott of the elections angered İnönü's moderate group in the RPP. This group had argued in favour of multi-party politics against the extremists' claim that such an experiment would be dangerous and lead to instability. The political behaviour of the Democrats—their press campaign and tours of the country—seemed to justify the extremist position. Elections, if contested by both parties, could rectify this and even strengthen the Republicans. However, the Democrats refused to play the game according to Republican rules.

The political strategy of the DP began to pay dividends. Immediately after the municipal elections, which the opposition parties boycotted, the ruling party passed further liberalizing measures in preparation for the general election. A law introducing direct elections was passed, the universities were given administrative autonomy and the Press Law was liberalized. But along with these concessions came a warning from Republican moderates against 'Democratic subversion'. It was significant because it came from İnönü's mouthpiece, Nihat Erim, who stated that 'if the situation which was causing deep disturbances in the social structure continued, it might be necessary to cover the blessings of freedom for a while and to establish authority from top to bottom'.[31] The effect of such warnings made the Democrat leadership more cautious. It was widely acknowledged that in those days İnönü could have had the new party closed down by simply sending a few gendarmes to the DP headquarters. The people were quite accustomed to see parties come and go and were unlikely to be aroused to make a protest.

Developments after the Election of 1946

The date for the general election was set for 21 July; despite earlier threats to abstain, the Democrats decided to participate, although they described their decision as 'a sacrifice'. Boycott of the election could have meant the closure of the party, and, at the very least, would have involved the loss of Assembly representation and a platform for propaganda. In the campaign the Democrats introduced a new tactic, that of trying to entice İsmet İnönü away from his party by offering him an above-party role in the political structure. Thus they declared that, in constituencies where the RPP put up the 'National Leader' as its candidate, the Democrats would do the same.[32] They wanted İnönü to become an above-party president—a role that would involve his giving up the leadership of the RPP and opting out of politics. In return, of course, they held out the possibility of his presidency's being continued if they came to power. This approach was intended to appeal to İnönü's ambitious character and his desire to break new ground in Turkey's history.

The 1946 election campaign embittered the political atmosphere. The Republicans hoped to have a campaign devoid of controversy and therefore ordered the RPP organization to avoid topics that would raise the political temperature.[33] The Democrats, however, thrived on controversy, their only substitute for real and pressing matters. On the same day as the Republican directive was put out they issued a brochure entitled 'Documents on Interference, Pressure and Irregularities: the Municipal Elections', which implied that similar practices were likely to take place in the general election.[34] These fears were not groundless, for in spite of the RPP directive to the party organization, the bureaucracy—with its links to the RPP—was indulging in pressure tactics against the Democrats. The press of this period is full of reports of such pressures as well as of Democrat complaints, and the Republican Party found it difficult to deny responsibility because most people continued to regard state and party as one. That way of looking at things was no longer totally accurate because the party was the creation of the state and not *vice versa*; and although the party depended on the state apparatus the reverse had ceased to be true. The state was quite capable of reversing its alliance, and, as we shall see, that is what happened.

The election was held on 21 July and resulted in an overwhelming victory for the Republicans, who won 390 seats out of 465, with 65 Democrats and 7 Independents.[35] According to general opinion at the time it was not conducted fairly, and this sowed the seed of a bitter and unfortunate political legacy, for the Democrats were able to point to it to justify their own excesses in the 1950s. It also alienated a large number of Republicans, who had expected fair play from their party under İnönü's leadership. Even officers in the armed forces felt estranged from the Republicans and began to sympathize with the Democrats.

Reform of the RPP: Moderates v. Extremists

The Republicans gave a sigh of relief, grateful that they had been guaranteed another four years in power. But the election proved a good lesson and they decided to carry out a programme of reform in the party and in the country so as to guarantee their position for the future. The opposition party had been dealt with; it was now a question of dealing with their own extremists, who were keen to end the multi-party experiment. Hence İnönü's words immediately after the election: 'Now we are entering a new phase in the national life of Turkey. ... It is a prime duty for both sides to forgive and forget the irritating words of the election days, and to introduce order in the nation and to open a period of striving.'[36]

Kemal Karpat has observed that the period between the election of 21 July 1946 and İnönü's multi-party declaration of 12 July 1947 was the most important period for the establishment of the multi-party system in Turkey.[37] It was a period of struggle between the moderates and extremists in the RPP, the former pressing for competitive politics and the latter demanding the continuation of a monoparty system and a policy of radical changes implemented from the top. The moderates triumphed and the opposition parties continued to have 'freedom of action and equality with the Republican Party'.[38]

The appointment as Prime Minister of Recep Peker, a die-hard monoparty man, seemed to suggest that the Republicans had opted for a policy of radical reform under the auspices of the state. A radical policy was urgently needed to solve the post-war economic crisis, and this, noted Necmettin Sadak, called not for a few passing decisions and measures but a long and continuous programme co-ordinated by the state.[39] In his cabinet, Peker retained only four ministers from the previous ministry, and he seemed determined to carry out the task with great vigour.

However, his government's first measures were of the kind Sadak had warned against. 'The Decisions of 7 September' (*7 Eylül Kararları*) were intended to remove restraints from the economy and bring about stability. The Turkish lira was devalued, import facilities were eased, and banks were permitted to sell gold. These measures led to a further increase in the cost of living and the price of imported goods rose sharply. If 100 is taken as the figure for 1938, in August 1946 it was 386·8 and immediately after the September measures it rose to 412·9.[40] The only people to benefit from these measures were the businessmen, who were able to take advantage of the situation by speculating and hoarding. 'The gap between the living standards of various social groups sharpened, and the existing antagonism toward the government increased.'[41]

These measures would logically have come from a *laissez-faire* Democrat Party government. But it was the aim of the RPP government to wean away some of the opposition's support and to dilute its criticism, and such measures would influence the business community in the RPP's favour. Ironically, however, they served the opposition well and for the first time it had real bread and butter issues to use against the government.

The Democrats criticized the rising prices, and at first were surprisingly silent about the September measures. But with the opening of the new session of the Assembly they introduced a motion of censure. The Republicans felt ideologically betrayed and accused the Democrats of not giving their economic policy a chance to work. The motion was defeated and it was another month (during the budget debate) before the Democrats were able to voice further criticism of the economy in the Assembly. Meanwhile they missed no opportunity to attack the government in their numerous public meetings. This strategy angered the Republicans, who considered such tactics a travesty of multi-party politics and claimed that the Assembly was the proper forum for criticism. Adnan Menderes's criticism of the budget brought an unrestrained response from the government benches, both against the opposition and against him personally. The opposition was accused of describing the situation in black terms and inciting the people to revolt. Premier Peker stated that the government intended to put an end to the opposition's tactics of inciting people to rebellion and disobedience. As for Menderes's opinions, he dismissed them as the 'expression of a psychopathic soul'. The Democrats responded by staging a walk-out and boycotting the Assembly for eight days.[42]

The situation was serious. Some Republicans, for example Nihat Erim, expressed the view that the opposition had abandoned its duty when it walked out of the Assembly; the implication was that the DP may as well be banned. Later Erim was to make similar threats, proposing the creation of another opposition from amongst Republicans, if the Democrats refused to play the game.[43] İnönü's intervention, however, resolved the crisis. In October he had made speeches promising to play the role of an above-party president and encouraging the development of the opposition. He called a meeting with the opposition leaders and assured them that there would be no recurrence of such incidents in the future. With this promise the Democrats returned to the Assembly. However, Premier Peker's position had been weakened by İnönü's gesture of appeasemement.

The crisis ended as a setback for the extremists in the RPP, and the Democrats emerged more confident of their position. This newly won confidence was in evidence at the first congress of the Democrat Party which opened at Ankara on 7 January 1947. From the opening speech of Party Chairman Celâl Bayar, the Democrats took the offensive against the government and made new proposals. They called for the amendment of the electoral law so that elections would in future be supervised by an independent judiciary and not by the partisan bureaucracy. They asked that the offices of President of the Republic and Party Chairman be vested in different persons, not in one person as was the case with İnönü. And they wanted all laws they considered unconstitutional and anti-democratic to be abolished.[44] These three demands were incorporated in the 'Pact of Freedom' (*Hürriyet Misakı*), and the Party's Central Committee was instructed to submit them to the National Assembly. If these proposals were rejected the Central Committee was authorized to boycott the Assembly.

Spurred by the DP challenge, the RPP Supreme Council (*CHP Büyük Divanı*) met on 16 January to consider reform of the party. By the 27th it had decided in principle to make changes in the party's programme and regulations, to begin reforming the party organization and the way in which it functioned, and to deal more closely and productively with matters relating to the press and information, social organizations, and economic measures. These decisions were applauded by progressive-minded Republicans as 'the first important turning-point in the history of the Republican People's Party'.[45] There was another ominous development which few people took seriously at the time but which Mehmed Ali Aybar commented on, namely the Supreme Council's decision to permit religious instruction in schools. Aybar noted that while the Republicans were trying to outdo the Democrats in being liberal they were also turning to religion for political ends. 'This party which has boasted up to this moment about its revolutionism (*inkilâpçılık*) and secularism has found its salvation by embracing religion at the most critical period of its political life.'[46]

Both parties were going through a period of internal dissension.

In both cases this took the form of the extremist group challenging the policies of the moderate leadership. In the Republican Party the extremists wanted an end to İnönü's policy of appeasement. The extremists among the Democrats demanded that the Bayar-Menderes group give up its 'policy of collusion'. Under constant pressure from their extremists, both parties were forced occasionally to adopt harsh policies towards each other. This pressure, however, also brought together the moderates in the two parties and resulted in brief periods of honeymoon.

In February 1947 a group of DP extremists led by Dr Mustafa Kentli, one of the founders of the İzmir organization, proposed making Marshal Fevzi Çakmak leader of the DP. Çakmak (1871-1950) had a great reputation and following in the country. He was an associate of Atatürk during the national struggle and became, after Atatürk, the most respected general in the armed forces. He was appointed the only marshal in the Turkish army and remained Chief of the General Staff for twenty-three years, until his retirement in 1944. His association with the DP gave great prestige and confidence to the party and won it respectability with the armed forces. He was regarded as İnönü's implacable rival and his supporters considered that if he became leader the extremists would be able to pursue a policy of provocation and force the RPP to show its true autocratic colours. The Bayar-Menderes group was naturally embarrassed by this proposal. They could not oppose it openly and therefore Bayar issued an ambiguous statement in which he praised Çakmak's contribution to the party and at the same time launched an attack on the government in order to appease the extremists in the DP.[47]

Once again elections provided the occasion for raising tension between the parties, and this tension continued into May 1947 when the Istanbul by-elections (6 April) and the elections of the village leaders (30 May) took place. The Democrats boycotted the elections and even threatened to withdraw from the Assembly if the Republicans persisted in their anti-democratic practices. The Democrat Party's propaganda campaign brought a response from the government and a confrontation between Bayar and Premier Peker. While this confrontation was taking place, however, the moderates in both parties were negotiating a compromise. A delegation from the National Assembly which included two Democrats, Fuad Köprülü and Enis Akaygen, left for England on 10 May. It also included İnönü's confidant Nihat Erim, and he and Köprülü discussed inter-party relations and agreed on the need for compromise on both sides. Knowing that his conversations with Erim would be faithfully reported to the President, Köprülü again played on İnönü's vanity and hinted that there was no question of anyone else being president while İnönü was alive.[48]

The conciliatory discussions between the moderates isolated the extremists of both parties, and particularly the group led by Premier Recep Peker. There were meetings between Bayar and İnönü, and, at the Sıvas Provincial Congress of the Democrat Party, Bayar revealed that he and İnönü had even arrived at an agreement on the rules of the game. He said that he had complained to İnönü about the pressure the Republican government was putting on the opposition party and İnönü had promised to have all action lifted.[49] Bayar's claim amounted to a confession from the government that it was guilty of unconstitutional and anti-democratic practices. Peker claimed that he was astounded to read Bayar's speech in the press and denied all the latter's claims concerning government pressure.

Charges and counter-charges continued into July, increasing the tension daily. Again İnönü intervened to end the crisis. On the evening of 11 July 1947 he read a statement over the radio contradicting Recep Peker's accusation that the DP sometimes acted as a revolutionary organization. The opposition party, declared İnönü, was acting within a legal political framework and must be permitted to operate under the same conditions as the RPP. As President, he said, he would serve both parties impartially.[50] İnönü had cut the ground from under Peker's feet; only a day earlier Peker had accused the Democrats of seeking to come to power through revolutionary means! This had indeed been a decisive moment to intervene on behalf of the opposition. If İnönü had supported his Premier it is possible that the Democrats would have been left with no alternative but to abandon the struggle in the Assembly. Many of the young Democrats like Samet Ağaoğlu and Mükerrem Sarol were disillusioned with the experiment in democracy as conducted by the Republican Party. They were willing to turn elsewhere, perhaps to the army.[51]

Moreover, the political strife between the parties was not providing a suitable environment for the badly needed economic stability and recovery. Forestalling the politicians, businessmen in the two parties had been attempting to bring about a reconciliation. Üzeyir Avunduk, vice-chairman of the Ankara Chamber of Commerce and chairman of the DP's Ankara branch, and Vehbi Koç, Turkey's foremost industrialist and chairman of the Ankara Chamber of Commerce, acted as mediators. No doubt both men were concerned about the fact that the American business community would have no confidence in Turkey, hence no investments, until the Turkish government could guarantee political stability.[52] Another element may have influenced İnönü's decision—America's growing interest and involvement in Turkey, culminating in the Marshall Plan. İnönü was particularly conscious of Turkey's image in the West and was often angered by the opposition's attempt to bring internal affairs to the attention of Europe and America. But he had learned, as had Necmettin Sadak, soon to be Foreign Minister, that America's principal concern was with regional and internal stability and not with democracy or multi-party politics. Sadak had spoken to the most influential American and British statesmen and that was their view. The stability of the Middle East was of vital importance and they did not object to the character of the régime so long as it was strong. They were even anxious lest party politics weaken Turkey.[53] İnönü's intervention was undoubtedly the best way to restore political stability, at least temporarily. Significantly, the Turkish-American Agreement on Aid was signed one day after İnönü's statement of 12 July.

This 12 July Declaration, as it is called, should have led to the immediate resignation of Prime Minister Peker, but Peker refused to go down without a fight. He tried to regain his prestige and neutralize İnönü's hostility by taking his case to the party's Assembly Group. On 26 August 1947 he came before the Group, explained his policy, and asked for a vote of confidence. He received an overwhelming vote, with only 35 votes against him. But in a party accustomed to unanimity that was as good as a vote of no confidence. The leader of 'the Thirty-five' was Nihat Erim but 'in fact the one behind him who was truly responsible was naturally İnönü'.[54] Peker resigned on 9 September and his departure was considered the defeat of the 'single-party mentality' in the Republican Party and the triumph of İnönü's moderates.

Republican Moderates in Power

Hasan Saka, the new Prime Minister, was a statesman of experience and liberal tendencies. Unlike Peker, he was a civilian who had been educated in Paris and who had taught law and economics at the Faculty of Political Science in Istanbul. He had been in turn Minister of Finance, the Economy, Trade, and Foreign Affairs, and as Premier he was considered well qualified to deal with the economic problems. The cabinet included many new faces and 'there was not anyone who was recognized as a single-party man'.[55] On 14 September İnönü set out on a tour of the country. He was accompanied by a Democrat member of the Assembly and he made speeches appealing to the provincial bureaucracy and party organization to be impartial and just towards the opposition party. On his return to Ankara on 26 September İnönü was welcomed at the station by Fuad Köprülü and a DP deputation, a departure from earlier tactics.

In spite of all the progress they had made, the Republican moderates were not entirely satisfied. The promises of greater party democracy remained unfulfilled; it seemed impossible to break the grip of the pro-Republican bureaucracy. Menderes had diagnosed the situation correctly when he noted that the 'People's Party, founded by the government within the structure of the State and steeped for a long period in the bureaucratic mentality of the single party, was now, over and over again, going through birth pangs in order to acquire the identity of a party'.[56] The RPP could have acquired a new identity at the Seventh Congress of the party, which opened on 17 November, but it failed to do so. Measures to make the party more democratic were passed but these measures did not live up to the hope expressed before the Congress. Nadir Nadi, a neutral and acute observer of the political scene, concluded that in spite of the reforms and the lip service paid to them, 'in the end the politics of the *status quo* had as always come out on top'.[57]

Another way to transform the Republican Party was to modify and reinterpret the six principles, the 'ideology' of the party. Thus emphasis on the revolutionary-radical aspect of the principle of *inkilâpçılık* was reduced and evolutionary development was stressed.[58] This was considered a step towards democracy in that reforms would no longer be imposed from the top, and only those reforms acceptable to the people would be implemented in future. The interpretation of étatism was made more flexible so as to remove discrimination against the private sector. And in order to maintain consistency with the right to private property, recognized as a fundamental principle in both the constitution and the party programme, the Party Congress decided to amend the land reform law of June 1945 by limiting its scope. The basis of nationalism was made linguistic, cultural, and territorial rather than racial, a move in the direction of a more liberal policy for the minorities, as well as a counterweight against 'foreign ideologies', namely communism and fascism. The discussion on secularism had been most heated and controversial and on this principle, too, the Congress decided to abandon the party's militant policy against Islam. A tendency in this direction had attracted attention even earlier and General Sadık Aldoğan, a DP firebrand, asked tauntingly: '... the People's party and its governments, which did all kinds of moral harm to innocent people, have accepted the teaching of religion in schools in order to repair their broken hearts. ...Rascal, whom are you fooling? Who is going to believe you now?"[59] The motive behind these promises of reforms was to bring the party even closer in doctrine to the Democrats, meet many of their criticisms, and regain the people's confidence. But Sadık Aldoğan was right: the people were not to be won so easily.

A Split in the Democrat Party

The political honeymoon, while expedient for the Republicans, was undermining the position of the Democrats. They were losing their dynamism, which depended on an aggressive policy towards the RPP, and hence their popularity. But perhaps the most immediate consequence for the Democrats was the increasing tension between the moderates and extremists in the party. The extremists had earlier denounced the party as a work of collusion; now they were describing it as a puppet opposition. İnönü is said to have encouraged the split by hinting that relations between the two parties could be consolidated if Bayar would only expel the extremists in his party.[60] This was done in the middle of 1948; however, as we shall see, the result was not the consolidation of inter-party relations.

Dissension within the Democrat Party had been smouldering for over a year. In January 1948 it burst into flame with the resignation of Kenan Öner, leader of the Istanbul organization. He accused the party leadership of dominating the party and repressing internal opposition, especially groups hostile to İnönü. He claimed that Bayar and İnönü had a secret agreement, that they were guilty of collusion—which explained why the RPP tolerated the Democrats. And finally, he alleged that İnönü had even given financial assistance to the leaders to establish their party.[61]

The conflict took the form of a struggle for authority between the Central Committee, dominated by Bayar's group, and the Assembly Group, composed mainly of people who resented central control reminiscent of the People's Party. The Central Committee considered party discipline vital and since it controlled the party machine, especially the Disciplinary Committee, it was able to have dissidents expelled. In March five deputies were expelled; and six members of the Central Committee, who resigned in protest, were also expelled from the party. There was already talk of another party and this was confirmed by Mustafa Kentli who also put forward, for the first time, the ideas of an upper chamber and a supreme or constitutional court.[62] These proposals were adopted by the Republicans after their defeat in 1950, but became a reality only after 1960. A group of DP dissidents in the Assembly calling themselves the Independent Democrats announced their existence on 10 May, while another group founded a new party, the Nation Party (NP—*Millet Partisi*), on 20 July 1948. A year later the Independent Democrats merged with the new party. The immediate consequence for the Democrat Party was that its strength in the Assembly was cut in half, but it became more unified.

Hasan Saka's Second Cabinet, June 1948

The improved political climate which had coincided with the formation of the Hasan Saka cabinet seemed to do nothing to alleviate the economic situation. Responsibility for the failure to implement the promises was placed on individual ministers. The role of the minister was particularly important in a highly bureaucratic system which did not have a momentum of its own and which tended to come to a halt if ministers were incompetent or lacked dynamism. This also explains why career bureaucrats were appointed ministers; it would have been virtually impossible for an outsider to work the machine. Hasan Saka resigned on 9 June and was asked to form a new cabinet. His new team was composed of ministers he considered capable of carrying out his programme, and included figures such as Nihat Erim (Public Works) and Cemil Sait Barlas (Trade), younger and ambitious men destined to play important roles in Turkish politics. However, the inclusion of Cavit Oral (Agriculture), a wealthy landowner from Adana, meant that a conservative policy would be pursued on the land question. Kasım Gülek, a new face in the first Saka cabinet with the portfolio of Public Works, was moved to the Ministry of Communications. It was these men who were expected to be responsible for carrying out economic development.

The Democrats were not impressed by this new cabinet. Bayar expressed the view that it would not be able to change the economic situation, which was deteriorating day by day. Menderes put forward similar views at the Kütahya Congress.[63] The Democrats were perhaps correct in their predictions, but their hostility was guided more by the pressure of their extremists than by a cool and rational analysis of the economic situation. They criticized but offered no alternative proposals; their motives were purely political. On 16 July they again decided not to contest by-elections because the Election Law had not been amended to their satisfaction, even though the government had repealed some of the anti-democratic laws. The Democrats nevertheless used the election campaign for their propaganda and in October launched an offensive against the Republicans. Politically the RPP was doing better after the split in the Democrat Party and the creation of the Nation Party; its problems continued to be economic. Even in his second term, Hasan Saka was unable to handle the problem of removing economic hardship from the daily lives of the people. This brought constant criticism from both the opposition and from his own party, and on 14 January 1949 he resigned for the second time.

The Günaltay Cabinet

The appointment of Semsettin Günaltay was the last straw for Republican extremists. He was a professor of history, with a reputation for Islamist sympathies, and the extremists believed that he was capable of turning his back on Kemalism. As a protest against Günaltay's appointment, the nationalist poet Behçet Kemal Çağlar resigned his seat in the Assembly and left the RPP. There were rumours that there would be a split and that the extremists would form a new party to be called the Kemalist Party.[64] The split in the RPP was avoided and Günaltay began to implement a programme or reform which he hoped would appease the opposition, win over a sullen and dissatisfied population, and lead the Republican Party to victory in the coming general election.

One of Günaltay's first announcements was the decision to adopt an overall economic plan to deal with Turkey's problems. A committee consisting of Necmettin Sadak, Nihat Erim, Nurullah Sümer and Tahsin Banguoğlu, with Günaltay as chairman, was set up. It was announced that a planning office would be established and placed under the Prime Minister, and its functions would be to co-ordinate the plans of the various ministries.[65] Even though this proposal did not get off the ground it does show the direction in which the RPP was moving. In February 1950 a commission to reform the electoral law was formed under the chairmanship of Nihat Erim, who said that opposition views would be given importance and the principles accepted in Western democracy would be taken as models.[66] Günaltay also began to implement his liberal policy towards organized religion, which later gave him the claim to boast of himself as the liberator of Islam in Turkey.[67]

At the same time government increased its repressive activities against the Left. The Turkish Left was neither big nor organized. Some socialists took advantage of the relative political freedom after 1945 to emerge into the open, but their activities were restricted to an appeal to the intelligentsia, of which they were themselves members. Some even founded political parties. The most famous of these was the Socialist Workers and Peasants Party of Turkey, founded on 19 June 1946 by Dr Şefik Hüsnü Değmer, and closed down by the martial law authorities on 16 December.[68] The Republican régime had always been hostile to the Left and Stalin's aggressive designs on Turkey in 1945 did not encourage the Turkish government to adopt a more tolerant attitude towards the Left. During the Cold War, in which Turkey soon came to play an active part through the Truman Doctrine, the Marshall Plan, and later the North Atlantic Treaty Organization all those with socialist sympathies were seen as fellow-travellers and potential traitors. It was in this climate that the socialist writer Sabahattin Ali was murdered on 2 April 1948, allegedly by someone working for the police.[69] It was also in 1948 that four professors were forced out of Ankara University as the result of a 'witch hunt ... to liquidate all possible leftist influence in the schools'.[70] Both the Republicans and the Democrats were agreed on the need to crush the Left and this task was duly accomplished in the early 1950s.

The rest of the period up to the election was devoid of any new political issues and the Democrats found themselves reverting to their old tactics of trying to create issues in order to keep political tension as high as possible. They were always able to embarrass the RPP by harping on its repressive past, so deeply engraved on the consciousness of the Turkish people, or on the prevailing economic destitution, about which the RPP had been able to do little. The Democrats pursued a policy of cautious radicalism, which amounted to being cautious in action and radical in words. Thus during their Second Congress they opposed amendment of the constitution, which undoubtedly needed to be amended if it were to meet the requirements of a society in the throes of establishing multi-party politics and democracy. But the Democrats claimed that it was democratic in spirit but autocratic in implementation. At the same time the party stated that 'any infringement upon the Election Law was equivalent to a violation of the individual's natural rights which placed the citizens in a position of self-defence'.[71]

The Election of 1950

For the first time since the founding of the Democrat Party the political initiative had passed to the Republicans. It was they who took the offensive, denouncing the activities of the Congress as subversive; and Nihat Erim, now Deputy Prime Minister, even claimed that it was the Republicans alone who were sincere about the experiment in democracy.[72]

The boycott of the by-elections in October 1949 did not affect the Republicans as it had done in the past. By 16 February 1950 the Election Law no longer remained an issue, for it had been amended in a form acceptable to the Democrats. By this date the unofficial election campaign was in full swing and the Republicans were confident that they had accomplished enough to win by a comfortable margin. They felt so sure of victory that they went as far as to offer the Democrats representation in the next Assembly. There were even unofficial meetings between members of the two parties to discuss this, though no acceptable agreement was reached.[73]

Perhaps the Republicans had good reason for their optimism. They had successfully restored multi-party politics and also begun to meet some of the spiritual longings and material needs of the people. As the comparison of the two election manifestos shows, there was hardly any difference between the programmes of the two parties. The RPP was willing to remove the six principles from the constitution if it was re-elected and it bent over backwards to appease the private sector and the clericalists in order to compete with the Democrats and the Nation Party. This mood of optimism symbolized the single-party, élitist mentality and reflected the view that the voter should be grateful for the reforms bestowed from the top and forget the oppression that accompanied them. It was precisely this memory which the Republicans were not able to eradicate, an impossibility while İsmet İnönü led the party. However hard the party tried to change its image, with İsmet Pasha at the helm the link with the past remained as strong as ever.

This was all to the advantage of the Democrats and they exploited the so-called 'Pasha factor' (*Paşa faktörü*) thoroughly. But although they kept the pressure on the Republican Party, they unobtrusively began to direct their fire less and less at the bureaucracy, differentiating between the two. This was extremely important because a hostile bureaucracy would have been a threat to the DP's electoral chances and a brake on its programme if it came to power. Therefore the bureaucracy had first to be neutralized and then won over. The Democrat hierarchy accomplished this by promising that the issue of the *ancien régime* would not be raised: *devr-i-sabık yaratmıyacağız* (we will not question the past). The bureaucracy would not be held responsible for the sins of the past, for which the party alone was to blame. In this way the bureaucracy severed its links with the RPP and began to play a neutral role. Without its neutrality it is doubtful whether the

Democrats could have won the 1950 election: the influence of the official had always been great in Turkish history. The non-partisanship of officials gave heart to the DP voter and increased the prestige of the party; a party that could neutralize the bureaucracy, the people argued, was worth voting for. The election took place on 14 May 1950. The people, sensing the historic moment, came out in overwhelming numbers—almost 90 per cent of the registered voters—and voted İnönü's Republican People's Party out of power.

NOTES

1 The best accounts of these early developments are to be found in Kemal Karpat, *Turkey's Politics: the Transition to a Multi-party System* (1959), 32 ff., and Bernard Lewis, *The Emergence of Modern Turkey* (2nd edn., 1968), 239 ff.

2 The text of the 1924 constitution, the later amendments, and the modern Turkish translation of 1945 are all given in Şeref Gözübüyük and Suna Kili, *Türk Anayasa Metinleri* (Ankara, 1957), 101-23. For an English translation of the 1945 version as well as the amendments to the 1924 constitution see Geoffrey Lewis, *Turkey* (2nd rev. edn., London, 1959), 201-14.

3 The quoted passage that follows is an excerpt from the official translation of the programme of the RPP, reproduced in Donald Webster, *The Turkey of Atatürk* (Philadelphia, Pa., 1939), 308-9.

4 CHP, *Dördüncü Büyük Kurultayı Görüşmeleri Tutulgası* (Ankara, 1935), 45.

5 Lewis, *Emergence*, 381-3; Karpat, *Politics*, 395.

6 Lewis, *Emergence*, 383.

7 *CHP Tüzüğü* (Ankara, 1938), 3; Fahir Giritlioğlu, *Türk Siyasi Tarihinde Cumhuriyet Halk Partisinin Mevkii*, i (1965), 139.

8 Karpat, *Politics*, 395. On the period 1939-45 see Mahmut Goloğlu, *Milli Şef Dönemi* (Ankara, 1974).

9 Frederick Frey, *The Turkish Political Élite* (1965), is a detailed examination of how this alliance was reflected in the assemblies of the Republic from 1923 to 1957. Lewis, *Emergence*, 474, gives a breakdown of the 1943 Assembly: 'Among the 453 deputies elected to the Assembly in 1943, 127 were public servants of various kinds, 67 members of the armed forces, 89 lawyers, and 59 teachers. Only 49 were merchants, 45 farmers, 15 bankers, and 3 industrialists.' A word of caution: although 89 representatives identified themselves as lawyers (*hukukçu*) this only means that they had all been to law school, not necessarily that law was their profession. In many cases they were probably wealthy landowners.

10 Giritlioğlu, *Halk Partisi*, i, 148-52; Karpat, *Politics*, 391.

11 Yıldız Sertel, *Türkiye'de İlerici Akımlar* (1969), 57-8; Hershlag, *Turkey: the Challenge of Growth* (1968), 132-3; Lewis, *Emergence*, 297-8, and 472-3.

12 Kâzım Öztürk, *Cumhurbaşkanlarinin Türkiye Büyük Millet Meclisini Açış Nutukları* (1969), 379.

13 Conversation with Hikmet Bayur, Istanbul, 1971. See also Karpat, *Politics*, 91 and *passim*. Karpat's is still the most detailed account in English of the period 1945-50.

14 For an excellent account and analysis of these reforms see Lewis, *Emergence*, 256-79.

15 Lewis, ibid., 474-5; see also Reşat Aktan, 'Analysis and Assessment of Land Reform Activities in Turkey', *SBFD, xxvi/3 (1971), 89-93*.

16 Necmettin Sadak, 'On Yedinci Madde', *Akşam*, 27 May 1945. A sociologist by training, Sadak was foreign minister in the last three Republican cabinets. See also Karpat, *Politics*, 118.

17 For a brief discussion of the land reform bill see *Ayın Tarihi*, May 1945, 28-50. For more detailed discussion see the parliamentary minutes in *Büyük Millet Meclisi Tutanak Dergisi*.

18 *Cumhuriyet* and *Akşam*, 21-30 May 1945.

19 *Cumhuriyet*, 13 June 1945 and Karpat, *Politics*, 145.

20 Hıfzı Oğuz Bekata, *Birinci Cumhuriyet Biterken* (1960), 10.

21 *Cumhuriyet*, 8 July and 23 Aug. 1945; Tarık Zafer Tunaya, *Türkiye'de Siyasi Partiler, 1859-1952* (1952), 638-45, and Türkiye Cumhuriyeti İçişleri Bakanlığı, *Türkiye'de Siyasi Dernekler* (Ankara, 1950), 107-25.

22 Necmettin Sadak, 'Bir iyi haber: Celâl Bayar'ın kurmak üzere olduğu parti', *Akşam*, 3 Dec. 1945; Karpat, *Politics*, 147.

23 'Yeni Parti', *Tanin*, 5 Dec. 1945. The same sentiment was expressed by former Democrats with whom the author spoke.

24 See Celâl Bayar's statement of 13 Mar. 1946 in *Cumhuriyet*, 14 Mar. 1946.

25 *Cumhuriyet*, 30 Apr. 1946; Karpat, *Politics*, 153-4.

26 *Ayın Tarihi*, May 1946, 7-15; Karpat, *Politics*, 154-5. In theory, the abolition of this article also permitted socialists to organize political parties. That was not so in practice. In fact, the persecution of the Left in Turkey increased after political liberalization, and Articles 141 and 142, which made it illegal to conduct 'communist propaganda', were used to persecute the Left.

27 See İnönü's election speech of 17 July 1946 in *Ulus*, 18 July 1946, and Suna Kili, *Kemalism (1969), 157-8*.

28 *Vatan*, 23 May 1946; the text of the article is given in Şükrü Esirci, *Menderes Diyorki!* i (n.d. [1967]), 19-22.

29 Even İnönü's son-in-law Metin Toker writes that had he been able to vote in the 1954 election he would have voted DP. See Toker, *İsmet Paşayla 10 Yıl, 1954-1957,* i (1965), 15. In a conversation with the author, Turhan Feyzioğlu also affirmed that the Democrats retained their popularity until as late as the second half of 1954. The reasons for their unpopularity after this period will be discussed later in this work.

30 Samet Ağaoğlu even had to write *İki Parti Arasında Farklar* (1947), in order to try to demonstrate that there were in fact differences between the parties.

31 Nihat Erim, 'Demokrasi Gaye midir, Vasıta mıdır?', *Ulus*, 30 May 1946. See also Ahmed Emin Yalman, *Gördüklerim ve Geçirdiklerim*, iv (1945-1971), (1971), 72-4.

32 *Cumhuriyet*, 16 June 1946. The Election Law allowed a candidate to stand in more than one constituency; important political figures stood in two or three in order to secure election in at least one.

33 *Cumhuriyet*, 25 June 1946, quoting a RPP directive to the party organization.

34 Ibid.

35 *Ayın Tarihi*, July 1946, 5; Karpat *Politics*, 164.

36 *Ulus*, 25 July 1946.

37 Karpat, *Politics*, 169. In fact, İnönü's declaration was broadcast on the radio on the evening of 11 July but—from its publication in the press the following day—came to be known as the declaration of 12 July.

38 Ibid.

39 Necmettin Sadak, 'Geçici tedbirler değil, Sürekli ve esaslı bir iktisat programına muhtacız', *Akşam*, 11 Aug. 1946.

40 *Cumhuriyet*, 29 Nov. 1946.

41 Karpat, *Politics*, 174.

42 *Cumhuriyet* and *Vatan*, 19 Dec. 1946. Yalman, *Gördüklerim*, iv, 9 and 104; Karpat, *Politics*, 174-5, and Metin Toker, *Tek Partiden Çok Partiye* (1970), 222-8.

43 Nihat Erim, 'Meclisi Terketmek Vazifeden Kaçmaktır', *Ulus*, 19 Dec. 1946.

44 Esirci, *Menderes*, 39-43; Tunaya, *Partiler*, 650-1; Karpat, *Politics*, 182.

45 *Akşam*, 21 Jan. 1947.

46 Article in *Hür*, 1 Feb. 1947, text given in Mehmed Ali Aybar, *Bağımsızlık Demokrasi Sosyalizm* (1968), 87-9.

47 *Cumhuriyet*, 10 and 11 Feb. 1947.

48 Cihad Baban, *Politika Galerisi* (1970), 428-9; Toker, *Tek Parti*, 257, 266, 341-6.

49 *Vatan*, 28 June 1947.

50 Text of İnönü's statement in Esirci, *Menderes*, 99-102 and in the press of 12 July 1947 and *Ayın Tarihi*, July 1947, 14-16. See also Cem Eroğul, *Demokrat Parti* (1970), 34-5 and Toker, *Tek Parti*, 258 ff.

51 This sentiment was expressed to the author in conversation he had with former Democrats. It was only on Celâl Bayar's insistence that they did not abandon the experiment and Bayar refused to countenance the use of non-democratic methods to attain power.

52 Toker, *Tek Parti*, 256, and Eroğul, *Demokrat Parti*, 32, n. 80.

53 Necmettin Sadak, 'Girişilen harekette dış endişeler asla yer tutmaz', *Akşam*, 16 July 1946. The Democrats, on the other hand, always tried to exploit Western public opinion to their advantage.

54 Toker, *Tek Parti*, 300.

34   The Turkish Experiment in Democracy

55 Yalman, Gördüklerim, iv, 119.
56 Esirci, Menderes, 94-7, where the full text of the speech is given, and Cumhuriyet, 2 Oct. 1947.
57 Cumhuriyet, 5 Dec. 1947.
58 Kili, Kemalism, 160-61.
59 Quoted by Hüseyin Cahit Yalçın in 'Şeriat İsteriz', Tanin, 3 Oct. 1947.
60 Eroğul, Demokrat Parti, 38. İnönü was referring to men like Kenan Öner, Sadık Aldoğan, and Ahmet Tahtakılıç.
61 Karpat, Politics, 211-15. Karpat cites Kenan Öner's letter published in Yeni Sabah, 17 Jan. 1948.
62 Cumhuriyet, 9 May 1948.
63 For Bayar's views see Cumhuriyet, 13 June 1948 and for Menderes's views, Esirci, Menderes, 151-6.
64 Cumhuriyet, 21 Jan. 1949 and Karpat, Politics, 220.
65 Cumhuriyet, 31 Jan. 1949 and E. J. Benice, 'Günaltay Kabinesi ve Kalkınma Planı', Son Telgraf, 1 Feb. 1949.
66 Cumhuriyet, 11 Feb. 1949.
67 In the Assembly, when his party was accused of being against Islam, Günaltay retorted, 'I am the Premier of a government which has opened the Faculty of Divinity (İlâhiyat Fakültesi) to teach the high principles of Islam in this country.' Cumhuriyet, 9 June 1949, quoted in Ayın Tarihi, June 1949, 27-31.
68 Türkiye Cumhuriyeti, İçişleri Bakanlığı, Türkiye'de Siyasi Dernekler (Ank., 1950), 341-64.
69 Kemal Sülker, Sabahattin Ali Dosyası (Istanbul, 1968), 81 and passim.
70 Karpat, Politics, 372-3. The professors expelled were Pertev Naili Boratav, Niyazi Berkes, Adnan Cemgil, and Behice Boran. Boratav and Berkes emigrated to France and Canada respectively.
71 Karpat, ibid., 232-3.
72 Erim's statement on the occasion of the anniversary of the Declaration of 12 July. Ulus, 13 July 1949.
73 The Democrats exposed these secret negotiations in 1955. See Toker, Tek Parti, 348-50; Karpat, Politics, 239; Yalman, Gördüklerim, iv, 208.

CHAPTER II

THE MENDERES ERA 1950-1960

In many respects, the Ninth Grand National Assembly will have in our history a unique place. It is for the first time in our history that, as a result of a full and free expression of the national will, this distinguished Assembly has come to a position where it can shape the nation's destiny.

We shall remember that historic day [14 May 1950] as the day of victory not only for our party but for Turkish democracy.

Adnan Menderes, speech in the Grand National Assembly, 29 May 1950

Inter-party Relations in 1950

THE Democrats had succeeded in wresting political power at the polls from the well-entrenched ruling party, a rare accomplishment in the politics of developing countries. But the election results created an identity crisis for the two parties since both had to adapt to new roles for which there was no precedent in Turkish politics. Despite rumours of military intervention (described in chapter 6 below), the transfer of power was carried out smoothly. The overwhelmingly Democrat Assembly elected Celâl Bayar as President, and he, in turn, appointed Adnan Menderes as his Prime Minister. The new government was announced on 22 May.[1]

Adnan Menderes (1899-1961) was an affluent landowner from Aydın, a prosperous and developed province in western Anatolia. He entered politics in 1930, joining the recently formed opposition party, the Free Republican Party. When this party was disolved a year later he joined the RPP and was elected representative for Aydın. Menderes remained in the party until his expulsion in 1945. He was a founder-member of the Democrat Party, and the destinies of the two became intimately linked.

Menderes had come to the notice of Celâl Bayar during the 'Free Party experiment'. The latter was struck by his dynamism and his acute awareness of Turkey's problems. Menderes, he recalled, understood the psychology of the people, especially the Turkish peasant, and possessed the qualities necessary for leadership. When Bayar decided in 1945 to form an opposition party he invited Menderes to be one of the founders. Later, he decided that if his party came to power at the general election of 1950 Menderes would be his Prime Minister. Only Menderes, he felt, had the personality and outlook to provide the modern and progressive leadership the country so badly needed in order to catch up with the developed West.[2]

The initial mature behaviour of the parties and the professions of goodwill towards one another proved deceptive. In fact, their relations in the Assembly and articles in party periodicals revealed unresolved tensions. The first confrontation was not long in coming. On 29 May Menderes presented his programme and this was followed by a debate during which the programme was criticized and defended. On 2 June Menderes answered his critics' charges and the Republicans sought the right to reply, in accordance with the regulations governing the procedure of the Assembly. However, Refik Koraltan, its Chairman, denied the opposition this right, and the Républicans walked out of the House in protest. The government received a vote of confidence, though there were 192 abstentions.[3]

The scene in the Assembly on 2 June was a bad omen for future relations between the parties. The press noted that this incident had virtually been a repeat performance of a debate which had taken place four years earlier on 14 August 1946. On that occasion Recep Peker had read his programme and the Democrats had requested an adjournment before the debate so that they could study the programme and prepare their criticism. The Chairman had rejected the request and the DP opposition had staged a walk-out. Before leaving the Assembly, Menderes had protested: '...if discussions are opened in this manner it means that we are not being given the opportunity to participate.'[4] There were other occasions when Republican governments had contravened parliamentary practice; now the Democrats were emulating their example.

Relations between the parties became even worse when, on 6 June, the government purged the high command of the Turkish armed forces, replacing the Chief of the General Staff and other senior officers with men not associated with the RPP and therefore more politically reliable.[5] The Democrats were very sensitive about their standing with the military, convinced that the commanders would not be totally loyal to the government while İsmet İnönü led the opposition. They reacted sharply when pro-RPP newspapers tried to exploit the purge for political ends. These newspapers (*Ulus* and *Hürriyet*), the Democrats claimed, were carrying out a campaign designed to inflame feelings in the armed forces against the government. When the opposition continued its offensive and demanded an explanation for the changes in the armed forces, Menderes denounced these tactics as a campaign to subvert the army and the nation, a campaign which the RPP had opened when the Democrats had not even been in power a month. 'All our efforts', he said, 'are directed to cementing democracy in our country. If the RPP wants to enter into a successful partnership, it must expel those craving for power [*iktidar hastaları*, literally power-sick] from the leadership. It is the "power-sick" who want to spoil the [political] atmosphere. They have attacked and taken the offensive, using a polemic designed to show the distortion of political stability in the country....'[6]

Menderes's *iktidar hastaları* was a reference to İnönü and his followers in the RPP and manifested the deep fear of İnönü which most Democrats harboured. It was this factor, the Pasha factor (*Paşa faktörü*), which bedevilled inter-party relations in the decade under discussion and long after. İnönü-phobia was based on the conviction that İsmet Pasha had not really accepted DP rule and was determined to undermine the Democrats at the first opportunity. The Democrats felt insecure so long as İnönü was active in politics. Not only did İnönü make them feel insecure, he also brought out a sense of inferiority in a way they could not explain. The real cause of their insecurity was that, although they had acquired political power at the polls, they felt uncertain about their hold over the state—especially the central and provincial bureaucracies—the armed forces, the judiciary, and even the universities and the press. All these institutions, especially the armed forces, the Democrats imagined, still retained some loyalty to İsmet Pasha and the RPP. Unable to depend on the state, the Democrats emphasized their dependence on the 'national will' (*milli irade*), which became a fetish with them and their successors.

It is difficult, in the light of the overwhelming majority they enjoyed, to understand the Democrats' preoccupation with the opposition during these ten years. In not one of the three assemblies—1950, 1954, and 1957—did the opposition come close to challenging and bringing about the fall of the DP government. In these three assemblies the RPP, the largest opposition party, had 69, 31 and 178 seats, respectively, as compared to 408, 503 and 424 seats ·held by the Democrat Party. What, then, did the Democrats fear?

In fact, the DP oligarchy, sometimes described as the Bayar-

Menderes group, was more concerned about its standing with its own party than with the opposition. Menderes was always more apprehensive of his own supporters, who had the power both to challenge him and overthrow him. The preoccupation with İnönü and the RPP, although it was real enough, was also diversionary and provided an element of unity in a party far from united. As we shall see in the next chapter, Menderes had to spend much time and energy maintaining a hold on his own party.

Another factor which requires serious consideration in the discussion of democracy in Turkey is the attitude of the majority party towards the idea of opposition in general and opposition parties in particular.[7] Historically, opposition of any sort had been equated with hostility, in the minds of both rulers and ruled. With the introduction of constitutional government, the Chamber of Deputies, the Senate, and political parties in 1908, it soon became evident that traditional political atti⁺ ides would continue to persist—and in such a political climate the opposition fared badly. When multi-party politics were restored in 1945 there had been no substantial change in political attitudes. The Republicans, then in power, did not expect the opposition parties to provide serious and constant criticism. They expected them to be the junior partners in government, providing mild criticism which would act as a safety valve and an element of stability in political life. The continued existence of a legal and active opposition bewildered and demoralized the supporters of the RPP, just as it increased support for the Democrats. The extremists in the RPP were aware of this and considered closing down the DP, but in the end the views of the moderates were able to prevail.

In power, the attitude of the Democrats to opposition was somewhat different from that of the Republicans. The Republicans, as the ruling party for over a generation, suffered from a sense of guilt in its dealing with the opposition. Even the legitimacy of Republican governments was in doubt since they had never come to power through free and honest elections; they had never received a mandate from the people. The Democrats, however, saw themselves as the new force in ᴸTurkish history which would take the 'revolution' to its final stage. They were confident that history was on their side and that their first task was to remove the RPP from power since that party under İnönü had become the principal obstacle to progress.

The Democrats believed that this obstacle had been removed by their victory at the polls, which they regarded as the culmination of the political revolution. Significantly, they described their electoral triumph as a 'white revolution'. But this was only the beginning, for they intended to progress from the political revolution to a thorough-going social and economic transformation, for which they had the mandate of the 'national will'. Thus, they became impatient and frustrated with the RPP opposition, which, they claimed, had virtually lost its *raison d'être* and which ought now to permit the new government to get on with the task of moving the country forward. Instead, the opposition continued to harass the government by indulging in politics and nothing but politics. Its positive contribution after six months had been nil, and Menderes expressed his anxiety about an opposition that had not brought a single constructive question before the Assembly. He hoped the Republicans would soon get a grip on themselves.[8]

The Democrats' view of themselves and their attitude towards the opposition seemed to be confirmed by their continuing triumphs at the polls, at least during the first seven years. The municipal elections of 3 September 1950, the first test to be held since the general election, were a landslide victory for the Democrats. Of the 600 municipalities held by the Republicans, 560 passed under Democrat control.[9] In October the Democrats won the provincial elections (*Genel Meclis Seçimleri*) in 55 of the 67 provinces[10] and this pattern continued until the general election of 2 May 1954, when the Democrats increased their representation in the Assembly from 408 (1950) to 503 and their percentage of the vote from 53·59 to 58·42 per cent. The Republican representation was reduced from 69 to 31 and their percentage of the popular vote from 39·98 to 35·11 per cent.[11]

Each electoral success made it even more difficult for the Democrats to accept and tolerate criticism, and Nihat Erim complained in the columns of *Ulus* that 'ever since the Democrat Party came to power, its first government has not been able to make itself get used to criticism.'[12] The concepts that criticism should be tolerated and that it should be constructive would have to become rooted in Turkey's political culture before multi-party politics could suceed. Immediately after the municipal elections of 3 September 1950 Menderes made a remark which summed up the attitudes of his party: 'On 14 May the Turkish nation eliminated the People's Party from power; on 3 September it [the nation] eliminated it from opposition.'[13]

Some former Democrats, in their conversations with the author, had difficulty in explaining why their preoccupation with the opposition continued even though they had realized that there was no threat to their power. They agreed, in retrospect, that this had been their party's major error, for it had diverted them from more pressing problems. What the élite of the DP could not deal with rationally was even more confusing for the party's rank and file. The rank and file had expected the victory of their party to reduce the RPP to total political impotence. To their surprise and bewilderment, the RPP—symbolized by İnönü— was still active and criticizing the new government with vigour.

This was the political climate in which Menderes began his rule. Throughout this decade inter-party strife, which became more bitter with time, remained a constant factor. Taken out of the context of relations between members within the parties, this factor is surprisingly incongruous since both parties had much in common and few areas of disagreement. Had Turkey been a developed country, where the function of the party system was to maintain the *status quo* or to bring about regulated change, the two parties might have functioned admirably. They differed about as much as the Republican and Democratic parties in the United States and had more in common than the Labour and Conservative parties in Britain. But they were not operating in a society in which the ruling class was united on the maintenance of the *status quo*; the Turkish ruling class was agreed on the need for change so long as the basic structure of society remained unaltered.

In spite of a broad area of agreement, the parties failed to agree on the nature and the pace at which the country ought to be transformed. The Republicans favoured a slower and steadier transformation in which bureaucratic–military groups within the power structure would not suffer unduly and would be given time and opportunity to be absorbed into the emerging capitalist society. The Democrats, on the other hand, had not considered the implications of their socio-economic programme. Their primary impulse was to develop the country as rapidly as possible, for they believed that once the country had gained sufficient momentum they would be able to eliminate errors and iron out the problems. Their only concern was to implement the programme for which they had a national mandate and which the opposition was hindering. By playing at politics it was distracting both the government and the nation from the urgent tasks ahead.

Much to the surprise and annoyance of the government, İnönü even criticized its decision to send a battalion of Turkish troops to Korea without consulting the opposition: 'The conformity of views between the Government and the opposition party over major national issues is a fundamental requirement in order to achieve unity in the country.'[14] The Democrats would have agreed but they objected to the way in which the Republicans exploited the issue. Some weeks later İnönü began to complain of the existence of instability and political insecurity in the country. The entire state structure, from the army to the lower levels of the bureaucracy, felt threatened. Commenting on the measures the Democrat Party had introduced against the Left, İnönü said that 'The accusation of communism and the threat to expel a citizen from the country is a direct attack on the principle of the rule of law. It is enough to put an end to every kind of political activity.'[15] Two days later the Ministry of Finance announced that it was investigating the finances of the RPP in order to see how much money the party had appropriated from the state treasury during its twenty-seven years in office, and how much it owed to the state.[16] It soon became clear that the government intended to seek 'compensation' of about TL 50 million, a sum which was expected to cripple the party.[17]

Analysing inter-party relations, Nadir Nadi, the editor of *Cumhuriyet,* noted that although eight months had passed since the Democrats came to power the two parties had failed to establish normal relations. He held the Republicans responsible because they had not given the new government an opportunity to perform its task; they had begun to attack the government without waiting to see its performance. They should have waited until the 1951 budget had been introduced before launching their campaign. For their part, the Democrats were criticized for reacting immaturely towards the opposition,[18] and for carrying out measures designed only to please the people. It was one thing to serve the people, wrote Nadir Nadi, and another to please them. The Republicans, in their last years in power, had sacrificed principles in order to cultivate votes and had thereby lost the opportunity to serve the people. He advised the Democrats not to do the same[19]—a sound and prophetic warning which was repeated often but which went unheeded. The budget debates in February 1951 reminded Nadir Nadi of inter-party relations in the years after 1946: he pointed out that, even though the ruling party (*iktidar partisi*) had come 'to power with the genuine wish of the people and with a large majority', it did 'not have the psychological excuse from which the People's Party suffered in the late 1940s.'[20]

Religious Reaction and Kemalism

This period of bitter relations between the government and the opposition coincided with what is described as the 'religious reaction', marked by the vandalizing of Kemal Atatürk's busts and statues, insolent behaviour towards women in the small towns of Anatolia, and demands for the restoration of Islamic practice in Turkey and an end to militant secularism. At the Democrat Party provincial congress in Konya, for example, some delegates demanded that the right to wear the fez and the veil, and to use the Arabic script, all three abolished by the Kemalist reforms of the 1920s, be restored.[21] These proposals were rejected by the party. But religious reaction had become issue number one for the RPP, much to the embarrassment of the DP leadership, though it hardly improved the RPP's image with the voter. The Republicans were able to renew their claim that they, members of the party of Atatürk, were the real guardians of his reforms. Menderes retorted that the real guardian of the reforms was the Turkish nation and the government began to take action against the Right.[22] The Ministry of the Interior issued a communiqué to all provincial governors ordering that measures be taken to protect Atatürk's statues, and investigations were opened against reactionary and clericalist publications such as *Büyük Doğu, Sebilürreşad* and *İslâmiyet,* which were charged with the exploitation of religion for political ends.[23]

The RPP's constant clamour about religious reaction and the Atatürk reforms seems to have been designed as a strategy to slow down change and to maintain the *status quo* for as long as possible. The DP leadership was embarrassed by the accusation of anti-Kemalism which was levelled against the party, but knew of no way to deal with it adequately since the accusation could never be satisfactorily defined. Many Democrats, especially men like Bayar, were able to make as good a claim to Kemalism as any Republican. In fact, they claimed that their aim was to make Kemalism a living ideology, as it had been before Atatürk died in 1938. On the fourteenth anniversary of Atatürk's death Menderes wrote that the task confronting Turkish society was not merely to preserve Atatürk's achievements (as the Republicans desired) in their original form and character, but to develop those achievements in accordance with the aims and motives which had governed them at the outset. Under the Democrats, the Turkish nation was experiencing the joys of such progress and Atatürk could rest eternally with a blessed soul.[24]

According to a DP interpretation of Kemalism—also shared by many Republicans—Atatürk had carried out his programme of reforms in order that Turkey should become Westernized within the capitalist system based on free enterprise. These were the 'aims and motives' of the reforms which Menderes referred to. This policy had been practised until the early 1930s, when it was found that both internal conditions and the world situation did not permit the continuation of this experiment. It was only then, perhaps encouraged by the Soviet example and aid, that the Kemalist régime decided to introduce active state intervention and planning into the economy. But even then, the aim was to create an economy which was viable and a class of private entrepreneurs capable of taking over. When this class was sufficiently developed, the state enterprises would be transferred to it and a free market economy established. This was the transformation the Democrats sought to carry out and they saw it as being perfectly in keeping with the original aims of Kemalism.

The Democrats asked for political peace, implying an opposition which shared the same fundamental principles, so as to implement this programme. But the RPP, complained Menderes, refused to make political peace and insisted on attacking the government. The opposition's initial accusation had been that the Democrats were not keeping their election promises, but statistics had given a lie to this accusation and the Republicans had been forced to drop it.[25]

The Republicans did not end their campaign of vilification, however. Instead they began to propagate the myth that there was 'no political tranquility and security in the country, that a partisan administration was in power which was doing great damage to the administrative structure of the country. Citizens were not receiving equal treatment and were being dealt with according to their alleged political convictions. The administration was so partisan that everyone in public service was under the control of a kind of political commissar. Not even the judiciary was left untouched and measures were being taken which would render the independence of the judges null and void. The mentality of the administration made it impossible [for the opposition] to work within the context of the National Assembly.'[26]

During their first year of office the initiative was entirely in the hands of the Democrat Party. It met the opposition's warnings of religious reaction and the threat to reform by passing an act, popularly known as the Atatürk Law, on 25 July 1951. The new law was designed both to protect Atatürk's statues and his reforms and at the same time to prevent the 'defamation of the DP government'.[27] Economic conditions also favoured the government. Nature in 1950 and 1951 had been kind and the country enjoyed a bumper harvest, both in grain and cotton, which assured the Democrats of the rural vote in the by-elections of 16 September 1951. The urban working class vote, still very small and therefore of no great political consequence, had been virtually secured by the passage of the 'paid weekly holiday law' in August. Later in the month the government sent to various ministries for examination the draft of a bill which would give unionized labour the right to strike. This bill became the carrot dangled before the working class but it was never passed by the Democrats during their ten years in office.

The Democrats become Autocratic

At this stage the Republican campaign carried no conviction for the voter, with the result that the Democrats won 18 of the 20 seats contested in 15 out of 17 provinces.[28] Success at the polls was followed by a 'foreign policy triumph'. In October 1951 the members of the North Atlantic Treaty Organization agreed in principle to accept Turkey's entry into NATO. In the climate of euphoria, the Republicans decided to maintain a low profile, but that was a temporary tactic and they resumed their campaign of castigation.

The RPP policy of constant criticism did not square with the DP interpretation of democracy and the Democrats concluded that the Republicans were not willing to play the game according to the rules. Deputy Premier Samet Ağaoğlu is said to have stated that 'Democracy is the régime of numbers. In this régime the wishes of the masses are carried out. We, as the responsible ones in power, are obliged to take into consideration the wishes of the mass of the people and not the shouts and criticisms of a handful of intellectuals.'[29] This view was consistent with, and complemented, the idea of the national will and was equally vague. It made the actions of a majority government democratic and legitimate, provided those actions were assumed to serve the people. The people had the ultimate power to judge the action and rectify an error at the next elections. Thus at the conclusion of the debate during which the Bill enabling the government to confiscate much of the property of the RPP was passed, Menderes said: 'If the nation declares that we have made a mistake, we will pay the price like men at the elections in three months' time.'[30]

It is on the basis of this cliché of the national will, repeated *ad nauseam* during the ten years, that many people have sought the principal philosophical differences between Democrats and Republicans. The Democrats were described as the populist, rural party and the Republicans as élitist, urban and supported by the intelligentsia.

The view that the majority party received its mandate from the people whom it served led the Democrats to conclude that they had the right to monopolize and to use for their own purposes all the institutions of the state. This was the mentality of a monparty régime and was out of place in a multi-party system in which most state institutions ought to be neutral in relation to political parties.

The Democrats disregarded this principle and considered all institutions to be at the service of the party in power. When the Republicans accused the government of monopolizing the state radio—instead of providing equal time to the opposition— Menderes replied that this practice was completely democratic because the controlling authority of the radio, which was an organ of the state, was the government. The radio was not common property and it would not be shared with the opposition parties. 'For the last time, they [the opposition] must realize this. We are making all possible efforts to eliminate party politics from the radio and make it an objective instrument voicing the opinions of the state.'[31]

As a result of this attitude the Democrats slowly began to lose the confidence and support of those elements affected by this policy, who may be broadly categorized as the intelligentsia. They retained the support of the broad mass of the Turkish people— hardly affected by their policy towards the radio, the press, the judiciary, or the universities. The intelligentsia had supported the Democrats during their years in opposition precisely because the RPP had become too rigid and monopolistic in its control of state institutions. They had hoped that the Democrats would restore to the system the dynamism and flexibility it had originally had. They found, however, that the Democrats were guilty of the same sin as their predecessors, with the added disqualification of being able to find precarious legitimacy for their acts in the national will.

This explains why İnönü and his party were beginning to regain some support and popularity by mid-1952.[32] The role played by İnönü in these first two years was designed to make him appear the guardian of the state and its values, with only intermittent concern for the voter. The Democrats attributed to İnönü's personality and leadership the RPP's refusal to compromise with them, and they calculated that, if they could undermine his image and position in the party, the opposition would crumble. They were correct in viewing İnönü as the symbol of the opposition. Their task, however, was not an easy one.

The Democrats believed—as did many Republicans—that while İnönü remained leader, the RPP could not acquire the new personality that was necessary for multi-party politics. İnönü was too deeply implicated with the past, and the party could not be liberated from the one-party mentality until he and his faction had been purged.[33]

Over the country as a whole, İnönü's image in opposition still cast a great shadow. Since Atatürk's death İnönü had all but replaced him in the public mind. During the war years, when he used the title *Milli Şef* (National Leader), he was almost guilty of establishing the cult of personality. He travelled round the impoverished country in the luxurious 'White Train' and in the city in a car surrounded by a motorcycle squad, a practice Celâl Bayar discarded. Furthermore, İnönü permitted statues of himself to be erected in public places, his picture to be printed on postage stamps and paper money, and his name to be given to streets, squares, and schools. The Democrats passed a law forbidding the erection of statues of the living as well as the use of their names for streets, squares and schools! Soon afterwards the İnönü banknotes were removed from circulation.[34]

For the Democrats, the relationship between their party and the RPP could be summed up in one word: İnönü. Speaking at a party rally in Istanbul, Mükerrem Sarol, a prominent Democrat and Menderes's confidant, told his audience: 'We have nothing to give or take from the Republican People's Party; the problem is the İnönü problem. If there were no İnönü, there would be nothing between us we could not resolve. ...'[35] This view was inevitable in a political system as ideologically limited as the Turkish, in which political parties became personality parties rather than parties based on doctrines and ideology. The DP became a personality party (*kişi partisi*) by 1954, and the RPP did not stop being İnönü's party until 1972, when it dropped İnönü. It now seems to have become Ecevit's party.

In the last quarter of 1952 two factors contributed to make inter-party relations even more bitter. First, the Republicans chose to exploit differences in the DP caused by the challenge to the Bayar-Menderes leadership. This infuriated Menderes. Secondly, the government's policy of inducing rapid growth produced serious social and economic problems. In the long run the second factor was more serious because the effects of the unbalanced and unco-ordinated economic policies were only beginning to be felt and became more acutely serious with the passage of time. This involved very basic questions such as rising prices, shortages of basic commodities, and inflation, issues which the man in the street understood and with which the opposition could reach large numbers.

İnönü, sensing a serious division in the DP and hoping to force an early election, embarked on a campaign tour of Turkey in September 1952.[36] This tour prompted Menderes to ask: 'What is the purpose of their rallies? Are they forming a new party or preparing a national uprising? Is it patriotism to keep the nerves of the people on edge as though we were on the eve of elections ...?'[37] The tension kept on rising. On 7 October Republicans were attacked by DP supporters and RPP buildings were stoned. Next day the governor of Balıkesir refused İnönü permission to hold a meeting in the town on the grounds that public order would be threatened. İnönü responded by cancelling the remainder of the tour, claiming that the government had made it impossible for the opposition to exercise its political rights.[38]

The attempt on the life of Ahmed Emin Yalman, one of Turkey's foremost journalists, on 22 November 1952 shocked the intelligentsia and brought the problem of the religious reactionaries to the forefront. The young schoolboy responsible was said to be a member of the Islamic Democrat Party, and Yalman was chosen as the target because he was a 'Jew and a mason'.[39] For the moment the two parties were forced to adopt moderate policies towards each other. Even the RPP's attempt to introduce a question in the Assembly on the Balikesir affair ended without incident. In spite of the exchange of harsh words on 29 November, the parties were headed for a period of honeymoon. The beginning of the honeymoon was marked by the Prime Minister's appeal to the 'conscience, common sense and patriotism' of the Republicans and the proposal to collaborate against 'religious reactionaries, communists and other lunatics who are the enemies of freedom.'[40]

The DP-RPP truce lasted into July 1953, one of the longest periods of amicable relations between the two parties. Beneath the calm, however, the government continued its investigation of the RPP's wealth. In Manisa, Menderes stated that the RPP was 'a political organization worth 250 million Turkish liras. Not even the capital of our national bank is so large. Is this a party, a bank or an American style trust or cartel...? Where did they acquire all this....?'[41]

However, the government's decision on 8 July to close down the Nation Party brought the truce to an end. The pronouncements at the Nation Party's Fourth Congress were considered a threat to the Atatürk reforms and the party was accused of exploiting Islam for political ends. As though to confirm the government's accusation, a group of forty members led by Hikmet Bayur walked out of the congress when their proposal that the party remain faithful to the Atatürk reforms was rejected.[42]

Instead of supporting the government, the RPP issued a communiqué denying the rumour that there was any agreement between the party and the government on this issue. This came as a surprise since the 'RPP, as the heirs of Atatürk, might have supported government action against a party seeking to undo the Revolution. Instead it decided to condemn the action as the infringement of domestic liberty, and to use it as a weapon against the government. ...'[43] Thereafter relations between the two parties began to deteriorate rapidly.

The Election of 1954

With a general election less than a year away, relations were bound to deteriorate. Political truce would have been disastrous for the opposition, whose very existence depended on controversy. The approaching election explains the RPP position on the closure of the Nation Party. The Nation Party votes could go to a sympathetic RPP—and that was precisely the accusation Hikmet Bayur made against the Republicans.

In preparation for the general election in 1954, the Democrats began to tighten their grip on the political situation in the country. On 16 July the Assembly Group of the party held an extraordinary meeting and decided unanimously to ask the government to prepare Bills designed to protect the established judicial, social, and political order. These Bills were to be submitted to the Assembly before the recess and the Assembly would remain in session until they had been debated and passed.[44] The amendments of the Universities Law, which forbade university professors from participating in politics, and the Law to Protect the Freedom of Conscience and Assembly were passed on 23 July and the Assembly went into recess.[45] A few days later Kasım Gülek, the Republican Party's Secretary-General, denounced these laws as anti-democratic measures designed to win the elections by devious means.[46]

By the end of October Menderes had virtually declared war on the opposition. He claimed that the Republican campaign was 'as disgusting as the broadcasts of Moscow' and gave a warning that his party had examined the situation carefully and in a spirit of patriotism and had decided that such an opposition was destructive and subversive. The relations between the opposition and the party in power, he said, were not those of criticism, discussion—or even struggle—but only of enmity. The situation could not be permitted to continue in this manner and the DP had decided to pay back in the same coin.[47]

The meaning of Menderes's warning soon became clear. The question of the RPP property came before the National Assembly on 9 December. After bitter debate, the Assembly voted to confiscate all Republican Party property which was not indispensable for the continuation of party activities. Apart from the material loss, which was substantial, this decision was a great blow to the prestige of the RPP. After the vote, İnönü made a speech in the Assembly denouncing the decision in the strongest terms, and the RPP Group walked out.[48]

The Republican Party was in total disarray. This was apparent from its electoral campaign, in which it was able to raise neither issues nor enthusiasm. The Republicans emphasized their claim that the DP was heading towards a dictatorship; the confiscation of RPP property proved this, and the possibility of a fair election was therefore ruled out. In January 1954 İnönü proposed that a Constitutional Court be established to act as a check on the Democrats' unconstitutional activities. Nadir Nadi pointed out that this contradicted İnönü's earlier ideas and his policy during his years in power. Besides, this demand could not be met in the short time before the election in May.[49]

In February, soon after the Republican Nation Party (RNP) was founded as the successor to the dissolved Nation Party, İnönü established a loose electoral alliance with this party. When he was accused of wooing the conservative, religious vote by this action, he explained that the co-operation was designed to give the opposition strong representation in the Assembly, and the agreement did not concern the party's principles or programme.[50] In April İnönü adopted a radical posture, criticizing the government's economic policies, especially the Law on Foreign Capital Investment and the Oil Law, both of which were denounced as exploitation and reminiscent of the capitulations.[51] All these shifts and turns had no beneficial effect on the electorate and proved disastrous at the polls, especially with the Democrats steering a sure and steady course.

For the Democrat Party, victory at the polls presented no serious problem. The party's record during the first four years seemed to speak for itself. The good harvests, foreign credits, and the government's investment in public works gave an air of prosperity to the country and contradicted the opposition's propaganda.[52] Nor could citizens with vivid memories of Republican autocracy take seriously the RPP's propaganda concerning the lack of freedom and security. The average citizen felt freer in 1954 than he had done five years earlier.

The Democrats, however, were not taking any chances with the opposition's propaganda. On 8 March 1954 the government amended the Press Law and prescribed punishment for journalists whose writings were deemed harmful to the political and financial prestige of the state or invaded the private lives of citizens.[53] Furthermore the party in power was in a position to reward its supporters materially.[54] The programme of public works and factory construction had also been undertaken with an eye to the electorate. That is why the opposition had described the numerous foundations for cement and sugar plants as 'election factories'.[55] On 2 May the Turkish people went to the polls and showed their overwhelming appreciation of the ruling party;[56] just as, three years later, they would make known their reservations.

The New Menderes

It was natural that the magnitude of this electoral victory should influence the prevailing political climate. The Democrats' populist image was reinforced and any doubts about the élitist character of the opposition were removed. Before the election Menderes had sometimes spoken of the years 1950-4 as a transitional period which would come to an end with the 1954 election. After that, a new era of stability would open in which the opposition would come to terms with the national will and begin to play the role of friendly critic and junior partner to the majority party. If, on the other hand, the opposition chose to continue its old truculent policy, the party in power would have a formidable majority in the Assembly and the support of the national will in the country to carry any policy.

The metamorphosis in Menderes and the DP after the elections was also widely noted. Ahmed Emin Yalman, who saw Menderes immediately after the victory, was told quite frankly:

The elections have clearly revealed how much the citizens like the road I have taken. So far I have attached value to consultations with you journalists. Metaphorically speaking I used to seek your advice on whether to use aspirin or optalidon as a cure for nerves. Now the people's lively confidence makes it obvious that there is no further need for such consultations. I am going to have the final word and use aspirin or optalidon as I please.[57]

The impression of one-man government was inevitable after an electoral victory to which Menderes had contributed so much. He now thought he could disregard the press and the universities—two bastions of the intelligentsia—and rule on his own. He alienated both, and the consequences in the party were great. Liberal academics in the party such as Fethi Çelikbaş, Feridun Ergin, and Turan Güneş became disillusioned with the DP under Menderes only after 1954. Other academics who had been sympathetic to the DP struggle for democratic politics (for example, Turhan Feyzioğlu, who was not a member of the party and whose father was a Republican) also became lukewarm towards the Democrats.

Fezioğlu joined others to air his discontent by writing in the Ankara weekly *Forum*.[58]

The marriage of grass-roots politicians and the intelligentsia could not last indefinitely. Liberalism became fashionable in the academic circles of Ankara and Istanbul in the late forties and fifties, just as socialism would become fashionable in the early sixties. Those who went as students to Britain and America returned home infatuated with Anglo-Saxon liberal ideals, which they planted in the universities. The fraudulent elections of 1946 had convinced the Turkish intelligentsia that parliamentary democracy could be achieved only with a DP victory and therefore the Democrats received the whole-hearted support of the intelligentsia.[59]

Many of the academics who supported the Democrats were interested primarily in political liberalism, of which economic liberalism was seen as a logical extension. In western Europe the process had matured in reverse; political liberalism had been the outcome of economic liberalism. While in opposition the Democrats had been sincere about liberalism, both political and economic. In power, however, their principal concern was the economy. In this respect they shared the aspirations of the Republicans: both wanted to achieve material progress that would transform Turkey into a 'Little America'.[60]

Factions in both parties reached the conclusion that political liberalism would act as a brake on economic expansion. In opposition the Democrats had been very hostile to this view, held by the Republican extremists. In power, Menderes found that the RPP extremists had not been so wrong after all and that political liberalism did distract the government from the task of economic expansion. By 1954 the Turkish liberals had learned their lesson: liberalizing a régime was not the same as transforming it into a liberal régime.

Menderes soon discovered that the political problems he had faced during his first term had been aggravated by the election results. The opposition was now weaker than before; the RPP's representation in the Assembly had dropped from 69 to 31. The party was demoralized and hardly in a position to exercise the functions of opposition. The Democrat Party's strength had increased to 504 seats, but internally this weakened rather than strengthened the party. Opposition to the Menderes-Bayar group began to crystallize and Menderes became more determined to establish his supremacy over the party.

Menderes told the Assembly on 24 May that the programme he was presenting was not new; it was already well known to the party and one which had been explained and defended throughout the country during the election campaign.[61] The cabinet he had presented on 17 May, however, was very different in character from the earlier ones. This was the first uncompromisingly 'Menderes cabinet' because the election had been won not by the party but by Menderes. Confident of his power, he decided to carry out a major reconstruction of the cabinet and the party. He felt free to bring in trusted friends like Mükerrem Sarol who were not popular with the party. In his new cabinet Menderes introduced seven new ministers and shuffled four.[62] The Assembly Group's reaction to this cabinet was such that it nearly led to the fall of Menderes in December 1955.

The threat came from within his own party; but again he concentrated his verbal fire on the opposition. In his programme he warned the opposition that

... we will not permit the continuation of the preceding period with all its serious mistakes, its irrational, corrosive and dishonourable quarrels, its false political struggle based on lies and slander as though nothing had happened on 2 May. [Applause and shouts of 'bravo' from the left.] The results of the last elections are of great significance and their extremely important and continuing consequences will be felt on the destiny of the country. The recent elections most definitely separate the proceeding transitional period from the one which is now beginning.

This is how we understand the meaning of 2 May.[63]

Measures against the Opposition

Menderes's task of consolidating his position in the party and the country would have been made easier had the economic troubles caused by four years of haphazard policies not begun to surface. Rising prices, spiralling inflation, shortage of goods and black-marketeering forced the government to announce in July that it would curtail commercial credit to importers in order to prevent the speculative hoarding of goods and that it would take other measures to combat inflation and profiteering.[64] The government introduced other devices such as foreign exchange controls and amended its very liberal foreign trade regulations. But all these were insufficient to check the economic crisis that was building up. To make matters worse, Turkish agriculture, which had seemed tremendously dynamic until 1953, began to show signs of stagnation. Production had increased because of an increase in the acreage cultivated and good weather, not because of greater yields per acre. In 1954 the harvest was below average and by the end of the year Turkey was forced to import American wheat.[65] In

October, airlines operating in Turkey raised the price of tickets by 25 per cent if they were bought in Turkish liras.[66]

The opposition now had an issue which affected the lives of ordinary people. Menderes, however, refused to acknowledge the existence of a serious economic situation, let alone a crisis. He saw the problems as minor, capable of being resolved by adequate legislation. He blamed the opposition for constantly harping on these issues and painting a picture which was bleaker than the reality. In fact, the opposition's criticism had turned into something like a self-fulfilling prophecy and made the task of the government more difficult.[67] The failure of the economy became one more reason why Menderes felt he had to silence the opposition.

The Press Law had already been tightened on 8 March 1954, before the general election in the following May. On 30 June the Assembly amended the Electoral Law so that a candidate rejected by one party could not stand for another in a coming election, thereby checking the tendency to defect. It became obligatory for government officials to resign six months before an election if they wished to contest it. Opposition parties were forbidden to put up mixed lists, a measure that nullified the possibility of electoral co-operation between them. Finally, the state radio would no longer be used by the opposition parties although the party in power would continue to use it.[68] On 5 July the Assembly passed a new law which empowered the government to suspend, and, after a period of suspension, to retire employees of the state, including professors and most judges who had either twenty-five years of service or were over sixty. This ended the bureaucracy's independence of the executive.[69]

The effect of these measures was to increase Menderes's unpopularity amongst the intelligentsia, a trend which continued until his fall on 27 May 1960. At the same time, however, his repressive legislation had made his position impregnable to legal attack. 'Today', concluded İnönü in a parliamentary debate, 'there is no force in the Assembly Group, in public opinion, nor in the press which can stop the Prime Minister from the road he has taken and push him towards moderation.'[70]

In the summer of 1955 the Cyprus question had come to dominate Turkish politics and the government exploited the issue to cover up its own deficiencies. The RPP all but gave up its function of opposition; on 26 August, three days prior to the opening of the London Conference on Cyprus, the Republicans declared that they were putting aside unilaterally the debate on internal politics as a sign of solidarity with the government.[71]

The Istanbul riots of 6/7 September exposed the pent-up

tensions in Turkish cities. It was rumoured that these riots were organized by the government to demonstrate to the London Conference how strongly the Turkish people opposed *enosis*, the unity of Cyprus with Greece. But this organized demonstration of high school and university students spontaneously degenerated into a riot—the rebellion of the Istanbul '*lumpenproletariat*, the bootblacks, porters, apartment janitors and mendicants— ex-villagers barely subsisting amidst the relative luxury and wealth of the city.'[72] This mob pillaged both Greek and Turkish stores in a fit of 'merciless hostility to wealth'. This was the first mass reaction against the DP's 'never-seen-before development'.[73]

The government was visibly shaken by the turn of events and immediately declared martial law in Turkey's three main cities, Ankara, Istanbul, and İzmir. Martial law enabled the government to tighten its political control and check dissent. But dissension within the Democrat Party rose sharply as the result of the riots and the Minister of the İnterior, Namık Gedik, resigned on 10 September 1955. In the next two months, Menderes's position had been so totally eroded that he was prepared to resign, so demoralized was he by the barrage of criticism from within the Assembly Group. But he was persuaded to go before the Group and to offer the formula of seeking a vote of confidence for himself while his cabinet resigned. The Group accepted this compromise and Menderes survived.[74]

Menderes emerged temporarily chastened from this experience. But the long-term effect of the compromise proved to be disastrous for Menderes, the party, and the nation. He came to see himself as indispensable; the entire cabinet could be sacrificed, but not Menderes. In accepting this compromise the Assembly Group had violated the principle of cabinet responsibility, so necessary for democratic government. The dissidents in the party lost all hope of being able to democratize the party from within and decided to go into open opposition. On 20 December 1955 they officially announced the formation of the Freedom Party (*Hürriyet Partisi*).[75]

The reconstituted cabinet and its programme were both indicative of the new and chastened Menderes.[76] It included ministers who had the approval of the Assembly Group; men close to Menderes, for example Sarol, had been dropped—Sarol was even sent before the Disciplinary Committee accused of activities which created discord and destroyed unity in the party.[77] The programme was so full of compromise, meeting almost all the demands of both the DP dissidents and the opposition, that İnönü asked rhetorically: 'Is it their programme or our list of demands?'[78] İnönü also noted that 'Adnan [Menderes] is playing for time. He will not implement any of it.'[79] Within a short time İnönü's assessment was proved correct and 1956 went down as the year of Turkey's retreat from democracy, when the ruling party destroyed democratic institutions.[80]

There is an intimate relationship between the deteriorating economic situation and politics. As prices rose and shortages increased, the public became more responsive to the criticisms of the opposition; Menderes responded by taking measures to isolate the public from politics. After the repressive measures, political activity outside the framework of the Assembly virtually became impossible. The law against public meetings made it difficult for a population whose literacy level was low to learn the views and criticism of the opposition. Those who were literate were left face to face with a muzzled press. Only discussion in the Assembly remained free, and later the government put pressure on the press to stop publishing reports of Assembly debates.[81]

The runaway inflation forced the government to resort to the National Defence Law, first introduced on 18 January 1940 when the country had had to face the hardships of wartime neutrality. The Law of 6 June 1956 gave the government broad powers of intervention in controlling prices and the economy. The passage of this law suggests that Menderes was not dogmatically committed to *laissez-faire* practices, as is often suggested. His economic position, while committed to capitalism, was 'pragmatic' and nearer that of the RPP than the liberal Democrats who had formed the Freedom Party. Freed from their influence and pressure, Menderes was quite willing to turn to controls.

With the emergence of the Freedom Party as an important force, the political situation became fluid. Menderes was able to re-establish his hold over the Democrat Party without serious difficulty. But the character of the party changed significantly with the liberal wing in opposition. The DP became Menderes's party and there was no longer anyone with national stature, except possibly Sıtkı Yırcalı, capable of challenging his leadership. Ideologically, the party remained committed to free enterprise; but now, like its leader, it was closer to the Republicans than to the Freedom Party.

In 1956 the opposition, in spite of the burden of legislative repression, became more confident and aggressive. Initially, the Republicans declined in influence and prestige and by December the Freedom Party had become the chief opposition party, with 32 members in the Assembly.[82] But the Freedom Party lacked the national organization necessary to transform it into an effective opposition party and its strength was therefore ephemeral.

The Election of 1957

The sense of political uncertainty which existed throughout 1956 could be resolved only by a general election. The Democrats, aware that they were losing ground and popularity in the country, postponed by-elections on 11 July and local elections on 1 September.[83] Despite these signs of the DP's reluctance to go to the country, by the end of the year rumours of an early election were strong.

On 5 January 1957 Menderes again denied such a possibility.[84] The first sign that he intended to hold a general election in 1957 was the government's announcement in May that the buying price of grain had been raised.[85] This was bad economics because it stimulated purchasing power in the countryside and increased inflation. But it was good electoral politics since it virtually guaranteed the rural vote. The increasing chauvinism over Cyprus—especially while the Soviet Union supported Makarios, and the growth of the Left in neighbouring Syria also strengthened the hand of the Democrats. By seeking a consensus on foreign policy they forced the opposition parties to accept a more passive electoral campaign.[86]

Only on 4 September did the Democrats announce that the general election would be held on 27 October, but an unofficial campaign had been in full swing throughout the summer. The opposition parties had been holding consultations to consider the question of co-operation and unity. This time they seemed to be making progress and were able to issue a joint proclamation of principles on 4 September. The Democrats, seeing this as a possible threat to their electoral chances, decided to present a Bill that would prevent opposition unity.[87] In the Assembly, Minister of State Emin Kalafat denounced 'the joint proclamation of the three opposition parties, who wanted to form a hostile front against the legitimate government in the guise of co-operation, as a document of subversion.'[88] However, the Democrats need not have worried, for in the end the opposition parties were unable to find a formula for co-operation, the RNP and the FP blaming İnönü and the RPP for the deadlock.[89]

In this election the Democrat Party still held the advantage. In spite of inflation the government pleased rural voters, who constituted the majority of the electorate, by paying a higher price for produce and establishing a moratorium on farm debts. The government distributed funds for schools and mosques and used the state radio for party propaganda; speaking in Kayseri, Menderes claimed that under his rule 15,000 mosques had been built in seven years.[90] The tension over Cyprus and the confrontation with Syria and the Soviet Union also helped. But in spite of all these positive advantages it was doubtful whether the Democrats would be able to win a majority as they had done in the past.

By the summer of 1957 economic hardship had become a reality though it affected the towns more than the countryside, and the poorer provinces of central and eastern Anatolia more than the prosperous west. Had the elections been held according to schedule, in May 1958, the story might have been different both in relation to further economic deterioration and opposition unity.

The opposition parties emphasized economic hardship and the lack of freedom, but they offered no appealing alternative. The RPP was the only opposition party with a national following. But during its seven lean years in opposition it had failed to eradicate its authoritarian image and win public confidence. It had succeeded only in regaining the support of the intelligentsia. Of the other two parties, the RNP was too parochial and the Freedom Party too vague and ill organized.

Nevertheless, the election of 27 October 1957 was a major setback for the Democrats. They still won an overwhelming majority in the Assembly: 424 seats as compared to 178 (Republican) and four each for the RNP and the FP. Perhaps more significant than the seats was the relatively low turnout of voters. Only 77·15 per cent of the eligible voters voted, as compared to 88·75 per cent in 1954 and 89·06 in 1950. The Democrats received 47·90 per cent of the vote—whereas in 1950 and 1954 they had won more than 50 per cent—and thus lost the right to claim the mandate of the national will. The Republican vote had risen from 36 to 41 per cent, an increase which gave the party greater confidence.[91]

Instability Continues

Menderes had held an early election in order to restore political stability and calm but the results produced only greater instability and tension. There had been some violence on election day and the Republicans began to question the legality of the election and the honesty of the results.[92] On Republic Day (29 October) there was an anti-government demonstration in Gaziantep and troops were called in to disperse it. Menderes was in a state of panic. He sent his Defence Minister Şemi Ergin to Gaziantep to investigate, telling him 'There is a rebellion (*ihtilâl*) in Gaziantep. The people have attacked the Government.'[93] On his return to Ankara, Ergin found soldiers and tanks at strategic points in the capital. This, Menderes told him, was because the Assembly would meet that day and perhaps the People's Party would seize the Assembly or there might be a rebellion. 'As a matter of fact', noted Ergin, 'once this anxiety gets into those who rule the country, it does not augur well for the future.'[94] Menderes's anxiety was not without some basis, for prior to the elections there had been rumours of military conspiracy and intervention.[95]

Menderes was unable to announce his new cabinet until 25 November, almost a month after the election.[96] During this period there was hardly any governmental activity, though the Assembly Group of the DP was busy discussing the policy of the new government. On 14 November the Group asked the government to take action against officials who had supported the opposition, and proposed more stringent press laws which would forbid 'harmful articles and pictures' as well as legal measures against the opposition.[97] On 19 November it voted unanimously to request the Assembly to investigate the opposition's activities before and after the election to see if they had been subversive.[98] By December there was even talk of amending the rules and regulations of the Assembly in such a way as to make opposition within it virtually impossible and to prevent reports of its proceedings from reaching the public. The amendments were passed on 27 December: sovereignty, which the constitution invested unconditionally in the people, passed into the hands of the government.[99]

These amendments marked the end of the freedom of speech, even in the Grand National Assembly. There were bitter discussions, but when the opposition members saw that their arguments had no effect on the government benches they decided to stage a walk-out in protest (25 December). Not even all Democrats were happy with these measures and many stayed away from the discussions; on the day of the vote only 381 out of 424 were present.

In this climate of political repression and increasing economic hardship came the first hint of military conspiracy against the government. On 17 January 1958 the press reported the arrest of nine officers in Istanbul on the charge of fermenting rebellion in the army. In spite of a long investigation, including torture, the authorities were unable to uncover anything; of the nine, all were released except the informer, who was sentenced to gaol. But the government had received a scare and became even more nervous and truculent. The Minister of Defence Şemi Ergin was forced to resign and was replaced by Ethem Menderes, who was very close to the Prime Minister though in no way related to him. Adnan Menderes did not give this incident very much importance because he was convinced that the armed forces as a whole remained untainted by conspiracy and he was misled by the support for the régime from the senior officers.[100]

The DP and the State

By the beginning of 1958 the government had become totally isolated from virtually all the institutions of the state. First, it had been the press and the judiciary, followed by the civil bureaucracy in the 1957 election, and finally the army and the universities. The Ministry of Education had had trouble with some professors in 1957 and after the amendment of the Assembly regulations the conflict became more acute. Hüseyin Naili Kubalı, Professor of Constitutional Law at Istanbul University, denounced the measures of 27 December as unconstitutional and declared that journalists were not bound by law to obey them.[101] Tevfik İleri denounced the professor's riposte against the measures as inter-ference in everyday politics and a violation of the Universities Law.[102] The following day it was announced that the Senate of Istanbul University would consider the Kubalı case and on 1 February Professor Kubalı was suspended.[103] This marked the beginning of a serious confrontation between the government and the universities, bringing together the two ingredients which played an important role in the overthrow of the Democrats: the army and the intellectuals.

Despite the government's measures, the economic situation did not improve in 1958 as Menderes had expected. Not only did the restrictive legislation fail to provide relief to the consumer, it had the effect of alienating important supporters of the government like the cotton farmers and the businessmen. The cotton farmers protested against the decision to freeze prices; the İzmir Chamber of Commerce criticized the measures to fix prices and regulate distribution and proposed that they be lifted, since competition was the only way to curb inflation and overcome shortages.[104] Unable to cope with the economy, Menderes decided, under foreign pressure, to introduce a stabilization programme on 4 August 1958. This involved a *de facto* devaluation of the Turkish lira from 2·80 to 9·025 to the US dollar. With this concession came the announcement of a $359-million credit from Turkey's allies which bolstered the government's financial position and was described by the opposition as a 'life belt' thrown to Menderes by the Western powers.[105]

The revolution in Iraq on 14 July 1958 added a new dimension to Turkish politics. It made a deep impression on the DP leaders, who now came to see military intervention backed by popular support as a potential threat to their power. It created in their minds a veritable revolution phobia. The opposition was seen in a new light, as being inevitably designed to subvert the government. Less than a month after the Iraqi revolution, the Assembly Group of the Democrat Party issued a communiqué accusing the RPP of attacking the Assembly, the ruling power (the government), and the Turkish nation. The communiqué ended with these words: '... it is evident that a democratic administration cannot work with such an opposition productively or in a state of security.'[106] The Assembly Group which issued this communiqué also decided to look into the RPP's activities when the Assembly reopened on 25 August, and, if it was deemed necessary, to take appropriate measures. This was the first hint of investigating the Republican Party.[107]

Menderes's Balıkesir speech of 6 September 1958 is considered by the Republicans as the beginning of a campaign of active repression against İnönü and his party.[108] It was also the first occasion on which Menderes used the word 'revolution' in the context of Turkish politics.[109] The direction that Menderes was intending to take became clear when he spoke at the party's İzmir Congress. He said that 'just as precautions are being taken against commercial profiteers under the National Defence Law it is becoming necessary to take precautions against profiteers in politics.' He then singled out the Republicans for criticism, and warned them that if they again threatened the bureaucracy, as they had been doing, it would mean curtailing democracy (*Demokrasiye Paydos*).[110] Finally, on 12 October Menderes appealed for the creation of a 'Fatherland Front' (*Vatan Cephesi*) against the 'front of malice and hostility' being created by the Republicans.[111] Menderes, attracted by General de Gaulle's example, was himself in search of a new type of populist régime.

In spite of the threats of repression, the RPP was gaining confidence and assuming the offensive. The Freedom Party, which had briefly challenged the RPP's claim to be the principal opposition party, dissolved itself and the majority at its Extraordinary Congress voted to merge with the Republicans.[112] The Republicans needed to make no great efforts to increase their popularity; the government's continuing economic setbacks took care of that. At the same time the RPP was changing its image and acquiring a new identity. The Fourteenth Congress (12–15 January 1959) marked the beginning of a new orientation in the party, towards a greater concern for economic welfare and social justice and away from abstractions, which had been its primary concern throughout the 1950s.[113] Soon after the campaign to establish the Fatherland Front and isolate the opposition 'Everyone, irrespective of party affiliation was urged to stand against the policy of subversion and destruction which endangers national security, leads our fellow-countrymen to fratricide and speaks ill of the efforts made for the good of the nation.'[114] The government used the carrot and the stick in its campaign, promising to reward those who supported the Front and punishing those who did not. Villages were promised roads, credits, and mosques; and a village which had voted Republican had its electricity cut.[115] This 'populist' campaign was a failure because it could not arouse any genuine enthusiasm.

Menderes's survival in the aircrash at Gatwick on 17 February 1959 introduced a new element into the political situation: the Menderes personality cult and religion, the one complementing the other. Menderes's escape was indeed a piece of good fortune in a tragic crash which took the lives of fourteen members of the delegation. In Turkey the escape was presented as a miracle and Menderes was portrayed as one chosen by God.[116] Religion had been exploited by both parties throughout the multi-party period, but now the exploitation became explicit and uncontrolled. The RPP was accused of atheism and of being anti-Islam while the DP projected an image of religiosity. The Democrats, unable to offer material rewards as they had done in the past, found it useful to offer spiritual ones. The opposition now had another issue to use against the ruling party, but one which did not find a response in the majority of the voters though it did stir the Kemalist sentiment in the armed forces.

The Democrats Lose the Initiative

The political initiative had passed to the Republicans. In spite of his victory in 1957 Menderes was uncertain about his strength in the country and the party. Dissension in the local organizations of his party had continued even after the expulsion and resignation of the leaders in 1955. In a number of provinces, where congresses should have been held at regular intervals, the party had postponed them year after year, knowing that each congress would expose new divisions. Menderes had tried to place his men in local organizations but this took time and planning and he was too preoccupied with problems at the centre, especially the economy.

The Democrat Party was in no position to hold elections in 1959 but on 25 March that is precisely what the Republicans proposed that it should do.[117] In April the Republicans launched a country-wide propaganda offensive, the climax of which was İnönü's tour of the Aegean region on 30 April. The tour had been well publicized and İnönü was met in Uşak by an enthusiastic crowd. The Aegean region was a Democrat stronghold. İnönü's arrival provoked a counter-demonstration and the police used tear-gas to clear the crowd. As İnönü's party was leaving Uşak for İzmir it was attacked by a large unruly mob and İnönü was struck on the head with a stone. This aroused bitter indignation throughout the country and was exploited to great effect by the Republicans.[118]

These incidents stretched the relations between the DP and the opposition parties to breaking point. The Republicans, unable to have the matter discussed in the Assembly, let alone investigated, resorted once more to a walk-out.[119]

Turkish politics were caught in a blind alley and the economy was in the doldrums. The stabilization programme of August 1958 had failed to halt inflation and 1959 was the year of rising prices. By the middle of June there was talk of an early election in order to resolve the political stalemate but the decision would depend on the prognostications of the experts on the performance of the economy.

These rumours of an election were sufficient to trigger off another tour of Anatolia by the Republicans designed 'to take the truth to the people in every corner of the country'.[120] But the economic situation did not permit an early general election and the government could not even risk holding by-elections in the prevailing atmosphere.[121] The opposition was therefore robbed of the right to hold public meetings—since these were now permitted only during an election campaign—and the political frustration increased. The policy of the government became more repressive but the RPP refused to be intimidated. Republican members of the Assembly continued to tour the country, an activity which was denounced as subversive by some Democrats who even demanded the closure of the RPP.[122] There were rumours that the decision on closure had already been taken.[123]

The year 1959 had been disastrous for democracy in Turkey. For the press, which was considered the conscience and guardian of a democratic régime, it was a year of trial and tribulation during which more newspapers were closed down and journalists imprisoned than in any other year.[124] Political activity had become almost totally negative and non-productive, with the result that the average citizen was disillusioned and demoralized. Only the intelligentsia which supported İnönü and the RPP retained its enthusiasm for politics.

The Republicans claimed that the Democrats had taken them by surprise by holding an early election in 1957. They would not permit that to happen again and were therefore conducting an unofficial campaign, calculating that there would be a general election in 1960. The government could do little to check the opposition's activities, except to threaten more repressive measures. But this created the danger of escalation, bringing with it the threat of political turmoil and military intervention. However, by February 1960 there were rumours of further restrictive measures such as the requirement of official permission to hold press conferences and reduction of the period for election propaganda from 45 to 17 days.[125] However, the possibility of an early election was ruled out after the 1960 budget was voted on 1 March and next day the Assembly went into recess until 4 April.[126] Republican calculations based on an early election had been upset and a few days later the party made a declaration that 'it was now impossible for the two parties to overcome their differences.'[127]

The Road to Military Intervention

The resignation of Vehbi Koç, the head of a vast commercial and industrial empire, from the RPP was symbolic of the turn the political situation was about to take. In his letter of resignation Koç wrote: 'I decided to resign from the RPP [which he had supported since its foundation] once it was clear that the inter-party conflict would be renewed with greater violence. I decided that when that happened I would not be in either party and would devote myself to work and activity that I am convinced will be of benefit to the country.'[128] He had sensed that the political situation would become worse and wanted no part in it.

The Republican declaration that 'it was now impossible for the two parties to overcome their differences' was a correct evaluation. In spite of the similarities in the programmes and ideologies of the two parties there was no agreement on the implementation of the programme. Electoral politics dominated the thinking of both parties. The Republicans, convinced that they would win the next election, pressed the government to hold it as soon as possible. But they issued a warning that unless the next election was fair, and held in an atmosphere of freedom, there could be a revolution.

Some newspapers were even comparing the situation in Syngman Rhee's South Korea with that in Turkey.

On 2 April 1960 Minister of Justice Esat Budakoğlu resigned and next day Celâl Yardımcı was appointed in his place. Yardımcı was very close to Menderes and Bayar and he is said to have been given this portfolio because Menderes could rely on him to carry out a programme of reform.[129] It is possible that Menderes wanted to fill such a key position as the Ministry of Justice with a person who would not question a policy of greater restraints against the opposition. Yardımcı's appointment coincided with the Kayseri incident, in which the train taking İnönü to Kayseri was stopped by the authorities and İnönü was asked to return to Ankara. He refused and was permitted to go after a delay of three hours, but this matter aroused great indignation.[130] The government was again embarrassed but reacted aggressively by accusing the RPP of conspiratorial activities, for which it claimed to have documentary evidence.[131] Next day the DP Assembly Group accused the opposition of instigating a military revolt and subversion, and requested that an Assembly Committee of Investigation be set up to establish the facts about the activities of the opposition.[132]

In spite of the accusation of the Assembly Group, *Cumhuriyet* was able to report that 'Adnan Menderes does not favour new tough measures at the moment; he defends the view that the country needs a period of tranquillity, not a period of darkness.'[133] Nevertheless, after a brief but acrimonious debate, an Assembly Committee of Investigation was set up on 18 April to investigate the Democrat charges that the opposition had transgressed legal limits. The Committee, made up entirely of Democrats and therefore hardly impartial, was given extraordinary powers which superseded those of the Assembly and the Courts, thereby violating the constitution itself. Using its powers, the Committee recommended the suspension of all political activity for three months and of all reporting of Assembly debates on the matter being investigated until the Committee had completed its work. On 27 April a Bill was passed empowering the Committee to censor the press, to suppress newspapers, to issue subpoenas, and to impose sentences of up to three years' imprisonment on anyone who resisted or hampered its work.[134]

The creation of the Committee immediately sparked off a demonstration in Ankara, on 19 April, which was dispersed by the police. On 26 April law professors denounced the authority granted to the Committee as unconstitutional. Next day the Assembly passed a law which increased the powers of the Committee, and it was during the discussion of this matter that

İnönü was suspended for twelve sessions for having 'used words inciting the people to revolt and to resist the laws, and openly attacked the Turkish nation and army and the integrity of the Grand National Assembly'.[135] The Republicans responded by staging demonstrations in İstanbul and Ankara, using their youth organizations.[136] The government declared martial law in both cities, and next day, when the demonstrations continued, the universities were closed down. The press, forbidden to report the domestic situation, wrote about the fall of Syngman Rhee in South Korea and the restoration of democratic freedoms there. The implications were clear and the Turkish intelligentsia took encouragement from this, especially when it was learned that the American government had not supported the Rhee dictatorship. Writing after the event, Celâl Bayar noted that 'the flowing out of the university into the street on its own did not signify anything.... It could be only a signal shot. If at the back there were crowds of people ready to come into the street, if there were trained militia forces, then it would mean there was a danger of revolution.'[137]

There was none of this in the wake of the student demonstrations. The people remained surprisingly passive and Menderes was confident that peace would soon be restored, and that those instigating the demonstrations would 'come to their senses by crashing their poor heads against the unshakeable rocks of law and order.'[138] By 3 May the situation had stabilized and the martial law authorities reduced the curfew hours and permitted public places like coffee houses, bars, cinemas, and night clubs to stay open after the curfew.[139]

It was more difficult to normalize the political situation and to establish a working relationship with the opposition. The question was: could the government do so before the army intervened? The threat of military intervention had become a reality by early May. İnönü had told foreign journalists that 'an oppressive régime can never be sure of the army' and Foreign Minister Zorlu had replied that the 'Turkish officer is fully aware that the army should not interfere in politics'.[140]

We now know that military plans to overthrow Menderes were in an advanced stage by May; Republicans and Democrats had some inkling of this and the Investigating Committee was scrutinizing the army. But Menderes decided to turn to the public in order to shore up his position. He addressed well-organized mass meetings in İzmir (15 May), Bergama (17 May), Manisa (17 May), and Turgutlu (18 May). He returned to Ankara on the evening of 18 May to celebrate the annual Youth Day on 19 May, and to receive Prime Minister Nehru, in Turkey from 20 to 24 May.

The demonstration of the War College cadets on 21 May struck a heavy blow to the prestige of the government. Student demonstrations could be dismissed as the activities of irresponsible youths but a demonstration by future officers of the armed forces was something else. The government introduced new martial law measures and Ankara was placed in a state of siege. The cadets' demonstration also alarmed the conspirators, who feared an investigation which might uncover their activities and this prompted them to act with greater urgency. It was then that they decided to overthrow the government on 25 May, before Menderes left for Greece. But on 24 May the visit to Greece was postponed and the next day Menderes opened a new tour with a speech in Eskişehir. He declared that the Investigating Committee had completed its work and was preparing its report. According to Tekin Erer, Menderes was going to announce elections for September in the same speech, but Hasan Polatkan persuaded him to keep this announcement for Konya.[141] If this was the beginning of normalization it came too late, for in the early hours of 27 May a group of officers of the Turkish armed forces carried out the *coup* and overthrew the Menderes régime.

Menderes, during his ten years in power, had failed to create a new balance within the ruling forces in Turkey. He had even failed to give his party a stable identity. The introduction of the multi-party system had destroyed the equilibrium of the political system which had been created to meet the needs of consensus politics under a single, populist party. This system was slowly eroded by the development of new groups within the ruling class, notably the business and commercial groups during the war, and it made way for competitive party politics in 1945. But none of these groups was strong enough to dominate the new politics, and the Democrat Party—even though it paid sincere lip service to liberalism—was a coalition united principally to destroy the single-party régime of the RPP.

Menderes came to power firmly convinced that free competition without any restraints from the government would produce rapid economic growth. Within a few years he found that this policy benefited small groups rather than the country at large, and he was forced to introduce measures restraining economic freedom, with the result that he alienated his own supporters. Menderes, the champion of a *laissez-faire* economy, was forced to reintroduce the National Defence Law, one of the most interventionist laws of the First Republic. Later, in 1958, he reverted to *laissez-faire* principles under the advice of American financiers. This zigzag policy left him without real support from any group except the landowners, his policy towards them having remained constant. By 1955 many businessmen had begun to support the opposition, with the result that in 1960 not even the businessmen were sorry to see him go.

Even in the days of opposition, when there was a great deal more unity, we saw dissension within the party which led to the formation of the Nation Party. But the imbalance in the political system affected not only the political parties but also the entire structure of the state. Initially the Democrats had concluded that the state would continue to serve the RPP and they had therefore attacked it as the ally of the Republicans. But within a few years they learned that the state apparatus was not naturally sympathetic to the Republicans and that it could be induced to remain neutral in the inter-party struggle and to serve the victorious party. What most state officials wanted was a guarantee that they would be left out of the political struggle and that there would be no reprisals against them if the Democrats came to power. The Democrats guaranteed this with the slogan 'we will not question the past' (*devr-i sabık yaratmıyacağız*). Secondly, the officials sought an autonomous status in political life—only then could the state provide a semblance of unity for a fractionalized ruling class in which the groups competed against one another—but Menderes did not fulfil that need either.

The salaried class which ran the state apparatus also suffered most acutely from Menderes's inflationary economic policy. This was especially true of members of the armed forces, with minimal opportunity to supplement their salaries as do other state officials and police (with bribes), and academics (by private commissions, consultancy work, journalism, and writing). Most of the salaried class suffered not only economically but also by loss of social status. Once again, Menderes's policies were too haphazard to absorb these elements into the new system he was trying to create. The result was his isolation from certain institutions of the state which ought to have served his government. The Democrats were aware of this shortcoming and tried to take measures against it throughout the ten years. The culmination of these measures was the Investigating Committee whose purpose was, *inter alia*, to investigate the civil bureaucracy, the judiciary, the armed forces, the police, and the universities. A government which did not control these institutions was doomed to failure and İnönü gave this warning on 27 April, exactly a month before the overthrow of the régime.[42]

68   The Turkish Experiment in Democracy

NOTES

1 Initially the cabinet consisted of: Adnan Menderes (Prime Minister); Halil Özyörük (Justice); Refik Şevket İnce (National Defence); Rüknettin Nasuhioğlu (Interior); Professor Fuad Köprülü (External Affairs); Halil Ayan (Finance); Avni Başman (National Education); General Fahri Belen (Public Works); Zühtü Velibeşe (Economy and Trade); Dr Nihat Reşat Belger (Health and Social Assistance); Nuri Özsan (Customs and Monopolies); Nihat İyriboz (Agriculture); Tevfik İleri (Communications); Hasan Polatkan (Labour); Professor Muhlis Ete (Management). See the Turkish press, 23 May 1950 and Kâzım Öztürk, *Türkiye Cumhuriyeti Hükümetleri ve Programları* (1968), 345-6, who lists the cabinet and all the subsequent changes. Samet Ağaoğlu and Fevzi Lütfi Karaosmanoğlu were brought in as Ministers of State in June and July 1950, respectively.

2 Conversation with Celâl Bayar. See also Celâl Bayar, *Başvekilim Adnan Menderes* (n.d. [1970]), 103 ff.

3 The Turkish press, 30 May and 1, 2, and 3 June 1950. That most of those who abstained were Democrats revealed the weakness of discipline and consensus within the party.

4 *Ayın Tarihi*, Aug. 1946, 5-12 and 18-36; *Cumhuriyet*, 4 June 1950 and Karpat, *Politics*, 171-2.

5 *Cumhuriyet*, 7 and 8 June 1950. This event and its implications are discussed in ch. 6 below.

6 *Cumhuriyet* and *Zafer*, 14 June 1950 and Tekin Erer, *On Yılın Mücadelesi* (n.d. [1963?]), 36.

7 For a historical discussion of this topic, but with contemporary politics in mind, see Şerif Mardin, 'Opposition and Control in Turkey', *Government and Opposition* i/3 (May 1966), 375-88. See also Lewis, *Emergence*, 221 f., 265 f., 279-81, and 306 ff.

8 See Menderes's Aydın speech in *Zafer*, 15 Nov. 1950.

9 *Ayın Tarihi*, Sept. 1950, 2-5 and *passim* for the coverage of the elections; Fahir Giritlioğlu, *Halk Partisi*, i, 288-9.

10 *Zafer* and *Cumhuriyet*, 16 and 17 Oct. 1950.

11 See below, pp. 107-12.

12 *Ulus*, 1 Aug. 1950.

13 *Cumhuriyet*, 5 Sept. 1950, quoted in Eroğul, *Demokrat Parti*, 70.

14 İsmet İnönü, *Muhalefet'de İsmet İnönü*, ed. Sabahat Erdemir, i, (1956), 18. The reason for the Democrats' anger was that foreign policy was considered to be a national concern, above party, and therefore not to be criticized in public. For more details of this incident see below, 390.

15 Ibid., 19-20 (İnönü's election broadcast of 28 Aug. 1950).

16 *Cumhuriyet*, 31 Aug. 1950.

17 *Cumhuriyet*, 1 and 7 Sept. 1950 and Şevket Süreyya Aydemir, *İkinci Adam*, iii (1968), 130 ff. This third volume of a long and interesting biography of İsmet İnönü covers the years 1950 to 1964.

18 Nadir Nadi, 'Partiler Arası', *Cumhuriyet*, 24 Jan. 1951.

19 Nadi, 'Tek Yol', *Cumhuriyet*, 28 Jan. 1951.

20 Nadi, 'DP'ye Düşen Vazife', *Cumhuriyet*, 25 Feb. 1951.

21 *Vatan*, 12 Mar. 1951.

22 *Cumhuriyet*, 18 Mar. 1951.

23 *Zafer*, 29 and 30 Mar. 1951. On the question of Islam and politics see ch. 13.

24 *Yeni Istanbul*, 10 Nov. 1952.

25 *Zafer*, 19 May 1952. For 'refutation by statistics' see Demokrat Parti, *Yeni İktidarın Çalışmaları; 22-5-1950—1-8-1951: DP hizmetinde bulunduğu Türk milletine hesap veriyor* (Ankara, 1951) and *Yeni İktidarın Çalışmaları; 22-5-1950—22-5-1952* (Istanbul, 1952). The Democrats were fond of producing such book-length publications and after a while they came to believe their own propaganda.

26 Report in *Zafer*, 3 June 1952 of a speech by Menderes at Manisa, in which he quoted from, but did not identify, a speech by İnönü.

27 *Milliyet* 26 July 1951 and Erer, *On Yıl*, 68-9.

28 Eroğul, *Demokrat Parti*, 75; Erer, *On Yıl*, 85-6. These by-elections were a serious setback for the Republicans because they had put up some of their leading personalities, including Necmettin Sadak and Lütfi Kırdar, both of whom were defeated. Soon afterwards Kırdar defected and became a Democrat Representative and Minister.

29 Yalman, *Gördüklerim*, iv, 238-9.

30 *Cumhuriyet*, 15 Dec. 1953.

31 Menderes's Antalya and Konya speeches, 13 Apr. and 22 May, respectively, reported over Ankara Radio on 14 Apr. and 23 May 1952 and monitored by the BBC. See the BBC's *Summary of World Broadcasts*, iv, no. 252, 18-19 (hereafter summarized as e.g. *SWB*, iv/252/18-19) and iv/263/31-2. For a full treatment of the radio question from the Republican point of view see Muammer Aksoy, *Partizan Radyo* (1960).

32 Yalman, *Gördüklerim*, iv, 270. Yalman quotes a contemporary dispatch he wrote from Samsun describing the trend towards İnönü.

33 See Fevzi Lütfi Karaosmanoğlu's statement of 4 Sept. 1950 in *Ayın Tarihi*, Sept. 1950, 13-14. This view was confirmed in the author's conversations with former Democrats, former Republicans, and present-day Republicans. It has been confirmed in practice by actual events since May 1972.

34 Erer, *On Yıl*, 78 and Ankara Radio, 25 Sept. 1952, in *SWB*, iv/298/24. Seyfi Kurtbek recalled that, while he was Minister of Communications (11 Aug. 1950 to 10 Nov. 1952), he had the İnönü postage stamps overprinted with the star and crescent because, while they were in circulation, Republicans continued to claim that İnönü was still the president and they produced the stamps as evidence. (Conversation with Kurtbek.) The same reasons would have applied to the removal of banknotes and other symbols of the İnönü era.

35 Quoted in *Cumhuriyet*, 16 Sept. 1952.

36 İnönü, *Muhalefet*, i, 121-51 reproduces the speeches İnönü gave during this campaign.

37 *Cumhuriyet*, 5 Oct. 1952; Yalman, *Gördüklerim*, iv, 273-4. This was perhaps the earliest occasion when Menderes implicitly accused the RPP

of planning a national uprising; he had often accused the opposition of dividing the nation. Later he would accuse it of fermenting revolution.

38 The Turkish press 8 and 9 Oct. 1952. For İnönü's statement see his *Muhalefet*, i, 151. This is considered a key incident in rallying the intelligentsia to İnönü.

39 *Cumhuriyet*, 24 Nov. 1952; Yalman, *Gördüklerim*, iv, 278-80;Çetin Özek, *Türkiye'de Gerici Akımlar* (1968), 179.

40 Menderes's appeal in *Zafer*, 28 Dec. 1952. See also Yalman, *Gördüklerim*, iv, 302.

41 Ankara Radio, 29 June 1953, in *SWB*, iv/377/17.

42 The Turkish press 30 June and 1 and 2 July 1953; Eroğul, *Demokrat Parti*, 88; Fürûzan Hüsrev Tökin, *Türk Tarihinde Siyasi Partiler ve Siyasi Düşüncenin Gelişmesi, 1839-1965* (1965), 87-8; Erer, *On Yıl*, 34. Conversation with Hikmet Bayur. The Nation Party was officially dissolved by court order on 27 Jan. 1954.

43 Bernard Lewis, 'Democracy in Turkey', *MEA*, x/2 (1959), 66; Giritlioğlu, *Halk Partisi*, ii, 12-13.

44 *Zafer*, 17 July 1953.

45 *Cumhuriyet*, 21-5 July 1953 and Giritlioğlu, *Halk Partisi*, ii, 14-15 and 18-20.

46 *Cumhuriyet*, 27 July 1953.

47 *Zafer*, 25 Oct. 1953.

48 The Turkish press, 15 Dec. 1953. The text of İnönü's speech is in *Muhalefet*, i, 224-5. It is worth noting that the Democrat Party was deeply divided on the issue of dispossessing the RPP.

49 *Cumhuriyet*, 5 Jan. 1954.

50 İnönü, *Muhalefet*, i, 247. The RNP was founded on 10 Feb. 1954. See Tökin, *Türk Tarihi*, 88-9. For a discussion of the social basis of this party see Muzaffer Sencer, *Türkiye'de Siyasal Partilerin Sosyal Temelleri* (1971), 243-8.

51 İnönü, *Muhalefet*, i, 250-4 and 259-62.

52 See Demokrat Parti, *Kalkınan Türkiye* (1954), a 205-page book the party distributed in order to present its case in figures and achievements.

53 The Turkish press, 9, 11, and 13 Mar. 1954; Eroğul, *Demokrat Parti*, 94-5, and Giritlioğlu, *Halk Partisi*, ii, 24.

54 For example the Democrats promised to sell to the consumer for only 20 kuruş a kilo wheat which the state had bought at 30 kuruş a kilo. See *Cumhuriyet*, 22 Apr. 1954.

55 See Menderes's indignant speech in the Assembly on 18 Nov. 1953 in Menderes, *Adnan Menderes'in Konuşmaları*, ed. Mustafa Doğan, i (1957), 243. Eroğul, *Demokrat Parti*, 96 lists a number of such projects.

56 In 1954 there were almost ten million registered voters; of these 88·63 per cent voted: 57 per cent Democrat, 35 per cent Republican, and 5 per cent Republican Nationalist. The DP victory was overwhelming: of the 67 Provinces they failed to win a majority only in Ankara, Bingöl, Gümüşhane, Erzincan, Muş, Urfa, Adana, and Uşak. The electoral system made their success seem even more spectacular: with 57 per cent of the vote the Democrats had 93 per cent of the seats (504), while the

Republicans had only 5·5 per cent of the seats (31) with 35 per cent of the vote. See the Turkish press, 23 May 1954; Eroğul, *Demokrat Parti*, 96; Ecvet Güresin, '1950 ve 1954 seçimlerini tetkik ederek vardiğimiz neticeler ve illerin durumu', *Cumhuriyet*, 25-28 Sept. 1957; and CHP, *Seçim Neticeleri Üzerinde bir İnceleme* (1959). There is a useful commentary on the elections in *MEJ*, viii/4 (1954), 321-2.

57 Yalman, *Gördüklerim*, iv, 317. See also Baban, *Politika*, 74.

58 Conversation with Professor Turhan Feyzioğlu.

59 Conversations with Professor Turhan Feyzioğlu and Professor Aydın Yalçın.

60 President Bayar became notorious for using this phrase in the 1957 election campaign. But the same phrase had passed unnoticed when used by Deputy Premier Nihat Erim eight years earlier: 'If we do not run into any external calamity, I am very hopeful for the immediate future of the country. In the near future Turkey will become a little America ...' (*Cumhuriyet*, 20 Sept. 1949.) Bayar told his audience: 'In our country we work following the stages of American progress. We are so hopeful that after 30 years this auspicious country will become a little America with a population of 50 million'. (*Zafer*, 20 Oct. 1957.) Bayar's prognostication about the population seems destined to come true.

61 The Turkish press, 25 May 1954 and Öztürk, *Hükümetler*, 391-424.

62 The new Menderes cabinet reads as follows: Fatin Rüştü Zorlu (Deputy Prime Minister and State); Mükerrem Sarol (State); Osman Kapani (State); Osman Şevki Çiçekdağ (Justice); Ethem Menderes (National Defence); Namık Gedik (Interior); Professor Fuad Köprülü (External Affairs); Hasan Polatkan (Finance); Celâl Yardımcı (National Education); Kemal Zeytinoğlu (Public Works); Sıtkı Yırcalı (Economy and Trade); Dr Behçet Uz (Health and Social Assistance); Emin Kalafat (Customs and Monopolies); Nedim Ökmen (Agriculture); Muammer Çavuşoğlu (Communications); Hayrettin Erkmen (Labour); Fethi Çelikbaş (Management). See the Turkish press, 18 May 1954 and Öztürk, *Hükümetler*, 389-90, who also lists all subsequent resignations and appointments.

63 Öztürk, *Hükümetler*, 396-7.

64 *Cumhuriyet*, 3 July 1954 and *MEJ*, viii/4 (1954), 459.

65 *Cumhuriyet*, 16 and 17 Nov. 1954.

66 Ibid. 21 Oct. 1954.

67 Ibid. 24-7 Oct. 1954. Kasım Gülek was proposing isolating economic problems from politics and holding 'above-party' consultation on the economy. Even Democrats like Professor Feridun Ergin were now criticizing the government's policy. See Eroğul, *Demokrat Parti*, 127.

68 B. Lewis, 'Democracy', *MEA*, x/2 (1959), 67-8; Giritlioğlu, *Halk Partisi*, ii, 21-2; Eroğul, *Demokrat Parti*, 115-16. The measure against the high bureaucrats was prompted by the fact that many of them had stood on the Republican ticket in the 1954 election, lost, and then returned to their former posts. This had angered Bayar. See Toker, *İsmet Paşa*, i, 15 ff.

69 The Turkish press, 5 and 6 July 1954; B. Lewis, as in preceding note; Giritlioğlu, 16-17; Eroğul, 116-17.

70 *Cumhuriyet* and *Zafer*, 22 May 1955. İnönü's speech is given in his *Muhalefet*, i, 323-8, and Menderes's reply in his *Konuşmalar*, ii, 136-53. See also Toker, *İsmet Paşa*, i, 63 and 70-3.

71 *Cumhuriyet*, 27 Aug. 1955.

72 Frank Tachau, 'The Face of Turkish Nationalism', *MEJ*, xiii/3 (1959), 262-72.

73 Ibid. and Toker, *İsmet Paşa*, i, 105 (quotation). There were also riots in Ankara and İzmir.

74 See below, 90, where this incident is discussed more fully.

75 Tökin, *Türk Tarihi*, 89-119, and M. Sencer, *Sosyal Temeller*, 249-55.

76 The cabinet was presented in the Assembly on 8 Dec. and the programme on 14 Dec. See Öztürk, *Hükümetler*, 427-38. Adnan Menderes was Prime Minister and Defence Minister until Şemi Ergin's appointment on 28 July 1957; Mehmet Cemil Bengü, Şemi Ergin, Emin Kalafat and Celâl Yardımcı (State; the post of Deputy Prime Minister had been abolished); Hüseyin Avni Göktürk (Justice); Ethem Menderes (Interior); Professor Fuad Köprülü (External Affairs); Nedim Ökmen (Finance); Ahmet Özel (National Education); Muammer Çavuşoğlu (Public Works); Fahrettin Ulaş (Economy and Trade); Nafiz Körez (Health and Social Assistance); Hadi Hüsmen (Customs and Monopolies); Esat Budakoğlu (Agriculture); Arif Demirer (Communications); Mümtaz Tarhan (Labour); Samet Ağaoğlu (Management; he also became Minister of Industries when the portfolio was created in Sept. 1957).

77 *Cumhuriyet*, 3 Dec. 1955. Conversation with a former Democrat.

78 Toker, *İsmet Paşa*, i, 146. It was also a very short programme.

79 Ibid.

80 *The Economist*, 14 July 1956 and Alp Kuran, *Kapalı İktidar* (1962), 139-40.

81 Kuran, ibid. The government amended the Press Law on 7 June, the Law on Meetings and Association on 27 June. It brought the judiciary under its control by retiring 16 judges on 3 May and six more on 12 June. The measure to prevent the press publishing Assembly debates of an 'offensive nature' was passed on 27 Dec. 1957. See Baban, *Politika*, 204-11, where he reproduces contemporary articles he wrote criticizing these measures. B. Lewis wrote: 'One of the major causes of these restrictions was the mounting economic crisis.... And in a period of economic strain, political controversy inevitability becomes more tense, more acrimonious—and more dangerous'. 'Democracy', *MEA*, x/2 (1959), 69.

82 *Cumhuriyet*, 5 Dec. 1956.

83 Eroğul, *Demokrat Parti*, 138 and *Cumhuriyet*, 12 July and 2 Sept. 1956.

84 *Zafer*, 6 Jan. 1957 and *Cumhuriyet*, 26 Dec. 1956 for the rumours.

85 *Cumhuriyet*, 18, 20 and 21 May 1957.

86 See Defence Minister Şemi Ergin's statement: 'Any foreign feet desecrating our homeland, whose soil reeks with the blood of our martyred ancestors, will be broken to pieces, not only by our army, but

tooth and nail by our men and women.' Ankara Radio, 14 Oct. 1957, in *SWB*, iv/376/12.

87 *Cumhuriyet*, 5 and 6 Sept. 1957; Yakup Kadri Karaosmanoğlu, *Politikada 45 Yıl* (1968), 225 ff.; and Toker, *İsmet Paşa*, i, 207 ff.

88 *Zafer*, 9 Oct. 1957.

89 *Cumhuriyet*, 21 Sept. 1957; Eroğul, *Demokrat Parti*, 142; and B. Lewis, 'Democracy', *MEA*, x/2 (1959), 71.

90 *Cumhuriyet*, 20 Oct. 1957.

91 For the best analysis of the 1957 election see Karpat, 'The Turkish Elections of 1957', *Western Political Quarterly*, xiv/2 (June 1961), 436–59. See also Eroğul, *Demokrat Parti*, 144 and CHP, *Seçim Neticeleri*, 5 ff.

92 İnönü, *Muhalefet*, ii, 167–75; and Toker, *İsmet Paşayla 10 Yıl*, ii (1957–60), 13–15.

93 Excerpt from Şemi Ergin's diary, quoted at the Yassıada Trials and given in *Cumhuriyet*, 10 Sept. 1960.

94 Ibid. Ethem Menderes also noted the sense of fear among the Democrats. See excerpts from his diary in Cumhuriyet, 11 Oct. 1960.

95 Abdi İpekçi and Ömer Sami Coşar, *İhtilâlin İçyüzü* (1965), 57–67 and Ali Fuad Başgil, *27 Mayıs İhtilâli ve Sebepleri* (1966), 159 ff. The latter is a translation of *La révolution militaire de 1960 en Turquie* (1963).

96 The last cabinet included the following: Menderes (Prime Minister); Tevfik İleri, Emin Kalafat, and Muzaffer Kurbanoğlu (State); Esat Budakoğlu (Justice); Şemi Ergin (National Defence); Dr Namık Gedik (Interior); Fatin Rüştü Zorlu (External Affairs); Hasan Polatkan (Finance); Celâl Yardımcı (National Education); Ethem Menderes (Public Works); Abdullah Aker (Economy and Trade); Dr Lütfi Kırdar (Health and Social Assistance); Hadi Hüsmen (Customs and Monopolies); Nedim Ökmen (Agriculture); Fevzi Uçaner (Communications); Hayrettin Erkmen (Labour); Samet Ağaoğlu (Industries); Sıtkı Yırcalı (Press, Broadcasting, and Tourism); Medeni Berk (Construction); Sebati Ataman (Co-ordination). The last three portfolios were new and reflected the government's concern for the economy. The Ministry of Industries was set up in Sept. 1957 and in the new cabinet it absorbed the Ministry of Management. See Öztürk, *Hükümetler*, 441–2.

97 *Cumhuriyet*, 15 Nov. 1957. The government passed two decrees on press advertising and the supply of newsprint on 25 and 26 Nov., making the press virtually dependent on the government. See the Turkish press, 26 and 27 Nov. 1957 and the *MEJ*, xii/1 (1958), 87.

98 The Turkish press, 20 Nov. 1957.

99 Ibid. 28 Dec. 1957; Eroğul, *Demokrat Parti*, 156–7; Kuran, *İktidar*, 134–41; and Toker, *İsmet Paşa*, ii, 29. See also Nadir Nadi, 'İç Tüzük Değişikliği', *Cumhuriyet*, 12 Dec. 1957 for some of the implications of this measure.

100 Conversation with a former Democrat. On the Democrats' relations with the military see ch. 6 below.

101 *Cumhuriyet*, 2 Jan. 1958 and Toker, *İsmet Paşa*, ii, 42 ff.

102 *Zafer*, 6 Jan. 1958.

103 *Cumhuriyet*, 2 Feb. 1958 and T. Z. Tunaya, *Siyasi Müesseseler ve Anayasa Hukuku* (1969), 172-81.

104 *MEJ*, xii/1 (1958), 87; and *Cumhuriyet*, 23 Nov. 1957 (cotton farmers' protest) and 1 May 1958 (Chamber of Commerce report).

105 Toker, *İsmet Paşa*, ii, 100-3; Z. Y. Hershlag, *Turkey*, 147; Richard D. Robinson, *The First Turkish Republic* (1963), 194; and *Cumhuriyet*, 4 Aug. 1958 and following.

106 *Zafer*, 12 Aug. 1958.

107 Erer, *On Yıl*, 341-2; and Eroğul, *Demokrat Parti*, 160-61.

108 İnönü, *1958 de İnönü* (1959), the preface. This book was issued by the RPP Research Bureau.

109 *Zafer*, 7 Sept. 1958; Şevket Süreyya Aydemir, *İkinci Adam*, iii, 377-8.

110 The Turkish press, 22 Sept. 1958; Aydemir, *İkinci Adam*, iii, 379-88; and Eroğul, *Demokrat Parti*, 162.

111 The Turkish press, 13 Oct. 1958. Sabiha Sertel, *Roman Gibi* (1969), 335, observes that the idea of the Fatherland Front was not original to the Democrats and that some Republicans had proposed it in Dec. 1945.

112 Tökin, *Türk Tarihi*, 89; Baban, *Politika*, 369 and 371-2.

113 See ch. 4 below.

114 Speech of Server Somuncuoğlu, Minister of Press, Broadcasting and Tourism, to the Budget commission. Ankara Radio, 4 Feb. 1959, in *SWB*, iv/774/13.

115 *Cumhuriyet*, 12 Feb. 1959.

116 'At the head of the nation is a leader who has been appointed by the Prophet, nay by God himself; he is Menderes'. Himmet Ölçmen, Representative for Konya, quoted in *Cumhuriyet*, 9 Mar. 1959.

117 *Cumhuriyet*, 26 Mar. 1959.

118 CHP, *İnönü'ye Atılan Taş ve Akisleri* (1959). In a survey covering 52 towns and 6,120 people, *Cumhuriyet*, 1 Jan. 1960 reported that the Uşak Incident was considered the most important event of 1959.

119 *Cumhuriyet*, 12 May 1959.

120 *Cumhuriyet*, 14 June 1959.

121 On 20 July the Assembly postponed the by-elections *sine die* and went into recess. See *Zafer*, 21 July 1959.

122 In a DP meeting in Diyarbakır a member of the National Assembly shouted: 'Close down the RPP, that nest of sedition and evil.' *Cumhuriyet*, 14 Sept. 1959, quoted in Eroğul, *Demokrat Parti*, 168.

123 Nadir Nadi, 'Kapansa ne olur?' *Cumhuriyet*, 23 Sept. 1959.

124 See the chronology in *Vatan 1960 Yıllığı* (1960), 5-28 and *passim*.

125 *Cumhuriyet*, 10 Feb. 1960.

126 Ibid., 2 Mar. 1960.

127 Ibid., 12 Mar. 1960.

128 Ibid., 13 Mar. 1960. See also Koç's own account in his autobiography *Hayat Hikâyem* (Istanbul, 1973), 150-1.

129 Conversation with a former Democrat.

130 The Turkish press, 4 Apr. 1960, and İnönü, *Muhalefet*, iii, 74-5.

131 *Zafer*, 6 Apr. 1960.

132 *Milliyet*, 8, 9 and 13 Apr. 1960; Başgil, *27 Mayıs*, 118-20; Erer, *On Yıl*, 394-5; and Eroğul, *Demokrat Parti*, 173-4.
133 14 Apr. 1960.
134 *Resmi Gazete*, 28 Apr. 1960 and the Turkish press, 19 Apr. 1960 and following. See also Nuri Eren, *Turkey Today—and Tomorrow* (1963), 37; Başgil, *27 Mayıs*, 120-1 and 128 ff.
135 Ankara Radio, 28 Apr. 1960, in *SWB*, iv/320/c/2-3. İnönü's speech did not appear either in the minutes of the debate or in the press because of the censorship. It was published only after the revolution of 27 May. See İnönü, *Muhalefet*, iii, 92-7.
136 Karaosmanoğlu, *45 Yıl*, 232-5.
137 Bayar, *Başvekilim Menderes*, 170.
138 Ankara Radio, 29 Apr. 1960, in *SWB*, iv/322/c/2-3; and *Cumhuriyet*, 30 Apr. 1960.
139 Ankara Radio, 3 May 1960, in *SWB*, iv/325/c/1.
140 *The Times*, 7 May 1960 and İnönü's interview of 6 May in İnönü, *Muhalefet*, iii. 100-3.
141 Erer, *On Yıl*, 9. The report of the Investigating Committee has recently been published by the man who wrote it. See Nusret Kirişçioğlu, *12 Mart, İnönü-Ecevit ve Tahkikat Encümeni Raporum* (1973). See also George Harris, 'The Causes of the 1960 Revolution in Turkey', *MEJ*, xxiv/4 (1970), 438-54.
142 '...But you cannot succeed. Was Syngman Rhee saved? ... He had the army, the police and the administration in his hands. You do not have the army, the administration or the university, or even the police in yours. How can this be an oppressive régime? How can it succeed?' See İnönü, *Muhalefet*, iii, 96.

CHAPTER III

ADNAN MENDERES
AND THE DEMOCRAT PARTY

The Democrat Party is a party which has discovered how to overcome the country's backwardness, the economic ruin to which it was destined and how to solve ... the problem of its progress.

Adnan Menderes, speech in the Grand National Assembly, 18 November 1953

Actually this was the party of people who, without giving the matter much thought, were opposed to the single-party system. Although at that time, as is the case today, the country had a thousand different problems which sought solution, those who were gathered round that table were not in a position to occupy themselves with these thousand and one problems.

Cihat Baban, *Politika Galerisi*, 416-17

Menderes as Prime Minister and Party Leader

WITH the founding of the Democrat Party in January 1946, the overthrow of the monoparty régime became the rallying cry of the majority of DP followers. The party's 'historic duty' was to establish a liberal, democratic régime—the original aim of the Turkish revolution that had been debased by the extraordinary circumstances of the thirties and the forties.[1] Ousting the RPP and the monoparty mentality was the immediate task, and the fervour with which the Democrats pursued it is reminiscent of national movements struggling for independence against a colonial power. Former Democrats tend to look back to this brief period of political struggle as the glorious days of the party, when its aims were noble and clear. Indeed, in his contacts with some of them, the author often had difficulty in steering their conversation away from this period to the more confused years of government, which ended in disaster for the party and its leaders. That outcome is more readily understood if one sees the DP as a movement embracing a variety of conflicting and contradictory interests united around a common goal, rather than as a political party with narrower interests and identification. The breadth of its interests was a great asset in opposition but proved to be a handicap in power since the unity provided by the common goal dissolved into factionalism once that goal had been accomplished. For the Democrats to have been successful in the framework of competitive party politics, the broad-based movement would have had to be transformed into a party with a narrower base.

The pressing question after the victory at the polls in 1950 was who should form the new government. The party was not a 'personality party' like the RPP, even though Celâl Bayar was its accepted leader. It was too rich in powerful figures to be transformed into a personality party without its very foundations being shaken. That is why political manoeuvres immediately after the electoral victory set the pattern for the future.

Celâl Bayar was the least controversial figure in the top echelons of the leadership. He was the founder of the party and acceptable to almost everyone as President of the Republic, or Prime Minister/Party Chairman. There were, however, differences of opinion as to whether he should be President or PM/Party Chairman. Those who wanted Bayar to accept the premiership and party leadership hoped that an independent and non-partisan person like Ali Fuad Cebesoy, the retired general, would become President and that the tradition of an above-party presidency would be established. Cebesoy was ideally suited to such office. He had been forced into political retirement in the mid-twenties by his differences with Kemal Atatürk. But after the latter's death in 1938 he was rehabilitated by İnönü and brought into the cabinet in 1939. Cebesoy was elected Chairman of the Assembly in 1947 and remained in the RPP until shortly before the election of 1950. In the election he stood as an independent for Eskişehir on the DP list and he was clearly under the impression that the Democrats would make him President if they came to power. He was even considering marriage so as to be able to fulfil his ceremonial functions more adequately. However, the inner circle of the party decided that Celâl Bayar should be President, and Ahmed Emin Yalman was given the delicate task of breaking the news to Cebesoy and persuading him to accept the Ministry of National Defence. Cebesoy refused.[2]

Had Cebesoy become President and Bayar Prime Minister, there can be little doubt that the fortunes of the party would have been very different. Bayar's leadership in the party was firmly established and he alone could have provided the stability necessary to enable the DP to acquire a new identity. Few aspiring leaders in the party had the confidence to chalenge his leadership. His Apollonian personality would have provided greater continuity and stressed the values of order and proportion rather than the intensity of emotion witnessed under Menderes. But the Democrat Party had been formed precisely in order to end the bureaucratic continuity and to provide a new dynamism.

Adnan Menderes's appointment as Prime Minister did not enjoy the same consensus. It was not a foregone conclusion since there were men like Professor Fuad Köprülü who felt they had a stronger claim because of their age and experience. Köprülü's position as the man immediately next after Bayar seemed established when he succeeded Bayar as acting party leader as soon as the latter was elected President on 20 May. Between 1946 and 1950 he had deputized for Bayar whenever the occasion arose. He expected to become Prime Minister or at least to remain at the head of the party and when he was given neither position he was extremely disappointed. 'I am an intellectual,' he told Yalman, 'I do not have an eye on office but it would have been more suitable for me to be Prime Minister for a while and thus to groom Adnan Menderes. Though this did not happen, I ought to have been given the leadership of the party along with the Foreign Ministry.'[3]

Not only did Adnan Menderes become Prime Minister; he was also elected party leader: all power was therefore concentrated in his hands. This concentration of power was designed to avoid conflict between members of the party in the government and the party administration. Conflict, noted Celâl Bayar, had been the sad experience of the Committee of Union and Progress (1908-18), in which Bayar had been active, as well as of the RPP during its last years in power.[4] In both cases the party had dominated the government and the Prime Minister had been subordinate to the party leader. In order to avoid placing governmental power in irresponsible hands the Democrats opted for centralization. This provided for a smooth and efficient process of decision-making, by-passing both the state and the party bureaucracies. It was also in keeping with the DP's dynamic philosophy of government.[5] But in making this choice, the Democrats removed one of the principal checks on the irresponsible exercise of power by the Prime Minister. Menderes would now be able to silence criticism in the party by taking his critics into the cabinet. This became his strategy and in pursuing it Menderes was following an impeccable democratic tradition, namely that of Great Britain.[6]

The First Cabinet

The first Menderes cabinet was well received by the press as the cabinet of moderates.[7] Of its 15 ministers only 6 (Menderes, Köprülü, Polatkan, İleri, Özsan, and Velibeşe) could be considered truly party men. The rest were either technocrats or former bureaucrats who had joined the party only recently. They were included in the cabinet to reassure the old régime that the new government did not intend to rake up the past, a promise the DP had made before the election in order to neutralize the state apparatus. Furthermore, all were men with no independent standing in the party. They lacked the popularity and local support in their constituencies to be elected without the party's promotion of their cause. Therefore if they wished to remain in the cabinet, or even be re-elected, they had to be absolutely loyal to the Prime Minister: the alternative was to be pushed into the political wilderness.

Menderes formed his first cabinet without taking into account the power structure in the party. This was a tactical error which had to be rectified before opposition in the party consolidated round some prominent Democrat who had been left out. During the rest of the year Menderes made a number of important changes designed to weaken the dissidents. Samet Ağaoğlu was appointed Minister of State and Deputy Prime Minister on 5 June. Fevzi Lütfi Karaosmanoğlu was brought into the cabinet on 11 July as Minister of State in charge of Marshall Aid. On 11 August Tevfik İleri replaced Avni Başman at the Ministry of Education and Seyfi Kurtbek, a retired colonel, took over İleri's portfolio of Communications. In September Dr Ekrem Hayri Üstündağ replaced Dr Belger as Minister of Health and Social Assistance and in December Hasan Polatkan was moved from the Ministry of Labour to Finance and Hulusi Köymen to Labour. At the Ministry of Public Works the independent-minded General Fahri Belen was replaced by Kemal Zeytinoğlu.[8]

These changes made Menderes's position in the party more secure by neutralizing influential and politically independent figures like Karaosmanoğlu, Üstündağ, and Köymen. These men controlled the party organizations in Manisa, İzmir and Bursa, respectively, and Karaosmanoğlu in particular was capable of challenging Menderes. Ağaoğlu, with his dynamic personality, was too dangerous a figure to leave outside the government, where he could criticize it. The other men who were removed from the cabinet (Başman, Belger, and Belen) were too independent for Menderes but they were no threat to him outside the government.

At the same time, Menderes was able to bring in men like İleri and Polatkan who were personally devoted to him. By the end of the year Menderes's position in the party seemed secure. A vote of confidence (375 for and 58 against) at the conclusion of the budget debate on 28 February 1951 confirmed this. Therefore, on 8 March, Menderes tendered his resignation to President Bayar claiming that he needed to form a new cabinet according to the needs of the day.[9]

The resignation took few people by surprise because the first cabinet had been criticized as weak or unco-ordinated, and the need for a stronger team was almost universally recognized. Having stabilized his position, Menderes naturally wanted to strengthen his cabinet to carry out reform. He was expected to make key changes in such ministries as Agriculture, Management (*İşletmeler*), the Interior, Education, and Justice, bringing in men like Sıtkı Yırcalı, Ethem Menderes, and Ahmed Hamdi Başar. However, he made no significant changes and merely replaced three ministers and reshuffled six others.[10]

The party's reaction to the new team was one of disappointment. This was not the cabinet of action or reform and those who expected the government to amend the anti-democratic laws realized that Halil Ozyörük (Minister of the Interior)—he was Minister of Justice in the first cabinet—was not the person to introduce democratic laws. Menderes himself agreed that there would be no change of policy in the wake of the newly reconstituted cabinet; nor would he give up the leadership of the party, as was rumoured. His immediate concern, he said, was to improve relations between the parties.[11] Yalman drew the right conclusions from the events of these last few days: 'Nothing has changed. Premier Adnan Menderes, confident in his native intelligence, intuitive power, fine eloquence, and all his other qualities, has taken the road to monopolizing power.' Then Yalman gave a prophetic warning: 'Yet thousands of historical examples show that it is impossible to assume and carry the burden of today's leadership and administration in this manner.'[12]

Dissension within the Party

Menderes's position with the DP Assembly Group was still precarious and the meeting on 27 March to discuss his new programme was expected to be acrimonious. Menderes was criticized for making too few changes and for being lenient towards the reactionaries who were vandalizing Atatürk's statues, busts and pictures; and four men close to him (Hasan Polatkan,

Sıtkı Yırcalı, Fatin Rüştü Zorlu, and Mükerrem Sarol) were accused of peddling political influence. When the Group voted on 29 March there were 61 negative votes, and this group of dissidents came to be known as 'the Sixty-one'.

A prominent member of 'the Sixty-one', claims that initially the dissidents had constituted about 150 members but that the number had dwindled to 61 because of various pressures. He said that, although the dissidents were not a homogeneous group, they were mainly Democrats who had entered politics for the first time after 1946, having had nothing to do with the RPP period. They had formed local DP organizations almost spontaneously once the party had been announced and therefore felt independent of the past as well as of the founders of the party. They saw the present DP hierarchy in many ways as a continuation of the RPP and criticized it for not offering a genuine alternative in terms of policy and programme.[13]

Rıfkı Salim Burçak thought that this interpretation of 'the Sixty-one' was only partially true, though he seemed to confirm it implicitly. He thought that one of the factors of continuing dissension in the party was the spirit of opposition in which the party had been formed in 1946. This had been carried into the post-1950 period and may have been stimulated by the complaints of local organizations and constituents, which their representatives voiced in the Assembly Group. He added that the question of personal ambition was also a factor.[14] Moreover, the dissension in the Group was complemented by criticism of the DP hierarchy at numerous local congresses. At the Balıkesir Congress on 21 April, for example, there were complainst againts the government for not fulfilling its promises, for neglecting the peasant, and for not purging officials who were partisans of the RPP. There was even a proposal for amending the party regulations so that the premiership and party leadership would be invested in different persons.[15] Şemsettin Günaltay, who had seen similar days himself, could afford to gloat over the troubles of the DP: 'Today the Democrat Party is in a *cul-de-sac....* It is obvious that the Premier and his ministers, who are going from one congress to another, are not able to carry out their day-to-day duties. Everywhere the authority of the state has been shaken and theft and brigandage have increased.'[16]

Menderes found it easier to deal with his immediate rivals in the party than with the pressure from below, which came from those who had not been involved in politics until they joined the DP. Many of them had suffered under Republican rule and they joined the DP principally because they thought the party was dedicated to the destruction of the RPP and all that it represented. They viewed the victory as a fresh start and not as a continuation of any legacy. Therefore they vigorously opposed the policy of 'not questioning the record of the *ancien régime*', which the DP hierarchy had inaugurated. Not only did they want to question that record, they wanted to obliterate the very remnants of its influence.

In terms of numbers it is difficult to estimate the strength of this group. They were particularly strong in the provincial bodies. In the first post-election Assembly this group's influence was significant because the central organization still did not have full control at all levels and the majority of the candidates had been nominated locally. As yet, Menderes did not have the influence 'to put up an ass and have it elected,' a claim he allegedly made when at the peak of his power and influence in the mid-fifties.

For the general election of 1950 the DP had permitted its local bodies to nominate 80 per cent of the candidates, reserving for the centre the remainder. This was a departure from earlier practice, under which candidates were selected by a small inner circle of the party. On this occasion candidates were chosen from amongst people who had local standing and who were members of the local élites. Their approach to politics was parochial rather than national, and they lacked any understanding of party discipline. All this was more true of the Democrats than of the established Republicans. The hard-liners in the DP were therefore to be found in the Assembly or the local organizations rather than in the party's central body.

In spite of all that is said about the populist and grass-roots character of the DP, the party was in fact founded by a small group of former Republicans in the Assembly who then took the party down towards the base. Very rapidly, they succeeded in creating a mass organization which accepted their programme of opposition but was to some extent at odds with them once in power.

The leaders had not had time to forge an organization at the provincial level which was totally loyal to them or even understood their aspirations. In some cases (especially in the Marmara and Aegean regions) men of local standing had been approached and asked to set up organizations.[17] In other cases, when people learned that an opposition party had been formed in Ankara, they wrote to Bayar and offered to set up a local branch in their district.[18] Such Democrats were concerned principally with the destruction of the Republican Party régime and they did not differentiate between party and the state. Many such Democrats were bewildered by the government's conciliatory policy towards the RPP and by the inclusion of former Republican administrators like Halil Özyörük in the cabinet. They had expected their government to begin purifying the bureaucracy straightaway and when this did not happen they communicated their grievances to the party.

Soon after the government was formed, Menderes's private secretary (*Başbakanlık Özel Kalem Müdürü*) Basri Aktaş recalled the thousands of letters and telegrams sent by ordinary Democrats urging Menderes to take immediate measures against the 'Republican' bureaucracy.[19] The DP oligarchy, conscious of the 'national will' which had brought it to power, felt a moral obligation to placate this demand, at least with a polemic against the Republican Party and the bureaucracy. But they did not go beyond words and there were no major changes in the bureaucracy. But this pressure from below also found expression in provincial bodies of the party and here its disregard could have serious consequences.

The hostility towards the bureaucracy was soon expressed both in the Assembly and at provincial congresses. On 21 June the question was debated in the Assembly and the bureaucracy was denounced by Democrats in the most bitter terms. It seemed, from Samet Ağaoğlu's words, that the government agreed and intended to carry out a purge:

Almost all the grievances in the country have their basis in the nightmare of the state official. One of the natural results of the long years of no control [over the bureaucracy] in the single-party system is that nothing was ever done in time. The country has witnessed a change in systems and a competitive system [*mukabili sistem*] has been established. Because of the single-party period in which responsibility was passed by one official to another and the system had no checks, our laws are full of formalism. If this is eliminated everything will move rapidly.

Those guilty of crimes such as embezzlement and corruption will not be employed in state service ... and the [bureaucratic] mentality which can rationalize 'I acquired the secret from the *Mesnevi*. If I stole I stole public property' will be destroyed.[20]

The provincial congress were also marked by the spirit of revenge against the state apparatus still intimately identified with the Republicans. At the İzmir Congress in July, Menderes and Ağaoğlu were again confronted with denunciations of the bureaucracy, and the government was accused of not having acted according to the expectations and demands of its supporters. It had disregarded the 'national will'. So tense and emotional was the atmosphere that one speaker took off his shirt to expose the marks of corporal punishment inflicted by the gendarmes.[21] This pressure from below became an important factor in regulating the ruling party's relationship with the Republicans. While the government could not meet the popular demand to purge the bureaucracy of former Republicans, it could appease its supporters by adopting an aggressive policy against the RPP.

The party oligarchy regarded the pressure from its rank and file as a nuisance but not as an immediate threat to its position. It did not intend to carry out a thorough purge of the bureaucracy since that would have paralysed the government. Menderes had already replaced the few provincial governors and officials who were too deeply committed to the former ruling party to be able to serve the new one. He wanted to put aside what he considered trivial issues and begin to deal with the real task of government, the development of the country.

Menderes's harsh threats and polemic against the Republicans did not appease or win over all dissident Democrats. His deeds, on the other hand, convinced many that he intended to maintain the *status quo* and to work through the existing institutions. Many felt that the party leadership had betrayed them by straying from the promises it had made.

As a protest against this policy, Nazım Öner, Representative for Diyarbakır, resigned from the party on 16 October 1950. He had already written an open letter to the Prime Minister in August and accused the government of failing to carry out the reform of the administrative machinery, so anxiously awaited by the nation.[22] His letter of resignation amplified his grievances. He informed Menderes: 'I am resigning from your party since my conscience does not permit me to go on working any longer among the founders and rulers of a political party which is gradually departing from its professed programme, regulations and the dictates of the Constitution, and which has no regard for the Freedom Pact....'[23]

Menderes was cautious in his dealings with individual dissidents as well as with dissent in the provincial party organizations. He was feeling his way and trying to avoid direct confrontation, all the while strengthening his position in the local bodies by supporting his own protégés. He went from congress to congress in order to establish his authority. But in August 1951 the local organizations were still strong enough to nominate their own candidates for the by-elections in September.[24] For the moment the local leaders were able to have their way with both the centre and the provincial bureaucracy, intimidated by the threats to its existence. This was a complete reversal of the situation that prevailed before 1950 and these local leaders were aptly described by Nadir Nadi as *Parti*

Ağaları, the party lords.[25] But Menderes did not permit this situation to last very long.

The Democrats held their Third Congress from 15 to 20 October 1951. It coincided, not accidentally, with the successful conclusion of negotiations for Turkey's entry into NATO, which strengthened the party's position in the country and Menderes's position in the party. Menderes and the party leadership were criticized but he was re-elected chairman unopposed. In return, he sacrificed Halil Özyörük, the unpopular Minister of the Interior, and replaced him with Fevzi Lütfi Karaosmanoğlu. Furthermore, he accepted the congress's proposal for a law to purge the bureaucracy of those who had supported the Republicans after 1946. The dissidents were unable to make any headway against Menderes, and, with the congress behind him, he was able to deal with them more firmly.[26]

The Assembly Group remained the only check on Menderes's authority, but it, too, turned out to be ineffective. On 2 November this body elected Refik Şevket İnce as its leader. İnce was respected in the party as a man of integrity, with great political experience and moderate views. Earlier in the year he had resigned from the cabinet, and, even though he did not disclose his reasons, it was known that he was opposed to Menderes's arbitrary behaviour in cabinet. There were even rumours that he and Karaosmanoğlu were considering forming a new party.[27] İnce could therefore be expected to stand up to Menderes and to uphold the integrity of the Group against incursions by the government. Under his leadership the Group could begin to function as a watchdog over the government.

However, by June 1952 İnce's influence in the Group had declined while Menderes's prestige had increased, and the Group failed to support İnce against Menderes. On 12 June it announced that there would be no by-elections in 1952. As İnce had not been consulted about this matter he resigned, and in his letter of resignation criticized Menderes in very strong terms. He complained of Menderes's indifference towards the Group and his arrogant manner towards himself. He accused the Premier of avoiding Group meetings, stating that the Group had to invite him to attend in order to express its grievances.[28] On 17 June the Group repudiated İnce's claims by an overwhelming majority, alleging that his letter of resignation represented only his own views and not those of the Group.[29]

İnce's resignation was not an isolated incident; it was the culmination of a chain of events which began with the expulsion from the party of Abdurrahman Boyacıgiller, Representative for Zonguldak, for violating discipline.[30] About the same time,

Menderes dispatched Hüsnü Yaman to investigate local organizations and to purge them of anti-Menderes factions.

İnce's resignation did not come as a surprise. Indeed it gave substance to the rumour, just mentioned, that he and Karaosmanoğlu were going to resign in order to form a new party. The revelation of his reasons for resigning was significant because for the first time a Democrat of stature had criticized Menderes in public. Earlier such matters were considered internal affairs to be discussed and resolved within the party. The dissidents' decision to bring the conflict before the public suggested that they were about to give their campaign a new direction.

Menderes Consolidates his Position

It is clear that the Democrat Party had reached a turning-point in its internal development. Hereafter Menderes gave up his policy of compromise and consensus and went about the task of fortifying his position in a more determined manner. This was reflected in the strengthening of the cabinet and the extension of control over the provincial organizations. It was a difficult task, accomplished only after the 1954 election, which became the testing ground for the factions. If Menderes could be dislodged because of the party's performance at the polls then the party could remain united under a new leader. If he emerged unscathed, then the dissidents would have to challenge him openly.

In the two years prior to the general election of 1954 the initiative was entirely with Menderes. The economy was booming because of the exceptionally bountiful harvests and massive government investments in agriculture and public work. The future seemed bright and in this climate of optimism and euphoria neither the opposition parties nor the DP dissidents were able to raise issues which appealed to the voter. For the moment Menderes was in full control.

At the Consultative Congress (*İstişari Kongre*) the dissidents were clearly told that the party was not a hotel where people could come and go as they pleased. Menderes served notice on those whose ideas, opinions, and organizations did not coincide with those of his own faction but 'who exploit us by being with us only nominally.'[31] It is at this point that the DP began to be transformed from a movement into a political party—a process, however, which remained uncompleted when Menderes was overthrown.

Apart from cabinet changes, the year 1953 was not particularly eventful. Menderes, however, did not remain idle. He was busy eroding the power of local groups and replacing them with his own followers. He was able to do this by exploiting the rivalries among the prominent landowning families in certain provinces, supporting one against the other. In some cases he broke the power of a traditional local group opposed to him by pitting against it a 'progressive, modernist group' composed of merchants and professionals from the town. In Seyhan (Adana), for example, the General Administrative Council of the Democrat Party was abolished by the central organization on a technical point and replaced by a new body. The new council was led by Ömer Başeğmez, a merchant who imported machinery and therefore depended on government licences. The council included a surgeon, a lawyer, the president of the Adana branch of *Türkiye İş Bankası*, and two landowners.[32]

By the spring of 1954 Menderes was sufficiently confident of his strength to override the electoral list of the provincial bodies and put up his own candidates in the coming general election. When the DP list was published in the press on 12 April the reaction from many provinces was one of surprise and bewilderment. Bayar and Menderes were flooded with telegrams from all those who had been left out of the list even though they had won the nomination of their local organizations.[33]

The composition of the 1954 Assembly and the DP Assembly Group was substantially different from that of 1950. For one thing Menderes brought back the more familiar ex-state officials and kept out the men of local standing. Even amongst candidates of local standing, 50 per cent of those elected in 1950 failed to be re-elected in 1954. One can only presume that many of these were replaced by Menderes's protégés.[34]

Menderes's position had become almost invulnerable both at the centre and in the provinces. However, he still faced the opposition of such personalities as Karaosmanoğlu and a group of liberals who had begun to criticize his anti-democratic policies, especially those against the press.

The day after his cabinet received its vote of confidence Menderes introduced a measure designed to consolidate even further his power in the party. A commission composed of men loyal to Menderes was formed to consider amendment of the party regulations—its purpose being to amend the regulations so as to make the party easier to control.[35] Soon afterwards the dissidents began to be purged. Four members of the Assembly were expelled on 9 July and for the rest of the year the press continued to report expulsions from the DP.[36]

The 'Right of Proof' and Menderes's Critics

There were periodic rumours of a cabinet reshuffle. They became more prevalent after the unexpected resignation of Fethi Çelikbaş (Minister of Management), who allegedly resigned because of his differences with Menderes over coal policy.[37] This resignation was considered significant because Çelikbaş was said to be the spokesman for the liberal, *laissez-faire* private sector and was very close to the banker-businessman Kâzım Taşkent, who had resigned from the Assembly on 26 February 1953, but who was still very influential behind the scenes.[38] The resignation also symbolized the parting of the ways between Menderes and the *laissez-faire* lobby, for Menderes had finally accepted the view that the Turkish economy needed state controls in order to overcome the inflation and shortages. This policy was opposed in the party and it was around Çelikbaş that the opposition to the Menderes-Bayar oligarchy began to take shape. The issue to which they rallied was not, however, the economy, but an amendment of the Press Law designed to give journalists the right to prove their assertions in court.

The 'right of proof' (*ispat hakkı*) issue provided the dissidents with a platform on which to rally the party against Menderes. But its appeal, inside and outside the party, was limited and amongst rank and file voters it was a non-issue. However, by the middle of 1955 the dissidents were in a position to challenge Menderes. Rumblings of this were felt at the İzmir Congress (21 March), in the Istanbul organization in May, and at the Manisa Congress (29 May). In July the dissidents found a leader for their cause when F. L. Karaosmanoğlu declared that he favoured the recognition of the right of proof for the press.[39] Even Fuad Köprülü is said to have been won over by the *İspatçılar.*[40]

For Menderes 1955 was a troubled year. In spite of his overwhelming victory in the 1954 election the dissidents refused to acknowledge his supremacy; on the contrary, opposition within the party became more vocal. The economic situation continued to deteriorate and the government's policy was criticized in the provincial congresses—which explains why Menderes was keen to have these congresses postponed when ever possible. It is noteworthy that the liberals did not exploit the government's economic problems, probably because they had been responsible for the policies that gave rise to them, and Menderes could have counter-attacked with effect. The Cyprus issue, however, came to Menderes's rescue, making criticism of the government seem unpatriotic at a time when there was a need for national unity.

The Istanbul riot of 6/7 September 1955, allegedly sparked off by the bombing of Atatürk's birthplace in Thessaloniki, gave the government the excuse to impose martial law over the cities of Istanbul, Ankara, and İzmir. The view of those who claimed that martial law had been imposed in order to silence opposition seems to have some justification.[41] The incident of 6/7 September did not meet any of the conditions of Article 86 of the constitution under which martial law was proclaimed. There was no threat of war, nor insurrection, nor any conclusive evidence of the existence of powerful and active conspiracy against the country or the Republic. But martial law was proclaimed, and was approved by the Assembly, and of course involved the restriction of immunity of person and dwelling, of the freedom of the press, of correspondence, of assembly and of association.

Martial law enabled Menderes to checkmate the opposition temporarily but it also demonstrated the weakness of his government. It was a confession that he could no longer control the situation by normal means. This probably did more to undermine his position than all the criticisms of his opponents. The immediate result was the increase of dissension within the DP; Namık Gedik, the Minister of the Interior, was made the scapegoat and he resigned on 10 September.[42]

The dissidents took the offensive early in October. They raised the issue of the 'right of proof' and presented an amendment proposal to the General Administrative Council of the party. But the Council refused to be swayed and the dissidents were asked to withdraw their proposal. There was a rumour that those who had signed it would be expelled from the party.[43] The proposal was not withdrawn and nine dissidents were sent before the Disciplinary Committee and expelled, while ten resigned in protest and sympathy.[44] The Menderes-Bayar oligarchy always retained control over the Disciplinary Committee and this paid rich dividends in dealing with opponents. With the expulsion of their leaders the dissidents had been disarmed for the General Congress which opened on 15 October 1955.

The dissidents had made a tactical error by taking the offensive prematurely and presenting Menderes with the opportunity to expel their leaders. They had intended to challenge him at the Congress by proposing Ekrem Üstündağ as Chairman of the Congress against Menderes's candidate Rauf Onursal, and then having Karaosmanoğlu challenge Menderes for the party leadership. But after the expulsions Menderes had the field to himself and was able to dominate the Congress completely. He was re-elected Party Chairman and the General Administrative Council consisted of men loyal to him.[45]

With his triumph complete, Menderes brought before the Assembly Group a proposal, accepted by the Congress, on the drafting of a law to require any Representative who left his party to resign his seat in the Assembly.[46] The Parliamentary Group, however, rejected it and Nadir Nadi wrote: 'If such a proposal had emerged from the Grand National Assembly in the form of a law, the Turkish Republic would have taken a terrible step in the direction of totalitarian régimes and away from the Western democracies.[47] The Democrat Party had come full circle: established to combat the single-party régime, it was now behaving like the supporter of such a régime.

Immediately after the Congress, Menderes began to reorganize the party in provinces where his hold was weak, dismissing members of the opposing faction and replacing them with men loyal to himself.[48] Fevzi Lufti Karaosmanoğlu complained that even state officials were being dismissed from their posts because they were said to be his men.[49]

The Assembly Group and the 'Sarol Formula'

Menderes's relationship with the Assembly Group remained unpredictable and this body continued to show signs of independence. In the elections of Assembly officers, the remaining dissidents challenged Refik Koraltan's bid for re-election to the Chairmanship of the Assembly by putting up against him Fahri Belen, and Belen received 147 votes to Koraltan's 198. The dissidents succeeded in electing Şemi Ergin as one of the three Deputy Chairmen, and Menderes's candidate Tevfik İleri was defeated by Burhanettin Onat in the election for leader of the Assembly Group.[50] The Group had shown its strength and ability to stand up to the General Administrative Council. The question was how long it would remain united and maintain its independence.

Tension in the party continued, marked by resignations and defections. On 19 November 1955 'the Nineteen' held a press conference and announced their decision to form a party. On 22 November the Group confronted the government with its most serious crisis. At the time Menderes was away in Iraq and perhaps the Group was encouraged by his absence. Ironically, his absence may have saved him because the Group was unable to maintain the pressure for the entire week the crisis lasted. The Group criticized the government's economic policy in strong, even violent terms and demanded an explanation from, and the resignations of, three ministers who were accused of corruption.[51] The meeting, which lasted four hours, was adjourned until Menderes could be present; had he been in Turkey he would have been forced to confront the crisis head on.

Menderes returned to Turkey on the 24th, but flew to Istanbul, appearing before the Group in Ankara only on 29 November. Again the government was attacked bitterly and Menderes accepted the need to resign, now that he had lost the support of his Group. But Mükerrem Sarol proposed that he allow the cabinet to resign and seek a vote of confidence for himself. After all, Sarol argued, the Group was against the ministers and not against Menderes personally. The other members of the cabinet opposed the 'Sarol formula', arguing that Menderes ought to resign with the cabinet so as not to violate the principle of cabinet responsibility. Sarol responded that the very existence of the party was at stake, and if Menderes resigned the Democrat Party was in danger of fragmentation. It was difficult to think of anyone who could replace Menderes and still keep the party together. Menderes accepted Sarol's arguments and went before the Group to seek a vote of confidence for himself, throwing himself on the generosity of the Group. 'I am not resigning. At this moment your power is so great that if you wanted to you could even change the Constitution. I am placing myself entirely at the disposition of the Group.'[52]

Why the Group accepted this formula by such an overwhelming majority is a matter of speculation; only nine, claims Sarol, voted against. To have rejected Menderes's proposal would have meant finding a new Prime Minister and the Group was not in a position to do so, especially now that men like Karaosmanoğlu were no longer in the party. Furthermore, in spite of all the bitter criticism, this whole business was seen as a family affair and it is doubtful whether the Group wanted to create a major institutional crisis. They would much rather have settled for the resignation of a few ministers but the situation had got out of control and many were thankful that Menderes was offering such a flattering compromise. In a sense, the entire crisis lacked substance because the Group was not united about the direction it wanted to take. It had succeeded in scaring Menderes temporarily but it had also exposed its immaturity, its indecisiveness, and its dependence on him.

For the moment Menderes was chastened by this experience and the Group continued to press its advantage and requested the liberalization of the régime. It recommended to Bayar that the constitution be amended and that a bicameral parliamentary system be introduced with speed; that all anti-democratic laws passed since 1950 be abolished immediately; that the Electoral

Law be amended to prevent repetition of the kind of malpractices witnessed in the local elections of 13-15 November 1955; that a campaign against the rising cost of living be instituted in order to overcome the hardships caused by the lack of certain goods; that the investigations into the conduct of the former ministers (Yırcalı, Polatkan, and Zorlu) be executed with speed and the results made public; and, finally, that journalists be given the right of proof and universities be guaranteed complete autonomy.[53]

Meanwhile, Menderes, unable to use many of his former colleagues, was hard pressed to form a cabinet.[54] He announced his new ministery on 8 December and presented its programme to the Assembly Group on 13 December. The programme met nearly all the demands made by the Group and received its overwhelming approval, with 343 votes in favour, 37 votes against, and seven abstentions.[55]

Members of the Assembly did not take Menderes's promises at face value and some criticized him severely. Ziya Termen (Representative for Kastamonu), who made the most critical speech, concluded: 'Menderes promises in the programme to fight corruption. This promise has remained unfulfilled for five and a half years. The expulsion of "the Nineteen" on account of Adnan Bey's caprice demonstrates that a party may actually be formed in this country because of the mistake of one individual. He himself is the hero who wanted to impose the İskât law. So far many promises of this sort have been made but they have never been fulfilled, even partially. That is why we do not trust the promises made today.'[56]

The programme was read in the Assembly on 14 December; although, when it came up for discussion two days later, İnönü delivered his most scathing attack on Menderes so far, the latter's response was moderate. The Group having approved the programme, the Assembly's vote of confidence was a foregone conclusion.[57] Meanwhile there were resignations and defections from the DP—the prelude to the official founding of the Freedom Party on 20 December 1955.[58]

The DP Assembly Group had done its worst and Menderes was still on his feet. It was caught in an impasse and the initiative had passed to Menderes. It became the victim of its own policy since it could not renege on the two votes of confidence it had given Menderes in two weeks. Thus Menderes rejected the Group's proposal to hold an investigation of the Incident of 6/7 September (see page 54 above); and, although the request to investigate the activities of Zorlu, Polatkan, and Yırcalı was accepted in principle, Menderes never permitted the investigation to develop.[59]

Menderes's Counter-attack

By the end of January 1956 he began to remove those critics
who had not already resigned and at the same time to purge
dissident local DP organizations, which he now had to secure
against Freedom Party inroads. Nor did he carry out any of his
promises to liberalize the régime or amend the Press Law. The
demand for 'right of proof', the very symbol of the dissident
struggle, was rejected by the Justice Commission on 20 April.[60]
Menderes's triumph over the Group, which had humiliated him the
previous year, was complete when his nominee Dr Namık Gedik
was elected Group Leader on 5 June by 152 votes, defeating
Rüknettin Nasuhioğlu (90 votes) and Osman Kapani (18 votes).[61]
On his appointment as Minister of the Interior in December,
Gedik was succeeded by Hayrettin Erkmen, another loyal
Menderes man.[62]

If Menderes had succeeded in establishing his mastery over the
party by the end of 1956, his power was not without some
qualifications. It is true that he had succeeded in ousting those
men who were capable of threatening his position. But at the same
time he was unable to establish his control over the local DP
organizations, and the strength of local influences was often
reflected in the composition of his ministries. It was weak in the
first (1950–1) and third cabinets (1954–5), when the DP had just
emerged from an electoral victory and Menderes felt he could take
liberties. This was especially true of the third cabinet, which
Menderes formed after his *personal* electoral victory in 1954 with
almost total disregard for the party. The first ministry may have
been the work of inexperience. But the second (1951–4) and fourth
(1955–7) manifested Menderes's attempts to appease local
interests and pressure groups.

However, such appeasement was only a partial solution to the
problem of dissidence at the local level and Menderes's other
remedy was to postpone congresses, in total violation of party
regulations. There was no General Congress after October 1955
and very few provincial congresses were held. The Istanbul
organization had not held a congress for two and a half years when
the party issued a communiqué announcing that it would hold one
on 23 August 1957.[63] On 2 August the press announced that
Menderes would open the election campaign with a speech at the
congress but a few days before it was due to open, it was
postponed with no reason given.[64] The Istanbul organization was
ridden with factionalism and in July Fuad Köprülü's son, Orhan
Köprülü, had been forced to resign his chairmanship because of his

differences with the local administrative council.[65]

There was talk of an early election in the autumn of 1957. The DP's General Administrative Council's announcement that it would be held on 27 October triggered off a number of resignations from the party. The most important was that of Fuad Köprülü, one of the four founder-members of the party. He had already resigned as Foreign Minister on 19 June and his son's resignation from the party was seen as a prelude to his own resignation. He resigned on 7 September and made a statement to the press: 'I am leaving today's Democrat Party which has completely lost its old identity and given up its programme.... It is the patriotic duty of every Turkish citizen who has faith in the democratic order to put aside all differences and to co-operate in order to achieve this aim [namely to overthrow Menderes].'[66]

Two Representatives for Konya, Rüştü Özal and Muharrem Obüz, who resigned on 6 September, were even more critical and their criticism was not as politically motivated as Köprülü's. 'Today, the Democrat Party has succeeded in making people forget all its past services because of the ambitions [of its leaders] and their uncontrolled and arbitrary rule. There exists a situation in which very great and mortal damage could be done, first to the existence of the party and secondly, to the country. Because the regulations and the programme have not been implemented, not even the unity of ideals remains in the party.'[67]

While there were many defections from the DP during September, the party also made some gains. Muammer Alakant, who had joined the Freedom Party, resigned from it. Although he did not rejoin the Democrats until 19 February 1960, his resignation from the FP implied that the private sector had little faith in that party; this was a gain for the Democrats. Kasım Küfrevi, a Representative with great local influence in eastern Anatolia, as he came from a family of Kurdish *Şeyhs*, rejoined the DP on 20 September. He was put in charge of the party propaganda campaign in the province of Kars.[68]

Just as Menderes did not trust many of the local organizations to hold congresses, so he did not trust them to put up reliable lists of candidates. Thus, according to information leaked to the *Cumhuriyet,* the party would not permit fifteen provincial organizations to make nominations.[69] When the party organizations saw the electoral lists, they found that 140 Representatives were not included, and that led to more resignations. Commenting on the DP list, Nadir Nadi noted that although there was a large turnover in personalities, the mentality remained unchanged. Out of a list of about 600 candidates, there were many ministers, ambassadors, and so on who personified the old monparty period. If the DP won this election that would be a direct step towards the restoration of the single-party system.[70]

The 1957 election left Menderes weaker in the Assembly, for the chief opposition party now had 178 Representatives, compared to about 30 in the years 1954 to 1957. But Menderes's position in the party had been strengthened. Many of the Representatives who had opposed him had left the party before the election and those he did not trust were not permitted to run. Thus, after the 1957 election, his position—on paper at least—was more secure than ever before. Yet Menderes continued to fear that a vocal opposition would set an example to his own rebels, despite the fact that the amendments to the Assembly regulations, passed on 27 December 1957, applied as much to DP members as they did to opponents, making opposition from any quarter virtually impossible.[71]

Challenge from 'the Mountain'

In spite of his dominant position, since Menderes took almost four weeks to form his cabinet it seems clear that he had failed to establish a consensus. Because of the secrecy with which his task was accomplished we do not know what problems Menderes ran into. Metin Toker, who is never at a loss to account for the shortcomings of the Democrats, can only put forward the inexperience and immaturity of the leader (*iptidailikler*).[72] The reason were far more complex and there is a hint of this in the various guesses published in the press before the final cabinet was announced. On 24 November, for example, *Cumhuriyet* gave a list in which Sıtkı Yırcalı was Minister of State. Two days later Yırcalı was listed as Minister of Press and Tourism, and Muzaffer Kurbanoğlu, who had not appeared on the earlier lists, was named Minister of State.[73] If Menderes had to deal with dissension, now it was only at the individual level from men like Sıtkı Yırcalı or Şemi Ergin, and neither was capable of rallying the opposition against him.

Menderes's last cabinet proved as unstable as the earlier ones and during the thirty months it was in power, ministers were shuffled around seventeen times.[74] He continued to use ministerial appointments as a way to control possible rivals and trouble makers, and, to a lesser extent, to appease pressure groups. The resignations of three key ministers (Sıtkı Yırcalı, Samet Agaoğlu, and Emin Kalafat) in September 1958 suggested that all was not well.[75] In fact, there was a strong group of moderates known as the *Yaylacılar*, who, like 'the Mountain' of the French Revolution whose name they adopted, sat in the upper benches of the Assembly and some of them belonged to the party's Assembly Group. They were unhappy with Menderes's autocratic methods and decided to challenge him in the Group, and possibly in the DP General Congress, which was expected to be held in 1958.

Their first challenge came when Şemi Ergin opposed Refik Koraltan in the election for the chairmanship of the Assembly hoping to end this monopoly which went back to 1950. But the *Yaylacılar* failed to defeat Koraltan though they were successful in having Âtıf Benderlioğlu elected leader of the Assembly Group; in other elections for party office their candidates were also defeated.[76] The following year Sıtkı Yırcalı decided to stand against Koraltan and Menderes took this challenge very seriously. He first tried to persuade Yırcalı to stand down and then made a determined effort to undermine his chances of success. Yırcalı was defeated, but managed to win 121 votes as compared to 228 for Koraltan.[77]

These attempts to defeat Koraltan were serious because the dissidents were attempting to oust one of the founding fathers of the party. Samet Ağaoğlu warned Yırcalı in a bitter debate just before the election that, by challenging one of the founders, he was threatening to fragment the party. It was especially dangerous prior to a general election, should there be one in 1960.[78] Had Yırcali defeated Koraltan, Menderes's position would undoubtedly have been weakened, giving courage to potential rebels. But this was the last open attempt by the dissidents to challenge the Bayar-Menderes duumvirate before it collapsed on 27 May 1960.

Too much of Menderes's time and energy, during the decade he was Prime Minister and party leader, were devoted to maintaining control over the party. This was bound to happen in such a broad-based and loosely knit formation as the DP, whose original purpose had been the overthrow of the Republican Party. In contrast to the RPP, the DP had been set up on the basis of greater freedom and democracy at the local level, and this had led to its rapid growth and success. But in power those virtues proved to be obstacles to the ruling oligarchy, and Menderes had had to clip the wings of his party organization. Dissension had continued, nevertheless, and by the spring of 1958 he considered reforming the party from top to bottom, replacing the democratic structure—which had already been eroded—with a hierarchical one. Menderes wanted this to be carried out after the General Congress and to be completed before the end of the year.[79]

In August 1958 there was talk of abolishing party establishments at their grass-roots level, namely at the level of the village (*ocak*) and the sub-district (*bucak*). These rumours came as a surprise to many Democrats because that was where the strength of the party lay. But Menderes claimed that political hostility between the opposition parties and the Democrats had now seeped through to the lowest levels and was dividing the country. The lower-level bodies had become so influential that they interfered with the working of the local bureaucracy, undermining its efficiency and neutrality. Finally, politics at the village level were even interfering with productivity. However, if the *ocak* and *bucak* organizations were abolished, noted Nadir Nadi, it would mean the elimination of the peasant from politics since the parties would no longer be able to make contact with him at the lowest level.[80] Once again the peasant would be left at the mercy of local forces, the landowner and the Şeyh, as he had been during the RPP period.

There was too much dissension in the provincial organizations for Menderes to be able to hold local congresses, let alone a general congress. It is doubtful whether the local forces released by the multi-party system would have surrendered their newly acquired influence without a struggle. Menderes never put them to the test. But the military régime which overthrew him carried out his plan and abolished these bodies by administrative decree.[81]

Menderes's policy towards both the opposition parties and his own dissidents suggests that he had reached an impasse. About the same time as the party was considering a thorough reorganization, Menderes, disillusioned with democracy as it had functioned in Turkey since 1950, threatened to impose 'a new form of democracy' (*yeni tarz demokrasi*) which would require closing down the opposition parties.[82] Soon after this he proposed to establish a 'Fatherland Front' in order to restore unity to the nation and counteract 'subversive activities'. All the signs seemed to lead away from multi-party politics back towards the rule of one party.

It would be easy to place all the blame for this state of affairs on the Bayar–Menderes duumvirate, but, in fact, the reasons for it were far more complex. Menderes came to power at the head of a diverse coalition of forces—businessmen, landowners, small-town artisans and traders, professionals and intellectuals, and even bureaucrats—all united by their opposition to the RPP. In power, Bayar and Menderes were concerned with Turkey's development and the need to catch up with the West in as short a time as possible. They found they could not please all the pressure groups which supported them. Menderes's governments were in some sense *interim* governments, formed at a time when the ruling class was in flux and no group had as yet emerged to dominate the political scene—a process that began in the mid-sixties and is still going on.

If any group benefited from Menderes's policies it was the landowners; his policy towards them remained constant and the rural vote became the foundation of his electoral success. The businessmen were content with him until the mid-fifties, when he was forced to reconsider *laissez-faire* policies and adopt controls to stabilize the economy. It was then that many of them switched their allegiance to the RPP, and by 1960 the Democrats were even accused of extorting money from businessmen no longer willing to make voluntary contributions to party funds.[83]

Those who had supported the Democrats because of their hostility towards the state apparatus were disillusioned by Menderes's reconciliation with former Republican bureaucrats. The bureaucracy generally remained suspicious because of his policy of subordinating the state to the party, though Menderes himself was convinced that he had won the loyalty of the state by rewarding bureaucrats and army officers. Although Menderes's position in the party lacked underpinning from the organization, his charismatic personality, which acquired greater force throughout the decade, held the voter captive, and that in turn tied the party to him.

NOTES

1 Ağaoğlu, *İki Parti*, 4-5; and conversations with Ağaoğlu and other former Democrats.

2 Yalman, *Gördüklerim*, iv, 220; Bayar, *Başvekilim Menderes*, 106-7.

3 Yalman, as previous note and Orhan Cemal Fersoy, *Adnan Menderes* (1971), 103.

4 Fersoy, as previous note, 251.

5 Conversation with Ağaoğlu. See also Samet Ağaoğlu, *Arkadaşım Menderes* (1967), 90; and Bayar, *Başvekilim Menderes*, 108.

6 See Richard Crossman, *The Myths of Cabinet Government* (Cambridge, Mass., 1972), 30 ff.

7 See above, 68, n. 1.

8 These changes are listed in Öztürk, *Hükümetler*, 345.

9 *Zafer*, 9 Mar. 1951.

10 The Turkish press, 10 Mar. 1951 and Öztürk, *Hükümetler*, 369-70. The composition of the cabinet was as follows: Menderes (Prime Minister); S. Ağaoğlu (Deputy PM and State); Refik Şevket İnce (State); Rüknettin Nasuhioğlu (Justice); Hulusi Köymen (National Defence);

Halil Özyörük (Interior); Professor Fuad Köprülü (External Affairs); Hasan Polatkan (Finance); Tevfik İleri (National Education); Kemal Zeytinoğlu (Public Works); Professor Muhlis Ete (Economy and Trade); Ekrem Hayri Üstündağ (Health and Social Assistance); Professor Rıfkı Salim Burçak (Customs and Monopolies); Nedim Ökmen (Agriculture); Seyfi Kurtbek (Communications); Nuri Özsan (Labour); Hakkı Gedik (Management).

11 *Cumhuriyet*, 11 Mar. 1951.

12 *Vatan*, 11 Mar. 1951, Quoted in Yalman, *Gördüklerim*, iv, 242.

13 Conversation with a former Democrat.

14 Conversation with Rıfkı Salim Burçak.

15 *Cumhuriyet*, 22 Apr. 1951. See also the reports on the congress in Bursa (12 May), Manisa (17 May), Adana (28–9 May), and Ankara (3 June) in Turkish newspapers of the following day.

16 *Cumhuriyet*, 18 June 1951.

17 For example, Hulusi Köymen in Bursa. Conversation with his son, Feridun Köymen.

18 Cemal Özbey, in his *Demokrat Partiyi Nasıl Kapattırdım* (1961), 18, claims that his relatives were involved in such activity in Malatya province.

19 Conversation with Basri Aktaş.

20 *Cumhuriyet*, 22 June 1950. Ağaoğlu understood the mentality of the bureaucracy perfectly, having resigned from it in 1945. His reference to 'Mesnevi' is an allusion to the *Mesnevi-i Manevi* of Celâleddin Rumi, a thirteenth-century classic on Sufi lore.

21 *Anadolu* (İzmir), 15 July 1950, reproduced in *Ayın Tarihi*, July 1950, 5–6.

22 *Cumhuriyet*, 23 Aug. 1950.

23 Ibid., 17 Oct. 1950. The Freedom Pact referred to certain principles accepted at the first congress of the DP in Jan. 1947. These principles included: the amendment of anti-constitutional laws and the separation of the Presidency from the Party Chairmanship. See Karpat, *Politics*, 182 and Esirci, *Menderes*, 38–43.

24 *Zafer*, 13 Aug. 1951.

25 *Cumhuriyet*, 7 Sept. 1951. Before 1950 the bureaucracy had dominated the local bodies. The local party boss was often the provincial governor.

26 The Turkish press, 15–21 Oct. 1951. See also Fahri Belen, *Demokrasiden Diktatörlüğe* (1960), 62–6; Yalman, *Gördüklerim*, iv, 250; and Eroğul, *Demokrat Parti*, 77–8.

27 *Cumhuriyet*, 29, 31 Mar. and 1 Apr. 1952.

28 Ibid. 15 and 16 June 1952.

29 *Zafer*, 18 June 1952. F. L. Karaosmanoğlu resigned on 7 Apr. and as usual he refused to disclose his reasons even though his rivalry and differences with Menderes were an open secret. See *Cumhuriyet*, 8 and 9 Apr. 1952.

30 *Cumhuriyet*, 8 Feb. 1952.

31 *Cumhuriyet*, 8 Feb. 1953.

100   *The Turkish Experiment in Democracy*

32 Ibid., 26 Feb. 1954; dissension in the DP organization at Seyhan had been rife since 1951. See Yalman, *Gördüklerim*, iv, 247. There is a need for studies on the character and composition of the provincial organizations of the parties, and until we have such studies our views are bound to remain impressionistic. George Prather of the University of California, Berkeley, has undertaken such a study of the DP (1946–54) and I am indebted to him for confirming some of my impressions. It is to be hoped that his study will soon be published.

33 *Cumhuriyet*, 13 and 14 Apr. 1954.

34 Baban, *Politika*, 74; Howard A. Reed, 'Revival of Islam in Secular Turkey', *MEJ*, viii/3 (1954), 279; and Frey, *The Turkish Political Élite*. Frey examines the changing character of the 'political élite' from 1920 to 1957 and provides useful insight.

35 *Cumhuriyet*, 28 May 1954. The comission consisted of Âtıf Benderlioğlu, Osman Kavrak, Samet Ağaoğlu, Rauf Onursal, Zühtü Velibeşe, Hüsnü Yaman, and Kâmil Gündeş.

36 Ibid., 10 July, 5 Sept., 6, 9 and 13 Nov. and 19 Dec. 1954.

37 Ibid., 7 and 8 Dec. 1954. See also newspapers for 25 Oct. and 18 Nov. 1954.

38 Conversations with former Democrats. Samet Ağaoğlu replaced Çelikbaş as Minister of Management. For a well-documented polemic against Fethi Çelikbaş and his 'anti-national capitalist' position see Muammer Aksoy, *Sanayi Bakanı Çelikbaş'ın, Rejime, Hukuka ve Memleket Menfaatlerine Aykırı Tutumu* (1963).

39 *Cumhuriyet*, 22 July 1955; Toker, *İsmet Paşa*, i, 77–80.

40 Toker, ibid., 76.

41 Belen, *Demokrasi*, 42–4.

42 Zafer, 11 Sept. 1955; Toker, *İsmet Paşa*, i, 106 ff. and Eroğul, *Demokrat Parti*, 127.

43 *Cumhuriyet*, 9 Oct. 1955.

44 Eroğul, *Demokrat Parti*, 127–8; Baban, *Politika*, 387 ff. Those who were expelled or resigned came to be known as 'the Nineteen' and they included some very prominent Democrats like F. L. Karaosmanoğlu, Fethi Çelikbaş, Ekrem Hayri Üstündağ, Raif Aybars, Ekrem Alican, Enver Güreli, and Turan Güneş. The result was that opposition to Menderes was left without leadership.

45 The Turkish press, 15–19 Oct. 1955; Eroğul, *Demokrat Parti*, 128.

46 *Zafer*, 19 Oct. 1955; Baban, *Politika*, 184 and 189; Toker, *İsmet Paşa*, 119. (The law was known as the 'Silence Law' (*İskât Kanunu.*) Before the congress there was even talk of abolishing the grass-roots organizations of the political parties, the *ocaks* and *bucaks*.

47 'Bravo Gruba', *Cumhuriyet*, 1 Nov. 1955. Commenting on the same trend, *The Economist*, 26 Nov. 1955 wrote: 'Paradoxically, the present Turkish government, which in its foreign policy shows a lively sense of the need to guard against Communist totalitarianism, in its domestic policies is showing a grave tendency to slip towards authoritarian rule.'

48 *Cumhuriyet*, 23 Oct. 1955 and Eroğul, *Demokrat Parti*, 129. The provinces where Menderes was faced with hostile organizations were

Diyarbakır, Urfa, Elazığ in eastern Anatolia, Adana and Mersin in the southeast, and Edirne, Kırklareli, Tekirdağ, Istanbul, Kocaeli, Bursa, Manisa, İzmir, and Burdur in the Thrace-Marmara-Aegean region.

49 *Cumhuriyet*, 30 Oct. 1955. For the atmosphere prevailing in the party at this time, see Baban, *Politika*, 186.

50 *Zafer*, 31 Oct. 1955; Belen, *Demokrasi*, 57-60; and Nadir Nadi, 'Bravo Gruba', *Cumhuriyet*, 1 Nov. 1955.

51 *Cumhuriyet*, 23 Nov. 1955. The ministers were: Sıtkı Yırcalı (Economy and Trade), Hasan Polatkan (Finance), and Fatin Rüştü Zorlu (Foreign Affairs).

52 Erer, *On Yıl*, 260. Ahmed Hamdi Başar, *Yaşadığımız Devrin İçyüzü* (1960), 114, gives a slightly different version of the quotation and Menderes is alleged to have told the Group that it possessed the power to restore even the Caliphate. See also Sevket Süreyya Aydemir, *Menderes'in Dramı* (1969), 257-8.

53 *Cumhuriyet*, 6 Dec. 1955.

54 See n. 10 above, Menderes brought in nine new ministers.

55 *Cumhuriyet* and *Zafer*, 14 and 15 Dec. 1955.

56 *Cumhuriyet*, 14 Dec. 1955. The *İskât* 'law' refers to the proposal that a Representative who changed his party should be required to resign his seat in the Assembly. See above, 90.

57 See the Turkish press, 15-17 Dec. 1955. The text of the programme is in Öztürk, *Hükümetler*, 429-61, İnönü's criticism in his *Muhalefet*, i, 342-58.

58 See above, 54-5. Among those who defected from the DP to join the new party were Dr Yusuf Azizoğlu and Muammer Alakant.

59 See the Turkish press, 11 and 17 Jan. 1956. The investigation ended in June and the Assembly found the three men innocent of the charges levelled against them. See *Cumhuriyet*, 21 June 1956.

60 *Cumhuriyet*, 21 Apr. 1956.

61 *Zafer*, 6 June 1956.

62 *Cumhuriyet*, 26 Dec. 1956. Erkmen was related by marriage to Samet Ağaoğlu.

63 *Cumhuriyet*, 23 and 26 July 1957.

64 Ibid., 21 Aug. 1957.

65 Ibid., 5 and 19 July 1957; Eroğul, *Demokrat Parti*, 141. Orhan Köprülü joined the Freedom Party on 23 Aug.

66 *Cumhuriyet*, 8 Sept. 1957; Eroğul, *Demokrat Parti*, 140-41.

67 Ibid., 7 Sept. 1957.

68 Toker, *İsmet Paşa*, i, 67. According to some former Democrats known to the author, Muammer Alakant had strong connections with business circles and was considered 'Kâzım Taşkent's man'. In 1959 he became president of the board of directors of the Central Bank.

69 26 Sept. 1957. These provincial organizations were: İzmir, Manisa, Burdur, Zonguldak, Çankırı, Ankara, Kırşehir, İçel, Gaziantep, Adıyaman, Diyarbakır, Elazığ, Erzurum, Kars, and Van.

70 *Cumhuriyet*, 9 Oct. 1957.

71 See above, 58.

72 Toker, İsmet Paşa, ii, 17.

73 Cumhuriyet, 26 Nov. 1957. For the cabinet see 73 above, n. 96. It is worth noting that this ministry came to include three Republicans who defected to Menderes: Lütfi Kırdar, Server Somuncuoğlu, and Sebati Ataman.

74 See Öztürk, Hükümetler, 441-2.

75 Toker, İsmet Paşa, ii, 111-12.

76 Ibid., 138, and Cumhuriyet, 1 and 14 Nov. 1958.

77 Cumhuriyet, 1 Nov. 1959. For pre-election manoeuvres see ibid., 16, 22 and 25 Oct. and Toker, İsmet Paşa, ii, 191-5. According to a former Democrat, Sıtkı Yırcalı's aim in challenging Koraltan was to restore democracy in the party.

78 Cumhuriyet, 1 Nov. 1959.

79 Ibid., 13 Apr. 1959.

80 Ibid., 27 Aug. 1958 and N. Nadi, 'Tuhaf Gerçekler,' ibid., 28 Aug. 1958.

81 Resmi Gazete, 6 July 1960; MER, 1960, 444.

82 Menderes's İzmir speech in the Turkish press, 22 Sept. 1958; Eroğul, Demokrat Parti, 172.

83 Hıfzı Oğuz Bekata, Birinci Cumhuriyet Biterken (1960), 34, put down a written question in the Assembly in Mar. 1960. For the government's reply to such allegations see Deputy PM Medeni Berk's statement in Cumhuriyet, 28 Mar. 1960. See also Toker, İsmet Paşa, ii, 214. According to Cumhuriyet, 14 June 1960, during the last few months before Menderes's fall, private firms made contributions totalling more than TL 25 million; between 1 Mar. and 13 Apr. 1960, TL 3,385,000 were deposited in the Yeni Cami branch of İş Bankası. All the big firms in Istanbul contributed: Yapı ve Kredi Bankası gave TL 500,000; Osmanlı Bankası TL 200,000; Akbank TL 250,000; and Eczacıbaşı TL 50,000. For financial contributions in İzmir see Cumhuriyet, 15 June 1960; also 9 Aug. and 15 Sept. 1960 for further revelations.

CHAPTER IV

THE REPUBLICAN PEOPLE'S PARTY IN OPPOSITION

The discipline of the barracks dominates the [Republican] People's Party. This must be replaced immediately by democratic discipline. Otherwise the Party will lose a great deal.

Halil Menteşe's statement to *Cumhuriyet*, 28 August 1946

The leader of the Republican People's Party has not remained faithful to any idea. Very often he has destroyed what he built up in his lifetime.

Turhan Feyzioğlu, *Yeni Tanin*, 3 May 1968

The Search for a New Identity

ON 14 May 1950 the Republican People's Party became the chief opposition party after twenty-seven years in power. Unprepared for this new role, the Republicans were faced with the problem of changing their identity in order to meet their new responsibilities, and that proved to be a painful process. The initial reaction of the party to this generally unexpected defeat was paralysed shock. The Republicans accepted defeat and promised to extend the hand of friendship to the new government. They expected to enjoy freedom of speech—and therefore of criticism—but undertook not to concentrate their fire on personalities. They pledged themselves to be tolerant/and asked for toleration in return; and they offered to join the Democrat Party in opposing communism and reaction.[1]

İsmet İnönü, Chairman of the RPP, told Ahmed Emin Yalman that his party would not exploit the inexperience of the Democrats; on the contrary, they would give them all the help and support necessary. 'For the first two years there will not be any bitter criticism from us and we shall begin our duty of opposition only after that.'[2] The Republicans rationalized their new role by claiming that between 1945 and 1950 they had supervised one phase of a great revolution—the transfer of power via the ballot box; now it was their duty to see the new phase through, namely the establishment of the new government on a secure and democratic base.[3]

Behind this façade of confidence and moderation the party was demoralized and in disarray. The election had been disastrous and had involved the defeat of many leading Republicans. With nearly 40 per cent of the vote, the party had only 14 per cent of the seats. The Assembly Group was weak in comparison with the party's General Administrative Council (*Genel İdare Kurulu*), which consisted of the most influential men—former ministers like Cavit Oral, Nihat Erim, Kemal Satir, Cemil Sait Barlas, and Necmettin Sadak. Many of these politicians had a vested interest in adopting a hard line towards the party in power and keeping up the pressure, since moderation would lead to their eclipse. Political observers foresaw the important role which these Republicans outside the Assembly would play in formulating policy, but few would have guessed the extent of their influence. Initially it was they who instigated the RPP to adopt an aggressively critical attitude towards the Democrats—which poisoned relations between the parties.

To some extent the leaders used this aggressive policy in order to counteract the demoralization. Until the party was revitalized and reformed an active policy of criticism would give the illusion of vitality. The danger was that the leaders might take the illusion for the reality and forgo reform. This was the question dogging the RPP: would it be able to reform, and transform, itself into a serious opposition?

The RPP had never been a political party in the true sense of the word. It had originated as a coalition of conflicting groups united in a national struggle against foreign aggression and the internal allies of that aggression, and the coalition had been retained throughout the twenty-seven years in power. This alliance of social forces had functioned more or less smoothly during the monoparty period but was found totally lacking once multi-party politics were introduced.

Democratic life [noted Necmettin Sadak] means the struggle of ideas and differences in principles and views. So far we have not witnessed this.... For four years [1946-50] there has only been the conflict between government and opposition....

... Today these conditions and circumstances [of the monoparty period] no longer exist and the party's old sources of power have been exhausted. It is no longer possible to continue with the old mentality and outdated principles. New conditions call for a rejuvenated structure and new qualities.[4]

The adoption of ideas and principles different from those of the Democrats was essential both for the vitality of democratic life in Turkey and for the future of the RPP. Failure to accomplish this task would mean that political life would degenerate into a repeat performance of the 1946–50 period. In order to acquire new ideas and principles the Republicans had to have a social base for their party which was substantially different from that of the Democrats. this called for a new leadership and the transfusion of fresh blood into the party.

There was a hope that the old guard led by İnönü, which was held responsible for the fiasco at the polls, would be discarded at the coming General Congress in June. There was even political gossip that, if the old guard was not ousted, a 'progressive-liberal' group led by Necmettin Sadak, Vedat Dicleli, and Cemil Sait Barlas would break away and form a new party.[5] There was talk of transforming the RPP into a peasants' party and concentrating on such problems as the uplift of villages, public health, roads, and education.[6] This reflected the views of those Republicans who believed that Turkey was an agrarian nation and ought to remain such. A much larger segment of the peasantry ought to own land and thus become a prosperous and productive class, which would in turn make the country self-sufficient and independent. Whatever little industry the country required, would be restricted to handicrafts and the state sector. It was this group which had supported the moderate land reform bill in 1945.[7]

Reforms of the Eighth Congress 1950

The future of the party was left to be decided at the Eighth Congress, which opened on 29 June 1950 and lasted five days. In spite of all the hopes expressed before the congress, very little was accomplished by way of reforming the party and giving it a new image and identity, although one group went so far as to ask İnönü to step down from active leadership so that the party could be rejuvenated. But by and large, the Republicans were too demoralized and insecure to be able to dispense with İnönü's historic personality at the helm. They believed that only he could keep the party from falling apart and his supporters described him appropriately as the sun around which the RPP revolved.[8] İnönü could keep the party together but only at the price of keeping it unchanged.

İnönü was re-elected Chairman unopposed, though fifty delegates voted against him. However, he was not left with all his former powers. He lost the prerogative to appoint the Secretary-General, who was now elected by the congress. The size of the Party Council (*Parti Divanı*) was reduced to thirty, all to be elected by the congress; and the Party Council was given the task of supervising day-to-day activities in between congresses. Whereas previously İnönü alone had been responsible for the party's course of action, the formulation of policy now became the responsibility of a committee to consist, among others, of the Party Chairman, the Secretary-General, and the leader of the Assembly Group.[9]

The result of these amendments was the creation of dual power between the Chairman and the Secretary-General, who was responsible to the congress and no longer to the Central Committee. This would have been only a paper reform if the Congress had elected İnönü's protége Nihat Erim as the Secretary-General; but it elected Kasım Gülek, who had entered the party only in 1940 and who, by the late forties, was considered a rising star with great ambition. In electing Gülek, the Congress passed over men of the old guard like Şemsettin Günaltay and Faik Ahmet Barutçu.[10] In spite of İnönü's attempts to revert to the previous system, further congresses refused to surrender their right and Gülek remained Secretary-General until 1959—almost always at odds with his leader. Gülek's great contribution was to sustain the morale of the party's rank and file, with the result that during the first four years in opposition the Republicans were able to retain their traditional vote of between 35 to 40 per cent. Without his energy and drive, without his 'American style' flamboyant campaigning it is quite possible that the Republican vote in the country would have been reduced.

Apart from these minor and marginal changes, the RPP remained substantially the same after the Eighth Congress. 'It seems', lamented Nadir Nadi, 'that the People's Party will continue to be İnönü's party just as it has been so far.'[11] Like so many others, he saw this as a setback for democratic politics in Turkey: for while İnönü continued to lead, it was impossible to abandon the traditional socio-economic base deeply entrenched in the landowners of central and eastern Anatolia and the civilian-military intelligentsia. Thus the party failed to shed its old mentality and adjust to the new political environment. Further-more, İnönü's re-election, noted Nadir Nadi, made a mockery of the abolition of the title 'Permanent Party Chairman' (*Değişmez Genel Başkan*) by the 1946 Congress. All these were but changes on paper.[12]

The repercussions of İnönü's continued leadership were, as we noted in chapter II above, disastrous for inter-party relations, and probably for the RPP as well. In 1965 İnönü himself expressed doubts about the wisdom of having continued in politics after the defeat. 'If in 1950', he told Ecvet Güresin, 'I had not been anxious about the new trials the nation had to undergo in order to establish the democratic régime, the most suitable decision would have been to end my political life.'[13]

The Party in Disarray 1951-1955

During the next four years the RPP was plagued with defections and resignations; such was the sense of disillussionment and hopelessness that entire local organizations went over to the Democrats. There were even rumours that prominent Republicans like Şemsettin Günaltay, the former Prime Minister, were considering resignation. Günaltay denied this but soon afterwards Feridun Fikri Düşünsel left the party, complaining that nothing in the party had changed and that the leaders 'think that it can still be run according to the methods of the period of happiness'.[14] Düşünsel's resignation was significant because he had been a member of the RPP since its inception. Moreover, he was very influential in the eastern provinces, especially among the Kurdish population, and his resignation implied the weakening of the party's influence in that region. Other resignations of Representatives from eastern Anatolia followed (and this accounted for the loss of some of these provinces, which had traditionally voted Republican, at the general election of 1954).

The by-elections of 16 September 1951 demonstrated the continuing decline, despite Kasım Gülek's claim that the party was gaining in strength as the 'opportunists' were purged. Out of the seventeen provinces involved in the by-elections, the Republicans won only in Sivas and Sinop, and their defeat in Istanbul was especially humiliating as they had put up their strongest candidates there, including Necmettin Sadak and Dr Lütfi Kırdar, who was the former Mayor and Governor of Istanbul.[15] Again İnönü's leadership was blamed for the electoral set-back and there were rumours that he would resign. There were hints in the press that a struggle between the reformists and the old guard was being waged, and Gülek's official denial of İnönü's impending resignation suggested that the old guard had won again.[16]

Ever since the establishment of the Democrat Party the RPP had been floundering, zigzagging to keep up with the Democrats. The result was that its supporters were totally confused about the party's position on any issue. During its last four years in power the RPP had compromised over some of its fundamental principles, for example étatism and laicism, to the point where its position was hardly different from that of the Democrats.

The leadership decided to rectify this situation at the Ninth Congress (26–30 November 1951) by retracing its steps and once again proclaiming the RPP as the party dedicated to the protection of the Kemalist reforms. The congress admitted that the party had betrayed its principles and lost all contact with the people (halk). In trying to restore this contact it had made too many concessions of principle and violated the Kemalist tenet 'In spite of the people, for the people' (Halka rağmen halk için). The return to emphasis on the Kemalist reforms, it was hoped, would restore the party's credit with its traditional following and terminate the doctrinal confusion. The party had to define its position within the very narrow ideological spectrum of Turkish politics in such a way as to provide an alternative to the DP. But a direct retreat to an old position did not prove to be adequate.[17]

The ideological position adopted by the Ninth Congress did not bring the expected unity and harmony. Resignations continued and by April 1952 there was again talk of a peasants' party. Günaltay was again mentioned as being involved, but this time he was supported by Cavit Oral, a landowner and press lord, and the venture was taken more seriously.[18]

Günaltay and Oral denied any involvement in such a scheme. They proposed that an extraordinary congress be held to amend the party's programme in order to enable it to provide an ideological alternative to the Democrats. Günaltay met İnönü on 27 May and after the meeting he told the press that he was not leaving the party, although he was unhappy with its regulations because they kept alive the spirit of the old order. The Chairman's duties had to be defined and that required the convention of a congress.[19]

The Tenth Congress opened a year later on 22 June 1953. Meanwhile the Günaltay commission had prepared a new programme redefining the position of the RPP on issues such as étatism and laicism. The Tenth Congress continued on the path taken in 1951 and returned more explicitly to the fold of Kemalism. The party retraced its origins to 'The Society for Defence of the Rights of Anatolia and Rumelia' (founded on 3 March 1919), and in the programme the term 'Kemalism' was replaced by 'Atatürk's Path' (Atatürk Yolu). The terms 'social' and 'economic' were also inserted into the programme to stress the party's growing concern with such issues. The six principles of

Kemalism, towards which the party had been lukewarm during its last years in power, were redefined and given greater emphasis. However, the programme accepted at the Tenth Congress did not merely look back; it also contained proposals which were new. Clause VIII recognized the need to establish a bicameral system, to secure the inviolability of the constitution in order to establish a balance among the forces in the state structure, and to guarantee political freedoms. Clause IX defended the principle of secure elections and the security and independence of the judiciary, as well as the freedom to found unions and occupational organizations. The workers were promised the right to strike. Clause X proposed that the régime should work under the guarantee of a Constitutional Court.[20]

The party's ambiguous attempts to redefine its position only increased the cynicism of its rank-and-file supporters. These proposals lacked sincerity and credibility, coming from a leadership which had had ample opportunity to implement them while in power. To make matters worse, İnönü asked the congress to give up its right to elect the Secretary-General and restore this power to the party Chairman. Such a move, claimed İnönü, would enhance unity but the delegates regarded it as a return to the one-party mentality and rejected the proposal.[21]

The Tenth Congress also ended in the defeat of the group which had sought to turn the RPP into a peasants' party. Cavit Oral, one of the leaders of this group, resigned in September, giving as his reason 'the direction that the party was taking and the policy adopted by the clique which dominates the party leadership and administration today'.[22] With the departure of this group the RPP became more open to new influences, which, however, only made themselves felt after the 1954 election.

The process of transformation proved to be very slow. With İnönü in command there could be no elimination of those whose views were outmoded and who wanted to take the party in a direction completely out of keeping with the times. İnönü assumed the role was of mediating between the reformers and the conservatives, without adopting an explicit position himself. Only in this way could he guarantee his own leadership, because at the last moment he would always lean towards the winning side.

In preparation for the coming general election an extraordinary congress was convened in Ankara on 25 February 1954. The aim of the Central Committee was to retrieve the privileges it had surrendered to the local organizations during the period of weakness, guilt, and remorse which followed the election of 1950. The Committee wanted back the right to nominate 20 per cent of the candidates on the electoral list, a right it had surrendered at the Tenth Congress.

The arguments of the Central Committee were interesting because they illustrated the élitist mentality which took for granted the infallibility of its judgement concerning what was good for the party and the country. The Central Committee argued that it was the best judge of candidates for the Assembly since it was not swayed by the parochialism of the local organizations, which tended to nominate persons with local, but not necessarily national standing.

The provincial delegates refused to surrender the newly won right and argued that this progressive reform had yet to be tried out in an election. Past experience had already demonstrated the Central Committee's failure to nominate winning candidates. Given another opportunity, it was likely to nominate old, discredited ministers, high officials, and other candidates who would have neither the support nor the confidence of the constituencies—which, if successful, they would be supposed to represent. The Central Committee was accused of being dominated by a handful of politicians determined to restore their hegemony over the party. Besides, there were far too many people in the party who were deeply entrenched and whose only concern was their own candidature. Such people prevented the Central Committee from exercising its choice freely even if it wanted to.[23]

In 1954 the RPP was still a divided party in search of a new equilibrium and social base. Apart from its internal weakness, it had been weakened by the government's confiscation of much of its wealth and was in no condition to face the Democrats in an electoral contest; hence the disaster which took place at the polls on 2 May 1954.[24]

The announcement of the election results marked the beginning of another internal crisis. Clearly the four years in opposition had been wasted and not only had the party failed to make any gains, it had lost yet more seats. İnönü's leadership was criticized and there were renewed demands for his retirement. Şemsettin Günaltay claimed that the nation had supported the Democrats because it feared that a Republican victory would mean the return of İnönü and the old régime. He wanted İnönü to announce that, if the Republicans were ever returned to power, he would not take office of any kind.

However, Günaltay did not wish İnönü to leave the party since that could well mean the disintegration of the RPP and the total domination of political life by the Democrats.[25] This was the party's dilemma: it could not be thoroughly reformed while İnönü was leader but it felt too insecure to do without him. For the next eighteen years the instinct for survival prevailed. The party organization again rallied to İnönü and on 6 May he issued a statement claiming that there was no substance to the rumours of dissension.[26]

In this period of renewed soul searching the Party Council, consisting of the most influential members, met on 10 June 1954. There were demands for a complete overhaul and the Council decided to hold a general congress in July to implement the reforms necessary to revitalize the party. It was proposed that in future the congress would choose the Party Council, which would then elect the General Administrative Council. The Administrative Council would elect the Secretary-General, putting an end to the division of power. İnönü's group argued that the division of power had undermined discipline and weakened the party. Kasım Gülek, whose position was threatened, claimed that this innovation had introduced democracy and was the only way of transforming the party by involving the people at grass-roots level.[27]

A five-man reform commission was set up and was asked to present its proposals to the congress. It produced some radical proposals, which the congress rejected. Barlas, for example, declared that the RPP was a party which had accomplished its historic mission but it must not look only to its past. He proposed that they create a party based on a specific economic doctrine and stop taking credit for the benefits and assuming responsibility for the misfortunes of the twenty-seven years before 1950. Otherwise, he predicted with great foresight, the party may not come to power for another twenty years.[28] If one judges from Barlas's other writings, he was proposing that the RPP transform itself into a social democratic party on the European model—one that would offer the kind of opposition the British Labour Party offered to the Conservatives, the DP in the Turkish context.[29] But Barlas's views were too radical for the time and the prevailing mentality. They smacked of 'socialism', which was synonymous for many Turks with communism, and therefore anathema.

The other members of the commission also proposed changes that would weaken the authority of the congress, but it refused to be swayed. It retained the right to elect the Secretary-General, rejecting the proposals of the Party Council, and Kasım Gülek was re-elected, defeating İnönü's candidate Ferit Melen by 295 to 169 votes.[30] But the size of the Party Council was reduced from sixty-seven (one delegate for each province) to thirty, which made it a more manageable body. The extremist faction, which proposed withdrawing from the Assembly and boycotting all elections until the Democrats decided to abide by the rules of democracy, was kept in check and the Republicans decided to temporize. To abandon the Assembly and boycott elections would mean proclaiming the impossibility of a lawful political struggle and it was still too early for such a drastic decision.[31]

The RPP was too weak and demoralized to pursue an active and aggressive policy inside or outside the Assembly. Four years of stagnation had left their mark and important figures, people close to İnönü, were defecting to the DP. Dr Behçet Uz, a former RPP cabinet minister, resigned on 14 February 1953 and Menderes made him Minister of Health in his 1954 cabinet.[32] The resignation of Server Somuncuoğlu had 'the effect of a bomb explosion on the party'. As well as being deputy leader of the Assembly Group, Somuncuoğlu was very close to İnönü, and his resignation resulted in acrimonious debate, revealing the existence of serious differences. Somuncuoğlu refused to discuss the inner politics of the RPP but he told the press that 'under existing conditions it is impossible for the Republican People's Party to continue its opposition duties'.[33]

The party was now divided between those who wanted to continue in opposition and those who wanted to throw in the towel and collaborate with the Democrats. Gülek was for continuing the struggle; Nihat Erim was against. İnönü stood by the ringside to await the turn of events before taking action. On 2 August, in the columns of his paper *Halkcı*, Erim launched his campaign for collaboration between the RPP and the DP. By the end of the year he had established contact—on behalf of İnönü, he claimed—with the Democrats and this marked the beginning of a brief period of co-operation between the parties.[34]

The Republican policy of conciliation was prompted partly by the opportunism of individual Republicans and partly by the desire not to hamper the growth of an anti-Menderes faction, slowly taking shape within the DP.[35] This was an intense period in Turkey's foreign relations, marked by the signing of the Baghdad Pact on 24 February 1955, and diplomatic manoeuvres to broaden it by including Egypt. Cyprus was also becoming an explosive issue and Menderes welcomed co-operation with the Republicans. The Administrative Council of the RPP gave a lunch for Prime Minister Menderes on 26 March and both sides promised to work together for the national good.[36] There were meetings between İnönü and Menderes in April but nothing of any substance emerged, since Menderes was unwilling to repeal his repressive laws and İnönü was unwilling to lead a puppet opposition party.[37]

The year 1955 was the turning-point for both the Democrats and the Republicans. The fortunes of the DP began to decline from the peak they had reached in 1954 and those of the RPP began to rise from the trough. The cause of these phenomena was the same: increasing economic difficulties. The government's failure to halt inflation and overcome the shortage of essential goods on the market gave the opposition parties an issue with which they could reach the people. At the same time its defence of the liberal freedoms—of the press, the judiciary, and political activity—slowly restored to the RPP its old standing among the intelligentsia. Moreover, the party had become stable by the middle of 1955, having lost most of the dissident elements. İnönü was once again recognized as the unchallenged leader and there were no more demands for his retirement.

The Republicans had done virtually nothing positive to regain their position and had benefited only from the mistakes and set-backs of the Democrats. The RPP was still without an ideology and it remained a personality party, İnönü's party. This may not be a matter for surprise. Turkey in 1955 was not a country in which ideas and programmes gave direction to political trends. The fate of political parties depended on their leaders, and on the influence of local élite groups upon the voters. İnönü made no attempt to alter this and his party remained a party of directives from the top.

With the Democrats divided, the initiative passed to the opposition parties. In order to allow this initiative to be exercised more effectively, Osman Bölükbaşı, leader of the RNP, a small right-wing party with limited support amongst the petty bourgeoisie of central Anatolia, began to hold consultations with İnönü about possible unity and common action against the DP.[38] These periodic meetings took place throughout 1955 and were prompted by the desire for self-preservation rather than common principles. By August the parties had agreed to boycott by-elections and to concentrate their attack on Menderes rather than the DP as a whole, since attacks on the party were likely to rally the DP dissidents. Just as the Democrats had concentrated their fire on İnönü, the opposition parties were concentrating their fire on Menderes.[39]

The decision to boycott elections was a departure from İnönü's policy of waging a political struggle according to the rules. He had always advocated contesting elections as a means of maintaining democracy and had forced extremists in the party to toe this line. But in August 1955 İnönü argued that Menderes's position was declining and that a victory in normally contested elections would strengthen it. A boycott, however, would focus attention on the grievances of the opposition parties and undermine the prestige of the ruling party.[40] This was precisely the way in which the Democrats had reasoned while in opposition.

The founding of the Freedom Party in December 1955 eclipsed the RPP temporarily and the FP acquired the status of the principal opposition party in the Assembly. But this was an artificial phenomenon caused by DP defections, and the Freedom Party lacked the organization and the following to be able to achieve success in an election. However, between 1956 and 1957 it was able to shoulder the main burden of opposing the government.

There was increased talk of co-operation and unity between the three opposition parties in 1956. On 29 June they even began to boycott the Assembly as a protest against the government's anti-democratic legislation, but returned on 11 July without having achieved any purpose. There was little ground for unity while leaders like Karaosmanoğlu and Bölükbaşı did not trust İnönü. The Freedom Party went so far as to ask İnönü to announce to the nation that he would not become President if the opposition parties won the next election. Needless to say, İnönü refused to make such a promise.[41] There could hardly be unity based on such distrust.

But the RPP revival was slowly gaining momentum and İnönü knew that time was on his side. All those groups which had supported the Democrats since 1946 were slowly returning to the RPP, which provided the only political alternative to the Democrats. The press and the bureaucracy were disillusioned with Menderes.[42] The liberal intelligentsia, although it had become hostile to Menderes, was still suspicious of İnönü and found refuge in the Freedom Party. Professor Turhan Feyzioğlu's entry into the RPP on 7 June 1957 was symbolic of the change in the attitude of the intelligentsia and it is not surprising that İnönü welcomed him with open arms.[43] Perhaps most important of all, the RPP began to receive money from businessmen who had thus far supported the DP, but now considered it wiser to support both. Metin Toker recalled that 'a year earlier [1954] no one turned round to look at the RPP and extended a helping hand. But now [1955] big merchants and businessmen consider it wise to invest in the opposition. That is why the RPP began to come alive not only politically but also financially. As a matter of fact, this climate continued until the 1957 election in which the RPP's represen-tation in the Assembly increased sixfold.'[44]

İnönü could now afford to formulate his party's policy in

isolation and in total disregard for the opposition partners. His initiative in establishing a working relationship with Menderes during the budget debate in February 1957 isolated the other parties, especially the FP, and aroused their suspicions.[45] During the next few months the Freedom Party took the brunt of the government's wrath while the RPP established its reputation as a 'responsible party'. İnönü was again in complete command and was able to have this policy of cordial relations with the majority party accepted unanimously in the Party Council, even though there was much resistance to it.[46]

By the summer of 1957 the parties were actively preparing for an early general election and the opposition parties again opened discussions on the question of unity. The Republicans, confident that they could win the election alone, were divided about the need for unity and co-operation with the small parties. It was mainly the local bodies which opposed these talks, while the central organization supported them. But even the central body was willing to consider unity only if the other two parties would subordinate themselves to the RPP.

By September it was evident that the three opposition parties— RPP, FP, and RNP—had not been able to find a formula for united action at the polls. But they did issue a joint communiqué on 4 September stating, *inter alia*, that if they came to power with the necessary two-thirds majority, they would convert the Assembly into a constituent assembly within six months, lay the foundations of a new régime, and hold a fresh general election. The constitution would be revised on the basis of two chambers instead of one; a Constitutional Court with the power to test the legality of laws would be set up; there would be proportional representation, and the right of unionized workers to strike would be recognized.[47]

It is doubtful whether this communiqué full of liberal promises swayed voters away from the Democrat Party. But we know that the serious economic situation, especially the spiralling inflation, affected almost every one. A peasant, asked why he was a Republican, replied: 'Because salt is expensive, cigarettes are expensive, horse shoes, nails..., everything is expensive.'[48] But even the economic crisis proved insufficient to induce an electoral victory for the opposition parties. In fact, the FP and the RNP were reduced in the Assembly to only four seats each. The Republicans, however, increased their representation from 31 to 178 and their percentage of the votes from 34 to 40 per cent. The party had finally emerged from the doldrums.[49]

İnönü Rejuvenates the Party 1957

The RPP was given a face-lift and rejuvenated temporarily by the injection of young blood at the centre. It had succeeded in capturing the imagination of the intelligentsia and at the time of the 1957 election a totally new and refreshing atmosphere prevailed. People like Turhan Feyzioğlu, Bülent Ecevit, Ali İhsan Göğüş, Osman Okyar, Doğan Avcıoğlu, and Coşkun Kırca all joined the party at this time and gave it a new outlook. It was they who set up the RPP Research Bureau after the election and introduced a more modern and rational approach to politics.

Although the superstructure of the party had been altered, its foundations remained the same. The Republicans had not been able to break into the DP stronghold in the Thracian-Marmara-Aegean regions, the most prosperous and developed provinces in Turkey. They had succeeded only in regaining much of the territory lost to the Democrats in 1950 and 1954 in central and eastern Anatolia, where the basis of society was still very traditional. The only province the Republicans won in 1957 west of Ankara was Uşak. Their success in Ankara was itself noteworthy, for it demonstated the alienation of the bureaucracy from the Democrat Party.[50] The RPP continued to be supported by the traditional landowners and failed to win the votes of newly emerging groups like the capitalist farmers of the west, the entrepreneurs, or even the workers.

In terms of doctrine, the RPP had finally adopted a liberal position. In its election manifesto all the promises made in the joint communiqué of 4 September were repeated and amplified. The manifesto promised to give unionized industrial and mineworkers the right to strike, and all those in the bureaucracy the right to form unions; to repeal anti-democratic laws, and to put an end to partisan administration. On the economic front the Republicans promised to repeal the National Defence Law passed by the Democrats to check inflation and overcome shortages.[51] This was the only hint that they gave of adopting a more liberal approach to the economy. Their aim, however, was to win over the private sector. But the RPP's contribution to the debate on the economy was perhaps the most barren aspect of its role in opposition. In this area, too, it offered no clear alternative to the Democrats.

After the 1957 election the RPP became the sole opposition party in the Assembly to have an Assembly Group. Its position continued to improve as the economic situation deteriorated. By the spring of 1958 İnönü was confident that his party would win the next election, irrespective of whether the Election Law was amended or not.[52] The Republicans were convinced that the tide had turned. By the end of 1959 and the beginning of 1960 we are told that the public was begging İnönü to save the country from Menderes.[53] We shall never know whether the Republicans would have defeated Menderes in an electoral contest; on the yardstick of their performance in the elections of the sixties, it seems doubtful that they would have done.

The Freedom Party thesis seems closer to the truth. They claimed that the Democrats could have been defeated in 1957: what had happened, they said, was that many voters, fearing for democracy if the RPP came to power on its own, had given their votes to the Democrat Party as a purely negative measure. If the co-operation talks between the Freedom Party and the Republicans had not broken down and if the two parties had fought the elections together, the story might have been different.[54] It was probably not so much fear of the RPP but of the RPP led by İsmet İnönü. The memory of İnönü's rule was too deeply embedded in the Turkish psyche to be uprooted even after his twenty years in opposition. This seems to be borne out by the fact that soon after he gave up the leadership of the party in 1972 its fortunes began to improve.[55]

Throughout 1958 and 1959 the RPP's position improved in inverse proportion to the decline in the position of the DP. The liberal forces in the party were augmented when, on 24 November 1958, the Freedom Party decided to dissolve itself and merge with the Republicans.[56] At the Fourteenth General Congress (12-15 January 1959) many former members of the FP joined the RPP and eight of them were elected to the Party Council.[57]

The growing spirit of liberalism found expression in the 'Proclamation of Primary Aims' (*İlk Hedefler Beyannamesi*), which reiterated the party's promises to reform the régime as soon as it came to power. 'Our constitution', stated the programme, 'will be amended in accordance with a modern understanding of democracy and society, and in accordance with a system of the state based on the principles of the sovereignty of the people, the rule of law, social justice, and security.'[58] These sentiments were closely in keeping with the spirit of the times and many of them found expression in the new régime established after the collapse of the Democrat Party.

The voices in the party that had called for İnönü's retirement from politics had been silenced by the revival and the success at the polls. As political repression increased in the late fifties İnönü came to be seen as protector rather than as leader of the party. It was as though only İnönü stood between Menderes and the RPP.

But in spite of this dependence on him, İnönü was not able to exercise absolute control over the rank and file. He was never permitted to amend the regulations under which the congress elected the Secretary-General. The day after the Fourteenth Congress met, the Party Council reaffirmed that the congress would elect the Secretary-General and on 15 January Kasım Gülek was reelected.[59] İnönü was forced to work with Gülek until September, when the latter resigned because of an indiscreet letter he had written to Colonel Fens, Chairman of the NATO Parliamentary Group. In this letter, Gülek is said to have sought for himself—in place of a party colleague whom he maligned—an invitation to the NATO parliamentary conference in London. The letter caused a minor scandal when it found its way back to Turkey.[60] Gülek was succeeded by İsmail Rüştü Aksal with whom İnönü established a close working relationship, much to the detriment of the Democrats in assembly debate.

The Republican People's Party had finally arrived. Now it was capable of playing the role of an opposition and providing an alternative to the Democrats. But the two parties failed to agree on the rules of the democratic game, and finally the army intervened and destroyed democracy in order to save it. Just as the 1950 election created a new political climate in Turkey so did the military *coup* of May 1960 and the interim régime that followed. Once again the RPP became an anachronism, this time the Republicans were forced to seek a new identity suited to the politics of the Second Republic.

NOTES

1 'Muhalefete Geçerken', editorial in *Ulus*, 18 May 1950, cited in Bayar, *Başvekilim Menderes*, 149-50; Erer, *On Yıl*, 36-7.

2 Yalman, *Gördüklerim*, iv, 219. See also İnönü's communiqué of 24 May 1950 in his *Muhalefet*, i, 8.

3 Faik Ahmet Barutçu, interviewed in *Cumhuriyet*, 26 May 1950.

4 'C. Halk Partisinin İkinci Vazifesi', *Akşam*, 28 June 1950.

5 *Cumhuriyet*, 17 June 1950. See also Aydemir, *İkinci Adam*, iii, 85-103.

6 *Cumhuriyet*, 25 June 1950.

7 See Behice Boran, *Türkiye ve Soyalizm Sorunları* (1968), 32-3. Their image of Turkey, resembling the Gandhian vision for India, was anachronistic for Turkey in 1950. It had little appeal and they were denounced at the congress as neo-fascists.

8 *Ulus* and *Cumhuriyet*, 29 and 30 June 1950; Giritlioğlu, *Halk Partisi*, i, 269-73; Aydemir, *İkinci Adam*, iii, 95-6. İnönü's opponents accepted

the analogy but replied that 'like the equatorial sun İnönü shines ['burns' in the original] a little too much'.

9 Osman Faruk Loğoğlu, 'İsmet İnönü and the Political Modernization of Turkey, 1945-1965', unpublished PhD thesis (Univ. of Princeton, 1970), 135.

10 Giritlioğlu, *Halk Partisi*, i, 273.

11 *Cumhuriyet*, 4 July 1950.

12 Ibid.

13 'İnönü Anlatıyor', *Cumhuriyet*, 22-25 Mar. 1965; the quotation is from the issue of 22 Mar.

14 *Ulus*, 24 Mar. 1951 and *Cumhuriyet*, 28 Mar. 1951 (quotation).

15 *Zafer*, 17 Sept. 1951 and Eroğul, *Demokrat Parti*, 75.

16 *Cumhuriyet*, 20, 29 and 30 Sept. 1951.

17 The best account of the congress is to be found in the daily press, especially in the party's official organ *Ulus*, 26 Nov.-1 Dec. İnönü's speeches are given in his *Muhalefet*, i, 78-83. See also Giritlioğlu, *Halk Partisi*, i, 298-9; Tunaya, *Partiler*, 602-5.

18 *Cumhuriyet*, 12, 30 April and 21, 22 May 1952.

19 Ibid., 28 May 1952; see also issues of 25 and 26 May.

20 Giritlioğlu, *Halk Partisi*, i, 302; Kili, *Kemalism*, 169-75. At this congress the Republicans set up a youth wing, marking the involvement of the young, particularly students, in politics. See Nadir Nadi, 'Partiler ve Gençlik', *Cumhuriyet*, 2 Apr. 1953. The Democrats denounced this practice as a fascist measure but announced the formation of their own youth organization in Jan. 1954. See Democrat Parti, *Genç Demokratlar Teşkilâtı ve Esasları: Gençlik ve Siyasi Eğitim*, DP Neşriyatı 5 (1954).

21 *Ulus*, 26 June 1953.

22 Ibid., 8 Sept. 1953. Cavit Oral (b. 1904) joined the DP and was elected to the Assembly in 1954. He lost his seat at the election in 1957 and became President of the board of directors of Sümerbank. In 1961 he joined the Justice Party, was elected Representative for Adana, but resigned in May 1963 and became an Independent.

23 *Ulus*, 25-28 Feb. 1954; Giritlioğlu, *Halk Partisi*, i, 309-11; Aydemir, *İkinci Adam*, iii, 102-3.

24 For the election results, see above, 70, n. 56.

25 Toker, *İsmet Paşa*, i, 29.

26 İnönü, *Muhalefet*, i, 291.

27 For reports of this meeting see the Turkish press, 10-14 June 1954.

28 *Cumhuriyet*, 4 July 1954; Celâl Bozkurt, *Siyaset Tarihimizde Cumhuriyet Halk Partisi* (n.d. [1968?]) 81-2. The commission consisted of Nihat Erim, Turgut Göle, Şevket Raşit Hatipoğlu, Cemil Sait Barlas, and Cemal Reşit Eyüboğlu.

29 See Cemil Sait Barlas, *Sosyalistlik Yolları ve Türkiye Gerçekleri* (1962) and the views expressed in *Pazar Postası*, a paper Barlas published in the fifties. I am grateful to his son, Mehmet Barlas, for bringing this paper to my attention.

30 *Ulus*, 31 July 1954.

31 The Turkish press, 26-31 July 1954. İnönü's congress speeches are

reproduced in his Muhalefet, i, 296-306. See also Aydemir, İkinci Adam, iii, 158-60; and Giritlioğlu, Halk Partisi, i, 316-17.

32 See above, 71, n. 62. After leaving the RPP on 14 Feb. 1953, Dr Behcet Uz (b. 1893) was elected Representative for İzmir in 1954 and became Minister of Health and Social Assistance. Earlier he had been a prominent Republican, holding posts in various cabinets of the forties.

33 Cumhuriyet, 24 June 1954. Toker, İsmet Paşa, i, 13-14, claims that Menderes encouraged defections from the RPP by 'buying off' those close to İnönü, with the intention of demoralizing the party. Somuncuoğlu, he says, was blackmailed with the threat of an investigation of his business accounts.

34 Cumhuriyet, 31 Dec. 1954 and 1 Jan. 1955. Mükerrem Sarol told the author how he had been approached by Erim and how he put Erim in touch with Menderes. At this point Erim was defending Menderes's repressive measures in RPP councils as well as in public, and this gave rise to serious differences between İnönü and Erim. See Toker, İsmet Paşa, i, 47-50.

35 See above, ch. 3.

36 Cumhuriyet, 27 Mar. 1955 and Toker, İsmet Paşa, i, 60.

37 Menderes reassured his group with the words: 'Will the laws passed by the Assembly be amended at their [Republican] requests? Never!' (Zafer, 11 May 1955). Kasım Gülek aired his own suspicions: 'The government longs for only a puppet opposition. But they will never see us in that role' (Cumhuriyet, 28 May 1955).

38 Cumhuriyet, 26 Nov. 1954, reported what seems to have been the first meeting.

39 Toker, İsmet Paşa, i, 82-6 and 92; Eroğul, Demokrat Parti, 120.

40 Toker, as previous note.

41 Ibid., 167.

42 Cemal Tüzün, Democrat Representative for Kocaeli, claimed that only 5 per cent of the state officials supported the DP while 95 per cent supported the opposition parties (Cumhuriyet, 7 Jan. 1959). Orhan Eyüboğlu (at the time of writing, Secretary-General of the RPP) was himself an ex-official—he had resigned from the bureaucracy in disgust in the mid-fifties, begun practising law, and then joined the RPP. See 7 Gün, iv/50, 22 Aug. 1973, 15-16.

43 Cumhuriyet, 8 June 1957; Toker, İsmet Paşa, i, 184; and conversation with Turhan Feyzioğlu. Feyzioğlu was more realistic than many other Turkish intellectuals. He never joined the Freedom Party because he knew it would never be an effective political force.

44 İsmet Paşa, i, 101 and 152 ff.

45 Cumhuriyet, 26 and 27 Feb. 1957.

46 Ibid., 25 Mar. 1957 and Nadir Nadi's editorial, 'Hep Oy Birliği', ibid., 26 Mar.

47 The Turkish press, 5 Sept. 1957; B. Lewis, 'Democracy', MEA, x/2 (1959), 70-71; Karaosmanoğlu, 45 Yıl, 225-6; and Toker, İsmet Paşa, i, 204-6.

48 *Cumhuriyet*, 4 Mar. 1957, quoted in Joseph Szyliowicz, *Political Change in Rural Turkey—Erdemli* (1966), 159.

49 See above, 57.

50 The RPP won in the following provinces: Adana, Ankara, Çankırı, Elazığ, Erzincan, Gümüşhane, Hatay, Kars, Malatya, Maraş, Mardin, Ordu, Sivas, Toket, Tunceli, Urfa, Uşak, and Van. Both the RPP and the DP won seats in Bingöl, Muş, and Niğde. The Freedom Party won in Burdur and the RNP in Kırşehir; the Democrats captured the remaining forty-four provinces. *Cumhuriyet*, 31 Oct. 1957; Toker, *İsmet Paşa*, i, 220.

51 *Ulus* and *Cumhuriyet*, 11 Oct. 1957. See also Karpat, 'The Turkish Elections of 1957', *Western Political Quarterly*, xiv/2 (1961), 436–59.

52 Toker, *İsmet Paşa*, ii, 60.

53 Ibid., 127 and *passim*.

54 This issue was discussed at the Freedom Party congress on 14 and 15 Mar. 1958. See the Turkish press, 15 and 16 Mar. 1958.

55 See *Yankı*, 121 and 132, 9 July and 30 Sept. 1973, 4 and 9, respectively, and the Turkish press in the months before the 1973 election.

56 Tökin, *Türk Tarihi*, 89; Baban, *Politika*, 369 and 371–2.

57 *Cumhuriyet* and *Ulus*, 17 Jan. 1959. The eight who joined the RPP were Fevzi Lütfi Karosmanoğlu, Turan Güneş, Enver Güreli, Cihat Baban, İbrahim Öktem, Emin Paksüt, Feridun Ergin, and Muammer Aksoy.

58 *Cumhuriyet* and *Ulus*, 15 Jan. 1959; Kili, *Kemalism*, 175–8; Toker, *İsmet Paşa*, ii, 143–4.

59 *Cumhuriyet*, 12 and 16 Jan. 1959.

60 Ibid., 28 and 29 Sept. 1959; Toker, *İsmet Paşa*, ii, 179–84.

CHAPTER V

THE ECONOMY UNDER
THE DEMOCRAT PARTY

A democratic economic policy may be defined as a system which is based on private property, which defends the economic freedom of the individual, and which considers private enterprise to be fundamental. Today's government, while remaining within the framework of this general definition, accepts the principle that the State may be given certain duties in the economic sphere. The government believes that the fundamental duty of the State is to encourage, regulate and supervise economic activity, and, at the same time, to create broad and secure working conditions for private enterprise by providing every possible legal and economic opportunity.

President Celâl Bayar, speech to the Grand National Assembly, 1 November 1952

The Democrat Party government believed that it would be a totally democratic act to participate in international trade and economic relations and to prepare the necessary climate and conditions for such participation. It was to be expected that a democratic régime and a democratic mentality would not confine the country to its shell but would make Turkey a part of the free and democratic world both economically and politically.

Refik Korkud, *Demokratik Rejim Matbuat-Muhalefet Hürriyet Suistimali* [Ankara, 1959]

Étatism and the Opposition 1945-1950

IT is noteworthy that the founder of the first party to challenge the monopoly of the Republican People's Party was an industrialist, not a politician. Nuri Demirağ, who founded the National Development Party (*Milli Kalkınma Partisi*) in August 1945, was a firm believer in free enterprise and sharply opposed to the

Republican Party's policy of state intervention or étatism. According to Demirağ, his party was founded 'in order to end the thousand and one miseries, calamities, and injustices that the people suffered from the étatist administration'.[1] It attracted little support and was soon eclipsed by the Democrat Party.

Demirağ did succeed in establishing the fact that opposition to the Republican Party was not merely political in the narrow sense, but was also concerned with economic issues related to developing the country materially, for which the prerequisite was political power. In the struggle waged by the Democrats, this aspect was often lost amidst such political issues as the Electoral Law or the amendment of anti-democratic laws. Yet the economic question had become the primary concern of both the RPP and the opposition parties.

Turkey had been impoverished by the prohibitive but vitally necessary armed neutrality she had been forced to maintain throughout World War II. The war was even more costly for the belligerents; in one sense, however, Turkey's plight was worse since she lacked the economic infrastructure necessary for a quick recovery. This foundation had to be laid before the country could begin to move forward.[2]

All parties recognized the seriousness of the economic situation and the need to take immediate steps to remedy it. There was no significant disagreement over economic doctrine and many Republicans understood that étatism had never been an economic system to be pursued dogmatically. It had been introduced in order to overcome years of economic backwardness, the result of bad government in the past. Its purpose had never been to oppose private enterprise; in fact, one of the aims of étatism had been to help the private sector and encourage its growth so that, one day in the near future, it would be capable of replacing the state as the dominant factor in the economy.[3] The problem, claimed Sadak, was that the limits of étatism had never been defined and this sometimes brought it into conflict with liberal economic concepts. The state had failed to designate separate functions to the two sectors—the incipient cause of insecurity in the private sector. If the functions and responsibilities of the two sectors were defined, Turkey would be on the way to establishing a mixed economy.

Sadak's interpretation of étatism was correct in theory. But the domination exercised by the bureaucracy over the economy undermined the original goals of étatism. It established the supremacy of the state sector, giving the bureaucrats a vested interest in maintaining the *status quo*. Menderes diagnosed the situation correctly when he told the Assembly that:

124   *The Turkish Experiment in Democracy*

The political views and opinions which found expression in the single-party domination of the former government were also reflected in its economic and financial policies....

Thus, in time it emerged as an interventionist, capitalist, bureaucratic, and monopolist state. It is natural for this kind of state to put the country in debt by constantly increasing expenditure and preventing the development of our economic resources by making business and production stagnant.[4]

Even Sadak had noted that the bureaucratic wing of the RPP wanted to convert étatism from 'state socialism', in which the primary motive of state economic enterprises had not been profit, to 'state capitalism'. In this case the state would compete with the private sector and that would be worse than the system being replaced.

Étatism was in the process of serious modification by the late forties and the introduction of the Marshall Aid programme in 1947 gave it more of a nudge than the politics of the opposition parties. American aid was followed by American criticism of Turkey's economic policies and the government was not slow to take note. As relations developed and Ankara became more dependent on American aid and investment, it realized that the 'internal régime should be more palatable to the United States in order to assure better understanding and to justify economic assistance'.[5] The members of the numerous American economic missions who came to advise the Turkish government usually belonged to the private sector and they naturally tended to direct the Turkish government away from étatism. The activity of Max Thornburg, who directed a study of the Turkish economy in 1948, was significant 'for his conviction that the curtailment of étatism and the favouring of free enterprise ... must be a prerequisite of American aid [and this] had an impact on a wide and influential audience',[6] both Turkish and American.

There is an intimate relationship between politics and economics and the Democrats were convinced of the impossibility of establishing democracy without free enterprise. The idea that political democracy would be insecure until the state sector had been subordinated to the requirements of the private sector was merely the other side of the communist doctrine that political power can be consolidated only by liquidating the private ownership of the means of production. For the Democrats it was not the state ownership that was loathsome but the fact that these state enterprises were run by an 'interventionist capitalist, monopolist bureaucracy', which had little concern for the private sector. The political system needed to be changed in order to restore the hegemony of the politician over the administrator.

Between 1946 and their defeat in 1950, the Republicans took numerous measures to establish a liberal economic system in Turkey. The 'Measures of 7 September' 1946 were the first step in this direction.[7] At the end of November Prime Minister Peker told the press that all the government's economic measures were based on the principle of competition and the free liberal system.[8] While the Democrats preached the virtues of free enterprise, the Republicans were slowly dismantling the structure of state ownership. The process was cautious because there was a struggle in the party between the étatists and the liberals, which ended in a liberal victory. By the time the Democrats came to power a number of economic adjustments and commitments had already been made and these formed the foundations of the economic policy of the Democrat Party. There was no fundamental difference in the election manifestos of the two rivals.[9] In the West, however, it was the DP which was proclaimed the champion of free enterprise.

The DP's Approach to Étatism

There was a difference in the way in which the two parties *executed* their policies and this became apparent soon after the Democrats assumed power. The DP, being a new party, had no ties with past policies and there were no factions pulling in different directions. Therefore it was able to pursue the capitalist path of development without any significant restraints or inhibitions. The Democrats had acknowledged that they were trying to accomplish exactly the same task as the Republicans, but they believed that they were capable of accomplishing it more efficiently.[10]

The economic policy of the party was explained by Professor Muhlis Ete, who became Minister of Management and Minister of Economy and Commerce in Menderes's first two cabinets. In an election broadcast in May 1950 he criticized Republican economic policies for being out of line with economic principles and promised that his party would be more consistent:

In our opinion the government's economic policy rests on private property, protects the individual's economic freedoms, and regards private enterprise as fundamental in the economic sphere.

However, to regard private enterprise as fundamental in the economy of the country must not be understood as meaning that there would be no state enterprises and co-operatives....

Our understanding of étatism takes more the form of 'organizing by the state' than 'running by the state'; the state's economic policy or its interest in the economy should take the form of measures necessary to encourage, protect and co-ordinate the development of the various branches of the economy.

State establishments and enterprises should be devoted to public service and to activities which are monopolistic by nature and which private enterprise and capital will not be able to handle.

We believe that, in an economic régime which rests on private property and personal freedom, the true owner of the economy is the individual or private enterprise in the form of companies. Our thesis is that the state's duty is not to be inside the economy but above it.

Consequently the state should not be involved in enterprises which are not of a public character. It should begin, gradually and according to a programme, to turn over all other enterprises ... unless they are in public service and basic industry to private enterprise and co-operative groups.

In order to have a firm and established economic policy applicable to the country's economic structure and relationships, we propose to create an economic research centre composed of economists recognized either for their academic standing or their success in business. . . .[11]

Muhlis Ete presented the broad theoretical outlines of his party's economic policy; Menderes presented the policy his government intended to follow. The basic principles remained the same. Menderes's policy statement was naturally more specific, and the emphasis was on economic expansion. In order to achieve this, the government intended to:

(a) Increase as much as possible that part of the budget which has the character of investment and direct all our other means exclusively into the sphere of production.

(b) Take all measures which will make private enterprise feel secure, both legally and in reality, and to help it to grow rapidly.

(c) Facilitate the flow of capital that exists in the country into fields of active production.

(d) Create the conditions in which it would be possible to benefit as much as possible from foreign enterprises, capital and techniques and to carry out all that is necessary to accomplish this.

(e) Bind to a plan the appropriations from the State budget which will be earmarked as investment funds for the purpose of economic expansion; the plan will be made with concern for the natural conditions of the country.

(f) Protect production from the damaging intervention of the State as well as all sorts of bureaucratic obstructionism ...[12]

Menderes reiterated most of the party views on private enterprise that had been expressed earlier by Ete. Turning to the government's commercial policy he declared:

In the field of trade, when internal and external conditions do not force our intervention, our policy will be to leave trade to the free and normal forces [of the market].

We strongly believe in the necessity of providing, under all conditions, firm stability to our foreign trade régime.[13]

Such were the broad theoretical and practical outlines of the government's economic policy with regard to the modern sectors of the economy, industry, and commerce. (The 'traditional' agrarian sector is discussed below.) It was intended to be as liberal as conditions permitted, with a clear break from the past in its execution.

By philosophy and temperament the Democrats were alien to bureaucratic procedures, which they associated with the old régime. They came to power on the anti-state platform and they sincerely felt obliged to carry out their electoral promises. Furthermore, they held the monoparty state apparatus responsible for many of the ills of the country and were convinced that if they could rectify these it would begin to move forward. Their antipathy towards the state was an inherent aspect of multi-party, competitive politics—in which the leaders of the party in power, rather than state officials, monopolize patronage and use it to pay back political debts or to reward their supporters. It was against the spirit of private enterprise and individual initiative, principles proclaimed by the Democrats, to work through the bureaucracy. Therefore the concept of planning, which is a bureaucratic process *par excellence*, was anathema to them. In fact, they often used the term 'plan', though never in the sense of an overall economic plan; more in the sense of a programme.

General Fahri Belen, who was Minister of Public Works in the first Menderes cabinet, recalled that his ministry had been placed on a 'plan footing' by the previous administration. There were studies and schemes for railway construction, roads, dams, and waterways which Belen wanted to use as the basis for his own programme. But his proposals were obstructed in the cabinet. As a military man Belen was well disposed to planning and working through the bureaucratic structure. But not so his civilian cabinet colleagues. He was told by Prime Minister Menderes that the five year plan he was preparing for his ministry was based on a communist principle.[14]

Belen also observed that Menderes permitted only limited contacts and negotiations between ministries and foreign firms. The negotiation of foreign contracts was supervised by a Minister of State, which made the process political rather than professional and technical. This practice was partly dictated by Turkey's growing economic relations with the West, especially the United States. American experts had criticized the policy of state intervention in economic affairs and emphasized that '... free enterprise in the developmental sector must be a prerequisite of American aid.'[15] This, Kerwin noted, had an impact on a wide and influential audience, both Republican and Democrat, and the bureaucracy soon felt the impact. Initially, these experts were satisfied with the concession of dealing directly with politicians rather than state officials; later they stipulated that American business would deal directly with its Turkish counterpart.

The victory of the DP was marked by the establishment of the supremacy of the party over the state, the domination of politics over administration. This is what Fahri Belen meant when he wrote: 'In every enterprise, more than planning there was the smell of votes ...'[16] The Democrats—and the same would probably have been equally true of the Republicans—began to give priority to economic projects that would also have a favourable political impact and guarantee votes in the next election. No wonder the opposition parties described the cement and sugar factories built by the Democrats as 'election factories', in view of their uneconomic locations.[17]

The Private Sector Fails to Respond

Menderes was under the illusion that the creation of liberal capitalism, as distinct from the RPP's state capitalism, was only a matter of legislation. If he passed measures de-étatizing the enterprises which were neither in public service nor constituted basic industry, businessmen and industrialists would then do the rest and in no time a private sector would come into being. On 6 July 1950 Muhlis Ete announced that the government would begin by de-étatizing the Sümerbank construction industry, which consisted of cement and brick factories. This would be followed by the textile industry. Various choices were offered to potential investors. They could buy enterprises outright or go into partnership with the state. The government was also willing to enter into joint operations with private-enterprise companies national or foreign, or to rent some undertakings to local and foreign capital.[18]

In August the Industrial Development Bank of Turkey (*Türkiye Sınai Kalkınma Bankası*) was founded to facilitate this transfer of state enterprises and the development of the private sector. Its capital of TL 12·5 million was put up by the major national and foreign banks, the International Bank of Reconstruction and Development (IBRD) granted a loan of $9 million, and Marshall

Aid provided TL 37 million. The stated goal of the bank was 'to found private industry, to encourage the participation of foreign and local capital in industry, and to make an effort to transfer to private hands the shares and securities on which Turkish industry is dependent and to retain them there.' The bank extended long-term credit to industrial firms wishing to renew or expand their productive capacity or to inaugurate new production units. It provided technical and managerial advice and guidance to firms and administered the Marshall Aid Counterpart Funds on behalf of the private sector.[19]

Analysing Menderes's policy in 1951, Bernard Lewis wrote:

Present government policy seems to be, not to abolish *étatisme* entirely, but to reduce it progressively and limit it eventually to those forms of economic activity which are specially suited to State ownership, or, what is perhaps the same thing, which are unattractive to private capital. . . .

. . . The central question here is—has the planned reconstruction of Turkey under *étatisme* gone far enough to permit its restriction or abandonment, without danger of a relapse into the old conditions or some form of economic colonialism? . . . Certainly the attempt, in the middle of the twentieth century, to turn back and catch up on the missing chapter of nineteenth-century liberal capitalism in Turkish history is not without its perils.[20]

This was, indeed, the central question that had to be answered before liberal capitalism could be fostered in Turkey. The Democrats found that the social class which embodies the values of the private entrepreneur was very small and underdeveloped. To the extent that such a stratum existed, its activities were hampered by the prevailing social attitudes and values. Thus, in spite of all their good intentions, the Democrats had difficulty in implementing their programme. They were unable to find a suitable formula for limiting the activities of the state sector, and the businessmen lacked confidence to lead the way. Anxious about the new government's policies, they were cautiously biding their time. The commercial groups did not come up to Menderes's expectations in purchasing the state enterprises offered to them; nor did they dramatically increase their investment in new industrial ventures. Thus throughout the ten years the private industrial sector grew very slowly.

The Democrats were committed to the development of liberal capitalism, but their commitment to the rapid expansion of the economy was even greater. Disappointed by the response of private capital, they once more reverted to the state sector as the more likely field for industrial expansion. State enterprises were modernized and their productive capacity expanded;[21] even the bureaucracy in charge of the state sector doubled in ten years.[22] Writing in the *Cumhuriyet* (7 May 1952), Nadir Nadi observed that the realities of power had taken the edge of the DP's liberalism. However, although the government was unable to turn over to the private sector as many state enterprises as it had initially planned, some progress had been made: Minister of Management Sıtkı Yırcalı, referring to the positive results of the opportunities given to the private sector, stated that while the state-owned Sümerbank had once catered for 70 per cent of the country's needs, it now catered for only 30 per cent. That was an indication of the extent to which private enterprise had grown.[23]

Dependence on Foreign Capital

This time the emphasis on étatism was not as extreme as in the thirties. Unlike their predecessors who had hoped to use the state sector in order to develop private enterprise, the Democrats assigned a limited role to the state. They intended to rely on foreign capital to fulfil the task of inducing rapid growth in the private sector. Once again, DP policies had been anticipated by the Republicans: on 22 May 1947 the Peker cabinet had sanctioned a decree facilitating the investment of foreign capital in Turkey, and when that proved insufficient to attract investors the Republicans passed the first Law to Encourage Foreign Capital Investment on 1 March 1950.[24]

The Democrats, as in everything else they did, accelerated the process of encouraging foreign capital investment. They felt sure that foreign money would pour in as soon as a government sympathetic to private enterprise came to power. However, as with the response from local investors, they were disappointed with the response from abroad. But they were optimistic and believed that it was only necessary to change the psychological climate in the country in order to attract large doses of foreign capital—which they regarded as vital for the Turkish economy.[25] President Bayar told his audience of bankers and financiers at the Calvin Bullock Forum in New York:

> We observe that no matter how great an effort we exert, our own financial and technical resources are not enough for the exploitation of our sources of wealth with the required speed.... A speedier opening of our resources for production is necessary. This will become possible through the influence of foreign capital.[26]

On 2 August 1951 the Democrats took the first step to stimulate the entry of foreign capital by liberalizing the Law to Encourage

Foreign Investment in Turkey. The amended law offered greater incentives to foreign investment in Turkish industry, in the exploitation of energy resources (excluding oil) and minerals, public works, and communications. Moreover the investor was allowed to transfer 10 per cent of his annual profits in foreign exchange to the country of origin.[27]

Even at the time, it was clear to many that the terms of this law were still not sufficiently attractive to draw capital in large enough quantities to make a substantial difference to the economy.[28] The government soon became aware of this and decided to liberalize its policies further: the bait dangled before the foreign investor was the exploitation of Turkey's oil resources. Sıtkı Yırcalı announced that the government would conclude agreements with foreign firms willing to pool their capital and technical know-how with Turkey. This was an important concession because the government was abandoning the principle of retaining vital resources such as oil as the monopoly of the state.[29]

The response from the US Embassy was immediate and favourable. Ambassador George McGhee, an oilman from Texas, welcomed this change in attitude and said that it would constitute a good example for the elimination of difficulties inherent in the oil policies of several other countries. 'The fact that the country which for the last 30 years had carried out oil prospecting under state monopoly was now inviting foreign firms to participate provided a new example of joint enterprise.'[30] On 22 January 1953 *Cumhuriyet* reported that an agreement to build an oil refinery had been reached with a firm in California.

Clarence Randall, Chairman of the US House of Representatives Commission on Foreign Trade Policy, and President of the Chicago Inland Steel Company, arrived in Ankara on 26 August 1953. He held discussions with the government on how to attract foreign capital and announced to the press that the law on foreign investment needed to be amended again. The new law must end all restrictions on the activity of foreign capital, which ought to have the same rights as local capital. There ought to be no restrictions on the transfer of foreign exchange, and efforts should be made to facilitate the handling of Turkish stocks on stock exchanges abroad. An organization to publicize investment possibilities in Turkey was needed; the government should limit state enterprise; and it should allow state enterprises, local entrepreneurs, and foreign capitalists to operate 'under equal conditions based on the principles of free competition'.[31] *Ulus* commented that whereas President Truman had used the state to further American relations with foreign countries, President Eisenhower preferred private capitalists to achieve the same end.[32] The government's liberal declarations brought immediate results. On 10 September the World Bank agreed to give Ankara credit worth $9 million, to be placed in the Industrial Development Bank of Turkey to finance private industry.[33]

The Law to Encourage Foreign Investment was amended on 18 January 1954 and the Oil Law was passed on 7 March.[34] There was great optimism in the country and many felt that Turkey had reached the turning-point on the road to development.[35] There was hope that the capital necessary for reconstructing the country would come from outside and that Turkey would soon join the ranks of the developed world. 'No national economy', declared Menderes, 'had developed without foreign capital. Therefore we considered it our patriotic duty to pass the Law to Encourage Foreign Investment.'[36] The Democrats had been deceived by the spectacular economic recovery Europe had made with the help of large injections of American aid and investment. They naïvely believed that the same process would be reproduced in Turkey and that they would be able to avoid the painful aspects of industrialization and economic development. They were convinced that Turkey's economic progress depended, not on the slow process of creating a strong foundation, but on expanding certain key sectors of the economy whose rapid growth would have side effects that would soon encompass the entire economic life of the country.

Despite all the encouragement and concessions, foreign investment remained disappointingly low, insufficient to make a dent in the problem of Turkey's development.[37] It neither provided the capital necessary to develop and exploit her resources; nor did it create jobs to ease the increasing unemployment. Nevertheless the influence of foreign capital in Turkish industry was totally out of proportion to the amount invested. It marked the beginning of the period of partnership between foreign and local enterprises which resulted in the dwarfing of local capitalism by the stronger and more developed partner. The development of a national Turkish industry was virtually impossible—but that became apparent only in the sixties.

The Agrarian Sector

Industry had always been the stepchild of the Turkish economy and the emphasis had invariably been placed on agriculture and commerce. This was due to the political strength of the commercial bourgeoisie in the towns and of the landowners in the countryside;

the relative weakness of the industrial sector was self-perpetuating. From the very foundation of the Republic, the Kemalists established a régime based on a tacit alliance between the modernizing bureaucracy, the commercial bourgeoisie, and the landowners. It is not surprising, therefore, that when étatism was introduced in the thirties it affected only industry and not agriculture or commerce. The government made no serious attempt to regulate commercial or agricultural activity, even though the various governments of the Republic were aware of the need to introduce land reform in order to correct some of the social and economic imbalances.[38] Both merchants and landlords grew even stronger with time, especially in the war years when they amassed considerable fortunes: their political influence increased along with their economic strength, and this found expression in the policies pursued by the two major parties in the post-war period.

The Democrats made agriculture the cornerstone of their economic policy, natural enough in a country 80 per cent of whose population was employed on the land and in which 50·5 per cent of the gross national product (GNP) came from agriculture.[39] But, as with industry, the Democrats made no attempt to create an infrastructure for Turkish agriculture by introducing intensive irrigation works or building enough fertilizer factories. This would have required a long-term programme and the Democrats were concerned with a rapid increase in production. In the short run their policy was most successful and during the years 1951 to 1954 production rose sharply. However, improved practices accounted for only 7 per cent; the increased acreage sown accounted for 36, the weather for 32, mechanization for 10, and transportation for 10 per cent of the increase in production.[40] The government believed that, by increasing purchasing power in the agricultural sector it would stimulate a demand for industrial and consumer goods which would benefit the economy as a whole.

The Democrats were committed to maintaining the existing structure of land ownership and therefore made no attempt to implement the Law for Providing Land to the Farmer (*Çiftçiyi Topraklandırma Kanunu*), passed in 1945 and amended in March 1950. According to their Minister of Agriculture Nihat Iyriboz, the 'Land Law the former administration passed was harmful and provided no benefits. Since former times the system of tenant farming [or share-cropping, *ortakçılık*] has been in practice. Under this system the wealthy landowner provided the small farmer with credit in kind and in cash. The Land Law ended that and created conflict over land between the landlord and the tenant. Now, we shall encourage tenant farming and also try to give land to the landless as soon as possible.' And he went on to promise that 'The big landlord will be protected and the Land Law will be brought to life. We shall provide aid to set up big estates and encourage the development of animal husbandry.[41]

It was hardly possible to reconcile the protection of the landlords and the creation of big estates with bringing the Land Law 'to life'. The government did distribute about 1·8 million hectares to about 360,000 families between 1947 and 1962, but only 8,600 hectares were taken from private land. Almost all the land distributed belonged to the state and was already in use as grazing.[42]

The losers from this scheme were largely the landless or near-landless peasants who had used the communal grazing lands. And in many cases the families who acquired land did not in fact benefit, because, as Yaşar Kemal reported: 'The peasant is again share-cropping on the lands distributed by the government; *he provides the land, the ağa provides the tractor.*'[43] In the past, the *ağa* (landlord) had provided the land and the peasant his labour!

A Western anthropologist who visited Turkey in the early fifties observed: 'The machine thus replaces implements and animal power [which the tenant had provided, and the] higher cost of investment is mentioned [by the landlord] to justify the change in the relation to the tenant. As the tenant usually does not get more land, he has less work to do but, getting less [work, he] is impoverished. The next step, already taken by some landlords, is to cultivate their land with hired "operators" (usually U.S. trained) and to terminate the relations with the tenants. These can now only get temporary work as agricultural workers in peak times and rely upon the government for resettlement [in other regions].'[44]

Land reform, however, was not merely a question of social justice; the needed increase in agricultural productivity depended upon it. The existing system of land tenure encouraged absentee landlordism and tenant farming; although it seemed to meet with the approval of the Minister of Agriculture, it did not stimulate either the owner or the tenant to make the land more productive. The large size of the estate guaranteed an adequate income to the big landowner and he had no incentive to invest more in order to increase productivity. The tenant, who tended to become a farm labourer once mechanization was introduced, was unlikely to see benefits from increased productivity either.[45]

The dramatic change in Turkish agriculture was provided by extensive mechanization, particularly the use of the tractor— sometimes, indeed, it was overused. The availability of Marshall

Aid funds facilitated the import of farm machinery which
continued to increase each year during the period 1948-57:[46]

Year	Tractors	Harvesters
1940	1,066	57
1948	1,750	994
1952	31,415	3,222
1957	44,144	6,523
1962	43,747	6,072

The tractor made it possible for new lands to be brought under
cultivation, and the area sown increased from 13,900,000 hectares
in 1948 to 22,940,000 hectares in 1959. The most rapid expansion
took place in the years 1950 to 1956, when the area under
cultivation increased from 14,542,000 to 22,453,000 hectares.[47]

These were the 'golden years' of the Menderes decade, when
Turkey became an exporter of grain. But an 'economic miracle'
based on such flimsy foundations was doomed to collapse, and the
stagnation had already begun to set in by 1955. In the four years
(1950 to 1953) the country witnessed a rapid growth of the
economy at an average rate of 13 per cent per annum. This was
due largely to the booming agrarian sector. In 1954 the rate of
growth dropped to 9·5 per cent and exposed the haphazard nature
of the economic régime. These years of plenty were followed by the
lean years of spiralling inflation (1956-9), when prices rose about
18 per cent a year.[48] By the end of the decade the average rate of
growth had flattened out to a mediocre 4 per cent per annum. In
spite of this indifferent rate of growth, the Democrats succeeded in
altering social and economic relationships in the countryside. This
was especially true in the areas where there was wide-scale
mechanization, as in the Çukurova region of southeast Anatolia
and in the Aegean-Marmara region.

Yaşar Kemal described vividly the transformation wrought by
farm mechanization in his native Çukurova. By late 1952 the
tractor had replaced the ox for ploughing and not an inch of land
remained uncultivated. But increasing prosperity and growing
poverty went side by side. Those with plots too small to make the
use of a tractor economically feasible, found they could no longer
live by farming. A few became drivers or mechanics on the big
estates, while the vast majority became agricultural labourers or
migrated to the towns. 'After this,' observed a villager, 'no one
without sufficient land can live in Çukurova.' But it was also
already clear that the infrastructure for mechanized farming was
lacking and Yaşar Kemal predicted correctly that the lack of spare

parts and mechanics would turn Çukurova into a 'graveyard of tractors'.[49]

As a result of migration, landowners were able to increase the size of their holdings, while at the same time rural unemployment, always a problem in Turkey, now reached serious proportions. The peasant migrants in the towns began to pose new problems for the government. As early as January 1951 it was estimated there were over a million unemployed in the towns as a consequence of rural migration.[50] One of the outcomes was an increase in urban crime and the *Cumhuriyet* proposed introducing limits on travel to, and residence in, big towns.[51]

The Democrats supported their policy of mechanization with a generous extension of credit to landlords. These credits, extended through the Agricultural Bank, increased from TL 112 million in 1945 to TL 412 million in 1950 and TL 2,392 million in 1960.[52] Originally, the credit scheme had formed a part of the Land Law of 1945. Its function was to provide credit to peasants who were to benefit from land distribution, so that they would be able to use their newly acquired land productively. But the credits came to be used mainly by prosperous landlords to purchase tractors and farm machinery. In 1951 the International Bank mission warned the government against extending credits before farmers had been taught how to use them productively. 'But', writes Eren, 'the general tendency in Turkey to minimize the human element, and to expect material factors to operate automatically prevailed. Generous agricultural credits were supplied without the indispensable concomitant: education for increased productivity. Naturally, they were squandered either in over-capitalization such as the purchase of uneconomic tractors, or radios, new clothes, furniture—items unrelated to increases in the output of the farm.'[53]

The IBRD mission to Turkey presented its report to Bayar in June 1951. Its proposals for developing agriculture were long term and stressed the training of personnel, experiments with seed, use of fertilizers, etc., in order to increase productivity. The Democrats did not adopt these proposals; they claimed that time was lacking and they preferred policies which gave quick results.[54]

The Democrats encouraged production in another way, namely by instituting an agricultural price policy unduly favourable to the producer. At the same time, agricultural incomes were not taxed, with the result that the landowners prospered and accumulated considerable wealth.[55] The Soil Products Bureau bought crops at inflated prices. The sum paid to farmers, wrote *The Economist*, increased from TL 22,800,000 in 1949 to 1950 to TL 519,165,000 during the 'last seven months'[56] [of 1954]. The result was an

increase in the inequality of incomes in the agrarian sector, and a
concomitant increase in consumption—and therefore a constantly
growing demand for consumer goods. This policy, which amounted
to a farm subsidy, was a drain on the exchequer and increased the
already high inflation of the mid-fifties. Since it was political in
character, the government could not abandon this policy without
risking defeat at the polls.

The Commercial Sector

The policy of quick and substantial returns, which the DP
government applied to foreign trade and to agriculture, was also
applied to internal trade. Such a policy reflected the predominance
of the spirit of profit over the spirit of enterprise in the Turkey of
Menderes. Its negative implications for the growth of a rigorous
entrepreneurial class were noted by Sabri Ülgener.

A policy based on all kinds of restrictions (import licenses, etc.)
provided non-professional persons, rather than the businessmen with the
opportunity to make large profits. This, too, encouraged the retainment of
the old concept of value. The policy pursued during these fifteen years
[1946-60] discouraged the spread of the idea that profits can be *earned* as
a result of long and arduous work. Instead, it fostered the belief that
business can be conducted [only] through personal contact and influence.
Thus, making money in the quick way and spending it just as easily
became very attractive.[57]

In Turkey there was an articulate and disgruntled business
community with a developed sense of group consciousness but
lacking what might be described as 'the spirit of capitalism'. Ever
since the founding of the Republic its members had formed a
strong political lobby, whose interests the government always took
into account. This group, composed of politicians, bureaucrats,
and even military officers, left the arduous task of establishing
industry to the state and concentrated its attention on the more
profitable activity of banking and commerce.[58] By the end of the
Second World War this lobby was stronger than ever. Kâzım
Taşkent, who, according to some former Democrats, directed this
lobby within the DP, founded the Yapı ve Kredi Bankası on 9
September 1944, a bank which continues to play an important role
in the economic and political life of the country.[59]

The groups which derived most benefit from the government's
economic policies were therefore the wealthy landowners, the
bankers, and the merchants. The liberalization of foreign trade,
which the Republicans began in 1946, was continued by the

Democrats, who believed that their programme of development called for a great increase in imports, of which the country had been long starved by the former government. They began the process of deficit financing of imports which soon liquidated the gold reserves accumulated by their cautious Republican predecessors.[60] Moreover, they incurred a huge foreign debt and began to find it increasingly difficult to obtain new credits abroad.

The value of the American dollar, which was maintained at TL 2·8 between the two devaluations of 1946 and 1958, while the market value was between TL 10 and 12, made importing foreign goods a very profitable business,[61] But Menderes, speaking in December 1955, rationalized the existence of the artificial rate of exchange in another way and refused to envisage devaluation:

> With respect to the protection of the value of our money, our decision is that we shall never consider any change in the value of our money despite all sorts of propaganda to the contrary. ... Because any change in the value of our money will mean the increase of the cost of capital to be invested in production in the country, the creation of an artificial pressure on prices in the domestic markets, the decrease of the value of national labour, the decrease of the purchasing power obtained through the sale of our products and our exports, an increase in the weight of our obligations to foreign countries, and an increase of our burdens.[62]

Only a small group with the political influence to acquire the cheap foreign exchange and the import licences was able to take advantage of this policy. Otherwise this policy was detrimental to industry and the export trade, both of which had to be subsidized by the government. It discouraged the *bona fide* businessman who lacked political influence and encouraged the influential profiteer and speculator.

Inflation 1954–1960

The shortcomings of the foreign trade policy had become evident to Menderes as early as 1952, and in September that year the government began to reconsider its policy of liberalization.[63] But the measures the government took were directed against the symptoms rather than the causes. By 1954 it had decided to limit imports to essential commodities and raw materials and attempted to curb speculation by asking importers to deposit payments within a period of five months with the Central Bank. It issued a decree fixing permissible profit margins and set up an office to control prices. Restrictions were placed on foreign travel and foreign exchange, and there were even rumours that the government intended to restrict agricultural credits and tax farm incomes; but these remained rumours.[64]

In spite of such measures, shortages of goods, profiteering and speculation continued unabated. By the middle of 1955 the government began to consider extraordinary measures of control, including the National Defence Law which was passed on 18 May 1956 after much soul-searching in the Democrat Party. This law, which violated almost all the promises the party had made earlier, gave the government the power to regulate the economy, along with increased power to regulate the distribution and pricing of goods and services.[65]

The economy was now in crisis. The lack of foreign exchange led to the drying up of almost all imports, and the lack of raw materials forced factories to operate at half their capacity. Even General Electric was threatened with closure.

In spite of radical legislation, the Democrats could not restore stability and confidence by piecemeal measures. They were victims of their own naive economic philosophy, believing that growth was the same as development. Their policy of cheap farm credits, government-supported prices for farm produce, and virtual tax exemption of agricultural incomes created a class of prosperous landowners and brought dynamism to the countryside. But this prosperity stimulated consumption and created a demand which the economy was incapable of meeting.[66] It also led to an increase in the price of food and an overall inflation which dislocated the entire economy and affected almost all sections of the population, especially those on fixed salaries and wages.

Menderes was never able to consider measures which would be unpopular with the rural electorate and his agricultural policy was the source of the country's economic troubles. The price he paid to the farmer was twice as high as the world price, causing a great loss to the treasury. The easy credits not only stimulated consumption, but left little for reinvestment and widened the economic gap in rural society. The failure to tax farm incomes discouraged productivity and at the same time robbed the state of revenue. Menderes's success at the polls in May 1954 convinced him of the validity of his policies, which he believed had been endorsed by the electorate.[67] The appeasement of the Turkish farmer came to be seen as the way to guarantee political success. It is not therefore surprising that Menderes's announcement on 19 May 1957 that he was going to put up the purchase price of wheat was interpreted as the signal for an early general election.[68]

By the late fifties the Democrats had lost control over the economy. None of their measures had produced the expected stability and confidence. The result of the 1957 election was a rude shock and there was little doubt that the set-back for the DP was brought about by the failure of its economic policy.

Menderes was convinced that his problems were temporary and that all he needed was a little time before the economy began to deliver the goods. He was convinced that his investments would begin to pay off and he hoped to buy time with the help of his foreign allies, especially his friends in Washington. In late July 1958 the Western powers announced their programme to rescue the Turkish economy and the Menderes government. They agreed to provide Ankara with a loan of $359 million and the consolidation of the $400 million debt. Of this sum, America agreed to provide $234 million, the European Economic Union $100 million, and the International Monetary Fund $25 million.[69]

This was indeed a 'rescue operation' which provided the vital injection of foreign exchange into Turkey's anaemic economy. But, along with this injection, the Western powers put pressure on Menderes to carry out measures 'to stabilize' the economy. The most important of these measures was the *de facto* devaluation of the lira from TL 2·80 to TL 9·025 to the dollar.

Despite the great optimism in Turkey and abroad, the effects of this credit were only temporary. According to Professor Hershlag, 'This "rescue operation", which constituted a major deviation from previous policies, might have proved successful and restored confidence and stability, if other supplementary measures—such as better choice of priorities, improvement in efficiency, reduction of external deficit, and consolidation of foreign debt—had been also put into effect successfully.... Following slackening production and increased deficits on current account in 1959 and 1960, the economically and politically undermined government was unable to hold its own.'[70]

By late 1958 Menderes was no longer politically capable of taking the necessary measures to stabilize the economy. If anything, the political struggle against the opposition parties forced him to disregard unpopular schemes in view of ever-impending elections. When Menderes was overthrown in May 1960 the Turkish economy was in collapse and one of the principal tasks of the régime that took over was to restore it to health.

NOTES

1 Tunaya, *Partiler*, 641. See above ch. 2, and Lewis, *Emergence*, 383. Nuri Demirağ (1886-1957) began life as a banker. In 1936 he set up an

aircraft factory and became an important figure in industry. He entered politics in 1945, and was elected Representative for Sivas in 1954.

2 If the figure for 1938 be taken as 100, between 1938 and 1945 Turkey's national income dropped from 100 to 77; her *per capita* income from 100 to 69, and agricultural production from 100 to 74, reflecting the general economic decline of the war years. See OECD, *Country Reports on the Organisation of Scientific Research: Turkey* (Paris, 1964), 19 and *passim*.

3 Necmettin Sadak, *Akşam*, 16 Dec. 1945. For the debate on étatism see Korkut Boratav, *Türkiye'de Devletçilik, 1923-1950* (1962).

4 Menderes's programme speech of 29 May 1950 in Öztürk, *Hükümetler*, 348-9.

5 Robert Kerwin, 'Private Enterprise in Turkish Industrial Development', *MEJ*, v/I (1951), 24. Kerwin arrived in Turkey in 1948 to study Turkish industry. He joined the International Bank for Reconstruction and Development in 1950 and wrote a PhD thesis 'Étatism and the Industrialization of Turkey' (1956).

6 Kerwin's article (as previous note), 24. See also Max Thornburg and others, *Turkey: an Economic Appraisal* (1949). Thornburg was Chairman of the Board of Engineers of the Standard Oil Company of California, Vice-President in charge of Middle Eastern and Far Eastern subsidiaries, and Petroleum Adviser to the US Department of State. In 1956 Menderes employed him as his adviser on economic affairs.

7 Karpat, *Politics*, 172-3; Erhan Bener, 'Foreign Trade Régime of Turkey', in ESSCB, *Foreign Trade and Economic Development* (1970), 174-5.

8 The Turkish press, 1 Dec. 1946; *Ayın Tarihi*, Dec. 1946, 226-7.

9 For the RPP manifesto see Bilsay Kuruç, *İktisat Politikasinin Resmi Belgeleri* (1963), 114-15; for the DP manifesto see *MEA*, i/5 (1950), 149-50, and *Ayın Tarihi*, May 1950, 53-61.

10 Celâl Bayar used the analogy of cooks using the same ingredients to make a *helva*; one of them would outdo the others, and that one, claimed Bayar, was the DP. (Conversation with Bayar.)

11 Kuruç, *İktisat*, 117; *Ayın Tarihi*, May 1950, 70-2.

12 Öztürk, *Hükümetler*, 351-4; Kuruç, *İktisat*, 118-19.

13 As previous note.

14 Belen, *Demokrasi*, 20.

15 Kerwin, 'Private Enterprise', *MEJ*, v/I (1951), 24.

16 Belen, *Demokrasi*, 17.

17 Menderes, *Konuşmalar*, i, 243; Eroğul, *Demokrat Parti*, 96; and see above, 49-50.

18 *Cumhuriyet*, 7 July 1950. The clumsier term 'de-étatize' has been used in preference to 'denationalize' because the Turks themselves, until recently, preferred to use *devletleştirmek* (to étatize) rather than *millileştirmek* (to nationalize), unconsciously revealing the gulf between state and nation.

19 *Cumhuriyet*, 5 Aug. 1950; Osman Okyar, 'Industrialization in Turkey', *MEA*, iv/6-7 (1953), 214-15; and Eroğul, *Demokrat Parti*, 69.

20 'Recent Developments in Turkey', *IA*, xxvii (1951), 328 and 329.

21 Okyar, Industrialization, *MEA*, iv/6-7 (1953), 215-16 and his article 'Hususi Teşebbüs Mevzuunda ne Yapılacaktı, ne Yapıldı', *Cumhuriyet*, 9 June 1957.

22 C. H. Dodd, *Politics and Government in Turkey* (1969), 50. See also Sadun Aren, *Ekonomi El Kitabı*, 3rd edn. (1972), 159 where development of the state and private sectors during the period 1950-60 is compared.

23 Ankara Radio, 15 Nov. 1952, in *SWB*, iv/312/24. Menderes gave somewhat different and more detailed information: 'While the Sümerbank met 60 per cent of our textile requirements in 1938, now it can meet only 40 per cent.' Ibid., 8 Jan. 1953, in *SWB*, iv/328/24.

24 Aren, *Ekonomi*, 81-2; Kenan Bulutoğlu, *Türkiye'de Yabancı Sermaye* (1970), 154-5.

25 *Cumhuriyet*, 13 and 16 May 1951. Conversations with former Democrats. The same attitude still prevails among the members of most political parties, including the RPP, but time and experience have made for a little more caution.

26 Ankara Radio, 26 Feb. 1954, in SWB, iv/445/21-2; Recep Bilginer and Mehmet Ali Yalçın, eds., *Türkiye Reisicumhuru Celâl Bayar'ın Amerika Seyahatleri* (n.p., n.d. [1954]), 150-2.

27 The Turkish press, 2 Aug. 1951; Bulutoğlu, *Yabancı Sermaye*, 155-6; Robinson, *Republic*, 314.

28 Doçent Dr Mehmed Oluç, 'Yabancı Sermaye Teşvik Kanunu ile Hariçden Sermaye Akını Beklemiyelim', *Cumhuriyet*, 14 Aug. 1951.

29 Reported over Ankara Radio, 29 Nov. 1952 in *SWB*, iv/318/19-20 and Nadir Nadi, 'Hükümetimizin Yeni Petrol Siyaseti', *Cumhuriyet*, 1 Dec. 1952.

30 Quoted on Ankara Radio, 7 Dec. 1952, in *SWB*, iv/320/22.

31 Ankara Radio, 29 Aug. 1953, in *SWB*, iv/394/19; *Ulus*, 29 Aug. and *Cumhuriyet*, 30 Aug. 1953.

32 *Ulus*, 29 Aug. 1953.

33 *Cumuhuriyet*, 11 Sept. 1953.

34 Bulutoğlu, *Yabancı Sermaye*, 155-6; Hershlag, *Turkey*, 152-4. This amendment coincided with President Bayar's state visit to America (27 Jan. to 27 Feb. 1954). One of the aims of this visit was to procure more aid and investments.

35 See, for example, Nadir Nadi, 'Yabancı Kapital' and 'Köşeyi Dönen Türkiye', *Cumhuriyet*, 13 and 14 Jan. 1954.

36 *Cumhuriyet*, 4 Oct. 1956. Menderes made his statement in order to refute the Republican Party's accusations that the Democrats were selling Turkey to the foreigners and restoring the régime of the capitulations.

37 Bulutoğlu, *Yabancı Sermaye*, 157-62; see especially the table on 158 giving figures for foreign investment during the years 1951 to 1960.

38 Kuruç, *İktisat*, 3, 44, 45, 46, 51, 79, 81, cites eight occasions on which the government proposed land reform between 1929 and 1943. See also Aren, *Ekonomi*, 143-6. The government's attitude towards industry may be judged from the fact that there was no Ministry of Industries until 1957.

39 Menderes's programme in Öztürk, *Hükümetler*, 356. This point was emphasized in every programme and presidential speech. In the years 1950 and 1952 industry provided 11·9 per cent of the GNP and services 37·6 per cent. See Aren, *Ekonomi*, 47.

40 H. Chenery and others, *Turkish Investment and Economic Development* (1953), cited in Osman Okyar, 'Agricultural Price Policy: the Turkish Experience', in ESSCB, *Agricultural Aspects of Economic Development* (1965), 290-1. See also Eren, *Turkey Today—and Tomorrow*, 103.

41 Statement to the press, *Cumhuriyet*, 12 Sept. 1950. On the question of land reform see Reşat Aktan, 'Land Reform', in ESSCB, *Agricultural Aspects*, 317-34; Suat Aksoy, *Turkiye'de Toprak Meselesi* (1970); Muzaffer Sencer, *Türkiye'de Köylülüğün Maddi Temelleri* (1971). For another view on this question see A. J. Meyer, *Middle Eastern Capitalism* (1959), ch. v, 'Turkish Land Reform: an Experiment in Moderation', 65-79.

According to Sencer (172-5), *Ortakcılık* (tenant farming or sharecropping), to which Nihat İyriboz refers, used to be widely prevalant in many parts of Turkey, especially in east and southeast Anatolia. In this system the landowner supplied the land, sometimes with implements, draught animals, and seed, and the tenant worked the land and owed the landlord a share of the produce. The share differed from one region to the next, according to local conditions and the agreement between landlord and tenant. In some regions the landlord's share was half and the system came to be called *yarıcılık*. Under the *marabacılık* agreement the landlord took as much as two-thirds or three-quarters of the produce. The tenant had no security of tenure and the agreements were renewable annually, after the harvest.

42 See Aktan, 'Land Reform', in ESSCB, *Agricultural Aspects*, 26; Aksoy, *Toprak*, 65-7; Sencer, *Türkiye'de Köylülük*, 91 gives an annual breakdown of land distribution for the years 1947 to 1962. Land distribution was a political gesture which was appreciated by most segments of the rural population and probably raised expectations. But its practical effect was negligible.

43 *Cumhuriyet*, 23 June 1955 (Yaşar Kemal's italic). The term *ağa* means more than the mere ownership of land. It has connotations of feudalism and is applied to men who sometimes own entire villages, and exercise great local power and authority over the peasantry. The word has pejorative overtones and is associated with an outmoded form of agriculture in which share-cropping is used rather than wage labour. This became less true after the introduction of mechanization in agriculture. The *ağas* were a very important factor in competitive politics because all parties sought their favour since they could deliver large blocks of votes.

The army, after overthrowing the DP, tried to break the power of the *ağas* in parts of eastern Turkey by removing 'fifty-five *ağas* to compulsory residence in western Turkey, and [by] the confiscation for future distribution of their lands. Breaking the power of these owners of large lands and often many villages, who exercised virtually feudal role over large numbers of peasants, had been one of Atatürk's chief efforts in eastern Turkey, but much of the old order still remained in 1960—and does today 1963.... The effectiveness of the *ağas'* political power became clear when the coalition government ... let them return and restored all their land and property that had not yet been distributed.' Walter Weiker, *The Turkish Revolution 1960-1961* (1963), 144-5; see below, 216.

44 Wolfram Eberhard, 'Change in Leading Families in Southern Turkey', in Louise E. Sweet, ed., *Peoples and Cultures of the Middle East*, ii (New York, 1970), 246-7, n. 13. Eberhard's essay was originally published in *Anthropos*, IL (1954), 992-1003.

45 Aktan, 'Land Reform', in ESSCB, *Agricultural Aspects*, 23.

46 Aksoy, *Toprak*, 71; his table is based on government figures. Sencer, *Türkiye'de Köylülük*, 117. Eren, *Turkey Today—and Tomorrow*, 113-14, quotes from an FAO report on Turkey in 1959 which suggests that the tractors imported by the government were not suitable for Turkish conditions.

47 Sencer, *Türkiye'de Köylülük*, 110. See also D. Kayran, 'The Plan and the Agricultural Sector', in S. İlkin and E. İnanç, eds., *Planning in Turkey* (1967), 116-17, in which there is a table showing changes in the pattern of land use in the years 1950-60.

48 Korkut Boratav, *Gelir Dağılımı* (1969), 186. See also Gülten Kazgan, 'Structural Changes in Turkish National Income, 1950:60', in Taufiq M. Khan, ed., *Middle Eastern Studies in Income and Wealth* (London, 1965), 148-67.

49 'Çukurova'da Traktör Dostları ve Traktör Düşmanları' and 'Çukurova'da Traktör Oburluğu', *Cumhuriyet*, 11 and 21 Nov. 1952. Many of Yaşar Kemal's reports on Anatolia in the years 1951-8 have been collected in *Bu Diyar Baştan Başa* (1971). See also Reşat Aktan, 'Zirai İstihsalde Makine Kullanılması Hadisesinin Ekonomik Analizi', *SBFD*, ix/1 (1954), 11-44; R. Robinson, 'Tractors in the Village—a Study in Turkey', *Journal of Farm Economics*, Nov. 1952, 451-62; W. H. Pine, 'Some Land Problems in Turkey', *Journal of Farm Economics*, May 1952, 263-7; K. Karpat, 'Social Effects of Farm Mechanization in Turkish Villages', *Social Research*, xxvii (1960), 83-103. Farm mechanization did succeed in creating a new group in the rural social structure: the tractor drivers and mechanics. These people with their modern training and indoctrination acquired a vested interest in the new agriculture and they became the articulate spokesmen of change in rural Turkey.

50 *Cumhuriyet*, 6 and 16 Jan. 1951.

51 'Asayiş Meselesi', ibid., 15 Dec. 1951. The urban population increased from 18·5 per cent of the total population in 1950 to 25·2 per cent in 1960. See Ruşen Keleş, *Türkiye'de Şehirleşme, Konut ve Gecekondu* (1972), 8 and *passim*. Fehmi Yavuz, 'Planning the Development of Villages and Cities', ESSCB, *Social Aspects of Economic Development* (1964), 38, gives different figures. He writes that the urban population rose from 25 per cent (1950) to 31·9 per cent in 1960. Both agree that the increase was about 6·8 per cent. Louis Dollot, *La Turquie Vivante* (1957),

23, gives population figures for some of the major cities and towns for the years 1927, 1950, and 1955.

52 Aksoy, *Toprak*, 67–73 and Boratav, *Gelir*, 128.

53 Eren, *Turkey Today—and Tomorrow*, 115. See also Howard A. Reed: 'Although sold relatively cheaply, these tractors still cost between ten and twenty thousand Turkish liras, roughly $3,500–$7,000, which is a fabulous sum to the average peasant whose normal cash income before the recent boom seldom exceeded $250 annually. This means that the wealthy peasants, or a relatively small number of absentee landlords, have bought most of the tractors and the farm equipment which they, themselves, use to good advantage and also rent, at about four dollars per acre, to their neighbours....' See 'A New Force at Work in Democratic Turkey', *MEJ*, vii/1 (1953), 38.

54 See International Bank for Reconstruction and Development, *The Economy of Turkey* (1951). For a penetrating critique of this report see Ömer Celâl Sarç, 'International Bank Report on Turkey', *MEJ*, vi/x (1952), 336–40.

55 See Okyar, 'Agricultural Price Policy: the Turkish Experience', in ESSCB, *Agricultural Aspects*, 281–320.

56 'Progress in Turkey's Villages', *The Economist*, 20 Mar. 1954. This wealth filtered down to other layers of rural society, creating a sense of prosperity and well-being unknown in the past. The Democrats also opened up the countryside with a road construction programme sponsored by the US government, ending centuries of isolation. See Daniel Lerner, *The Passing of Traditional Society* (1964), 111–66.

57 Sabri Ülgener, 'Value Patterns of Traditional Societies: the Turkish Experience', in ESSCB, *Social Aspects*, 132–3. See also Thomas Balogh, *The Economics of Poverty* (New York, 1970), 195–6.

58 The founding of the Türkiye İş Bankası is a good example; members of the Turkish establishment looked upon it as a source of quick fortunes. See the cover story 'İş Bankası Savcılıkta', 7 *Gün*, i/16, 27 Dec. 1972, 12–19; 7 *Gün*, i/7, 25 Oct. 1972, 17–21; *Yeni Ortam*, 9 Oct. 1973, 5; and Doğan Avcıoğlu, *Devrim Üzerine* (1971), 104–5. Bayar, who was the founder of İş Bankası, was sometimes accused of promoting its interests when he founded the DP.

59 *Cumhuriyet*, 10 Sept. 1973 on the occasion of the twenty-ninth anniversary of the bank. Banks have mushroomed and expanded during the multi-party period and their political influence is considerable, simply judging by their representation in the political parties and the cabinets. Unfortunately, there is no study that I know of which examines their role. The Turkish Left, however, has given it great emphasis; see, for example, the *Proleter Devrimci Aydınlık* (no. 36, 30 Mar. 1971), which announced the formation of the Erim cabinet with the headline: 'The Big Bourgeoisie has formed the New Government: Akbank and Has Holding have gone—Koç Holding and Yapı ve Kredi Bankası have arrived.'

60 Memduh Yasa, 'The Development of the Turkish Economy and Foreign Trade', in ESSCB, *Foreign Trade and Economic Development* (1970), 48–50.

61 Kemal Kurdaş, 'Basic Factors Impeding a Rapid Growth of the Turkish Economy', in ESSCB, *Capital Formation and Investment in Industry* (1963), 22.

62 Quoted in Hershlag, *Turkey*, 145.

63 Memduh Yasa, 'The Development of the Turkish Economy and Foreign Trade', in ESSCB, *Foreign Trade and Economic Development*, 49.

64 *Swiss Review of World Affairs*, iv, Oct. 1954, 16–18.

65 The debate on the Bill began on 7 May 1956; see the Turkish press 8–18 May 1956.

66 *The Economist*, 20 Mar. 1954; Reed, 'New Force', *MEJ*, vii/1 (1953), 33–4; Paul Stirling, 'Two Turkeys', *The Listener*, 29 Apr. 1954.

67 Menderes's statement in the Assembly on 24 May 1954 in Öztürk, *Hükümetler*, 391.

68 See above, 56 and *Cumhuriyet*, 18, 20, and 21 May 1957.

69 The Turkish press, 4 Aug. 1958; *The Economist*, 9 Aug. 1958 ('A Rescue Operation'); and Hershlag, *Turkey*, 147.

70 Hershlag, *Turkey*, 147.

CHAPTER VI

MILITARY RULE
MAY 1960—SEPTEMBER 1961

We shall continue our efforts to bring our heroic army to a position consonant with the needs of today and capable of meeting every kind of aggression. This will be accomplished by using all material and moral resources in proportion to the strength of our economic and financial potential [Applause]. In fact, one of the main goals of our economic measures and development is to maintain, with our own means, a large army as soon as possible.... As has been our practice so far, military appropriations will increase in proportion to the growth in our national income.

Adnan Menderes's programme speech before the Grand National Assembly, 24 May 1954

The clique in power after 1954 trampled on all the rights of the people. They deceived the nation and dragged the country into economic and social ruin. Moral values were forgotten and people were made oblivious of them. The institution of the state was transformed into an appendage of the party organization. The pride of the Turkish Armed Forces, which are the only organized force in the country, was hurt on every occasion; the uniform which is the real legacy of our history brought shame to those who wore it ...

Orhan Erkanlı, interview in *Cumhuriyet*, 20 July 1960

The DP and the Armed Forces

FROM the very beginning of the multi-party period, the role of the armed forces became a major concern for the Democrats. They expected the army to be sympathetic to the Republican People's Party, especially while İsmet İnönü, a former general greatly respected in military circles, remained its leader. Moreover, the RPP was intimately identified with the state, to which the army was bound to be loyal. Loyalty in Turkish political culture tended to mean hostility, at least potential and latent, to the opposition.

The Democrats were aware of their isolation from the state and therefore tried to counterbalance İnönü's influence by recruiting the retired Marshal Fevzi Çakmak and other generals. Çakmak, who had been Chief of the General Staff until January 1944, enjoyed an awe-inspiring reputation and prestige in the armed forces. Before the general election of 1946 both parties competed to secure him as their candidate. Çakmak turned down five Republican offers and finally agreed to stand as an independent for Istanbul on the DP list.[1] This was a political triumph for the new party, whose leaders hoped that the Marshal and the other fourteen retired generals who were standing as DP candidates would be an insurance against action by the state.

The election of 1946, rigged on behalf of the governing party, introduced a new element into Turkish politics, namely junior officers willing to act on behalf of the Democrats. This was not so surprising in view of the fact that there had been disaffection in the army as early as the late thirties, most probably following the death of Atatürk, the charismatic and historic leader of the Turkish Republic. Of all the institutions of the Republican period, the army had changed least. It had retained the equipment, strategy, and mentality of the First World War and the War of National Independence. The army, indeed the country as a whole, had been totally unprepared for the years of armed neutrality during the Second World War. Except for the senior officers, its members had suffered great deprivation during the war, along with the urban population—again, with the exception of state officials and businessmen. Alparslan Türkeş, who was a young officer at the time, wrote:

During this period, the administration, with the *Milli Şef* [National Leader] and his accomplices in the lead, adopted a patronizing and belittling attitude towards the army and the officers and the generals who led it. The rising cost of living and the struggle to survive was humiliating and suffocating to the officers. Everywhere officers were treated like second class human beings. In Ankara, people had labelled basement flats 'Staff-Officer flats'. In places of entertainment officers were nicknamed 'lemonaders' because they did not have the money to order expensive drinks and compete with the black-marketeers and profiteers; the sons of this sacrificing nation were described by such names . . .[2]

Men like Türkeş hoped that the fall of the İnönü régime and the rule of the Democrats would bring better days. But when they witnessed the fraud of the 1946 elections they became convinced that the Republicans would not relinquish power unless they were forced to do so. Many in the Democrat Party were also pessimistic about the future of multi-party politics, especially after the Republicans had turned down the proposal for proportional representation. Some of the younger members in the party, among them Samet Ağaoğlu, Mükerrem Sarol and Tevfik Ileri, had come round to the view that it was not possible to conduct a legal political struggle while the single-party mentality was dominant in the RPP. The idea of military intervention against the government appealed to them and they went so far as to make contact with some army officers who were willing to act on their behalf.[3]

But Bayar was totally opposed to any such scheme. He related to this group the anecdote of how Atatürk had been asked by some generals during the national struggle to dissolve the Assembly for the course of the war of independence. They complained that the Representatives were constantly criticizing the army and making derogatory statements about the officers which the generals found difficult to tolerate. Could the Assembly be shelved until a more appropriate time? they asked. Atatürk refused to countenance this and told them that they had better get used to criticism because to criticize was one of the functions of the Assembly. Bayar also refused to consider any form of political struggle which was extra-legal, and invited those who wanted to conduct such a struggle to leave the party. This unambiguous attitude, noted Sarol, naturally alienated those officers who sought an initiative for such an adventure from the Democrat Party.

Since the proclamation of martial law on 23 November 1940 the armed forces had played an active political role. The Democrats knew that this worked against them, in so far as it inhibited their propaganda campaign, and they finally had martial law removed in December 1947. But they continued to keep a watchful eye on the activities of the military High Command. The publication of New Year greetings from the Chief of the General Staff, General Salih Omurtak, to President İnönü brought a sharp protest from Köprülü. The greetings had concluded with the words: 'May Almighty God grant that our Great Leader will shine for ever with glory and honour upon our armed forces and our beloved Turkish nation.'[4] Köprülü held İnönü responsible for the publication of the message, which, he said, reflected the spirit of the old 'One Leader, One Party, One Nation' system and was against the spirit of democracy.[5]

The Democrats were convinced that, ever since the general election of 1946, İnönü had been encouraging the army to demonstrate in some way or other its opposition to the new party.

İnönü, claimed Celâl Bayar, had visited every army command between 1946 and 1950 in order to carry out propaganda against the Democrats. But the army had refused to respond.[6] Seyfi Kurtbek, who retired as a colonel, joined the Democrats and served as Minister of Communications and later Defence, also recounted a story bearing on the relations between the army and the RPP. The source of the story, claimed Kurtbek, was Nihat Erim, who was Deputy Prime Minister at the time.

Some months before the election of 1950 Erim met General Tınaztepe, Commander of the First Army (Istanbul). Tınaztepe expressed his apprehension about multi-party politics and the damage they were doing to the nation. The Democrats were exploiting the situation and Tınaztepe felt that it was time for the army to act. Erim returned to Ankara and reported his conversation to İnönü. İnönü took the matter seriously enough to return with Erim to Istanbul and held a meeting with Tınaztepe and other generals.

İnönü is alleged to have told the generals that they were not to worry about the political system, that the changing situation in the world had made it necessary to introduce multi-party politics and that the army should not see this as a threat to the régime. If one day the régime was threatened they could rest assured that he would 'ring the bell' and call in the army.[7]

Purge in the Army, June 1950

After the Democrats won the general election of 1950 they were apprehensive about the military's reaction. The commanders gathered in Ankara in May soon after the election, and the Democrats felt threatened. The commanders usually met in the capital twice a year (in February and July) to hold the military council meetings, so there was no reason for them to be there in May. Celâl Bayar sought information from the authorities and was told that the generals had come on military business but that they were being asked to return to their commands.[8] Later the DP leaders learned that the generals had visited İnönü and offered to intervene and annul the results of the election. İnönü had rejected this offer.[9]

The matter did not end there. On 6 June the Menderes government carried out a purge in the military High Command, removing the Chief of the General Staff and the commanders of the army, navy, and air force, as well as other generals of doubtful loyalty to the new government.[10] The immediate cause of the purge is said to have been information which a colonel gave to Menderes warning him of a military *coup* planned for 8/9 June. Menderes saw Bayar and they decided on immediate counter-measures.[11] The colonel's warning may indeed have triggered off the purge. But it is unlikely that Menderes would have felt secure in the saddle while İnönü's classmate and comrade in arms, Abdurrahman Nazif Gürman, was Chief of the General Staff. It was natural that Menderes should place men loyal to him, or at least politically neutral, in responsible positions. He did the same in the civil administration, but not as dramatically.

The pro-Republican press exploited this event politically and carried out a campaign designed to inflame feelings in the armed forces against the DP. *Hürriyet* of 9 June published a story concerning officers who had visited İnönü after the elections and offered their services to him. This, alleged *Hürriyet*, was the reason for the purge.[12] Naturally the government denied the story as implausible and told the RPP that it should not exploit a measure which it was normal for a new government to take.[13]

The Democrats had warded off any immediate threat that might come from the High Command. But they continued to feel the same uneasiness towards the armed forces as they felt towards the rest of the state apparatus. Their discomfort *vis-à-vis* the army was perhaps greater because the army was intimately linked, in the popular mind, with İnönü and the RPP. The only way to resolve this was by reforming the military institution and creating a new instrument suitable for democratic politics. This is what the Democrats decided to do. As early as 20 June 1950 the new Chief of the General Staff, Nuri Yamut, announced that democratization would soon be introduced into the army to end the rigid stratification which existed between the various ranks and to establish a more liberal atmosphere.[14]

Kurtbek's Reform Programme

The reform of the Turkish armed forces was long overdue. Both parties recognized this, although it was the Democrats who virtually made it a part of their programme. The DP's views on the issue were expressed in the Assembly discussion of the defence budget on 23 February 1949. Their spokesman Kemal Zeytinoğlu proposed that the army be reformed and modernized, and that the defence budget be prepared on the basis of economic principles, avoiding wastage and extravagance. Next day Prime Minister Günaltay reassured the military High Command that no one should expect the Republicans to carry out so rash an act as the sudden reform of the army.[15]

The DP's reformist policy was unpopular with the generals but popular with the junior officers (colonels and below), who were anxious to see the army modernized and opportunities for promotion made flexible. One of the architects of the party's scheme to create a new military institution was Colonel Seyfi Kurtbek. In 1948, while he was head of the National Mobilization Section of the General Staff, he made unofficial contact with the Democrats. He hoped that the new party would accept his radical reform proposals and put pressure on the government to adopt them. Thereafter he kept Celâl Bayar informed about military affairs and finally decided to resign his commission in order to enter politics. He was not interested in a political career but came to the conclusion that the only hope he had of implementing his military programme would be from a political base. He joined the Democrat Party in April 1950 and was elected Representative for Ankara in May.[16]

Seyfi Kurtbek entered the first Menderes cabinet as Minister of Communications on 11 August 1950 and was appointed Defence Minister on 8 November 1952. He came with a reputation as a radical reformer and there was great apprehension in the ranks of the generals, who sensed that they would be retired or at least forced to give up their power. All the opponents of military reform began a whisper campaign against Kurtbek. The principal theme of this campaign was that Kurtbek was preparing the ground for a military takeover, using the reform programme as a cover to place his men in strategic positions. They described him as an ambitious and dynamic officer who had considered 'staging a *coup* against the dictatorship of İsmet İnönü as early as 1938', while he was only a major. He was even compared to Enver Pasha, War Minister in 1914, who had also purged the army in order to capture power.[17]

But the pressures for reform were also strong. By 1952 Turkey was a member of NATO, and NATO commanders who dealt with the Turkish Armed Forces also wanted to see the system changed and rationalized. The division of power between the Defence Ministry and the General Staff was not clearly demarcated. Marshal Çakmak's long tenure as Chief of the General Staff had established the supremacy of the latter over the Minister, and that tradition was maintained even after Çakmak had gone. Kurtbek wanted to alter it, and, in accordance with the needs of a democratic state, bring the military under civilian control.

Bayar and Menderes were also anxious to have the military institution reformed; they had brought Kurtbek into the cabinet for that very purpose. On 3 May 1953 there was a cabinet meeting at which President Bayar presided. Kurtbek's entire reform programme was discussed and given the seal of approval. Menderes was delighted with it and described it as the second *Nizam-i Cedid*, a reference to the 'New Order' of Sultan Selim III (1789-1807). Bayar compared it to a surgical operation which many vested interests would oppose, but encouraged Kurtbek to resist all pressures and carry it out, promising to give him full support.[18] Seyfi Kurtbek was never able to implement his programme; one day Menderes sent a message to him and advised him to postpone the reforms for the time being. Kurtbek understood that his programme was being politely shelved and tendered his resignation on 27 July 1953.[19]

The whisper campaign had had its effect, sowing the seeds of distrust against Kurtbek in the minds of Menderes, Bayar, and those close to them. That is one theory. It is more likely that Menderes was unwilling to challenge the generals directly and at the same time leave himself open to attack from İnönü and the opposition parties. The relatively minor purge of June 1950 had been embarrassing and Kurtbek's programme was to be much more thorough-going. By temperament Menderes was not the man to face any problem head on when he could circumvent it. In this case, he was more concerned with the loyalty of the officers than with reform for its own sake. To secure their loyalty and co-operation he was willing to do without reform and sacrifice his minister.

Thus, Menderes appeased the generals but at the same time he lost the opportunity to establish firm control over the military institution. Inevitably he had undermined the authority of all the Defence Ministers who succeeded Seyfi Kurtbek, and the *de facto* control of military affairs was in the hands of the generals. Menderes's own relationship with the army seemed to be established on firm foundations. Many generals, including Chief of the General Staff Nuri Yamut and Tahsin Yazıcı, the 'hero of Korea', retired from the army and joined the Democrat Party before the 1954 election.

Junior Officers and the Democrats

The Democrats had good reason to feel confident of their generals and because of this they neglected officers of lower rank. But after Turkey joined NATO in 1952 the character of the armed forces began to change and these officers acquired an importance they had never had before. This was especially true of the staff officers, who had the mental flexibility to learn the science of modern atomic and nuclear warfare; the old generals, trained in the post-World War I era, could hardly cope. Membership of NATO therefore divided the Turkish armed forces on technological lines; Menderes's compromise with the generals accentuated this by dividing them on lines based on rank and socio-economic status. Menderes's success in winning the loyalty of the commanders became evident a few years later, when the military conspirators experienced difficulty in finding a senior general to lead their plot.

Unrest among junior officers began in the mid-fifties. This coincided with the beginning of the inflationary trend in the Turkish economy and the general disillusionment with the Democrats in the large urban centres. Menderes had not come up to the expectations of these officers. The *Milli Şef* system had been changed but it had not been replaced by anything substantially different. In fact, the system looked very much the same, with the generals—the so-called Pashas—again being feted while the rest of the army was neglected. The neglect seemed worse when the army of Turkey was compared with those of her NATO allies. The government's disregard of the material welfare of the armed forces was a serious political error. Inside NATO, the Turkish soldier became aware of his material backwardness. In contrast, other sectors of Turkish society, especially business, seemed to be thriving. Thus, traditional discipline was undermined.[20]

The army in the multi-party system did not enjoy the same political or social prestige as it had enjoyed earlier. This was not due to any sense of indifference on the part of the Democrats. Judged by Menderes's programmes, Bayar's presidential speeches, and the military budget, the army was far from neglected. But there is no doubt that the military institution came lower down the list of priorities of a government determined to develop the country than of a government concerned with maintaining stability. The Democrats did not view the army as an institution which promoted economic growth. They saw it as an instrument of foreign policy and one which ought to be financed substantially from NATO and American coffers. They often complained that the military budget was causing considerable hardship to the economy, throwing it off balance and increasing inflation. They wanted the Allies to pay more of the cost of the army which guarded NATO's eastern flank.[21]

In the context of democratic, competitive politics, the army was just another pressure group competing for scarce resources. But this was not the view the military had of itself. The Democrats wished the army to be patient, to wait for the economy to expand. Once the size of the cake had grown there would be more for everyone, especially for the army—for which Menderes is said to have had special affection.[22] Other sectors had priority: the country needed roads, electricity, water, industry, and welfare for the majority of the people.

If the Democrats had implemented such a programme, instead of merely paying lip service to it, there is little doubt that the junior officers would have waited patiently for their turn to receive benefits. But in spite of all the good intentions, all they saw was the gap between the rich and poor growing bigger, with the lower middle class, to which they belonged, on the declining side of it. The Democrats had introduced a fundamental change in values, from the mythical moral (*mânevi*) values of Turkish society to the materialistic (*maddi*) values, which were 'alien' yet praised and encouraged by the Democrats. In this scheme the soldiers found themselves being demoted in the social structure in which they had once been virtually supreme. The government did not increase salaries to keep up with the ever-rising cost of living, with the result that a young officer in 1954 found it difficult to marry and enjoy a modest standard of living on his meagre salary.

Discontent in the armed forces, however, acquired a political direction only within the context of the inter-party struggle. It was but natural that the armed forces should become infected by the political controversies raging among the politicians and that they should begin to articulate their grievances in terms similar to those of the opposition parties. Thus indirectly there is a strong relationship between unrest in the army and the activities of the RPP.

The Nine Officers Incident 1957

By September 1957 the involvement of some officers in the inter-party struggle was openly manifested by announcements in the press that officers were retiring and joining the RPP. It was already common for retired officers, usually generals, to join the ruling party; but their joining the opposition heralded something new, and, from the point of view of the Democrats, something dangerous. Staff Colonel Cemal Yıldırım retired and joined the RPP.[23] His example was followed by other officers and such moves received considerable coverage in the Turkish press, much to the joy of the Republicans and the alarm of the Democrats.[24] The political situation had deteriorated so gravely that there was talk of intervention before the 1957 election; lack of agreement among the conspirators was responsible for its postponement.[25] Some claim that the leaders of the Democrat Party intended to use the army if they lost the election. But the soldiers were in no mood to be used for such a purpose and the Republicans had been assured that they had nothing to fear from the military.[26]

If the DP did not know of the goings-on in the army, it learned of them soon enough. In late December 1957 nine serving officers were arrested in Istanbul and accused of conspiring against the government. The arrests were made public on 16 January 1958 and the Ministry of Defence issued an official statement denying that there were large-scale arrests or extensive plotting in the armed forces.[27] The officers were tried, and released, since nothing could be proved against them; only the informer was sentenced to jail.

The significance of this entire event lies in the way in which the government reacted to it. According to Celâl Yardımcı, who was Minister of Education at the time, President Bayar wanted the government to carry out a thorough investigation and uncover whatever disaffection there was, so as to put an end to any further conspiracies. Menderes was lukewarm to this idea because he did not want to show undue concern; he wanted to bury the matter as quietly as possible.

Again it was a question directly related to Menderes's personality: he wished to avoid confronting the problem lest it turn out to be more serious than he was led to believe, or rather wanted to believe. Minister of Defence Şemi Ergin and the commanders played down the significance of the incident, claiming that there was no need for a long and thorough investigation. They argued that such an investigation would antagonize the armed forces and create unrest. Menderes agreed with this diagnosis and reasoned that any pressure on the army, especially if it led to a purge, could alienate the armed forces just as the suspension of Professor Hüseyin Naili Kubalı had alienated the universities and the intelligentsia. He was also reassured by the fact that no high-ranking officers were involved, believing that while they were on his side the government was secure. Menderes refused to conduct a complete investigation of the armed forces and offered to resign rather than preside over one. Bayar, who would have been happier to see the matter cleared up, relented and stopped pressing for an investigation.[28]

Behind Menderes's reluctance to pursue the matter was the sense of insecurity about the loyalty of state institutions to the DP government. This is evident in the constant fear he had of antagonizing the armed forces. This fear was not unfounded, but the Democrats felt helpless because they did not know how to deal with it. Şemi Ergin, who was Defence Minister until 19 January 1958, knew of the existence of a conspiracy because he had been approached by the conspirators and asked to become its civilian head.[29]

Yet what could Ergin do? The Democrats simply did not have complete control over the army and a serious investigation might have exposed that. There was an investigation of sorts, followed by a trial. Faruk Güventürk, one of the conspirators, recalled: 'The trial judges Turgut Lüleci, Ârif Onat and Cemal Tural were exposed to all kinds of pressures and threats. But they did not compromise their dignity and honour.... Cemal Tural even said: "they can pension me off but they cannot soil my conscience." '[30] Tural, who was a major-general and president of the tribunal, accurately reflects the attitude of the generals upon whom Menderes was relying; it was very much a question of 'us' and 'them'.

The Conspiracy takes Shape

The arrest of the officers and the limited investigation that followed was nevertheless a temporary set-back for the conspirators. Not knowing how serious the investigation was going to be, they decided to be cautious and gave up their activities until the pressure was off.[31] However, when it became clear that the investigations were not leading anywhere, conspiratorial activity was renewed with greater secrecy and fervour. At this point the conspirators decided to find a powerful and high-ranking officer to lead the movement. Unless they found such a figure and acquired control over the Personnel Office (*Erkân Şubesi*), they would not be able to succeed in their efforts or accomplish their aims.[32] The adoption of this important decision had great repercussions, as we shall see, after the armed forces captured power in 1960.

It was not easy to find a general who was willing to collaborate with the conspirators. General Necati Tacan, who had recently been appointed Commander of the Land Forces, was approached and agreed to lead the anti-DP movement. Unfortunately for the conspirators, the general died of a heart attack in the summer of 1958 and the search for a leader started anew. Again they decided to approach the Commander of the Land Forces, and Cemal Gürsel, who had succeeded Tacan, accepted the leadership.[33] With Gürsel's help the conspirators began to occupy such key strategic positions as that of Chief of the Army Personnel Office and even the command of the Presidential Guard.[34] The ease with which they accomplished this is surprising and points to the weakness of military intelligence in the fifties. Yet military intelligence did sense that something was amiss and at the beginning of May 1960

General Gürsel was put on terminal leave and departed for İzmir on 4 May.

This was a heavy blow to the conspiratorial organization. The junior officers were in a state of panic. The time for action was approaching yet they knew it could prove fatal to carry out the *coup* without the support of a general. They considered generals Sıtkı Ulay, Fahri Özdilek, Cevdet Sunay, and Cemal Madanoğlu as possible replacements for Gürsel. Ulay was considered a government man and rejected; Özdilek and Sunay were approached but refused to join, though neither exposed the conspiracy. Sunay was the Deputy Chief of the General Staff while Özdilek was Martial Law Commander in Istanbul and both were therefore suitably placed to lead a *coup*. The last to be approached was Mandanoğlu, who was only a major-general and Chief of Logistics on the General Staff, with no active command position. After some thought he accepted almost apologetically, exclaiming: 'I have balls but no brains', to which one of the conspirators allegedly replied 'Don't worry, we have both.'[35]

Again, it is worth noting how some generals learned of the conspiracy but agreed not to inform the government. Fahri Özdilek, Cevdet Sunay, and Sıtkı Ulay were considered loyal officers, having been promoted only in August 1959.[36] According to former Democrats, both Ulay and Özdilek were very close to Menderes and even described as Menderes's men. Yet their behaviour suggests that they felt greater loyalty to the army than to the government.

Were the Democrats aware of the danger from the army? The answer must be an emphatic 'yes'. Ever since the founding of the party they had been apprehensive of the army's attitude towards multi-party politics, and, once in power, they periodically warned the opposition parties not to try to involve the armed forces in politics. The exposure of the 'Nine Officers' Conspiracy' was alarming, and the overthrow of the Iraqi monarchy by General Abdul Karim Kasim on 14 July 1958 increased the tensions. It is not surprising that Menderes spoke—for the first time on 6 September 1958—of the RPP's trying to provoke in Turkey a revolution of the Iraqi type; thereafter allusions to revolution became fairly common in the political struggle between the two parties.[37]

In the same year there were also military takeovers in Pakistan and the Sudan. The signing of the Bilateral Agreement with the United States on 5 March 1959 was partially a guarantee against such eventualities.[38] The Republicans objected to this agreement precisely because the government could request military intervention from Washington whenever it wished to do so in order to prevent 'internal, unarmed aggression'. Ecevit pointed out that no European state had a bilateral agreement with the US against an internal threat and that such agreements, with their sinister implications, were operative only with Arab states like Lebanon.[39]

Intervention, 27 May 1960

The situation for the DP government was ambiguous. The High Command seemed loyal and there were no ambitious generals ready to take over. In spite of this, the government was never at ease. Yet when the storm finally broke on 28/29 April 1960, with student demonstrations in Istanbul and Ankara, the army's support for the government was most encouraging. Pressure had been building up throughout 1959 and 1960 and these demonstrations provided the perfect opportunity for military intervention. Martial law was declared in Istanbul and Ankara on 29 April, with Generals Özdilek and Namık Argüç named as the respective commanders. The demonstrations were brought under control by firm measures even to the extent that the police and the military opened fire.

In communiqué number 15 Fahri Özdilek announced that, since most of those who were demonstrating were of such a tender age as to be considered children, tolerance had been shown during the first two days. But that state of affairs would not be permitted to continue, especially in view of the NATO Foreign Minister's Conference, due to open on 2 May.[40] Next day the demonstrators were dispersed by force and there were many arrests. But after 2 May the tension subsided and the opportunity for military intervention seemed to have disappeared. On 3 May curfew hours were reduced and General Gürsel was given terminal leave until his retirement the following June; the hopes of the conspirators seemed dimmer than ever.

The government continued to be apprehensive about military intervention and on 6 May Foreign Minister Zorlu told journalists that 'The Turkish officer is fully aware that the army should not interfere in politics.' On the same day İnönü denied that his party had any connection whatsoever with the military but made the ominous point that 'an oppressive régime can never be sure of the army'.[41]

The writing was on the wall but the government could do no more than offer belated concessions to the soldiers. Fifteen days before the *coup* officers were promised new and higher pay scales.[42] The government promised to improve their conditions of service and to look into the question of providing reasonably priced, comfortable quarters for them.[43] When the War College cadets held their silent demonstration in Ankara on 21 May, the government met their demand and released officers who had been arrested, including a Colonel İsmail Atak.[44] The conspirators were unaware of the timidity and indecision of the Democrat Party, and were furious with the organizers of the cadet demonstration, which threw them into panic and a state of despair. They were sure that the government would now be forced to take serious counter-measures in an effort to crush dissension in the army.[45]

Again the government temporized, reassured by the COGS, General Rüştü Erdelhun that the demonstration was not to be taken as a measure of the preparation for a rebellion.[46] During these critical days Menderes was busy addressing large public meetings in western Anatolia and trying to reassure himself by drumming up mass support in the country. It is even said that he did not believe that the army would act against him.

There was no one in the government with the will to take decisions; this marked the total bankruptcy of DP rule. Defence Minister Ethem Menderes turned down General Namık Argüç's proposal to move the armoured brigade from Konya to the capital. He claimed there was no need for that, though such a move would certainly have demoralized the conspirators.[47] The politicians, not the army, had lost the will to defend the government. For just as the government had 'no stomach for fratricidal conflict', so it is doubtful whether the conspirators would have moved against the government had they expected stiff resistance which men like Argüç were willing to provide. Thus when the military intervention took place in the early hours of 27 May there was hardly any resistance from loyalist troops and the *coup* was accomplished with the minimum of bloodshed.

Honourable fellow countrymen! Owing to the crisis into which our democracy has fallen, in view of the recent sad incidents, and in order to avert fratricide, the Turkish armed forces have taken over the administration of the country. Our armed forces have taken this initiative for the purpose of extricating the parties from the irreconcilable situation into which they have fallen, ... [and will hold] just and free elections as soon as possible under the supervision and arbitration of an above-party and impartial administration, ... [They will hand] over the administration to whichever party wins the elections.

This initiative is not directed against any person or class. Our administration will not resort to any aggressive act against individuals, nor will it allow others to do so. All fellow-countrymen, irrespective of the parties to which they may belong, will be treated in accordance with the laws ...[48]

The National Unity Committee

This radio announcement on 27 May by the officers who had just seized power was noteworthy for its stress on the purpose of their action: to extricate 'the parties from the irreconcilable situation', to set up an above-party administration, hold free elections, and hand back political power to the winning party. There was a sense of relief in the country because the political parties had become trapped in a political blind alley and this intervention seemed to provide the escape. The Democrats had feared a pro-İnönü *coup*, but those who recognized Colonel Türkeş's voice reading the first announcement over the radio knew that it could not be pro-İnönü.[49] Yet the announcements that officials, ministers, and members of the Assembly were being taken into custody were not so reassuring. Only time would clarify the character of the intervention.

The participants did not themselves know the direction their movement would take. During the period of preparation the discussions had been purposely vague, since debate on the specific could only divide. There were a number of loose factions among the conspirators: one faction wanted to overthrow the Democrats and hand over power to İnönü; another sought to eliminate corrupt politicians, hold elections, and restore power to the politicians; yet another wanted the armed forces to retain power so that they could carry out structural reform before restoring parliamentary democracy. The second group, which included the senior officers, was the most influential and the radio declaration was representative of its views. In fact, the situation was fluid and immediately after the take-over other forces began to influence events.

One of the early communiqués of the self-proclaimed National Unity Committee (*Milli Birlik Komitesi*) announced that the task of preparing the new constitution had been entrusted to a group of professors, distinguished by their learning and legal expertise, headed by Rector Sıddık Sami Onar of Istanbul University. At the same time activities by all political parties were banned, with the promise that any violation of this order would be severely punished.[50] The communiqué was signed by General Cemal Gürsel, 'Chairman of the NUC and the Commander in Chief of the Turkish Armed Forces'.

It is important to remember that at this early date the NUC

existed only in name and had yet to be given substance. Gürsel, who had been flown from İzmir on the morning of the *coup*, was declared the leader of the NUC. But when Orhan Erkanlı, who belonged to the Istanbul group, arrived in the capital on the night of 29 May, he found only confusion at the Prime Minister's Office where the NUC was holding its deliberations. He found that he knew only a few officers present, since their organization had been secret; there was agreement neither on ideas nor principles. It was decided that they would pick a body of six to eight officers to select those who would constitute a twenty-member NUC. In their heated discussions, which lasted about seven hours, they found it impossible to restrict themselves to twenty and ended up with a committee of thirty-eight. Gürsel, with his amiable qualities and absence of Bonapartist tendencies, was made Head of State, Prime Minister, C.-in-C., and Chairman of the NUC and he was given more power on paper than even Atatürk had ever held. But this only disguised the crisis of authority in the NUC. Gürsel was viewed as a figurehead and not as the leader, who had still to emerge.[51]

The stated goals of the armed forces in seizing power were to extricate the parties from their political impasse by holding a free election supervised by an impartial administration, and to restore power to the party which won the election. This may have been the original purpose, but the creation of the Constitutional Commission under Professor Onar, on 27 May, altered the character of the movement and nudged it in a different direction. It may not be too extravagant to suggest that the professors transformed the *coup* into a revolution. The first report of the Constitutional Commission, presented on 28 May, provided the military with an entirely new and legalistic motivation for overthrowing the Democrats:

It is not right to regard the situation in which we find ourselves today as an ordinary political coup d'état. The political power which should represent the conception of State, law, justice, morality, public interest and public service and should protect public interests had for months, even years, lost this character, and had become a material force representing personal power and ambition and class interests.

The power of the State, which before all else should be a social power bound by law, was transformed into an instrument of this ambition and power. For this reason this political power lost all its moral ties with its army ... with its courts and the bar, with its officials who wanted to be loyal to their duties, with its universities, and with its press which represents public opinion, and with all its other social institutions and forces, and fell into a position hostile to the State's genuine and main institutions, and to Atatürk's reforms, which are of extraordinary value and importance if Turkey is to occupy a worthy place among the nations of the world as a civilized State.

After giving an account of the misdeeds of the Democrat Party, the report continued:

A class which engaged in such arts, which have no relationship whatsoever with laws and rights and our conception of State, could not be considered a social institution any longer. . . .

From the viewpoint of legality, the situation is the same. The legality of a Government lies not only in its origin, that is to say in its coming to power. Legality is possible only by its observance of the Constitution which brought it to this position, and its existence in an order of legality by co-operating with institutions such as the public opinion of the nation, the army and scientific and judicial institutions.

The report then gave an account of the Democrats' failure to do that, which lost them their legitimacy, and turned to the position of the Assembly:

Because it was prevented by the political power from being a real organ of legislation and was converted into a party group serving personal and class interests, the Grand National Assembly, which ought to have represented the nation, was actually placed in a state of dissolution. In such circumstances, the army, the administration and all forms of other State institutions lost their fundamental characteristic of representing the conception of the State and the quality of being a factor of balance among the institutions mentioned above. Thus the former Government lost its political authority a long time ago.[52]

Such a state of affairs may well have justified military intervention and the actions of the NUC. But the new situation called for the recreation of state and social institutions as well as political authority and legal government. This necessitated the following measures:

1. The formation of 'a provisional Government which will conduct public services according to desirable democratic requirements wanted by the nation,... which will protect human rights and freedoms, take care of public interests and maintain the administration.'

2. The preparation of a constitution that 'will ensure the materialisation of a state of law, set up State organs, and ensure that State social institutions are placed on a democratic basis and on principles of right and justice, to replace the [existing] Constitution of the State which has been neglected and rendered inoperative.'

3. The drafting of an election law that 'will permit the expression of the true will of the nation and prevent the corruption of political

power by precluding the establishment of absolutism by a majority.[53]

If the NUC accepted the professors' report it would mean giving up the initial claim that the intervention had been impartial. It would also mean agreeing to carry out radical reforms, instead of simply handing back power to the civilians. Initially many Democrats were led to believe that they would be permitted to function as a party as soon as the corrupt elements had been purged. After being taken into custody with other Democrats, Sıtkı Yırcalı was released along with a number of other Democrats and told by General Madanoğlu that he would be permitted to lead a purified DP.[54] But he was taken into custody again on 31 May, an act which marked the change in policy prompted by the professors' proposals. Within a day, all members of the Assembly belonging to the DP—save a few who escaped abroad—were arrested. Later Professor Hüseyin Naili Kubalı admitted that he was one of those who had proposed that all the Democrat Representatives be arrested—as proof that, in the matter of arrests, the revolution was not acting arbitrarily. Had only some Democrats been taken into custody, the influence of those left free would soon have secured their release. Moreover, this policy gave substance and direction to the *coup*, transforming it into a revolution.[55]

On 12 June the Constitutional Commission's Provisional Constitution defining the powers of the NUC was made public and went into effect two days later. According to this document, the NUC would exercise the right of sovereignty on behalf of the Turkish nation until the Grand National Assembly took over again after a general election had been held and the new constitution was in force. The NUC would exercise legislative power directly and executive power through the cabinet appointed by the Head of State and approved by the NUC. The NUC had the right to dismiss ministers, but only the Head of State could appoint them. Only the judicial function was left independent of the Committee though it retained the right to approve or veto the death sentence.

The NUC consisted of the President and thirty-seven other members whose signatures were appended to the Provisional Constitution. Members could withdraw from the NUC but could be dismissed only if a court of law judged that they had violated their oath; membership also became null and void if a member was convicted of treason or other crimes. But an investigation could be opened against a member only if four-fifths of the Committee voted for it. Debates of the Committee would be held in secret session and neither the discussion nor the decisions would be made public. In the Committee all the members were to be equal, regardless of the rank they held. The document was signed by all the members, whose names became public for the first time.[56]

Moderates and Radicals in the NUC

From the outset, the Committee was divided between those who wanted to restore power to the civilians as soon as possible and those who wanted to carry out reforms which would alter the political structure of the country before party politics were once more permitted. The latter scheme would involve military rule for at least four years, and longer if necessary. The first group, led by Gürsel and the generals, came to be known as the moderates; the second group, consisting of junior officers up to and including the rank of colonel, came to be designated the radicals or extremists.

The element of hierarchy naturally entered into the division, for the senior officers could not easily adapt themselves to the idea of sharing power with captains and majors. Politically the positions of the two groups focused on İnönü and the RPP. The moderates were, in fact, proposing that power be handed to the RPP since that was the strongest political organization after the Democrat Party had been dissolved. The radicals, on the other hand, had no desire simply to surrender power to the Republicans. They had hoped that a purged and purified DP would be able to compete, but as that was no longer possible, they preferred the military to retain power until a new political climate had been created in the country.

Initially the senior officers did not take the challenge very seriously. They calculated on the acceptance of Gürsel's proposal that officers who had taken part in the *coup* should return to their units, and assumed that Gürsel and a junta would be left in power. But the junior officers who had planned the *coup* rejected the proposal. They formed the Committee and asked the professors to furnish the Provisional Constitution which legally guaranteed the existence of the NUC until elections were held and the Assembly and a new government could take over.[57]

This marked the end of the first round in the struggle for power, which continued until fourteen of the junior officers were expelled on 13 November 1960. Initially the position of the radical group was strong. Its members were able to exert considerable influence in the sphere of policy making, and Colonel Alparslan Türkeş, perhaps the only member of the Committee with any plan for the future of the country, became Gürsel's Under Secretary. In this office he came to be regarded as the real power behind the scenes, manipulating the father-like personality of Cemal Gürsel.[58] Major

Orhan Erkanli became the Deputy Secretary-General of the NUC, an influential and strategic post since everything passed through his hands before it was implemented. In the Committee, the majority was with the radicals in so far as most members felt no urgency about handing back power to the civilians.

The situation was, nevertheless, one of tension. The senior officers controlled the executive, with Gürsel (Prime Minister), General Kiziloğlu (Interior), General Özdilek (Defence), and General Ulay (Communications).[59] Moreover, Major-General Madanoğlu was the Commander of the Ankara Garrison and Commander of the 28th Division, and Colonel Osman Köksal was in charge of the Presidential Guard, the only two active commands held by members of the Committee. The radicals, on the other hand, had given up their army careers and no longer had immediate relations with the armed forces, though some of them did retain contact with active junior officers like Dündar Seyhan and Talât Aydemir who had taken part in the conspiracy but had, for various reasons, not become members of the NUC. Therefore, radicals still constituted a threat to the generals. The junior officers had successfully overthrown the government without the help of their senior colleagues; there was no reason why they should not do that again, this time against the generals. Both groups, therefore, lived in fear of a *coup* by the other.

The generals were the first to take the initiative against their rivals in the Committee. On 21 September members (with the exception of Gürsel's immediate group—Madanoğlu, Ulay, Özdilek, Köksal, and Acuner) set out on a propaganda tour of Anatolia in order to explain the May revolution to the people. The next day Türkeş, who had become the *de facto* leader of the radicals, was dismissed from the Prime Minister's Office. He was replaced by Hilmi İncesulu, a civilian administrator who had served as a provincial governor.[60]

The news of Türkeş's dismissal was interpreted as a minor purge and Orhan Erkanlı, perhaps fearing for his own position, rushed back to the capital with other members also cutting short their Anatolian tour.[61] But there was nothing the radicals could do except use their majority in the Committee and have it pass a rule that, with the exception of Gürsel, its members could not hold public office.[62]

By September the National Unity Committee had begun to discuss the question of establishing a Constituent Assembly (*Kurucu Meclis*) which would take over the legislative function from the Committee. Those who wanted the Committee to remain in power were opposed to this proposal and felt confident that they could stave it off, since, to be adopted, all measures had to pass the NUC with a four-fifths majority. The moderates knew that they could never muster such a majority; but at the same time they realized that the activities of the Committee were making the radicals unpopular both in the armed forces and the country at large. The retirement of the 235 generals and 5,000 officers in August, the threats to reform the press, and the purge of 147 professors from the universities in October alienated many members of all these groups—which had supported the NUC since 27 May. Furthermore, the responsibility for these measures was placed on the radicals rather than on the Committee as a whole. The press, in particular, became more critical and exploited the theme of continuing division in the NUC. By the beginning of October there were reports that the radicals, who wanted to retain power, had elected a leader. But this was denied by Gürsel, who declared that there was no division in the Committee, which was 'fully united around its leader'.[63]

Relations in the Committee continued to deteriorate and the final test between the factions became a question of time: one group was determined to demilitarize politics while the other was just as determined to prevent this. The question hinged on whether the NUC would permit the creation of the Constituent Assembly. The radicals repeatedly emphasized that they would never permit the Committee to pass the necessary measure. Nevertheless, on 3 November Gürsel invited Professor Turhan Feyzioğlu to draft a constitution for the Constituent Assembly and on 6 November told a crowd in Zonguldak, 'Don't believe the gossip you hear about our heading for a dictatorial régime; our goal is democracy and no one can turn us from this road.'[64]

By the end of October the Committee was paralysed with dissension. Such a state of affairs could not be permitted to continue indefinitely. There are some hints that a small faction around Türkeş proposed overthrowing the moderates, but that other radicals like Erkanlı rejected the proposal because they did not believe they had the means to carry out a *coup*. Nevertheless, Erkanlı's resignation on 11 November and his departure for Istanbul aroused Madanoğlu's suspicion and convinced him that this was the prelude to a *coup*. The generals took no chances and decided to purge the radicals before they had time to act.[65]

On the morning of 13 November Gürsel's pre-recorded message announced the dissolution of the original NUC and the reconstitution of a new Committee of twenty-three members.[66] Meanwhile the fourteen members who were purged had already received Gürsel's letter of dismissal and were either taken into custody or placed under house arrest, only to be flown out of the country to sinecures at Turkish embassies around the world.[67]

With the ousting of 'the Fourteen', the NUC was able to establish a consensus. Gürsel and the generals had not been able to remove all those who opposed their policies, otherwise they would have been left in a minority. Their main concern was to restore complete authority over the Committee and set in motion the policies which would demilitarize politics within a short time. The law to establish the Constituent Assembly was accepted by the Committee on 7 December and the draft bills were published and became law on 16 December.[68] The Constituent Assembly held its first meeting on 6 January 1961 and began to share legislative duties with the NUC. The first major step towards civilian rule had been taken.

The removal of 'the Fourteen' had been greeted with a great sigh of relief by the Turkish bourgeoisie, threatened by their collectivist radicalism. But the response in the armed forces, especially among the junior officers, was one of frustration and anger. 'The Fourteen' had represented a radicalism created by a lack of faith in the ability of the politicians and the established institutions to solve the country's problems, and this radicalism was to be found throughout the military. So long as 'the Fourteen' were active in the NUC the radicals felt that they had an indirect voice in policy making and the future shape of the country. One consequence of their dismissal was the re-establishment of conspiratorial groups within the armed forces.

The Armed Forces Union

Senior officers with active commands were aware of this danger and tackled it by forming an umbrella organization designed to embrace and control all dissident elements in the armed forces. This organization, known as the Armed Forces' Union (AFU— *Silahlı Kuvvetler Birliği*), included General Cemal Tural, who was both the Commander of the First Army and Istanbul's Martial Law Commander, as well as other generals and officers of different rank. Chief of the General Staff Cevdet Sunay himself decided to maintain contact with it so as to bring it under his control.[69]

If one purpose of the AFU was to act as a watchdog over the junior officers, another was to keep an eye on the activities of the NUC. After the purge of 'the Fourteen', Madanoğlu had emerged as the strong man of the Committee and it was feared that he might try to assume power directly. Soon after the *coup* of 13 November two members of the Committee, Mucip Ataklı and

Emanullah Çelebi, visited Tural in Istanbul and reported that Gürsel was contemplating another *coup* in order to establish a 'Directory' (*Direktuar*) with Köksal, Okan, Ulay, and Madanoğlu.[70] Had such an attempt been made, the Armed Forces Union would have intervened to prevent it. But, for the moment, most of the members of the Union shared with the Committee the desire to restore power to the civilians. To this end they gave full support to the NUC.

The AFU became the real power and guarantor of the restoration of parliamentary rule. The members of the NUC had virtually entered politics, accepting in principle life-seats in the Senate, offered to them by the Constituent Assembly.[71] General Sunay, on the other hand, assured the people that 'Our armed forces today, determined to overcome every obstacle, intend to hand over democracy safely to the great Turkish nation.... [They] are successfully conducting the organizational work of the third stage of the revolutionary action of 27 May....'[72] But the final realization that power had shifted from the NUC to the military command came only when the Tansel Incident broke over the Committee's head.

On 3 June 1961 Ankara Radio announced that Lieutenant-General İrfan Tansel, Commander of the Air Force, was being sent to Washington as head of the Military Mission. Major-General Süleyman Tulga had been appointed Acting Commander.[73] The appointment was legal enough since Gürsel was Head of State, Prime Minister, C.-in-C. of the Armed Forces, and President of the NUC. But Tansel was one of the leaders of the Armed Forces Union and if he could be posted abroad into virtual exile so could the others. Therefore the AFU could not permit this appointment and still retain its prestige and authority. The Union presented Gürsel with an ultimatum and told him to reinstate Tansel in his old post. Gürsel was also asked to remove Cemal Madanoğlu from the post of Martial Law Commander of Ankara and Osman Köksal as Commander of the Presidential Guard. Some generals whose names were listed in the ultimatum were to be retired and the Minister of Defence, General Muzaffer Alankuş, removed from the cabinet. Finally, the NUC was told not to interfere in military appointments, promotions, or dismissal nor to remove any other member from the Committee.[74]

The ultimatum was accepted and on 8 June General Sunay issued an order stating that Tulga had resigned and that it had been 'considered advisable to retain Lieutenant-General İrfan Tansel as Commander of the Air Force'.[75] Madanoğlu and Köksal relinquished their posts and Madanoğlu even resigned from the

Committee, though his resignation was not accepted. Officers were retired according to the details of the ultimatum and on 11 June, for the first time, Sunay participated in a meeting of the NUC, a practice he continued thereafter.[76]

By mid-summer Turkey was once again back on the road to multi-party politics. The restoration of political parties had been authorized on 12 January 1961 and new parties began to emerge the following month. In spite of the activities of the supporters of the former DP against the interim régime, the military guardians permitted the parties to begin political activities on 1 April. But warnings against reactionaries were constantly made by Gürsel and on 9 May the Istanbul martial law command announced the arrest of certain 'degenerate persons' who had succumbed to the subversive influence of foreign ideologies and wanted to revive the dissolved Democrat Party.[77] On 27 May the first anniversary of the *coup*, the Constituent Assembly accepted the new constitution and the Electoral Law; Sunday, 9 July, was set as the date for the referendum on the constitution.

It was during this period that the supporters of the successor parties to the old DP, especially the Justice Party (JP—*Adalet Partisi*), began to carry out propaganda against the constitution and the military régime. General Cemal Tural issued a communiqué on 28 June whose purpose was to intimidate the JP, and in the NUC there were some who even wanted to close down the party.[78] The referendum was held and the new constitution received only lukewarm support from the voters; almost 40 per cent voting against it.[79]

The political climate was tense. Ever since 15 October 1960 the trials of the former Democrats were being conducted on Yassıada, an island in the Sea of Marmara, in the full light of publicity, and their influence on national politics had been unsettling. The tension increased more as the country anxiously awaited the verdicts.[80]

The stage had been cleared for a general election, however, and on 21 July the Constituent Assembly voted to hold it on 15 October 1961. Provocations against the régime continued to increase but there is also very little doubt that the military was doing its utmost to weaken the JP in order to improve the RPP's chances of winning the election. It is not therefore surprising that only members of the neo-Democrat parties were harassed and prosecuted by the authorities. The military had decided that the future of Turkish democracy could be secured only with a Republican victory.

One way of accomplishing this was by fettering the election

campaign and forcing the parties to agree on a type of propaganda which suited the Republicans best. On 31 August the party leaders began their round-table conference under military auspices and issued on 5 September a joint declaration in which they promised: (1) not to question or exploit for political purposes the Revolution of 27 May; (2) to protect Atatürk's reforms; (3) not to exploit Islam for political ends; (4) not to exploit the verdicts of the Yassıada trials.[81] Next day the press lords held their own round-table conference and also promised to behave responsibly.

The verdicts of the Yassıada trials were announced on 15 September. Of the fifteen death sentences, the NUC refused to commute only those of Menderes, Zorlu, his Foreign Minister, and Hasan Polatkan, his Finance Minister. The two latter were executed on 16 September and Menderes a day later.

Why the NUC insisted on carrying out these executions is still the subject of puzzled debate. There were pressures, foreign and internal, to commute them and restore the country to the path of conciliation; and this would have been a propitious step. But there were too many pressures within the armed forces, not exactly calling for blood, but pointing out that the NUC and the commanders had erred in their decision to hold an early election. Ever since the restoration of 'normal politics', the forces opposed to the 27 May movement had shown brazen disregard for the régime. The large abstentions and the negative vote in the referendum had been a rebuff, no matter how the NUC chose to interpret it, and in spite of its almost total monopoly of the propaganda campaign on behalf of the constitution; thereafter the anti-NUC forces had continued to challenge the Committee with impunity. 'In spite of all the pressures', noted Erkanlı in his report of 15 July, 'people are enlisting in the new parties. The new parties, proclaiming themselves to be heirs of the DP either openly or secretly, are attempting to win votes.... The chances of an election are declining all the time. Now a new threat is being heard: "If the [Republican] People's Party does not win the election, the army will not hand over power...." This propaganda is creating a bad and demoralizing effect on the people.'[82]

To those who disagreed with the policy of early demilitarization it was still not too late to reverse this process, which began on 13 November 1960 with the purge of 'the Fourteen'. The army's suspicion of competitive politics grew parallel with, and perhaps in reaction to, the neo-Democrat forces which were active once more. By September 1961 some factions were again willing to intervene to check the growth of these forces. The Yassıada verdicts coincided with this interventionist mood and the executions were designed to appease these extremist elements in the army. This was in keeping with the generals' policy of appeasing extremists by making timely concessions, and, at the same time, retaining the programme of political democratization. Two days after the execution of Menderes, General Sunay issued a communiqué in which he promised that 'The Turkish Armed Forces will maintain a neutral and apolitical posture in order to realize the ideal of democracy in this final stage of the electoral phase.'[83]

There were other reasons for carrying out the executions. Amongst them was the rationale for the *coup*, which the professors had provided for the military; and that the executions were required to demonstrate the necessity and legality of the intervention. It is also widely believed in Turkey that the armed forces wanted to destroy the Menderes 'myth of immortality', which grew after he survived the Gatwick air crash of 1959. They believed that commutation of his sentence would be used as propaganda against the armed forces: it would be said that 'they found him guilty but even the Army can't kill him'.[84]

The executions appeased the extremist, interventionist wing of the armed forces, if only temporarily. Had the 1961 election resulted in a sound defeat for the neo-Democrat parties and a victory for İnönü's RPP, the army might have settled down to the role of a cautious and passive guardian of the newly elected régime. But the results justified the prophecy of those who had warned against the danger of handing back power to the civilians without changing the social and political structure. The Republicans received only 36·7 per cent of the votes and 173 seats. The neo-Democrat parties, the Justice and the New Turkey Party (NTP—*Yeni Türkiye Partisi*) received 34·8 and 13·7 per cent of the votes, and 158 and 65 seats, respectively. The fourth party, the Republican Peasants' Nation Party (RPNP—*Cumhuriyetçi Köylü Millet Partisi*), which was closer to the neo-Democrats than to the Republicans, polled 14 per cent of the votes and won 54 seats.[85] These results were interpreted, in the country and outside, as a victory for Menderes and a vote of censure against the régime of 27 May. In such a political climate it was improbable that the army would return to barracks and watch events take their course.

NOTES

1 *Vatan*, 27 June 1946 and a selection of articles from the Turkish press in *Ayın Tarihi*, June 1946, 60-2; Karpat, *Politics*, 160.

2 Alparslan Türkeş, *1944 Milliyetçilik Olayı* (1968), 20-1; and also

conversations with Türkeş and Seyfi Kurtbek. These impressions are confirmed by others who experienced these times. But it is noteworthy that junior officers made similar accusations against the Menderes régime. See Orhan Erkanlı, *Anılar ... Sorunlar ... Sorumlular* (1972), 171-2.

3 Conversation with former Democrats. Seyfi Kurtbek told the author that Celâl Bayar had learned from some officers that the DP had won Çanakkale in 1946 because the army, which had an important base there, had supported it. See also George Harris, 'The Role of the Military in Turkish Politics', pt 1, *MEJ* xix/1 (1965), 63-6.

4 The text is in *Cumhuriyet*, 2 Jan. 1948.

5 Fuad Köprülü, 'Gafletten Gaflete', *Kudret*, 4 Jan. 1948.

6 Conversation with Celâl Bayar.

7 Conversation with Seyfi Kurtbek. Unfortunately I was unable to confirm this story with Nihat Erim, despite a number of attempts on my part to see him.

However, in July 1949, Erim did go on a tour of western Anatolia and the Democrats accused him of holding a secret meeting on 14 July with the commanders in İzmir (*Cumhuriyet*, 15 July 1949). A few days later, Bayar spoke in İzmir and remarked: 'Information leaked to us about the secret meetings suggests that a dangerous game is being played.' (Ibid., 19 July 1949.) Menderes denounced Erim's tour as a preparation for using the army and the administration to perpetuate the RPP's rule. (Esirci, *Menderes*, 191-2; and Eroğul, *Demokrat Parti*, 49-50.) So serious was the debate on the army and politics in July 1949, that Defence Minister Hüsnü Çakır issued a statement reminding the press that it was illegal to discuss the army in debates on internal politics. (*Cumhuriyet*, 26 July 1949.)

8 Conversations with Celâl Bayar and Seyfi Kurtbek.

9 Ibid.; Ahmet Taner Kışlalı, *Forces Politiques dans la Turquie Moderne* (n.d. [1970]), 15. Toker, *İsmet Paşa*, ii, 32 writes that İnönü has denied this incident. Seyfi Kurtbek said that he had made arrangements with officers sympathetic to the DP to take counter-measures against possible action by the commanders.

10 The Turkish press, 7 and 8 June 1950; Aydemir, *İkinci Adam*, iii, 45-9; Eroğul, *Demokrat Parti*, 67.

11 Erer, *On Yıl*, 33 ff.

12 See also *Ulus* for the days following 7 June 1950.

13 *Zafer*, 11 June 1950.

14 Mümtaz Faik Fenik, 'Askerlikte Büyük İnkilâp', *Zafer*, 21 June 1950.

15 *Cumhuriyet*, 24 and 25 Feb. 1949. Nihat Erim, who was Deputy PM and Minister of State at the time, told Kurtbek that the Republicans would reform the army after they won the 1950 election. Asked why they did not do so immediately, Erim replied that the generals purged would join the opposition parties and weaken the RPP. Kurtbek replied that if all the old generals joined the DP, the party would sink and go under. Conversation with Seyfi Kurtbek.

16 Conversation with Seyfi Kurtbek. See also Harris, 'The Military', pt 2, *MEJ* xix/2 (1965), 169.

17 Conversation with Kurtbek; Aydemir, *İkinci Adam*, iii, 52-4.

18 Conversation with Kurtbek; Aydemir, *İkinci Adam*, iii, 54.

19 Conversation with Kurtbek. Other former Democrats with whom the author discussed this question claimed that Kurtbek was too junior in rank to be able to inspire confidence in the army and carry out reforms. They said that the programme was not carried out because of Menderes's intervention. Menderes did not want to antagonize the generals and preferred to let the situation drift.

20 Conversation with Samet Ağaoğlu. These impressions were confirmed in conversations with a variety of people.

21 In relation to its national income, Turkey has spent more on the armed forces than almost any other NATO member. In the early fifties her military spending rose as follows: $248 million (1950); $273 million (1951); $307 million (1952); $386 million (1953). See *The Economist*, 15 Nov. 1952 and 19 Dec. 1953.

22 This was the view of all the former Democrats I saw. Those who claim that Menderes was contemptuous of the army base their claim on a widely quoted statement attributed to him: 'If I want, I will have the army run by reserve officers.' This is quoted by İpekçi and Coşar, *İhtilâl*, 27, but without any reference. I have been unable to trace its origin. When confronted with this statement after his overthrow, Menderes denied ever making it. See Erkanlı, *Anılar*, 347.

23 *Cumhuriyet*, 14 Sept. 1957.

24 See, for example, *Cumhuriyet*, 17, 18, 19, 20 and 22 Sept. 1957.

25 İpekçi and Coşar, *İhtilâl*, 57-67; Başgil, *27 Mayıs*, 159 ff.; Harris, 'The Military', pt 2, *MEJ* xix/2 (1965), 172-3; and Ergun Özbudun, *The Role of the Military in Recent Turkish Politics* (1966), 31-2.

26 Toker, *İsmet Paşa*, ii, 31 ff. writes that İlhami Sancar, who later became Defence Minister, was the Republican approached by the conspirators. İpekçi and Coşar, *İhtilâl*, 61-3 state that the conspirators wanted to contact İnönü directly but that he was cautious, fearing that if the Democrats ever found out they would close down the party. However, he knew what was going on in the armed forces and was kept informed.

27 Ankara Radio, 16 Jan. 1958, in *SWB*, iv/453/6; *Cumhuriyet*, 17 Jan. 1958; İpekçi and Coşar, *İhtilâl*, 69-100.

28 Conversation with a former Democrat.

29 İpekçi and Coşar, *İhtilâl*, 63-7; Yalman, *Gördüklerim*, iv, 355. According to some former Democrats, Ergin even covered up for the conspirators.

30 Güventürk quoted in *Cumhuriyet*, 1 July 1960; Toker, *İsmet Paşa*, ii, 37. Harris's conclusion that the 'outcome [of the investigation] allayed the government's fears of the military so successfully that thereafter the DP leaders found it difficult to credit conspiracy in the armed forces', is not borne out by later events. Harris, 'Causes', *MEJ* xxiv/4 (1970), 446.

31 Erkanlı, *Anılar*, 13; İpekçi and Coşar, *İhtilâl*, 101-2.

32 This strategy is attributed to Colonel Sadi Koçaş. See İpekçi and Coşar, *İhtilâl*, 102.

33 Ibid., 104-8.

34 Ibid., 109–11.

35 This account is based on conversations with Alparslan Türkeş. But it does not differ in substance from İpekçi and Coşar, İhtilâl, 149–59 and Erkanlı, Anılar, 160.

36 Cumhuriyet, 30 Aug. 1959.

37 Zafer, 7 Sept. 1958; Fahri Belen, 'Ordu ve Politika', Cumhuriyet, 19 Apr. 1971. See also Aydemir, İkinci Adam, iii, 377–8 and Toker, İsmet Paşa, ii, 113.

38 The text of the agreement was published in the Turkish press, 6 Mar. 1959 and is also given in George Harris, Troubled Alliance (1972), 221–3, and Haydar Tunçkanat, İkili Anlaşmaların İçyüzü (1970), 173–7. See also Aydemir, İkinci Adam, iii, 328.

39 Cumhuriyet, 6 Feb. 1960.

40 Ankara Radio, 1 May 1960, in SWB, iv/323/c/3; and Sabahat Erdemir, ed., Milli Birliğe Doğru, i (1961), 275. See also Bediî Faik, İhtilâlciler Arasında bir Gazeteci (1967), 48–52.

41 The Times, 7 May 1960 and İnönü, Muhalefet, iii (1959–60), 100–7.

42 Cumhuriyet, 10 May 1960.

43 Zafer, 25 May 1960.

44 Sıtkı Ulay, Harbiye Silâh Başına (1968), 79.

45 Conversation with Alparslan Türkeş.

46 Ulay, Harbiye, 86.

47 Notes from Ethem Menderes's diary quoted in Kim, 20 Sept. 1966, 5; Namık Argüç, who was martial law commander in Ankara, received a ten-year sentence at the trials.

48 Ankara Radio, 27 May 1960 in SWB, iv/345/c/1; Erdemir, ed., Milli Birlik, 293.

49 Erer, On Yıl, 16–17.

50 Communiqué no. 13, 27 May 1960 in Erdemir, ed., Milli Birlik, 298.

51 Erkanlı, Anılar, 18–21; Dündar Seyhan, Gölgedeki Adam (1966), 87–8. Gürsel had already become PM and Acting Defence Minister on 28 May when the cabinet was announced. The cabinet, designed to be non-partisan in character and composed of officers, bureaucrats, technocrats, and professors, represented the traditional alliance of the military-civilian intelligentsia. For the list see Öztürk, Hükümetler, 465–6 and Weiker, Revolution (1963), 139–40, nn. 36 and 37.

52 Ankara Radio, 28 May 1960, in SWB, iv/347/c/4–6; the Turkish press, 29 May 1960.

53 Ibid.

54 Conversation with a former Democrat. İpekçi and Coşar, İhtilâl, 265–6; Erkanlı, Anılar, 79; and MER 1960, 434–5.

55 Kubalı's statement in Cumhuriyet, 14 Dec. 1961. Concerning the influence of the professors on Madanoğlu, see Erkanlı, Anılar, 79 ff. and 162.

56 Ankara Radio, 12 June 1960, in SWB, iv/358/c/1–4; Resmi Gazete, 14 June 1960; İpekçi and Coşar, İhtilâl, 291–301; and Weiker, Revolution, 119.

57 Erkanlı, Anılar, 294–6.

58 Weiker, *Revolution*, 125-7. Türkeş favoured forming a political party in order to contest elections but this proposal was rejected by the NUC. See *Cumhuriyet*, 16 June 1960.

59 In the reformed cabinet of Aug. 1960, Ulay became Minister of State and Özdilek was replaced by General Muzaffer Alankuş as Defence Minister. See Weiker, *Revolution*, 139-40, n. 37.

60 *Cumhuriyet*, 23 Sept. 1960.

61 Yalman, *Gördüklerim*, iv, 373.

62 *Cumhuriyet*, 29 Sept. 1960.

63 Ankara Radio, 1 Oct. 1960, in *SWB*, iv/453/c/3; *Cumhuriyet*, 2 Oct. 1960.

64 İpekçi and Coşar, *İhtilâl*, 492 and 491 ff. Faik, *Gazeteci*, 86-7.

65 İpekçi and Coşar, *İhtilâl*, 490-502 and Erkanlı, *Anılar*, 153-7.

66 Ankara Radio (7.30 a.m.), 13 Nov. 1960, in *SWB*, iv/489/c/1; the Turkish press, 14 Nov. 1960.

67 Erkanlı, *Anılar*, 157-9. Gürsel told a foreign journalist: 'Let "the Fourteen" thank God that I was involved in this business. Otherwise all of them would have been shot. I prevented that.' Quoted in Türkeş, *Milliyetçilik*, 115.

68 The Turkish press, 8, 12, 15, 16, and 17 Dec. 1960.

69 Faik, *Gazeteci*, 97-106; Erkanlı, *Anılar*, 142. *The Economist*, 21 Oct. 1961, is obviously referring to this body when it speaks of the *Ordu Şûrası*.

70 Faik, *Gazeteci*, 101. İpekçi and Coşar, *İhtilâl*, 504-5 also write that Gürsel had considered dissolving the NUC.

71 Gürsel's press conference,'*Cumhuriyet*, 3 Mar. 1961.

72 Ibid., 8 Mar. 1961.

73 Ankara Radio, 3 June 1961, in *SWB*, iv/W112/A/5; Weiker, *Revolution*, 136-7.

74 Faik, *Gazeteci*, 117.

75 Ankara Radio, 8 June 1961, in *SWB*, iv/W113/A/4, and *Cumhuriyet*, 9 June 1961.

76 *Cumhuriyet*, 12 June 1961; Faik, *Gazeteci*, 119; Weiker, *Revolution*, 137. The Tansel Affair became public only in late 1962. See *Cumhuriyet*, 8 Dec. 1962, 5.

77 *Cumhuriyet*, 10 May 1961.

78 *Cumhuriyet*, 29 June 1961 (communiqué) and Baban, *Politika*, 249-55. Baban was a member of the cabinet.

79 *Cumhuriyet*, 12 July 1961; Yalman, *Gördüklerim*, iv, 379; *The Economist*, 15 July 1961. This was the first time that army officers exercised their newly acquired right to vote. See Kışlalı, *Forces politiques*, 21. For an analysis of the referendum see Weiker, *Revolution*, 165-6.

80 Weiker, *Revolution*, 25-47 gives an excellent summary of the trials.

81 The Turkish press, 6 Sept. 1961.

82 Erkanlı, *Anılar*, 184.

83 *Cumhuriyet*, 21 Sept. 1961.

84 Weiker, *Revolution*, 45.

85 Ibid., 163 and *Türkiye Yıllığı 1963* (1963), 208-9.

CHAPTER VII

THE FAILURE OF
TUTELARY DEMOCRACY 1961–1971

We believe that our national and most sacred duty is to support and assist the Armed Forces to accomplish, in peace, their noble task of safeguarding the country and defending democracy within the framework of their hierarchy and command, away from every political influence and movement. (Cries of 'Bravo' and prolonged applause.)

... We will take the necessary measures so that the personnel of the Armed Forces who operate under arduous and difficult conditions will be able to enjoy a standard of living suitable to the honour and pride of their vocation. (Applause from the left.)

Süleyman Demirel, programme speech in the Assembly, 3 November 1965

Abortive Coups 1962–1963

THE indecisive results of the general election of 1961 brought Turkey to the brink of another crisis. The army was divided as to the action it should take, and certain factions led by officers like Talât Aydemir wanted to annul the election results, abolish political parties and the NUC, and establish the rule of a military junta.[1] These groups were undoubtedly influential and potentially dangerous, but the commanders around Sunay were aware of the threat and therefore took timely measures to counter it. The method they used was to convince the interventionists that the High Command would act if the political situation warranted action. The generals had learned from the experience of the 27 May movement the danger of losing contact with junior officers and giving them the chance to act independently. If the army had to act politically it was better for the High Command to lead. The function of the Armed Forces Union was to keep one step ahead of the junior officers so as to retain the initiative. This became the

178 The Turkish Experiment in Democracy

pattern for the next ten years and it culminated in the 'coup by memorandum' on 12 March 1971.

Immediately after the election the AFU treated the threat of intervention by the lower ranks seriously enough to take immediate measures to defuse it. One of Gürsel's first acts was to issue a communiqué praising the patriotism of 'the Fourteen' and making it public that there was no longer any reason to keep 'the Fourteen' outside the country.[2]

On 21 October Colonel Dündar Seyhan met some of them in Brussels to discuss the political situation in Turkey. Seyhan, who was representing the AFU, had brought a message from General Sunay asking 'the Fourteen' to delay their return. 'We want you to return to Turkey and the last communiqué is proof of this. But the situation is very confused as the election results have not been reassuring to a large section of the army. In order to rebel again, the interventionists are in search of a leader and they want you to return, recognizing you as the leaders. Your return to Turkey under these conditions would lead to major incidents. We are in search of stabilizing formulas and you can help us ... ; for the moment please listen to me and do not come back.'[3] Those members who were present agreed to postpone their return and went to Paris, where they gave a press conference stating that political events had proved them right.[4]

On the same day as Seyhan began his discussions in Brussels, ten generals including Cemal Tural, Martial Law Commander and Commander of the First Army (Istanbul), and twenty-eight colonels signed in Istanbul the '21 October Protocol'. They threatened to intervene in order to entrust the revolution to the true and competent representatives of the nation, to prohibit all political parties, and to annul the election results as well as abolish the NUC. The decision to intervene was to be implemented by 25 October.[5]

What was the rationale behind this protocol? According to Colonel Aytekin, one of the signatories and Cemal Tural's staff officer:

If intervention took place after 25 October, Parliament would have convened and its legality have been established. If intervention took place after Parliament convened, a new responsibility for revolution would have to be assumed. Yet in the three days before us a state of revolution already exists. During this period any intervention would be accepted as another act of the ongoing revolution. Apart from this, there is another reason which is very important. Any intervention which takes place after the Assembly is in session will be a very bloody affair. This time it will not be possible to halt the young officers. But if intervention were carried out within the hierarchical framework an attempt from below can be prevented and the lives of many politicians saved.⁶

The protocol had the desired effect on the neo-Democratic parties. On 24 October the party leaders were summoned by the army commanders to the President's residence at Çankaya, where they signed a protocol of their own. They agreed not to have the Assembly pass laws reinstating officers retired by the NUC and not to seek an amnesty for the Democrats sentenced at Yassıada. They also promised to have General Gürsel elected President of the Republic, and to accept İnönü as Prime Minister.⁷ The two chambers convened on 26 October and Gürsel was duly elected President. Professor Ali Fuad Başgil, a stubborn supporter of the Democrat Party, had been forced to stand down as a candidate for the presidency and even to resign from the Senate.⁸

The armed forces had restored parliamentary democracy as they had promised. But they were unable to extricate themselves from politics, finding themselves in the ironic position of having to undermine democracy in order to save it. They had become guardians of two contradictory legacies: that of the 27 May movement and of multi-party democracy, both of which they were committed to defend. The first involved establishing a consensus which all parties would agree to respect and which the army would enforce, if violated. The second implied giving the parties autonomy in politics, even though this might clash with the legacy of 27 May. This contradiction created tensions which bedevilled Turkish politics throughout the sixties and into the seventies.

Even before the election the army had been sensitive to the criticism and political exploitation of 27 May. The commanders had forced the party leaders to make a joint declaration on 5 September promising not to question the revolution and its consequences. But the neo-Democratic parties would have acted out of character had they abided by this declaration. In the election campaign the revisionist propaganda paid rich dividends and the policy continued to be practised in the period of coalitions, finding expression in the amnesty question.

The constant exploitation of the amnesty question unsettled the coalition governments, and, to make matters worse, the interventionist faction of the armed forces interpreted this as a provocation. On 20 December, for example, Mucip Ataklı, a former member of the NUC and now a Life Senator, gave warning that an amnesty might trigger off another revolution: 'There is an attempt to show those who carried out the revolution as tyrants and those who caused it as the oppressed. Those who look back with nostalgia to the period of oppression and the rule of gangsters must realize that the forces which carried out the revolution will not hesitate to prepare a more terrifying one for those people.'⁹

Certain sections of the armed forces had been provoked sufficiently to begin considering a second *coup*. Extreme statements by politicians and rumours circulating in the press, claimed İnönü, were creating instability. 'On the one hand, there is a wind blowing to the effect that a second revolution is imminent; on the other hand an atmosphere is being created to the effect that efforts are being made to take revenge for 27 May.... It is out of the question to deny that such an atmosphere exists.... [But] neither of these two possibilities is likely to happen. The atmosphere in question is absolutely unjustified and artificial.'¹⁰ İnönü had sensed the mood of the times correctly, though he probably played down the possibility of a *coup* in order to avoid alarming the audience he was addressing. Intervention by the army was widely expected and this accounted for its failure when it came.

On 9 February 1962 members of the AFU met in Istanbul to discuss the unstable situation. As in October 1961, they signed a protocol declaring their intention to act by a certain date, in this case not later than 28 February. Once again the initiative was retained in the hands of the AFU generals in Istanbul, and not allowed to pass to the 'colonels' junta' in Ankara. Chief of the General Staff Cevdet Sunay, however, refused to support the protocol; moreover, the air force also opposed intervention by the army. There was now an ambivalent situation: on the one side there was the AFU's commitment to intervene, though this had been undermined by the attitude of Sunay and the air force. On the other side was the Ankara junta, which was totally isolated and open to governmental reprisals. It had been manoeuvred into a corner from which there was no escape. İnönü knew this and decided to call its bluff by assigning members of this group to new posts where they would cease to be a threat. In order to prevent this the Ankara junta raised the standard of revolt.¹¹

The abortive *coup* of 22 February 1962 was led by Colonel Talât Aydemir, Commandant of the War College. He had been a member of conspiratorial groups in the mid-fifties, but on 27 May he was in South Korea and was therefore unable to participate in the *coup* or to play a role in the military régime that emerged. This is said to have rankled and made him bitter, and he was one of those who believed that it would be a serious error to hand back power to civilians too soon. During the period of the National Unity Committee he was an influential member of the Ankara group within the AFU. He disliked the results of the 1961 election and believed that the army ought to intervene; when this was not done he continued to talk of intervention. His constant and open threats were designed to undermine the morale of both the government and the armed forces so that when the *coup* was attempted there would be no serious resistance. He cannot have expected to overcome any serious opposition from the regular army by means of the forces at his command, namely the cadets from the War and Gendarmerie Colleges and some armoured units from the Ankara garrison. The authorities had no difficulty in suppressing this half-hearted *putsch* and Aydemir himself went to the headquarters of the Chief of the General Staff to surrender.[12]

For the moment, the abortive *coup* strengthened Premier İnönü's hand *vis-à-vis* his coalition partners and political opponents. But in fact it was the High Command which became even more influential than it had been. Article 111 of the new constitution provided for the establishment of the National Security Council (NSC—*Milli Güvenlik Kurulu*) consisting of 'the Ministers provided by law, the Chief of the General Staff, and representatives of the armed forces'. The President, or in his absence the Prime Minister, was to preside over it, and its function was to assist the cabinet 'in the making of decisions related to national security and co-ordination'. These functions were in themselves broad enough to give great power and influence to the High Command. But in March 1962 a new bill increased the powers of the Council, enabling it virtually to interfere in the deliberations of the cabinet, through regular consultations and participation in the preparatory discussions.[13] This led to rumours of differences between the Defence Ministry and General Sunay, but they were denied by the Ministry.[14]

İnönü found it impossible to have any controversial measure passed by the Assembly without support from the High Command. The Justice Party refused to sanction an amnesty for the rebels of 22 February unless it was also extended to the former Democrats, and the very existence of the coalition was threatened.[15] The extremists in the JP wanted their members to leave not only the government but also the Assembly.

Once again Sunay came to the rescue. 'It's an ugly trick to mix the military amnesty with the other.... This is not something people with good intentions would do. Those people with bad intentions want to bring the nation and the army face to face.'[16] This warning was sufficient and next day both the JP and the NTP agreed to vote for the amnesty bill and the crisis was over.[17] The only concession they received in return was a pardon for those who were ill amongst the convicted Democrats. A month later the same Assembly declared 27 May 'Freedom and Constitution Day', making it a national holiday, though of the 157 Justice Party representatives, 117 voted against the motion.[18]

With the High Command committed to supporting him, İnönü decided to resign on 30 May in order to end the impasse in the cabinet—the extremists in the JP had made it impossible for the cabinet to deal with problems which plagued the country, especially the stagnant economy. Once again it was not easy to form a coalition without prodding from the army. On 19 June İnönü consulted Sunay and Gürsel. The party leaders were called in next day and the press reported that there were now signs of a three-party coalition.[19] On 24 June the usual protocol was signed by the leaders of the RPP, the NTP, and the RPNP, and by Necmi Öktem on behalf of the Independents. Next day İnönü announced his Second Coalition.[20]

The army was totally engaged in politics; the question that troubled the politicians was how to bring about a divorce. İnönü's answer was to have the government and the constitutional order functioning smoothly, to establish the absolute sovereignty and prestige of the Assembly, and to end all activities likely to provoke the army.[21] But that was easier said than done, and İnönü was guilty of wishful thinking if he believed that the High Command wanted to withdraw; for within its ranks there was a certain amount of ambivalence concerning total withdrawal from the political arena.

Political stability proved elusive. The Justice Party, now in opposition, continued to exploit the amnesty issue and the anniversary of Menderes's execution on 17 September 1962 became the occasion for demonstrations. This was precisely the kind of incident which provoked a response from the army. Groups describing themselves as the 'National Revolution Army' (*Milli Devrim Ordusu*) and the 'National Forces' (*Kuvayi Milliye*) distributed leaflets in Ankara and Istanbul warning the 'reactionaries' that they would be given no quarter when the revolution came.[22]

That all was not well in the armed forces became clear on 2 December 1962 when İrfan Tansel, Commander of the Air Force, announced that he was retiring eleven officers because they were involved in politics and took their orders from Life Senator Mucip Ataklı. One of those dismissed was Halim Menteş, Commander of the Bandırma air base, who had been active in the AFU and was said to be very close to Talât Aydemir and Dündar Seyhan.[23] There were hints of a relationship between the Republicans and this 'air force junta'. The Justice Party tried to uncover this relationship by raising the question in the Assembly on two occasions (12 and 14 December), but on both occasions it was rejected. İnönü claimed that he did not want to make military affairs an issue for debate and that is where the matter ended.[24]

'The Fourteen' began returning to Turkey in this political climate. In their final meeting in Brussels they failed to reach agreement on a common programme of action and decided to work as individuals. Orhan Erkanlı returned in August and Orhan Kabibay in October 1962. But the arrival of the charismatic Alparslan Türkeş on 23 February 1963 aroused the greatest interest.[25] Türkeş declared his intention to enter politics 'within the framework of the constitution and the law' in order to emphasize that he would keep away from conspiratorial groups in the army. But there is no doubt that his return stimulated such activity. The *coups* in Iraq (8 February, leading to Kasim's overthrow) and in Syria (8 March) must also have provided a stimulus to conspirators in the Turkish armed forces.

In the year and a half that had lapsed since multi-party politics were restored, the parties had failed to settle down and had not even begun to deal with the problems which weighed so heavily on the country. Amnesty was still the principal political and emotional issue. The government, not strong enough to resolve the problem conclusively, continued to make gestures which led to demands for more from the neo-Democrats. One such gesture was the conditional release of Celâl Bayar on 23 March. His journey from Kayseri, where he had been interned, to Ankara became a triumphant procession and a protest against the revolution. Enraged youths who considered themselves the guardians of Kemalist Turkey reacted by attacking the JP headquarters and right-wing newspapers.[26] Bayar was taken back into custody and the National Security Council decided that he would reside in a place chosen by the government and measures would be taken to deal with disorders.[27]

Again there were those who claimed that İnönü had created this crisis in collusion with the High Command, that he was demonstrating to the opposition parties that amnesty would not bring tranquillity; on the contrary it could result in another *coup* that would bring about the demise of civilian rule.[28] It is doubtful whether İnönü would have taken such a risk for such minor gains. A sudden rise in political tension was usually manifested in a rise in conspiratorial activity, and this occasion proved to be no exception. The Defence Ministry announced on 22 April the arrest of five officers engaged in activities similar to those of Aydemir, and promised further arrests. Next day five naval officers were taken into custody in Istanbul, accused of being members of the 'Kemalist Army' and inciting army units to revolt.[29]

The anniversary of the student demonstrations which sparked off the revolution of 1960 was 28 Aptil. Senator Mücip Ataklı used this occasion to propose that a 'legal revolution' (*Hukuki ihtilâl*) be carried out. 'The aim of this revolution ought to be to carry out much-needed reforms and to gather into one camp all those groups of our countrymen who are now divided. [To bring this about we must] make changes in the constitution and the electoral laws, end the activities of the parties for a certain period, and purge the mentality which is alien to Kemalist thought. If Parliament can show common sense it may be able to save the country and the régime.'[30] If Parliament refused to show common sense, implied Ataklı, there were worse prospects ahead.

This proposal reflected the general dissatisfaction with parliamentary democracy and the general desire to accelerate from above the process of social, economic, and political change which was believed to be impeded by party politics. It did not reflect any impending crisis; in fact since the excitement in April the situation had calmed down. Then, unexpectedly, on 14 May İnönü made a cryptic statement before his Assembly Group: 'The situation is most urgent. I repeat: it is most dangerous and critical. Anything may happen. Take great care. Keep calm. I am struggling very hard and making every effort [to master the situation]. At the moment I am not going to tell you anything more. Under the existing conditions I am trying to do what I can.'[31]

The press reported that a group calling themselves the 'Young Kemalist Army of the Turkish Republic' had sent a communication to the Senate rejecting Ataklı's proposal for reform. İnönü recalled the Deputy Premier Ekrem Alican from Erzurum and consulted President Gürsel and General Sunay. Members of the Assembly and Senators were asked to remain in Ankara and to maintain national unity. The cabinet held an extraordinary meeting and the chief of security, İhsan Aras, arrived in Ankara.[32] The country had been told that a dangerous situation existed but İnönü refused to explain, even in the Assembly, where the danger came from. It is more surprising that he was not pressed for an explanation. During the past three years the country had become accustomed to living in the extraordinary atmosphere of an impending *coup*. There was no reason to doubt İnönü's warning; but at the same time no reason to take it seriously either. In the Senate, Mucip Ataklı repeated his proposal for a 'legal revolution' and proposed vesting Premier İnönü with exceptional executive powers similar to those vested in General de Gaulle in 1958.[33]

Talât Aydemir's abortive *coup*, which took place on the night of 20/21 May 1963, had no connection with İnönü's 'dangerous and critical situation'. On 2 June İnönü admitted that 'in spite of the prevailing gossip I did not anticipate the events of 21 May'.[34] Aydemir's action was expected, only the timing came as a surprise. The government knew that Aydemir was plotting with some of 'the Fourteen', and General Memduh Tağmaç, who was Deputy Chief of the General Staff, testified at Aydemir's trial in July that he, Tağmaç, had prevented a *coup* taking place as early as 31 March.[35] This would have been a more appropriate timing for a *coup*, since Bayar's release and the incidents that followed had raised the temperature in the country.

Aydemir's rebellion, with no substantial support within the armed forces, was doomed to fail. It began just after midnight with the capture of the Ankara radio station. Aydemir was able to hold his own until first light when jets from the Eskişehir base buzzed the city and strafed the War Academy with gun fire, forcing the cadets to surrender. By dawn the rebellion had collapsed. Talât Aydemir went into hiding but was captured about noon. The curfew was lifted at 2 p.m. though the government took the precaution to proclaim martial law for one month in the cities of Ankara, Istanbul, and İzmir.[36] Martial law, although proclaimed initially for one month, was not lifted till 21 July 1964 and assured the commanders an open and legal right to intervene if the political situation called for it.

For the moment, however, Aydemir's second try marked the end of overt political activity by the junior officers. All these activities of the past three years had been the remnants of the 27 May movement and it was some years before new movements, with their roots in the sixties, began to emerge. The High Command was in full control but its position in the political structure was ambiguous. The Turkish armed forces, stated Sunay, were at the command of the government. But they were also an element of equilibrium and stability in the life of the nation.[37]

The 1961 Constitution and Radical Politics

The claim that power had been restored to the politicians without a fundamental change in the political and socio-economic structure was essentially correct. The Democrat Party was dissolved but nothing was done to prevent the return of neo-

Democrats. Since the socio-economic basis of power remained unaltered the old political forces were bound to come to the front.

Nevertheless Turkey of the sixties was different from the Turkey of the previous decade. The responsibility for this lay not so much with the army which carried out the *coup* but with the intelligentsia, especially the professors who drafted the constitution of the Second Republic. This constitution radicalized politics and held forth the promise of a liberal and democratic Turkey if it was faithfully implemented. This became the principal contradiction, because the neo-Democrats and conservative Republicans were determined to prevent its implementation. However, the constitution did permit groups who had been tightly controlled before 1960—the workers and the radical intelligentsia—to wage a political struggle against the entrenched forces.

The 1961 constitution was radically different from its predecessor. It provides for a bicameral parliament. The lower chamber, the National Assembly, consists of 450 members elected every four years by a system of proportional representation. The Senate consists of 150 members elected for a term of six years by a straight majority vote, with one-third retiring every two years; the former members of the NUC, who became Life Senators; and 15 members nominated by the President for six years. The two chambers together constitute the Grand National Assembly (under the previous unicameral system, that was the name of the single chamber).

The President is elected for a term of seven years by the Grand National Assembly, in plenary session, from among its own members, by a two-thirds majority. He appoints the Prime Minister, who chooses the rest of the cabinet, and the cabinet is responsible to the National Assembly.

A noteworthy innovation which proved a great annoyance to some future governments was the Constitutional Court. Its principal function was to review the constitutionality of legislation but it was also endowed with power to act as a high council for the impeachment of Presidents, ministers and certain high officials 'for offences connected with their duties'. It has become one of the most important and controversial institutions of the Second Republic.

Perhaps more important than the new institutions were the explicit guarantees of freedom of thought, expression, association and publication, as well as other democratic liberties, contained in the new constitution. In addition, it promised 'social and economic rights, with provision both for the right of the State to plan economic development so as to achieve social justice, and the right of the individual to the ownership and inheritance of property, and the freedom of work and enterprise'. In theory, the state was given the right 'to plan economic development so as to achieve social justice'. In practice, the forces which controlled the state and whose interests it served obstructed any advance towards social justice until they were forced to give way. This was the kind of contradiction which made the politics of the Second Republic interesting as they had never been in the last decade of the First.

After a decade of struggle, the trade unions were given the right to strike, but within limits to be determined by legislation. 'Other clauses in the constitution [sought] to safeguard the secularist Kemalist reforms from reaction, and the democratic basis of government from a new dictatorship.'[38]

The revolution of 27 May and the 1961 constitution introduced liberal politics without the underpinning of a structural base. For the first time in decades a party, the Workers' Party of Turkey (WPT—*Türkiye İşçi Partisi*), which openly represented interests clashing directly with those of the ruling classes, was allowed to function, albeit under great pressure from various quarters. Its influence on Turkish politics during its ten years of existence was totally out of proportion to its size and representation in the Assembly.[39] Thanks to the freedoms guaranteed by the constitution, intellectual societies (*fikir kulüpleri*) with radical, leftist tendencies were organized in the universities to debate and publicize Turkey's problems. The publication of political literature—especially in translation—flourished and speeded up the politicization of the bourgeois intelligentsia and even the working class.

These developments alarmed the government but it was not possible to reverse the process while the new constitution was in operation. Within a short time the government was using the 'threat from the Left' as the excuse for prolonging martial law. In August 1963 Defence Minister İlhami Sancar told the Assembly that members of an extreme leftist group who were conspiring to free Aydemir and his friends had been arrested.[40] The following month the press reported that the National Security Organization was being reorganized as the National Intelligence Organization (*Milli İstihbarat Teşkilâtı*, the notorious *MİT*).[41] The main function of this organization was to keep track of conspiracies in the armed forces and radical, leftist activity elsewhere. The preoccupation with the reactionary Right was a hangover from the past and persisted in the intelligentsia. But successive governments concentrated more on the growing Left, which they diagnosed as the real threat to the existing order.

One of the factors making for the instability of the RPP-led coalitions was that the neo-Democratic partners viewed İnönü and his party as being too radical, too leftist for their taste. The Republicans were held responsible for the new constitution and for the concept of a planned economy, still under discussion in the early sixties. In each case the parties which formed a coalition with the RPP tended to become tainted pink in the eyes of their supporters. This led to dissension in the JP during the First Coalition, and the New Turkey Party (NTP—*Yeni Türkiye Partisi*) and the Republican Peasants' Nation Party (RPNP—*Cumhuriyetçi Köylü Millet Partisi*) seemed to suffer from the same ailment during the Second.

The Second Coalition collapsed immediately after the results of the local elections became known in November 1963. The Justice Party did well while the other two neo-Democrat parties suffered setbacks, which they blamed on their collaboration with İnönü. These two parties withdrew from the coalition, and İnönü, who was attending President Kennedy's funeral in Washington, resigned on 2 December. The fact that Ragıp Gümüşpala, Chairman of the JP, was asked to form the new government was most significant. It meant that the Justice Party had acquired respectability in the eyes of the commanders, who no longer viewed a JP-led government as 'counter-revolutionary'.[42]

Gümüşpala failed to form a cabinet and the task was given to İnönü once more. The small parties refused to enter a coalition and finally İnönü formed a cabinet with Independents. The Cyprus crisis, which threatened to break into open hostilities with Greece, came to his aid.[43]

Throughout 1964 the Cyprus question monopolized the attention of the country, forcing the opposition parties to show 'national solidarity' in the face of an external problem. No one wanted a cabinet crisis and İnönü was able to pressure the Assembly into passing the budget and other fiscal measures by threatening to resign.[44] The Cyprus crisis also exposed Turkish isolation in foreign affairs, making the Turks feel particularly bitter against their allies in NATO, and the Turkish press attacked the United States for the first time. No one had supported the Turkish thesis at the UN and in the months that followed there were hints that the government might be forced to consider a reorientation of its foreign policy.

The Cyprus dispute served to obscure internal political problems and the socio-economic crisis, which continued as before. The Senate elections of 7 June were a clear victory for the JP, exposing the fact that the policies of the new régime had not acquired any substantial support among the electorate. The main effect of this political instability, now aggravated by the threat of war and martial law, was felt in the economy. However, the first year of the five-year plan, 1963, produced a 7·2 per cent increase in the gross national product, 0·2 per cent higher than the target. The 1964 harvest was also above average, but the economy was too depressed to react immediately to these stimuli.[45]

In this climate of uncertainty, the High Command adopted a 'wait and see' attitude. The politicians were left alone so long as they behaved themselves but the commanders were always vigilant. They noted the growth of extremism in the JP after the death of General Gümüşpala. The struggle for the party chairmanship encouraged some groups to curry favour with the extremists in the party. Chief of the General Staff Cevdet Sunay drew the politicians' attention to the attacks being made by certain parties—a veiled reference to the JP—on the 27 May revolution, the army, and the commanders. The country, he warned, was being divided into two hostile camps; the army was being shown as an institution opposed by the people and the commanders and officers were unhappy with this situation. Should such provocations persist there was danger of armed revolution. The parties were asked to communicate their views on the prevailing situation by 22 November.[46]

The party leaders issued a communiqué swearing fidelity to the 1960 revolution and promised to abstain from acts likely to provoke the army.[47] One of the results of Sunay's letter was that Süleyman Demirel, a moderate who could be expected to establish better relations with the commanders, was elected the new leader of the Justice Party on 29 November. On 10 December his meeting with the Life Senators, known as the National Unity Group, suggested that under his leadership the JP would try to pursue a conciliatory policy towards the 27 May revolution and its military guardians.[48]

The days of the Third Coalition were now numbered. Confident of his strength in the country and tolerance within the High Command, Demirel issued a warning that the JP would bring down the government as soon as it secured the necessary 226 votes.[49] Sunay made no attempt to deter Demirel from taking the step designed to bring about İnönü's fall and create political instability. Demirel then began to plan openly to engineer the resignation of the government. The occasion chosen for this was the debate on the budget, which, when it came to the vote, failed to obtain a majority and İnönü tendered his resignation.[50]

On this occasion there was no crisis. The High Command had come to accept the Justice Party and there was no longer any question of forcing İnönü upon the country for the fourth time. The man chosen to form the caretaker government until the general election in October 1965 was Suat Hayri Ürgüplü, who, in 1961, had been elected Independent Senator from Kayseri on the JP list. The government, he announced on 20 February, was a four-party coalition with the Justice Party as the senior partner.[51]

The policy of the new government began to veer to the right, following the line laid down at the last congress of the JP. Ürgüplü promised to fix the boundaries for the state sector in order to allay the anxieties of private enterprise, and Trade Minister Mâcit Zeren also stressed that the government believed in a mixed economy in which private enterprise was the dominant strain.[52] Gone—except for lip service—was the emphasis on social justice which had been one of the dominant themes of the new régime. In keeping with this new trend was Demirel's reliance on foreign capital 'for the rapid, balanced, and stable development' of Turkey. The Republicans were not opposed to foreign investment; they were more cautious and wanted to retain control of such primary resources as oil. While İnönü led the coalitions there had even been talk of nationalizing the oil industry. Demirel made it clear that he was opposed to such measures. 'Are we to seize the property and areas of the foreign oil companies?' he asked indignantly, and added: 'For us it is unthinkable to withdraw and unlawfully seize rights that were ceded by law ...'[53]

The policy of the Fourth Coalition towards the Left also became more stringent and repressive. Earlier governments were by no means favourable to the Left and the meetings of the Workers' Party had often been attacked by armed gangs and its publications banned by local officials. But such measures had never been executed openly with governmental sanction—state officials had operated against the Left with a sense of guilt, knowing that they were acting against the constitution, which permitted socialism. Demirel had no such qualms. Addressing the meeting of the Turkish Chambers of Commerce and Industry and the Union of Bourses, he said the government would not permit class struggle and that the time had come to unite against the 'group of perverted minds' who wanted to create it.[54]

To this, Mehmet Ali Aybar, the leader of the Workers' Party, replied: 'If the Deputy Prime Minister wants to prevent class struggle, let him nationalize oil immediately, give land to the landless, tax everyone according to his capacity, pass the unemployment insurance law. In short let the constitution be implemented perfectly and in its totality. Otherwise the true implications to emerge from the words "to prevent class struggle" will be simply to maintain today's rotten system on its feet.'[55] Events proved Aybar's evaluation to be correct. On the same day as his statement was published in the press, the cabinet demanded new measures against the 'extreme Left' [*aşırı sol*]. The parties were determined to prevent the WPT from contesting the general election.

The election campaign was fought by the Justice Party on the emotional slogans of anti-Communism and Islam. Demirel's Samsun speech of 29 June illustrated the theme: 'We are the enemies of communists. We have decided to combat communism without giving way.... We have decided to combat extreme leftist tendencies.... Communism will not enter Turkey because our population is 98 per cent Muslim. We must be able to call ourselves a Muslim nation.'[56] The Republicans, unable to make headway against such propaganda, appealed to President Gürsel and Prime Minister Ürgüplü: 'The charges of leftism and communism which Justice Party leader and Deputy Premier Demirel continues to throw around in an irresponsible way are dividing the people into hostile camps. I urge that you intervene urgently in order to save the country from being dragged into a civil war ...'[57]

The High Command was no longer willing to intervene and the Republicans were forced to fend for themselves as best they could. The JP propaganda was particularly effective because the Republicans had introduced the 'left-of-centre' slogan as a part of their campaign to win back the intelligentsia from the Workers' Party, and to project a new progressive image of themselves. But the use of the term 'Left' was enough to damn them in the eyes of a population conditioned to give a Pavlovian response. Nor was the voter sophisticated enough to understand Professor Erim's explanation that, although Sweden, Norway, France, the United Kingdom, and Germany had left-of-centre governments, they were not communist countries. Professor Feyzioğlu defended his party's policy from another angle. The RPP was not an irrational enemy of communism; its enmity was logical because a left-of-centre policy was the best antidote to communism.[58]

The Justice Party and the Army

The Justice Party confounded all predictions and won an overwhelming majority with 52·9 per cent of the vote and 240 seats. The system of proportional representation, whose aim had been to prevent the domination of the Assembly by one party, had not worked. The result was disastrous for the RPP, which polled only 28·7 per cent of the vote, the lowest in the multi-party period.

But proportional representation enabled it to have 134 Representatives in the Assembly. The parties of the Right—the Nation Party, the RPNP, and the NTP—lost their voters to the JP and between them succeeded in polling only 12·2 per cent of the votes and winning 61 seats. The Workers' Party, which had aroused great interest, did not fare as well as many had prophesied. But it did obtain 3 per cent of the votes and 15 seats, a respectable performance for a party with very limited financial means, which had suffered from official repression throughout its existence. In spite of its limited representation, the Workers' Party played an important role in opposition, one which changed the character of political debate. It introduced the ideological dimension, absent among parties which differed in emphasis rather than substance.

Many Turks showed their unhappiness and disillusionment with the system by refusing to vote. The turnout for the election—71·3 per cent of the registered voters—was the lowest since 1950. It declined from 88·6 per cent in 1954 to 76·6 per cent in 1957 and rose again to 81·0 per cent in 1961. But the period of coalitions, with all the bickering over such issues as amnesty while the economy stagnated, had alienated many potential voters. Throughout the sixties voter participation continued to decline and in the 1969 election the percentage of registered voters who bothered to exercise their civic right had dropped to 64·3 per cent.[59]

The initial response to the JP victory was one of relief that the country had left behind the period of unstable coalitions. Moreover, the army had acquiesced in a neo-Democrat party coming to power on its own. This time there was no meeting of the Armed Forces Union followed by a protocol. Demirel must take the credit for this, for it was he who consciously made an attempt to win over the commanders. It is not surprising that the largest number of retired officers elected to the Assembly was from the JP.[60]

The government had become sufficiently confident of the army to propose a partial amnesty bill which would apply to the former Democrats as well as to those who had participated in Aydemir's abortive *putsch* of 1963. There was not a word of warning from the High Command, though the National Unity Group in the Senate issued a statement denouncing the measure. They described it as an attempt 'to destroy the principles laid down in the preamble of the constitution' and warned the government that it was exhausting the legality it had acquired through the elections.[61] The Justice Party was no longer intimidated by the threats of former soldiers, knowing that they had no following in the army. In the

Assembly its Representatives even taunted the military critics by heckling: 'Go on, carry out another revolution.'[62]

The government's standing with the High Command improved even further when Cevdet Sunay was elected President. Cemal Gürsel, who had been ailing for many years, was sent to America for treatment in February 1966. It was clear that he would not be able to resume his duties and the parties soon arrived at a consensus to elect Sunay. He resigned from the army on 14 March and was appointed to the Senate. Next day Cemal Tural replaced him as Chief of the General Staff.[63] Sunay was elected President on 28 March by 461 votes; his opponent Alparslan Türkeş received only 11.[64] Abdi İpekçi noted the difference in the JP's attitude: in 1961 the party had opposed Gürsel's candidature strenuously; in 1966 it led the way to Sunay's election. Sunay may not have been Demirel's man but it helped Demirel if it appeared as though he were.[65]

Within a short time, Sunay came to be identified with the Justice Party and its policies and there was even a whisper campaign by the opposition parties suggesting that Sunay and the High Command had 'sold out' to Demirel. Sunay repudiated this in his speech of 19 May, declaring that 'the Turkish armed forces ... and ommanders are not the tool of one policy or another. ... In tnis connection and as the President of the Republic who gave his word of honour to the nation in the Grand National Assembly and before his great nation that he would maintain strict impartiality, I reject strongly and with loathing all tendentious and slanderous statements against me.'[66]

Three days later Osman Bölükbaşı, the leader of the Nation Party, aired the entire controversy in public. In a radio broadcast made during the campaign for the partial Senate elections, he declared:

In no country run really democratically and where the national will is respected has a person leading the army become President of the Republic in the way Cevdet Sunay has done. It is not even possible to imagine such a thing in those countries....

We are sure there is not a single citizen who finds it compatible with democracy and national sovereignty or who considers it normal and constructive. No citizen can but feel anxious about the future of our country and democracy if electing the Chief of the General Staff for President becomes a custom, and a kind of 'heir to the throne tradition' is created.

In view of such a picture, how can the world believe that democracy exists in Turkey? Let Demirel, if he dares, address the nation, give his reasons, and enlighten the nation about the calculations he made and save it from anxious thoughts. President Sunay must also explain why he accepted the Presidency.... We ask Demirel: What happened to your national will, to democracy which emerges from the ballot box in the case of Sunay's election?... Has the Justice Party made secret calculations? We hear the JP propagandists throughout the country claim that the wily Demirel has taken the army in hand. The Turkish army is nobody's tool. If the JP has sought safety in the election of General Sunay as President it should remember that 27 May has proved how unsound is the security based on individuals.[67]

Bölükbaşı had raised important questions about Turkish democracy which went unanswered, but he was wrong—and Sunay right—to think that the army was being manipulated by Demirel. Politicians, like soldiers who prepare for future wars on the basis of the last one, still thought in terms of the Democrats and the army. But the situation had changed radically since the fall of Menderes.

The Army's New Role

During the Democrat period there had been no ideological differences between the parties; only the difference of emphasis on how to implement the same ideology. In that situation the majority party had tried to make the army its instrument, and the opposition parties had endeavoured to use the army against the government. In neither case was the nature of the régime threatened. But after 27 May 1960 the army became an autonomous institution, recognized as the guardian of the new régime it had set up. It was sucked into both the political life of the country and its socio-economic life. New legislation improved the economic status of military personnel and their social status rose accordingly. Junior officers were no longer taunted by landlords or waiters and they began to live in the best residential areas. Retired officers were recruited into the upper levels of the bureaucracy or into private and state enterprises and generals were sent abroad as ambassadors. The creation of the Army Mutual Assistance Association (*Ordu Yardımlaşma Kurumu*, better known by the acronym OYAK) in 1961 brought the military directly into business and industry and within a few years OYAK became one of the largest conglomerates in the country, described by some as the third sector.[68]

Therefore in the sixties the military was more concerned to defend the régime than a particular party. Its primary concern was stability and it was willing to intervene against any party which undermined or threatened this. The High Command was naturally antagonistic to a socialist party like the WPT which sought a change of régime, just as it was sympathetic to parties like the JP which promoted the existing order of private enterprise. The commanders, who had become a privileged group with a major stake in the *status quo*, no longer needed to link their fortunes with those of a party leader like Demirel. It was party leaders who tried to link their fortunes to those of the commanders.[69]

But the Demirel government failed to provide the country with the much-needed stability. His own party was divided politically between his group and the followers of Sadettin Bilgiç, whom he had defeated for the leadership. Demirel was therefore as preoccupied with consolidating his position in the party as with the problems facing the country. The economy continued to stagnate, with prices and unemployment constantly rising. Tension over Cyprus continued and Turkey's isolation amongst even her allies increased the xenophobia in the country. Hostility towards the United States after revelation of the Johnson-İnönü correspondence over Cyprus became more marked and spilled over into criticism of the Demirel government—which was denounced, especially by the Left, as a puppet government.

The military High Command had to deal with a political situation which was becoming ideologically polarized. The workers were becoming increasingly militant and a minority had broken away from the moderate trade union federation, *Türk-İş*, and formed the militant Confederation of Revolutionary Workers' Unions (*Devrimci İşçi Sendikaları Konfederasyonu* or DİSK). The universities had become politicized, especially on the issue of a non-aligned Turkey independent of NATO and the United States. If one judges by the clandestine leaflets, this sentiment had also found its way into the armed forces. The leaflets issued by 'The Committee of Free Officers' (January 1966) and 'National Liberation Committee' (March 1966) called for unity and action against 'this anti-national government policy' and America, which had made Turkey into her satellite.[70]

The General Staff issued a warning to 'opponents of the present regime' that the 'exploitation of the name of the armed forces for such underground activities designed to disturb the unity, concord and solidarity among Turkish citizens is tantamount to treason against the country'.[71] The High Command recognized that the struggle against opponents of the régime was ideological and in April Cemal Tural, the new Chief of the General Staff issued a circular that the book *Komünizmle Mücadele Metodları* (Methods of Combating Communism) must be read throughout the armed forces.[72] Supporters of the Right, who had already taken the offensive against radicalism, were naturally encouraged to attack the Left with greater vigour.

By May 1966 the political situation had become sufficiently grave for President Sunay to consult party leaders, Senators, and the commanders. There was talk in the press of possible military intervention and Sunay's aim was to warn the parties and nudge them towards moderation.[73] The appeal for moderation came just in time for the partial Senate election campaign which began on 15 May, and succeeded in persuading the politicians to be a little more moderate than they would normally have been. These election results marked no change since October 1965; if anything, the JP and the TWP improved their positions—with 56·29 and 3·92 per cent of the vote, while the votes cast dropped to 54 per cent of the registered voters.[74]

The situation calmed down after the election and a more confident Justice Party decided to postpone legislation to amend the Election Law and introduce the amnesty bill. In return, the opposition parties agreed to withdraw all censure motions and permit the Assembly to deal with more vital legislation. But the division on the Right was too deep and only an amnesty for the former Democrats could help heal the wound. The first sign that amnesty was on the way was the pardon for Celâl Bayar on 8 July. The amnesty law was passed on 3 August and included all political prisoners save those who had violated Articles 141 and 142 of the penal code, namely those guilty of 'communist propaganda'. The National Unity Group opposed the bill and appealed to Sunay to veto it. There is said to have been some opposition among the commanders, and Sunay's personal secretary, Cihat Alpan, sought the approval of the generals before taking it to Istanbul for Sunay's signature.[75]

Both major parties were too involved with internal dissension to be able to give undivided attention to national affairs. Demirel was occupied with pressure from his party's right wing which was alarmed by the impact of a burgeoning capitalist economy on the small Anatolian merchants and artisans, who found it difficult to survive against the competition. The RPP was torn with the dissension caused by the very slight turn to the left. In both parties the right-wing factions broke away to form parties of their own. Turhan Feyzioğlu and his friends left the RPP and formed the Reliance Party (RP—*Güven Partisi*) in May 1967; the JP retained its unity until 1970, when the Democratic Party (DP—*Demokratik Parti*) was formed.[76]

The government's offensive against 'the Left' continued unabated. It was as though the country was faced with an imminent threat of subversion and revolution but nothing could have been farther from reality. Persecution of the Left had taken place under the coalition governments, but Demirel's government became hysterical. The intelligentsia was the principal target and writers and artists were constantly harassed; some were prosecuted under Articles 141 and 142 of the penal code for disseminating communist propaganda. Such was the hysteria that the police went so far as to prosecute a 15 year old schoolboy for writing an essay on Atatürk and Lenin![77] Minister of Industries Mehmet Turgut appealed to the private sector to combat the enemies of capitalism.[78]

The government's repressive policies brought a response from the intelligentsia, especially the students, who were a new political factor in the sixties. Politics had entered the university, and the factory, and on occasion spilled out into the street. By the mid-sixties student demonstrations were a fact of political life. The government, having learned the folly of using the army against demonstrators, had created a riot squad, euphemistically described as the 'Community Police' (*Toplum Polisi*), which was specially armed and equipped to deal with demonstrators. Street politics created a permanent atmosphere of crisis and were therefore an element of instability. The parliamentary régime, unable to control the situation, was discredited and again there were rumours of military intervention. President Sunay in his New Year message confirmed the rumours. But he stated categorically that the armed forces would neither be instruments nor spectators of such events.[79]

In November 1966 General Tural issued an order to the armed forces to prepare themselves for the struggle against subversive activities, by which he meant activities of the Left. The order was made public on 23 January 1967. It caused great political turmoil and was severely criticized as a threat to freedom of expression and democracy. However, Demirel supported Tural, stating that the government knew of the order; and the Assembly Group of the Justice Party even demanded an end to all criticism of the Chief of the General Staff, as well as new measures against 'anarchy'. Tural defended his action on 1 February, claiming that what he had done had been common practice during the Atatürk period and that the army was duty bound to awaken the nation whenever necessary, and that was all he had done.[80]

The implications of Tural's logic were dangerously clear. Abdi İpekçi warned his readers that the creation of the myth of a communist menace could be the prelude to a military take-over that would be justified on the grounds of saving Turkey from communism.[81] The Workers' Party brought a motion of censure against Tural but it was defeated in the Assembly; even the Republicans voted against. Such was the atmosphere in the Assembly that when Behice Boran of the TWP tried to speak she was shouted down with cries of 'Throw her out of the country', 'To Moscow, to Moscow'.[82] Encouraged by this show of support from the politicians, Tural repeated his call on 1 March. The military High Command's political allegiance had been stated openly. It was totally committed to the existing régime and no longer pretended to stand outside or above politics.

For some time the Right had been claiming that the 1961 constitution was 'closed to socialism'. This question aroused great emotions and fears on both sides, and Sunay's support for the interpretation that the constitution was closed to socialism, as well as communism and fascism, strengthened the position of the Right.[83] His comment sparked off a constitutional controversy which inflamed political feelings. Ever since the beginning of the Second Republic, political debate had focused on the interpretation and implementation of the constitution; the form of the new republic depended entirely on this. Sunay's statement was partially supported by the Constitutional Court's compromise decision that the constitution was open to only 'limited socialism'.[84] This was an important decision, for if it was enforced, it would restrict the political spectrum to parties of the centre and the Right which shared a similar ideology. It would therefore be a step back towards the politics of the fifties.

Under Demirel's leadership the economy began to pick up and expand, but at the cost of constantly rising prices and spiralling inflation. The emphasis was now on industry and foreign investment, preferably in collaboration with local capital. The government retained the principle of low wages in order to keep down the cost of industrialization and provide the investor with a handsome margin of profit. However, this principle was impossible to reconcile with the concept of social justice, especially for a working class growing more politically conscious and militant. But the economy did not expand rapidly enough to absorb the ever-growing work force, which, fortunately for Demirel, found an outlet by temporary emigration to Europe. According to Mehmed Ali Aybar, the WPT's research showed that, by the beginning of 1968, the economy had started to slow down and this trend was expected to continue for the rest of the year, becoming more pronounced, with a strong possibility that 1969 would be the year of intense crisis. Turkey, he predicted, had entered a period of economic retrogression similar to that of the years 1954 to 1957.[85]

If Aybar's prediction was accurate the political implications would be grave.

Another significant feature of the late sixties was the extraordinary degree of radicalism espoused by Turkish youth. Turkish universities were undoubtedly affected by the world-wide trend, especially by the student insurrection in Paris in May 1968; their students, concerned with local problems, demanded that the government deal with them. They called for, among other things, reform of the archaic system of education, of land ownership which was both unjust and inefficient, and the end of an alliance with the West, which, they believed, restricted their country's freedom of action. Because of the continuing frustration over Cyprus, anti-imperialism became the most emotional issue, an issue of great embarrassment to a government totally committed to the United States. This was particularly true when the students began to demonstrate against the visiting Sixth Fleet or American dignitaries like Dean Rusk.[86]

Young people on the Right were also active in the 1960s; if anything they were better organized than those on the Left. The government was sympathetic, and they were dealt with more leniently than the radicals. Their platform was a virulent anti-communism and their principal target was the WPT, whose meetings they attacked and disrupted, especially before any election. They claimed to be anti-imperialist, but the imperialism they opposed was Russian imperialism, which was no longer seen as an obvious threat in Turkey.

The political situation in Turkey had polarized and Demirel observed that the 'polarization of ideological movements is a fact of life in our world. Certain ideological movements have spread through various foreign countries as fashions do. In our country they have been pushed to such extremes as to be repugnant.' This, he declared, was brought about by too much freedom in the Turkish political system and he warned that 'Freedom of thought, expression and criticism ... should not be allowed to stretch to such a limit that an ideology could threaten those freedoms.'[87] Hereafter Demirel began to stress the existence of 'too much freedom' with proposals to rectify the situation by amending the constitution.

The government's position in the Assembly was still secure but turmoil in the universities, the factories, and sometimes in the streets created the potential for military intervention and this was an unsettling factor for Demirel. There were some who encouraged the junior officers to act in order to fulfil a 'national duty'. But there was no response, at least none that we know of. The only echo was a circular from cadets at the Naval War College which threatened the reactionaries and enemies of Atatürk's reforms with violence.[88]

The High Command remained quiet. In the circumstances President Sunay's New Year message was unusually mild. He regretfully observed that the students were drifting away from their original attitude under the provocation of a small minority which had no discipline and hampered educational activity. He reproached young people for the breakdown of discipline and asked them to stop acts of disruption in educational institutions.[89] A week later, totally disregarding Sunay's appeal, students demonstrated against the American ambassador, Robert Komer, who was visiting the Middle East Technical University, and burned his car.[90] İnönü, a good judge of the times, predicted that Turkey had entered a stormy period. His evaluation was based not on student activity, but on the militancy of the workers. 'We are seeing the first sign of this in the Sümerbank strike. It is difficult to understand a misunderstanding that goes on so long.'[91]

Still there was no response from the High Command, though the National Security Council met more frequently and received greater publicity. The High Command may have been suffering problems within its own ranks and was too divided to act. General Tural was showing signs of political ambition. But he was isolated and lacked the ability to deal with the collective power of the High Command. His term as the Chief of the General Staff ended on 11 March 1969 and he was replaced by General Memduh Tağmaç.[92]

A general election was due in 1969 and as the summer drew to a close the parties began to prepare. The restoration of civil rights to former Democrats was still an issue which aroused emotion and was worth many votes for the party which seemed to support the measure. Demirel was bound to exploit the issue but this time İnönü also decided to make political capital out of it when the Bill came before the Assembly on 11 May. And with the support of the RPP it was passed on 15 May.[93]

The commanders, however, opposed the restoration of rights and made that clear to the parties. However, instead of holding Demirel responsible for introducing the Bill, they blamed İnönü for helping it to pass. They had no objections to Demirel exploiting the issue in order to tap the former DP vote; but they did not like İnönü using the same weapon. Neither Demirel nor the commanders wanted political rights restored since the return of the former Democrats to the political arena would undermine Demirel's position, not İnönü's. But all was not lost, for the measure had yet to go through the Senate. The parties, apprehensive of military intervention and in no position to challenge the military domination, decided to withdraw the Bill on the advice of their respective leaders.[94]

The general election of 12 October brought no change; not that any was seriously expected. No opposition party offered an alternative to Demirel's Justice Party. The RPP was still recovering from the damage done to its old identity by the left-of-centre controversy. The WPT was torn by internal squabbles and factionalism, and by 1969 it had become too respectable for the 'revolutionary' youth who had supported it in 1965. The main element of interest was again the electorate. This time it showed its displeasure with the parties and the politicians by registering the lowest vote (64·3 per cent) of all the elections held since 1950. Demirel's share of this reduced vote was down by 6·4 per cent to 46·5 per cent, lower than the DP vote in 1957. The RPP and the WPT also lost votes and with the ending of the national remainder system the WPT's representation in the Assembly was reduced to two.[95]

The election was a setback for the small parties, confirming the hold of the centrist, conservative Justice Party. The poor performance of the Republicans and of the Workers' Party alienated a large section of the intelligentsia—especially the radicals and the Left—from the system. They had hoped that a change of government might lead to the implementation of reforms promised in the constitution, but Demirel's victory made that improbable. Demirel, now weaker than ever in the party and faced with a split, was unlikely to take any risks with an unpopular policy. Before the election an army officer had noted that a JP victory would be useful because the party's continued failure to solve problems would mobilize 'fresh forces' to put an end to the present system.[96]

The Régime under Pressure

After the 1969 election Turkey was led by a weak government under siege from every side. The majority party was divided by internal factionalism and its leader discredited. The opposition parties, disillusioned with the system in which they performed so badly, were in no mood to compromise with the government—an attitude that aggravated the instability. The general economic situation continued to decline rapidly, and 1970, with one of the most severe droughts of recent years, was declared the year of crisis. The universities were paralysed by student agitation and violence and the factories by worker militancy and strikes. Even the traditionally 'apathetic peasant' stirred himself and occupied land legally not his own. The mass media, especially the influential Turkish Radio and Television, constantly highlighted the shortcomings of the government and the ruling party. On 11 February 1970, within months of his electoral triumph, Demirel was forced to resign when JP dissidents voted against the budget and in so doing brought the government down. Sunay reappointed him Prime Minister but he was never able to recover from this set-back; after 11 February it was downhill all the way for Demirel.[97]

The unstable political environment encouraged adventurism in the armed forces, prompting the National Security Council to step in and issue a warning. On 27 March it took the unprecedented step of issuing a strong statement against the disorders in the universities and threatened counter-measures which paid scant attention to university autonomy. The NSC had gone beyond its consultative and advisory duties assigned by the constitution. But its members were not deterred by mere legality when the existence of the régime was at stake.[98]

That there were rumblings in the army is borne out by a communiqué from the General Staff revealing the arrest of two colonels charged with inciting the armed forces to carry out a military revolution.[99] There were reports of repressive counter-measures to uproot any conspiracy. Officers were forbidden to visit other units, and the press reported that about 700 colonels had been retired.[100]

The High Command's measures confirmed its commitment to the government. Demirel, confident of the generals' support, ridiculed the talk of revolution: 'Is the nation', he asked, 'to be frightened of its armed forces—the apple of its eye—charged with protecting the unity of the country, its régime and independence? These fears are as out of place as they are laughable.'[101] But Demirel was virtually dependent on the commanders for his very survival, and imposition of the 'Yahya Khan formula' in Turkey seemed only a question of time. After the massive workers' demonstration in Istanbul and Kocaeli on 15/16 June, which the government described as a dress rehearsal for revolution, martial law was declared. According to Mehmed Ali Aybar, this was the first step towards the 'Yahya Khan formula'.[102]

Even the commanders were having difficulty in maintaining a consensus in the face of the politicians' failure to maintain order and introduce reform. Some of them lost their patience and wanted to impose a solution from the top. The first indication of this was the Batur memorandum presented to the commanders. Muhsin Batur, a member of the NSC, had recently become Commander of the Air Force. He had the reputation of being a young, innovative, and reformist commander who was unhappy with the political situation. In his memorandum Batur concluded that an orderly parliamentary régime could be maintained only if a radical programme of reform was introduced immediately and backed by the armed forces.[103]

However, no reforms were introduced and on 24 November Batur presented a second memorandum, this time only to Sunay, proposing that the NSC be broadened to include all ranks of officers from lieutenants to generals (rather like the Armed Forces Union), and that a Constituent Assembly be set up to examine objectively the country's problems. His memorandum stated that, because of the prevailing political and socio-economic crisis, unrest in the armed forces had reached a dangerous level, and he advised that immediate measures be taken.[104] Sunay informed Demirel of the situation and set out on a tour of the military commands to feel the pulse of the armed forces for himself.

The other commanders held back and decided to find a solution to the crisis within the context of the existing political structure. On 4 January 1971 Sunay began discussions with party leaders and learned that they would not collaborate with him in order to rescue Demirel. The opposition leaders were disappointed to find that the aim of Sunay's consultations was only to protect Demirel and to throw the army's weight behind him.[105] Demirel met Sunay again on 8 January and when he left the meeting assured the press that the régime was in no danger.[106] On 22 January the NSC met again and reaffirmed its support of the government.[107]

In the new year law and order declined dramatically, almost inviting military counter-measures. Urban guerrilla activity in the form of bank robberies and kidnappings, followed by the government's measures against the universities whence the guerrillas were said to be operating, increased the tension. There were attempts to divide the army and involve it in anti-governmental activity. The commanders were alarmed by propaganda which sought to create the image of an alliance between the government and the High Command in the service of the United States. Such propaganda had already been partially successful in planting the notion that the Turkish Army was purely a 'NATO army' and in holding the commanders responsible for this. The implications of such propaganda were dangerously subversive and the commanders saw the threat. Chief of the General Staff Memduh Tağmaç issued a warning that

... A group of miserable persons who have been trying for some time to drag our country into the dark pit of their ideology have now directed their attacks at destroying the national belief, unity and reputation of our armed forces which is the greatest source of security for the State. Those who have not observed anything like the present indecent defamation of the Turkish armed forces, which have represented the honour and dignity of the great Turkish nation since its foundations, are now witnessing with admonition and disgust the attacks, which consist of repulsive expressions such as 'corrupt', 'fascists' and 'lackeys', against the forces and commanders—the symbols of the national sanctuaries.

It is not possible any more to determine how much longer the armed forces will patiently resist the hostile attacks of these lackeys. In conducting their fundamental duty within the Constitution and democratic system, the armed forces deem imperative a return to the course of Atatürk's reform through concerted action by all State organs to achieve a categorical and speedy solution to ideological clashes, destruction, sabotage and intimidation, which aim at the complete collapse of the country. The Turkish armed forces will oppose any such view and concept, and confront all activities which might drag the country into calamities....[108]

Even after the NSC meeting of 24 February there was no indication that Demirel would soon be dismissed. After the meeting he told journalists that the government was not even considering martial law in order to deal with the 'anarchic situation'.[109] Yet within the week something occurred which forced General Tağmaç to describe the situation as critical. On 3 March he addressed 300 officers and ordered them to steer clear of the incidents—bank robberies, kidnappings, student violence—and stated that the army must remain united. The army, he promised, would be the final arbiter if the situation required it, but such a situation had not yet arisen.[110]

A week later, on 10 March, Tağmaç called an extraordinary meeting of the Supreme Military Council (*Yüksek Komuta Konseyi*). We do not know exactly what was discussed but we do know that there was a demand for Demirel's dismissal. The deliberations continued the following day but no decisions were made public. Evidently the decision to remove Demirel had been taken, and Sunay was informed of it immediately after the meeting.

On 12 March President Sunay and the Chairmen of both chambers received a memorandum signed by Chief of the General Staff Memduh Tağmaç and the Commanders of the Land, Sea, and Air Forces, acting on behalf of the armed forces. The memorandum demanded the formation of a strong, credible government capable of implementing the reforms envisaged by the constitution. Unless this was done immediately the armed forces would assume power. Knowing that the basis of his power had been removed, Demirel resigned, but not without protest. 'It is not possible', he wrote in his letter of resignation, 'to reconcile the memorandum with the constitution and the rule of law [literally, legal state]. In view of this I am submitting, with respect, the resignation of the government.'[111]

The motives for this intervention, and its timing, are still far from clear. The memorandum held the Assembly and the government responsible for driving 'our country into anarchy, fratricidal strife and social and economic unrest', with the consequence that the 'future of the Turkish Republic is . . . seriously threatened . . .' This was the justification for the intervention. If these were the reasons then they had existed for a year or more and therefore the timing becomes significant. It seems that the memorandum was prompted by information that officers, including generals, outside the circle of the High Command, were going to intervene. There had been inklings of such intervention as early as Batur's first memorandum; it is said that Batur was even asked to lead such a movement.[112]

Generals close to the High Command were again approached by the conspirators and told of the impending intervention. The generals informed the High Command—which may explain Tağmaç's meetings with the officers and commanders, designed to establish a consensus and bring into play the armed forces as an institution rather than a cabal. This was the technique used by the commanders ever since the formation of the Armed Forces Union in 1961. The memorandum of 12 March forestalled action from below. Having defused the movement by taking a step which seemed radical and reformist, the commanders gained the initiative and dealt with the insurrectionist officers and their civilian allies in their own good time.

NOTES

1 Yalman, *Gördüklerim*, iv, 385; and Türkeş, *Milliyetçilik*, 119.

2 Ankara Radio, 16 Oct. 1961, in *SWB*, iv/771/c/2; *Cumhuriyet*, 17 Oct. 1961.

3 Quoted in Erkanlı, *Anılar*, 187. See also Türkeş, *Milliyetçilik*, 117-21.

4 *Cumhuriyet*, 31 Oct. 1961. Those present at the Brussels meeting were Alparslan Türkeş, Orhan Erkanlı, Orhan Kabibay, İrfan Solmazer, Numan Esin, and Mustafa Kaplan.

5 The text of the protocol is in Faik, *Gazeteci*, 174-5, but see also 172-6; Dündar Seyhan, 'Gölgedeki Adam', *Milliyet*, 21 June 1966; Yalman, *Gördüklerim*, iv, 385-6.

6 M. Emin Aytekin, *İhtilâl Çıkmazı* (1967), 79.

7 *Milliyet*, 25 Oct. 1961; Faik, *Gazeteci*, 168 and *passim*.

8 *Milliyet*, 26 and 27 Oct. 1961; Faik, *Gazeteci*, 161 ff.; Baban, *Politika*, 257 ff.

9 *Cumhuriyet*, 21 Dec. 1961; *MER 1961*, 575–6.

10 İnönü's speech to industrialists and businessmen, *Cumhuriyet*, 2 Feb. 1962.

11 Faik, *Gazeteci*, 188–94; Aytekin, *İhtilâl*, 181–8. Talât Aydemir, who led this revolt, told his own story. See his *Ve Talât Aydemir Konuşuyor* (1966), 116–43.

12 There is considerable literature on the Turkish army in politics. Apart from the works cited in nn. 3, 5, 6, and 11 above, see also Can Kaya İsen, *Geliyorum diyen İhtilâl* (1964); Erdoğan Örtülü, *Üç İhtilâlin Hikâyesi* (1966); Walter Weiker, 'The Aydemir Case and Turkey's Political Dilemma', *MEA*, xiv/9 (1963), 258–71; Kemal Karpat, 'The Military and Politics in Turkey, 1960–64: A Socio-Cultural Analysis of a Revolution', *American Historical Review*, lxxv/6 (1970), 1654–83.

13 *Cumhuriyet*, 31 Mar. 1962. Conversation with Seyfi Kurtbek who had become one of the leading figures in the Justice Party. See Article III of the bill; the text is given in *MEJ*, xvi/1 (1962), 215–38.

14 Ankara Radio, 3 Apr. 1962, in *SWB*, iv/914/c/1.

15 The Turkish press, 6, 7, 8, 11, and 21 Apr. 1962.

16 Ibid., 24 Apr. 1962.

17 Ibid., 25 Apr. 1962.

18 Ibid., 27 May 1962 and Avni Elevli, *1960–1965 Olayları ve Batırılamıyan Gemi 'Türkiye'* (1967), 289.

19 *Cumhuriyet*, 20 and 21 June 1962. The fourth volume of Toker, *İsmet Paşa*, deals with the years 1961–4 from İnönü's perspective.

20 *Cumhuriyet*, 25 and 26 June 1962. The cabinet is given below, 228, n. 19.

21 See İnönü's speech following the vote of confidence in the Assembly, *Cumhuriyet*, 8 July 1962.

22 *Milliyet* and *Cumhuriyet*, 6–10 Oct. 1962. Faik, *Gazeteci*, 231 suggests that Turhan Feyzioğlu (Minister of State) and Life Senator Ekrem Acuner were responsible for these leaflets. In a conversation with the author, and in a further private communication, Feyzioğlu ridiculed Faik's allegation in the strongest terms.

23 The Turkish press, 3 and 4 Dec. 1962 and 5 Dec. for Mücip Ataklı's reply. See also *TY 1963*, 44–6.

24 Faik, *Gazeteci*, 226–47 devotes a chapter to this incident in order to establish a relationship between the RPP and the eleven officers.

25 Erkanlı, *Anılar*, 191–2 (Brussels meeting). Türkeş's return received wide coverage in the press on 24 and 25 Feb. 1963. See also *The Economist*, 2 Mar. 1963. Türkeş was arrested in May 1963 in connection with Aydemir's abortive *coup*. This, he claims, destroyed his chances of taking over the Justice Party. On 31 Mar. 1965 he and four other former exiles joined the RPNP, which he took over in June. Under Türkeş the party began to change its character, acquiring fascist, populist overtones, and he even organized para-military youths to use against the Left. In

1969 the name of the party was changed to the Nationalist Action Party (NAP—*Milliyetçi Hareket Partisi*). Since 1965 Türkeş has been Representative for Adana.

26 *Cumhuriyet*, 22–5 Mar. 1963.
27 Ibid., 27 Mar. 1963.
28 *The Economist*, 30 Mar. and 6 Apr. 1963.
29 *Cumhuriyet*, 23 and 24 Apr. 1963.
30 Ibid., 29 Apr. 1963.
31 Ibid., 15 May 1963.
32 Ibid.
33 *Cumhuriyet*, 17 May 1963.
34 Ibid., 3 June 1963. Toker, *İsmet Paşa*, iv, 88 says that they were caught unaware. See also the works listed in n. 12 above.
35 *Cumhuriyet*, 4 July 1963.
36 The Turkish press, 22 May 1963; *TY 1964*, 69–107.
37 Sunay's statement to the French press cited in *Cumhuriyet*, 21 July 1963.
38 The quotations are from Bernard Lewis, 'Dustūr: Turkey', in *EI²* (1966). The text of the constitution is given in *MEJ*, xvi/1 (1962), 215–38 with comments by Kerim Kâmi Key. The same issue of *MEJ* includes İsmet Giritli, 'Some Aspects of the New Turkish Constitution'. Giritli was one of the professors responsible for drawing up the constitution. See also Münci Kapani, 'Outlines of the New Turkish Constitution', *Parliamentary Affairs*, xv (1961/1962), 94–110; Joseph Szyliowicz, 'The 1961 Constitution—an Analysis', *Islamic Studies*, ii/3 (1963), 363–81; Robert Devereux, 'Society and Culture in the Second Turkish Republic', *MEA*, xii (1961), 230–9. Perhaps the best analysis of the 1961 constitution is Mümtaz Soysal, *Anayasanın Anlamı* (1969), 58–144.
39 On the Workers' Party see Kemal Karpat, 'Socialism and the Labour Party of Turkey', *MEJ*, xxi/2 (1967), 157–73; and excerpt from *Türkiye İşçi Partisi Kimlerin Partisidir?* (Istanbul, 1962) translated in Karpat, ed., *Political and Social Thought in the Contemporary Middle East* (1968), 358–60; Kışlalı, *Forces Politiques*, 103–12; and the party's programme: *Türkiye İşçi Partisi Programı* (1964).
40 *Cumhuriyet*, 20 Aug. 1963.
41 Ibid., 5 Sept. 1963. A more efficient intelligence service has played a major role in keeping track of and disarming conspiracies in the army.
42 See the Turkish press, 3 Dec. 1963 and following.
43 *Cumhuriyet*, 26 Dec. 1963 and Toker, *İsmet Paşa*, iv, 135–40 and *passim*. The cabinet is given below, 230, n. 44.
44 *Cumhuriyet*, 20 and 21 Mar. 1964. The Cyprus question is discussed in ch. 14 below.
45 The economy is discussed in ch. 10 below.
46 Sunay's letter to the Chairman of the Assembly, Fuad Sirmen, was delivered on 12 Nov. and published in the press on 18 Nov. 1964, also in *TY 1965*, 244–6. See also his statement to *Kim*, 3 Dec. 1964.
47 *Cumhuriyet*, 23 Nov. 1964.
48 Ibid., 11 Dec. 1964. According to Seyfi Kurtbek, it was Demirel's

policy to appease the commanders, but he practised this policy with circumspection so as not to alienate the extremists in the party.

49 *Cumhuriyet*, 19 Dec. 1964; Toker, *İsmet Paşa*, iv, 141 ff.

50 *Cumhuriyet*, 12-14 Feb. 1964. See below, 223.

51 Ibid., 17 Feb. 1965; *TY 1965*, 308-9. For the cabinet see below, 230, n. 57.

52 For Ürgüplü's programme see the press, 27 Feb. 1965 and Öztürk, *Hükümetler*, 583 ff.; and for Zeren's statement, *Cumhuriyet*, 13 Mar. 1965, 7.

53 Ankara Radio, 16 May 1965, in *SWB*, iv/1862/c/3-4.

54 *Cumhuriyet*, 30 May 1965.

55 Ibid., 31 May 1965.

56 *Son Havadis*, 30 June 1965. For Demirel's election speeches see his *Seçim Konuşmaları* (1966, published by the JP Central Committee).

57 Deputy Secretary-General Suphi Baykam's telegram, *Cumhuriyet*, 1 July 1965.

58 *Milliyet*, 8 Aug. (Erim) and 22 Aug. 1965 (Feyzioğlu).

59 See Nermin Abadan, 'Turkish Election of 1965', *Government and Opposition*, i/3 (1966), 335-44, and her very detailed study *1965 Seçimlerinin Tahlili* (1966). The official results were given in the press on 15 Oct. 1965.

60 J. C. Hurewitz, *Middle East Politics: the Military Dimension* (1969), 505, n.9.

61 *Milliyet*, 17 and 18 Jan. 1966.

62 Ibid., 3 Feb. 1966. By 1966 so confident was the JP of its standing with the generals that some of its members assaulted retired General, former Minister and Senator, Sıtkı Ulay in the Assembly (the press, 7 May 1966). Compare this with the Nuri Beşer incident of January 1962 when a Justice Party Representative 'insulted the army' while intoxicated. He was expelled from the party, had his parliamentary immunity removed, and was sentenced to one year's imprisonment with hard labour and four years of provincial exile in Tatvan.

63 *Cumhuriyet*, 14-16 Mar. 1966.

64 Ibid., 29 Mar. 1966. Brigadier General Cihat Alpan replaced the civilian Nasır Zeytinoğlu as the President's personal secretary, *Cumhuriyet*, 10 Apr. 1966. Alpan is said to have been very influential politically, acting as liaison between the commanders and Sunay. See *Ortam*, 2, 26 Apr. 1971. *Yankı*, 148, 20 Jan. 1974, 4, claimed that 'there is a widespread belief that Alpan was the brains behind every important decision of the presidency'.

65 *Milliyet*, 30 Mar. 1966.

66 Ankara Radio, 19 May 1966, in *SWB*, iv/2169/c/1-2.

67 For reports see *Cumhuriyet* and *Milliyet*, 23 May 1966.

68 OYAK will be discussed in the context of the economy in ch. 10 below. As for retired officers in the bureaucracy and other sectors, a few examples will suffice. Admiral Fahri Korutürk, who is President today, was sent to Moscow and Madrid; General Kızıloğlu to the Vatican; General Tansel to Ottawa. Colonel Agasi Şen became director of Turkish

Airlines after he left the post of personal secretary to Gürsel. This tendency has been accelerated since 12 Mar. 1971 and needs to be studied with some care.

69 On 29 June 1966 the press reported that houses were being built for the commanders in Çankaya, the most fashionable embassy district of the capital. See İlhami Soysal, 'Komutanlarimizin Yuvası', *Akşam*, 29 June 1966.

70 *Ulus*, 20 Jan. 1966 and *Cumhuriyet*, 5–6 Mar. 1966.

71 Ankara Radio, 12 Mar. 1966, in *SWB*, iv/2112/c/1.

72 *Cumhuriyet*, 29 Apr. 1966.

73 The Turkish press, 13–14 May 1966.

74 Ibid., 7 June 1966. For an analysis of the results see Cavit Orhan Tütengil, 'Seçim Sonuçları', *Cumhuriyet*, 19 June 1966, 2.

75 *Cumhuriyet*, 20 July and 1, 3, 4, 7, 8, and 10 Aug. 1966. The Bill became law when it was published in *Resmi Gazete*, 9 Aug. 1966.

76 Muzaffer Sencer, *Sosyal Temeller*, 304–12 (Güven Partisi) and 373–81 (Demokratik Parti).

77 *Cumhuriyet*, 9 and 10 Mar. 1966. The schoolboy Gürbüz Şimşek was defended by Muammer Aksoy and acquitted on 30 Sept. See *Cumhuriyet*, 1 Oct. 1966.

78 Ibid., 28 Sept. 1966.

79 Ibid., 1 Jan. 1967; *MER 1967*, 511.

80 *Cumhuriyet* and *Milliyet*, 31 Jan., 1 and 2 Feb. 1967; *MER 1967*, 512.

81 *Milliyet*, 5 Feb. 1967. A few months later, when the Greek army overthrew George Papandreou, the Turkish press noted that the junta had intervened against a left-of-centre government, similar to the type İnönü and Ecevit wanted to set up. See the press, 22 Apr. 1967 and following.

82 The Turkish press, 10 Feb. 1967; *MER 1967*, 512.

83 Ankara Radio, 27 May 1967, in *SWB*, iv/2478/c/3–4. For a criticism of Sunay's statement see Nadir Nadi, 'Niyetler İyi Olsa da', *Cumhuriyet*, 30 May 1967, reproduced in Nadir Nadi, *27 Mayıs'tan 12 Mart'a* (1971), 344–5; and *MER 1967*, 512–13.

84 *Resmi Gazete*, 25 July 1967 and the press, 26 July 1967.

85 Ankara Radio, 18 May 1968, in *SWB*, iv/2776/c/2–3. Professor Besim Üstünel corroborated this view a year later, claiming that the economy was heading for a situation similar to that of 1958 (*Cumhuriyet*, 3 May 1969). In Aug. 1970 the Turkish lira was devalued by 66 per cent.

86 The Turkish press, 20 and 21 Apr. 1966; *MEJ*, xx/3 (1966), 382.

87 Ankara Radio, 23 Mar. 1968, in *SWB*, iv/2731/c/1–2.

88 *Milliyet*, 3 and 4 Nov. 1968; Tevfik Çavdar, *Türkiye 1968* (1969), 122. See also İlhan Selçuk, 'Harbiye Konuştu', and Sezai Orkunt, 'Deniz Subaylarının Bildirisi Üzerine', *Cumhuriyet*, 4 and 9 Nov. 1968, respectively. Both articles are reproduced in *VY 1969*, 407–13.

89 *Cumhuriyet* and Ankara Radio, 1 Jan. 1969, in *SWB*, iv/2964-/c/1–2.

90 The Turkish press, 7 Jan. 1969. The university was closed down until 10 Feb.

210   *The Turkish Experiment in Democracy*

91 *Cumhuriyet*, 26 Jan. 1969. This was the longest strike in Turkish history.

92 *Ulus*, 12 and 18 Mar. 1969. *Yankı* 18, 4 July 1971, 5 claims that General Faruk Gürler refused to support Tural. Gürler was Under-Secretary at the Defence Ministry and a very popular general in the army.

93 The perss, 11-16 May 1969.

94 Ibid., 22 May 1969; *The Economist*, 31 May 1969. Just before the election Tural announced that the armed forces had played no role in preventing the passage of the Bill, implying that Demirel alone had been responsible. Demirel refused to join issue (*Cumhuriyet*, 29-30 Aug. 1969).

95 The official results were published in the press, 19 Oct. 1969. For an analysis of these elections see Michael Hyland, 'Crisis at the Polls: Turkey's 1969 Elections', *MEJ* xxiv/1 (1970), 1-16.

96 Sami Kohen in the *Christian Science Monitor*, 10 Oct. 1969.

97 A good account of the internal dissension in the JP in 1970 is given in *Milliyet 1970* (1971), 30-48. This will be discussed more fully in the next chapter.

98 On the criticism of the NSC statement see Bahri Savcı, 'Büyük Hastalık', *Cumhuriyet*, 6 Apr., and the panel discussion in *Milliyet*, 12 Apr. 1970. There was also a response from a clandestine group in the armed forces. See İlhan Selçuk, 'MGK Bildirisi ve Devrimci Ordu Gücü Karşı Bildirisi', *Cumhuriyet*, 5 Apr. 1970.

99 *Milliyet*, 26 May 1970 and Sami Kohen's report, *Christian Science Monitor*, 19 June 1970.

100 *Cumhuriyet*, 27 July 1970. The actual figures, 56 generals and 516 colonels, were announced on 28 Aug. Some members of the National Unity Group in the Senate were also thought to be involved in the conspiracy and the government tried to have their parliamentary immunity lifted, but failed. However, they were unable to escape so easily after 12 Mar. 1971. See *Madanoğlu Dosyası* (1973), the indictment prepared by Süleyman Takkeci, a martial law prosecutor.

101 *Cumhuriyet*, 29 May 1970.

102 Aybar's interpellation in the Assembly on 22 June 1970 in Mehmet Ali Aybar, *12 Mart'tan Sonra Meclis Konuşmaları* (1973), 5-26. The term 'Yahya Khan Formula' (*Yahya Han Formülü*) enjoyed wide currency in Turkey during 1970 and 1971. It was used to describe the anticipated open domination of the politicians by the commanders, as was the case in Pakistan. Fahri Özdilek, leader of the NUG in the Senate, had already asked Sunay to replace Demirel but Sunay refused (*Cumhuriyet*, 9 June 1970). He told Kemal Aydar that he would never use this formula (interview in *Cumhuriyet*, 14 June 1970).

103 *Le Monde*, sélection hebdomadaire, 9-15 July 1970; *Yankı* 129, 9 Sept. 1971 (cover story), 5-10.

104 *Yankı*, as previous note. This memorandum was published in the press on 12 Dec. 1970.

105 See the statements of the NUG, İsmet İnönü and Dündar Taşer (NAP) in the press, 6-7 Jan. 1971.

106 *Cumhuriyet*, 9 Jan. 1971.

107 Ibid., 23 and 24 Jan. 1971.

108 Ankara Radio, 6 Feb. 1971, in *SWB*, iv/3605/c/1; see also *Cumhuriyet*, 6 Feb. 1971. For examples of attacks on the army see Tayfur Ketenci, *Türk Silâhlı Kuvvetleri ve Aşırı Sol* (n.d. [1971]).

109 *Cumhuriyet*, 25 Feb. 1971.

110 Ibid., 4 Mar. 1971. For a description of this period, see my article, 'The Turkish Guerrillas: Symptoms of a Deeper Malaise', *NME*, 55 (Apr. 1973), 13–16.

111 See the Turkish press, 11–13 Mar. 1971 and *Milliyet 1971* (1972), 42–64.

112 Uğur Mumcu's article in *Devrim* 50, 29 Sept. 1970, partially quoted in Metin Toker, *Solda ve Sağda Vuruşanlar* (1971), 80.

CHAPTER VIII

THE COALITION GOVERNMENTS 1961-1965

In Turkey today it is impossible to differentiate between the parties by claiming that this party is on the right path and that party is on the wrong path, or by reaching the conclusion that if that party is closed democracy will be saved. In varying degrees, all parties are on the wrong path. None of them has taken up the country's genuine problem. The manner in which the leaders of the parties argue with one another is not very different from that in which arguments between rival groups in a village coffeehouse take place....

The new parties have brought nothing new to the country, and the old parties have been unable to liberate themselves from their traditions. In my view this is the weakest feature of the matter. In this country there are millions of independent citizens who belong to none of the parties. Watching this struggle of the blind, they are becoming pessimistic; they cannot look with confidence to the future. ... The success of the democratic experiment depends on an alteration of these situations ...

Editorial from *Akşam* quoted over Ankara Radio, 7 August 1961

Republican People's Party-Justice Party

ON 10 November 1961 İnönü was given the task of forming his First Coalition. The task was difficult, for not one of the parties wanted to serve under him. They made this clear in their consultations with President Gürsel after the election, and only the threat of a political crisis likely to provoke military intervention persuaded the Justice Party of the necessity to work with İnönü. *Cumhuriyet* of 10 November reported that the JP had decided, as a final resort, to collaborate with the RPP in forming a government. But there was to be much bargaining before the ministry finally took shape.

The new government was announced on 20 November and the

portfolios were divided evenly between the two parties, each receiving eleven ministries.¹ Perhaps the most significant shortcoming of this cabinet was İnönü's failure to persuade the JP Chairman Ragıp Gümüşpala to accept a post, for he would have strengthened its position politically. Without Gümüşpala, the Justice Party's commitment to the ministry was a weak one.

The first concern of the government was to revive the economy, which had been stagnating for two years. This called for political stability, something for which coalitions are not the best institutions. To make matters worse the summer of 1961 had been dry, resulting in a poor harvest, and in eastern Anatolia there was even the threat of famine.² In industrial areas workers were agitating for the implementation of the right of collective bargaining and the right to strike, promised by the new constitution. On 31 December they staged a massive rally in Istanbul in order to stress their demands. But for the moment they had to be satisfied with promises, since the government was still too preoccupied with playing politics to deal with their problems.

The environment was such that the future of parliamentary democracy was in question. There was an influential group in the armed forces and the intelligentsia which was convinced that only a closed régime could protect the Kemalist reforms, carry out new reforms envisaged in the constitution, and withstand the onslaught of neo-Democratic revanchisme. Their principal fear was that the neo-Democrats would in time assume power and create a revanchist régime. The prophets of doom were predicting that democracy would not work.

Against this background, İnönü made a radio broadcast on 17 January 1962 categorically opposing the imposition of a closed régime:

> To think that Atatürk's reforms can only be protected by a closed regime is a great mistake.... Reforms achieved under a closed regime can survive only if they can withstand storms emerging under a democratic regime. If we had not adopted a democratic regime it would not have been known whether or not Atatürk's reforms would survive. Under a democratic regime these reforms have been debated. Such debates still occur....

> I want to tell you of two definite things: While this operation is being conducted I will never allow the creation of a closed regime that will abandon the democratic regime whatever its nature may be. I will never take part in such a closed regime. I will stand and fight against it. Similarly, whatever the cost, I will never make any concessions to anybody regarding Atatürk's principles, the Western way of life, the freedom of expression and thought which constitutes the basis of our Republic....

The coalition Government [he concluded] represents fraternity among citizens. Co-operation in our political life is constantly progressing. This will reduce causes of anxiety and finally eliminate them. We have confidence in the future.[3]

In view of the AFU's protocol of 9 February, which gave the political parties until 28 February to form a coalition, even the JP extremists realized the wisdom of supporting İnönü, at least temporarily. The Assembly Group, which had earlier opposed the coalition, now declared that it stood behind Gümüşpala and the government.[4] Moreover, the party leadership began to expel the extremists from its ranks in order to show its good faith to the army. The JP tried to emphasize that only a régime 'based on the people's vote', not on the army, and representing 'the people's will', could ensure the survival and development of democracy.

İnönü manipulated the threat of military intervention with consummate skill and succeeded in subduing the Justice Party's aggressiveness. The tension created by Talât Aydemir's abortive *putsch* strengthened İnönü's hand even further, and when he entered the Assembly on 23 February, having outwitted Aydemir, 'something rarely seen in our political life took place. The entire chamber, including political rivals and even enemies, rose and gave [İnönü] a standing ovation, expressing its admiration.'[5] The Assembly then conveyed its 'profound appreciation, gratitude and sentiments of confidence to the Honourable President Gürsel, the Honourable Prime Minister İnönü and members of the cabinet, to all the patriotic commanders and officers ... [for having] once again saved the Turkish people from a historic tragedy'.[6] The neo-Democrats had received a scare and decided that it was wiser to have political stability, even if that meant collaborating with İnönü, than to provoke military intervention. Inadvertently Aydemir had succeeded in creating a political consensus where none had existed before.

In the cynical atmosphere which prevailed in Ankara at the time, there were rumours that İnönü had permitted the Aydemir adventure in order to strengthen his position politically and to crush reactionary tendencies.[7] Avni Doğan, a Republican cabinet minister, is alleged to have said: 'If I have any anxiety it is that İnönü is planning to use the troublemakers in the army and their preparations in order to create the conviction among his JP coalition partners that they can survive only under his wing.'[8] Five years later General İrfan Tansel, who had been Commander of the Air Force in 1962, confronted İnönü with a similar charge but İnönü refused to enter into any controversy.[9]

For the moment İnönü was master of the situation. On 25 February the government and all the parties issued a joint communiqué reaffirming their loyalty to the revolution and the constitution. Next day the Assembly began to consider measures to protect the revolution, passing them on 3 March in the form of the Law to Prevent Certain Activities Aimed at Destroying Constitutional Order, National Security and Tranquillity. The aim of this measure was to deter, with the threat of imprisonment, neo-Democrat extremists from praising the fallen régime and criticizing the new one.[10]

But the unending political crisis, focused around the question of amnesty, only disguised the serious differences between the RPP and the neo-Democrats over socio-economic issues such as planning and the reforms, the role of the private sector, rights for the workers, and the question of the 'social state' (*sosyal devlet*) which the 1961 constitution promised to create. İnönü had been temporizing since October but now that his position was strong he decided to force the other parties into a subservience which would permit the government to act.

On 26 April he conferred separately with the leaders of the coalition parties on current problems and the state of the coalition. He asked them to accept certain conditions necessary to keep the coalition alive. He demanded a positive vote for the government's economic and financial measures and warned them that they must not propose laws which would burden the budget, nor deviate from the fundamentals of the programme. In order to bring about general tranquillity they must introduce sincere and beneficial measures and ask for a general amnesty only after that had been achieved. They must give up opposition within the coalition as well as attempts to make political capital. Finally they must give an affirmative vote to government Bills.[11]

İnönü was under pressure from the younger group in his party, which was demanding that he begin to deal with the real problems facing the country rather than manufactured ones such as the amnesty issue.[12] The planners, who had been entrusted with the task of reviving the economy, objected to concessions being made to the rich, notably the failure to require a declaration of wealth, which they considered essential for the reform of the tax system.[13] But the neo-Democrats refused to meet İnönü's conditions and in the Justice Party they even demanded the resignation of their leader, Ragıp Gümüşpala, because of his willingness to compromise.[14] It was precisely on the essentials that İnönü could obtain no concessions: therefore on 30 May 1962 he decided to resign, hoping that the new coalition would be more accommodating.[15]

RPP-NTP-RPNP-Independents

The situation was a little more promising than it had been six months earlier. The New Turkey Party was willing to join a coalition under İnönü, and, with the Justice Party split between extremists and moderates, it was possible to find a working majority in the Assembly. Gürsel invited İnönü to form a new government on 4 June, and İnönü began consultations on the same day. Once again he ran into old problems: How much control, he was asked, would the state exercise over the economy and how much freedom would the private sector have?[16]

Having failed to make any headway, İnönü gave up his attempt on 18 June. But military pressure was brought to bear and on 24 June (the 25th day of the governmental crisis) the RPP, the RPNP, and the NTP as well as Independents (mainly former Justice Party Representatives) agreed to form a coalition government.[17] The protocol they signed made it manifestly clear that İnönü had 'agreed to compromise on their social [and economic] programme and to accept private enterprise as an equal partner. The chairman of the New Turkey Party [Ekrem Alican], an ardent defender of private enterprise, was made Deputy Premier in charge of economic affairs, including the State Planning Organization . . .'[18]

The Second Coalition was announced on 25 June and *The Economist* noted that it was difficult to see how a cabinet in which feudal landlordism, big business, and religious fanaticism were all represented would carry out reforms. In spite of the growing labour movement and increasing working class militancy there was still no trade union representation in the Assembly, let alone the cabinet.[19]

The ideological inclinations of the new government became clear when it proposed legislation, passed by the Assembly on 10 September, permitting the fifty-five *ağas* (big landowners and tribal chiefs of eastern Anatolia) to return to their old place of residence.[20] The *ağas* had been banished from those regions, where they exercised great power and influence, and settled in other parts of the country by the National Unity Committee. Initially 254 of them were arrested but later 189 were released and only 55 were 'resettled' in western and southwestern Turkey. This had been the first attempt by any modern Turkish government to break the power of the feudal landowners of eastern Turkey and was described by *Ulus* as 'one of the most important social reforms we have carried since the time of Mahmud II' [1808-39].[21] Yet with one stroke İnönü erased this important measure, thereby weakening the possibility of land reform, so vitally necessary for economic development. Politically the government's decision meant the restoration of the *status quo ante* in eastern Anatolia, and the neo-Democrat parties, especially the JP and the NTP, began to make grand preparations in the east to greet the returning *ağas*. *Cumhuriyet* (15 September 1962) reported that both parties were competing to enlist their support.

There was a sharp reaction to all the concessions the government had made to the Right, which inevitably undermined the possibility of radical reform. Within the RPP there was a demand for İnönü's resignation both as Prime Minister and Party Chairman. Ferda Güley claimed that it was essential to eradicate the conviction that this régime could not function without İnönü. At the same time a new leader acceptable to all factions in the party must be elected during his (İnönü's) own lifetime. Others also criticized his leadership, but İnönü stated categorically that he did not contemplate resigning and that he would continue the struggle until success had been achieved.[22]

A few days later (26 September), the principal technical advisers at the State Planning Organization (SPO) resigned collectively because the government had diluted the plan so as to make it ineffective. They had had disagreements with Deputy Premier Alican and İnönü had always backed him up. Under such conditions, they argued, their work would serve no purpose.[23] At the beginning of October there were anti-İnönü demonstrations in Ankara and demands for his resignation; ironically, it was the Justice Party which rallied round İnönü and decided to support him.[24] The RPP was demoralized and even the editor of the party paper *Ulus*, the renowned novelist Yakup Kadri Karaosmanoğlu, resigned from the party in disgust, declaring that the Republicans were making many inroads into Atatürk's principles.[25]

Later he recalled that İnönü had told him at the time that 'I am only "touching up" Atatürk's principles.' 'He was constantly making concessions and "touching up",' said Karaosmanoğlu. 'He destroyed the plan. They brought the economic plan to a miserable state, following the views of those Melens (and I don't know who else), and those reactionary economists. It was the only thing which could have raised this country; all hope rested in the implementation of this plan point by point. And he [İnönü] eliminated all those who produced the plan. He transformed it into something which was artificial and inapplicable.'[26]

The political parties were steadily moving to the right. This was as true for the RPP as it was for the JP. At the JP General Congress (30 November–2 December) the extremists defeated the moderates and took control.[27] At the RPP's Sixteenth Congress, too, İnönü and the conservatives retained complete control and Kemal Satır became Secretary-General. There were protests and resignations over the establishment of İnönü's 'absolute personal dictatorship', but as yet there was no power which could shake it. It would be another ten years before that could happen.[28]

Not surprisingly, this swing to the right was marked by a more active policy of repression against the Left. No Turkish government had ever tolerated the Left. However, the 1961 constitution permitted—for the first time—the existence of a legally constituted socialist party like the Workers' Party of Turkey. More important than the legal right was the existence of a liberal and hopeful atmosphere after 27 May 1960, which allowed ideological debate and the organization of the Left.

The first group to take advantage of the new freedom was focused around the weekly *Yön*, founded in December 1961. Strictly speaking, this group ought to be described as being composed of non-Marxist, left-wing radicals. There were some convinced socialists in its ranks but the leadership always remained in the hands of radicals like Doğan Avcıoğlu, who came from the left-wing of the RPP. It was an élitist movement of intellectuals, who, instead of seeking mass support, flirted with the interventionist radicals in the army, hoping to come to power on the point of a bayonet. Their aim was 'to improve, consolidate and preserve rather than drastically change the basic structure of the social system'.[29]

Socialism in the Turkey of the early sixties came to be represented by the Workers' Party of Turkey. This party was founded on 13 February 1961 by a number of trade unionists who sought to use it as a vehicle for working class representation in the Assembly. But the party was of no consequence until its leadership was assumed by Mehmet Ali Aybar, a socialist of long standing, in February 1962.[30] It was he who gave the party a personality, attracting to it the intelligentsia, especially young lecturers and students at the university, who became its life blood. At the same time, however, Aybar and his associates took care that their party did not become the monopoly of the intelligentsia, cut off from the working class, and they guaranteed working class participation by allotting to it 50 per cent of all positions in the party administration.

The Workers' Party developed slowly and was no immediate

threat to the established system. Yet by November 1962 its meetings, even inside the city of Istanbul, were being attacked by organized mobs and its supporters manhandled by the police. In order to protest against the violation of their constitutional rights, the leaders sent a delegation to meet İnönü, who assured them that the rights granted by the constitution would be extended to them as well.[31]

But it was not only repression of the WPT which marked the swing to the right. What was more symptomatic of the change was the prosecution of intellectuals for translating articles like Jean Paul Sartre's 'Marxism and Existentialism', or the banning of the translations of Graechus Babeuf's writings.[32] In this atmosphere the Assembly set up an all-party Commission to Combat Communism (*Komünizmle Mücadele Komisyonu*) on 11 January 1963. This was followed later in the year by the countrywide reactionary organization known as the Association to Combat Communism (*Komünizmle Mücadele Derneği*).[33]

The politicians were going in a diametrically opposite direction to that of enlightened opinion in the country. One of the results was the total disillusionment of youth with the traditional parties. Large numbers resigned from the RPP in January 1963 and began joining organizations like the WPT and the Socialist Cultural Associations (*Sosyalist Kültür Dernekleri*), recently founded by three former planners—Torun, Erder, and Atilla Karaosmanoğlu— and the *Yön* group.

The concessions to the Right did not produce either social stability or reform. The only piece of legislation of any consequence by this government was the Labour Laws, granting the rights of collective bargaining and strike to the unions and the right of lock-out to the employers.[34] 'All these measures and policies', noted Minister of Labour Bülent Ecevit, 'contribute a great deal to Turkey's immunity against such ideologies and doctrines as might threaten her independence, as well as her internal peace and democracy.'[35] In place of hope there emerged a sense of pessimism amongst those who had placed their faith in the ability of a Republican government to carry out peaceful change. In this climate Talât Aydemir attempted his second abortive *coup* on 20/21 May 1963. For the first time, people saw this not as just another military *coup*, but as an attempt by a 'Turkish Nasser' to seize power in order to carry out an extensive programme of reform.

İnönü's policies did, however, succeed in providing governmental stability. There were no longer constant rumours regarding the collapse of the coalition, and it lasted, with minor changes, until December 1963. The principal reason for the collapse of the Second Coalition was the poor performance of the RPP's coalition partners in the local and municipal elections of 17 November 1963. Between them, the New Turkey Party and the Republican Peasants' Nation Party succeeded in polling only 9 per cent of the vote (NTP 6·5 and RPNP 2·6), while the Justice Party polled 46·2 per cent and the Republicans 37·5.[36] According to a survey conducted by *Cumhuriyet* before the elections, the JP was expected to obtain only 31·35 per cent, the RPP 36·58, and the coalition partners 13·16.[37] The two minor parties drew the conclusion that their electoral set-back had been caused by their alliance with İnönü. They decided to withdraw from the coalition, and İnönü, faced with their defection, resigned on 2 December 1963.[38]

Republican People's Party-Independents

The elections had also been a setback for the RPP, which within two years had declined to the status of the second party. The party was losing ground because the voters held it responsible for the prevailing climate of socio-economic and political uncertainty. Republicans like Barlas therefore proposed that the party stay out of any future coalition and leave the task of government to the JP.[39]

Moreover, it was no longer appropriate for the RPP to form a new ministry. President Gürsel recognized the logic of the situation and asked Gümüşpala to form a government. The situation was contradictory; his Justice Party had become the first party in the country but it was still the second in the Assembly. A general election would alter that situation but it was still almost two years away. The minor parties could not go into a coalition with the JP, precisely because they were so ideologically close to it that they would risk being swallowed up and losing their identity and independence. Unable to form a ministry, Gümüşpala wrote to Gürsel asking that an early general election be held to enable the country to extricate itself from the blind alley of coalitions.[40] In all this, a point that was not lost on political commentators was the armed forces' willingness to accept a cabinet led by a neo-Democrat party. This was a fact of great significance for the immediate future.

With Gümüşpala's failure to form a government, the President appointed İnönü as Prime Minister on 16 December and his party's Assembly Group gave him full authority to negotiate a new coalition. Next day Kemal Satır, the party's Secretary-General, stated that if a government could not be formed an immediate general election would become an urgent necessity.[41] He hoped that, after their experience in the local elections, the small parties would fear being wiped out in a general electoral contest and would therefore agree to collaborate with the RPP. Barlas again stressed the need for the JP to take part in government if reforms were to be carried out and the plan implemented. Otherwise the cabinet would again be a weak one, intended to mark time until the next general election, still two years away.[42] But İnönü was able to reach a working agreement neither with Gümüşpala nor with the small parties. When these negotiations broke down, he announced on 23 December that he would form a cabinet with the Independents, of whom there were 33 in the Assembly, giving the government only 208 votes, 18 short of a majority.[43]

İnönü presented his new cabinet on 25 December amidst the rising tension of the Cyprus crisis, which threatened to burst into open hostilities, between Turkey and Greece.[44] He told the Assembly that his principal concern would be the crisis; therefore, temporarily at least, internal political conflicts were shelved and a sense of national solidarity was created. But it was only skin-deep and controversies were not forgotten.

The government's programme was read on 30 December, and the subsequent discussion on it seemed to presage defeat. Out of an Assembly of 441—nine seats were vacant—the government needed 221 votes to survive, and it commanded only 208. The opposition parties seemed determined to overturn the cabinet and it is noteworthy that the commanders made no threatening noises. However, on 2 January the Republicans issued a warning that, if the government failed to receive a vote of confidence, they would not join any coalition that might subsequently be formed. Faced with the possibility of a new crisis, especially while tension over Cyprus continued, the New Turkey Party decided to vote in favour. Next day the Third Coalition received its vote of confidence, 225 for and 175 against.[45]

The government was preoccupied with Cyprus throughout 1964, which distracted it from such vital tasks as reforming the economy. Not that it was in any position to inaugurate serious reform: the parties of the Right, which dominated the Assembly, had stressed on many occasions that they were not in sympathy with the reforms promised by the constitution. On 9 February the JP declared that it regarded land reform as a violation of the property rights guaranteed by the constitution.[46] But not even the Justice Party sought to create a governmental crisis so long as İnönü did not raise controversial issues. Aware of his weakness, İnönü was cautious and the Third Coalition continued to limp along, always at the mercy of the opposition.

It was also in 1964 that conservative and reactionary forces took courage and emerged once more to challenge the new régime. On 21 February Mesut Suna, described in the press as a man of anti-reformist, even reactionary tendencies, tried to assassinate İnönü.[47] There was a revival of religious groups like the *Nurcular* (the Nurists), or followers of Saidi Nursî (1873-1960), who had always opposed the secularist reforms of the Republic. As in the past, this revival was marked by vandalism of Atatürk's statues and desecration of the Turkish flag. One consequence of such activity was always to distract the government and the country from the task in hand, in this case the reforms, and involve the mass media in an emotional controversy destructive of unity and beneficial only to the conservatives. Such a controversy exposed the deep gulf between the reformist intelligentsia and the population at large, which was taught to see reforms as the instruments eroding their popular culture.

By May a new factor had emerged which embittered the already tense relations between the government and the opposition, especially the Justice Party: this was the question of Turkey's place in the Western alliance. İnönü felt betrayed by what he considered America's unfavourable stand towards Turkey in the Cyprus crisis. Turkey was totally isolated when the issue was debated at the United Nations and this stimulated a neutralist trend in the press. İnönü had gone as far as to make bitter statements about the American position and when foreign policy was debated in the Assembly on 5 May it was noteworthy that the Justice Party spokesmen were alone in supporting America rather than their own government.[48] Even after the veiled threats of the Johnson Letter, in which President Johnson threatened not to defend Turkey from a Soviet attack, and whose contents were secret, known only to the government, members of the Assembly, and Senators, the opposition refused to support the government. A few days before he left for Washington to hold discussions with President Johnson, İnönü sought a vote of confidence in the Assembly in order to strengthen his negotiating position. A secret debate on foreign policy opened on 15 June. On 18 June, the day before the vote, Gürsel wrote to the parties asking them to act responsibly on this important issue. Next day İnönü was saved from defeat by only four votes.[49] Two days later he left for Washington, hardly in a position to claim that he enjoyed the overwhelming confidence of the country.

The contents of the Johnson Letter were leaked to the press, with the result that popular sentiment turned against the United States. Even the government which had reaffirmed that there would be no fundamental change in Turkey's foreign policy nevertheless began to mend its fences with the Soviet Union.

For the rest of the year there was no change in the relations between government and opposition; if anything, the government's position continued to decline. The Justice Party blamed the cabinet's weakness for its feeble foreign policy, and Osman Bölükbaşı called for a national government. By the end of 1964 Süleyman Demirel, the newly elected leader of the JP, was stating openly his scheme to overturn the government as soon as he had secured 226 votes.[50] The people, he told a joint meeting of the Assembly and the Senate Group, are grumbling about the economic and financial distress; they are discontented with the pressures put on the family, authority, and the established order by the extreme Left. The people are bitter about the exploitation of 27 May and the principal institutions of the Turkish state against themselves. They are complaining about the suspicion some people want to cast on the Assembly and the institution of the vote, about the one-sided use of the Precautions Law (*Tedbirler Kanunu*)— which should have been applied impartially against the Left and the Right—and about irresponsible policies.[51]

The Justice Party became more aggressive in its call for an early general election and on 25 January it decided, subject to discussion in the Assembly Group, to defeat the government over the budget.[52] Immediately after this decision Demirel began to consult other opposition leaders to seek their support for his scheme and for a cabinet led by the JP. By 9 February agreement had been reached and İnönü had stated that he would resign if his budget was defeated. Only support from the army could save İnönü, and none was forthcoming. On 11 February Prime Minister İnönü saw President Gürsel and told him: 'I am waiting calmly.' Next day the budget was defeated as Demirel watched from the gallery, and İnönü resigned as Prime Minister for the last time.[53]

Few people were sorry to see the demise of the Third Coalition. As a government led by the RPP it had no moral *raison d'être* after the party's defeat in the local and municipal elections. Such a weak government was incapable of a vigorous policy, and, to some extent, Demirel had been correct in attributing a vacillating foreign policy to its feebleness. It would have been interesting to see how a Justice Party government would have dealt with the Cyprus crisis and the role İnönü might have played in opposition; later Demirel was able to claim that he had inherited the crisis and that the policies of his predecessor limited his own freedom of action.

İnönü's defeat was nevertheless remarkable for the unity of action by the opposition and for the speed with which Demirel was able to achieve this unity, for it was no easy task to secure the 226 votes he had often spoken of. The nationalist radicals and the Left smelt an 'American rat' in this affair; and the press recalled how Ambassador Raymond Hare had visited Demirel and Hasan Dinçer before the vote. The pattern of US policy in the under-developed world was being established for Turkey as well.[54] At the time, as George Harris argues, İnönü rejected any possibility of American involvement in his fall. In July 1966, however, he taunted the 72 Republican Representatives who were opposed to his left-of-centre policy with the words: 'The Americans found a Prime Minister to replace me.... Apply to the Americans, perhaps they will find you a party leader.'[55] Whatever the truth of the matter, the 'American factor' had now become an integral part of Turkish domestic politics.

Fourth Coalition: JP Rule by Proxy

President Gürsel proposed a four-party coalition with the RPP in opposition. The problem was to find a leader for such a government. Gürsel suggested Kemal Kurdaş, a former official of the ministry of finance who had resigned because of differences with Menderes and gone to work for the International Monetary Fund in Washington. Recalled after the *coup* of 27 May 1960, he had become one of the 'brains' in the National Unity government. Gürsel rejected Demirel because of his youth—he was only 41—and because he did not want him to get burnt out so soon. The Justice Party proposed Professor İhsan Doğramacı, the rector of Ankara University. But finally Suat Hayri Ürgüplü, the Independent Senator from Kayseri elected on the JP list, was asked to form a cabinet.[56] In this way the military was able to save face by keeping its word that power would not be surrendered to the JP. But this was only a technicality, for the JP dominated, if it did not actually control, the cabinet.[57]

The policy of the Fourth Coalition was outlined in the four-party agreement and in the government programme which was read in the Assembly on 26 February 1965. The government promised, among other things, to maintain the sovereignty of the constitution based on the principles of Atatürk, and as the legitimate basis of 27 May and the national will; to combat extremist trends in the country, to pass the land reform law, to base economic policy on the principle of a mixed economy and the development plan, and to seek to establish good relations with neighbouring states.[58]

The government, made up of parties of the Right, did not intend with any sincerity to implement such a programme. All these parties believed that only the Left constituted a threat, and that the 'extremist trend' lay there. They were opposed to any serious land reform; as for planning, Demirel, the chief protagonist of the private sector, assumed charge of the SPO. The Republicans criticized the programme as being 'far from sincere' and stated that 'those who were criticizing until yesterday the principles defended by the RPP have proposed a programme full of ideas resembling those principles'.[59] The main purpose of this coalition was not to carry out reform but to act as night watchman and lead the country into a general election. During its brief interlude of eight months, Turkey had a taste of what government would be like under Demirel.

As the elections drew closer, the Justice Party began to whip up a 'red scare' throughout the country. In Samsun, Demirel denounced 'the leftists', i.e. the left-of-centre Republicans, for creating widespread unrest and dissatisfaction. Their goal, he accused, was to bring about a complete change in the established social order, and they were trying to accomplish this under the guise of reformism and progressivism. They assailed private ownership, wealth, profits, reputations; in short everything. And the goal of the 'extreme left' (a reference to the Workers' Party) was communism.[60]

The cunning aspect of Demirel's theme was its ability to identify 'reformism and progressivism' with the Left, and in the public mind this came to include the RPP which was in process of adopting the 'left-of-centre' slogan. Such was the nation-wide outcry against the Left that President Gürsel was forced to make a statement to the effect that 'There is no communist presence in the country to the extent that one would suppose from the clamour being raised about it. Some "erring persons" have been hired by others to raise this clamour and politicians are also participating in the effort.'[61] Coinciding with the campaign against the Left was the campaign to woo the religious sentiment of the voter. These became the major themes of the general election of 1965.[62]

The RPP warning that the Justice Party's inflammatory statements would divide the country and provoke violence was confirmed in Bursa when the Workers' Party rally was attacked by a mob of thousands chanting 'death to the communists'. There were physical attacks on the delegates, six of whom were seriously wounded. Such attacks, said Aybar next day, had been going on for the past three and a half years but under the Fourth Coalition they had become more frequent, and in Bursa the attack was fully organized. These were not merely attacks on the WPT but on democracy in Turkey.[63]

However, instead of intimidating the WPT, such assaults tended to strengthen it, drawing to its ranks the angry and disillusioned intelligentsia. Already the radical youth organizations were moving from debate to activism in the face of such violence; and in preparation for the coming election, they are said to have spent TL 35,000 to set up the TWP's centres in 46 provinces.[64]

The cabinet discussed Aybar's charges of attacks on his party, but Premier Ürgüplü claimed not to perceive a dangerous situation and concluded that the 'Bursa incident is not contagious'.[65] The attacks on the Workers' Party continued and Aybar denounced the government as an extreme right-wing government full of members of the Justice Party, and called for an independent and neutral caretaker government during the pre-election period.[66]

The socialists were not alone in coming under rightist pressures. Even the headquarters of *Türk-İş*, the Confederation of Turkish Trade Unions close to the establishment, was raided by the police. The union had prepared a black list of members of the Assembly who were hostile to organized labour, and asked its members not to vote for them.[67] The police raid was sanctioned by the courts, as being in conformity with Articles 37 and 122 of the Election Law, and the President and Secretary-General of *Türk-İş* were prosecuted.[68]

The participation of the WPT changed the very character of the 1965 election campaign, lifting it to a new plane. The party, represented by a group of intellectuals, was alone in raising fundamental issues concerning the country's social and economic future. The priority, however, was to liberate the country from the hold of the Americans and to do this Aybar called upon the Turks to wage the second war of independence, exploiting the nationalist and anti-American sentiments aroused by the Cyprus issue. It was only after the country had become independent once again that the problems of development could be taken in hand.[69] Aybar claimed that 'being dependent [on America] means being deprived of the power to carry out all these tasks' [land reform, industrialization, etc.] that are meant to benefit the nation and the people.[70]

The Republicans also attacked the United States by innuendo but only for supporting Demirel and the JP: 'Now we see that the Central Bank is releasing America's blocked account to be used any time, in any place, and for any purpose. Would those concerned tell us whether this will or will not be used in the direction of influencing the election?'[71] Two days before the election, the JP was accused by Orhan Apaydın, a former member of the party, of receiving money from foreign companies.[72] Commenting on the campaign, the press noted that the character of the general election was coloured by the fact that the WPT was gaining ground. While there was poor attendance at the RPP and the JP rallies, especially in the big towns, the WPT meetings were well attended by enthusiastic crowds. This had forced the Republicans to direct their attacks on the Justice Party in order to acquire a radical image. The JP adopted a more moderate position towards its principal rival in order to concentrate on the Workers' Party, which seemed to be weaning workers away from the JP and members of the intelligentsia away from the Republicans.[73] 'What is certain', wrote Nadi, 'is that our people believe more every day that the twenty-year-old régime of the *status quo* has led us to impasses. They have come to believe that democracy in form alone will do no good. This rapid awakening of the people is very promising.'[74] The optimistic forecasts of the liberal commentators reflected their own wishful thinking rather than the mood of the voters. The election results showed—in spite of the low turn-out for Turkey—that a majority of the voters were tired of ineffective coalitions and preferred a return to the nearest option to the old order. That is what they thought Demirel's Justice Party offered.[75]

The election results were the final blow to the original 27 May movement, demonstrating that a new régime which commits itself to far-reaching change only on paper is destined to be overwhelmed by the old order as soon as it restores competitive politics. This had already been demonstrated in 1961. In 1965 the voter showed the ineffectiveness of an electoral law designed to prevent the overwhelming victory of a single party.

NOTES

1 The composition of the First Coalition was as follows: *RPP*: İsmet İnönü (Prime Minister); Turhan Feyzioğlu and Avni Doğan (State); Sahir Kurutluoğlu (Justice); İlhami Sancar (Defence); Selim Sarper (External Affairs); Şefik İnan (Finance); Hilmi İncesulu (Education); Emin Paksüt (Public Works); Bülent Ecevit (Labour); Fethi Çelikbaş (Industries). *JP*: Âkif İyidoğan (Deputy Prime Minister and State); Necmi Öktem and Nihat Su (State); Ahmet Topaloğlu (Interior); İhsan Gürsan (Trade); Dr Suat Seren (Health and Social Assistance); Şevket Pulatoğlu (Customs and Monopolies); Cavit Oral (Agriculture); Cahit Akyar (Communications); Kâmuran Evliyaoğlu (Press, Broadcasting, and Tourism);

228   The Turkish Experiment in Democracy

Muhittin Güven (Construction and Resettlement). See Öztürk, Hükümetler, 491-2.
2 Ârif Nihat, 'Açlıkla Mücadele Eden Doğudan Raportajlar', Cumhuriyet, 24 Dec. 1961 and following; TY 1962, 341.
3 Ankara Radio, 17 Jan. 1962, in SWB, iv/848/c/1-3.
4 Milliyet, 24 Jan. 1962 and 17 Feb. 1962.
5 Yalman, Gördüklerim, iv, 393; Toker, İsmet Paşa, iv. 77. For a discussion of İnönü's exploitation of the threat of military intervention against his coalition partners, see Karaosmanoğlu, 45 Yıl, 269-72.
6 Milliyet, 24 Feb. 1962.
7 [David Hotham], 'Angry Young Turks', The Economist, 3 Mar. 1962.
8 Avni Doğan quoted by Faik, Gazeteci, 206 and 210-11.
9 Cumhuriyet, 22 Feb. 1967.
10 The law was passed in the Assembly on 3 Mar., in the Senate on 5 Mar., and was published in Resmi Gazete, 7 Mar. 1962. The text is also given in TY 1963, 29-30. The liberals saw this as a setback for freedom and democracy; see Feridun Ergin, 'Hürriyete Şal Ortmek', Cumhuriyet, 5 Mar. 1962.
11 Cumhuriyet, 27 Apr. 1962.
12 Ibid., 11 May 1962.
13 Ibid., 13 May 1962, reporting the planners' press conference.
14 Milliyet, 28 May 1962.
15 Ibid., 31 May 1962; The Economist, 9 and 16 June 1962. The JP claimed to be surprised at the resignation, seeing no reason for it.
16 Cumhuriyet, 17 June 1962; Toker, İsmet Paşa, iv, 76 ff. Osman Bölükbaşı, the leader of the RPNP, did not want to join a coalition and decided to leave the party. He and 29 other members of the RPNP resigned and formed the Nation Party (NP) on 14 June. See the press, 13-15 June 1962 and TY 1963, 187.
17 Cumhuriyet, 25 June 1962.
18 Kemal Karpat, 'The Turkish Left', JCH i/2 (1966), 183.
19 30 June 1962. The composition of the Second Coalition was as follows. RPP: İsmet İnönü (Prime Minister); Turhan Feyzioğlu and Hıfzı Oğuz Bekata (State); İlhami Sancar (Defence); Sahir Kurutluoğlu (Interior); Şevket Raşit Hatipoğlu (Education); İlyas Seçkin (Public Works); Orhan Öztrak (Customs and Monopolies); Bülent Ecevit (Labour); Fethi Çelikbaş (Industries). YTP: Ekrem Alican (Deputy Prime Minister and State); Raif Aybars (State); Dr Yusuf Azizoğlu (Health and Social Assistance); Mehmet İzmen (Agriculture); Rifat Öçtem (Communications); Fahrettin Kerim Gökay (Construction and Resettlement). RPNP: Hasan Dinçer (State); Abdülhak Kemal Yörük (Justice); Muhlis Ete (Trade); Celâl Karasapan (Press, Broadcasting and Tourism). Independents: Necmi Öktem (State); Feridun Cemal Erkin (External Affairs); Ferit Melen (Finance). See the press, 26 June 1962; Öztürk, Hükümetler, 515-16; TY 1963, 255-61.
20 Cumhuriyet, 11 Sept. 1962.
21 Quoted by Ankara Radio, 18 Oct. 1960, in SWB, iv/467/c/1; MER 1960 and 1961, 450-1 and 528, respectively.

22 *Cumhuriyet,* 23 Sept. 1962.

23 The Turkish press, 27 and 28 Sept. 1962; *TY 1963,* 39–41; Toker, *İsmet Paşa,* iv, 93–8. Those who resigned included Osman Nuri Torun (Under-Secretary and principal adviser at the SPO), Atilla Karaosmanoğlu (head of the office of economic affairs), Nejat Erder (head of the office of social affairs), and Ayhan Çilingiroğlu (head of the office for co-ordination).

24 *Cumhuriyet,* 3 and 10 Oct. 1962.

25 *Cumhuriyet,* 15 Oct. 1962. Falih Rıfkı Atay, another committed Kemalist and member of the RPP since its founding, resigned on 10 Dec. for virtually the same reasons.

26 'Zoraki Diplomat'ın Dedikleri', *Cumhuriyet,* 7 Dec. 1970; Ferit Melen was Finance Minister. See also *Yankı* 138, 11 Nov. 1973, 18.

27 The Turkish press, 30 Nov.–3 Dec. 1962.

28 Ibid., 14–20 Dec. 1962.

29 Kemal Karpat, 'Socialism and the Labour Party of Turkey', *MEJ* xxi/2 (1967), 159. See the 'Declaration' published in the first issue of *Yön,* 20 Dec. 1961, 12–13, reproduced in Karpat ed., *Social Thought,* 334–8, and Karpat, 'On *Yön* and Statism', ibid., 342–56. For the Marxist Left's criticism of the Yön movement see Dr Hikmet Kıvılcımlı, *27 Mayıs ve Yön Hareketinin Sınıfsal Eleştirisi* (1970).

30 Aybar (b. 1910) was politically active in the forties, editing newspapers like *Hür* and *Zincirli Hürriyet* in which he criticized the single-party régime. He was also a doçent (reader) at the Istanbul Law Faculty. He took over the Workers' Party in 1962 and remained its leader until 1970, and was expelled from the party in Feb. 1971 for his 'revisionist views'. He was Representative for Istanbul from 1965 to 1973, when he was not re-elected. He was elected chairman of the Sosyalist Parti founded in Ankara on 30 May 1975.

31 *Cumhuriyet,* 23 Dec. 1962. The attacks took place on 11 Nov. at Beyazit and 9 Dec. at Şişli.

32 *Cumhuriyet,* 5 Jan. 1963 and the monthly *Sosyal Adalet,* Nov. 1964, 3. Vedat Günyol, who translated Babeuf's writing jointly with Sabahattin Eyüboğlu, has given a full account of the Babeuf case in *Devrim Yazıları—Babeuf Dosyası* (Istanbul, 1974).

33 *Milliyet,* 12 Jan. 1963 and Süleyman Genç, *12 Mart'a Nasıl Gelindi* (1971), 25–30.

34 *Resmi Gazete,* 24 July 1963 which was declared 'Workers' Day' by the unions. The law is also given in *TY 1964,* 145–92. See also Toker Dereli, *The Development of Turkish Trade Unionism* (1968), 111–18 and ff.

35 Opening statement at the Second Annual Conference of the ESSCB, 4 Aug. 1963. See ESSCB, *Social Aspects,* xv–xxi.

36 *Cumhuriyet,* 22 Nov. 1963.

37 Ibid., 8 Nov. 1963.

38 *Milliyet,* 3 Dec. 1963; Toker, *İsmet Paşa,* iv, 135–40.

39 C. S. Barlas, 'Milli Koalisyon Değil, AP Hükümeti', *Cumhuriyet,* 25 Nov. 1963.

230   The Turkish Experiment in Democracy

40 *Milliyet,* 15 Dec. 1963.
41 Ibid., 18 Dec. 1963.
42 Barlas, 'AP'nin Koalisyona Girmesi Şarttır', *Cumhuriyet,* 19 Dec. 1963.
43 *Ulus,* 24 Dec. 1963.
44 See the Turkish press, 26 Dec. 1963. The composition of the Third Coalition was as follows. *Republicans:* İnönü (Prime Minister); Kemal Satır (Deputy PM); Vefik Pirinçcioğlu and İbrahim Saffet Omay (State); Sedat Cumralı (Justice); İlhami Sancar (Defence); Orhan Öztrak (Interior); İbrahim Öktem (Education); Ârif Onat (Public Works); Fenni İslimyeli (Trade); Dr Kemal Demir (Health and Social Assistance); Turan Şahin (Agriculture); Muammer Ertem (Industries); Bülent Ecevit (Labour); Ali İhsan Göğüş (Tourism and Information); Celâlettin Uzer (Construction and Resettlement); Lebit Yurdoğlu (Rural Affairs); Hudai Oral (Energy and Natural Resources). *Independents:* Malik Yolaç (State); Feridun Cemal Erkin (External Affairs); Ferit Melen (Finance); Mehmet Yüceler (Customs); Ferit Alpiskender (Communications). See Öztürk, *Hükümetler,* 549-50.
45 See the Turkish press, 31 Dec. 1963-5 Jan. 1964.
46 *Son Havadis,* 10 Feb. 1964.
47 The Turkish press, 22-4 Feb. 1964; *MEJ* xviii/2 (1964), 236; Toker, *İsmet Paşa,* iv, 111.
48 *Cumhuriyet,* 6 May 1964. The question of foreign policy will be discussed in ch. XIV below.
49 The Turkish press, 16-20 June 1964.
50 *Cumhuriyet,* 15 Dec. 1964.
51 Ibid., 13 Jan. 1965.
52 *Son Havadis,* 26 Jan. 1965.
53 The Turkish press, 5-14 Feb. 1965; Toker, İsmet Paşa, iv, 141-7.
54 *Cumhuriyet,* 12 Feb. 1965; *Sosyal Adalet,* Mar. 1965, 1-2; Harris, *Alliance,* 131-2.
55 *Cumhuriyet,* 28 Apr. 1967 quoted in Genç, *12 Mart,* 62.
56 *Cumhuriyet,* 15-17 Feb. 1965.
57 The Fourth Coalition was announced on 20 Feb. and it was made up of Independents, the JP, the NTP, the RPNP, and the MP. *Independents:* S. H. Ürgüplü (Prime Minister); Hasan Işık (External Affairs); Orhan Alp (Public Works). *JP:* Süleyman Demirel (Deputy PM and State); İhsan Gürsan (Finance); Cihat Bilgehan (Education); Macit Zeren (Trade); Dr Faruk Sükan (Health and Social Assistance); Ahmet Topaloğlu (Customs and Monopolies); İhsan Sabri Çağlayangil (Labour); Ali Naili Erdem (Industries); and Mehmet Turgut (Energy and Natural Resources). *NTP:* Şekip İnal (State); Turhan Kapanlı (Agriculture); Mithat Şan (Communications); Recai İskenderoğlu (Construction and Resettlement). *RPNP:* Mehmet Altınsoy (State); Hasan Dinçer (Defence); İrfan Baran (Justice); Seyfi Öztürk (Rural Affairs). *MP:* Hüseyin Ataman (State); İsmail Hakkı Akdoğan (Interior); Ömer Zeki Dorman (Tourism and Information). See the Turkish press, 21 Feb. 1965 and Öztürk, *Hükümetler,* 581-2.

58 *Milliyet,* 21 and 27 Feb. 1965; Öztürk, *Hükümetler,* 583–605; and *Sosyal Adalet,* Mar. 1965, 1–2.

59 *Cumhuriyet,* 1 Mar. 1965.

60 Ankara Radio, 12 June 1965 in *SWB,* iv/1884/c/1; and *Son Havadis,* 12–16 June 1965 where other speeches are given.

61 Interview in *Cumhuriyet,* 18 June 1965; also Ankara Radio, 19 June 1965, in *SWB,* iv/1890/c/1.

62 The question of religion and politics will be discussed in ch. 13 below.

63 *Milliyet,* 5–6 July 1965.

64 Genç, *12 Mart,* 24.

65 *Milliyet,* 8 July 1965.

66 Ibid., 15 July 1965.

67 Ibid., 20 Aug. 1965.

68 *Vatan,* 24 and 25 Aug. 1965.

69 Aybar's broadcast on Ankara Radio, 25 Sept. 1965, is reported in *SWB,* iv/1971/c/1–3.

70 Ibid. Though a member of the neo-Democratic NTP, Minister Recai İskenderoğlu seemed to share Aybar's view. He was quoted as saying: 'We are a dependent country from the political, military, economic and judicial point of view, entirely dependent on the USA. Turkey's problem is therefore independence. First the USA does not set us free. Secondly men who have sold themselves to the USA do not allow it.' See Mehmet Kemal's column in *Vatan,* 15 Sept. 1965.

71 Deputy Secretary-General Suphi Baykam's statement in *Cumhuriyet,* 13 Sept. 1965.

72 Ibid., 9 Oct. 1965. For a detailed account of accusations against American interference in the elections, see Harris, *Alliance,* 133–4.

73 Abdi İpekçi's editorial in *Milliyet,* 21 Sept. and Nadir Nadi in *Cumhuriyet,* 22 and 23 Sept. 1965.

74 *Cumhuriyet,* 22 Sept. 1965.

75 For the election results see above, 191–2.

CHAPTER IX

THE JUSTICE PARTY AND THE REPUBLICAN PEOPLE'S PARTY 1965-1971

The Justice Party has emerged from the bosom of the Turkish nation ... Like everything which has emerged from the bosom of the Turkish nation up to the present, it is beautiful, vivacious and full of life.

Süleyman Demirel, at the Justice Party Congress, 28 November 1964

If only the Justice Party on the right of centre would put up a wall against the extreme Right as the Republican People's Party ... has done against the extreme Left, democracy would have the opportunity of a continuous existence.

Bülent Ecevit, *Cumhuriyet,* 28 October 1966

Süleyman Demirel's Justice Party

EVEN before the Democrat Party was officially dissolved, the military rulers of Turkey became aware of the problem of the 'five million' DP voters in the country. As soon as parliamentary democracy was restored its future would be in their hands. Some members of the National Unity Committee proposed that the Committee form a party with former Democrats who had been independent of the Bayar-Menderes group in order to harness this vote. There were various reports that such an organization would be called the National Unity Party (*Milli Birlik Partisi*) or the Revolution Party (*İnkilâp Partisi*). But the senior officers, who wanted to restore power to the civilians, insisted on the principle that the NUC was above politics and intended to remain so.[1]

The ban on party activities, imposed on 27 May 1960, had been partially lifted on 13 January 1961. The formation of new parties was permitted and within a month at least fourteen were registered, though most of them proved ephemeral. The most

JP and RPP 1965–1971

233

important of the new parties was the Justice Party, created under the leadership of Ragıp Gümüşpala, a retired general.[2]

The NUC had decided against forming a party of its own, but at the same time it had not relinquished its aim of trying to guide the new parties in a direction that would not be revanchist. It therefore encouraged former dissident Democrats like Ekrem Alican to form one of the new parties. Alican had been expelled from the DP in 1955 and become a founding member of the Freedom Party. After the May revolution he entered the cabinet as Finance Minister and resigned on 24 December 1960 in order to make preparations for new political activity. In February he announced the formation of the New Turkey Party, which was set up as successor to the DP of the early years, before it abandoned democracy and liberalism. The party represented the 'intellectual', élitist, and urban wing of the former DP and included high bureaucrats, professors and professionals. At the same time, some of its electoral strength was based on alliances with local landowning élites in eastern Anatolia. Initially it seemed as though the NTP would inherit the 'five million Democrat votes' and become the successor party. But precisely because of the élitist nature of its leadership and its limited popular base the party failed to achieve this position. Too many former Democrats, still loyal to the deposed leadership, had neither forgotten nor forgiven the expulsion of these men, and finally, their merger with the 'enemy', the RPP. Therefore the role of successor party (*miras partisi*) passed almost automatically to the other new organization, the JP.[3]

The formation of the Justice Party was announced on 11 February 1961. Its leader, Ragıp Gümüşpala, had been Commander of the Third Army at the time of the *coup* of 27 May. Contrary to the rumours about him—that he had been pro-Menderes and opposed to the revolution—Gümüşpala had communicated his loyalty to General Madanoğlu in Ankara within hours of the *coup*.[4] He was appointed Chief of the General Staff on 3 June and retired in August, in accordance with the rejuvenation programme in the armed forces. Nothing more was heard of him until the founding of the JP, when his leadership came as no surprise since many other retired generals were also taking to politics.

There seems little doubt that initially the JP enjoyed the full confidence of the NUC. General Sıtkı Ulay revealed a few days before the general election of 1965 that the army had laid the foundations of the Justice Party and entrusted the duty of leading it to an honourable soldier.[5] It must have seemed a good idea to the High Command to counter the threat of revanchism by placing men loyal to the régime at the head of the political parties. But there were three elements in the JP: the retired officers led by Şinasi Osma, Gümüşpala's former aide-de-camp and Secretary-General of the party; the members of the Peasants' Party founded in 1952 who had merged with the JP; and the former Democrats.[6] The latter were the most vital element. It was they who enabled the JP to acquire a countrywide organization in the shortest possible time by reforming the defunct DP organizations at the provincial and local levels. In İzmir, for example, the JP committee was composed mostly of former DP members of the town council, and retired General Mehmet Ali Aytaş, a DP supporter, was appointed chairman of the committee.[7]

Within a short time members and adherents of the dissolved party had become the principal element in the JP, making it difficult for Gümüşpala to steer the party in the direction of moderation that the military desired. The party soon ran into trouble with the authorities over the question of opposition to the new régime. We have already seen how the armed forces reacted to what they considered provocation from the JP (chapter 7 above) and the policy of the party during the coalition period (chapter 8). It is quite possible that the armed forces would have closed down the JP had it not been for Gümüşpala's moderating influence—one of the principal advantages the former Democrats saw in his leadership.

Competition for Party Leadership 1964

Gümüşpala died on 5 June 1964, two days before the partial Senate elections, which his party won by a comfortable margin. He had been the unchallenged leader and his death threw open the whole question of the leadership. Sadettin Bilgiç, the younger brother of Sait Bilgiç, a former hard-line Democrat who had served in the Investigating Committee in April 1960, was considered the most likely successor. He was made acting chairman until the question was decided at the general congress.

Bilgiç, however, was not the only candidate. The group of retired officers in the party wanted to elect a man who would be able to win the confidence of the armed forces. Tekin Arıburun, a former Air Force Commander and President Bayar's aide-de-camp, seemed a good choice. As a former officer he would be acceptable to the High Command; his service with Bayar would appeal to the former Democrats.[8] By September, new personalities were introduced into the contest. The extremists were preparing Professor Ali Fuad Başgil to oppose Bilgiç, while the younger group had put up Süleyman Demirel.[9] By the beginning of November, Demirel had become Bilgiç's only serious rival. At the Ankara Provincial Congress it was reported that former Democrats were turning against Bilgiç, who had adopted the slogan 'new party—new policies'. Demirel had become the candidate of those who wanted continuity, unity, and moderation and it was on those slogans that he campaigned.[10]

The General Congress began on 27 November 1964 and after much debate between the three candidates (Bilgiç, Demirel, and Arıburun) Süleyman Demirel was elected by an overwhelming vote of 1,072 as against 552 for Bilgiç and 39 for Arıburun. Demirel's victory was a great surprise since Bilgiç had been the clear favourite. He was strong in the organization, described as courageous and a man of principles who followed a direct course instead of zigzagging. His firm reaction to Sunay's warning to the JP regarding the increase of reactionary activity[11] had strengthened his position in some quarters, but had also shown him to be inflexible. He had been supported by the conservatives but even that group let him down. Moreover, he was not supported by the party's 'intellectuals', who considered him a traditional politician out of touch with the times.

Demirel, in contrast, was considered more modern, a man who 'knew about economics' and also had the characteristics of a leader. His support came from the party's Senators and Representatives and he was put forward as Menderes's man, which won him the favour of the Democrat faction. It is likely that this faction considered that he would be easier to manage than Bilgiç—both came from Isparta but Bilgiç also had a political base there and could therefore afford to be independent. Because of his experience in business and management, he is said to have had the confidence of big business, Turkish and foreign. Demirel's one handicap in seeking to lead a party which depended on the votes of the religious-conservatives was his personal secular background. He was attacked as a freemason, which was almost as bad as being a communist in the eyes of religious Right. But this did not turn out to be a serious obstacle and Demirel was able to counteract it by stating: 'I am not a mason; I was born into a family that does not sit down to breakfast before reading the Holy Qur'an.'[12]

It is also probable that General Sunay's letter of 12 November 1964, cautioning the parties—especially the JP—not to criticize the 27 May revolution or the armed forces, was timely and benefited Demirel. The delegates, intimidated by the threat of military intervention, decided to vote for the moderate and flexible Demirel. If anyone could improve the party's standing with the military it was he.

Süleyman Demirel

Süleyman Demirel was forty-four years old when he became Chairman of the Justice Party and was young by Turkish standards for such a position. He was born into a lower middle class family in the western Anatolian village of İslâmköy in the province of Isparta. As is quite common in Turkish society, Demirel had changed his status through education. He entered İstanbul Technical University in 1942 and graduated in 1949 with a diploma in engineering. Between 1950 and 1960 he worked for the Department of Hydraulic Works, becoming the director in 1955. During these years he was in close contact with Menderes and that cost him his post after the *coup*. For the next eighteen months Demirel was forced to do his military service, which he had managed to delay for so long. After that, unable to return to state service, he worked independently. During these years he established contacts with speculators like Mıgırdıç Selefyan and foreign firms like Morrison-Knudsen, which employed him for a while. These liaisons were used against him politically and he was even given the sobriquet 'Süleyman Morrison'.[13]

Demirel epitomized the new Turkish politician. He did not come from the traditional 'military-bureaucratic intelligentsia' which had dominated politics in Turkey since the *Tanzimat* period in the nineteenth century. He was a technocrat, the 'dam king', who rose to power on his own merit. He was a leader with whom the 'ordinary Turk', especially the ambitious rural migrant who lived in one of the new shanty towns, could identify himself, for he symbolized the self-made man. This proved a great asset in elections, and Demirel was able to reach this type of voter because he was an insider while leaders like İnönü, and even the socialist Aybar, remained outsiders.

Demirel's first task as party leader was to allay all suspicion in the armed forces concerning the alleged revanchism of the JP and generally to win their confidence. He met the Life Senators, who were the most vocal and ardent guardians of the 27 May revolution, and assured them that he was not a crypto-Democrat, that he did not depend on the former Democrat group in the JP, and that he had his own programme and his own cadres.[14] Seyfi Kurtbek noted that, as proof of his good faith, Demirel abandoned the practice of visiting Bayar (in prison at Kayseri) as soon as he became Chairman. Later, when he became Prime Minister, he gave up all attempts to bring the military under civilian control and opted for the policy of virtual autonomy for the armed forces, leaving their administration to the commanders. Thus the subordination of the military to the Prime Minister and the Defence Minister became a fiction. The General Staff, claimed Kurtbek, went as far as to prepare the Defence Ministry's budget, the Defence Ministry became the General Staff's secretariat, and the minister became a cipher. Kurtbek may have exaggerated Demirel's role in the growing autonomy of the army and Demirel may have merely acquiesced in the *de facto* situation.[15] Be that as it may, within a short time Demirel succeeded in winning the confidence of the High Command and established a working relationship which lasted until 12 March 1971.

Demirel's election was only the first step in the establishment of his control over the party. The process was not an easy one and he always had to take care not to fragment the JP by unconsidered action. Since its founding, the JP had been divided into a number of factions virtually immune to party discipline. It was Demirel's task to give it an identity and end the factionalism. In December he struck a further blow at the Bilgiç group by not permitting its leader to be elected deputy chairman.[16]

But Demirel was cautious. With a general election in October 1965 he had to strive for unity and prepare the party for power. We have already seen how he forced İnönü to resign and then became the dominant partner in the Fourth Coalition. Demirel now adopted a moderate and conciliatory position whose aim was to avoid controversy in the party. He may have told the NUG that he was independent of the DP faction, but he had to make full use of it and its following in the country in order to win votes. In July 1965 the JP abandoned its emblem of the lette.s AP on either side of an open book of laws and replaced it with a prancing white horse, using 'a semantic and symbolic device to identify it with the moribund Democrat Party. It thus convinced the majority of the electorate of its loyalty to the old order.'[17] At the same time the JP began putting up relatives of former Democrats as candidates. For example, Bayar's daughter, Nilüfer Gürsoy, Menderes's son, Yüksel Menderes, Koraltan's son, Orhan Koraltan, Samet Ağaoğlu's wife (Nermin) and sister (Süreyya), Namık Gedik's wife, Melâhat—all these, as well as relations of Polatkan and Yardımcı, were fighting the election on the JP slate.[18]

Except for its constant proclamations against the Left, Demirel's party refused to commit itself ideologically. 'We are against all "isms" including liberalism and capitalism,' announced Demirel to the press. 'We are not for any diehard ideology or system. We establish our economic view in accordance with the conditions of the day.'[19] The election manifesto emphasized national unity and the need for a strong state as its principal points. It called for the formation of a stable government, without which Turkey would head for anarchy. This led to questioning of the electoral system, based on proportional representation, which would have to be amended if coalition governments were to be avoided. The JP exploited the country's desire for stability.

'We are not a party dependent on any class. We are the nation with its peasant, farmer, worker, artisan, and merchant. As the Justice Party we shall defend the rights of all these classes.' The principal appeal was to the countryside, where 75 per cent of the population lived. The promise was of agrarian reform, i.e. the reform of outmoded farming techniques and the introduction of modern technology, rather than land reform which meant distributing land to landless peasants, and did not exclude agrarian reform. The Justice Party also promised aid and credits for the farmer, the artisan, and the craftsman.

The party appealed to the ambition and the drive of the man in the middle rather than the man at the bottom. This was true both in the countryside and in urban areas, where its promises found a ready response among the rural migrants of the shanty-towns who had left their villages in order to climb the socio-economic ladder.[20]

The promise of everything to everyone was the JP's prescription for electoral success, especially while the main rival was weak with internal dissension. But Demirel's victory ought not to be minimized and reduced to plain and simple exploitation of the 'ignorant masses'. In peasant societies there is a universal yearning for a leader who will be on 'your' side against local bosses, local exploiters such as the *ağas* and landlords, as well as the local representatives of the state. Demirel, like Menderes, seemed such a leader and people voted for him; there was no one else who could fit the bill.

Even after the electoral success, Demirel's control over the party was far from complete and he had to be cautious in dealing with the various factions. This became his major preoccupation for the next five years—until he was able to purge the dissidents, who then formed a party of their own.

However, with the election behind him, Demirel was at last able to state his policy in less ambiguous terms so as to prepare the country for economic stability and growth. On 12 October, two days after the election, he informed the press that under his government a declaration of wealth would no longer be required (thus making tax evasion impossible to control), that aid would be given to the private sector and all possible encouragement to foreign capital investment.[21] These promises were designed to win the confidence of private enterprise, which had been most

suspicious of the post-27 May régime. As though to emphasize the
change that had just been brought about by the election, the US
Agency for International Development (AID) also announced that
it would no longer funnel aid through the Turkish government,
preferring to deal directly with the private sector.[22] A few days
later an AID mission arrived in Ankara to discuss Turkey's needs
and promised that aid would be increased if internal resources
were mobilized. The press reported that Demirel's election had
made a favourable impression in the United States.[23]

Prime Minister Demirel

If Demirel was quick to bring confidence to the business
community and the armed forces, he was not able to do the same
within his party. The cabinet he picked was not the cabinet of
conciliation, and neither Sadettin Bilgiç himself nor members of his
group were given portfolios.[24] Without the Bilgiç group, the cabinet
was weak and had to face strong opposition in the Assembly
Group as well as in the party organization. There were even
rumours that this was only a temporary ministry and that Demirel
would make adjustments as soon as he had had time to settle
down. It was thought that the principal reason for Bilgiç's absence
from the cabinet was that he had wanted to be Deputy Prime
Minister, and Demirel had offered him only a Ministry of State.
Nor had Demirel considered men like Aydın Yalçın, Ahmet Dallı,
Ertuğrul Akça, and Cevat Önder who were said to be too
independent-minded for Demirel.[25]

From the very beginning the internal conflict was focused on
personalities: Süleyman Demirel and Sadettin Bilgiç. Demirel's
opponents accused him of wanting to be the sole leader of the
party. 'After the formation of the cabinet in 1965', remembered a
dissident, 'I said in the General Executive Council: "you must not
have the ambition to be the sole person with the mentality of 'I
know everything and I'll do everything'; you cannot have this in a
democracy. Actually you are not capable of doing this."'[26]

The immediate threat from the dissidents arose from the
possibility that the Assembly Group would not support the
cabinet's programme. Demirel was aware of the danger and in the
General Executive Council meeting of 31 October he sought
support for the government, admitting that the cabinet had not
been formed in the best possible way, but for the moment unity
and solidarity came first. Cevat Önder gave a warning that
'dictator-like behaviour' would not be tolerated and that the
Assembly Group would go so far as to unseat the government if

such behaviour continued. Demirel heard other criticism and promised to benefit from it. Next day his supporters won the Assembly Group elections and Bilgiç himself promised to vote for the cabinet.[27]

The government's programme made so many and such varied promises that few people expected it to be implemented. It promised to uphold the constitution, the Kemalist reforms and democracy, and to limit the duty of the state to 'safeguarding the security of life and property of the citizen, his freedom to work and to travel, and in preserving the security and peace of the country'. Demirel promised development through foreign aid and private enterprise, the same foreign policy as was being followed, and no radical reform outside the terms of the election manifesto. As for the reform of taxation, this would be reviewed and the declaration of wealth eliminated since it 'has caused widespread anxiety and insecurity among taxpayers'.

Demirel and the Justice Party were the representatives of capitalism in Turkey, but not, as Demirel kept emphasizing, the irresponsible, profiteering capitalism of the nineteenth century. 'The path of the modern Turkish state', the programme read, 'will be totally different from the methods of nineteenth century capitalism, which even the Western world abandoned a long time ago.'[28]

Nadir Nadi's comments on the programme were as perceptive as those of the experts and came more directly to the point:

... Just think, as a citizen yearning for development you are promised welfare and development whoever you are, from factory owner and landlord to farmer, worker, janitor, artisan and bureaucrat, and all this with no bother, no sacrifice, no hardship. We cannot believe that a national development movement can be realized without some sacrifice, hardship, and toil.... The Prime Minister does not explain how the necessary investment will be obtained for development. We have already witnessed that no constructive results can be obtained from foreign loans, foreign capital, or the private sector. Development can be achieved only with national effort.

Demirel claimed that to ask for sacrifices, to tighten belts would result in the destruction of freedoms. We do not believe this. On the contrary, governments coming to power with promises of economic development resort to the curtailment of political freedom when they realize that their promises are futile....[29]

Initially, Demirel was almost totally preoccupied with his political vulnerability in the party. He had got over the first hurdle of the vote of confidence but his position was still insecure. Commenting on 'Mr Demirel's Hundred Days', *The Economist* (12

February 1966) observed that the government had done nothing to carry out its economic programme and was therefore being criticized 'for putting the political cart before the economic horse'. The young and inexperienced Demirel was not capable of finding the quick solution to his political problems that would have allowed him time to tackle the large trade deficit, the huge foreign debt, rising prices, and increasing unemployment. However, under the circumstances it is not clear that anyone else could have done better. Instead he gave his attention to subjects which had been included in the programme but which had no priority.

In January 1966 he carried out a large-scale administrative reshuffle which involved about 500 senior officials. Then he introduced a bill to amend the Electoral Law, with the object of abolishing the 'national remainder system' (which had permitted the small parties to have representation in the Assembly), and of ending proportional representation. Finally he initiated an amnesty bill which would restore liberty as well as civil rights to all former Democrats, and it was this which generated the most tension.

The RPP responded to these measures by accusing the government of deliberately causing unrest by doing nothing about the rising cost of living and, at the same time, 'presenting one after another to the Grand National Assembly unnecessary draft bills which will eventually lead to bickering over the régime, and which will aggravate the economic situation all the more, instead of fighting the high cost of living'.[30]

The Justice Party Divided

Demirel, the man who had succeeded in reconciling the armed forces to JP rule, failed to reach the accommodation with his political rivals and opponents that would have enabled social peace to be established. This was the special characteristic of his five years in power.

The Justice Party still had not found its identity, and its problems resulted from the character of its establishment. It had been founded under abnormal circumstance and as a reaction to the extraordinary situation created by the 27 May revolution. It came to include a wide assortment of political types: secularist intellectuals and reactionary Islamists, officers and the anti-military, former Democrats of all hues and those new to politics. In economic terms the division was between those who wanted to continue with the nineteenth century brand of capitalism and those who wanted to adopt the twentieth century variety.

Initially the Justice Party had been an organization without a head, and this had resulted in factionalism and instability. Its organization had been inherited from the DP and it did not recognize any leader; hence the significance of the amnesty issue, since, for many JP supporters, the real leaders were in jail. But the party organization, having elected Demirel in 1964, found that he was determined to become independent of it by creating local bodies loyal to himself. The organization fought back and that is why the conflict took the form of the new men against the former Democrats. The conflict was more complex than it seemed.

The dissidents hoped to remove Demirel from the party leadership at the Third General Congress which opened on 27 November 1966. But on the 29th Demirel was re-elected with an overwhelming majority of 1,239 votes against 175 for his rival Kadri Eroğan. This was a victory not only for Demirel but also for the liberal wing. It was a defeat for the 'nationalist-sacredist' (*milliyetçi-mukaddesatçı*) faction led by men like Professor Osman Turan. Hereafter, the Justice Party began to lose its ultra-conservative, religious, 'caliphatist' (*dinci, hilâfetçi*) character (as the press described it) though that did not prevent it from exploiting religion for political ends.

In terms of party organization, the Central Committee became more powerful and authoritarian, and discipline was tightened. Demirel became more influential and acquired greater freedom to make appointments. The party was now in power and there could be no conflict between the government and the organization. In a sense it was a repeat of the DP experience—though Demirel was no Menderes, and found the situation difficult.[31]

At the end of 1966 Demirel's position seemed strong. He had mastered the party, established good relations with the military High Command thanks to President Sunay, and the economy had performed well, with a growth rate of almost 9 per cent. There was a strong feeling of optimism in the country. Demirel maintained his pressure on the dissidents, even expelling some, and by March 1967 he seemed to have subdued even Sadettin Bilgiç, the very symbol of opposition. The cabinet reshuffle of 1 April introduced seven new ministers, including Bilgiç as Minister of Communications.[32] The cabinet was now more balanced and representative of the party as a whole. Ministers said to be unpopular with the Assembly Group had been removed.

In 1967, however, the opposition to Demirel within the party became openly ideological. The right-wing faction led by Professor Turan accused him of 'sliding to the left', of falling into the hands of vested interest groups, and of operating under their directives. Economic policy was not conforming to the programme and was serving narrow interests rather than the mass of the people. As for the party's attitude to religion, this was the same as that of the RPP. Moreover the 'nationalist elements' (i.e. the right-wing youth movement) were being repressed while 'subversive currents' (the left-wing groups) were treated with indulgence.[33] Turan continued these accusations and in October he was expelled from the party for violating discipline.[34]

Osman Turan's criticism of Demirel's policy is significant as the manifestation of contradictions which began to emerge from the economic policies of the multi-party period. Large-scale modern capitalism, in some areas having the character of a monopoly, was finally being established and making its influence felt throughout the country. A small group of capitalists, big by Turkish standards, led by men like Vehbi Koç, Kâzım Taşkent, and the Sapancı family, had been able to take advantage of this trend. But it was the small independent tradesman, merchant, and artisan of Anatolia who found it difficult to survive the competition from this modern sector.

Demirel recognized their plight and told them to organize. They constituted a substantial sector and were therefore important politically. 'In our country', said Demirel, 'there are a million and a half tradesmen and artisans; this means about five or six million people. Self-sufficient, experienced, knowledgeable, and skilled people are a force in the democratic order. Today's small tradesman may be tomorrow's factory owner.'[35] In order to develop they were told to organize themselves and were promised generous credits to help them grow.

Only a handful of this one and a half million would survive the competition and become factory owners. The plight of the traditional Turkish soft-drink (*gazoz*) industry was an indication of what was more likely to happen. The modern soft-drink industry, led by such international giants as Coca-Cola and Pepsi Cola, had virtually driven the indigenous industry out of the cities and by 1966 was threatening the towns. The *gazoz* manufacturers sent a delegation to Istanbul to discuss their future with the Chamber of Commerce in the light of these developments. With a capital of about 60 to 70 million TL (6 to 7 million dollars at the 1966 rate of exchange), the industry would go bankrupt unless foreign investment in this field was stopped.[36]

It was too late and perhaps anachronistic to try to reverse the trend which all Turkish governments had followed since the founding of the Republic. The small man was the sacrificial lamb to be slaughtered on the altar of capitalism. Six months later, when the Confederation of Turkish Tradesman and Artisans held its

Fifth General Congress, its members had accepted their lot and asked only that the government provide them with social security and rights similar to those of unionized workers.[37]

There was nothing that any party which believed in developing the economy through capitalism could do for these people. Yet they did constitute a pressure group, and were politically conscious and therefore influential in elections. All parties competed for their votes and when this group became unpredictable in its voting behaviour it became an element of instability in Turkey's parliamentary democracy.

Yet in the party Demirel's position remained strong. At the Fourth General Congress which opened in Ankara on 29 November 1968 he retained full control—although the internal opposition was becoming better organized to challenge him. In January 1968 the former Democrats had formed a political club known as *Bizim Ev* (Our Home), led by Celâl Bayar, whose ostensible aim was to agitate for the political rights of its members.[38] In fact it soon turned into a pressure group against Demirel, with the aim of undermining his position in the party. The question of restoring political rights to former Democrats, which Demirel side-stepped with consummate skill, led to the resignations from the JP of Bayar's daughter and Samet Ağaoğlu's wife. Bayar also issued a directive asking former supporters of the DP not to vote in the general election of October 1969.[39]

Demirel won the election but his vote had been reduced; the people who benefited were the Independents, who received 5·6 per cent of the votes. Equally alarming for Demirel was the drop in the votes cast, from 71·3 to 64·3 per cent of the registered voters. And in spite of his dominance and his electoral victory, which made his control over the party stronger, Demirel was losing the confidence of those whose interests he claimed to serve: the business community.

One of the outcomes of the rapid social and economic transformation in Turkey was the fragmentation of the parties which subscribed to capitalism. In the late sixties all the parties except the WPT, and perhaps the Unity Party (*Birlik Partisi*), supported capitalism but they differed in their approach. The RPP, for example, upheld the view that the capitalist ought not to be directly involved in politics, which should be left to the party and the state. The JP, on the other hand, believed in the direct participation of the capitalist in the struggle for political power and the formulation of policy. This was perhaps the major difference and it made the JP less bureaucratic in its approach to both politics and economics. The Justice Party spoke for big business; the RPP tried to represent the entire spectrum, and ended up representing no one. The position and fortunes of the small parties depended on the success or failure of their bigger brothers; reflecting the needs of the tradesman and artisan, such parties acted as their spokesmen against 'the capitalist'. The position of small parties like the RPNP and the NP has always been vague and ambiguous. But under the leadership of Alparslan Türkeş the RPNP, renamed the Nationalist Action Party (NAP) on 9 February 1969, tried to become a militant, Poujadist party, opposed to monopoly capitalism and unions alike.[40]

The fragmentation of the Right was Demirel's failure. He also proved incompetent in dealing with working class militancy that led to strikes, and with student agitation which paralysed universities and often spilled into the streets, creating an atmosphere of anarchy and instability. He had failed to silence the nationalist and left-wing clamour, manifested in bloody demonstrations against the visiting US Sixth Fleet, for an independent foreign policy. Nor had he been able to curb the spiralling inflation which created tension and insecurity in all sectors of Turkish society. Unable to deal with the situation, Demirel blamed the institutions of the Second Republic for his problems. Having amended the Electoral Law, which, he claimed, created political instability, he turned his attention to the constitution, whose liberal character (he argued), was exploited and abused by the Left; the Constitutional Court, whose vigilance made it virtually impossible for the Assembly to legislate; and the TRT, which had become a state within a state.

As early as May 1968 there were signs that Turkey's businessmen were beginning to have grave reservations about Demirel's policies. At a meeting of the Union of Chambers (of Commerce and Industry) on 18 May 1968, Demirel's policies were criticized by a group of representatives led by Necmettin Erbakan, who claimed that 'Turkey had come to be an open market for Europe and America'. After much acrimonious debate the president of the Union, Enver Sırrı Batur, declared that 'this economic order will not be altered'.[41]

A year later on 24 May 1969 Professor Erbakan, with the votes of the Anatolian merchants, defeated Batur in the election for the presidency of the Union of Chambers of Commerce and Industry.[42] More important than this set-back for Demirel was a speech made by Vehbi Koç, Turkey's leading industrialist. He expressed alarm at the growing economic crisis, which, he said, would threaten the régime unless measures were taken. He confessed that he had lost faith in JP rule.[43] What was needed, suggested Koç, was a viable alternative for Demirel's JP. It could be another political party,

and if none fitted the bill, a bureaucratic-technocratic, above-party
government would be an alternative.[44]

Emergence of the Democratic Party

After the general election, the tide began to turn rapidly against
Demirel. The composition of his new cabinet suggested that the
compromise he had concluded in April 1967 had broken down and
that the dissidents were out of his control once more.[45] This was
confirmed three days later when the party's Assembly and Senate
Groups met jointly to discuss the government's programme and
146 dissident members refused to participate.[46] By the end of
December there were reports that Ferruh Bozbeyli, Chairman of
the Assembly, would challenge Demirel's leadership at the next
congress.[47] Disciplinary measures leading to the expulsion of two
dissidents in January 1970 brought the crisis to a head. Some of the
leading dissidents, all members of the General Executive Council,
walked out of the meeting where the matter was being discussed.[48]
On 4 February five of them, plus Cihat Bilgehan, resigned from the
General Executive Council, and exactly a week later Demirel's
draft budget was defeated in the Assembly, and this defeat forced
him to resign.[49]

The principal charge against Demirel was that under his
leadership the JP had become a party dominated by his clique:
therefore he had to be replaced as Party Chairman. President
Sunay, however, asked Demirel to form a new cabinet and he
presented exactly the same cabinet as that which had just been
forced to resign. With 41 dissident Representatives capable of
voting against the government, Demirel's position was always
threatened. The dissidents had demonstrated their power; it was
now a question of undermining Demirel's position and defeating
him at the congress to be held in October. Meanwhile, they
launched a campaign to discredit him by accusing him of corrupt
practices, of peddling influence to obtain large credits for his
brothers.[50] Judged by the outcome of the Fifth General Congress,
the campaign against Demirel did little damage and he maintained
his hold over the party.[51]

The dissidents had only one card left to play in order to force
Demirel's resignation: to succeed in persuading the Assembly to
investigate the charges of corruption against him. This request had
already been rejected by the JP majority and then overruled by the
Constitutional Court. The motion came before the Assembly again
on 16 December and after a seventeen-and-a-half hour debate it
was defeated by 309 votes to 276.[52]

As early as the summer of 1970 the dissidents had spoken of leaving the JP and forming a new party. But they intended to do so only if they failed to dislodge Demirel, preferring to capture the party and maintain unity. When that proved impossible, they announced the formation of the Democratic Party (DP— *Demokratik Parti*) on 18 December, the day after the motion to open an investigation against Demirel was defeated. Ferruh Bozbeyli, who had resigned as Chairman of the Assembly on 19 October and from the JP on 13 November, was elected Chairman.[53]

The dispute in the Justice Party was not merely the result of hostility to Demirel or a struggle for leadership. It was also the result of a decade of development marked by rapid social and economic change in the commercial and agrarian sectors, which had been dominant throughout the fifties and were now being forced to make way for the expanding industrial sector.

The dissidents, as İsmail Cem's analysis shows, belonged to the declining sectors, essentially the landowners and provincial notables who opposed Demirel's schemes to speed up the modernization of the economic structure by such measures as land or agrarian reform and the taxation of farm wealth. If Demirel was permitted to carry out such reforms, these groups would become as anachronistic as the Anatolian tradesmen and artisans. It is therefore not surprising that there was an attempt to bring these elements together to form a political coalition against Demirel's 'twentieth-century capitalism'.[54]

After the founding of the DP there were defections from the Justice Party and Demirel was left without a majority in the Assembly. His position had been completely eroded and he had become a 'factor of instability'. As early as 13 January 1971 President Sunay expressed privately the view that 'it would be useful if Demirel withdrew for a while, for he had brought the entire establishment against him.... [but Sunay said that he] had only the power to recommend.' The commanders, looking at the examples of 27 May and the situation in Greece, said they would certainly not give up democracy, so Demirel's government was permitted to linger on for another two months.[55]

As the weeks went by it became clear that Demirel had virtually lost all authority. He was totally eclipsed by events and forced into the background, in the shadow of the commanders. It is worth noting that, when the urban guerrillas released the four American servicemen they had kidnapped, Ambassador William Handley thanked opposition leader İsmet İnönü and not Premier Demirel. This was not lost on the press.[56] In February Demirel spoke to the correspondent of the *Frankfurter Allgemeine Zeitung* of the possibility of an early general election, which would give him a new mandate to rule.[57] But there was to be no spot election. Even after the split in the party there were reports of groups who wanted Demirel to resign. The candidate who was expected to replace Demirel was Defence Minister Ahmet Topaloğlu, who would be acceptable to the armed forces. There was a meeting on 8 March 1971 at which this question was discussed but Demirel was able to retain control, dismissing the remaining dissidents led by Aydın Yalçın as political opponents bent on destroying party unity.[58] Four days later the Commanders presented their memorandum to President Sunay and the Chairmen of the Assembly and the Senate, and Süleyman Demirel was forced to resign. The political future of Demirel and of his party were in grave doubt in the period that followed.

Evolution of the 'New' RPP

The 'Old Guard' Persists, 1960–1965

The *coup d'état* of 27 May 1960 froze political activity and with it the developments which had been taking place in the RPP since 1957. There was much elation in the party, for overnight it had been transformed from a party threatened with investigation and possible closure, to a party exercising indirect but dominant influence on the policies of the interim régime. Some members of the National Unity Committee, notably Türkeş, were opposed to İnönü but they were soon ousted from the Committee, and even while they were there the party was able to exercise influence through the civilians (professors and technocrats) most of whom were sympathetic to the RPP's policies and ideas. Many of the features of the Second Republic (the bicameral parliament, proportional representation, the Constitutional Court, and economic planning) had been proposed by the RPP. This was no accident since the Constituent Assembly, which played the major role in determining the shape of the Second Republic, was dominated by Republicans. If the Republicans suffered any setback from the *coup*, it was their failure to have an early general election before the country had had time to recover from the shock of 27 May.

With the military in power, İnönü was able to establish absolute control in the party. He was a factor of strength and stability but his leadership also made for conservatism and stagnation. However, the party could not entirely ignore the dynamism generated by the 27 May movement; therefore as soon as political activity was permitted again it began recruiting students and youths as well as retired officers and academics; the enrolment of youth into the party proved particularly significant.[59] But, apart from those moves, the Republicans made no attempt to change the character of their party. The emphasis on officers and academics suggests that they wanted to strengthen the element of the traditional 'civilian-military intelligentsia' in the party.

The proceedings of the Fifteenth General Congress (24-8 August 1961) amply demonstrate that little had changed in the upper levels of the RPP. A Republican sympathizer observed that, 'Citizens in search of peace and stability expected many things from the Fifteenth Congress, which was meeting at a time when the one-and-a-half year old revolutionary régime was coming to an end and the general election was approaching. It was expected that the Republican People's Party would take power at the coming general election and the citizens were waiting with curiosity to see the new policy which the party would adopt.' He continued, 'The Congress opened ... in Ankara on Thursday 24 August 1961 and destroyed all hope from the very first day. It began and ended as a demonstration of personal rivalries.'[60]

The rivalry Giritlioğlu refers to is the İnönü-Gülek rivalry we witnessed in the fifties. Gülek, having been ousted as Secretary-General in 1959, was determined to make a comeback. He began to prepare the ground for the contest with İnönü by publishing a newspaper, the *Tanin*, in which he carried out his propaganda. But he was no match for İnönü, even though his supporters dominated the congress. İnönü's threat to resign, along with his implied ultimatum of 'either me or Gülek', clinched the issue. He was re-elected Chairman and his candidate İsmail Rüştü Aksal was elected Secretary-General, defeating Gülek by 957 votes to 335; Gülek was not even elected to the General Administrative Council.[61]

The party had been weakened by the behaviour of the factions and even İnönü became a factor of discord rather than unity. The revolution may have ushered in a new era for Turkey but not for the RPP, which continued in its old ways. The results of the 1961 general election demonstrated the voters' coolness towards the RPP, which did worse in this election than in 1957.[62]

The three years of the İnönü-led coalitions caused even more damage. The constant dilution of the reforms to which the party was committed undermined its standing, and large numbers of its younger supporters defected to the Workers' Party. During these years the RPP was divided and confused, unable to do anything to revive its fortunes with the voters, as the local elections of November 1963 proved. The party's rank and file was at odds with the party organization and with the government. During the years in opposition, the leadership had promised to implement a broad and radical programme of reform as soon as it came to power. The rank and file now pressed for action but the RPP coalitions were unable to implement such a programme. Not only had the government failed to carry out the major reforms, land reform for example, but the country was actually moving towards greater conservatism. The party acquired the reputation of the rhetorical reformer: always promising reforms, it was in fact successfully sabotaging them. That is why, later on, the party in opposition was often exposed to the Justice Party retort: 'Why are you criticizing [our proposal]? Earlier you also delayed this law.'[63]

The set-back in the local elections (November 1963) and the partial Senate election (June 1964) forced the RPP to reconsider its policies in order to project an image which would differentiate it from the JP and provide an alternative to the socialism of the WPT. Once more the party reverted to the rhetoric of its old reformist, Kemalist image. It proclaimed itself the party of reform. 'Those who are not on the side of reform', Turhan Feyzioğlu told his audience in Konya, 'are people opposed to the well-being of the Turkish nation.... As our name proclaims, we are the People's Party. We believe in social justice. The only way to defeat communism is by implementing social justice. We are opposed to backward ideas which are so unaware of the world as to believe that it is sinful even to talk of social justice.' In Bursa, Kemal Satır, the party's Secretary-General, stated that 'an office boy paying tax on 200 liras while someone who earns hundreds of thousands pays nothing is no different from putting dynamite under social justice'.[64]

The Seventeenth Congress of 16-18 October 1964 was intended to be a point of departure. It was to be an 'intellectual congress' and for the first time the Youth and Women's wings of the party participated. The most significant feature was the declaration entitled 'Our Ideal of an Advanced Turkey' (İleri Türkiye Ülkümüz), which was adopted by the congress. The declaration was drawn up by Turhan Feyzioğlu and Bülent Ecevit, the two rising stars of the RPP, with the intention of modernizing the party's principles and bringing them in line with contemporary needs. It dealt with such topics as land reform, social justice, social security, economic development, 'democratic' étatism, education, secularism, the fine arts, nationalism, and youth. Only through the proper socio-economic policies, read the declaration, would the 'extreme Right' and 'extreme Left' be countered.[65]

Observers followed the proceedings with great interest to see how İnönü's party would react to the challenge of the sixties, and what measures would be taken to revitalize its moribund structure. The results were not reassuring. The congress repeated tired clichés and promised reforms which it had failed to carry out while in power. The election of Kemal Satır as Secretary-General, with Sırrı Atalay and Cihat Baban as his deputies, suggested that the party intended to retain its conservative character despite its lip service to reform.[66]

The Party Moves Left of Centre

After İnönü's government was defeated in February 1965 the party became more radical and the general election in October became its principal concern. There was, however, a strong reaction in the party against the 'turn to the left'. According to a conservative Republican, Bülent Ecevit's speech before the party's youth congress in May, with its reference to nationalization, was a clear indication of the new orientation. The enrolment of three of 'the Fourteen' was an open invitation to radicals to join the party.[67] But the reaction was also an indication of how the opposition parties would be able to exploit the RPP's reformism, especially once it adopted the slogan 'left of centre' (*ortanın solu*) to describe its position in Turkey's political spectrum. The Republicans were immediately put on the defensive.

The term 'left of centre' was introduced to the public in İnönü's statement published in *Milliyet* on 29 July 1965. The controversy which resulted from this proved extremely costly at the polls on 10 October. The opposition parties, especially the JP, immediately began to use the slogan as a weapon against the RPP. In logic reminiscent of *Alice in Wonderland*, being left of centre was explained as being in the centre of the left, while the jingle '*ortanın solu, Moskova yolu*' (left of centre is the road to Moscow) was intended to arouse the anti-communist response conditioned by the word 'Moscow'. It could not have been otherwise in a country where 'democrat' was symbolized by the 'white horse'.[68]

The Republicans were caught by their own ruse, designed to undermine the position of their socialist rival, the WPT. They were forced to explain 'left of centre' and that proved particularly difficult in the countryside, where counter-propaganda using traditional factors like religion and private property was far more effective. Few people outside the urban areas were comforted by the thought that Sweden, Norway, France, the United Kingdom, and Germany were not communist but were ruled by 'left-of-centre' governments.[69] Ali İhsan Göğüş, one of the younger men İnönü had brought in to rejuvenate the party, tried to explain that 'the word "left" is not an indication of communism as some people claim [and] communism can be prevented by using rational means not by shouting "may the communists perish!" Left of centre is not a matter of Ahmet and Mehmet, it is the issue of solving the problems of this country.'[70] Finally, three days before the election, İnönü decided to moderate his party's position by stating over the radio that 'the State, the Constitution and the RPP are all left of centre'.[71]

The election was a disaster for the party but there was now no turning back. Not only had the party made clear its intentions about pursuing a radical policy; it had also brought to the forefront younger radicals like Bülent Ecevit to represent such a policy. Initially the slogan had been accepted only as a talisman for the election, since the conservative elements, after successive electoral failures, could offer no alternative. The electoral defeat, worse than any other the Republicans had suffered, discredited the slogan and the policy it represented and left the party torn with dissension.

The situation of the RPP after its adoption of the left-of-centre stance was similar to its position twenty years earlier after it had passed the land reform bill. In both cases the forces of the *status quo* were mobilized in order to curb the rising tide of reformism. On the first occasion, dissension had led to the formation of the DP; in 1965 events had yet to unfold. But the forces of the *status quo* took the initiative and tried to reverse the radical-reformist trend in the party.

The first spokesman for this group was Tahsin Banguoğlu, the RPP Senator for Edirne, who held İnönü responsible for adopting the slogan and leading the party to defeat. 'Not to see such open realities one has to be senile [İnönü was 81] or be influenced by a group of profiteers around oneself. Some officials of the party have lost themselves to such a degree that they seem willing to risk taking Turkey behind the Iron Curtain. But it should not be forgotten that what the Turkish nation rejected was the wrong policy of İnönü at the end of his days and not the Republican People's Party. The party will continue to fulfil its historic mission.'[72]

İnönü did not intend to resign; he had declared in Trabzon before the elections: 'I will not give up politics until the reforms have been carried out.' And after the election he reaffirmed this in an interview with Mehmet Barlas.[73] Had İnönü left the party at this point there would have been a bitter and uncontrolled struggle for power between the radical and the conservative factions, with victory in the balance. His presence assured a gradual evolution instead of a sudden shift in one direction or the other.

Although the slogan 'left of centre' was used before and during the election campaign it is doubtful whether its effect on the electoral fortunes of the party was as serious as the critics claimed. The RPP was unlikely to win the election in 1965. In spite of its political record, the supporters of the *status quo* considered it too progressive; and the radicals were disillusioned with it for being progressive in words, conservative in action. The decision to introduce the slogan was regarded as an investment that would pay off, not in 1965, but in 1969 or even 1973. For the moment it was a question of defeating the conservatives in the party and establishing a consensus around the new orientation.

Few people recognized or understood the fact that İnönü had been forced to adopt this slogan by the political changes of the sixties. After the founding of the WPT the Republicans had to define their position in the political spectrum. The 30 or 40 per cent of the total vote which the party had traditionally received was no longer guaranteed, since many votes were now going to the JP or the WPT. İnönü recognized the danger that the country, especially its intelligentsia, might swing to the Left if one of the major parties did not provide an alternative.[74]

İnönü visualized a threat to Turkey from the Left represented by the WPT, and the extreme Right, as yet not politically organized, but manifesting itself in the JP. He was willing to make his party the bulwark against the Left if only Demirel would agree to do the same thing on the Right. 'The party in power outspokenly expresses its identity. This is an improvement. I see it as right-wing. I tell them: "You protect our right wing [from extremists] and I will protect the left wing and then there will be no fear in the country." Will it [the Justice Party] be able to protect itself from this [the Right]? They have not done so so far. From the Nurist to the reactionary everyone joins the Right. Compared to them we are a left-wing party. There is a threat on our left also; but we will protect ourselves from that....'[75]

The debate in the party continued to rage into 1966. The opponents of the left-of-centre policy spoke in pragmatic terms, arguing that the country was too backward and conservative, and unprepared to accept such a radical departure. Others claimed that the people did not understand what the term stood for. And they were probably right: the Republicans were not clear about this either—on 2 December 1965 *Cumhuriyet* reported that twenty-seven different definitions of left of centre had been offered in the party. There were also the opportunists who proposed that the RPP ought to come to power first by using other, more popular slogans and then implement a 'left-of-centre' policy.[76]

İnönü, however, refused to abandon the slogan; he was wise enough to recognize that such a step would be disastrous for the credibility of a party whose sincerity was already in question. But he became more moderate in his statements and emphasized that his party was not becoming Marxist or socialist and that they were opposed to communism. He reassured the capitalists that the RPP was not opposed to their interests either. 'The private sector was used against us in the last election.... The ignorance of the private sector is that it considers our measures on taxation and other things are against it. But it is wrong. A country has to make sacrifices for development.'[77]

The criticism had its effect and the slogan was virtually dropped in the campaign for the partial Senate elections of 5 June 1966. However, the party fared no better than in the general election. But as Ecevit has demonstrated with election statistics, this had little to do with slogans, for the JP was also losing votes, even though it had won the election. The voters were obviously disillusioned and angry with the traditional parties.[78]

The RPP's Central Committee had accepted the left-of-centre slogan but there was still opposition in the party, especially in the Assembly Group and in some provincial organizations. The struggle continued until one of the factions was eliminated and both factions prepared for the General Congress in October 1966, when the question would be resolved.

Secretary-General Ecevit 1966

The Eighteenth Congress proved to be one of the most active of recent years. It was marked by a struggle between the Central Committee and the organization, which ended in a victory for the left-of-centre Central Committee. İnönü, challenged by Kasım Gülek for the leadership, defeated him by 929 votes to 230; perhaps more important for the future was the election of Bülent Ecevit as Secretary-General.[79]

Ecevit was born in Istanbul in 1925, the son of a doctor who was also a Republican member of the Assembly. After finishing his schooling at Robert College in 1944, he was sent to the Turkish Embassy in London to work in the press attaché's office. He returned to Turkey and joined *Ulus*, the RPP's official organ, in

1950. During the years of turmoil in the party he demonstrated the ability to work with all factions and in 1957 he was a member of the young group brought into the party's inner circle to inject new blood. He was elected one of the Representatives for Ankara and played an important role in the party's newly established research bureau. But at this time he was overshadowed by the more charismatic and sparkling personality of Professor Turhan Feyzioğlu.

In 1961 he was appointed to the Constituent Assembly; and later in the year, when İnönü formed his first coalition government, Ecevit was given the portfolio for Labour. He won for himself the reputation of being the friend of the unions and the new labour legislation was passed during his ministry. But it is worth remembering that it was Ecevit who had the American trade unionist, John Thalmayer, virtually expelled from Turkey for campaigning against the exploitation of Turkish workers by Turkish and foreign concerns. Ecevit has been dismissed by his rivals as a romantic, out of touch with political reality; but examination of the facts reveals that, on the contrary, Ecevit's political judgement has often proved to be superior to that of his critics. Nowhere has he demonstrated this better than in his handling of the left-of-centre slogan.

Most Republicans saw the slogan as a way to give the RPP a new radical image so that the voters would see it as an alternative to the Left. Ecevit, however, saw 'left of centre' not only in those terms but also as a policy that could change the character of the party, transforming it into an organization capable of meeting the challenge of the sixties and the seventies within the existing socio-economic structure. If the party was to win elections it had to broaden its electoral base by winning the vote of the peasant and worker, even if that meant losing the support of the shortsighted and anachronistic landowner. There was also an urgent need to rectify the imbalances caused by the changes of the previous twenty years; unless this was quickly accomplished there was a serious risk of breakdown and anarchy. Reform of the social and economic structure was also the only way in Turkey to make capitalism viable, for it had to be rendered more productive and more equitable than the prevailing nineteenth century variety.

A 'left-of-centre' policy, as Ecevit visualized it, would provide a new equilibrium which would act as the antidote to violent social change. To those who dismissed his schemes of land reform, promoted with the slogan 'land to the tiller and water to the user' as communist, he gave the example of Chiang Kai-shek's Taiwan, where land reform had been the foundation of an 'economic miracle' under capitalism.[80] Social peace could be guaranteed only if those sections of the population (peasants, workers, and the class of independent merchants and artisans) adversely affected by large-scale capitalism were given some protection and security. The new policy was designed to do that, appealing at the same time to the industrialist and entrepreneur to behave responsibly and in the national interest. It claimed to be opposed to 'isms' and parties representing the interests of specific classes; Ecevit described Demirel's Justice Party as the only true class party in Turkey, with the state in the role of mediator in the conflict of interest groups. In many respects this new doctrine was a return to the Kemalist principle of populism, which recognized no class struggle and saw classes as complementing one another.[81]

The results of the Eighteenth Congress—official acceptance of the left-of-centre position and the election of its proponents to party bodies—sharpened the conflict in the party. The right-wing group numbering 76 (appropriately called 'the Seventy-six') and led by Turhan Feyzioğlu, took the offensive, denouncing the new trend as leftist and socialist. These denunciations were far more dangerous than accusations from outside the party and had to be countered before serious damage was done. On 22 December Tahsin Banguoğlu, the most outspoken critic of the new policy, was expelled from the party. Next day he introduced a new line of attack which was potentially more subversive than the accusations of leftism. He described the new policy as anti-Kemalist. He told the press that he was a Kemalist and refused to become an 'İnönüist' that the 'left-of-centre' policy was a form of crypto-socialism which had nothing to do with Atatürk, and therefore that the party might as well become socialist.[82]

Out of 'the Seventy-six' there emerged 'the Eight' to lead the struggle against Ecevit. Had İnönü decided to remain neutral, Ecevit might have been defeated. But he threw his weight behind the Secretary-General and picked up the gauntlet thrown down by 'the Eight'. 'Their movement is against me and I shall do whatever is necessary.'[83]

The position of the dissidents was weak; they were accusing the party of becoming socialist, a charge that was hardly convincing in the light of İnönü's reaffirmations to the contrary: 'I am telling you again, I am announcing it to the whole country. The name of the RPP is the Republican People's Party. It is not a socialist party. It will not be a socialist party....'[84]

It is difficult to avoid the conclusion that these charges of socialism were merely a subterfuge used in an attempt to force the party to retain its old identity, which suited many of its die-hard and conservative supporters. Feyzioğlu's leadership of the conservative group is not easy to understand, since his earlier politics had been liberal. One possible explanation for this *volte face* may be that pride and ambition had been injured when he was bypassed in the leadership of the party by Ecevit. Feyzioğlu's role in Turkish politics since 1967 remains an enigma.

The issue was decided in favour of the İnönü-Ecevit group at the Fourth Extraordinary Congress which met on 28 April 1967. The division of forces remained the same as it had been at the General Congress: the central organization supported İnönü and Ecevit while Feyzioğlu found support in the Assembly Group and some provincial organizations. İnönü asked for the amendment of Articles 45, 46, and 50 of the party regulations so that the Party Executive would have complete control over all members, including Representatives and Senators, and the Disciplinary Committee would be able to expel members of the Assembly. He asserted that the party needed unity and allegiance to a single programme; under present regulations that was not possible.

Next day Feyzioğlu challenged the demand for such arbitrary powers, claiming that they were against the principles of the party. İnönü was introducing a DP practice and one used by socialist parties on the Continent, though not in Britain. But İnönü's amendments were passed and the dissidents' fate was sealed.[85]

Feyzioğlu and his seven friends left the RPP before they could be expelled, and other resignations followed. These ex-members held a meeting on 1 May and decided to form a new party whose official date of establishment was 12 May 1967. It was named the Reliance Party (RP) and Turhan Feyzioğlu was unanimously elected party leader.[86] In 1945 radicalism in the RPP and the threat of reform had led to fragmentation and the formation of the DP. Almost a generation later, the same threat brought virtually the same response, which suggests that very little had changed in the past 22 years.

The departure of Feyzioğlu and his followers did not leave the RPP a monolithic party united round the left-of-centre slogan. Many stayed on out of personal loyalty to İnönü; they realized that while İnönü continued to lead the RPP it would continue to follow a moderate and conservative path. Besides, if all dissidents of the Right left the RPP, Ecevit's group would be able to dominate by default and there would be no one to dilute the radicalism. For the moment, however, there was internal calm while the different factions took stock of the new situation.

Faced with constant criticism from the JP and the new Reliance Party that it was a leftist organization, the RPP began to attack the Workers' Party. Moreover, as the Republicans had claimed all along, the aim of their new orientation was to wean away the intelligentsia from the WPT by providing a radical alternative. The new policy began to pay dividends and the party recovered some of the support it had lost earlier to the JP and the WPT. The results of the local and partial Senate elections of 2 June 1968 showed that the Republicans were beginning to make gains in the prosperous and modernized regions while they were losing strength in regions dominated by the landowners, who had traditionally supported them. This was significant because every party that had won elections in the multi-party period had always carried the prosperous regions of Thrace, Marmara, and the Aegean.[87] This trend may have been encouraging but the actual results still left the Republicans far behind; of the 58 Senators elected, only 13 were Republican while 38 belonged to the JP and one each came from the Nation and Reliance Parties.[88]

The RPP still had a long way to go, and under İnönü's leadership it was doubtful whether it would grow in the direction that would enable it to provide a genuine alternative. During these years the party spoke with two voices: İnönü's and Ecevit's. İnönü emphasized the anti-left, anti-communist aspect of the new policy, presenting it as 'an insurmountable wall of defence... against communism'.[89] Ecevit, on the other hand, shared his leader's views but spoke of radical reform and a transformation of the existing order, needed to guarantee democracy and social peace.[90] The two voices were contradictory, for Ecevit's reformist schemes could not be undertaken while the RPP continued to represent the traditional pressure groups such as the landowners and the bureaucracy.

Thus in spite of lip service to the new policy, the party remained a 'personality party' rather than a 'party of ideas'. This became clear at the Nineteenth Congress when the 'left-of-centre' policy was all but renounced, no doubt with an eye on the general election, only a year away. The avoidance of a pre-election split was one of the objectives of the congress and it was achieved at the expense of the radical group, which made all the concessions. That was a mistake, argued Mümtaz Soysal, for the new identity of the party had had an impact on supporters, dissipating apathy and creating a sense of vitality, with the result that the RPP had again been attracting the young and the thoughtful. 'When an image and a concept, whatever their actual value, are identified with the personality of an individual [a reference to Ecevit] who assumes the responsibility for making them a reality, they become a persuasive power, almost a concrete agent in attracting votes.'[91]

The Party's Dual Character

The RPP ought to have concentrated on keeping alive its new personality and purged all those who tarnished it by their associations with the past. But the congress did the reverse. The Ecevit group made concessions, believing that time was on their side and that their first task was to keep the party intact. They forgot that the provincial organizations and the voters were more radical and less opportunistic. 'The recent congress', concluded Soysal, 'could have been used as an opportunity to strengthen convictions that the party would remain steadfast in its new course. The opportunity was missed. Now, groups of this or that colour, by-products of the congress, appear more out of place or incongruous than ever in comparison with the concrete and worthy ideas expressed in the policy statements.'[92]

As the general election drew near, the party turned more and more to its traditional politics. In May 1969 İnönü did a somersault and supported the government's motion to restore political rights to former Democrats. It was only a political tactic to counteract Demirel's manoeuvre. But this unprincipled approach to politics by a party which had always claimed the monopoly of principles—to the extent of being self-righteous—shocked public opinion and led to resignations.[93] İnönü did not stop at that; he took the logical step and held meetings of reconciliation with Celâl Bayar, designed to draw Democrat votes to the RPP.[94] Three weeks before the election, the party organ *Ulus* (20 September 1969) published a banner headline: 'A General Amnesty when the RPP Comes to Power.'

The party's campaign strategy was to avoid controversy, and a secret circular instructed its officials to keep away from disputes on past political differences and resentments; to eschew speeches which could be interpreted as being against the national will; and to avoid controversial words like 'progressive' and 'reactionary', and topics such as religion and secularism. Instead the party should put forward the thesis of 'reform from the economic and social point of view', describing opponents as 'social conservatives' rather than 'reactionary' or 'anti-Atatürk'.[95] Ecevit's radical promises of 'land to the tiller, water for the user' were in marked contrast to the general tone of the campaign, and increased the confusion and cynicism of the voters.[96] The result was that the RPP's support in the country remained virtually static, dropping from 28·7 per cent of the votes in 1967 to 27·4, while the JP vote dropped from 52·9 to 46·2 per cent.[97]

Just as the partisans of the 'left-of-centre' slogan had been blamed for the party's performance in the 1965 election, they could blame the conservatives for shying away from the slogan and losing votes in 1969. The conflict between the two factions came out into the open, with the conservatives accusing Ecevit of criticizing Atatürk. Ecevit, while claiming to be a Kemalist, had never made it a secret that Kemalism ought to be updated and he pointed out that some of Atatürk's reforms, the hat reform for example, had alienated the people. Ecevit had also argued that the party's policy of secularism had been rigid and aggressive and had failed to understand the mentality of the people.[98] The confrontation between the radicals, now totally identified with Ecevit, and the conservatives again began to take shape. İnönü remained neutral, though each faction was banking on his support.

The first encounter took place in the Party Council meeting on 26 and 27 March 1970 and the conservatives met a reverse when Erim failed to be re-elected to this body. Ecevit, determined to consolidate his position, called for an extraordinary congress.[99]

The Twentieth Congress met on 3 July and after three days of debate Ecevit again emerged triumphant. This time İnönü backed him up and succeeded in preventing further fragmentation. In the party elections Ecevit's supporters won the majority of the positions. Only İnönü stood between Ecevit and the control of the party; but, as Ecevit must have realized, İnönü was a formidable rival.[100]

It is doubtful whether Ecevit intended to challenge İnönü's leadership so soon. For the next eight months they continued to work together as Chairman and Secretary-General—as they had done for the past four years—at cross purposes but not in conflict. This arrangement might have lasted even longer but for the military intervention.

As the social, economic, and political situation continued to deteriorate, Ecevit began to hope that the Justice Party, unable to deal with the problems, would crumble and that a general election would be held at which the RPP would gain office. In December 1970 he even sent a directive to the provincial organizations to prepare themselves for the JP's collapse and the RPP's assumption of power. Demirel denounced this as psychological warfare.[101] The military intervention on 12 March 1971 upset the party's calculations of coming to power *via* an early general election, just as the *coup* of 27 May 1960 had done. İnönü's reaction to the Commanders' memorandum which led to Demirel's resignation was cautious and ambiguous, but he decided to describe their action as democratic. Ecevit's group reacted less opportunistically and Haluk Ülman stated categorically in *Ulus* of 14 March that the memorandum could not be described as democratic, nor did it help the cause of democracy. What made matters worse was the armed forces' decision to appoint Nihat Erim as the 'above-party' Prime Minister, his claim to impartiality depending on nothing stronger than the requirement that he resign from the RPP before accepting office.

This appointment was a blow to Ecevit and the new policy. Erim had initially supported the left-of-centre policy and was described as one of its original partisans. In time, however, he had sided with the conservatives and had even led this faction against Ecevit. As Prime Minister of what was to be a national coalition he would have great power, which he could use on behalf of Ecevit's rival Kemal Satır. Had İnönü decided not to support the Erim government, Ecevit's position in the party might have remained tenable. Being a man of principle as well as sound political calculation, Ecevit resigned as Secretary-General on 21 March, the day İnönü proclaimed his support for the government.

One of the main features of the left-of-centre policy had been the abandonment of the party's 'alliance' with the armed forces and the bureaucracy. That, claimed the left-of-centre theoreticians, would restore the party's contact with the people and increase its chances of winning elections. Their desire to break down the barriers between the party and the people was made incapable of fulfilment by İnönü's decision, which immediately identified the RPP with the intervention, as in 1960. The only way to salvage the new policy, and prevent it from being devalued in the eyes of its supporters, was for the radicals to resign their party posts. Only then would they be able to continue the struggle; and, if they won, restore the policy designed to introduce radical reform.

NOTES

1 *Cumhuriyet*, 16 June and 1 Dec. 1960; Seyhan, *Gölgedeki Adam*, 96. Alparslan Türkeş told the author that he was engaged in forming a party with Ekrem Alican and Abdullah Gözübüyük, both cabinet ministers, when he was ousted from the NUC in Nov. 1960.

2 See *MER 1961*, 532 ff.; *TY 1962*, 326-32; Tökin, *Türk Tarihi*, 103.

3 On the NTP see Eren, *Turkey Today—and Tomorrow*, 68 and 98; *MER 1961*, 539-41; *TY 1962*, 331-2; Tökin, *Türk Tarihi*, 106-7; and Nimet Arzık, 'YTP Nasıl Kuruldu', *Yön*, 28 Feb. and 7 and 14 Mar. 1962.

4 Cemal Madanoğlu, *C. Madanoğlu İnkilâbı Anlatıyor*, ed. Cevat Oktay (n.d. [1960]), 16.

5 Refik Erduran's column in *Milliyet*, 5 Oct. 1965.

6 *Cumhuriyet*, 16 July 1961.

7 Ibid., 28 Feb. 1961 quoted in *MER 1961*, 537.

8 *Cumhuriyet*, 13 June 1964.

9 Ibid., 9 Sept. 1964.

10 Süleyman Demirel, *Adalet Partisi Genel Başkanlığına Adaylığımı Neden Koyuyorum?* (1964); *Son Havadis*, 9 Nov. 1964. This was the first time in Turkey's political history that the leadership of any party was decided by contest.

11 See above, ch. 7.

12 *Cumhuriyet*, 29 Nov. 1964. The second part of the quotation is not given in the party pamphlet, Adalet Partisi, *Adalet Partisi İkinci Büyük Kongresinde Genel Başkan Adaylarının Konuşmaları* (n.d. [1964]), 8. Conversation with Aydın Yalçın.

13 Demirel's official biographical sketch is given in his pamphlet, *Genel Başkan*, 8. For a more detailed and critical biography see *Ortam* 4, 21 June 1971, 12–15. Türkeş tried to discredit Demirel by giving out unflattering information about him after the *coup* of 27 May 1960. See *Vatan*, 5 Oct. 1965.

14 Conversation with Seyfi Kurtbek, who said that one of his sources of information was Orhan Erkanlı. Kurtbek was one of the deputy leaders of the JP and a member of the General Executive Council.

15 Ibid. Seyfi Kurtbek claims that all governments since 1961 have been responsible for increasing the autonomy of the armed forces, and not one has tried to bring the situation back to normal. The Assembly Group protested against the government's lack of control over the commanders. See *Cumhuriyet*, 6 Jan. 1966.

16 *Milliyet*, 21 and 22 Dec. 1964.

17 N. Abadan, 'Election of 1965', *Government and Opposition* i/3 (1966), 341. As Professor Abadan explains, in Turkish a white horse is '*kır at*'. The popular pronunciation of the word Democrat in Turkish is *Demirkırat*, which means a white horse made of iron. See *Cumhuriyet*, 22 July 1965.

18 *Cumhuriyet*, 21 July and 17 Aug. and *Milliyet*, 31 Aug. 1965.

19 *Vatan*, 15 Sept. 1965.

20 AP, *Seçim Beyannamesi* (Ankara, 1965), and the Turkish press, 19 Sept. 1965.

21 *Milliyet*, 13 Oct. 1965.

22 *Cumhuriyet*, 6 Nov. 1965.

23 Ibid., 17 Nov. 1965. During his visit to the US President Sunay was informed by a group of businessmen that 'Turkey has become an ally, especially on account of the economic policy followed by the JP government. In particular, the restoration of stability, within the short time that Premier Demirel has been in power, will make it possible to concentrate investment on a large scale in agriculture and tourism.' See *Cumhuriyet*, 14 Apr. 1967.

24 Süleyman Demirel (Prime Minister); Cihat Bilgehan, Refet Sezgin, Kâmil Ocak, and Ali Fuat Alişan (State); Hasan Dinçer (Justice); Ahmet Topaloğlu (Defence); Faruk Sükan (Interior); İhsan Sabri Çağlayangil (External Affairs); İhsan Gürsan (Finance); Orhan Dengiz (Education);

Ethem Erdinç (Public Works); Macit Zeren (Trade); Edip Somunoğlu (Health and Social Assistance); İbrahim Tekin (Customs and Monopolies); Bahri Dağdaş (Agriculture); Seyfi Öztürk (Communications); Ali Naili Erdem (Labour); Mehmet Turgut (Industries); İbrahim Deriner (Energy and Natural Resources); Nihat Kürşat (Tourism and Information); Haldun Menteşeoğlu (Building and Resettlement); Sabit Osman Avcı (Rural Affairs). See Öztürk, *Hükümetler*, 609-10; the Turkish press, 28 Oct. 1965. See below, n. 32.

25 *Cumhuriyet*, 6 Nov. 1965. Apparently Aydın Yalçın refused to enter Demirel's first cabinet because Demirel would not define the duties of the Ministry of State he was being offered. Professor Yalçın writes that he also disliked the general composition of the cabinet. He says that Ahmet Dallı was offered a post in the cabinet but was too ill to accept. (Private communication from Professor Yalçın.)

26 Kadri Eroğan's statement in DP, *72'ler Hareketi ve Demokratik Parti* (1971). See also *Milliyet*, 1 Nov. 1965 which reported similar accusations.

27 *Milliyet*, 1-2 Nov. 1965.

28 Demirel read the programme on 3 Nov. See the Turkish press, 4 Nov. 1965 and Öztürk, *Hükümetler*, 611-70. For a detailed and critical analysis by seven experts see *Cumhuriyet*, 6-12 Nov. 1965.

29 'Program', *Cumhuriyet*, 5 Nov. 1965.

30 *Vatan*, 20 Jan. 1966.

31 The Turkish press, 27-30 Nov. 1966 and the JP pamphlet, AP, *Adalet Partisi Üçüncü Büyük Kongresi: Raporlar* (1966).

32 The other new ministers were: Hüsamettin Atabeyli (State); Vedat Ali Özkan (Health); Ahmet Türkel (Commerce); İlhami Ertem (Education); Orhan Alp (Public Works); Turgut Toker (Rural Affairs). See *Milliyet*, 2 Apr. 1967 and Öztürk, *Hükümetler*, 609-10.

33 *Cumhuriyet*, 14 June 1967, quoting Osman Turan's speech.

34 *Milliyet*, 31 Oct. and 1 Nov. 1967.

35 *Cumhuriyet*, 11 Sept. 1966.

36 Ibid., 4 Dec. 1966.

37 Ibid., 31 July 1967, 7.

38 *Milliyet*, 15 Jan. 1968.

39 *Cumhuriyet*, 16 Sept. 1969.

40 Conversation with Alparslan Türkeş. A good example of the attitude of this group towards monopoly capitalism is given in one of their journals, *Yeniden Milli Mücadele*, 54, 9 Feb. 1971 quoted in Toker, *Sol ve Sağ*, 105: 'Finance capital is by its nature and purpose not national. Banks, insurance companies and financial trusts that are attached to it are the mortal enemies of the national economy. In fact there is a contradiction between finance capital and all the elements of the national economy. Finance capital is concerned with weakening and destroying the national economy in all its aspects by robbing the banks, manipulating the stock exchange and by various other swindles. It exploits all the possibilities in Turkey through puppet enterprises which speed up the productive economy. It makes the national wealth its own property by

264   The Turkish Experiment in Democracy

setting up plants which encourage luxury and waste (Coca-Cola, Fanta, etc.) and exploits the national wealth (the plunder of minerals). There is also a class of compradors which participates in these activities of this anti-national capital, reaping large profits and sharing in the crime. They are virtually traitors. Thus the struggle between the national and the anti-national economy is one between international capital and its accomplices against the nation. What is needed now is to establish the effect of these accomplices of the anti-national economy on our social groups and then to attack.'

41 *Cumhuriyet*, 19 May 1968.

42 See the chronology in Servet Ediboğlu and others, eds., *Salname 1390/1970 Yıllığı* (1970), 29–30, 36–9, and 45; and *Milliyet 1970*, 155–7.

43 Vehbi Koç's speech quoted by Kurthan Fişek, 'Odalar Birliği Kavgası', *Emek*, 16 June 1969, 3.

44 Ibid. This was prophetic in view of the developments following 12 Mar. 1971.

45 In this cabinet Demirel ignored the right wing of the party, which lost the portfolios for Finance, Interior, Communications, and Industries. Only four ministers (Atabeyli, Topaloğlu, Çağlayangil, and Özkan) retained their former ministries; others were reshuffled. Demirel introduced 15 new ministers: Gürhan Titrek and Turhan Bilgin (State); Yusuf Ziya Önder (Justice); Mesut Erez (Finance); Professor Orhan Oğuz (Education); Turgut Gülez (Public Works); Ahmet Dallı (Trade); Ahmet İhsan Birincioğlu (Customs and Monopolies); Nihat Menteşe (Communications); Salâhattin Kılıç (Industries); Necmettin Cevheri (Tourism and Information); Hayrettin Nakipoğlu (Building and Resettlement); Turhan Kapanlı (Rural Affairs); Hüseyin Özalp (Forests, a new ministry); İsmet Sezgin (Sport and Youth, a new ministry). See the Turkish press, 4 Nov. 1969 and *MEJ* xxiv/1 (1970), 69.

46 *Milliyet*, 7 Nov. 1969.

47 *Cumhuriyet*, 26 Dec. 1969.

48 *Son Havadis*, 8 Jan. 1970; *Milliyet 1970*, 30–48. Those who walked out included: Sadettin Bilgiç, Faruk Sükan, Mehmet Turgut, Cevat Önder, Ali Naili Erdem, Talât Asal, and Yüksel Menderes.

49 The Turkish press, 5, 12, 14, and 15 Feb. 1970; DP, *72'ler Hareketi*, also deals with this issue. See also *Milliyet 1970*, 30–48. The five were Bilgiç, Turgut, Sükan, Asal, and Menderes.

50 *Milliyet*, 16 Feb. 1970. *Günaydın*, an Istanbul tabloid, publicized the issue and demanded an investigation against Demirel.

51 The Turkish press, 22–4 Oct. 1970.

52 *Milliyet*, 17 and 18 Dec. 1970. See also Demirel's speech of 12 Nov. 1971 published as a JP pamphlet, *Soruşturma İstiyorum* (Ankara, 1971) and AP, *Soruşturmanın İçyüzü* (Ankara, 1971). For the dissidents' case see the DP pamphlet, *Demirel'den Hesap Soralım* (Ankara, n.d. [1971]).

53 *Cumhuriyet*, 19 Dec. 1970. DP, *72'ler Hareketi*, 88–90 gives the statement of the new party and the names of its 69 founders. See also *Milliyet 1970*, 157–8, and Muzaffer Sencer, *Sosyal Temeller*, 373–81.

54 İsmail Cem's and Ali Gevgilili's columns in *Milliyet*, 7 Mar. and 1

July 1970, respectively. Both are reprinted in *Milliyet 1970*, 39 and 42. Gevgilili notes that in 1945 the opposition to land reform was led by Adnan Menderes. A generation later his son Yüksel was in the ranks of the new DP. See also Besim Üstünel's discussion of Demirel's economic policy and its implications in *Ulus*, 13 Sept. 1970.

55 Aydın Yalçın reporting his conversation with President Sunay to the JP Assembly Group on 1 June 1971. See *Cumhuriyet*, 2 June 1971.

56 Ibid., 12 Mar. 1971. *Cumhuriyet* also reported rumours of a meeting on 11 Mar. between the commanders, Ambassador Handley, and Richard Helms, Director of the CIA. The meeting was allegedly held at the US Embassy.

57 *Cumhuriyet*, 18 Feb. 1971, quoting the interview.

58 *Milliyet*, 9 Mar. 1971. Conversation with Aydın Yalçın.

59 *MER 1961*, 533-4.

60 Giritlioğlu, *Halk Partisi*, ii, 236.

61 Ibid., 236-9; *MER 1961*, 534.

62 For the election results see above, 172. See also Karaosmanoğlu, *45 Yıl*, 258-63, who holds İnönü responsible for the party's failure; and Giritlioğlu, *Halk Partisi*, ii, 260-5.

63 Çetin Altan quoting Nuri Bayar in his book, *Ben Milletvekili İken* (1971), 195. Nadir Nadi, 'Eskisinin Kopyası', *Cumhuriyet*, 3 Feb. 1966, observed that Ferit Melen had criticized the JP—budget which was a copy of earlier budgets he himself had prepared while Finance Minister (1962-5). Nadi concluded: 'Although governments change in Turkey, social and economic outlooks remain the same, and the budget which reflects the government's policy does not vary from one government to another.'

64 Both quotations are from *Cumhuriyet*, 13 Apr. 1964.

65 Giritlioğlu, *Halk Partisi*, ii, 338-40; Kili, *Kemalism*, 188-90.

66 *Milliyet*, 21 Oct. 1964.

67 *Ulus*, 14 May 1965, reporting the statement of Kemal Karan, Representative for Amasya. The three who joined the RPP were Orhan Erkanlı, Orhan Kabibay, and İrfan Solmazer. Karan's reaction is an indication of the confusion between radicalism and leftism which exists in Turkey today. Not one of the three had any inclination towards socialism; Solmazer even defected to the Reliance Party in 1967.

68 The best discussion of this issue is in Bülent Ecevit, *Ortanın Solu* (1966), 11-13. See above, n. 17.

69 Nihat Erim's statement in *Milliyet*, 8 Aug. 1965. For the negative reaction of the rural population see *Cumhuriyet*, 25 Aug. 1965, 4, which was covering the election campaign.

70 *Ulus*, 27 Aug. 1965.

71 *Cumhuriyet*, 8 Oct. 1965.

72 *Dünya*, 12 Oct. 1965.

73 *Cumhuriyet*, 16 Oct. 1965 (Trabzon speech) and 19 Oct. 1965 (interview).

74 *Ulus*, 20 Nov. 1965, reporting İnönü's speech before the Party Council.

75 *Cumhuriyet*, 18 and 19 Dec. 1965.
76 Ecevit, *Ortanın Solu*, 56-63.
77 *Cumhuriyet*, 17 and 18 Dec. 1965 (quotation).
78 Ecevit, *Ortanın Solu*, 68 and 71-6.
79 *Ulus*, 22 Oct. (İnönü's election) and 25 Oct. 1966 (Ecevit's election); Kili, *Kemalism*, 190-4.
80 Speech at Kozan, *Cumhuriyet*, 27 Jan. 1967, and interview with Abdi İpekçi, *Milliyet*, 18 Jan. 1971. Author's conversation with Bülent Ecevit.
81 *Cumhuriyet*, 4 Oct. 1970.
82 *Cumhuriyet* and *Milliyet*, 23 and 24 Dec. 1966.
83 *Milliyet*, 4 Jan. 1967; *MER 1967*, 513-16. 'The Eight' were: Turhan Feyzioğlu, Emin Paksüt, Orhan Öztrak, Süreyya Koç, Ferit Melen, Turan Şahin, Fehmi Alparslan, and Coşkun Kırca.
84 *Akşam*, 5 Feb. 1967 quoted in Kili, *Kemalism*, 193.
85 *Ulus*, 29-30 Apr. 1967; *MER 1967*, 515; Kili, *Kemalism*, 194-8.
86 *Milliyet*, 13 May 1967. Ferit Melen was elected a deputy leader. Judged by its programme, the RP wanted to appear a moderate party, emphasizing nationalism and the need to avoid class conflict. But it soon abandoned its moderation and adopted a position on the secular Right, bitterly opposed to radicalism and socialism. Even the left-of-centrists were described as people 'who want to drive Turkey into a communist adventure by moves disguised as "socialism" or "leftism"'. (Ankara Radio, 16 May 1967, in *SWB*, iv/2468/c/3.) A few months later, eighty-six members from the Istanbul organization left the party, claiming that owing to the influence of the JP, it had become like the 'Association to Combat Communism' and that Feyzioğlu had become Demirel's shadow. Those who had complained of İnönü's dictatorship had set up their own Feyzioğlu-Melen-Kırca junta. (*Milliyet*, 11 and 12 Oct. 1967.)
87 CHP, *CHP XIX Kurultayı: Parti Meclisi Raporu* (1968), 22-8 gives a detailed analysis of the results and a projection of trends.
88 Ankara Radio, 5 June 1968, in *SWB*, iv/2715/c/3.
89 *Ulus*, 19 Feb. 1968.
90 The best account of Ecevit's position is to be found in his Assembly speech (15 Feb. 1968) criticizing the budget. A revised and enlarged version was published under the title, *Bu Düzen Değişmeli* (1968).
91 *Milliyet*, 6 Nov. 1968, 2.
92 Ibid.
93 *Cumhuriyet*, 12 May 1969. The resignations came from the younger group and included intellectuals like Nermin Abadan.
94 *Milliyet*, 15 May 1969 and Turhan Dilligil, *Bayar-İnönü Yakınlaşması* (Ankara, 1969). Pre-publication extracts from this book were serialized in the right-wing daily *Adalet*, 20 Sept.-6 Nov. 1969.
95 This circular, dated 26 July, was published in *Cumhuriyet*, 11 Aug. 1969.
96 *Cumhuriyet*, 15 Aug. and *Ulus*, 1 and 5 Oct. 1969.
97 For the results, see above, 201.
98 *Cumhuriyet*, 9 Dec. 1969. For a full exposition of Ecevit's views see

Atatürk ve Devrimcilik (n.d. [1970]). The title is based on Ecevit's speech of 11 Nov. 1969 to the Federation of Social Democratic Associations on the anniversary of Atatürk's death.

99 *Ulus*, 27 and 28 Mar. and 1 Apr. 1970.

100 *Ulus*, 2–7 July 1970 and CHP, *CHP XX Kurultayı: Parti Meclisi Raporu* (1970).

101 *Akşam*, 7 and 9 Dec. 1970.

CHAPTER X

THE POLITICS OF PLANNED ECONOMIC GROWTH 1960-1971

Transformation of agriculture is the crucial problem in developing economies. If farming cannot be transformed, there can be no genuine revolution of economic growth.... There is no doubt, however, that as agricultural methods are thousands of years old, agriculture is the most difficult sector to change. Yet it seems to be a safe rule to put down for developing communities that if you do not change agriculture, you will not change the economy.

Nejat Eczacıbaşı, opening statement at the International Conference on the Agricultural Aspects of Economic Development, Istanbul, 2 August 1964

The Workers' Party of Turkey rejects the view that the state will do what private enterprise cannot. Its notion of étatism is that private enterprise does what the state is not required to do in the interests of the public. State institutions and enterprises should not be used to enrich or give power to private capital. The goal of étatism planned by the people is to meet the increasing material and cultural needs of Turkish society and the Turkish working people and to raise the standard of living of the great mass of the people.

The WPT's pre-election declaration, 1 August 1965

Establishment of the State Planning Organization

THE economy which the National Unity government inherited from the Democrats was bankrupt. Ten years of inflationary policies had virtually exhausted the gold and foreign exchange reserves; the foreign debt stood at around $850 million; the terms of trade had been deteriorating for the past ten years, and exports were stagnating at about $300 million per annum. Under these conditions there was little room for manoeuvre.

Initially, the measures taken by the government amounted to little more than strict application of the economic stabilization programme of August 1958. (Menderes had introduced that programme; for political reasons, however—the measures would have been unpopular and lost his party votes—he had been unable to implement it.) The new government reduced expenditure in the budget by TL 500 million, cutting back on many projects. It placed TL 250 million worth of bonds in banks in order to raise revenues. Some investments in the state sector were cancelled, others were postponed, and this led to a saving of about TL 1,000 million a year.

There was also the problem of restoring confidence and reviving the private sector. The government hoped to do this by abolishing credit ceilings for exports and industrial investment. It also abrogated the National Defence Law of 1956 which had provided for government control over prices and the supply of goods. Thanks to these measures there was a marked improvement in the economic situation, though unemployment increased as a result of the deflationary policies.[1]

All these, however, were short-term measures whose aim was to deal with the existing crisis. The new régime was far more ambitious and intended to place Turkey on a new economic footing. That the economy was uppermost in the minds of the military rulers may be seen in the 'Fifteen Important Decisions taken by the Cabinet' on 20 June 1960, nine of which dealt with economic matters. They included the decision to establish a Planning Bureau to formulate investment policy; to examine funds earmarked for investment but still uncommitted; to carry out fiscal reform without raising taxes; to float a state loan called the 'Freedom Loan'; and to insert into the constitution a provision dealing with the issue of afforestation.[2]

The most important long-term decision was that setting up the Planning Bureau, which soon developed into the fully fledged State Planning Organization (SPO). The Turkish establishment had finally realized that unplanned economic growth involved too many risks for the socio-economic and political structure of the country. Under external pressure (see page 140 above), Menderes is said to have been coming round to this view and he had invited the Dutch economist Jan Tinbergen to report on the Turkish economy.[3] The military rulers, many of whom were staff officers, were fairly sympathetic to the concept of planning. Under their aegis the process moved along more rapidly than it would have otherwise done.

The SPO was created on 30 September 1960 by Law No. 91,

in which the institutional set-up of the new planning body was presented and provisions were made for the preparation of plans. . . .

... [The SPO] was an advisory body under the authority of the Prime Minister. Two bodies were to be in charge of the actual execution of the plan, namely:

1. The High Planning Council, with the Prime Minister or his deputy as chairman, three ministers appointed by the Cabinet, the Undersecretary for Planning, and three department heads of the State Planning Organization. The Council was to discuss and confront political and technical views, and to decide on planning strategy, later to be approved by the Cabinet and transmitted for elaboration to plan experts of the SPO.

The experts' proposals were to be re-examined by the Council and, if approved, submitted for final approval to the Cabinet and the Turkish Grand National Assembly.

2. The (Central) State Planning Organization was to undertake the task of the implementation of the Plan through its three divisional departments: (a) the Economic Planning Department; (b) the Social Planning Department; (c) the Co-ordination Department, mainly responsible for controlling the implementation of the plan.[4]

Not satisfied with this, the military rulers had the principle of a planned economy introduced into the 1961 constitution. Article 41 of the section headed 'The Regulation of Economic and Social Life' states that:

Economic and social life shall be regulated in a manner consistent with justice and the principle of full employment, with the objective of assuring for everyone a standard of living befitting human dignity.

It is the duty of the State to encourage economic, social and cultural development by democratic processes and for this purpose to enhance national savings, to give priority to those investments which promote public welfare, and to draw up development projects.

Article 129 states that:

Economic, social and cultural development is based on a plan. Development is carried out according to this plan.

The organization and functions of the State Planning Organization, the principles to be observed in the preparation and execution, and application and revision of the plan, and the measures designed to prevent changes tending to impair the unity of the plan, shall be regulated by special legislation.[5]

It will be clear from the above that planning was intended to be more than a remedy for economic stagnation and a formula for rapid growth. The planners would be concerned with increasing the GNP, but they would also want to see wealth distributed more equitably, so that the gap between the rich and the poor—which had grown under the DP—could be narrowed. The planners recognized that economic development would require structural changes in Turkish society. Therefore 'social planning' became established as a legitimate and indispensable part of the development effort, with a special 'Department of Social Planning'.[6] Had the planners thought purely in economic terms (if such were possible) they might have won the support and collaboration of businessmen and landowners. As it was, the talk of social change and social justice alarmed them and forced them into a continuous retreat and a mood of non-co-operation.

The Opposition of Vested Interests

Even before the creation of the SPO these circles had been disturbed by the radical talk and aspirations of some members of the NUC. On 4 July 1960 Cemal Gürsel addressed representatives of bankers, businessmen, and trade unions to assure them that '... we are not a Government of revolution, but a Government of reform, and we are provisional'.[7] But about the same time the NUC launched an 'education mobilisation programme' which identified ignorance, laziness, and illiteracy as its principal targets. This programme would require about TL 2,000 million altogether—about TL 200 million a year for the next ten years. To raise this sum the 'first thing considered is the taxation of the income from large estates, that is to say, the agricultural production of big landowners, in order to remove a great taxation injustice and at the same time find the money required for education....'[8]

Side by side with the landowners, the businessmen also felt insecure. There were rumours that the government intended to examine the accounts of business houses and to make the declaration of wealth obligatory. But the businessmen were told, this time by Istanbul's Governor, Refik Tulga, that there was no truth in these rumours.[9]

This atmosphere of insecurity and uncertainty resulted in a stagnant economy. The volume of money that was in circulation dropped, there was scarcely any new investment, stocks of goods remained unsold, production was reduced, and without doubt the only thing that rose was unemployment.[10]

The general recession in economic activity continued into 1961; the poor harvests of 1960 and 1961 made the situation worse. It was obvious that the private sector did not trust the interim régime and was waiting for the general election in October 1961 before making any move. The economic régime was, after all, open to political pressures. The SPO was only an advisory body under the authority of the Prime Minister; all measures had to have the final approval of the cabinet and the Assembly. In these bodies the landowners and businessmen would again be supreme. In the final analysis, planning under parliamentary rule was a political process.

The election campaign was the first step in the undermining of the process of planning. After the experience of the fifties, the planners intended to avoid inflationary financing, hoping to make taxation the main instrument of public saving. They believed that this was the only realistic way to finance the plan, even though progressive taxation would be difficult to introduce under the existing social structure and bureaucracy. And, as already stated, it would be an element in their scheme for social justice.[11]

However, politicians of all parties were promising the voters that they would reduce or even remove taxes if their party was voted in. Finance Minister Kemal Kurdaş, alarmed by this propaganda, described such promises as 'utter madness'. He issued a warning that another experience like that of the decade 1950-60 would open the way to five generations of misery for the Turkish nation; the reduction of taxation would cripple state investments and services. Although the tax burden could be more justly distributed, the chief point for consideration was not the reduction of taxation but how to invest its proceeds profitably.[12]

The reintroduction of party politics restored the primacy of the politicians, who began to sabotage the principles of the plan. Except for the ultra-conservative circles, where the plan was described as a blue print for a socialist society, the private sector generally approved of the idea of planning, though it disapproved of what it described as a diminished role for itself. The plan, argued the businessmen, gave undue importance to the public sector by holding it responsible for 60 per cent of the total investment; this could only mean the growth of the state sector at the expense of private enterprise. They complained that they had been consulted in neither the preparation of the plan nor its annual programmes. Nor had the plan set specific targets for public investment, with the consequence that the private sector could not identify the areas in which it was likely to face competition. This would therefore discourage private investment in certain areas in which the investors felt insecure.[13]

Basing its views on past experience, the private sector was simply voicing its fears of the domination of the economy by the state bureaucracy, recalling the years before the multi-party period. However, planning was not étatism, and, as we have noted, the ultimate control over the plan and the economy was in the hands of a party government and an elected parliament. The risk of 'economic tyranny' would arise only if a single party dominated the Assembly as the DP had done. But the new constitution and the Electoral Law were designed to prevent precisely such an eventuality.

If one judges by İnönü's radio broadcast of 30 September 1961, he and his party seemed committed to a planned economy. If the RPP came to power he promised that investment would be properly planned and he would never permit inflation. Investment in the state sector would be increased, and, at the same time, private enterprise would be given a new life. Taxation would be based on social justice and there would be planning in agriculture in order to increase production so that the peasant's standard of living could be raised. There had to be rapid industrialization and the state would provide aid to small artisans for modernization and to industrialists for expansion. Finally he promised that his party would disseminate the principle of social justice widely.[14]

Had the RPP won the 1961 election by a sufficient majority to form a government, İnönü might have tried to fulfil his promises. Even then, it seems doubtful whether his party, dominated as it was by the large landowners, would have permitted any tax on incomes from large estates. But as the leader of coalition governments formed in partnership with parties hostile to planning (as conceived by the planners), he was forced to make compromises from the very beginning.

İnönü gave priority to winning over the private sector. In four days of talks with businessmen and industrialists, he assured them that 'in actual practice the State and the private sector are not opposed to each other in our country. The important thing is what kind of a relationship should be established between the two. This can be achieved by the co-operation and the mobilization of the resources of both sectors.' In response to their complaint about the lack of consultation, İnönü promised that they would be consulted by the government before any new legislation was introduced; he would meet them at least once every three months.[15]

After the collapse of the First Coalition the private sector wrested more concessions from the state as the price for supporting the Second Coalition under İnönü. The protocol of 24 June 1962 signed by the coalition partners (RPP, NTP, RPNP, and the Independents) included a long section on economic policy. After the fashionable rhetoric of 'economic development within a democratic order', the protocol laid down certain guidelines for the state:

... the State must encourage private enterprise to increase its investments, and to divert them towards the fields necessitated by rapid and balanced development. However, this encouragement must be made through a financial and credit policy, and through the formation of a capital policy, and guidance and technical knowledge, and not through direct interference, which is incompatible with the economic and political order with which we identify ourselves.

... the State must refrain from unnecessary bureaucratic interference which obstructs and checks the form of private enterprise investment or the possibilities of private enterprise operating with stability and confidence. Frankness and decisiveness must form the basis of the State's economic policy, and the finance, currency, price, foreign trade, and investment policies and their implementation must be regulated by enabling private enterprise to be farsighted and to operate with a lasting sense of confidence.... The fundamental principle that must guide the work to be undertaken by the State, should be to make strategic investments, investments necessary for long-term development, and investments that private enterprise cannot undertake.[16]

The private sector had succeeded in having the principle of the mixed economy adopted, in which the state would undertake the unprofitable projects which subsidize private enterprise. This had been the role assigned to the state sector under étatism and it was a far cry from the concepts of the planners. Under these political conditions it was unlikely that the plan which the SPO was in the process of preparing would be acceptable to the cabinet and the Assembly. In April 1962 the government had already rejected the proposals of the British economist, Nicholas Kaldor, for taxing the incomes of large estates. Kaldor proposed taxing the potential average production of the land, leaving everything above this average untaxed so as to encourage productivity. Thus it would be agrarian inefficiency and the under-utilization of land that would be penalized. Had this proposal been accepted, it would have created nearly 2 per cent of investable funds for the plan. But the lobby of big landowners was too powerful and the government preferred to incorporate the agrarian sector into the income tax system, with large exemptions for medium and small plots of land.[17]

By August 1962 the First Five-Year Plan (1963-7) was ready for examination by the High Planning Council. Here it ran into objections from the cabinet. 'The draft [on Agricultural] Reform prepared by the SPO as an appendix to the plan was not even discussed ... because ... the ministers ... were opposed to it...' Another point of disagreement between the planners and the politicians was the proposed reorganization of the state economic enterprises so as to make them efficient, competitive, and profitable. 'This principle of reorganization, almost identical with the organizational pattern of the biggest international corporation, was also refused ... and deleted from the text.' Had the state sector been reorganized it would have become a competitor to the private sector and this was against the philosophy of the mixed economy. Finally, there were the differences over the issue of financing the plan, though 'the principle of a more balanced and economically sound method of financing had already been rejected during the discussions of the Five-Year Plan'.[18]

The government accepted the 7 per cent rate of growth, as well as other objectives of the plan. But political pressures forced it to reject the means necessary to achieve these objectives. In the words of Atilla Sönmez, such an 'attitude has meant, in effect, nothing less than a back-door return to the practices of the governments of unplanned years'.[19] As a result, some of the top officials of the SPO resigned. They claimed that the implementation of the plan had been endangered by the government's refusal to accept the measures necessary to finance it.[20] During the next five years the SPO was unable to stabilize its position within the administration and there was a high turnover of officials, especially at the upper level of the organization. There were four different under-secretaries, four heads of the Economic Planning Department, and three heads of the Co-ordination Department. There was a similar turnover among the technical staff, especially among the experts.[21] Moreover appointments, especially under JP rule, became political, designed to serve the party rather than the SPO. The result was that the discipline required for planning was never fully established and the SPO was unable to acquire a sense of identity.

The SPO had been reduced to what the conservative politicians had originally intended it to be: a bureau to plan government investment. It is true that there was a plan but it did not have much meaning when its purpose was to plan the public sector for the benefit of the private sector, which was by its very nature unpredictable. The SPO did not become the instrument of development that it might have been, aimed not merely at the physical growth of wealth within the established social structure, but at the peaceful transformation of the existing system. The SPO had thought in terms of an initial 15-year plan that would launch a rational struggle against every natural or social force impeding development.

The conservative politicians understood planning to mean 'growth planning', whose purpose was to achieve certain quantitative targets without altering the *status quo* in any drastic way. It was not to be an overall system of intervention. Its function was to be limited to the support—and therefore the development—of the private sector.

Thanks to the efforts of the SPO, the sixties were the golden years of Turkish capitalism. The Menderes decade had also been kind to the businessmen and industrialists but they had always been uncertain of the capricious behaviour of Adnan Menderes. The governments of the sixties, especially after the fall of İnönü in February 1965, all gave priority to their interests. But a number of factors stood in the way of the smooth development of Turkish capitalism. Perhaps the most important single factor was the land question.

The Question of Land Reform

The NUC had made public its intention to deal with the land question and in August 1960 the Ministry of Agriculture was asked to prepare a Land Reform Bill. The Bill was duly prepared and presented to the Constituent Assembly which, occupied with the task of framing the constitution, did not have time even to discuss it. As with planning, the question of land reform was included in the new constitution, whose Article 37 stipulated that:

The State shall adopt the measures needed to achieve the efficient utilization of land and to provide land for those farmers who either have no land, or insufficient land. For this purpose the law may define the size of the tract of land according to different agricultural regions and the types of soil. The State shall assist farmers to acquire agricultural implements.

According to Article 38:

The State and other corporate bodies, where public interest deems it necessary, are authorised, subject to the principles and procedures as set forth in the pertinent law, to expropriate the whole or part of any immovable property under private ownership, or to impose an administrative servitude thereon provided that the true equivalent value is immediately paid in cash.[22]

In a country like Turkey, almost 80 per cent of whose working population in 1960 was dependent on the land, a rational solution to the land question was vital for economic development.[23] Yet this vast work force provided only 40 per cent of the GNP. It was the defects in the agrarian sector which resulted in low productivity and became an obstacle to development. Land reform by itself would not solve all Turkey's economic problems. But there was no doubt that, by making agriculture a dynamic instead of a static sector, economic development would be accelerated and a suitable climate would be created for further progress and development.[24]

According to Hershlag, the land tenure system in Turkey during the sixties could be broadly classified into four major categories:

(1) old feudal land ownership devoid of modernization—in the south-east; (2) the modern management type of large absentee ownership, under wage-relations—in the west and north-east; (3) small and medium ownership, with a growing tendency towards large ownership through concentration of land sold by small peasants—in central Anatolia and in the Adana region, presenting the greatest menace to social equality; and (4) small fractioned and poor villages, the chief reservoir of rural wage earners ...[25]

The tendency of this system was to encourage absentee landlordism and share-cropping (see page 134 above), which discouraged both parties from improving the land. This resulted in low productivity, the depletion of natural and human resources, and a low standard of living. There was no incentive to channel capital, initiative, energy and know-how into the land, and this led to stagnation. Consequently one of the principal goals of any legislation related to the land was to guarantee security to the tiller and that is what the Land Reform Bill attempted to do. It laid down the ceilings to be established on land holdings—maximum holdings varied between 275 and 5,000 *decares*, and minimum holdings between 22 and 400 *decares*. Excess land was to be expropriated (with compensation) and redistributed against cash payments over 20 years. The size of holdings was to be determined according to the requirements of rational exploitation of the land, and the redistribution was to be effected according to the same criterion. Scattered and fragmented plots were to be consolidated and the conditions of share-cropping and tenancy regulated. At the same time the Bill spoke of promoting agricultural co-operatives in order to help the small farmer.[26]

The implementation of this Bill might have ended the situation in which 87·28 per cent of the landholders owned 51·34 per cent of the land while 12·72 per cent—mostly great landlords—owned 46·31 per cent. It might have helped to consolidate the 84 per cent of the holdings which 'are composed of small pieces of land and are separated into still smaller pieces'.[27] But this 'relatively mild reform bill', which contained 'no extreme changes that may upset the roots of society' and which respected 'individual rights of ownership' was too much for the landlords and wealthy farmers. They immediately joined forces and mobilized resistance to these measures through the Federations of Farmers' Organizations.

Since it was impossible to take an open stand against land reform, for it had the sanction of the constitution and the plan, the opponents of land reform tried to demonstrate that it would be harmful for the economy and that the government would be better advised to use its resources to reform agriculture in order to increase productivity. This could be done by land reclamation, irrigation, the increased use of fertilizer, improved seed, mechanization, pest control, increased credits, and other measures of this kind.[28]

There was no question of this Bill being passed by the Turkish Assemblies of the sixties, dominated as they were by conservative forces.[29] İnönü's attempts to have it pushed through were defeated in the Assembly on 11 February 1965, and under Ürgüplü the provisions of the Bill were made more lax. By 1967 the Demirel government had decided to have a new bill prepared. But not even Demirel succeeded in having a land reform scheme passed by the Assembly during his five-year tenure as Prime Minister. In the end his attempts to do so were partially responsible for the fragmentation of his party.[30]

Lop-sided Development

Without reforming the most important sector of the economy, it was virtually impossible to have balanced economic growth. And this proved to be the story of the sixties. The target of 7 per cent for the GNP was not achieved, and individual sectors diverged from the plan. Production in the agrarian and industrial sectors increased only about three-quarters as fast as planned; construction and service industries, which were more profitable, exceeded the planned rate of growth. 'In agriculture, neither new investment nor, more important, the dissemination of new techniques proceeded as rapidly as expected. Insufficient amounts of well-organized investment projects, foreign exchange, and domestic savings ... impeded the full achievement of the desired manufacturing capacity ...'[31] Nevertheless by the end of the decade the economy had again changed its character, and the change was marked by the emergence of what Turkey had lacked for so long, an industrial bourgeoisie.

Initially the private sector, alarmed by what it saw as the growing influence of the state under a planned economy, had held back investments and the economy had stagnated. But by 1963 it was clear that the state would not be permitted to play such a role and that it would act as a back-up to the private sector. The private sector was given complete autonomy in its investment policy, and the plan provided that if it 'does not invest in a field which is regarded as necessary in the Plan and this situation creates significant bottlenecks in the economy, the state or public enterprises will readjust their investment programs to assure realization of the necessary investment'.[32] Bulutoğlu wrote that if private savings did not increase sufficiently to meet the estimates of investment, the private sector would have to be provided with public funds or foreign capital in order to fill the gap. Otherwise, the private investment targets projected in the plan would not be realized.[33]

By 1964 the economy had begun to pick up. In 1963 agricultural production had been high, especially cotton and tobacco. Moreover, foreign capital was beginning to enter the country at a rate unknown before. In the years 1951-61 foreign capital entering Turkey had averaged about TL 12·2 million a year; between 1962 and April 1963 total foreign investment rose to TL 40·3 million, an increase of 229 per cent.[34] This trend continued for the rest of the decade and during the nine years 1960-8 foreign investment in Turkey amounted to TL 551,920,845, or about $61 million at the prevailing rate of exchange.[35] As under the Democrats, foreign capital continued to be regarded as one of the pillars of the economy.

The dependence on foreign capital implied an emphasis on consumer industry—for that is where most foreign investment was made—rather than the capital industry needed to build the infrastructure for an industrial society. An investigation of investment of foreign capital for the years 1951-65 showed that only 0·21 per cent went into agriculture, 1·25 per cent into mining, 0·92 per cent into construction, and 2·34 per cent into service industries, while 95·28 per cent was invested in manufacturing. A further breakdown of the investment in manufacturing showed that 26 per cent went into the plastics and rubber industry, 25 per cent into chemicals, 13 per cent into the electrical industry, and 11 per cent into processed foods, alcoholic beverages and tobacco.[36] The aim of such investment was to exploit local raw materials and relatively cheap labour, and to produce goods which would cater for local consumer demand. Such industries were in no way designed to produce goods for an export market in which they could hardly compete with foreign counterparts. This raises the important question of the ability of Turkish industry to survive within the Common Market once Turkey is integrated into the community.[37]

Foreign investors used their capital in partnership with local businessmen, setting up joint enterprises in conjunction with the state. 'The local investor provides the bulk of the capital; the foreign firm brings in the patent, most of the parts to be assembled, and some managerial and engineering skill; the whole affair comes under state protection, either by way of direct state participation in investments, or by important restrictions which make the product almost a monopoly item enjoying the benefits of non-competitive prices and low wages ...'[38] The result has been the creation of units which assemble prefabricated goods, employ relatively few workers, and produce maximum profits for investors. This kind of structure has been aptly described as the 'Trojan horse' of Turkish industry, serving both foreign and local investors.[39] Nevertheless, the growth of the industrial sector in the sixties was impressive. Its national product increased by 140 per cent in ten years—from TL 13 billion in 1962 to TL 31·2 billion in 1971. In the same period, the increase in the agrarian sector was only 42 per cent. According to the projections for the first six months of 1972, industry's share in the GNP was expected to be greater than that of agriculture, for the first time in Turkish history.[40] This is undoubtedly a turning-point in Turkey's road to economic development, opening up a number of possibilities for the future.

OYAK

However, one development needs to be singled out, since it has serious implications for Turkey's future development, both economic and political. This is the emergence of the armed forces as entrepreneur. The process began on 3 January 1961 when the Law of the Army Mutual Assistance Association was passed, setting up what soon became one of the largest industrial and commercial conglomerates in Turkey.[41] Under OYAK regulations, regular officers of the Turkish armed forces, who number about 80,000, are obliged to invest 10 per cent of their salaries in the fund, to be reimbursed at a later date. In this way OYAK has been able to accumulate capital which is then invested in all the most profitable branches of the economy. It is attached to the Ministry of Defence, but it is run like a corporation by civilian managers and technocrats.

The professed aim of this organization is to provide welfare for its members by supplying loans and other benefits. It has set up 'Army Bazaars', which, like the British NAAFI and the American PX, sell goods to the armed forces at discount prices. But the most notable feature of OYAK has been the rapid expansion it has undergone. Within a few years, the fund has come to have 'controlling interests in Turkish Automotive Industry, a company that assembles International Harvester trucks and tractors; MAT (*Motorlu Taşıtlar Ticaret Anonim Şirketi*), a truck and tractor sales firm; the OYAK Insurance Company; Tukaş, a food canning firm and a $3,000,000 cement plant. OYAK also holds 20 per cent of the $50 million Petkin Petrochemical plant ..., 8 per cent of the state-owned Turkish Petroleum, and 7 per cent of a $5·6 million tire factory owned mostly by Goodyear.'[42] Perhaps its most successful partnership is with Renault of France, in whose Turkish subsidiary OYAK-Renault the army has 42 per cent of the shares. According to the brochure OYAK published on its tenth anniversary, it had started with an initial investment of TL 8,600,000. By 1970 its investments had grown to TL 502 million, and altogether its assets in 1972 were estimated at $300 million.[43]

With such a large stake in the economy, the armed forces can no longer afford to be neutral or above politics. OYAK's links with foreign companies make it the natural ally of the kind of industrialization we have discussed above. But it is diversifying its investments rapidly, and since it has less limited interests than a privately owned organization, it is not unlikely that it will turn to the path of national industrial development. But whatever policy OYAK decides to follow, the impact on the economy and politics of Turkey will be considerable.

Consequences of Lop-sided Development

The economic transformation of the sixties did not take place without creating certain major problems, social, economic, and political. The main cause of these problems was the government's virtual abandonment of many of the restraints on the economy, which gave the private sector free rein. As early as November 1964, Demirel stated that, as a consequence of a government not qualified to run the country, the economy was under severe strains. 'In the first seven months of 1964 there have been 95 bankruptcies on the Istanbul market. The number of workshops which have closed down is 1,495'.[44] This was probably the result of measures taken to overcome the economic stagnation of the early sixties. By the end of 1964 the economy was out of the trough and the conditions for stability and balance were again restored.[45]

But the SPO's projections showed that, unless measures were taken to cut back the spending of the consumer and the state, inflationary pressures would increase in 1965 and prices would rise. It recommended that certain preventive measures be taken before the 1965 budget was introduced in the Assembly. But this was not done and later the budget was defeated by Demirel on the grounds that it 'did not establish a balance' and that 'a deficit of this dimension would open the way to inflation.'[46] İnönü resigned and İhsan Gürsan, the Finance Minister in the new government who belonged to Demirel's Justice Party, introduced the same budget with an additional deficit of TL 500 million. The government did not take a single one of the precautionary measures proposed in the SPO programme for 1965; on the contrary, a number of its decisions put aside all efforts to develop the Turkish economy with stable prices and balanced growth.[47] By the end of the year there was a marked rise in prices, especially of foodstuffs.

The first Demirel government, which came to power in October 1965, opted for development with inflation. This policy tended to burden the wage and salary earners and favoured the businessmen, making at the same time for more rapid, though unbalanced growth. In sacrificing social justice it undermined social peace. Not surprisingly, therefore, this period was marked by workers' strikes for higher wages.[48]

There was sufficient warning of the dangers of such a policy. The Union of Chambers of Commerce published a report in May 1966 appealing for economic stability. It proposed that, to counter all the pressures, Turkey must follow a stable financial and economic policy, stop wage increases exceeding the rate of increase in production and volume of imports, curb public expenditure as much as possible, finance investment with real savings, and, finally, establish a balance between resources and expenditure by obtaining the maximum income from taxes.[49] Even Finance Minister Gürsan, who must assume some responsibility for the inflationary policies, resigned and sent a memorandum to Prime Minister Demirel advising that measures be taken before the inflation became a threat to the régime.[50] But the government took no measures; the inflation continued to gather momentum and was accompanied by political and social disorders.

The Demirel government had made its economic choices and found it difficult to return to a safer road. For example, such was the dependence on foreign aid and capital investment, that, when the flow from the Western countries slowed down or became insufficient for Turkey's needs, the government was forced to turn to the Soviet Union and Eastern Europe, in spite of its ideological reluctance.[51] Even Demirel recognized the need to save Turkish industry from almost total dependence on foreign countries. 'If we look at the composition of our imports, we can see that 45 per cent of our investment goods, 45 per cent of the raw materials, and 10 per cent of the consumer goods are bought abroad. That is why one of the goals of the Turkey of 1970 is to end the total dependence of its industry on the world outside.'[52] The fact that Turkish industrial development was dependent on imports to such a large extent was perhaps the principal reason for Turkey's inability to industrialize. In short, Turkey had not been able to establish an infrastructure; she could not control prices since they depended on imports. Moreover, this connection with foreign capital also divided the private sector between those who benefited from the foreign link and those who did not, and who viewed it as a threat to the national economy. The political implications of this division have been noted elsewhere in the book.[53]

By March 1971, when the military High Command intervened, the Turkish economy was very different from what it had been ten years earlier. Despite the lack of structural reforms, even the character of agricultural production had undergone change: by 1969 the area of land cultivated by machine had risen to 30 per cent, with almost 100,000 tractors. The industrial sector, as we have already noted, had also been transformed. It had outgrown the domestic market and was in search of opportunities outside. In 1971 the Turkish economy was in a blind alley and it required structural reforms in order to break out. This was recognized by the Turkish bourgeoisie. But the political polarization between the representatives of the modern sector (Demirel's JP and segments of the RPP which supported Ecevit) and the traditional sector led by the parties of the Right (NRP, DP, etc.) prevented this taking place within the structure of competitive party politics. Democratic politics also made it difficult to control those forces (trade unions, radical students and workers and their political party, the WPT) which demanded social justice with economic growth. Thus one of the aims of the military intervention was to provide the political climate in which structural changes could be implemented so that Turkey might undertake a new phase of development. How far the High Command was successful in achieving these aims will be discussed in the next chapter.

NOTES

1 A. Sönmez, 'The Re-emergence of the Idea of Planning and the Scope and Targets of the 1963-1967 Plan', in İlkin and İnanç, eds., *Planning*, 35-7; *MER 1960*, 444-5.

2 Ankara Radio, 20 June 1960, in *SWB*, iv/365/c/1-2; *Cumhuriyet*, 21 June 1960; and Weiker, *Revolution*, 21-2. See also 'Plans to Overcome

Economic Difficulties', Ankara Radio, 13 June 1960, in *SWB*, iv/359 /c/2-3.

3 See above, 140; and Doğan Avcıoğlu, *Türkiye'nin Düzeni*, ii (Ankara, 1969), 498-9.

4 Hershlag, *Turkey*, 187; Eren, *Turkey Today—and Tommorrow*, 139-43; İlkin and İnanç, eds., *Planning*, 311-16 which reproduces Law No. 91 from *Resmi Gazete*, 5 Oct. 1960. See also Ibrahim Poroy, 'Planning with a Large Public Sector: Turkey (1963-1967)', *IJMES*, iii/3 (1972), 348-60.

5 İlkin and İnanç, eds., *Planning*, 310.

6 M. B. Kiray, 'On Certain Aspects of the Social Planning of the First Five-Year Plan', and O. N. Torun, 'The Establishment and Structure of the State Planning Organisation', in İlkin and İnanç, eds., *Planning*, 166-80 and 65-6, respectively.

7 Ankara Radio, 4 July 1960, in *SWB*, iv/378/c/4. It is worth noting that Gürsel's cabinets included representatives of big business, men like Daniş Koper (Public Works), Cihat İren (Trade), Kemal Kurdaş (Finance), Şahap Kocatopçu (Industries) and Orhan Mersinli (Communications). See Avcıoğlu, *Türkiye'nin Düzeni*, ii, 497.

8 Ankara Radio, 25 July 1960, in *SWB*, iv/395/c/1. On the same day *Cumhuriyet* reported that the NUC did not intend to leave a class or group which did not pay tax. Gürsel, however, told the press that only the large landowners would be taxed and this would affect only 10 per cent of the population. See *Ulus*, 18 Sept. 1960 and *MER 1960*, 449. These statements reflect the difference between the 'radicals' and the 'moderates' in the NUC.

9 *Cumhuriyet*, 1 Oct. 1960. But Law No. 139, introducing the declaration of wealth, was passed on 31 Dec. 1960. See İsmail Arar, *Hükumet Programları 1920-1965* (1968), 546.

10 Feridun Ergin, 'İşsizlik, Durgunluk', *Cumhuriyet*, 13 Oct. 1960.

11 Sönmez, 'The Re-emergence of Planning' and Kenan Bulutoğlu, 'Financing Turkey's Development Plan', in İlkin and İnanç, eds., *Planning*, 40 and 191-8, respectively.

12 *Cumhuriyet* and Ankara Radio, 12 Sept. 1961, in *SWB*, iv/742/c/1. Kurdaş was the new breed of manager-technocrat which began to emerge in the Turkey of the sixties. They believed in the modern, rational, twentieth-century brand of capitalism which the traditional Turkish businessman found difficult to understand.

13 İ. Öngüt, 'The Private Sector in the Five-Year Plan', in İlkin and İnanç, eds., *Planning*, 162.

14 Ankara Radio, in *SWB*, iv/761/c/2-4. For the RPP's economic programme see Ferruh Bozbeyli, ed., *Parti Programları*, vol. i, pt. 1 (1970), 65-72.

15 Ankara Radio, 1 Feb. 1962, in *SWB*, iv/863/c/1-3 and *Cumhuriyet*, 1 and 2 Feb. 1962.

16 Ankara Radio, 24 June 1962, in *SWB*, iv/979/c/1-3 and the Turkish press, 25 June 1962. See also the economic programme of the Second Coalition in Öztürk, *Hükümetler*, 521-33.

17 Bulutoğlu, 'Financing Turkey's Development Plan', in İlkin and İnanç, eds., *Planning*, 91 ff.; he cites N. Kaldor, 'Report on the Turkish Tax System', a confidential report to the Prime Ministry of Turkey, Apr. 21, 1962.

In 1969 Kaldor told Mehmet Barlas that the Turkish landlords were too powerful and made any land tax impossible. *Cumhuriyet*, 5 Sept. 1969.

18 Sönmez, 'The Re-emergence of Planning', in İlkin and İnanç, eds., *Planning*, 40-1.

19 Ibid., 43.

20 Wayne Snyder, 'Turkish Economic Development: the First Five-Year Plan, 1963-67', *Journal of Development Studies*, vi/1 (1969), 60-6. Poroy notes: 'Thus the failure to introduce institutional and structural reforms in the tax system contributed to the shortfalls of the planned goals.' 'Planning with a Large Public Sector', *IJMES*, iii/3 (1972), 357. On the resignations in the SPO, see above, 217, n. 23.

21 Torun, 'Establishment and Structure of the SPO', in İlkin and İnanç, eds., *Planning*, 70. Baran Tuncer, who resigned as head of the Department of Economic Planning on 4 Oct. 1966, wrote a memorandum to PM Demirel. 'He complained about the government's lack of interest in the Planning Organization, the non-implementation of SPO proposals, rejection of its written reports, and the constant postponement of meetings related to the plan, which should have been held regularly'. *Cumhuriyet*, 5 Oct. 1966.

Next day, Memduh Aytur, a former under-secretary at the SPO, commented: 'If the collapse at the SPO is not immediately halted, the country's economic and national credit will become a subject of grave doubt, both at home and abroad.' *Cumhuriyet*, 6 Oct. 1966.

22 *Constitution of the Turkish Republic* (Ankara, 1961). See also Aktan, 'Land Reform', in ESSCB, *Agricultural Aspects*, 27-8.

23 Sencer, *Türkiye'de Köylülük*, 81. By 1965 the population dependent on the land had been reduced to 75 per cent, and almost 70 per cent by 1969. See Eczacıbaşı's words at the head of this chapter.

24 Aktan, 'Land Reform', as cited in n. 22 above, 38; and Hershlag, *Turkey*, 'The Enigma of Agriculture', 207-15.

25 Hershlag, *Turkey*, 209. Hershlag acknowledges that this incisive analysis comes from Mübeccel Kıray.

26 D. Kayran, 'The Plan and the Agricultural Sector', in İlkin and İnanç, eds., *Planning*, 129-30; Aktan, 'Land Reform', in ESSCB, *Agricultural Aspects*, 28-30.

27 Kayran, as preceding note, 116. See also Minister of Agriculture Turan Şahin's statement in ESSCB, *Agricultural Aspects*, xiii.

28 Aktan, 'Land Reform', as n. 26 above, 30-2. This marked the beginning of the controversy between the 'land reformers' and the 'agrarian reformers'.

29 There were 40 Representatives who described themselves as landowners in the 1961 Assembly. But the majority of those who described themselves in terms of their education in law (*adliyeci ve hukukçu*) were

most probably landowners also. There were 158 in this category. See *TY 1962*, 226.

30 See above, 247; and Avcıoğlu, *Türkiye'nin Düzeni*, ii, 445-50 and 683-8.

31 Snyder, 'Turkish Economic Development', *Journal of Development Studies*, vi/1 (1969) 58. The growth rate of the economy as a whole averaged 6·3 per cent per annum during 1962-7 and dropped to 5·86 per cent in the years 1968-70. This was disappointingly low and many Turkish economists claimed that the economy could grow at 5 per cent a year without any real effort or 'planning' being necessary. With the rate of population growth close to 3 per cent, the actual growth of the economy was reduced further.

32 Öngüt, 'The Private Sector in the Five-Year Plan', in İlkin and İnanç, eds., *Planning*, 154 and 'The Development of a Capital Market in Turkey', in ESSCB, *Capital Formation and Investment in Industry* (1963), 140-1.

33 Bulutoğlu, 'Financing Turkey's Development Plan', in İlkin and İnanç, eds., *Planning*, 189.

34 Muhlis Ete (Minister of Trade), reported in *Cumhuriyet*, 1 May 1963.

35 Bulutoğlu, *Yabancı Sermaye*, 190 provides a table giving the annual breakdown. He also gives figures for the transfer abroad of profits by foreign investors. Between 1965 and Aug. 1969 TL 232,598,315 were transferred as profits.

36 Bulutoğlu, *Yabanci Sermaye*, 162; Aren, *Ekonomi*, 158-63.

37 Turkey's decision to enter the European Economic Community (EEC) is of great significance both politically and economically. The agreement, signed in 1963, provides for a transition period of 12 years beginning in 1970. During these 12 years Turkey will begin to withdraw protective legislation and place its economy on a competitive footing *vis-à-vis* its community partners. There is an ongoing debate on Turkey's future in the Common Market and the literature is scattered and vast. One of the best sources is Gülten Kazgan, *Ortak Pazar ve Türkiye* (1970). See also Aydın Köymen, *Ortak Pazar Gerçeği ve Türkiyenin Sanayileşme Sorunu* (Istanbul, 1974).

38 Mümtaz Soysal, 'The Policy of Mixed Industrial Enterprises in Turkey and its Socio-Political Consequences', *Development and Change*, i/2 (1969-70), 25.

39 Bulutoğlu, *Yabancı Sermaye*, 183 and Mümtaz Soysal, as preceding note.

40 Özlem Özgür, *Türkiye'de Kapitalizmin Gelişmesi* (1972), 177-8. The contribution of agriculture to the GNP decreased from 35·7 to 25·4 per cent in 1970. A billion (*milyar*) in Turkish usage = a thousand millions.

41 See Ordu Yardımlaşma Kurumu Genel Müdürlüğü, *Ordu Yardımlaşma Kurumu Kanunu* (Ankara, 1972); see above, 194 ff.

42 'The Army Conglomerate', *Time*, 11 Sept. 1972, 73. For a fuller inventory of OYAK's assets see *Ant*, 136, 5 Aug. 1969, 8-9. In spite of its

ten years in existence there is no comprehensive study on OYAK, at least none that I know of.

43 Ordu Yardımlaşma Kurumu, *Onuncu Yıl* (Ankara, n.d. [1971]); *Cumhuriyet*, 14 July 1971; and *Time*, 11 Sept. 1972, 73.

44 Demirel's speech in Adalet Partisi, *Adalet Partisi İkinci Büyük Kongresinde Genel Başkan Adaylarının Konuşmaları* (n.d., [1964]), 11. However, the number of millionaires was also increasing. In 1963, during a period of stagnation, there were 117 new millionaires compared to 86 in 1959, 58 in 1958, 53 in 1957, and 43 in 1956. See *Cumhuriyet*, 2 Jan. 1965.

45 Besim Üstünel, *Kalkınmanın Neresindeyiz* (1966), 100-1. This is by far the best book on the Turkish economy in the first half of the sixties, written by a professional economist who also understands politics.

46 Ibid., 101.

47 Ibid., 101-2. On İnönü's resignation see above, 223-4.

48 Dereli, *Turkish Trade Unionism*, 214-18.

49 *Cumhuriyet*, 22 May 1966.

50 *Cumhuriyet*, 1 Nov. 1966. While he was minister he had denied the existence of inflation.

51 F. A. Váli, *Bridge Across the Bosporus* (1971), 180. According to the Turkish-Soviet Agreement on Financial and Technical Aid, 26 Mar. 1967, Moscow agreed to build an oil refinery, an aluminium plant, a sulphuric acid factory, an iron and steel mill, and a lumber factory. Turkey agreed to pay back in goods. See *Cumhuriyet*, 8 Oct. 1970. Also see below, 409.

52 *Milliyet*, 25 Oct. 1970. The service chiefs began to express similar views about the armed forces' dependence on foreign arms and began to consider a domestic arms industry.

53 See above, 244; the industrialization of the sixties also sharpened the regional imbalance between western Turkey and the rest of the country, especially the east. The balance had always been in favour of the Thracian-Marmara-Aegean region and in the sixties industry was concentrated even more in this area. 'Istanbul now comprises 45% of all manufacturing plants in Turkey and produces 48% of the total net value added ...' Soysal, 'The Policy of Mixed Industrial Enterprises in Turkey and its Socio-Political Consequences', *Development and Change*, i/2 (1969-70), 25-6. See also the economic map at the end of Hershlag's *Turkey*, which shows the location of major industries, mineral deposits, and principal agricultural products.

CHAPTER XI

FROM MILITARY INTERVENTION TO GENERAL ELECTION MARCH 1971–OCTOBER 1973

Our community, which has a dynamic structure within the system created by the Constitution, has entered a phase of rapid structural and political change. ... The necessary structural and establishment changes were not made for various reasons, and solutions to problems always lagged behind incidents. This led to important friction between the communal structure and the State system. ... Ending this confused situation and the habits created by it is an important issue that must be solved by the Government. ... This will be possible by fulfilling without delay the necessary reforms in the way shown by the Constitution. Because of this, we are facing Turkish public opinion as a Government of reform and are presenting a programme in conformity with this character ...

Prime Minister Nihat Erim, reading his government's programme in the Assembly, 2 April 1971

The 12 March Memorandum

THOSE who were following events were not taken by surprise when the military commanders intervened and forced Premier Demirel to resign on 12 March 1971. But most observers failed to understand the character of the intervention. The liberal press saw it as an anti-Demirel measure and therefore welcomed it. No one was immediately able to discern which faction in the armed forces had acquired control. The intelligentsia hoped that it was the radical-reformist faction, which was hostile to Demirel and committed to the implementation of reforms included in the 1961 constitution.[1] The memorandum, which called for an end to 'anarchy and strife', and the implementation of reforms, seemed to justify this hope. It read as follows:

(1) The Parliament and the Government, through their sustained policies, views and actions, have driven our country into anarchy,

fratricidal strife, and social and economic unrest. They have caused the public to lose all hope of rising to the level of contemporary civilisation which was set for us by Atatürk as a goal, and have failed to realise the reforms stipulated by the Constitution. The future of the Turkish Republic is therefore seriously threatened.

(2) The assessment by the Parliament, in a spirit above partisan considerations, of the solutions needed to eliminate the concern and disillusionment of the Turkish Armed Forces, which have sprung from the bosom of the Turkish nation, over this grave situation; and the formation, within the context of democratic principles, of a strong and credible government, which will neutralise the current anarchical situation and which, inspired by Atatürk's views, will implement the reformist laws envisaged by the Constitution, are considered essential.

(3) Unless this is done quickly, the Turkish Armed Forces are determined to take over the administration of the State in accordance with the powers vested in them by the laws to protect and preserve the Turkish Republic.

Please be informed.[2]

Responsibility for the situation had been placed squarely on the shoulders of parliament and the government. It was their 'sustained policies, views and actions' which had 'driven our country into anarchy, fratricidal strife, and social and economic unrest'. The formation of a 'strong and credible government' within a democratic framework would 'neutralise the current anarchical situation' and lead to the implementation of the reforms envisaged in the 1961 constitution. That is all the Commanders demanded; if it was not carried out quickly, only then would they take over. These statements amply justified the optimism of the intelligentsia; for almost a decade it had been calling for this solution, and finally the military had stepped in to fulfil its hopes.

Süleyman Demirel resigned with the mildest protest. Thereafter he was most cautious, advising his party to be patient and to await the turn of events. He must have been relieved to learn that the intervention had been carried out to forestall another conspiracy in the armed forces which would probably have resembled the intervention of 27 May 1960. General Gürler, one of the strong men in the junta, is alleged to have telephoned Demirel soon after the memorandum was delivered and assured him that 'We did not do this against you, Süleyman Bey.'[3] Demirel viewed the military situation as a temporary setback and one which may have saved him from permanent disaster.

Initially İnönü's reaction to the memorandum was surprisingly harsh and honest. He told a joint session of his Assembly and Senate Groups:

If high-ranking military commanders are to decide when a Government is to be changed and what the short and long term tasks of newly formed Governments are, and particularly if they put forward suggestions and insist on their implementation as unavoidable measures, then we cannot imagine that parliamentary life can be feasible. Parliament represents constitutional order. It is the place where the procedures for censuring, overthrowing or forming Governments are decided. ...
We believe in a democratic regime. We came to Parliament with the intention of implementing reforms, but there are others who came with other intentions. They are in the majority. ... In these conditions what kind of a Government will be established for the purpose of implementing reforms? The commanders will have to intervene every day so that the Assembly will support the Government. If we have faith in democracy we must accept that a democratically formed Government will carry out these reforms in proportion to its powers.[4]

İnönü, with his vast political experience, had recognized the dilemma facing the armed forces. They had intervened, but with the example of the Greek military junta before them, they were reluctant to assume power directly. They were forced to retain an Assembly dominated by anti-reformist parties and to have reforms carried out by a so-called above-party government. This, İnönü noted, would require constant military interference and therefore an unstable situation. Yet as soon as it became clear that Professor Nihat Erim would form the new government, İnönü decided to support the new régime.

The Erim Governments

President Sunay began to consult party leaders on 15 March. But he excluded the leaders of the NOP, the NAP, the WPT, and the UP from the consultations. The major problem was to find a Prime Minister acceptable to the RPP, the DP, the NRP, and the JP as well as to the National Unity Group in the Senate. Nihat Erim, who had been the choice of the neo-Democrat parties in 1961 to lead the coalition instead of İnönü, seemed to be the candidate who was least controversial. He was officially asked to form a government on 19 March and after some difficulty he announced his cabinet a week later.[5]

Erim described himself as the leader of a national government resembling the Ramsey MacDonald government of 1931 in Britain. The comparison was more apt than Erim may have realized at the time. Like MacDonald, he too became the mere figurehead of a predominantly conservative régime, to be discarded as soon as he had served his purpose.[6] Far from being a national government intended to establish a political consensus, it was a cabinet of contradictions and disunity. Erim described the cabinet as a 'brains trust' (*beyin takımı*) of technocrats which would carry out the reforms. This was a tacit confession that reforms could not be carried out in a democratic régime. 'Fearing the weakness of democracy', noted Harold Macmillan on another occasion, 'men have often sought safety in the technocrats. There is nothing new in this. It is as old as Plato.'[7] Erim adopted the same device and for this purpose he brought in, among others, Atilla Karaosmanoğlu from the World Bank, Özer Derbil from OYAK, Ayhan Çilingiroğlu, a former adviser to the Portuguese government, İhsan Topaloğlu, ex-director of the Turkish Petroleum Company, and Şinasi Orel, a former staff officer who had been placed in charge of the SPO in 1960. They were expected to give the cabinet its dynamism and flair, and keep it on a radical path.

But side by side with the reformers, Erim had been forced to include conservative anti-reformists like Ferit Melen and Sait Ergin, who had been responsible for holding back reform in the coalition governments of the early sixties. The reformers objected to the inclusion of these two men. 'We are putting ourselves forward as a reform cabinet. But amongst us is a Sait Naci Ergin, who represents the bankers. There is a Melen whose personality is impossible to reconcile with our understanding of reform. In that case, let them stay and we will go.'[8] But Erim was able to prevail upon the reformers and they agreed to stay. From the very beginning it was clear that members of the cabinet would find it difficult to work together, especially with the conservatives dominant in the Assembly.

Erim presented his programme to the Assembly on 2 April and his government received a vote of confidence on 7 April. Erim spoke of reforms but stressed that they would be implemented only in an atmosphere of tranquillity and security, implying that the parties, especially the JP, would be consulted. The moderation appealed to the politicians. İnönü described it as a perfect programme. Feyzioğlu found that the programme was in keeping with the principles defended by his party. İlhami Ertem, speaking for the JP, found 'nothing original' in it and said that 'we were ahead of this programme'.[9]

However, the first conflict in the cabinet arose because of Erim's excessive desire to placate the JP. On 5 April during the discussions of the programme he promised that 'We will implement this programme together with you and the party leaders. We will consult often and I shall call upon the Honourable Mr Demirel. If he does not come to me I shall go to him. If he comes to me once I shall go to him twenty times.'[10]

Erim's sentiments may have been noble but the effect they had on the Assembly was as though 'the roof had fallen in'. His words would have been more appropriate under normal political circumstances, when the government was dependent on Demirel's votes. But Erim was supposedly at the head of a reform government backed by the armed forces. His words were interpreted as a sign of weakness by the anti-reformists in the Assembly and encouraged them to resist the government's measures. Ten members of the cabinet objected strongly to Erim's appeasement 'of the very circles who were responsible for today's situation' and sent in a collective letter of resignation.[11] Next day they withdrew their resignation when Erim promised to rectify the situation in the Senate.[12] But a division had emerged between those who believed that reforms could be pushed through despite opposition in the Assembly, and those—like Erim—who realized that the Assembly's support was vital. By the end of the year the first group had resigned in frustration. But the second group accomplished nothing either by working through the Assembly.

Reform or Law and Order?

.So far the headlines had been monopolized by the constant talk of reform. But the discerning eye could also see the new régime's concern with the questions of law, order, and stability. After all, the intervention of 12 March had been a preventive *coup d'état* designed to end the activities of radicals, civilian and military, who wanted to overthrow the government and implement reform.[13] The Commanders had thought it wiser not to confront these forces head on but to deal with them more circumspectly. The first sign that something was amiss in the armed forces came on 17 March, when the press reported the retirement of five generals, one admiral, and thirty-five colonels. Some of these officers had intended to intervene on the night of 9/10 March, but—in order to prevent bloodshed in the army—had been persuaded by the Chief of the General Staff and the Commanders not to act.[14] The Commanders had to deal with unrest not only in the armed forces but also in the civilian elements of the intelligentsia, which were held responsible for leading the armed forces astray. Demirel had found it difficult to handle opposition outside the Assembly within the framework of the 1961 constitution. He had often proposed amending some of its articles which gave 'too much freedom' or which were being 'exploited by irresponsible people'. But he had never enjoyed a two-thirds majority to amend the constitution. It was only logical that some of the Commanders, who had reached the conclusion that the post-27 May régime had proved unworkable, should want to modify the instrument which they believed was responsible.

The fresh outbreak of urban guerrilla activity in April 1971 created the atmosphere for the introduction of a repressive régime. The kidnapping and bank robberies by a group calling themselves the 'Turkish People's Liberation Army' enabled the government to give priority to law and order over reform. Rumours that military officers and cadets were directing this force were confirmed by government intelligence sources. Within a short time military intelligence, responsible to General Tağmaç, the COGS, was set up alongside MİT, both organizations taking away much of the initiative and power from the civilian government.[15] By 22 April the government, which was allegedly opposed to amending the constitution, had given way. Deputy Premier Sadi Koçaş, the armed forces representative in the cabinet, announced that 'from today we are declaring war on all those who come against the law'.[16] İsmail Arar, the cabinet's spokesman, said that the government wished to amend the constitution in order to have extraordinary powers at its disposal until lawlessness had been eradicated and reforms affected. 'We are giving priority to the problem of lawlessness rather than to reforms because individuals and organizations who oppose social injustice in the country continue to violate law and order without even waiting to see what our Government does. ... Amendments similar to what we are asking already exist in the constitutions of France, West Germany and Italy.'[17] With priority given to law and order, it was only a matter of time before the country was brought under martial law.

Martial law was proclaimed on 27 April in eleven of Turkey's sixty-seven provinces, namely Ankara, Istanbul, İzmir, Kocaeli, Sakarya, Zonguldak, Eskişehir, Adana, Hatay, Diyarbakır, and Siirt. The reason for martial law, claimed İsmail Arar, was to deal with 'a powerful and active uprising discovered against the Nation and the Republic'. The National Security Council, which had first discussed the question, had given four reasons: to check activities against the secular Republic; to put an end to ideological and bloody incidents; to stop divisive activities in the eastern provinces, and to afford a favourable position for possible action in Cyprus.[18]

It is difficult to see how a state with such deep roots as the Turkish Republic could be threatened by the kinds of activities that were outlined. It seems that the purpose of martial law was to terminate political activity outside the Assembly, just as the 12

March memorandum had shelved politics within it. During the first few days of martial law, political youth organizations were banned and political meetings or seminars of professional groups or trade unions were forbidden. Halil Tunç, the Secretary-General of Türk-İş, stated rather timidly that if workers' rights were narrowed down the reaction would be harsh.[19] On the 28th the newspapers Akşam and Cumhuriyet were suspended for ten days and bookshops were warned that they would be prosecuted for selling forbidden publications. Next day Çetin Altan (Akşam) and İlhan Selçuk (Cumhuriyet) were taken into custody and all the remaining left-wing or radical journals like İşçi-Köylü, Proleter Devrimci Aydınlık, Aydınlık, Türkiye Solu, Devrim, and Ant were proscribed, while militant rightist journals like Durum or Yeniden Milli Mücadele continued to be sold.[20] On 3 May the martial law authorities in Ankara forbade strikes and lockouts, and to all intents and purposes the same ruling was applied to all areas under martial law.[21] At one stroke the militancy of the workers had been extinguished. It is true that employers were forbidden to hold lockouts, but with passive workers they would no longer need to do so. The authorities promised to arbitrate between workers and employers; but arbitration implies the recognition of some justice on both sides to a dispute, and the stability of existing relationships on both sides which need to be readjusted through arbitration when they fall out of balance. By making the strike a legal offence the authorities established an unequal relationship, beneficial only to the employers. It is not surprising, therefore, that this class gave total support to the Erim government.

The full force of repression was felt only after 17 May, following the abduction by the urban guerrillas of Ephraim Elrom, the Israeli consul in Istanbul. This incident was a grave blow to the prestige of the state, and Sadi Koçaş told the Senate that the government would defend the honour of the state and demonstrate its presence. The same day he broadcast a warning to the guerrillas that if Elrom were killed the government would pass a law instituting retroactively the death penalty for kidnapping. The constitutionality of such a law was doubtful and it was challenged by the reformist faction in the cabinet led by Atilla Karaosmanoğlu.[22]

It mattered little what the civilian ministers thought, for the martial law commanders and the intelligence services were in full control. It was the turn of the intellectuals to be rounded up by the police and Cumhuriyet of 19 May reported that 427 persons had been taken into custody in 19 provinces. They included trade unionists, members of the WPT, writers of renown like Yaşar Kemal and Fakir Baykurt, and professors like Bahri Savcı, Bülent

Nuri Esen, Tarık Zafer Tunaya, and Mümtaz Soysal. This was most embarrassing for Professor Erim since many of those in custody were friends and colleagues; but there was nothing he could do. The idea of resigning does not seem to have crossed his mind.[23] All these measures did not save Elrom; if anything they drove his kidnappers into a corner. On the afternoon of 22 May the government announced a curfew in Istanbul from midnight to 3 p.m. the following day. During these hours a house-to-house search would be carried out by 30,000 troops in order to ferret out the guerrillas. Elrom's body was found at 5 a.m.; the autopsy showed that he had been killed soon after the announcement of the curfew the previous day.[24]

The struggle against the Left provided the backdrop for all other activity and for the next two years martial law was renewed every two months with regularity. For Erim and the military the amendment of the constitution became the primary goal. The amendments were to cover almost all the institutions of the state: the unions, the press, radio and television, the universities, the Council of State, the Constitutional Court, the Assembly, the Senate, and the Court of Appeal. The rights and freedoms provided by the 1961 constitution would have to be brought within certain limits so that 'the integrity of the State with its country and nation, the Republic, national security, and public order could be protected'.

When Erim made clarifications in respect of the amendments he stressed that 'everyone ought to bear in mind once and for all: that there is no going back to the period before 12 March.'[25] This was the crux of the matter: the new régime wanted to guarantee that Turkey did not live through another period of liberalization with all its risks. That is what Erim had meant when he said that the 1961 constitution was a luxury for Turkey, a luxury an under-developed country could ill afford on its progress along the road to capitalism.[26]

Constitutional Amendments

There was much discussion in the press on the question of the amendments. Those in opposition argued that it was not the constitution that was to blame but the politicians who had failed to implement it. Ecevit argued that constitutional amendments could be considered *after* the reforms—which had already been delayed ten years—were implemented. There had been a turning-point on 27 May which had opened up new horizons to Turkish society, and the freedoms it had brought must not be curtailed. To Erim's argument that the Turkish constitution was more progressive than the constitutions of some European countries, Ecevit replied that the government ought not to respond to this by making the Turkish constitution regressive. Rights and freedoms in Europe were more deeply rooted than in Turkey and therefore did not have to be guaranteed. In Turkey rights and liberties were new and had not taken root and that is why the constitution had to guarantee and protect them.[27]

Erim had himself called for a public debate on the constitution, but the debate was in fact academic. Opposition to this measure would not be permitted to have any influence. The parties of the Right (the JP, the DP, the NRP, and the NAP) were delighted with the proposed amendments. The Justice Party found that the changes were far more thorough-going than even it had dared to envisage and seemed to justify all that the party had claimed about the 'dangerous situation' months before 12 March. That is why Hasan Dinçer could state truthfully, though with a touch of understatement: 'There is some resemblance between the declarations of the Honourable Prime Minister Erim and the preparations we had made.'[28]

The opposition to the amendments was limited to mild criticism by Türk-İş, the Chamber of Architects, Fakir Baykurt's Turkish Teachers' Union, and other professional bodies. Even İnönü and the RPP decided not to offer serious opposition. Had there been no martial law there would have been opposition both vocal and active, especially from the students. But Turkey was in the grip of repression with thousands in custody. The Workers' Party of Turkey was dissolved on 20 July and since its leaders were in goal there was no one to raise the voice of protest. Only Mehmet Ali Aybar, who had been expelled from the WPT in February 1971, was able to use the parliamentary forum to protest. 'The proposed amendments of the Constitution', he declared, 'are against the philosophy and the basic principles of our current democratic Constitution; their aim is to proscribe socialism and for this reason they cannot be reconciled with the contemporary understanding of a democratic régime.'[29]

No one responded to Aybar's accusations, though Erim tried to reassure the country that, although the constitution was closed to socialism, it was still open to social democracy.[30] The Assembly passed the amendments on 6 September and the Senate followed suit on 20 September.[31] With the 'political reforms' out of the way the Erim government felt in a position to deal with the socio-economic reforms.

Defeat of the Reformers

Erim had come to power to carry out the reforms that would restore the equilibrium of the system, reforms which the democratic and liberal institutions of the Second Republic had not permitted. The sixties had been a period of rapid economic expansion and social change, and once again, as in the fifties, the socio-economic imbalances in Turkish society threatened the stability of the political régime. 'Had there been no inflation after 1954 there would have been no 27 May'; and no 12 March but for the spiralling inflation of the sixties. Once again it was the 'inflationist politicians who breast-fed the Marxist, Leninist and Maoist movements in Turkey', and became indirectly responsible for the breakdown which invited military intervention.[32]

In the sixties there had been lopsided economic development: the modern sector (especially those areas—dominated by foreign capital—that were concerned with the assembly of parts, mostly imported) had grown rapidly while the traditional sector, especially agriculture, had lagged behind. 'The JP's preoccupation to create a modern industrial society and a class of industrialists forced it to fight and retreat in its first encounter with the economic and political wills of the big landowners, the usurers, businessmen in league with foreign capital and having external connections, as well as the owners of real estate.'[33] Reform was badly needed to restore the balance. Although all segments of the power structure—the army, the parties, the bureaucracy, the universities, industry and commerce—recognized this, they were divided as to the nature and the degree of reform. Demirel had found it impossible to cope with this complex situation within the framework of democratic politics and that is why the army had intervened, intending to hold the ring while the necessary reforms were carried out.

Nihat Erim thought he had been given the power to push through the reforms. Initially he seemed determined to do the job. 'I am not a Prime Minister who came to power through election. ... My [cabinet] friends and I are not appeasers. We have not come here to conduct an administration of appeasement. ... No, we have no anxiety about winning an election to come.'[34] He promised to carry out the reforms envisaged in the 1961 constitution, especially those concerned with land, education, and tax. 'I am putting my greatest trust in Turkish public opinion ...; today, as you know, democracy means public opinion democracy, that is to say it is no longer ballot-box democracy ...'[35]

However, Erim was given the task not only of carrying out

reforms in order to restore stability, but also, at the same time, of speeding up the process of industrialization. In an early statement, before law and order and political reform became the principal issue, Erim declared that he would set up a new Ministry of Heavy Industry and Technology. 'Regardless of the name of the ministry, importance must be attached to heavy industry. Industrialisation is essential for Turkey and heavy industry has a great part to play in this. We have been saying that we must manufacture machines and must free ourselves from assembly industry [*montaj sanayii*]. So we have to make a start to achieve our goal.'[36]

The government programme expressed similar sentiments. It envisaged nationalizing natural resources in order to limit foreign controls in this area of the economy. It proposed modernizing agriculture in order to increase production and rural wealth, and a tax on agricultural wealth so as to free resources for industry. It also contained proposals to curb tax evasion so as to raise more revenue and introduce a greater degree of social justice.[37] Immediate measures had to be taken, noted Vehbi Koç, if Turkish industry was to survive the competition of the Common Market. He was even apprehensive that private enterprise in Turkey would be destroyed unless the reforms were carried out quickly. If private enterprise were to continue, the government would have to support all its initiatives; the scope of free enterprise in Turkey was limited and the state was the biggest partner of the private companies.[38]

Erim's programme appealed to the most developed sector of the Turkish economy, namely modern industry represented by men like Koç. For the rest, the possibility of reform was alarming, especially the talk of land reform, the land tax, and restrictions on foreign ties and capital. This alarm was compounded when Karaosmanoğlu was appointed Deputy Prime Minister in charge of the economy.

Atilla Karaosmanoğlu, an ex-World Bank bureaucrat, who served one of the principal institutions of the capitalist world, was regarded by the Turkish capitalists as a radical socialist, a threat to their very existence. His broadside against Demirel's economic policies aroused great controversy. He denounced the devaluation of August 1970 as a measure carried out under foreign pressure. The foreign debt of TL 3·4 billion incurred by the JP government did not justify the limited economic development accomplished. He exposed the fact that while $112 million had been invested in Turkey as foreign capital, $121 million had been transferred abroad as profits. The period of encouraging the private sector, he warned, was over. Agricultural wealth would be taxed and land reform implemented. At the present rate of development, he concluded tongue in cheek, Turkey would need 2,359 years to reach the level of the Common Market.[39]

Erim's programme of reform ran into strong opposition. The business community, except for the largest entrepreneurs and industrialists, still a small minority, considered the programme a threat to their very existence. Raif Önger, President of the Union of Chambers [of Commerce and Industry] of Turkey, claimed that the private sector was the guarantee of the country and its democracy. He stated that any attempt to remove this guarantee would shake the economy, destroy stability, and damage the well-being of the nation. Such was the situation. The government ought not to be opposed to private enterprise; on the contrary in ought to stand by its side.[40] The government's policy towards foreign capital, which Önger interpreted as being hostile, was also criticized. Any policy which insisted that Turks hold 51 per cent of the capital in a given enterprise was self-defeating in view of the country's need of capital investment for new technology. Önger stated his preference for the continuation of the open-door policy.[41]

The business community feared the growth of either monopoly capitalism in the hands of a few giant organizations or the re-emphasis on state capitalism; in either case they knew that they were threatened. The landowners were bitterly opposed to the government schemes for land reform and the tax on agricultural income. Together, the businessmen and the landowners provided formidable opposition to the Erim government.

Erim had already lost much of his prestige and credibility amongst the intelligentsia for carrying out the 'political reforms', a euphemism for the destruction of liberal democracy, before the socio-economic reforms. Before he could even begin to achieve these reforms, he sacrificed İhsan Topaloğlu, one of his principal reformist ministers. Topaloğlu had made a reputation for himself as the opponent of foreign control over Turkey's mineral resources. He was unpopular with the business community, which regarded his views as a discouragement to foreign investment. He had not received the support he had expected from Erim—in fact, there were rumours of serious differences—with the result that he resigned on 28 September.[42]

Topaloğlu's resignation was the more surprising, coming as it did immediately after a strong statement by the Commanders to the effect that the reforms would be carried out under their régime. 'The principle stipulated by the forces command is, in brief: Reforms will be categorically instituted because the second part of the second article of the memorandum refers to Atatürk's reforms and their implementation. As the forces command, we oppose

delays, time-wasting and avoiding reforms in one way or another.
... The forces command will follow the reforms to the very end ...
and will ensure that they are implemented.'[43]

Erim, encouraged by this support, believed that the reforms
would now be accepted by the politicians. Instead, he found
himself confronted with a cabinet crisis brought on by Demirel's
decision to withdraw JP ministers from the cabinet.[44] Demirel
claimed that the decision was not taken impulsively or without
reason. After the 12 March memorandum it had been decided to
set up an impartial and above-party government under a neutral
premier. However, the government's attitude during the past seven
months had been neither impartial nor above-party, and Erim's
speech of 29 September [when he invoked the Commanders'
support] was incompatible with his policy.[45]

Demirel's manoeuvre was interpreted in the cabinet as an
attempt to sabotage the reforms. The press described it as an
indirect assault on Erim's technocrats, designed to eliminate them
from the cabinet.[46] Erim himself was expected to resign; but for the
time being the crisis was put on ice until after Queen Elizabeth II's
state visit (18-25 October). On 12 October Erim rejected the
resignations of Özalp and Akçal and abolished the portfolio held
by Kitaplı.

The day after the Queen left the country Erim submitted his
resignation but it was rejected by President Sunay.[47] Two days
later Chief of the General Staff Memduh Tağmaç stated in his
Republic Day message that 'the dangerous situation' would not be
permitted to continue. But he softened his warning by reassuring
the anti-reformist forces that the commanders would not take over,
that they 'earnestly believe that the Turkish nation's most
authoritative organs, Parliament and the Government, will solve
the present crisis in a way best suited to our national interests ...,
[and they are] determined to support with all their might the
authoritative organs of the Government. ...'[48]

Demirel's concession, in order to meet the Commanders half
way, was to revoke the party's decision on its cabinet ministers.[49]
The cabinet crisis had been resolved to Demirel's satisfaction. He
had taken the measure of the armed forces and learned that his
party was indispensable to the political forces. During November
his position became ever stronger and on 3 December the press
announced that Mesut Erez, Demirel's Finance Minister, had been
appointed Deputy Prime Minister.

This was too serious a concession for the reformist technocrats
to accept, and eleven of them resigned collectively, forcing Erim to

do so on the same day.[50] Their letter of resignation to Erim was written in the following terms:

Our resignation is the culmination of a number of reasons which have been developing for over eight months. We took office in a government which was founded with the aim of implementing within the Atatürkist view-point reforms and a developmental drive needed by the country. And we have resigned in the belief that it is no longer possible to carry out these aims. Mesut Erez's inclusion in the cabinet was the last drop which made the glass flow over. But to link these resignations only to Mesut Erez's appointment to the cabinet would weaken the real reason for our resignations.[51]

The reformers resigned in frustration and disgust. Ever since 12 March there had been no progress towards reform and as time went on the anti-reformist forces became more confident. Land reform, which was considered vital if structural changes were to be introduced into the economy and society, had once again become bogged down in controversy. The measure was denounced as a leftist scheme threatening property rights guaranteed by the constitution. Bahri Dağdaş, Demirel's former Minister of Agriculture who defected to the DP, criticized the land reform bill as 'having been prepared according to Marxist-Leninist views to such a degree that the Workers' Party text seemed sugar-coated in comparison.'[52]

The opposition in the Assembly was so strong and so organized that it succeeded in having the discussion of the measure diverted from reform of the landholding system to the reform of agriculture.[53] By November the opposition had made such inroads into the proposal that even Atilla Karaosmanoğlu conceded that the Bill had been reduced to a state in which it could no longer be implemented.[54]

To many observers it had been clear that there would be no land reform while Professor Orhan Dikmen was Minister of Agriculture. *Devrim* had described him as the most reactionary member of the cabinet, the son-in-law of a Giresun notable (*eşraf*) who had been one of the saboteurs of the reform after the revolution of 27 May 1960. His appointment had even cast doubt in the minds of the technocrats concerning Erim's sincerity about reform.[55] Their worst fears had been confirmed..

Since land reform was said to be supported by influential capitalist circles, led by Vehbi Koç and Nejat Eczacıbaşı, its defeat was surprising. Yet it only confirmed the power of the traditional-conservative forces which had been dominant throughout the multi-party period. Erim's boast that he and the Commanders would not permit the reforms to 'degenerate' had been exposed. Nothing prevented the Commanders from intervening on behalf of the reforms except that they too were divided, and some had a stake in the existing system. The conservative forces had learned that the Commanders, intimidated by their experience after 27 May as well as by the bankruptcy of the Greek junta, were unwilling to step in and assume power. The initial euphoria for reform had been dissipated and the politicians had succeeded in wearing down the Commanders' enthusiasm.

When Erim announced his second cabinet on 11 December 1971 he abandoned the 'brains trust' and the idea of bureaucratic reform as a dismal failure. The second cabinet included no Karaosmanoğlus and no women, and the Ministry of Culture was quietly scrapped. The gimmicks Erim seemed so fond of were abandoned. The new cabinet included unrepentant conservatives like Melen, Ergin, and Dikmen or colourless bureaucrats who would not have an abrasive effect on the Assembly, as the 'brains trust' had had.[56] The reforms had not been abandoned: by this time Erim had come round to the view that he had a better chance of achieving them by appeasing the Assembly and the parties than by bullying them.

Turkey's business circles, in contrast to the industrialists, were delighted with the removal of 'the Eleven' from the cabinet. Naim Talu, President of the Central Bank, who became Minister of Foreign Trade in the new cabinet, held 'the Eleven' responsible for the inflation in the country. Turhan Feyzioğlu's NRP, using smear tactics, claimed that the ministers who had resigned had had close relations with the 'extreme leftists' then on trial.[57] The Chambers of Commerce throughout the country, with few exceptions, hailed the new cabinet and promised to give it their support.[58]

Erim's programme met most of the demands of the business community. It stressed a return to parliamentary democracy, protection of the interests of the private sector, encouragement of foreign capital investment, and support for NATO. The plans to nationalize the oil and borax industries were dropped. 'Efforts will be made to instil confidence in the private sector so that it may make investments commensurate with our economic development plans. We believe that the private sector should receive as much attention as the public sector does. We therefore expect the private sector to fully and expeditiously carry out its duties by giving serious consideration to the interests of the country. Our Government will introduce the necessary incentive measures which will ensure the rapid achievement of investments by the private sector and increase our exports.'[59]

The Right in Political Control

Erim's second term as Premier proved no more successful than the first and culminated in his resignation on 17 April 1972. For his part, Erim did his best to appease and conciliate Demirel but he was able to procure no concessions in return. The policy of depending on the JP's majority in the Assembly did not pay off either, and Erim was unable to have any of his schemes for reform enacted. Demirel, who had been ousted ten months earlier, had succeeded in becoming once again the dominant figure in Turkish politics. His influence on government policy was such that the Republicans claimed that they could see no difference between what might be a JP government and the Erim government.[60] The roles had been reversed and the RPP had once again become the opposition party. It was İnönü who began to oppose the martial law régime and the legislation for hanging political offenders; Demirel found both measures necessary.[61]

Erim's policy of appeasing the political Right seems to have been calculated to seduce this group in the Assembly into surrendering extraordinary power to the government. The continuing tension caused by urban guerrilla activity and the government's counter-measures created an atmosphere of ongoing crisis. Martial law was extended with regularity, but even after almost a year of military rule, 'law and order' had not been restored. Capital punishment for guerrilla activity was passed by the Assembly (although the measure was overruled by the Constitutional Court). Erim then proposed the establishment of special courts to deal with extremist activities once martial law was lifted, and this too was acceptable to most of the Assembly. However, it refused any concessions that would make the government in any way independent of the parties.[62]

Erim wrote to the party leaders on 18 March 1972, the day he left on an official visit to the United States, proposing certain changes in the legal code and the constitution so as to purge the bureaucracy and the universities of 'leftists', and suggesting that a 'State Security Court' (*Devlet Güvenlik Mahkemesi*) be set up.[63] The parties, with the exception of the RPP, had no objection to the establishment of a system which would have little in common with democracy, except in the most formal sense. But they objected strongly to a letter from President Sunay asking that political debate be halted temporarily until reforms had been carried out, and that the government be given the power to rule by *kararname*—edicts which would have the force of law.[64]

Erim tried to reassure the parties that Sunay's letter was no ultimatum and that the government had no intention of limiting political activity. He reiterated that neither Sunay, the government, nor the commanders wanted to implement the third clause of the memorandum of 12 March 1971 threatening intervention and military rule. All he wanted was to be given the power to rule by edict until the general election, due in October 1973.[65] The party leaders agreed to consider Sunay's requests and after a few days of deliberation answered with an emphatic and unanimous 'No!' They refused to surrender their power of control, claiming that the constitution prohibited government by edict. It was not possible for them to freeze the activities of the parties since the party was an institution which, according to the constitution, could not be ignored. Furthermore, silence would hardly be reconcilable with democracy.[66]

As far as Demirel was concerned this was the end of Erim as Prime Minister. There was no question of the JP supporting him any longer: 'here was someone who had been a law professor making a greater blunder than the one he was trying to put right.' His greatest sin was that 'he wanted to place the government above Parliament by ruling the country through administrative edicts' while claiming 'I will not be a Premier of an administration not supported by Parliament.' At the same time he tried to use the National Security Council to obtain a vote of confidence for himself by threatening to resign.[67]

The Democratic Party tried to bring about Erim's fall by introducing a question in the Assembly and not giving him a vote of confidence. But the wily Demirel knew it was more politic not to make the parties responsible for his resignation. The Assembly rejected the DP question on 10 April 1972, but all the foundations of Erim's power had already been sapped. His resignation was now a mere technicality and once again it was the visit of a foreign dignitary, this time Nicolai Podgorny, which delayed matters. Asked by a correspondent to comment on a foreign radio broadcast reporting that he had in fact already resigned and was merely waiting for Podgorny's departure to announce it, Erim replied 'no comment'.[68] Podgorny left on the 17th and Erim's resignation was announced the same day.[69]

Why had Erim been discarded? Essentially because over the past year his meandering course had left him without support in any quarter. He had started out a reformer supported by the intelligentsia and soon came to be hated by them for leading a government which acquiesced to torture in the execution of its repressive policies. He had started out relying on İnönü, and when that support proved inadequate, he turned to Demirel whom he had earlier attacked. Finally he had started out depending on the Assembly and ended up seeking to override it. In the end not even the Commanders were able to follow his course and this time when he threatened to resign, as he had often done in the past, they simply let him go.

Erim's departure did not become the cause of a political crisis; if anything there was a sigh of relief and a decrease in political tension. He was not even pressed to remain in power until a new Premier had been appointed. Ferit Melen, the Minister of Defence and spokesman for the Reliance Party in the cabinet, was made acting Prime Minister and it was only on 25 April that President Sunay began to consult political leaders about a new appointment.

Suat Hayri Ürgüplü was asked to form the new government on 29 April. This choice suggested that the Commanders had accepted Demirel's view that the country ought to have a government which would take the country to the polls. Ürgüplü was an experienced statesman who had played precisely the same role in 1965 and the party leaders found him most suitable. He promised to form a brand-new cabinet and to carry out all the reforms before the election. On 13 May he presented his proposed cabinet and Sunay rejected it without giving any reasons. Ürgüplü resigned.[70]

This was the first occasion in the annals of modern Turkish history that a President had rejected a cabinet. The rejection was all the more surprising since it came after the cabinet had been made public by Ürgüplü. Sunay had found the new ministry acceptable but it seems that the Commanders had raised objections. One can only speculate as to the objections, since they were not made public. Ürgüplü's cabinet, in contrast to those before and after it, was a genuine coalition consisting of all the principal parties (JP, RPP, DP, and NRP). It is conceivable that Demirel and the Commanders objected to the strong representation of the RPP and the DP in a cabinet which was to lead the country to a general election. Ürgüplü had given nine portfolios to the JP, five to the RPP, three to the DP, and two to the NRP. The remaining five ministers had no party affiliation.[71] Such a cabinet would have been difficult to manage, especially as the country prepared for the election. Ürgüplü was therefore asked to make some changes, but he refused to do that at such a late hour and preferred to resign.

Acting Premier Ferit Melen was now invited to form a government. The composition of his team suggests that there was some truth to the hypothesis that Demirel had objected to the inclusion of Democrats in the Ürgüplü ministry and Melen took care to leave them out.[72] It is noteworthy that the Prime Minister was not asked to resign from his party as Erim had been, nor required to be an Independent like Ürgüplü. Melen belonged to one of the smaller parties of the Right, one which had no hope of upsetting the balance in the election and this made him an acceptable candidate. The fact that he had been Defence Minister since 26 March 1971 suggested also that he was acceptable to the Commanders.

On the day he was appointed Melen stated that his priorities would be to prevent disorder—a reference to the guerrilla activities—and to implement economic, cultural, and legal reforms. Once again the emphasis was on the economy and he promised to decide on the strategy of the Third Five-Year Plan and put it into operation. The aim was to lead the way to economic growth and take serious and effective precautions to halt unemployment, already a very serious problem.[73]

In spite of the continuing talk of reforms, it was incongruous to expect Melen to execute such measures since he had spent the better part of his political life obstructing reform. The cabinet's programme, it was widely noted, neglected to emphasize reform and the government sought to identify itself with Kemalism, which in Turkey has become 'the last refuge of scoundrels'. Many members of the Assembly, noted *Yanki*, preferred to sip tea and coffee in the corridors rather than listen to Melen's thirty-page programme. Nothing fresh was expected from him and he was careful not to spring surprises. He promised to prepare the necessary climate for the election, wipe out anarchy, and fight against both communism and the extreme Right, as well as against 'divisive activities', the last being a reference to Kurdish separatism. He promised to take measures against the recurrence of anarchy. These would include land reform, as well as the reform of justice, administration, education, agriculture, the taxation system, and finance.[74]

Atilla Karaosmanoğlu, asked to comment on the programme, summed up his criticism by expressing scepticism about the possibility of reform:

It may be said that this programme is one which does not say what, why, how, or when anything will be done.... Everyone can see, in terms of political preferences, how far removed it is from openness and clarity. For example, those who read the sections dealing with financial, tax, educational and administrative reform will not understand what the government wants to do....

... There may be reasons for this. The main reason may be that this government may not want to carry out serious reforms. It will satisfy itself by describing whatever laws are passed by Parliament as 'the reforms'. Another reason for not stating openly the reforms to be carried out may be to avoid controversy over the support for the government by the parties which are in conflict [over the question of reform]. But I believe that a politician like Melen ... who has not expressed openly certain topics in the programme, will not take the initiative to carry out serious reform later on.[75]

In June there was again talk of constitutional amendment before the election. Melen had begun to hold consultations with the party leaders, and the Commanders were supporting him one hundred per cent. It was now made public that, throughout 1970, Chief of the General Staff Memduh Tağmaç had often warned Demirel that the constitution needed to be amended. But Demirel had complained that he lacked a majority in the Assembly to carry this out. No wonder people were claiming that the memorandum had served and vindicated the Justice Party; since 12 March 1971 the régime had done by extraordinary means—create 'law and order'— what Demirel had failed to do democratically.[76] All the party leaders except Ecevit, who had recently ousted İnönü from the leadership of the RPP, supported the idea of constitutional amendment. Ecevit argued that there was no need for amendments since the same needs could be met by special laws.[77]

The purpose of amending the constitution, said Turhan Feyzioğlu, was to facilitate the working of the Assembly; to create a situation in which threats to national existence, unity, and 'the free democratic régime' could be met without resorting to martial law each time. This would involve setting up special courts—the State Security Courts—to try serious political crimes against the country and the republic; and reforming the law governing political parties, which permitted the establishment of parties, notably on the Left, that were alien to the spirit if not the content of the constitution. 'What we want to do is not weaken the democratic régime but to protect and strengthen it. The goal is not to limit the freedoms unnecessarily but to enliven the free democratic order and to protect it from the threats of those who want a totalitarian dictatorship ...'[78] In spite of the lip service to democracy, the régime by its measures was in fact undermining it.

Bülent Ecevit argued that instead of having an extraordinary régime, as the supporters of the amendments were proposing, Turkey should return to a normal régime. There was no point in amending the constitution in such a harsh and undemocratic manner simply to be able to govern the country without martial law. To do so would be to sacrifice the substance of democracy in order to retain the semblance of it.[79]

Struggle for the Presidency

As Turkey entered 1973 virtually all the old problems remained unsolved. Martial law was still functioning, with no end in sight. The constitution, only partially amended, awaited further amendments. There was still talk of the reforms, but they were no closer to being implemented. The working class had been temporarily coerced into silence and passivity, but neither the strike and lockout law nor the laws on collective bargaining had been amended to the satisfaction of either the workers or the employers—whether both could ever be satisfied was doubtful. The universities were in the process of being purged of dissidents, and passified, but the law giving them a new status had not been passed. There was great bitterness within the intelligentsia, especially while some of its heroes—Mümtaz Soysal and Çetin Altan to mention only two—were being prosecuted and kept in jail. There was also the question of whether Sunay would remain President after his term expired in March or whether he would be succeeded by the Chief of the General Staff. Yet 1973 was election year and a great deal had to be done to prepare the country for the polls. It was widely recognized, however, that the future of Turkish democracy depended on the holding of this election and all political groups worked under this pressure.

The presidency was of great significance for the relations between the armed forces and the politicians and it was given much attention in the press and in political circles. The President was elected by the two chambers in joint session. But on both occasions in the sixties the Grand National Assembly had bowed to the wishes of the Commanders and 'elected' their candidate. Would it be the same again? There was some doubt about this. The politicians had learned from experience that the Commanders, dependent on them for the semblance of democracy, did not wish to intervene and assume power directly. In the battle of wills it was quite possible for the politicians to defeat the Commanders, especially now that Ecevit's RPP was in agreement with Demirel over restoration of the Assembly's supremacy.

The President was to be elected on 13 March and this meant that Prime Minister Melen would resign in order to enable the new President to appoint his own Premier. This is what the constitution required but it is worth noting that this procedure had not been practised in 1966 when Sunay replaced Gürsel. At that time Demirel had been Prime Minister and he had not resigned his office to be reappointed. However, unlike Melen, he had been the leader of the majority party. Melen came from a small party and lacked an automatic majority in the Assembly.

This was a strange anomaly for a system which purported to be parliamentary. The RPP was opposed to the cabinet. The JP was in the coalition but Demirel, simply temporizing, had often stated that his party was neither in power nor in opposition. There was still speculation that the Commanders might intervene if the Grand National Assembly failed to elect their candidate, but that was dismissed as highly improbable. The Commanders, who had not taken over at the very height of instability, were unlikely to intervene in total violation of the constitution.[80]

The Commanders attempted to have their candidate, General Gürler, elected President. He resigned his post as COGS and was appointed Senator on the presidential quota so that his candidature could be put forward. But in spite of all the pressures the politicians—though divided—stood firm and refused to elect Gürler. Demirel and Ecevit were agreed on not electing a general for the third time since 1960, but they could not agree on a civilian candidate as an alternative. Humiliated by the rejection of their candidate, the Commanders proposed amending the constitution so as to extend Sunay's term. But the Assembly rejected this proposal too. The politicians had called the High Command's bluff and the generals were left with no choice but to intervene or draw back. They decided to draw back and asked the Assembly to choose its own candidate, with the sole condition that he be acceptable to the armed forces.

The struggle of wills lasted from 13 March to 6 April, when the Grand National Assembly elected the retired Admiral, Fahri Korutürk, as President of the Republic. He was known as a moderate Senator who respected the political system; he had recently voted against the State Security Courts. The Commanders acquiesced because he had been one of them and could be relied upon to remain independent of the politicians.[81]

When, on 7 April, Ferit Melen resigned and Korutürk exercised his constitutional right to appoint his own Prime Minister, he chose Naim Talu, the Minister of Trade, former president of the Central Bank, and widely recognized as the representative of big business.[82] The government that Talu formed was a coalition of the Justice Party and the Republican Reliance Party (RRP—*Cumhuriyetçi Güven Partisi*).[83]

The general election was exactly six months away and the principal task of the new government was to prepare the country for it. There was still talk of reforms but it was now generally accepted that these reforms were political issues designed to consolidate the régime of law and order, and leave the social and economic reforms for future governments.

The last of the political reforms was the reform of the universities. This was the logical culmination of the repressive measures, since the universities were held responsible for 'corrupting young people' and inciting them to radicalism and socialist activities. Ever since the proclamation of martial law, professors like Sadun Aren, Mümtaz Soysal, and Uğur Alacakaptan had paid dearly for their politics.

However, the régime was determined not only to punish, but also to change the character of, the universities so as to preclude, or at least control, any future political activity within their walls.

The Universities Law, passed in June 1973, was 'designed to restructure the country's academic community in a way which would forestall further outbreaks of student unrest. ("Not reform, but chloroform", quipped one junior academic.)'[84] There was hardly a voice raised against this law and Professor Faruk Erem's dissent and resignation from the university was aptly described as the 'loneliness of the rebel academic' by the *Guardian Weekly* quoted above. Erem's principal target for criticism was the new University Supervisory Council, with the Prime Minister as its chairman, and to which all universities in Turkey were answerable for any of their actions. And if universities failed to take disciplinary measures against their members when the council recommended them, the new body would have powers to act itself. It would also be able to take over a university administration when it deemed this to have broken down. It was, as Erem commented, the end of university autonomy in Turkey: 'From now on, national politics will always have a decisive influence in university affairs.'[85]

By the summer of 1973 the post-12 March régime had carried out all the political changes. The constitution had been amended, special courts had been set up, the universities had been harnessed and blinkered, and the trade unions pacified. But not a single social or economic problem of basic significance, land reform for example, had been implemented. These problems were left to the new government which would come to power at the polls in October.

Parallel with the repression and the political reforms, and intimately linked with both, a new spectrum of political forces emerged in the period between March 1971 and October 1973. This may be the most significant development of this period and therefore merits discussion in some detail.

The New Political Spectrum

As we have seen, the Turkish establishment had been unable to cope with the effect of the Workers' Party on the political environment—not because the WPT was ever an electoral threat but because it had played a role totally out of proportion to its size in politicizing the country. Its influence on the unions and the youth movements had been particularly marked and the government had often sought to have the party and its members prosecuted for violation of the country's laws and of the constitution. The government's failure to solve economic problems, especially the galloping inflation which was blamed on constantly rising wages, made the closure of the WPT even more urgent; but each time the Constitutional Court had stood in the way, interpreting the laws and the constitution liberally and giving the party a new lease of life. On 12 March 1971 the public prosecutor announced that he was taking up the case against twenty-three members of the WPT for speeches they had made at the last congress, in which they had allegedly carried out communist propaganda and encouraged activities designed to divide the country. The last charge referred to the Kurds in Turkey, whose autonomy the WPT allegedly favoured.[86]

The case against the twenty-three opened on 29 June and they were found guilty and took the matter to the Constitutional Court. On 20 July the party was dissolved by a unanimous decision of the Constitutional Court, which found its officials guilty of violating the law on political parties and the constitution; forty-one of them were forbidden to found another party for five years.[87] The matter did not end there. The leaders were arrested again and tried by a military tribunal for their role in the so-called subversive activities and given draconian prison sentences, ranging from 15 years with hard labour for Mrs Hatko (much better known as Behice Boran) to terms varying between six and ten years for other party officials. The Constitutional Court had closed down the party, noted Altan Öymen, because of 'divisive activities' and not because of Article 141 of the criminal code which makes it illegal to wage a class struggle against the existing order. Yet twenty members of the WPT were sent to gaol by the military tribunal for violating this Article and not for 'divisive activities'. This contradiction could not be raised publicly, for the press had not been permitted to cover the trials and had to rely on press handouts.[88]

Defeat of İsmet İnönü in the RPP

From the viewpoint of Turkish democracy the closure of the WPT and the harsh treatment of its leaders was important because it meant that those operating the power structure had recognized its failure to reconcile socialism and democracy. Debate about whether the constitution was open to socialism had gone on throughout the sixties, and, as we saw, the Right had declared quite explicitly, with Sunay as their spokesman, that the constitution was closed to socialism. After 12 March Sunay's verdict was no longer a matter for discussion; with the closure of the WPT it was converted into a *fait accompli*. In theory it was possible for Turkish politics to revert to the narrow, non-pluralistic framework of the fifties; but Turkish society had witnessed too many major changes in the past generation for its politics to stand still. It was too dangerous to leave the vacuum created by the closure of the WPT unfilled. It is not surprising that Nihat Erim, in his capacity as Prime Minister, had proposed that a new socialist party be set up to take the place of the WPT. This was perfectly in keeping with the bureaucratic tradition of the power structure, but at the time no one on the left was in a position to take up Erim's proposal. The first socialist party—the Socialist Workers' Party of Turkey—announced its existence on 22 June 1974, almost three years after the closure of the Workers' Party. Initially, the response to the challenge from the Left came from within the RPP. In 1965 the party had adopted the 'left-of-centre' slogan and policy, but these had proved insufficient to rejuvenate and revive the old RPP. Under normal circumstances it is doubtful whether the party, with its entrenched leadership, would have been capable of making the transformation. The political crisis created by the memorandum of 12 March provided the Republicans with the opportunity to change their leaders and give the party a new character.

The party's reaction to the memorandum had been harsh, yet a few days later İnönü did a *volte face* and agreed to support the Erim government.[89] This was precisely the type of political opportunism which undermined the democratic process and made the voters doubt the RPP's sincerity. Most people with the slightest interest in politics believed that İnönü was supporting the government only because it was headed by his protégé Erim; the man in the street did not treat Erim's timely resignation from the party seriously and saw it only as a political manoeuvre.

On this occasion party discipline did not hold up and Bülent Ecevit, supported by other dissidents on the administrative body, resigned as Secretary-General. He refused to view the military intervention as an act against the Demirel government, which was already tottering. He saw it as a blow against the RPP, which, with its radical orientation, he thought, was capable of coming to power either at the polls, if the democratic system was not, undermined, or by means of the army if voters thought the party had abandoned the idea of gaining power by election. 'I cannot agree', he said, 'to the Republican People's Party coming to power or seeming to come to power by means other than the people's will.'[90]

İnönü's support for Erim again raised the spectre of collaboration between the RPP and the army. There were many cynics who believed in the equation: RPP + Army = power. But Ecevit and his supporters had come to see it as a formula for electoral disaster. Ecevit wished to purge the party of its élitist image and to create a new one, identifying it entirely with 'the people'. The lesson of the Democrat and Justice parties had not been lost on him. He recognized that the voters had supported those parties because they brought benefits and did not simply exploit the ignorance and emotions of the people, as Republicans were fond of claiming. The Republicans must abandon such simplistic notions as 'the people do not understand, that is why they do not elect us. . . . We are a party committed to reform and the people are reactionary; that is why we are not elected.' In Ecevit's view: 'It is necessary for us to give up claiming that only intellectuals know what is best, and to accept that the people know perfectly well where their interests lie. If so far people have not voted for the reformist forces this has not been because of backwardness but because they saw that the reformists were alienated from them.'[91] But it was impossible to carry out such changes while the party was led by İnönü and his coterie of sycophants—who were as determined to retain the old character as Ecevit was to change it. They had successfully resisted change for the past twenty years and seemed likely to do so again, especially with İnönü on their side.

Ecevit's resignation, under normal circumstances, would have marked the end of his political career within the RPP. Party supporters of the *status quo*, led by Kemal Satır, believed that this would come about and expressed their pleasure openly. It was true that Ecevit had the support of the İzmir and other provincial organizations, as well as the party's youth groups. But the central organization continued to support İnönü.[92] When the Assembly and Senate Groups discussed Erim's programme to determine whether to give him a vote of confidence, the party was divided and decided by a vote of 100 to 50 to support Erim. Ecevit argued for a negative vote, claiming that only then would the parliamentary régime be saved; otherwise the people would reconcile themselves to military rule. Ecevit's thesis was defeated but next day he received 27,000 telegrams of support.[93]

Ecevit's position on the constitutional amendments was again populist in character. Both he and İnönü were opposed to the amendments. But İnönü was able to reconcile the party's support for the measure on the grounds that 'Before us is a scheme proposed with good intentions. Let us show our own good will by compromising and helping to carry out some changes.'[94] Ecevit, however, refused to compromise. the 1961 constitution had been legitimized by a referendum; if important articles of this constitution were to be amended they had to be sanctioned by a new referendum.[95]

Ecevit's grass-roots politics threatened the conservatives, who dominated the party. They therefore took the offensive against him and his supporters. This was not something new. The difference was that in the past İnönü had protected Ecevit. Now he had to fend for himself. Ecevit was attacked for adopting a 'Marxist critique of Atatürk', for claiming that Atatürk had not carried out structural reforms. Ecevit's use of the slogan 'land for the tiller, water for the user' was denounced as undermining the state.[96]

The principal accusation against Ecevit was that he wanted to take the party to the left and make it a 'socialist party'. There was even talk of his leaving the RPP and forming a social democratic party by joining with the dissident trade union leaders inside Türk-İş. But Ecevit stated categorically that the RPP would not be divided and that he had never contemplated forming a new party.[97]

The attacks on Ecevit proved counter-productive and he continued to gain strength at the local level. By October 1971 İnönü began to complain that a campaign was being waged against him in certain provincial party organizations. In İzmir, which had supported Ecevit from the very beginning, İnönü's pictures were destroyed. He threatened to meet the challenge of the dissidents at the party congress, confident that he would triumph as he always had done in the past.[98] İnönü played the role of the neutral father observing a family squabble. This was how he had always run the party, keeping himself in reserve until the opportune moment when the squabble could be terminated with least damage to the 'family'. This time he permitted Kemal Satır, his former Secretary-General, to lead the conservative faction, but everyone knew that Satır was only İnönü's proxy.

By the beginning of 1972, however, İnönü was forced to enter the struggle for the party. Satır, with his tired politics, was no match for Ecevit—who was happier to have him as his antagonist than İnönü. Ecevit was continuing to win support at the provincial party congresses despite İnönü's communiqués. His group won in Adana (9 January), İzmir and Antalya (16 January), and Ankara on 23 January.[99] It was these set-backs which provoked İnönü to state openly that the conflict was between himself and Ecevit, and not between Satır and Ecevit. He blamed Ecevit for the factionalism, for conducting opposition from outside and creating the crisis.[100]

The battle had been joined, and, with İnönü openly ranged against Ecevit, few people gave any odds for Ecevit's chances of political survival, let alone victory. In February both sides argued their case before the party, but the issue had gone beyond words and had to be decided in the general congress which was scheduled to meet in July.[101]

The debate continued and Ecevit's faction kept winning at the provincial congresses and ousting the pro-İnönü administrative bodies. The desire to forestall further victories is most certainly one of the reasons why the central organization decided to call an extraordinary congress for 5 May to replace the general congress that would normally have been held in July. Having called the extraordinary congress, İnönü declared that there was no longer a need to hold any further provincial congresses.[102] Next day he invited the old provincial delegates who were loyal to him to attend the congress, not the recently elected supporters of Ecevit.[103] But Ecevit and his followers protested, and right up to the congress it was not clear who the *bona fide* delegates were.

The Fifth Extraordinary Congress of the Republican People's Party was to have opened on 5 May, but it was delayed a day because of İnönü's 'heart spasm'. With İnönü behind him, Satır was so confident of victory that he declared two days before the opening: 'I am not saying that we are going to win the congress. I am saying that we have already won it.'[104] However, the press was not so sure. *Milliyet*'s survey of the provincial leaders showed that they favoured Ecevit. The veteran journalist Bediî Faik wrote that Ecevit would win but that the party would disintegrate in the process.[105] Nevertheless, it was difficult to imagine a defeat for İnönü, and Ecevit did his utmost to isolate Satır from İnönü. Ecevit's faction never stopped repeating that it wanted to continue to work alongside İnönü and that İnönü was being misled by the Satır group. İnönü refused to be swayed and seemed willing to gamble for all or nothing.

The extraordinary congress had been called to resolve the question of the RPP's Party Council in which Ecevit's supporters were dominant, bringing it into conflict with İnönü. İnönü wanted the congress to pass a vote of no confidence against this body and then elect a new one which would collaborate with him. Normally this would have been a formality, but, as this congress was to show, the situation in the party and the country had changed. In spite of İnönü's historic personality and his honoured position, the delegates were determined to act independently. The first manifestation of this was the election of Sırrı Atalay—who was identified with Ecevit's policies—as chairman of the congress in preference to İnönü's candidate Hudai Oral. The door was never closed on İnönü until he closed it on himself by giving the party the option of choosing between himself and Ecevit. The congress opted for Ecevit by giving the existing Party Council a vote of confidence.[106] The next day İnönü resigned as Chairman of the party, a position he had held for more than thirty-three years. This marked the end of an era and the opening of a new one.[107] On 14 May the congress met again and elected Bülent Ecevit Chairman of the Republican People's Party.[108]

There was grave apprehension about the future of the RPP. Would it break up now that İnönü was no longer there to hold it together? This had been the justification, or the excuse, for retaining him as party leader since 1950. It was evident that İnönü's followers would defect as soon as it was opportune to do so, but that would in fact prove beneficial to a party trying to abandon its old identity and acquire a new one. The other question in everybody's mind was whether Ecevit would be able to control the left wing of his party or would it now take control and threaten the very existence of the RPP? There was even apprehension that the party under Ecevit would run foul of martial law and be dissolved. Ecevit was cautious and undoubtedly sincere about the political position he had in mind for his party. He had no intention of taking the party towards socialism; at most he would try to give it a social democratic colouring. In his judgement that was as far as the country was ready to go. The political spectrum would polarize, with the RPP on the left and a wide range of parties on the right.

Parties of the Right

The closure of the Workers' Party and the new orientation in the RPP were the two significant changes on the left and on the left of centre. There was nothing comparable on the right. In spite of all the prognostications following Demirel's humiliation on 12 March, he was able to retain his grip over the party. Almost all his serious rivals had already left the JP and formed a party of their own, the DP. Moreover, Demirel's policies had been vindicated by the activities of the post-memorandum governments, a factor which strengthened his position in the party. He therefore had little difficulty in meeting any challenges to his authority. As we have seen, he was able to exercise considerable influence on the various governments which found it difficult to function without his co-operation.

With the exception of the National Order Party the memorandum had little effect on the futures of the other parties of the Right. The DP refused to collaborate with the régime and played the role of the opposition on the right. Türkeş's Nationalist Action Party, never very influential under normal circumstances, was virtually in eclipse. Turhan Feyzioğlu's National Reliance Party seemed to be in the ascendent but this was illusory. The party provided the Defence Minister for the first two cabinets and the Prime Minister for the third, and this added to its importance. But the NRP could not supply an alternative to the Justice Party.

In July after the Twenty-first Congress of the RPP, the Satır Group defected and formed the Republican Party (*Cumhuriyetçi Parti*) which merged with Feyzioglu's NRP, becoming the Republican Reliance Party (RRP).[109] This should have strengthened the RRP, but, as we shall see, in the general election of 1973 the fortunes of the party actually declined.

Necmettin Erbakan's National Order Party suffered the fate of the Workers' Party and was dissolved on 20 May 1971 after a life of fifteen months. The Constitutional Court had found the leaders guilty of violating articles 2, 19, and 57 of the 1961 constitution, related to the secular character of the state.[110] But the leaders were not penalized in any way, and, at the time, many people interpreted the closure of the party as a demonstration of the government's 'even-handed policy' towards the 'extreme Left' and the 'extreme Right'. Other parties of the Right found its Islamist propaganda a threat to their votes, even though the news media treated the NOP as a joke.

For the next year and a half nothing was heard of this party or its members; Erbakan was said to have gone to Switzerland until the situation calmed down. But in October 1972 the party re-emerged under the transparent disguise of a new name, the National Salvation Party (NSP—*Milli Selamet Partisi*). For the moment Süleyman Ârif Emre, the ex-Secretary-General of the dissolved party, assumed the leadership of the new one; but it was clear that he was only the front man for Erbakan.[111] Initially, the NSP hardly made an impression on Turkey's political life. The intelligentsia continued to view it as the party of obscurantists determined to take Turkey back into its Islamic past. Few realized that religion had become a weapon in the struggle for economic domination.[112]

Erbakan knew better than most how the growth of capitalism was undermining the socio-economic basis of traditional society in Anatolia. By using traditional symbols, which were of necessity Islamic, he was soon able to mobilize support for the party. The NSP emphasized religion in a less vulgar way than the NOP had done. The image that began to emerge was of a party preaching 'Islamic socialism' rather than Islamic fundamentalism. The success of this propaganda became apparent when the NSP came out of the general election as Turkey's third party.

The Election of 1973

The unofficial electoral campaign began as early as the autumn of 1972, a full year prior to the polls. The Justice Party seemed the most likely winner and there was much speculation as to whether the Commanders would allow the man they had ousted to lead the country again. The failure of the High Command to have Faruk Gürler elected President or to extend Sunay's term was a success for Demirel, for both had played an active role in his fall. Neither, as President, would have found it politic to appoint Demirel Prime Minister, and Sunay had said as much. But with Korutürk's election to the presidency the way seemed clear for Demirel to come back to power via the ballot-box.

An obstacle that Demirel had to overcome was the fragmentation of the Right, marked by the proliferation of parties competing for the same votes. This was especially true for the Democratic Party, which would certainly corner some votes from the JP vote bank. The Reliance Party was now stronger on paper than it had been in 1969 and could hope for right-wing Republican votes. The Salvation Party was an unknown quantity but it was expected to seduce the 'religious vote'. The expectation was that the JP would still be the principal party, with the strength to pick and choose its coalition partner from among one of these parties.

There seemed to be absolutely no danger from the left wing of the political spectrum. The Workers' Party had been dissolved. The RPP was still in the process of finding its feet after İnönü's resignation as Chairman and the defection of the Satır group in July. İnönü's resignation from the party on 5 November 1972 suggested that he was throwing his weight against the RPP in the coming election.[113] Resignations followed and the RPP seemed weaker than ever. Moreover, Ecevit had begun to take care about how he used radical-leftist slogans, causing a certain amount of doubt about his sincerity amongst his adherents in the intelligentsia. Yet he must have known that they were a captive following with no other leader to turn to. It is significant that the Unity Party, which became the Unity Party of Turkey (UPT— *Türkiye Birlik Partisi*) on 28 November 1971, was cast in the role of the party of the Left. Mehmed Ali Aybar and seven other former members of the Workers' Party stood as Independents on the UPT tickets in the 1973 election. But the Unity Party lacked the organization and the national leadership to make any impression on the electorate. It was hindered by its reputation for being the party of the Shia minority in Turkey.

The results of the 1973 election were therefore a great surprise. Few had predicted an Ecevit victory, or, stated more accurately, a defeat for Demirel. The weekly *7 Gün*, which supported Ecevit, predicted a victory for Demirel with 190 seats, Ecevit running second with 173. The DP, NSP, RRP, UPT, NAP, and MP were expected to win 34, 29, 16, 7, 1, and 0 seats respectively.[114] The actual results revealed a far more serious fragmentation of the Right, reducing the JP to the second party with 149 seats. The Republicans won 185 seats but they were 41 short of the majority required to form a government. The National Salvation Party also performed better than predicted and won 48 seats, with the DP running close with 45. The Reliance Party, despite its merger with Satır's faction, did badly, winning only 13 seats compared to 15 in 1969; even the NAP improved its representation from one (1969) to three. The Unity Party succeeded in having only its leader Mustafa Timisi elected, and not one of the ex-members of the Workers' Party standing on its lists was successful.[115]

The election results were indecisive, as they had been in 1961. Since no party won a majority large enough to form a government, Turkey seemed destined, once again, to live through a period of unstable and precarious coalition governments. In 1961 the Justice Party—as yet without Demirel at the helm—had been the dark horse; this time it was Bülent Ecevit's Republican People's Party, revitalized and confident of the future. The electoral campaign had brought Ecevit into the limelight as the potential saviour of democracy in Turkey. He inspired trust and confidence, and came to be seen as the man who was capable of extricating politics from the blind alley of party squabbles and leading the nation 'towards bright days'—*Ak Günlere*, the title of his party's election manifesto. Ecevit had emerged as Turkey's hope for the future. However, before he could fulfil such expectations he had to consolidate his political position by winning the next general election conclusively. After the election of 1973 he applied all his energy and political acumen to the accomplishment of this task.

NOTES

1 See the Turkish press, 13 Mar. 1971 and following. The memorandum, issued in the name of the armed forces, was supported by the trade unions, including DİSK, the revolutionary workers' union'. Two law professors, Bülent Nuri Esen and Bahri Savcı, found the military intervention constitutional. See *Milliyet*, 15 Mar. 1971.

2 The memorandum was signed by the COGS General Memduh Tağmaç and the Commanders of the Land, Naval, and Air forces, General Faruk Gürler, Admiral Celâl Eyicioğlu, and General Muhsin Batur respectively. The text was broadcast over Ankara Radio, 12 Mar. 1971 (*SWB*, iv/3633/c/2) and published in the Turkish press, 13 Mar. 1971; and *Milliyet 1971*, 43.

3 This story was being circulated by an unidentified JP Senator. See Fikret Otyam's column in *Cumhuriyet*, 19 Mar. 1971.

4 Ankara Radio, 15 Mar. 1971, in *SWB*, iv/3636/c/2-3; *Ulus*, 16 Mar. 1971.

5 Nihat Erim resigned from the RPP in order to lead an 'above-party' government. The cabinet included five ministers from the *JP*: Doğan Kitaplı (State), Cahit Karakaş (Public Works), Haydar Özalp (Customs), Erol Akçal (Tourism), and Sezai Ergun (Sport); three from the *RPP*: Sadi Koçaş (Deputy Prime Minister), İsmail Arar (Justice), and İhsan Topaloğlu (Energy and Natural Resources); and one from the *NRP*: Ferit Melen (Defence). The DP refused to join the government. The remaining ministers were brought in from outside the parties and included: Atilla Karaosmanoğlu (Deputy Prime Minister in charge of the economy); Mehmet Özgüneş (State); Hamdi Ömeroğlu (Interior); Şinasi Orel (Education); Ayhan Çilingiroğlu (Industry and Trade); Dr Türkan Akyol (Health); Orhan Dikmen (Agriculture); Halûk Arık (Communications); Atilla Sav (Labour); Selâhattin Babüroğlu (Construction and Resettlement); Dr Cevdet Aykan (Rural Affairs); Selâhattin İnal (Forests); Özer Derbil (External Economy); Osman Olcay (External Affairs). See *Milliyet*, 27 Mar. 1971; Kurtul Altuğ, *12 Mart ve Nihat Erim Olayı* (1973), 8-35 and *passim*; and 'Chronology', *MEJ*, xxv/3 (1971), 386.

As well as the 'technocats', this cabinet also included Turkey's first woman minister (Türkan Akyol) and this was widely publicized. In July, Erim brought in Talât Halman as Minister of Culture, and the portfolio was abolished a few months later. In its inclusion of professors and technocrats the cabinet resembled the National Unity governments of the 1960-1 period. See 'Milli Birlik Hükümeti ve Erim Hükümeti', *Devrim*, 6 Apr. 1971.

6 See Erim's press conference in *Son Havadis*, 20 Mar. 1971, and his 'The Turkish Experience in the Light of Recent Developments', *MEJ*, xxvi/3 (1972), 249-51.

7 Quoted in Nora Beloff, *The General Says No* (London, 1963), 59.

8 Quoted in Altuğ, *Erim Olayı*, 21. Kurtul Altuğ was Erim's adviser on relations with the press. He has given a first-hand account of many important events.

9 *Cumhuriyet*, 9 Apr. 1971.

10 Altuğ, *Erim Olayı*, 37; *Yankı*, 81, 8 Oct. 1972, 13.

11 Altuğ, as in preceding note, 37–41.

12 Ibid., 41–8.

13 See Erim's statement to a visiting Israeli journalist in *Milliyet* and *Cumhuriyet*, 1 Aug. 1971 and his article cited in n. 6 above.

14 *Cumhuriyet*, 18 and 19 Mar. 1971. Retired Admiral Sezai Orkunt, the RPP Representative for Istanbul, was to be included in Erim's cabinet. However, his name was found on the list of the military conspirators who were planning the radical *coup* and who considered Orkunt to be sympathetic to them. See *Cumhuriyet*, 25 Mar. 1971.

15 Ibid., 11 Apr. 1971.

16 Ibid., 23 Apr. 1971 and the cover story on Koçaş in *Yankı*, 7, 18 Apr. 1971.

17 Ankara Radio, 23 Apr. 1971, in *SWB*, iv/3667/c/1. Seeking sanction for its measures by reference to European example was a favourite device of the Erim government. Critics likened this to the nineteenth century *Tanzimat* mentality (*Tanzimat Kafası*), which reflected a sense of inferiority *vis-à-vis* Europe.

18 *Milliyet*, 27 Apr. 1971. General Faik Türün, Martial Law Commander of Istanbul, told the press: 'We were on the verge of a civil war; this war had even begun. They called it "People's War"; I call it war against the people. Martial law was declared under these conditions.' (*Milliyet*, 6 May 1971.) The government continued to talk of an international conspiracy exploiting the left-wing organizations. But it has not produced any evidence so far. See Erim's statement to the foreign press, *Cumhuriyet*, 19 Oct. 1971, and his article cited in n. 6 above.

19 *Cumhuriyet*, 28 Apr. 1971.

20 *Milliyet*, 29 and 30 Apr. 1971 and *Yankı*, 10, 9 May 1971 are virtually devoted to the discussion of martial law measures.

21 *Milliyet*, 4 May 1971.

22 Altuğ, *Erim Olayı*, 68–77; *Milliyet*, 18 May 1971 and *Yankı*, 13, 24 May 1971, 4–5.

23 Altuğ, *Erim Olayı*, 79–80. COGS General Tağmaç expressed what was almost an article of faith on the Right that 'the anarchic trend which had brought the nation to the edge of an abyss had been half organized in the university.' (*Milliyet*, 7 July 1971.) Erim had consulted Professors Esen, Savcı, and Soysal on 8 May and Tunaya on 12 May about amending the constitution. (*Milliyet*, 9 and 13 May 1971.)

24 *Cumhuriyet*, 23 May 1971; *Milliyet 1971*, 116–21.

25 *Ortam*, 3, 14 June 1971, 4–10; *Cumhuriyet*, 9 and 10 June 1971.

26 *Milliyet*, 2 May 1971. Altuğ, *Erim Olayı*, 56–7 explains that Erim used the word 'luxury' in a statement to the foreign press. Erim's press secretary Altemur Kılıç translated this into Turkish as '*lüks*' and gave a press handout to Turkish journalists who made Erim's views public. Erim was most upset. The significance of this anecdote is that Erim presented two faces, one for home consumption and the other for export.

27 Ecevit's statement to *Milliyet*, 4 June 1971.

322   The Turkish Experiment in Democracy

28 *Cumhuriyet,* 11 June 1971.

29 Ibid., 18 Aug. 1971. See also Aybar, *12 Mart,* 87-207 for other parliamentary speeches protesting against the régime.

30 *Cumhuriyet,* 7 Sept. 1971.

31 Ibid., 6, 7, 13 and 21 Sept. 1971; *Yankı,* 26-28, 23, 30 Aug. and 6 Sept. 1971. See also Turkish State Information Organization, *The Turkish Constitution [As Amended]* (1972).

32 Cihat Baban, 'Pahalılık İşkencesi', *Cumhuriyet,* 30 Nov. 1971. Turkey was second to Iceland in the European 'inflation league table' for the years 1961-71, with an annual average of 7·5 per cent. See the *Guardian Weekly,* 110/8, 24 Feb. 1974, 6. *Akşam,* 13 Dec. 1971, citing a UN report, claimed that Turkey was seventh out of 72 countries in the world for rising prices between 1963 and 1970.

33 Ali Gevgilili, *Türkiye'de 1971 Rejimi* (1973), 231.

34 Interview with Kemal Aydar in *Cumhuriyet,* 9 and 10 Apr. 1971.

35 Ibid. This was in total contrast to the populist view of democracy held by people like Demirel and Ecevit.

36 Ankara Radio, 23 Mar. 1971, in *SWB,* iv/3643/c/1-3.

37 The Turkish press, 3 Apr. 1971; *Yankı,* 6, 11 Apr. 1971, 4 ff.; Gevgilili, *1971 Rejimi,* 239-42.

38 *Cumhuriyet,* 10 Apr. 1971; and 'Vehbi Koç İş Alemini Uyardı', *Yankı,* 7, 18 Apr. 1971, 17.

39 *Milliyet,* 15 Apr. 1971; *Yankı,* 8, 25 Apr. 1971, 4-6; *Ortam,* 1, 19 Apr. 1971, 8-10. *Ortam* described Karaosmanoğlu as the 'young revolutionary in the cabinet'.

40 *Cumhuriyet,* 9 Sept. 1971.

41 Ibid. Önger also claimed that the government's hostility to the private sector was causing investment to be held back and resulting in a stagnant economy. *Cumhuriyet,* 23 Sept. 1971. See also 'Raif Önger: 1972 Mart'ına Dikkat', *Yankı,* 29, 19 Sept. 1971, 20.

42 *Milliyet* and *Cumhuriyet,* 29 and 30 Sept. 1971; Altuğ, *Erim Olayı,* 139-49; and *Yankı,* 31, 3 Oct. 1971, warning that this was only the first resignation from among the reformers.

43 Gürler's statement of 28 Sept., following those of Admiral Eyicioğlu and General Batur. See the Turkish press, 28 and 29 Sept. 1971, and *Yankı,* 31 and 32, 3 and 10 Oct. 1971, which presented these statements as cover stories.

44 *Milliyet,* 6 Oct. 1971. The JP ministers resigned on 7 Oct.

45 Ankara Radio, 17 Oct. 1971, in *SWB,* iv/3817/c/1.

46 *Cumhuriyet,* 7 and 8 Oct. 1971; *Yankı,* 33, 17 Oct. 1971, 4-9.

47 *Milliyet,* 27 Oct. 1971; *Yankı,* 35, 31 Oct. 1971, 4-5.

48 *Milliyet,* 29 Oct., *Yankı,* 36, 7 Nov. 1971, 4-7 ('Tağmaç: Bir Buhranın Anatomisi'). Tağmaç was very close to Demirel and the JP, as were many other generals. After his retirement he was given a sinecure on the board of directors of the Industry and Development Bank. See *Yankı,* 114, 21 May 1973, 18.

49 *Milliyet,* 2 Nov. 1971.

50 *Milliyet,* 4 Dec. 1971; *Yankı,* 38, 12 Dec. 1971, 6-11.

51 Altuğ, *Erim Olayı*, 221-2. The longer statement which 'the Eleven' distributed to the press is given on 222-6. See also *Milliyet*, 5 Dec. 1971, and Gevgilili, *1971 Rejimi*, 336-9. Raif Önger expressed his sense of relief at the resignation of the 'reformers', declaring that 'God took pity on the Turkish nation and "the Eleven" resigned on their own and left'. *Milliyet*, 23 Feb. 1972. 'The Eleven' who resigned were: Koçaş, Karaosmanoğlu, Ömeroğlu, Derbil, Olcay, Orel, Babüroğlu, Akyol, Sav, Özgüneş, and Çilingiroğlu. See n. 5 above.

52 *Milliyet*, 26 Oct. 1971.

53 *Hürriyet*, 26 Oct. 1971. The distinction was between *toprak* and *tarım* reform.

54 *Milliyet*, 17 Nov. 1971; *Yankı*, 38, 12 Dec. 1971, 14-15.

55 *Devrim*, 6 Apr. 1971 and *Yankı*, 81, 8 Oct. 1972, 13.

56 The Second Erim Cabinet was still essentially a JP-RPP coalition with eight ministers from the JP: Doğan Kitaplı and İlyas Karaöz (State); Haydar Özalp (Monopolies); Rıfkı Danişman (Communications); Mesut Erez (Industry and Technology); Erol Yılmaz Akçal (Tourism); Bingöl Ersoy (Construction and Resettlement); and Adnan Karaküçük (Sport); four from the RPP: Ali İhsan Göğüş (State); İsmail Arar (Education); Mukadder Öztekin (Public Works); and Ali Riza Uzuner (Labour); one from the NRP: Ferit Melen (Defence). The rest were non-party appointees and included: İlhan Öztrak (State); Professor Suat Bilge (Justice); Ferit Kubat (Interior); Halûk Bayülken (External Affairs); Sait Naci Ergin (Finance); Naim Talu (Foreign Trade); Cevdet Aykan (Health); Orhan Dikmen (Agriculture); Nezih Devres (Energy and Natural Resources); Professor Necmi Sönmez (Rural Affairs); and Selâhattin İnal (Forests). See *Milliyet*, 11-12 Dec. 1971; *Yankı*, 39, 19 Dec. 1971, 7; 'Chronology', *MEJ*, xxvi/2 (1972), 178. For an analysis of the cabinet see Gevgilili, *1971 Rejimi*, 339-42.

57 *Milliyet*, 5-6 Dec. 1971; Altuğ, *Erim Olayı*, 222-6.

58 *Cumhuriyet*, 10 Dec., *Milliyet* and *Akşam*, 15 Dec. and *Yankı*, 39, 19 Dec. 1971, 2-21. At the twenty-seventh General Meeting of the Union of Chambers, Raif Önger boasted: 'When we took office the First Erim Government and "the Eleven" were in power. We launched a bitter struggle against "the Eleven". We established a beautiful dialogue with the Second Erim Government. Our collaboration is continuing in this direction'. *Toplum*, 9, 2 June 1972, 4.

59 Ankara Radio, 16 Dec. 1971, in *SWB*, iv/3870/c/3-8 and *Milliyet*, 17 Dec. 1971. See also Erim's discussion of his programme with Abdi İpekçi in *Milliyet*, 18 Dec. 1971.

60 *Milliyet*, 2 Feb. 1972; and Bedri Koraman's cartoon in *Milliyet*, 3 Feb. showing the transformation of Erim into Demirel.

61 *Milliyet*, 31 Jan. 1972.

62 See Demirel's statement in *Milliyet*, 15 Mar. 1972.

63 His four-page letter became public on 27 Mar. and the official text was published the next day. See *Cumhuriyet*, 27 and 28 Mar. 1972.

64 *Milliyet*, 4 Apr. 1972; *Yankı*, 55 and 56, 9 and 16 Apr. 1972, 4-5 and 12-13, respectively.

324   The Turkish Experiment in Democracy

65 *Milliyet*, 6 Apr. 1972; *Toplum*, 1, 7 Apr. 1971, 5-7.

66 *Yankı*, 57, 23 Apr. 1972, 6-7.

67 Ibid., 7-8.

68 Quoted in *Milliyet*, 13 Apr. 1972.

69 The Turkish press, 18 Apr. 1972; *Yankı*, 58, 30 Apr. 1972, 4-6; *Toplum*, 3, 21 Apr. 1972, 4-7.

70 See the Turkish press, 25 Apr.-14 May 1972.

71 *Milliyet*, 14 May 1972; *Yankı*, 62, 28 May 1972, 5; and *Toplum*, 7, 19 May 1972, 4-8.

72 The Melen cabinet was composed of eight from the JP, five from the RPP, two from the NRP, one presidential Senator, and nine non-party men. The *NRP* provided Ferit Melen (Prime Minister), and Fehmi Alpaslan (Justice). The *JP* provided: Doğan Kitaplı (State); Haydar Özalp (Monopolies); İlyas Karaöz (Agriculture); Rıfkı Danişman (Communications); Mesut Erez (Industries and Technology); Yılmaz Akçal (Tourism); Turgut Toker (Construction and Resettlement); and Adnan Karaküçük (Sport). The *Republicans* provided: İsmail Arar (State); Mukadder Öztekin (Public Works); Dr Kemal Demir (Health); Ali Riza Uzuner (Labour); Nuri Kodamanoğlu (Energy and Natural Resources). The *presidential Senator* was Mehmet İzmen (Defence). The *non-party* men were: Zeyyat Baykara and İlhan Öztrak (State); Ferit Kubat (Interior); Halûk Bayülken (External Affairs); Ziya Müezzinoğlu (Finance); Sabahattin Özbek (Education); Naim Talu (Trade); Necmi Sörmez (Rural Affairs); Selâhattin İnal (Forests). See *Milliyet*, 23 May 1972 and *Toplum*, 8, 26 May 1972, 4-5.

73 *Cumhuriyet*, 16 May 1972.

74 *Milliyet*, 30 May 1972; *Yankı*, 64, 11 June 1972, 4-5.

75 Interview in *Yankı*, 64, 6.

76 *Yankı*, 70, 23 July 1972, 11; see also nos. 69 and 71.

77 *Yankı*, 71, 30 July 1972, 4.

78 Ibid.

79 *Yankı*, 83, 22 Oct. 1972, 17.

80 Interview with Turan Güneş in *Yankı*, 101, 25 Feb. 1973, 5.

81 See the Turkish press, 12 Mar.-7 Apr. 1973. 'Soldier On' and 'Rebuff for the Generals', *The Economist*, 10 and 24 Mar. 1973, respectively. *Yankı*, 104-108, 18 Mar.-15 Apr. 1973; four of the five cover stories were devoted to the election of the President. There was fear of military intervention and on 28 Mar. Air Force jets buzzed the Assembly building.

82 *Yankı*, 109, 22 Apr. 1973 and 7 *Gün*, ii/33, 25 Apr. 1973. Both weeklies featured a cover story on Talu.

83 The Talu Cabinet consisted of 13 members of the *JP*: Nizamettin Erkmen (State and Deputy Prime Minister); İsmail Hakkı Tekinel (State); Sadık Tekin Müftüoğlu (Finance); Orhan Dengiz (Education); Nurettin Ok (Public Works); Ahmet Türkel (Trade); Ahmet Nusret Tuna (Agriculture); Ali Naili Erdem (Labour); Nuri Bayar (Industries); Orhan Kurumoğlu (Rural Affairs); İsa Bingöl (Forests); Celâlettin Coşkun (Sport); Ahmet İhsan Kırımlı (Tourism). The four from the *RRP* were: Kemal Satır (State and Deputy PM); İlhami Sancar (Defence); Vefa

Tanır (Health); Nebil Oktay (Construction and Resettlement). The rest were *non-party* men: İlhan Öztrak (State); Hayri Mumcuoğlu (Justice); Mukadder Öztekin (Interior); Halûk Bayülken (External Affairs); Fethi Çelikbaş (Customs); Sabahattin Özbek (Communications); Kemal Demir (Energy and Natural Resources). See *Cumhuriyet*, 16 Apr. 1973; *Yankı*, 110, 23 Apr. 1973, 4–6. Satır, Sancar, and Demir were former Republicans who defected from the RPP after Ecevit's victory.

84 *The Guardian Weekly*, 109/11, 8 Sept. 1973, 5. See also *Milliyet*, 20 and 21 June 1973; and *Yankı*, 116 (cover story) and 123, 10 June and 23 July 1973, 6–10 and 8–9, respectively.

85 *The Guardian Weekly*, as preceding note. *Cumhuriyet*, 26 July 1973 reported Erim's resignation with the headline 'A Terrible Period is about to Begin for the University'. See also *Yankı*, 125, 12 Aug. 1973, 20–2 (cover story).

86 *Cumhuriyet*, 13 Mar. 1971.

87 *Cumhuriyet*, *Milliyet* and *Akşam*, 30 June, 2, 12 and 21 July 1971; *Ortam*, 9, 26 July 1971, 14–15 and *Yankı*, 22, 26 July 1971, 7–8.

88 Altan Öymen, 'TİP yöneticileri hakkında karar'. *Cumhuriyet*, 29 Apr. 1973. For the Constitutional Court's statement see *Resmi Gazete*, 6 Jan. 1972. The sentences were published in the Turkish press, 27 Apr. 1973. See also *Yankı*, 111, 30 Apr. 1973, and *The Guardian Weekly*, 108/2, 12 May 1973, 6.

89 See above, 290.

90 *Ulus*, 22 Mar. 1971. See also Ecevit's interview with Abdi İpekçi in *Milliyet*, 26 Apr. 1971. Some people believed that Ecevit's rivalry with Erim dictated his policy. Erim as Prime Minister was expected to undermine Ecevit's position in the RPP. See 'Haftanın Raporu'. *Cumhuriyet*, 22 Mar. 1971. Ecevit was replaced by Şeref Bakşık as Secretary-General.

91 *Ulus*, 10 Nov. 1969 quoted by İsmail Cem, 'Aslına Rücû mu?', *Milliyet*, 20 Oct. 1971. Also author's conversation with Bülent Ecevit.

92 *Cumhuriyet*, 23 Mar. 1971.

93 *Milliyet*, 4 and 5 Apr. 1971.

94 İsmail Cem, 'İnönü ve Ecevit'. *Milliyet*, 30 July 1971.

95 Ibid. See also Ecevit's criticism in the Assembly, *Cumhuriyet*, 10 July 1971. Later, when the question of the death penalty for political offences came up, İnönü opposed it and Ecevit refused to take up a position, knowing that the death penalty was popular with the people. He adopted a similar position on the amnesty question, but later revised it and became the principal supporter of amnesty. See below, 336–41.

96 Cihat Baban, 'Atatürk'e Dönüş' and Ecevit's reply in *Cumhuriyet*, 31 July and 12 Aug. 1971, respectively.

97 Abdi İpekçi in *Milliyet*, 11 July; *Cumhuriyet*, 12 July and *Milliyet*, 16 Aug. 1971; *Ortam*, 8, 19 July 1971, 5–9. According to *Ortam* (17, 20 Sept. 1971; 3), the aim was to make Ecevit leave the RPP without a struggle but he refused to fall into this trap. With the WPT disolved, there was no longer any need to have Ecevit run the left-of-centre policies. A conservative figure like Kemal Satır could do the same thing and recoup

the party's losses on the right. Moreover, an RPP led by Satır would make an ideal coalition partner for the JP. In view of the composition of the Talu cabinet (n. 83 above), this was a sound analysis.

98 *Milliyet*, 15 and 16 Oct. 1971.

99 Ibid., 10, 17 and 24 Jan. 1972.

100 Ibid., 24 Jan. 1971 and *Yankı*, 44-45, 17 and 24 Jan. 1971, 4-6 and 5-7, respectively.

101 For a full exposition of the views of both sides see Kemal Satır, *CHP'de Bunalım* (Apr. 1972) and Bülent Ecevit, *Perdeyi Kaldırıyorum* (n.d. [Apr. 1972]).

102 *Milliyet*, 21 Apr. 1972.

103 Ibid., 22 Apr. 1972.

104 *Yankı*, 60, 8 May 1972, 4. This remark was widely quoted in the press.

105 Reported ibid., 5.

106 *Milliyet*, 7-8 May 1972. The pro-Ecevit *Toplum* gave the fullest account of the proceedings of the congress in its issue No. 6, 12 May 1972, 6-19. See also *Yankı*, 60 and 61, 8 and 15 May 1972.

107 *Milliyet*, 9 May 1972; *Toplum*, 6, 12 May 1972, 13.

108 *Milliyet*, 15 May 1972; *Toplum*, 7, 19 May 1972, 8-12.

109 The Republican Party was formed officially on 3 Sept. 1972 (*Cumhuriyet*, 4 Sept. 1972).

110 *Milliyet* and *Cumhuriyet*, 22 and 23 May 1971.

111 *Yankı*, 130, 10 Sept. 1973, 4-8.

112 See Gevgilili, 'Sanayi Toplumu Eşiğinde Lâyiklik', *Milliyet*, 10 Apr. 1971 reproduced in his *1971 Rejimi*, 245-7.

113 *Cumhuriyet*, 6 Nov. 1972; *Yankı*, 87, 13 Nov. 1972, 5-6.

114 *7 Gün*, iv/57, 10 Oct. 1973.

115 The official results were published in *Resmi Gazete*, 31 Oct. 1973, 23; see also *Yankı*, 136, 22 Oct. 1973, 4.

In these elections participation increased from 64·3 (1969) to 66·8 per cent. The RPP won 33·3 per cent of the vote; the JP 29·8; the NSP 11·8 and the DP 11·89. It will be noted that, between them, the five parties of the Right won 62 per cent of the votes. But it is doubtful whether a single party of the Right will be able to win such a majority as the JP used to achieve.

CHAPTER XII

THE EMERGENCE OF BÜLENT ECEVİT

I cannot look for a way to save myself while my countrymen are being knocked to the ground by stones as they listen to me. I shall march with the people against those who attack, and against those cowards who instigate murder by leading the attackers into the streets. We did not find democracy in the street, and we shall not abandon it there. Let those pathetic people with a yearning for fascism know this.

Some people may have fascist inclinations, but Turkey shall not become fascist. Even if those with fascist inclinations come to power for a while, they will not be able to bring fascism to Turkey. The Turkish people are freedom loving, people with self-respect, and too proud to live willingly under a régime other than democracy.

Those in government today are trying to destroy the state. They are undermining the high courts and the constitutional foundations [of the state], and they are planning to dress armed hooligans in police uniforms to attack us with state weapons. They are trying to bring anarchy to the country by going outside the institutions of the state [rule] of law.

Bülent Ecevit, speech in Istanbul, 28 June 1975

The Indecisive Election of 1973

THOSE who had expected the October general election to bring political stability to Turkey and produce a government capable of resolving some of the country's major economic problems, inflation and unemployment in particular, must have been sorely disappointed. Most people hoped for a strong government based on the 'national will'—not on the will of the generals—a determined government that would tackle the problem of rising prices and lay the foundations of a social welfare state (*sosyal refah devleti*).[1] For Behçet Osmanağaoğlu, who was chairman of the board of directors of the Istanbul Chamber of Commerce, a strong and stable government was vital if Turkey was to face up to pressing economic issues and implement the reforms necessary to prepare the country for entry into the European Economic Community.[2] Professor Esat Çam, a political scientist at the Faculty of Economics, Istanbul University, was of the opinion that 'the future of Turkish democracy is in large measure tied to this election'.[3] All the experts were agreed that this election must resolve the 'crisis of the régime' and provide Turkey with a 'brave and knowledgeable government'. Professor Ergin also gave a timely warning against the naïve view, widely prevalant in political circles, that once the 'problem of the régime' had been resolved the economic difficulties would disappear on their own. Research had shown that the ground for political crises was prepared by economic and social instability, and not the other way round.[4]

The results of the 1973 election did not give the winning party (the RPP) a sufficient majority to form a strong government. Instead, the country was forced to turn to a coalition govern- ment—an organism which, by its very nature, tends towards compromise and inability to take decisive and unpopular measures. Furthermore, for reasons explained below, all the parties found it politically expedient not to coalesce with certain other parties. For example, Demirel's Justice Party refused to form a coalition with Ecevit's Republican Party; not that Ecevit was obliging when Demirel attempted to form a government. Bozbeyli's Democratic Party would enter into an alliance neither with the RPP nor with the JP while it was led by Süleyman Demirel. Necmettin Erbakan, the leader of the Salvation Party, was willing to form a partnership with anyone provided the price was right. But he was deterred by fear of alienating his rank-and-file and fear of the defection of Salvationists in the Assembly and the Senate. Turkey was experiencing the longest ministerial crisis in its history so far: the coalition government did not emerge until 25 January 1974.

The reaction of the party leaders to the outcome of the election was mixed. Erbakan and Bozbeyli were delighted because their parties had emerged as important factors to be taken into consideration in any future coalition. The election had transformed them from small splinter parties into medium-sized parties, now third and fourth in the country. Of the other small parties, the Reliance and the Action Party remained much as they had been in 1969, while the Unity Party and the Nation Party were virtually wiped out. How did the two major parties fare?

For the Justice Party the 1973 election proved to be a major set-back. Its vote declined from 46·5 per cent in 1969 to 29·4 per cent, and its seats in the Assembly from 256 to 149. Most political commentators had predicted a JP victory, perhaps with a slightly smaller margin than in 1969, but no one had predicted such a rapid decline. The only hint of a possible set-back appeared in *Yeni Ortam* on 9 June 1973, when it was reported that some observers were comparing the situation with that before the 1950 general election, when state officials were competing to become Republican candidates. This time state officials were trying to find seats on the JP list. That particular connection had been disastrous for the Republicans and it could prove equally so for the Justice Party. At the same time, Demirel's record since 1969, especially on the economy, had lost him the confidence of voters, and, in the words of the DP deputy chairman Cevat Önder, 'the nation had eliminated Demirel'.[5] In a democratic party structure in which the party was not totally dominated by its leader, this electoral defeat might well have meant a change of leadership. But not so in Turkey. The Justice Party was Demirel's party and he had no intention of resigning. In fact, he had to pursue a more aggressive and uncompromising policy towards the other parties in order to retain a grip on his own. That also made the task of forming the coalition a little more difficult.

The 1973 election was generally hailed as a triumph for the RPP and a personal triumph for its leader Bülent Ecevit. It is to Ecevit's credit that he was able to revitalize the party by breaking away from its conservative base and leading it 'back to the people'. This meant weakening the RPP's alliance with the landowners, the commercial and industrial circles, and the military–civilian bureaucracy, and finding new allies who would support a social democratic régime modelled on those of Western Europe and Scandinavia. The allies Ecevit sought were in the westernized intelligentsia, the urban working class, the petty bourgeoisie of small-town Anatolia, and the peasantry, as well as amongst the nationalist wing of the commercial and industrial bourgeoisie. In fact, one of his aims was to convince the latter that social democracy was in their interest; for it was the only way to arrest the growing class conflict.[6] One means of convincing them was to win an election, come to power, and demonstrate the efficacy of his new populism.

Ecevit did not have very much time in which to reach the voters. Since martial law was not lifted until three weeks before election day the campaign was subject to severe restrictions and shorter than usual. Nevertheless, his simple and direct style caught the imagination of the voters, and everywhere he went he was met by huge crowds chanting '*Halkçı Ecevit*' ('Man of the People, Ecevit'). The almost too familiar appellation '*Karaoğlan*', applied to Ecevit by the masses, suggested that they saw him as a popular star rather than a politician. He accomplished what few politicians are able to, and established a rapport with his audience which convinced them he was seeking more than their votes. Because of the trust he generated, Ecevit was even able to raise money for his party's campaign directly from the people by selling the RPP's election programme and his own photographs, as well as other symbols of the party. Raising money in this way was something new in Turkish politics, though the Workers' Party had tried to do the same thing on a smaller scale and less successfully. And it gave substance to Ecevit's claim that 'We shall come to power indebted only to the people.'[7]

Ecevit had stood up to the military régime after the *coup* of 12 March 1971 and managed to survive. He had then challenged the power of İsmet İnönü in the RPP and successfully overcome that too. He seemed to be blessed with good fortune. At the same time he refused 'to behave like a politician'; his speeches were straightforward yet full of idealism, and he neither played political games nor indulged in verbal gymnastics as most other political figures did. The impact of his speeches was such that fragments from them were taken up as slogans:

A just and humane order with neither poverty nor restraints, neither oppressor nor oppressed.

I shall defend the Right's freedom of speech.

Wealth belongs to the people and so does the state.

We shall reverse the process of development that originates from the rich.

The nation has risen and is flowing to the RPP like a torrent.

The JP came to power with honest votes but became a government of the corrupt.

The takeover of [the landlord's] land is the peasant's struggle to live.

We shall halt communism with freedom.[8]

If one judges by the genuine enthusiasm for him, the nation had indeed risen and seemed to be flowing to Ecevit, who now personified the Republican Party. The party's supporters described themselves as *Ecevitçi* (Ecevitist) or said they were members of Ecevit's party. They carried huge banners stating 'Ecevit Is Our Hope.'[9] No wonder an English journalist who came to report the October election is said to have wired his paper: 'The Turkish election has been won by a party called Ecevit.'[10]

In the 1973 election stakes the JP had started as the favourite and the RPP as the outsider. During the race, especially towards the end, it seemed possible that the Republicans would win by a big margin. They did win, though the victory did not allow them the majority to form the government. Had there been a longer election campaign, Ecevit might have succeeded in turning the torrent of votes into a flood. The victory was a great achievement, nevertheless it was a little disappointing. Secretary-General Orhan Eyüboğlu admitted: '... we did not achieve our expectations. The votes won by the RPP are 5 per cent less than I had expected.'[11] The failure to win this 5 per cent made all the difference, paving the way for precarious coalitions.

Negotiations for a Coalition

The newly elected Assembly convened on 24 October and on the 27th President Fahri Korutürk gave Ecevit the task of forming a government. In fact, informal negotiations between the parties began as soon as they realized that the election results had made rule by coalition virtually inevitable. Those who wanted stability and the maintenance of the *status quo* proposed a coalition between the RPP and the JP. A government of the two major parties would enjoy an overwhelming majority of 334 votes in the Assembly and 121 votes in the Senate, whereas an RPP alliance with one of the other possible partners—the NSP or the DP— would provide only a fragile majority in the Assembly and a minority in the Senate. In such a situation the opposition parties would be able to turn back legislation passed by the Assembly and hinder the effective working of government. Moreover, an RPP-JP coalition was favoured by the conservatives because the Justice Party would keep Republican radicalism in check, and prevent Ecevit from extending the democratic environment by introducing such measures as a general and political amnesty, reducing the voting age to 18, or allowing greater freedom of speech and expression. But Ecevit was aware of the dangers of a partnership with the Justice Party. He announced at a press conference on 15 October that he was committed to reforming the existing order (*düzen*) and that he would make no concessions in order to form a coalition. Such concessions would lead to a loss of hope in the country, which would be harmful not only to the RPP but to the régime as well.[12]

One alternative to an RPP-JP government was a coalition of the parties of the Right, led by the Justice Party. Demirel may have lost the election but he seemed to hold the key to any stable government. However, he had decided that it would be to his political advantage to remain outside government, at least for the time being. He knew that whoever came to power would have to implement unpopular measures such as raising the price of home-heating oil and other essentials, prices which had been kept down for political reasons by the Talu government, in which the Justice Party had been dominant, with thirteen ministers. Unpopular measures which would affect the man in the street would not improve the standing of the coalition partners with the voters, and that could prove significant if the country was forced to hold an early election. The Justice Party had a better chance of regaining its popularity with the electorate in opposition than in power.

As early as 16 October, Demirel had made his intention very clear at a press conference: if there was to be a coalition government he wanted no part in it.

There was in fact a coalition ranged against the JP. The election has been a contest between the JP and this coalition. In this election the nation gave us the duty of opposition. It is possible for parties other than our own—namely the RPP, the NSP, and the DP—to form a coalition.

We do not desire a coalition with anyone. We shall be an example of an honest opposition in the state. We shall remove one of the shortcomings of Turkish democracy. We are accepting the nation's decision with respect. There is one thing we desire and shall continue to desire, namely that our nation should have a voice in the country...[13]

Demirel, who always claimed with pride that he never made decisions without consulting his party, had reached this important decision on his own.[14] Moreover, his decision foreclosed the possibility of a coalition other than one between the RPP and the NSP. The Democratic Party was too closely linked with former Democrats to form a government with the RPP; in any case they were ideologically too far apart to be able to work together.

There had been much speculation about partnership between the Republicans and the Salvationists and many political analysts accepted its feasibility. The election programmes of the two parties revealed that they had much in common. Both claimed to believe in a democracy that guaranteed the fundamental freedoms, a mixed economy, economic and social development with social justice, and an economic policy which benefited society as a whole and not only some of its groups. Both were committed to the protection of tradesmen and artisans and their small enterprises, and to étatizing mineral resources and oil, and companies which produced capital goods. Both sought working conditions that were humane and democratic, as well as social security, and opposed the exploitation of the people by 'big capital'.[15]

However, if the Republicans and the Salvationists had something in common, their differences were equally great, and perhaps fundamental. The Salvation Party claimed to be the party of the lower middle class, threatened by the ever-rising tide of the modern capitalist sector which made its members—the tradesmen and artisans—redundant. It therefore opposed the growth of modern capitalism, with its links to the outside world of the European Economic Community and NATO. The Salvationists claimed to want to preserve small-scale capitalism, and perhaps develop it into a national capitalism which could survive the competition of the Arab world but not that of the Common Market. That is why it was necessary to break all ties with the West and turn to the east. That was where the salvation of Turkey lay.

Ecevit's RPP did not subscribe to any such views. It was in no way opposed either to the capitalist system or to Europe or America; in fact, Ecevit wanted to emulate the example of some European social democratic régimes such as those of Sweden and Germany. He wanted Turkish capitalists to acquire a modern mentality which could look beyond high profits to the social welfare of the people. He wanted to open Turkish capitalism 'to the people' by creating a people's sector (*halk sektörü*) in which the small man could invest his money. Under Ecevit there was no question of Turkey leaving the Common Market or NATO; in each case he wanted to re-examine Turkey's relationship with these bodies and to make changes that seemed necessary.

Differences between the RPP and the NSP were also reflected in their social philosophies. Both parties were reacting to the same stimulus, namely, a rapidly changing social structure in which traditional values and forms were crumbling before the onslaught of a new way of life which manifested itself in an ever-expanding technology, whose roots lay in the alien West. The Salvationists looked inwards and offered their followers the comforts of traditional Islamic values and the creation of a firm faith as a shield against this challenge. The Republicans' prescription was an up-dated Kemalist nationalism in which social welfare became a powerful ingredient. The party under Ecevit attracted the intelligentsia, especially university students and professors, many of whom aspired to a socialist humanism. As individuals they were totally secular, with little regard for Islamic values, which they considered anachronistic. But as students of contemporary Turkish society they appreciated the significance of religious sentiments for most Turks and the role that could play in elections. Thus the RPP abandoned the militant secularism for which, under İnönü, it was renowned, and Ecevit made it clear that the party's hostility to Islam was a thing of the past.[16]

But it was not differences which prevented the two parties from forming a coalition, nor common goals which finally brought them together. Their political calculations counted for more than anything else, and the similarities in their programmes were only the rationalizations of pro-Republican intellectuals.

Both Ecevit and Erbakan needed to establish the legitimacy and respectability of their parties, a goal that could be accomplished by leadership of the government. The question of legitimacy was more important for Erbakan because his party, the National Order Party, had been closed down in 1972 for unconstitutional activities, an allusion to the party's exploitation of religion for political ends, and its hostility to the Kemalist ideology. What was true for the NOP was equally true for the NSP, and it was quite conceivable that the Justice Party, whose votes it had captured, would ask the courts to dissolve the Salvation Party. Already a JP candidate who lost the election had appealed to the High Election Council to annul the NSP vote. He claimed that the NSP was exactly the same party as that dissolved by the Constitutional Court.[17] The Kemalists in the armed forces and the bureaucracy also had little sympathy for Erbakan, and would have been happy to see his party shut down a second time. It was almost a question of survival that Erbakan find a role for his party in any coalition government; a coalition with the secular and Kemalist RPP would automatically enhance the image of his party.

For Ecevit the problem was not quite so serious. His radical rhetoric, especially his promise to change the existing order, had alarmed the conservative forces in the country, and political leaders such as Turhan Feyzioğlu and Alparslan Türkeş exploited his radicalism to foster a communist scare. The military High Command was said not to trust Ecevit, and after the election there was specuoltion as to whether it would permit him to govern the country. It was therefore important for Ecevit to form a government and prove that he was a cautious and responsible politician who understood the problems of his nation.

Despite the advantages to both parties, the coalition took almost three months to form. Ecevit offered a partnership to Erbakan on 30 October and on 6 November the NSP rejected the offer. However desirable such a partnership might be for the leaders, it would be difficult to sell to the party's representatives in the Assembly, as well as to the voters. There was even a danger that

Erbakan was losing control of his party, because his followers viewed an alliance with the RPP, which he had constantly denounced as godless, as gross political opportunism.[18]

Ecevit abandoned his attempt to form a government on 7 November and President Korutürk, after consulting the party leaders, appointed Demirel on the 12th. Erbakan was willing to support Demirel, but Ferruh Bozbeyli, the leader of the Democratic Party, was not, and the possibility of a coalition of the Right collapsed. The commercial and industrial community, supported by Fahri Korutürk, again proposed a JP–RPP coalition. But Ecevit rejected this proposal on 17 November, and Demirel confessed his inability to form a government. For the next few days Ecevit investigated the possibility of leading a minority government. But with local elections approaching in December, the leaders decided to await their results before attempting to form a government. 'The local elections', said Ecevit, 'have assumed the importance of a national election.... The knotty problems which have emerged in Ankara during the past month, will be resolved with the help of the people on December 9.'[19]

The results of the local elections did not resolve the problem, and President Korutürk decided to revert to the formula of a national coalition led by an above-party premier. The pro-RPP trend which had been evident in the general election was confirmed in these elections. The party won 39·5 per cent of the votes, while the JP won 33·9 per cent and the NSP only 5 per cent. But the local elections were also important for the Republicans because their supporters were able to come to power in 32 of the 67 provinces, and the party captured the municipalities of the four major cities—Istanbul, Ankara, Izmir, and Adana. That could prove most profitable in a future general election.[20]

On 15 December the President asked Naim Talu to form a coalition in which the RPP would have 9 ministers, the JP 7, the NSP and the DP 2 each, and the RRP one. Its task would be to prepare the country for an early general election.[21] The parties were reluctant to accept this formula, which, they said, negated the general election and was new, having been introduced by the régime of 12 March 1971. Erbakan refused to enter the coalition on the ground that Talu's appointment was unconstitutional. The RPP said it would enter Talu's government only if the election was held by May 1974 at the latest.[22] But the other parties were opposed to an early election since they did not expect to do as well as in 1973. Talu continued to negotiate with the party leaders into January and gave up the attempt to form a government on the 10th.[23]

The RPP-NSP Coalition

Meanwhile the Republicans and the Salvationists had been holding secret talks, and on 13 January 1974 Ecevit and Erbakan announced that they had reached agreement in principle to work together. The President asked Ecevit to form a government on 16 January and thereafter it was only a question of deciding on the particulars. On 18 January the parties began to prepare their 'joint protocol', a document that would present their intentions to the nation. It was signed on 25 January, when the names of the new ministers were made public.[24]

The RPP-NSP agreement, which virtually became the government's programme, laid the guidelines for a broad spectrum of issues—social, economic, and political—and pointed to the direction in which it wanted to take the country. As will be clear from the principal terms of the agreement, its implementation would have marked a beginning in the correction of the socio-economic imbalances in Turkish society, and restored a level of democratic freedom unknown since 12 March 1971. The two parties agreed to:

(1)   implement a general amnesty which would include those convicted of crimes of thought (*düşünce suçları* or *fikir suçlari*: explained in note 36 below) and forest offences, as well as former Democrats who had been deprived of civil rights, to whom they would be restored;

(2)   reduce the voting age to 18 years, except for high school students;

(3)   make public servants liable to prosecution not only for abuse of office, but also for dereliction of duty;

(4)   establish a more equitable system of taxation;

(5)   prevent waste in the bureaucracy;

(6)   legalize the ownership of *gecekondus*—homes built without permission by rural migrants—constructed up to the end of 1973;

(7)   accelerate technical education in secondary schools, and to abolish university entrance examinations;

(8)   support the co-operative movement in rural areas and to found a co-operatives bank which would be supervised by the Ministry of Rural Affairs and Co-operatives;

(9)   employ foreign exchange reserves for the development of the country in the best possible way; and to encourage co-operatives and 'people's enterprises' to use bank credits;

(10)   take measures to provide agricultural credits to the peasant to free him from the need to resort to middlemen and usurers;

(11)   establish a minimum price for agricultural produce, and to

announce it as early as possible in order to safeguard the producer from having to sell at very low prices;

(12)   ensure the efficiency of co-operatives in the marketing of agricultural produce, and to prevent artificial price increases;

(13)   find a solution to, and end, the unjust treatment of the opium poppy growers;

(14)   change the name of the Ministry of Agriculture to the Ministry of Food-Agriculture and Animal Husbandry [to reflect new and wider functions];

(15)   make the operation of public [state] enterprises more democratic, permitting employees to participate in their administration, and to share the profits;

(16)   formulate an industrial policy for the expansion of heavy industry—especially capital goods—and to set up a national armaments industry;

(17)   promote regionally balanced industrialization, in keeping with a geographical balance and social justice;

(18)   limit to a reasonable amount the transfer abroad of profits by foreign investors;

(19)   rely on water and coal to produce electrical energy;

(20)   place under state control the exploitation of underground mineral resources, including borax; to re-examine the Petroleum Law and amend those clauses which contravene national interests;

(21)   import through public companies or co-operatives those goods whose prices increase very sharply as a result of shortages;

(22)   introduce unemployment insurance, and give priority to old people without means, and cripples;

(23)   remain within the joint security system and the existing alliances, but at the same time to increase Turkey's ability to defend herself, and to place under state control joint Turkish-American bases and establishments.[25]

Ecevit presented his government's programme in the Assembly and the Senate on 1 February, and amplified the terms of the protocol. It was a cautious programme whose aim was to allay the fears and suspicion of the conservative business circles. They were pleased to learn that the new government intended to focus economic development around heavy industry, which the state would take in hand, leaving the more profitable light industry in private hands. Thus Turkey would acquire an industrial infrastructure necessary for the development and growth of the national economy. The programme also emphasized the government's commitment to a national armaments industry—something which the High Command had been calling for, and therefore a point which made the Command more sympathetic to Ecevit. On the whole, Ecevit's economic programme complemented rather than competed with the private sector. It did not even attempt to deal with the question of land reform, but concentrated on issues such as co-operatives and the efficient marketing of produce.

Despite this moderation, the conservatives remained rather suspicious and apprehensive of Ecevit's intentions. Their reasons must be sought in those parts of the programme in which the government promised to establish a democratic society, for example:

The two parties which form the government know that it will not be sufficient merely to broaden the freedoms in order to strengthen democracy and society. We believe that a régime of social justice covering the whole of society is as necessary as political rights and liberties and the freedom of thought and belief. We know that extensive social justice rooted in liberty cannot be considered in isolation from rapid and balanced economic development.

That is why we are determined to realize and secure democratic freedoms in the broadest sense simultaneously with extensive social justice and rapid economic development.

We believe that we shall be able to accomplish this aim by the road shown in our constitution.

... Our government is convinced that it can resolve these questions and difficulties, not with an escapist and evasive administration (*idare-i maslahatçılık*), but only by determined and courageous efforts and a force born from the coalescence of state and nation.[26]

No other government programme had dwelt on the question of democracy as did this one. It pointed out the shortcomings of the existing situation and promised to remedy them. That is what alarmed the conservatives and those who favoured the *status quo*. They viewed the restoration of democratic freedom—absent since 12 March 1971—as the end of 'law and order' and the return to what they described as 'anarchy' (*anarşi*), a situation in which workers would be able to organize and strike, in which student radicalism would emerge to criticize exploitation and the lack of social justice, and in which the special security forces would lose their power of repression. In their eyes, the restoration of democracy was all the more inappropriate at a time of world economic crisis, when Turkish workers in Europe might be forced to return home to join the ranks of the unemployed, raising their demands and making them more militant. It would be difficult to deal with the working class in a democratic environment, all the more so if an election was approaching and all parties were wooing the workers' vote. It was therefore essential to impede the implementation of this process of democratization. To accomplish this, the conservatives began to use the 'commandos' (*komandolar*) of Türkeş's mini-party to create unrest and disorder in the streets.[27]

Even as the coalition was in the process of being negotiated, the conservative press, led by *Son Havadis* and *Tercüman*, had tried to undermine the negotiations by claiming that the Salvationists were forming an alliance with the 'leftists'. This remained the principal propaganda theme even after the coalition had been formed, and the partnership was not expected to survive even a month. The purpose of the campaign was to undermine the NSP's conservative support and force the party to break with the Republicans in order to retain it. The other political parties were equally uncompromising in their attacks on the coalition, especially during the debate on the programme in the Assembly. They denounced the government as a government of the Left, to which every faction of the Left had tied its hope. Süleyman Demirel noted that 'extremist currents' (*aşırı cereyanlar*)—a reference to the Left—had not been mentioned in either the protocol or the programme, and there were no proposals for measures to combat those currents. He asked the government: 'Do you or do you not accept that Turkey is the target of an international communist attack?' Turning to the question of freedom, Demirel asked if communist propaganda would be included in the freedom of thought.[28] The spokesman for the DP was more explicit. He stated that 'The coalition government formed by Ecevit will go down in our political history as "Turkey's first leftist government" ', and that a 'leftist government programme was being presented to the public in a classic wrapper.'[29] The debate continued until 7 February when the government was given a vote of confidence.[30]

With Ecevit in power, a new political atmosphere began to prevail in the country. The general view was that the government would make serious efforts to implement its programme. The appointment of İsmail Cem İpekçi, a talented young journalist, to the post of Director-General of Turkish Radio and Television (TRT), reflected the mood to innovate. This appointment disregarded the requirement that an appointee to such a post ought to have served as a state official for 12—later reduced to 7—years, but Ecevit circumvented that by issuing a decree (*kararname*), a device introduced by the post-12 March 1971 régime.[31] In February the government began to prepare the Amnesty Bill, which was presented to the Assembly in March and passed on 14 May after bitter controversy and amendments.[32] In March the government permitted the opium poppy to be sown in six provinces, despite threats from the US government that, as a consequence, it might cut off aid to Turkey.[33] Under pressure from Washington, the Erim government had prohibited poppy cultivation in 1972. This decision had been very unpopular in the country, and became the symbol of Turkey's subservience to America. Its reversal by Ecevit was most popular for it was seen as restoring Turkey's dignity and independence, and it added to Ecevit's personal standing and prestige. Such was the sense of freedom and optimism that Mehmed Ali Aybar, the ex-chairman of the dissolved Workers' Party of Turkey, suggested that in view of Premier Ecevit's promise to establish a democratic society equal to any in Europe, the time was ripe to establish a new socialist party in Turkey.[34] Politics now revolved around Ecevit. The opposition parties, especially Demirel's Justice Party, were confused and in disarray, aware that if they did not reform themselves in keeping with the new populism, they would be submerged at the next general election. This fact was not lost on Necmettin Erbakan either.

Initially the relations between the coalition parties were most cordial. Observers were quick to note the co-operation between the leaders during the programme debate, and the failure of the opposition parties to split the alliance by their constant emphasis on Ecevit's domination and Erbakan's subservience—there was no doubt that Ecevit was dominating the coalition in every way and that Erbakan was living in his shadow. The Salvationists realized that if such a situation continued much longer their role in the government would be totally eclipsed and the party would lose votes both to the RPP and to the parties of the Right. They therefore decided to publicize themselves as being independent of Ecevit and his party. Erbakan could not afford to take chances with major issues such as amnesty, or such popular issues as opium cultivation, for to do that could endanger the coalition. He had to choose minor ways which would combine maximum publicity for the Salvationists with the minimum of irritation to Ecevit. Erbakan chose issues which focused on public morality, such as pornography in publications and in the cinema, an issue that would assure controversy in the press, irritate the intelligentsia, and appeal to the traditional values of the petty bourgeoisie.

The sculpture of a reclining nude entitled 'Beautiful Istanbul', which was set up in a busy square to celebrate the 50th Anniversary of the Republic, became the occasion for the first controversy. On 17 March, addressing his party's Istanbul Congress, Erbakan related the issue of pornography to the duties of the state: 'The state is obliged to behave well towards the nation. Whatever the nation wants will be done. It is necessary to remove ideas opposed to this from the heads of administrators.... The nation does not want films on TV which undermine morality.... The sculpture placed in Karaköy will be removed. This is what it means to coalesce state and nation. A government which says "I am going to retain this sculpture even if you do not want it" cannot stay."[35] The sculpture was removed on 19 March but the controversy continued, especially on the question of pornography and the Salvationists' crusade against it.

Erbakan and the National Salvation Party did receive more publicity as a result of such campaigns, and the coalition continued to function despite minor irritations. But it came close to collapse on 14 May when 20 members of the NSP defied party discipline by voting against granting amnesty to those who were in prison for violating Articles 141 and 142 of the penal code, i.e. those who had been found guilty of carrying out 'communist propaganda and encouraging class conflict'.[36] Ecevit called an emergency meeting of the Party Council to discuss the situation, and he was expected to hand in his resignation. But the Republican ministers decided that it was still too early for Ecevit to resign. They thought he ought to wait until the party had acquired sufficient prestige in the eyes of the people to be able to win the next election with a large enough majority to form a government. Moreover, Erbakan offered a face-saving formula to maintain the coalition, namely, to pass a decree releasing for six months all those who had been imprisoned for transgressing Articles 141 and 142. The government could then eliminate those articles from the penal code during the six-month period.[37] Both parties found it convenient to maintain the coalition, and despite constant friction it continued into July 1974 when a new chapter of the Cyprus crisis opened somewhat unexpectedly. As a result of his handling of this crisis, Ecevit acquired tremendous prestige in the country, and the party decided that the time had come to end the coalition and seek an early general election.

Ecevit and the Cyprus Crisis, July 1974

When the National Guard in Cyprus, supported by the military junta in Athens, overthrew President Makarios on 15 July 1974, relations between Ankara and Athens were already tense. The Turco-Greek tension had been caused by the mutually exclusive claims of the two countries to an area of about 10,000 square kilometres of sea-bed in the North Aegean Sea, said to be rich in hydrocarbon deposits and oil. The Greek government had granted licences to foreign corporations for the exploration of the sea-bed and the exploitation of any mineral discoveries. The Turkish government responded by issuing a concession to the State Petroleum Company in November 1973 for exploration of the Aegean sea-bed, parts of which coincided with the concessions granted by the Greek government. On 29 May the *Candarlı* sailed into the Aegean to search for oil, and during the weeks that followed there was sabre-rattling in the Turkish press, although the government continued to exercise restraint.

Soon after Ankara learned of the *coup*, Prime Minister Ecevit made a speech in which he described it as 'Greek intervention' and said that Turkey would take the necessary steps to protect her interests on the island. On 16 July Ankara delivered a note to the British government invoking the Zürich Treaty of 1960, signed by Britain, Turkey and Greece, to guarantee the independence of the Republic of Cyprus. The note proposed joint action by Anglo–Turkish forces and requested the British government to open negotiations within twenty-four hours. Meanwhile, troops had been mobilized and concentrated in the southern ports of Turkey, only fifty miles from Cyprus, ready for action. Internally, Ecevit had made 'Cyprus a national issue', keeping the party leaders informed of developments and constantly seeking their advice. He flew to London on 17 July to explain Turkey's position to Prime Minister Harold Wilson: Greek officers ought to be removed from the island and the *status quo ante* be restored, along with the establishment of a balance of forces between Turkey and Greece in Cyprus. Such action, argued Ecevit, could be accomplished by Anglo-Turkish co-operation; but Wilson refused to use force, hoping that the crisis could be resolved diplomatically.[38] Wilson's refusal to intervene jointly with Turkey gave Ecevit a free hand as the only guarantor power willing to act. Ecevit did not want the United States to become involved in this issue, arguing that the US was not a 'guarantor state'. But Secretary of State Henry Kissinger had already sent his Under-Secretary Joseph Sisco to Athens (19 July) and then Ankara. Sisco's goal was to restrain Turkey and Greece from going to war, but the offer he brought from Athens— the removal of Nikos Sampson as President of Cyprus and the abandonment of Greek ambitions on the island—was not convincing in Ankara, where it was feared that Turkish inaction, as past experience showed, could lead to a *fait accompli*. The Turks, having prepared the ground diplomatically, landed troops in northern Cyprus on 20 July and within two days were in command of the military situation. A cease-fire was established on 22 July, and on the 25th representatives of Britain, Greece, and Turkey met in Geneva to find a solution to the Cyprus problem. Meanwhile, violence in Cyprus continued, leading to violations of the cease-fire. On 14 August the Turkish army launched its second offensive on the island in order to consolidate earlier gains, and established the Attila or Şahin (Falcon) line, giving Turkish forces control of about 40 per cent of northern Cyprus. Thereafter there was a *de facto* partition, and a solution was left to negotiations which could continue for years.

If Turkish intervention—the government preferred to call it 'peace actions' (*barış harekâtı*)—transformed the situation of the Turkish Cypriots, it did the same for Bülent Ecevit's political standing at home. The decision to intervene had changed the 'idealist' into the 'man of action'. Metin Münir, who interviewed him on 17 August, described the popular reaction:

> Ecevit's handling of the situation has met with widespread approval in Turkey and has even led many Turks to compare him with Mustafa Kemal Atatürk—founder of the modern state of Turkey and the country's outstanding national hero.
>
> Almost overnight Ecevit has been transformed in many people's eyes from a well-intentioned, idealistic leader of a shaky coalition into a man of authority who could be looked upon to give the country new horizons and, more important, the unity which many Turks have felt lacking since the demise of their father figure.[39]

During the months before the crisis, the RPP-NSP coalition had indeed been precarious, and Ecevit had considered resigning but refrained from doing so because that was not the right time for action. By the end of August he had acquired tremendous prestige, which virtually guaranteed an overwhelming victory for his party if a general election could be held in the next few months. The coalition had also become more unmanageable because Deputy Premier Erbakan, realizing that all the prestige and glory was going to Ecevit, had begun to act independently of his partner. Thus while Ecevit wanted to offer higher interest rates in order to encourage and increase bank deposits, Erbakan began speaking of establishing an 'interest free' economic system, in keeping with Islamic principles which forbad interest on loans which did not incur any risk of loss.[40] His statements on Cyprus were more aggressive and expansionist, proposing partition while Ecevit maintained that partition had not been considered.[41] The right-wing press went as far as to claim that it was Erbakan who had persuaded the cabinet to intervene in Cyprus, and that Foreign Minister Güneş and other Republican ministers had voted against intervention. This was denied by Ecevit, who said that the decision had been unanimous. The NSP claim was all the more untenable since Turan Güneş was in China when the government decided to intervene.[42]

With the coalition partners pulling in different directions, the partnership was not expected to last long. Ecevit wanted to end the coalition and have an early general election while his prestige was high. He consulted party leaders, especially Ferruh Bozbeyli of the DP, and there was a rumour that Bozbeyli had agreed to have his party vote in the Assembly for an early election. It was not clear whether Ecevit would find another party that wished to join him in a coalition if he broke with the NSP. But it was believed that Ecevit had consulted President Korutürk and won him over to the possibility of a minority government which would take the country to the polls.[43] The question was how should the Republicans destroy this coalition while making the Salvationists bear the responsibility. They constantly snubbed their NSP colleagues in public—for example, by not permitting them to travel on Ecevit's helicopter, when he went to Elazığ to open the Keban Dam on 9 September. On the 13th Ecevit announced to the press that Orhan Eyüboğlu, who was Minister of State and Secretary-General of the RPP, would deputize for him while he went on an official visit to the Scandinavian countries. Deputy Premier Erbakan retaliated by refusing to sign the decree (*kararname*) sanctioning Ecevit's visit. On 16 September Ecevit announced that he had decided to postpone his visit, stating that it was his lack of confidence in the deputy premier which had not permitted him to hand over the premiership to Erbakan, especially during the Cyprus crisis. He said he was going to resign and he did so on the 18th.[44]

If Ecevit believed that the parties of the Right would permit him to form a new coalition and hold an early general election, he was sadly mistaken. No party was willing to form a government with the Republicans and agree to a December election, since the RPP was expected to win by a landslide.[45] The parties of the Right were still not able to agree on a leader under whom they would form a government, and they refused to allow Ecevit to form a minority government. Once again, therefore, Turkey was left with a government which did not have the support of the Assembly.

The Longest Ministerial Crisis

Bülent Ecevit and Süleyman Demirel took turns in trying to form a government but with no success. Finally, on 12 November, President Korutürk was obliged to appoint Professor Sadi Irmak as

Prime Minister and ask him to form an above-party cabinet. Irmak had been elected representative for Konya in 1943, served briefly as Minister of Labour in 1946, and returned to the Faculty of Medicine at Istanbul University after the defeat of the RPP in 1950. He returned to politics when he was appointed a presidential senator on 8 June 1974, and rather unexpectedly he found himself appointed Premier. All parties except the Reliance Party refused to provide ministers and Irmak was obliged to appoint state officials, technocrats, and professors to the cabinet, which he announced on the 17th. Eleven ministers were taken from the Assembly and the Senate, fifteen from outside, and the cabinet resembled the colourless above-party cabinets of the National Unity period of the early sixties.[46]

Neither Ecevit nor Demirel was willing to support the Irmak government, for neither would benefit from a stable political environment. Ecevit wanted a general election as soon as possible so as to exploit his role in the Cyprus crisis before it faded in the public mind. Demirel wished to delay the election as long as possible, and he wanted to form a coalition of the Right under his own leadership. His conservative rivals had hoped that he might be defeated as party leader—or at least that his position would be weakened—at the Seventh Great Congress of the Justice Party, which opened on 21 October 1974. However, Demirel emerged stronger than ever, having overcome all challenges. He was now better placed to lead a coalition of the Right.[47] Thus when Premier Irmak presented his programme to the Assembly and asked for a vote of confidence, he received only 17 votes.[48] Professor Irmak resigned on 29 November but the President asked him to continue in office until a new government could be formed. He remained Prime Minister until 31 March 1975, running the country with a cabinet which lacked the confidence of the National Assembly.

Formation of the Nationalist Front Government

By December all Ecevit's schemes for an early election had been frustrated by an Assembly controlled by parties which did not want an early poll. The initiative passed to Demirel who, on 2 December, announced that he was prepared to form a coalition of the Right. The parties which feared an early election most were the splinter parties (the RRP, the NSP, the DP, and the NAP) since they depended largely on uncertain floating votes. Therefore Demirel threatened to agree to an early election if he failed to form a government.[49] The small parties were in a dilemma: a general election could lead to their eclipse, yet an alliance with the JP could lead to their loss of identity and eventual absorption; and most certainly a loss of voters to the JP in any election. However, they could not continue to assume responsibility for sabotaging the formation of a government, under either Ecevit or Demirel, especially when Turkey needed a strong and stable government to deal with the Cyprus question, inflation, unemployment, and growing student unrest. In order to make it easier for the small parties to subordinate themselves to the JP in a coalition, Demirel adopted the idea of forming a Nationalist Front (*Milliyetçi Cephe*), an idea Celâl Bayar and Ferruh Bozbeyli had proposed in June and July 1974, and which Demirel had then rejected. The use of the term immediately reminded observers of the Fatherland Front (*Vatan Cephesi*) of 1957 and the polarization of politics which that had represented. In 1974 the right-wing parties began to create a similar situation, but this time the confontation was ideological, against the entire spectrum left of centre; they were creating 'a Rightist Front against the Left' (*Sola karsı Sağ Cephe*). The Nationalist Front was designed to bring moral pressure on all the parties of the Right—especially the DP—to band together in order to isolate the RPP as a minority party. If the scheme worked, Bozbeyli would either have to succumb and join the Front under Demirel's leadership, or he would split his party and an important segment of it would defect to the Justice Party. Demirel wrote to the leaders of the right-wing parties on 12 December to propose the formation of the Front. All of them except Bozbeyli responded favourably and in failing to do so he isolated himself from his own party. Demirel tried to weaken Bozbeyli further by attracting former Democrats (the Bayar faction) in the DP into his own party. But such was the DP antipathy towards Demirel, that Bozbeyli was able to maintain party unity for the time being. The proposal to join the Front was put to the vote in the DP's Assembly Group, and it was rejected by 20 votes to 15, although the Group offered to join a government not led by any party leader.[50]

The failure to divide the DP arrested the activities of the other four parties (JP, RRP, NSP, and NAP). A Nationalist Front without the DP did not command a majority in the Assembly, and the four parties simply had to wait their opportunity. It was only a question of time before the DP split—on the last occasion, only Bayar's intervention had prevented former Democrats from defecting to the JP. For the moment, the four parties began to work together in the Assembly. Professor Turhan Feyzioğlu, the intellectual and ideologue of the Front, prepared a programme to which the four parties subscribed: 'A free democratic régime,

nationalism, enmity to communism, opposition to the activities of
the extreme Left [i.e. the RPP], war on the high cost of living and
poverty, balanced development, and a change in the electoral
system which would provide for joint electoral lists.'[51] Newspapers
which supported the Front parties popularized the slogan 'Demirel
in Parlament, Türkeş in the Street' (*Parlamentoda Demirel,
Sokakta Türkeş*). As a manifestation of this 'division of labour', by
the beginning of 1975 right-wing violence in the street carried out
by Action Party 'commandos' had become almost a daily occuren-
ce. The aim of this violence was to emphasize the so-called danger
from the Left, and it gave the Nationalist Action Party an
opportunity to exert a political influence totally out of proportion
to its following in the country and its strength in the Assembly.

In the months after Ecevit's resignation the government was
paralysed, incapable of doing more than reacting to events. In
internal affairs it lacked the power to implement any long-term
measures and was limited to dealing with day-to-day problems.
Externally, it was unable to make any concessions that would lead
to a solution of the Cyprus question. Meanwhile the country
continued to mark time, the people became more cynical of
politicians and parties, and the politicians themselves continued to
attempt various manoeuvres to outflank their rivals. In the
circumstances, the military guardians were very patient and
seemed to be exercising great restraint. Perhaps activity in Cyprus
kept them occupied, for there were no threats of intervention, at
least none that we know of.

The ministerial crisis continued into March 1975. Ecevit and
Bozbeyli were again discussing the feasibility of an RPP–DP
coalition. But Bozbeyli knew his party would never accept such a
partnership. Ecevit then proposed a compromise: on 17 March he
informed President Korutürk that his party would support a DP
government led by Bozbeyli, on condition that it included non-
party technocrats who had the confidence of the RPP, and that it
took the country to an early election. Next day Bozbeyli accepted
these conditions and promised to hold the election on 12 October
1975; but he could not carry his party with him and the scheme
was abandoned. Bozbeyli and Ecevit then offered to support a
government led by Naim Talu, like the one he had led before the
1973 election. Korutürk, however, insisted on a 'democratic
formula', and again instructed Ecevit, as the leader of the largest
party in the Assembly, to form a government. Ecevit, knowing that
the attempt would be futile, politely refused. On the same day (19
March) the task was given to Demirel, who agreed to try again.[52]

As on the earlier occasion, Demirel's ability to form a government which enjoyed the support of a majority in the Assembly depended on whether the DP would support him. Initially it seemed as though it would not. This time, however, the party failed to maintain its unity. On 26 March *Yeni Ortam* reported that it had learned from reliable sources that Sadettin Bilgiç and ten other members of the DP had had discussions with ex-President Celâl Bayar, and had decided to leave the Democratic Party. Next day this report was denied by the party, but on 28 March nine members did in fact resign and promised to support Demirel's Nationalist Front government as Independents in the Assembly.[53] With thses nine votes Demirel was able to secure a total of 228 votes in the Assembly, quite sufficient to guarantee a vote of confidence. Why did 'the Nine' defect? It seems they wanted to prevent an early election, and that is what Bozbeyli had come round to offering his support. A Front government—possibly with a promise from Demirel—seemed the best guarantee against an early general election.[54]

Demirel announced his coalition government on 31 March.[55] It was composed of sixteen ministers from the Justice Party, eight from the NSP, four from the RRP, and two from the NAP. The Action Party had made the best bargain: of its three representatives in the Assembly, two of them were ministers. However, as was noted earlier, this party made its contribution in the streets, were it directed the violence against all opponents of the Right, and became the strong arm of the Nationalist Front.

The ministerial crisis had lasted 213 days, the longest in Turkey's political history. But its conclusion by the formation of the Front government did not promise long-term stability. The government was dependent in the Assembly on the votes of the Independents, representatives who were not responsive to any party discipline and who defected from one party to another for purely personal gain. Demirel had to exercise all his political skill to maintain the coalition intact.[56] Even as the new government was announced, four Independents declared that they would give a negative vote to the government if its programme was not in keeping with the principles of Atatürk.[57]

The formation of the government was, however, a personal triumph for Demirel. In the eyes of the public he had succeeded in overcoming the disgrace and stigma of having been overthrown by the armed forces in March 1971. Most commentators had forecast the end of his political career but here he was back in power, leading a coalition through which he would be able to undermine the electoral position of his partners, especially the NSP. Most important of all. Demirel had succeeded in destroying the momentum that Ecevit had built up during the Cyprus crisis and which he hoped would carry him to success in an early general election. But there was to be no early election; Ecevit had miscalculated when he resigned in the hope of an early poll. Time was on Demirel's side; the longer the election was delayed, the more time he would have to restore the unity of the right-wing vote which, until 1969, had gone into his party's vote bank.

Demirel presented his government's programme in the Assembly on 6 April. The Front government had taken those reforms out of the RPP programme which might help to enhance its standing with the electorate: the promise to lower the voting age to 18, extend health and unemployment benefits to workers, develop the provinces of eastern Anatolia, and to prepare schemes enabling workers to purchase shares in the firms that employed them. But perhaps the most important vote catcher in any future elections was the promise to reduce the price of artificial fertilizers. The price had risen sharply after the increase of oil prices in 1973 since many fertilizers are made from petro-chemicals. The rich landowners, who could afford to use fertilizers in the first place, were forced to pay more, and they were unhappy with the situation. It was their votes—and the votes of peasants dependent on them—that could be won by Demirel's concession. Moreover Demirel did not wait long to fulfil his promise. On 19 April the government announced that the prices of various types of fertilizer had been reduced by between 43 and 154 *kuruş* a kilo. By reducing the price, said Demirel, the government had subsidized the landlords with about TL 5 billion.[58]

In foreign policy, Demirel continued to support a federal bi-zonal independent state as the solution to the conflict between Turkish and Greek Cypriots. He promised to pursue Turkey's rights in the Aegean Sea with determination, and without making any concessions to Greece. Turkey would continue to be a member of NATO, and there would be a reassessment of her relations with the US if the American arms embargo established in February was not lifted.

For the rest, there was nothing new in the programme; the usual promises to halt high prices and inflation, encourage industry, broaden educational facilities, and increase sources of energy. But at the same time, Demirel declared that

...This government... will open a new chapter in the political, economic, social, and cultural life of Turkey.

This term will be a period of order, development, and effort. It will be a period in which a nationalism that is uplifting, unifying, and communal—

all of which [qualities] find expression in the Constitution—and in which the understanding of national togetherness will reign supreme in those who command the state. This term will not be one in which provocation to anarchy and civil strife is tolerated, but one in which brotherhood, respect for law, and the sovereignty of law will be encouraged and realized. We shall not exploit poverty [politically], but we shall pass serious measures in order to try to end the distress and suffering of the poor, and those with low incomes.

We shall deal affectionately with the problems of the young, who represent the future of our country. We shall protect freedom of thought and belief, but we shall definitely say 'halt' to anarchy and activities outside the law.[59]

Unfortunately, Demirel was unable to live up to these promises, and even the securing of a vote of confidence is said to have required coercion and intimidation.[60] There were accusations that the four representatives who were not in the Assembly for the vote had been kidnapped by supporters of the Front government and kept away by force. Immediately after the vote fights broke out in the Assembly and one representative even drew a pistol.[61] As far as Ecevit was concerned, he told his party's Assembly Group that the real struggle for democracy was just beginning. 'Put aside all your political preoccupations. It is the duty of all of us to save the young people and to do everything in our power... to protect their lives.'[62] At the time they were being killed and wounded in street violence.

The Threat of Fascism?

The creation of the Front government postponed the possibility of an early election, at least until after the partial Senate elections on 12 October. They would provide the testing ground for Ecevit's RPP and for the parties of the Right. But they were still six months away and they dictated the policies and activities of all the parties. In such circumstances, political peace and stability was virtually impossible both in the Grand National Assembly and the country at large. While the government removed officials who were either neutral or hostile to the Front, replacing them with its own supporters, the parties of the Right—even Bozbeyli said he would support the Nationalist Front in its struggle against communism—began to wage war against the RPP. During this period of tension there was an incident which aroused great controversy, some excitement, and a little amusement: Prime Minister Demirel was punched on the nose, suffering a minor fracture.

Demirel was attacked as he emerged from a cabinet meeting to give information to the press. A government communiqué identified the assailant as Vural Önsel, a young man of 34, who was described as a member of the RPP youth wing. The Minister of State, Seyfi Öztürk, speaking for the government, claimed that this had been an assassination attempt behind which stood Ecevit and the RPP. As it turned out, the assailant had no connection with the RPP. But the damage had been done—anti-RPP sentiment had been aroused amongst the supporters of the Right. The same night as the attack, bombs were thrown into the homes of two professors who supported Ecevit.[63] The RPP's press bureau issued a release on 15 May denying the party's involvment in the incident, and tried to counteract the hostile propaganda. Investigations had revealed, the release stated, that in 1970 Vural Önsel had 'succeeded in approaching and establishing friendly relations with Mr. Süleyman Demirel, Mr. İsmet Sezgin, and Mr. Necmettin Cevheri (all from the JP), and in the same year he was employed as editor for internal news with a periodical *Sancak*, to which present-day apologists for the National Front also contributed.'[64] At his trial a connection was established between Önsel and the Nationalist Action Party. There was much speculation as to what might have happened if Demirel had been killed. Some thought that the government, led by Türkeş (a man with fascist leanings), might have declared a state of emergency, had the Republican party dissolved, and established an openly fascist régime.[65]

Under the Nationalist Front government, the RPP was having to operate under very difficult circumstances. Demirel had begun to place his men in key positions in the bureaucracy, and the fact that he controlled the state news agency Anatolia Agency and TRT, gave him control over virtually all the media. One of the first changes he made was to remove İsmail Cem as Director-General of TRT and replace him with Professor Nevzat Yalçıntaş, a die-hard conservative. The rhetoric and the policies of the Nationalist Front encouraged the conservatives and reactionaries throughout the country to become more confident and aggressive. It is not that these people were capable of carrying out a counter-revolution and reversing the reforms of the past fifty years. But they could create a climate of tension and uncertainty which was demoralizing to the supporters of democracy, and which could provide the armed forces with an excuse to intervene. The situation was sufficiently serious as to provoke General Semih Sancar to threaten to break 'the hands of those who extended them towards the unity of the nation and the principles of Atatürk.'[66] But no action was taken against the Right, and the 'commandos' continued to disrupt and attack Ecevit's meetings at every opportunity.

The high point of these attacks came on 21 June, in the small town of Gerede, half way between Istanbul and Ankara. Newspapers reported that, on Friday 20 June, a wandering preacher arrived in Gerede and began to harangue the crowd, inciting people against the 'irreligious Republicans' and communists. The next day the bus carrying Ecevit and his party officials into the town where he was going to address a meeting was stoned by youths. Later, when Ecevit began to speak, the meeting was attacked by a mob that had congregated inside the mosque opposite the square where the meeting was being held. According to eye witnesses, Ahmet Çakmak, the JP representative for Bolu, the province in which Gerede is situated, gave the signal for the attack by firing a pistol. The gangs then attacked the meeting with stones and clubs and then withdrew into the mosque, hoping that the police and supporters of the RPP would chase them into the sanctuary, and thereby provoke a religious incident. There were even reports that NAP commandos had stoned the mosque and were even prepared to go so far as to burn the large prayer rug in order to arouse the indignation of religious people against Ecevit and his party.[67]

By all accounts the violence had been organized by the parties of the Nationalist Front. Whether Ecevit's life was threatened is not clear, though his bodyguards drew their pistols in order to protect him, and the *Sunday Telegraph* (22 June 1975) described the event as an attempt on Ecevit's life. But the Gerede Incident had immediate political repercussions. It reminded observers of the Topkapı Incident of 1960 involving İnönü, an event which had hastened military intervention. Members of the intelligentsia began to speak of possible civil strife which would lead to another intervention by the army. Some of them urged Ecevit to be cautious and to abandon his meetings for the time being in order to avoid provoking such incidents, whose outcome could be a military régime that would cancel all the democratic gains made since 1973. This was the kind of demoralization the Right hoped to bring about by the constant use of violence. If Ecevit could be intimidated to abandon his programme of tours and speeches, he would undermine his own popular support, with serious consequences for the elections.

Ecevit's response was to meet the challenge of the Right head-on. He announced a rally to be held in Istanbul on 28 June where he would speak out against the policies of the Nationalist Front. A massive crowd, estimated at around 200,000 assembled in Taksim Square to hear him.

Ecevit blamed the Front for provoking violent incidents each day all over the country. He described how it was manning the institutions of the state with its own followers and undermining the neutrality of the officials, especially in the security forces, and how it was dividing the people on the basis of religious sects and ethnic affiliations. This was an allusion to the Front's policy against the Shia, and the Kurdish- and Arabic-speaking people of eastern and southeastern Anatolia.[68] He told his audience how government bodies, such as the Anatolia Agency, were trying to undermine his popularity by publishing and distributing fabricated documents purporting to show that he and his party had links with extreme left-wing revolutionary groups in Germany. He pointed out that the courts had established the groundlessness of the Demirel government's accusations that leftist revolutionaries had burnt down the Istanbul Opera House and sabotaged three ferry boats. These accusations had been useful only for passing measures against the Left after the 12 March memorandum. Ecevit continued:

All these are the familiar methods of those with fascist inclinations. The major pitfall of such methods is this: one day, if there is ever a genuine threat from the extreme Left, people will find it hard to believe.

It would be far from the truth, even self-deception, to place the responsibility for these fascist manoeuvres on certain people one can identify within the government. The Justice Party wanted to heap its shame in Gerede on the National Salvation Party. If that is so, how to explain away the greater shame of two years ago in Isparta, on Demirel's home ground, where the incident was staged by those close to him?

A newspaper, published by someone very close to Mr Demirel, the organ of the Justice Party, even Demirel's mouthpiece, has been publishing unsigned articles for months... preparing the ground and the conditions for fascism.... it is not important who writes these articles, but who has them written, and whose thoughts they reflect. Even though we have warned them several times, this Demirelist paper goes on publishing these articles. It continuously encourages and puts pressure on the army to carry out a Rightist intervention. But our army will not fall into such a trap.

He [Demirel] was upset when he saw that we would not be silenced, intimidated, or cowed by these attacks and intrigues.... If I had been intimidated and silenced in Merzifon and Amasya, and if I had run away frightened from the guns, sticks, and stones in Gerede last week, or in Isparta two years ago, I would now be a serious statesman in the eyes of the JP official. But I am not Demirel and the RPP is not the JP. When my party is attacked, I do not pick up my hat and run as Demirel did, leaving my party colleagues behind.[69]

Towards the Partial Senate Elections

The Istanbul rally signalled the failure of the Nationalist Front's strategy of intimidating the RPP. Ecevit had not buckled under; on the contrary he had become more aggressive, counter-attacked, and mobilized many indifferent and wavering people against the Front parties. The failure of this strategy of force demoralized the coalition, and by the beginning of July differences between Demirel and Erbakan began to emerge into the open. There was speculation as to whether the coalition would survive much longer. Again, the fear of a general election kept the small parties hitched to the JP wagon. The partial Senate elections of 12 October would point the way to the future.

The three months before the elections were relatively quiet. The 'commandos' continued to attack RPP meetings, but there was no major incident except for the Elazığ Incident on 4 September, when Ecevit's bus was stoned, and the meeting was attacked in a manner reminiscent of Gerede.[70] Demirel was embarrassed by a financial scandal involving his nephew, Yahya Demirel, a scandal which received great coverage in the press. Meanwhile the government remained paralysed, unable to introduce any serious measures because of its weak position in the Assembly. Moreover it tended to avoid long-term remedies because they would require belt-tightening, and preferred to pass short-term measures with an eye to elections. Therefore, the economy continued to stagnate, with inflation uncontrolled and the rate of unemployment constantly increasing. All groups affected by the economic crisis—workers, peasants, state officials, artisans, businessmen, and industrialist—made conflicting demands on a government unable to act, but promising all things to all men. Instability had been going on for so long that the coming elections aroused little excitement—except among the politicians—because few people expected anything major to emerge from the results.

The results of the 12 October elections were significant nevertheless. The Republicans increased their representation in the Senate from 45 to 62, and with the support of 18 Life Senators and three Presidential Senators, they were able to muster 83 votes. The Justice Party's majority declined from 83 to 78, but it continued to enjoy a commanding position in alliance with its Front partners. Amongst the splinter parties, the NSP increased its seats from 3 to 5, the RRP went down from 7 to 5, the NAP from 2 to 1, and the DP lost the only Senator it had had.[71]

More significant for the future was the change in the pattern of voting since the general election two years earlier. The Justice

Party began to consolidate the vote that had been fragmented by the splinter parties such as the DP and the NSP. Thus the JP's percentage of the vote increased from 30·8 to 40·8, while that of the DP declined from 12 to 3·2, and of the NSP from 11·5 to 3·4. The Democratic Party had been virtually wiped out, and it was quite possible that the Salvation Party would go the same way. It was also noteworthy that the parties of the Right, which had won 65 per cent of the total votes in 1973, won only 55 per cent in 1975.

The Republican Party increased its percentage of the vote from 35·4 in 1973 to 43·9. This was a very significant increase because these were 'new' votes, unlike those of the JP, which had been won back. Ecevit had done well in the cities, winning overwhelming majorities in Istanbul, Samsun, and Trabzon, and this was the continuation of the trend which began in 1973, reversing the 'old RPP's' alliance with the landlords. Demirel, on the other hand, had done well in the countryside; perhaps his policy of reducing fertilizer prices had paid off.

Both Demirel and Ecevit claimed victory and each looked forward to the general election, when he would come to power with a majority sufficient to form a strong government. But the elections had shocked the small parties out of any complacency they might have had, and all of them were determined to prevent an early general election, in order to survive until October 1977.

The change in the voting pattern also reflected the dissatisfaction of the voters with coalition governments, and especially with the behaviour of the splinter parties, such as the Democratic Party, which had been able to prevent the formation of a government by refusing their co-operation. The voters seemed to be yearning for a stable government which a two-party system could supply. It is also worth noting that neither the exploitation of religion nor the exploitation of the 'communist menace' produced votes. The Salvation Party made great use of religious propaganda and yet its vote declined. The other parties spoke incessantly of the threat of communism, against which they stood as the bulwark. But the voters did not seem to be listening. General Faik Türün, the former martial law commander of Istanbul and self-proclaimed enemy of communism, stood as an Independent on the Justice Party ticket and suffered a heavy defeat. The voters had become more sophisticated over the years; they now voted for politicians who, they thought, would be able to fulfil some of their most fundamental and mundane demands. In this respect, the future lay with Ecevit's RPP. That was the only party in 1975 with a programme capable of providing for the greatest good of the greatest number in the context of capitalist development and social democracy.

NOTES

1 Feridun Ergin, Professor at the Faculty of Economics, Istanbul University, speaking at a forum on 'Turkey Before and After the Election', *Milliyet*, 7 Oct. 1973.

2 Ibid.

3 Ibid.

4 Ibid.

5 *Milliyet*, 16 Oct. 1973.

6 This changing relationship between the RPP and various social groups who used to be its allies, is the result of social and economic changes. According to Professor Çam, this is the result of the establishment of large-scale capitalist enterprises into which high state officials (including generals) have been drawn. For example, Memduh Tağmaç, COGS until Aug. 1972, and General Nazmi Karakoç, a former Commander of the Land Forces, both became members of the board of directors of Türkiye Sinai Kalkınma Bankası (*Yeni Ortam*, 1 Dec. 1973). As a consequence, the ties between the generals and bureaucrats have loosened, and so have the links of both to the RPP. (See *Milliyet*, 7 Oct. 1973.) On the participation of state officials in the 1973 election see Emin Çölaşan's '1973 Seçimlerinde Bürokrasi', in Emin Çölaşan and others, *1973 Seçimleri* (Istanbul, 1975).

7 *Milliyet*, 1 Jan. 1974, the issue which proclaimed Ecevit 'Man of the Year'.

8 Ibid. I have translated some of these rather freely in order to make them more intelligible in English.

9 *Yankı*, 135, 15 Oct. 1973, 5-6.

10 *Milliyet*, 1 Jan. 1974.

11 *Milliyet*, 16 Oct. 1973. At his press conference on 15 Oct., when the election results were still coming in, Ecevit was expecting to win about 40 per cent of the vote—which could have given his party as many as 250 seats in the Assembly. As we shall see below, the contention that a longer campaign would have improved the RPP's vote seems to be substantiated by the steady gains the RPP has been making in other elections.

12 *Milliyet*, 16 Oct. 1973.

13 *Milliyet*, 17 Oct. 1973. For Demirel's attitude after his election defeat see the cover story in *Yankı*, 136, 22 Oct. 1973, 7.

14 Abdi İpekçi, 'AP'nin Tutumu', *Milliyet*, 19 Oct. 1973. The Justice Party's Administrative Council took the decision not to enter any coalition only on 22 Oct. İpekçi supported the idea of an RPP–JP coalition and therefore did not appreciate Demirel's negative response. See his editorial in *Milliyet*, 16 Oct. 1973, where he put forward the proposal of an RPP–JP government.

15 Professor Ümit Doğanay's analysis in the discussion on 'The New Government and the Questions before It', *Milliyet*, 21 Oct. 1973. Professors Mümtaz Soysal and Uğur Alacakaptan also believed that the RPP and the NSP shared certain common aims and were therefore compatible partners. See their respective views in 'CHP-MSP uzlaşması', *Yankı*, 136, 22 Oct. 1973, 5, and 'Hak Avdet Etti ama', 7 *Gün*, 31 Oct. 1973, reproduced in *1974 VY* (1973), 353-5.

16 See Ecevit's message to the nation on the occasion of the Festival of Sacrifices (*Kurban Bayramı*) in *Yankı*, 249, 22 Dec. 1975, 10. He declared: 'I offer greetings for *Kurban Bayramı* which belongs to Turks everywhere and to the entire world of Islam.' The propaganda of the parties of the Right (Including the NSP) tried to keep alive the militantly secular image of the RPP.

17 *Milliyet*, 21 Oct. 1973.

18 Cover story in *Yankı*, 139, 12 Nov. 1973, 4-10. There was also great opposition to this coalition from the 'money bags' (*para babaları*), as Professor Velidedeoğlu described them. They feared that such a government would slow down the growth of the capitalist sector and encourage small businessmen in the 'people's sector'. See H. V. Velidedeoğlu, 'Faşizme Davetiye mi?', *Cumhuriyet*, 18 Nov. 1973 reproduced in *1974 VY*, 356-9; Mümtaz Soysal in *Yankı*, 139, 12 Nov. 1973, 5; and Oya Baydar, 'Ankara'da kaynayan kazan', *Yeni Ortam*, 2 Nov. 1973.

19 *Milliyet*, 30 Nov. 1973.

20 The Turkish press, 10-14 Dec. 1973. *Yankı*, 144, 17 Dec. 1973, 11-12 shows how the position of the parties changed since the local elections of 1968. The JP vote dropped from 49 to 34 per cent, while the RPP's vote increased from 27·8 to 30·4 per cent.

21 The Turkish press, 16 Dec. 1973, and *Yankı*, 144 and 145, 17 and 24 Dec. 1975, 4-8 and 6-10 respectively.

22 *Yeni Ortam*, 17 Dec. 1973, and *Yankı*, 145 (as in n. 21).

23 *Milliyet 1974*, 5.

24 The negotiations between the RPP and the NSP received much attention in the Turkish press, especially *Milliyet* and *Cumhuriyet*, 12-26 Jan. 1974, and the weekly *Yankı*, 148-151; 14 Jan.-4 Feb. 1974. See also *Milliyet 1974*, 23-9.

The full cabinet included 18 Republicans and 7 Salvationists. *Republicans*: Bülent Ecevit (Prime Minister); Orhan Eyüboğlu and İsmail Hakkı Birler (State); Hasan Işık (Defence); Selâhattin Cizrelioğlu (Health); Turan Güneş (External Affairs); Deniz Baykal (Finance); Mustafa Üstündağ (Education); Erol Çevikçi (Public Works); Orhan Birgit (Tourism); Mahmut Türkmenoğlu (Customs and Monopolies); Ferda Güley (Communications); Önder Sav (Labour); Cahit Kayra (Energy); Ali Topuz (Construction and Resettlement); Mustafa Ok (Rural Affairs and Co-operatives); Ahmet Şener (Forests); M. Yılmaz Mete (Youth and Sport). *Salvationists*: Necmettin Erbakan (Deputy PM); Süleyman Ârif Emre (State); Şevket Kazan (Justice); Fehim Adak (Trade); Korkut Özal (Food-Agriculture and Animal Husbandry, *Gıda-Tarım ve Hayvancılık*); Abdülkerim Doğru (Industry). This cabinet must have been one of the youngest, and the least experienced, the country had ever had. Only Ecevit and Işık had had previous cabinet experience.

25 This is only a brief summary of the protocol, which was 14 pages long. For the full text see *Milliyet*, 25 Jan. 1974. See also *Yankı*, 150, 28 Jan. 1974, 8.

26 For the text of the programme see *Milliyet*, 2 Feb. 1974. See also the discussion between Professor Gülten Kazgan (an economist), Nurullah Gezgin (chairman of the Istanbul Chamber of Industry), and Dr Erdoğan Teziç (a constitutional lawyer) on what the coalition was expected to do, in *Milliyet 1974*, 52-8.

27 Ali Sirmen, 'Hükümet ve iş çevreleri' (The Government and Business Circles), *Yeni Ortam*, 3 Feb. 1974. However, Ecevit's programme won him the support of the Left, and the RPP was described as 'a democratic and progressive organization in today's circumstances' and therefore deserving of support by socialists. See Oya Baydar, 'Sosyalizm çizgisi', ibid., 6 Feb. 1974. By the middle of March the activities of the NAP 'commandos' had become serious enough for Premier Ecevit to threaten counter-measures. See the press of 20 Mar. 1974 and *passim*; reports of 'commando' activity became a regular feature in the press.

28 *Milliyet*, 5 Feb. 1974. Demirel spoke for four and a half hours; Ecevit had read the programme in fifty minutes. See also *Yankı*, 152, 11 Feb. 1974, 4-7.

29 *Milliyet*, 5 Feb. 1974.

30 *Milliyet*, 8 Feb. 1974; 235 voted for, 136 against, 2 abstained, and 76 walked out of the Assembly; and *Yankı* (as in n. 28 above).

31 *Milliyet 1974*, 6; *Yeni Ortam*, 11 Feb. 1974. İsmail Cem replaced General Musa Öğün, who had been appointed to this post by the 12 March régime to purge 'the leftists and radicals' in the TRT. The Cem appointment was controversial and became the subject of a cover story in *Yankı*, 156, 11 Mar. 1974.

32 The passage of the Amnesty Law may be conveniently followed in the chronology of *Milliyet 1974*, 6-9, and the Turkish press of this period; see also *Yankı*, 159, 1 Apr. 1974, 4-10.

33 *Milliyet 1974*, 7; *Yankı*, 158, 25 Mar. 1974, 4-8 gives the full story of the politics of opium which led to Erim's prohibiting its cultivation, and Ecevit's lifting of the ban. See also the American view of the question, stated by a foreign service officer, in James W. Spain, 'The United States, Turkey and the Poppy', *MEJ*, 29/iii (1975), 295-309.

34 *Yeni Ortam*, 17 Feb. 1974. However, before Aybar could found a socialist party, Oya Baydar, lecturer dismissed from Hacettepe University in 1971, and Burhan Şahin, the leader of the Press Workers' Union, announced the formation of the Socialist Workers' Party of Turkey (Türkiye Sosyalist İşçi Partisi) on 22 June 1974. See *Yeni Ortam* and *Milliyet*, 23 June 1974.

35 *Milliyet*, 18 Mar. 1974. Erbakan's remarks about the sculpture and about pornographic films and publications were enthusiastically received by the audience. An investigation was opened to judge whether the sculpture was pornographic or not. If a panel of experts found it

pornographic, a case was to be opened against the sculptor and the Committee to Celebrate the 50th Anniversary. *Milliyet*, 21 Mar. 1974. Ecevit said he did not want to see the 'Beautiful Istanbul' affair as a political issue but as an issue of artistic freedom. See his recollections 'Ecevit Başbakanlık Dönemini Anlatıyor', edited by Altan Öymen, in *Cumhuriyet*, 13 July 1975.

36 The Turkish press 15 May 1974 and *Yankı*, 166 and 167, 20 and 27 May 1974, 4-10 and 4-12 respectively. The amnesty covered every category of criminal but excluded those who had been imprisoned for 'thought crimes' (*fikir suçları*) such as translating Marxist literature since this was considered communist propaganda under Articles 141 and 142. By coincidence, on the same day as the vote in the Assembly, a court sentenced translator Muzaffer Erdost to another seven and a half years for translating into Turkish Stalin's *The Problems of a Socialist Economy*. Earlier Erdost had been sentenced to a total of 30 years for translating other books on Marxism.

37 The Turkish press, 16-19 May 1974, *Yankı*, as cited in n. 36 above. On 1 June the RPP took the question before the Constitutional Court and asked it to annul clause 5 of the Amnesty Law. The Court did so on 2 July. See *Milliyet 1974*, 10 and 11.

38 The Turkish press 16-19 July 1974; *Yankı*, 175, 22 July 1974, 6-7. *7 Gün*, 2/vii, 22 July 1974, 4-11. In August Ecevit blamed Harold Wilson for not acting jointly with Turkey. He told his interviewer: 'You see, when the coup that was to end the independent state of Cyprus took place, I went to London uninvited and approached the United Kingdom Government about co-operating with us to save the crumbling state of Cyprus and to try to establish peace and security there but I was refused. And I remember telling our friends before leaving 10 Downing Street that I hoped they had no burden on their conscience over developments that might take place because of their refusal...' *The Middle East*, no. 3, Sept./Oct. 1974, 10. Ecevit's own recollections on the Cyprus crisis ('Ecevit Kıbrıs'ı Anlatıyor'), edited by Altan Öymen, began to be serialized in *Cumhuriyet* on 15 July 1975. See also *Cumhuriyet*, 18 July 1975.

39 *The Middle East*, as cited in preceding note, 6. The issue featured Ecevit on the cover with the caption 'Ecevit the New Atatürk?', though in Turkey Ecevit was hailed as the 'second Atatürk', the 'conqueror of Cyprus.'

40 *Yankı*, 181, 2 Sept. 1974, 6-7.

41 Ibid. Here is a typical Erbakan statement quoted in *Yankı*: 'When we decided to take action in Cyprus, our decision was made in defiance of the whole world. The action in Cyprus has determined a new position for our nation in the world. This new position is one we have deserved for a thousand years. Now our task is to have our rights on the island sanctioned by the nations of the world. Let those who approve, approve, and those who do not, not approve. The island is ours.' See also *Milliyet 1974*, 12 and *passim*.

42 *Yankı*, 182, 9 Sept. 1974, 4-5 and 10-11, and the editorial on 34. See Ecevit's memoirs in *Cumhuriyet*, 25 July 1975 and following.

43 *New York Times*, 17 Sept. 1975; *Yankı, 183, 16 Sept. 1974, 4-6.*

44 The Turkish press, 17-19 Sept. 1975; *Yankı*, 184, 23 Sept. 1974, 4-8.

45 According to Art. 108 of the constitution, only after the Assembly had unseated three governments consecutively with votes of no confidence, could the Prime Minister request the President to call a new general election.

46 The Irmak cabinet was composed of the following: Prof. Sadi Irmak (Prime Minister); Zeyyat Baykara (Deputy PM); Muhlis Fer, Salih Yıldız, and Mehmet Özgüneş (State) Mukadder Öztekin (Interior); Melih Esenbel (External Affairs); Hayri Mumcuoğlu (Justice); İlhami Sancar (National Defence); Prof. Bedri Gürsoy (Finance); Prof. Safa Reisoğlu (National Education); Vefa Tanır (Public Works); Prof. Halûk Cillov (Trade); Dr Kemal Demir (Health); Prof. Baran Tuncer (Customs); Prof. Reşat Aktan (Agriculture); Sabahattin Özbek (Communications); Turhan Esener (Labour); Mehmet Gölhan (Industry); Erhan Işıl (Energy); Selâhattin Babüroğlu (Construction and Resettlement); İsmail Hakkı Aydınoğlu (Rural Affairs and Co-operatives); Fikret Saatçioğlu (Forests); Zekai Baloğlu (Sport); Nermin Neftçi (Culture); Sadık Şide (Social Security); İlhan Evliyaoğlu (Tourism). Four were members of the Reliance Party and seven were Presidential Senators. The rest were brought in from the outside. See the Turkish press 18 Nov. 1974; *Milliyet 1974*, 188-9; *Yankı*, 193, 25 Nov. 1974, 7-9.

47 On the JP congress, see the Turkish press, 22-5 Oct. 1974; *Yankı*, 189, 28 Oct. 1974 (cover story: 'Demirel Again the Unrivalled Leader in the JP').

48 *Cumhuriyet*, 30 Nov. 1974; *Yankı*, 194, 2 Dec. 1974, 4-5. Of the 17 votes, 11 belonged to the Reliance Party, 3 to the NAP, 1 to the NSP, and 2 to Independents. 358 voted against.

49 *Milliyet*, 5 Dec. 1975.

50 Ibid., 13-16 Dec. 1974; 'Vatan Cephesinden Milliyetçi Cepheye', in *Milliyet 1974*, 143-55.

51 *Milliyet 1974*, 155.

52 *Milliyet*, 18-20 Mar. 1975; *Yankı*, 210, 24 Mar. 1975, 7-9, and 34.

53 *Milliyet*, 29 Mar. 1975; *Yankı*, 211, 31 Mar. 1975, 4-5. Among the nine who resigned were Celâl Bayar's daughter Nilüfer Gürsoy, and Adnan Menderes's son Mutlu Menderes. One of the nine, Hasan Değer, representative for Diyarbakır, joined the Republican Party on 4 Apr.

54 On 28 Mar. the Turkish press reported that Ecevit and Bozbeyli had reached an agreement to hold a general election on 12 Oct. 1975.

55 The four-party Nationalist Front government was made up as follows. *Justice Party*: Süleyman Demirel (PM); Seyfi Öztürk and Giyasettin Karaca (State); İhsan Sabri Çağlayangil (External Affairs); Yılmaz Ergenekon (Finance); Ali Naili Erdem (Education); Halil Başol (Trade); Nihat Menteşe (Communications); Selâhattin Kılıç (Energy); Lütfi Tokoğlu (Tourism); Nurettin Ok (Construction and Resettlement); Vefa Poyraz (Rural Affairs); Turhan Kapanlı (Forests); Ali Şevki Erek (Youth and Sport); Rıfkı Danişman (Culture); Ahmet Mahir Ablum (Social Security). *National Salvation Party*: Necmettin Erbakan (Deputy

PM); Hasan Akay (State); İsmail Müftuoğlu (Justice); Oğuzhan Asıltürk (Interior); Fehim Adak (Public Works); Korkut Özal (Food and Agriculture); Ahmet Tevfik Paksu (Labour); and Abdülkerim Doğru (Industry). *Republican Reliance Party*: Turhan Feyzioğlu (Deputy PM); Ferit Melen (National Defence); Dr Kemal Demir (Health); Orhan Öztrak (Customs). *Nationalist Action Party*: Alparslan Türkeş (Deputy PM); Mustafa Kemal Erkovan (State). See *Milliyet*, 1 Apr. 1975; *Yankı*, 212, 7 Apr. 1975, 5–7.

56 Even though the Front government was supported by four parties, it came to rely on the support of 14 Independents for a vote of confidence. Without the 14 Independents it could muster only 214 votes in the Assembly—JP (149), NSP (50), RRP (12), and NAP (3)—as compared to 219 for the opposition parties—RPP (187), DP (31), and UPT (1).

57 *Milliyet*, 1 Apr. 1975; see Abdi İpekçi's editorial on the situation.

58 See the programme in *Milliyet*, 7 Apr. 1975; and the government's decision to reduce prices, ibid., 14 and 20 Apr. 1975.

59 Ibid., 7 May 1975.

60 In the vote of confidence 222 voted for, 218 against, 2 abstained and 4 representatives were absent from the Assembly. See the Turkish press, 13 Apr. 1975; *Yankı*, 213, 14 Apr. 1975, 4–5.

61 *Milliyet*, 13 Apr. 1975.

62 *Yeni Ortam*, 13 Apr. 1975. On the same day *Yeni Ortam* reported a clash at Erzurum University in which five students were injured, two very seriously. Leftist students claimed they could no longer attend lectures because their lives were always in danger. *Milliyet*, 15 Apr. reported that two students from the school for chaplains and preachers (*İmam-Hatip Okulu*) in Kayseri province shot their teacher, exclaiming 'Stop a minute, it's our turn to do the reckoning.' On 14 Apr. the School of Pharmacy and Chemical Engineering in Eskişehir was occupied by members of the right-wing *Ülkü Ocakları*, and pro-RPP students could neither enter nor leave the building. *Yankı*, 217, 12 May 1975, 7, wrote that in Mar. and Apr. there were 57 incidents throughout the country, resulting in 4 killed, 132 wounded, and 498 taken into custody.

63 The Turkish press, 14 May 1975 and following; *Yankı*, 218, 19 May 1975, 4–7.

64 CHP Genel Merkez Basın Bürosu, 'Facts about the Incident Involving the Assault on Prime Minister Demirel: How were the Facts Manipulated?' Ankara, 15 May 1975.

65 Turhan Temuçin, 'Neden Olmasın?', *Yeni Ortam*, 6 June 1975. This conspiracy theory was made more plausible because Türkeş was said to have a large following among junior officers in the armed forces, who were willing to support such a régime. During the summer of 1975, the author heard both stories constantly while in Turkey.

66 The threat was included in his Chief of the General Staff's message to the nation on the fifteenth anniversary of the 27 May revolution. See *Cumhuriyet*, 27 May 1975, and *Yankı*, 220, 2 June 1975, 11.

67 The Turkish press, 22 and 23 June 1975; *7 Gün*, 10/147, 1 July 1975, 4–14; *Yankı*, 5, 224, 30 June 1975, 4–5.

68 On 23 June there was a demonstration against Deputy Premier Türkeş's visit to Diyarbakır, which became violent and almost led to the proclamation of martial law; Türkeş wanted to have martial law proclaimed. But the demonstration was provoked by Action Party 'commandos' who came to Diyarbakır 'like an occupation force', just before Türkeş's arrival, and shouted slogans in the streets: 'Flee, the Turks are coming.' Diyarbakır has a large Shia and a large Kurdish- and Arabic-speaking population, which objected to such chauvinism.

69 CHP Genel Merkez Basın Bürosu, 'CHP Genel Başkanı Bülent Ecevit'in Istanbul Konuşması', 28 June 1975. The text of the speech was also published in Cumhuriyet, 29 June 1975.

70 Cumhuriyet, 5 Sept. 1975; Yankı, 234, 8 Sept. 1975, 7.

71 Cumhuriyet and Milliyet, 13 and 14 Oct. 1975.

CHAPTER XIII

RELIGION AND POLITICS

*Every reactionary movement is a struggle for profits being carried
on by local and foreign circles, sometimes by themselves and
sometimes in collaboration...*

*... Local profiteers and foreign exploiters use the weapon of
religion to give a lofty and sacred appearance to the maintenance
of their economic hegemony.*

Bülent Ecevit, press conference in Bandirma, 2 August 1969

IT is paradoxical that in Turkey, where there have been no
organized Islamic pressure groups since the establishment of the
Republic, religion has played such an influential role in the politics
of the country during the last quarter century. For hundreds of
years Islam had been a pillar of the state and the Sultans exercised
both temporal and religious power. This made it imperative for the
Kemalists to deal decisively with the question of Islam; not to have
done so would have meant leaving intact a force around which
opposition to the new régime could rally. In the struggle between
the Kemalists and the Sultan-Caliph's forces, Islam was one of the
most potent weapons used against the nationalists by the old order.
On 11 April 1920 the *Şeyhülislâm* (the head of the religious
institution) Dürrizâde Abdullah Efendi, 'issued a *fetva* declaring
that the killing of rebels, on the orders of the Caliph, was a
religious duty...' The nationalists tried to counteract the effect of
this religious injunction by a *fetva* of their own, issued by the
pro-nationalist Mufti of Ankara. But this had only limited effect.
'Anti-nationalist riots broke out in many places, and irregular
forces of various kinds, encouraged and sanctified by the authority
of Istanbul, harried the nationalists even in the neighbourhood of
Ankara.'[1]
It was unfortunate for Islam in Turkey that it came to be
intimately identified with the forces more concerned to retain their
own power, even by collaborating with Great Britain, the

supporter of the Greek invasion, than to save the country from partition. Nevetheless Mustafa Kemal Pasha was most cautious in his dealing with the religious institution. He decided on an uncompromisingly secular policy only after he was convinced that his régime would always be threatened by the old order so long as Islam provided the slightest toehold.[2]

By the time Mustafa Kemal Atatürk died in November 1938 the secular republic seemed secure. The social, economic, and political reforms of the preceding years made it unlikely that there could be a counter-revolution and a restoration of the theocratic régime of the Sultan-Caliph. But the Kemalists knew that Islam was an important factor in Turkish politics and that it would be used against them unless precautions were taken to prevent that. The only way was to establish a moratorium on the subject.

Another factor which encouraged the secular policy was the new régime's commitment to the West. Secularism was recognized as one of the hallmarks of westernization, with the result that it soon became the new dogma of the ruling élite. During the first generation of the republic, the Turkish state, governed by the Republican People's Party, mostly ignored Islam, except of course to curb it when it was used by opposition groups. However, Islam remained the religion of 98 per cent of the population, and by ignoring it the government and the party became alienated from the people they ruled.

The introduction of multi-party politics in 1945 and the competition for votes forced the RPP and the opposition parties to reconsider their attitudes to religion. It was the RPP which had to take the initiative because many of its reforms during the past twenty years, bringing little direct benefit to the people, had made them apathetic and even hostile. As early as 1941, before the Republicans were concerned with the challenge of opposition, they permitted the reintroduction of military chaplains into the armed forces. With the advent of political competition, the RPP began to make other concessions over religion which it hoped would increase its popularity and influence voters in its favour.

The Democrats, recognizing that this change of policy could endanger their position, tried to protect themselves by continuing to accuse the Republicans of being hostile to Islam. Premier Şemsettin Günaltay could claim with ample justification that he and his party were liberating Islam in Turkey. A number of reforms were carried out and before the general election of 1950 the party, even according to İnönü's admission, was guilty of exploiting religious forces for political ends.[3] But the record of a generation of bureaucratic despotism could not be washed away with a few concessions; on the contrary, the concessions only served to arouse the suspicions of the people, making them doubt the sincerity of the Republicans, so long identified with unremitting and militant secularism.

Even without the introduction of multy-party politics it is probable that the RPP would have relaxed its militant secularism and adopted a more liberal attitude towards Islam. Such a change would have made the régime more popular and helped to bridge the gap between the bureaucracy and the people. But with multi-party politics the element of competition was brought in, inevitably making the issue political. Neither party was about to permit a counter-revolution, but, on the other hand, both parties had to pay a price for their votes. Before the 1950 election the Democrats could make only promises while the Republicans made the concessions; but it was the Democrats who won.

The Democrats and Islam

The Democrats continued the liberal policies of their predecessors towards Islam and their first measure was to amend Article 526 of the penal code, which forbad the *ezan* (the call to prayer) being made in any other language than Turkish. The Assembly simply lifted the prohibition, giving the *müezzin* the choice of singing the *ezan* in Turkish or Arabic, and most chose Arabic.[4] The decision to introduce this amendment, notes Belen, was taken over cocktails! Menderes wanted the cabinet to introduce the motion and opposed those who preferred it to be introduced by members of the Assembly, for the new Assembly could be denounced as reactionary while the government, full of accredited Kemalists, could not be attacked in the same way.[5] Other changes followed. On 5 July the ban on religious radio programmes was lifted and the Qur'an was recited over the radio. In October religious lessons in schools became virtually compulsory, since it was made necessary for parents who did not wish their children to attend such classes to furnish a letter to that effect.[6]

Initially the RPP did not oppose these measures and its Assembly members voted for amendment of the *ezan* law. If there was opposition to liberalization it came as much from DP circles as from the RPP. For example, *Cumhuriyet* of 9 July 1950 reported that there had been criticism within the DP about the lifting of the ban on religious radio programmes and there were rumours that questions would be asked in the Assembly Group. For the moment there was a bipartisan consensus on the Kemalist reforms and the

Democrat leaders considered themselves as committed Kemalists as any. Neither party was likely to raise objections to the '*fetva*' of the Director of Religious Affairs against communism. 'Islam', he declared, 'rejects communism absolutely, its ideology in any form and all its practices. Faith and the spirit are the most powerful weapons against communism. It is not possible for a genuine believer to reconcile himself to the ideas and practices of communism.'[7]

The victory of the Democrats released years of pent-up hostility against the Republicans and their twenty-seven years in office. We have seen, in chapter 3 above, how Menderes was forced to take note of this pressure from below and how it influenced his relations with the RPP. The supporters of the DP were *ipso facto* opponents of the RPP, and now that their party was in power they believed they were free to vent their feelings against policies they had always found objectionable and never accepted. By the beginning of 1951 there were reports of Atatürk's busts and statues being vandalized and insolent behaviour towards women in small towns. At the DP's Konya congress there were demands for restoration of the fez, the veil for women, and the Arabic script.[8] Religious sermons were used to attack the Republicans and 'in this way', writes Aydemir, 'the way was opened for daily politics to enter the mosque'.[9]

Competitive party politics made religion a political factor and all the parties tried to exploit it to their advantage. This did not mean, however, that any of the major parties would appease reactionary opinion to the extent of threatening the existing order. There was no question of desecularizing the state by undoing major reforms such as the Western code of law or the Latin script. Not even the Nation Party, while it was led by men like Hikmet Bayur, envisaged such changes.

The Republicans, however, claimed to be members of the party Atatürk founded and therefore constituted themselves the 'guardians of Atatürk's reforms'. The implication was that the other parties, particularly the DP, were delinquent in their obligation to protect these reforms and were even encouraging the reaction against them. The RPP, because of its élitist character and its divorce from the people, was always suspicious of any popular manifestation emanating from below. It failed to understand the popular but limited reaction against secularism expressed in attacks on Atatürk as well as reactionary demands to restore the fez or the Arabic script. It interpreted these outbursts as a fully fledged reactionary movement which threatened the very existence of the republican, secular state and called for harsh counter-measures. It would be sixteen years before any responsible member of the party was courageous enough to question the character of the Kemalist reforms and explain why they were not popular with the bulk of the Turkish people.[10]

Menderes was stung by the Republican criticism. He regretted the reactionary outbursts as much as they did. But at the same time he recognized that true restoration of the freedom of conscience was long overdue and he was only continuing a process begun by the RPP. He did not see the possibility of a counter-revolution as the result of the activities of a minority. He dismissed the Republicans' claim that they were the 'guardians of the Kemalist reforms' and told his interviewer that 'the real guardian of the reforms was the Turkish nation'.[11]

During the early years of his rule, Menderes's 'religious policy' was not marked by any extravagant concessions to the Islamist Right. For example, the Islamists wanted the freemason organizations to be closed down, yet under the Democrats freemasonry flourished, becoming more popular and open.[12] Many of the leading Democrats, including Menderes, were described as freemasons and some go as far as to say that the freemasons came into their own under Democrat rule. Nor did Menderes's government shy away from measures against reactionary activity, especially after it was accused of pandering to it. In March 1951 the Ministry of the Interior sent a circular to the provincial governors ordering them to take measures to protect Atatürk's statues, busts, and pictures. At the same time cases were opened against reactionaries like Necip Fazıl Kısakürek as well as the Islamist publications, *Büyük Doğu*, *Sebilürreşad*, and *İslâmiyet*.[13] Addressing the students who had demonstrated most energetically against the threat of reaction, Deputy Prime Minister Samet Ağaoğlu promised that 'reaction will be crushed wherever it raises its head'.[14]

The government was serious about checking reactionary tendencies and in June 1951 it began to round up the Ticanis, members of a religious order who were vandalizing Atatürk's statues and campaigning for a theocratic monarchy. Reports of their arrest became a regular feature in the press and on 27 June Kemal Pilâvoğlu, the *Şeyh* of the order was arrested.[15] He was sentenced to ten years in jail with hard labour and his order sank slowly into oblivion.[16]

The passage of the 'Atatürk Bill' on 25 July 1951, giving the government greater powers to deal with those who challenged the reforms, ought to have removed all suspicion concerning the government's intentions. In February 1952 the press announced that an all-party organization known as the Clubs of the Turkish Revolution (*Türk Devrim Ocakları*) would be set up to protect the Kemalist tradition and reforms. This organization included Hikmet Bayur from the Nation Party, Yavuz Abadan and Behçet Kemal Çağlar from the RPP, and Fethi Çelikbaş and Avni Başman from the DP.[17] Some days later the Islam Democrat Party (*İslâm Demokrat Partisi*) was closed down and the activities of its founder, Cevat Rıfat Atılhan, a notorious rightist, were placed under investigation.[18]

In the light of this activity it is difficult to justify the accusation that the Democrats were encouraging religious reaction. But it is also true that the government no longer had any inhibitions about Islam, and its attitude in the early fifties was expressed in *Zafer*, the DP's semi-official organ. Mümtaz Faik Fenik, who was very close to Menderes, wrote in response to an allegation made by *Dawn* of Karachi that Turkey had discarded her Islamic character:

This is not true since Islam is Turkey's religion, and ever since democratic freedoms were firmly founded here the Islamic character has manifested itself more than ever before. It must be pointed out that religion has been completely isolated from political affairs. It never occurs to any of us to use religion as a political instrument, either individually or internationally....[19]

The attempt on the life of Ahmed Emin Yalman, one of Turkey's most respected journalists, brought a sharp reaction from Menderes. The government, he declared, would crush those who attempted to intimidate intellectuals and politicians. 'In our democratic régime ... in which the will of the nation is sovereign, the will of individuals and their theocratic absolutism will never be allowed.'[20]

The immediate consequence of this incident was that the government stepped up its activities against the extreme, fanatical Right. The Democrats expelled Hasan Fehmi Ustaoğlu, the Representative for Samsun, who had published articles attacking laicism and the Kemalist revolution, and Necip Fazıl Kısakürek was sentenced to jail. Saidi Nursî, the leader of another religious group known as the *Nurcular*, was put on trial and in January 1953 the Nationalists' Association of Turkey (*Türkiye Milliyetçiler Derneği*), the right-wing, anti-liberal forerunner of the Association to Combat Communism, was closed down. The Ministry of Education under Tevfik İleri was said to be involved in this organization, which suggested that few institutions could function without the state's involvement. Finally, on 23 July 1953 'the Law to Protect the Freedom of Conscience' was passed to prevent religion from being used for political ends.[21]

During these years the DP was the centrist party. To the right of it was the Nation Party, which was currying favour openly with conservative opinion. To the left was the RPP, which had returned to its militant secularism—except before elections, when, like everyone else, it exploited religion. But one of its principal propaganda themes against the government was the impending threat of reaction. This was, as Menderes argued, the manifestation of an arrogant and élitist mentality totally out of touch with the people.

Alleging that there is reaction in the country is the same as alleging that you [the audience] are backward and illiterate and that you favour ideas from the Middle Ages. According to the allegations made by opposition circles, Turkish society is a backward society ready to turn to a religious reactionary movement that can be controlled only by the threat of bayonets. This is an insult to Turkish society.... In the Opposition's opinion there is only a handful of real human beings in the country; these are the intellectuals and reformers, and the rest of you are bigoted. In their opinion you are the enemies of reform and the followers of reactionary principles.[22]

Two weeks later in Adana he stated his own views on the issue:

The Turkish people are Muslims and will remain Muslims. No one has the right in this country to violate the freedom of conscience. Those who are true and sincere Muslims can rest assured of the freedom of conscience. It is the true and sincere Muslims who, while being united in their own religious convictions and beliefs, also know how to respect the conscientious religious convictions and beliefs of others. Religion should be spared, in accordance with the principle of the freedom of conscience, from any sort of oppression as a sacred institution. It would not be inaccord with our majority interpretation of the freedom of conscience to consider secularism as anti-religion or inimical to religion. Together with our decision to safeguard religion from any sort of oppression, our decision to prevent religion from being made the means of bringing pressure to bear on compatriots with different beliefs ... is also definite. This country cannot tolerate the turning of so sacred an institution as religion into the instrument exploited by the dregs of society and political pedlars.... Just as dragging the army into politics is a serious crime, so is trying to make a sacred institution like religion the vehicle and instrument of various aims, interests and political disputes.[23]

Menderes was speaking with an eye on the Nation Party which was divided between those, like Hikmet Bayur, who believed that the party ought to remain loyal to the reforms, and others who wanted to come out and adopt an openly reactionary position.

Should the latter group prevail, there was a danger that it would attract the right-wing of the DP into its ranks and Menderes wanted to avoid that, even if it meant closing down the NP.

He issued his warning in the Assembly on 28 February. 'Religious beliefs', he said, 'are not under pressure, so the political parties need feel no necessity to take this matter into their programmes. If there are any groups or parties doing so their aim is to establish pressure through religion and provide themselves with a demogogic weapon. As long as the parties do not openly pledge themselves not to mix religion with politics, the illegitimate use of this weapon ... amounts to a divergence from the course dictated by this country's interests. A day may come when it will be necessary not to let run free those who follow this dangerous course for the same reason that forced us to outlaw communism. ... To say that there is no danger of a reactionary revival in the country does not constitute a reason for giving free rein to efforts to create reaction...'[24]

The Nation Party did not heed Menderes's warning. On 8 July it was temporarily banned on the grounds that it was engaging in subversive activities under a religious cloak, and on 27 January 1954 it was dissolved by court order.[25]

The Issue becomes Political

During the first four years in power the ruling party had no need to use Islam as a crutch. It had established its reputation as the liberalizer of religion without sacrificing the Kemalist reforms. At election time both major parties tried to exploit Islam. The Republicans claimed: 'We reopened the mausoleums,' and the Democrats responded that the *ezan* in Arabic, religious instruction, and religious broadcasts were the work of the DP. Kasım Gülek promised that his party would always remain faithful to Islam. The Democrats counteracted this by distributing a photograph of Gülek in an academic gown and mortar board, claiming that this was the outfit of a Christian priest.[26]

Before the general election of 1954 it was the Republicans who had to use religion in order to increase their votes. Their position was ambivalent since they also claimed to be the guardians of the reforms. But they were very careful not to present this fact to the public. They used the tactic that had been used against them, and had thousands of photographs of President Bayar at a ball distributed throughout the country.[27] Most surprising of all was İnönü's decision to co-operate in the election with the newly constituted NP, now calling itself the Republican Nation Party

(RNP–*Cumhuriyetçi Millet Partisi*). It was inexcusable for a party claiming to be reformist (*devrimci*) to form an alliance with a group totally at odds with its philosophy.

The election was a disaster for the RPP and a triumph greater than that of 1950 for the DP; but it is doubtful whether religion played any significant role, save perhaps in Kırşehir where the RNP won all the five seats—because of the influence of the Bektaşi dervish order in the region.[28] The Democrats won the election on the basis of their record during their first term in office. They seemed to do best in areas, such as western Anatolia and the Marmara region, which had prospered most from the expansion of a market economy under their rule. The most conservative and tradition-bound areas in eastern and southeastern Anatolia, which still remained to be opened up, continued to vote Republican.[29]

It was only when the DP leadership began to lose ground on account of the worsening economic situation, as well as dissension within the party, that it began to exploit Islam more explicitly. The fragmentation which led to the establishment of the Freedom Party robbed the Democrats of their liberal and most secular wing and strengthened the Right. The results of the municipal elections of November 1955, in which neither the RPP nor the RNP participated, suggested that the tide was beginning to turn against the Democrats.[30] If the 'concessions' the government made to the Islamists before the general election of 1957 were designed to reap a rich harvest in votes, they were a miserable failure. The Democrats won the election but their percentage of the vote dropped from 56·6 to 47·3.[31]

If the concessions did not help the Democrat Party electorally, they did encourage the Islamist-traditional forces throughout the country, including those in the DP, to become more active. The peak year for the manifestation of Islam in Turkey was perhaps 1958 and it coincided with Turkey's worst year economically, when the government was forced to devalue the lira by almost 400 per cent. 'Why was 1958 different from other years?' asks Metin Toker, and he answers: 'This was related to conditions prevailing in the country. Hardship, shortages, the lack of goods, and high prices had all got worse. The people were unhappy with life and the pink hue disappeared with time. It is a historical fact that governments which bring hardship to their people, everywhere and in all ages, have tried to soften this by exploiting religion. In 1958 the DP had fallen into the sea and was in the state of embracing a snake...'[32]

Toker is probably correct in his diagnosis, and the increasing religious activity, both official and unofficial, may have had the effect of distracting the people from hard times. The radio broadcast the Qur'an, the *ezan* and religious programmes, while the Nurists carried out their anti-secular propaganda. By May 1958 such was the situation that Fuad Köprülü appealed to 'the Government and the opposition [to] work together against reactionary manifestations which will cause disputes and hatred among citizens and will drag the nation back into darkness and a morass of ignorance and fanaticism'.[33]

Investigations were opened but they led nowhere. The government was no longer willing to deal with the reactionaries as it had done in the early fifties. The 'Atatürk Law' was still on the statute book but it was totally ineffective. The government, claimed Ferda Güley, a Republican member of the Assembly, was turning a blind eye to the reactionary press that was actively campaigning against the RPP as the party opposed to religion.[34]

The Democrat Party had become identified willy-nilly with the resurgence of Islam. But after Menderes survived the air crash at Gatwick in February 1959, in which fourteen members of his party lost their lives, the identification became more open and bizarre. The hand of providence was seen in the escape, described as miraculous, and even Menderes is said to have come to believe this. Hundreds of sheep were sacrificed throughout Turkey, many allegedly financed by the DP and the government, and a new religious image was bestowed upon the Prime Minister.

The Islamists took advantage of the situation and the tempo of their propaganda against the reforms increased. To a large extent the government was exploiting this trend in its 'patriotic front' (*Vatan Cephesi*) campaign, making it seem like a religious and national duty to join the front. İnönü stated that these dangerous practices divided the nation, but he concluded that hostility to the reforms would never succeed.[35] A few days later the party's Assembly Group issued a communiqué denying that the RPP was against religion but warning that the exploitation of religion would be disastrous for the country.[36] The pattern of charges, denials, and counter-charges suggested that both parties were expecting an early election. But there was no early election, for on 27 May 1960 the DP government was overthrown.

Immediately after the DP came to power observers were quick to note the revival or the resurgence of Islam in Turkey. This was interpreted as a result of the DP's more easygoing policies, designed to win votes; and many observers, foreign and Turkish, asked whether the westernized Kemalist structure itself was not threatened by the concessions to the Islamists. This became the debate of the fifties and the sixties, assuming in retrospect a seriousness it did not warrant.

The intelligentsia reacted hysterically to the Islamic resurgence: its older members had witnessed the anti-national politics of the Islamists after 1908 and its younger members had been educated under the militantly secular Kemalist régime which lasted until 1945. The latter had been carefully screened against their Islamic past and taught to be apprehensive of any collective manifestation of religion. The intelligentsia, a privileged stratum in Turkish society, had guarded its privileges jealously and the Kemalist reforms had become the best guarantee of the *status quo* and privilege. It was naturally suspicious of any movement from below, believing that such a movement would undermine the entire system. To some extent this was true, but it was inherent in the multi-party system based on direct elections rather than the influence of Islam. In fact there was no question of an Islamic resurgence threatening the reforms since they were based not on mere legislation but on a generation of socio-economic change which had affected a significant minority in Turkey. It was conceivable to restore the fez to its former glory but virtually inconceivable to reintroduce the Ottoman script.

The Régime of 27 May and Religion

There was a widespread belief that the military régime of 1960, which replaced the Democrats, would mount an offensive against Islamic liberalization and restore the militant secularism of the earlier era. There were rumours to the effect that the *ezan* in Turkish would be restored and that mosques would be converted into barracks. But the National Unity Committee had no such intentions and it began to counter this propaganda by adopting a favourable attitude towards Islam, an attitude which any opposition in the context of competitive politics would have denounced as the exploitation of religion for political ends. As early as 2 June 1960 an unidentified spokesman for the NUC emphasized the part which prayer had played in the liberation of the Turkish nation. He concluded with the words: 'O Lord, deprive us never of the great and selfless who love their fatherland, their nation and mankind. Perpetuate the honourable Turkish nation that has brought us to these happy days.'[37]

The NUC was not totally agreed about its religious policy. There was a small minority, led by Türkeş, which wanted to substitute a nationalist ideology for Islam, not through legislative fiat but through education and propaganda. To this end an organization known as the Union of Ideals and Culture (*Ülkü ve*

374 The Turkish Experiment in Democracy

Kültür Birliği) was set up in June under the direction of Türkeş. It was to be a nation-wide, 'non-political', cultural organization 'whose purpose would be to promote the moral development of the Turkish people and youth in the light of free thought and positive science'. But it never got off the ground, especially after Türkeş was removed from the Prime Minister's office in September.[38]

The majority in the NUC wished to transform Islam into a national instrument of the state, taking it out of the exploiting hands of conservative interest groups and political parties: 'It is the greatest aim of the NUC to keep our sacred religion, which is the treasure of freedom and conscience, pure and unblemished, and to save it from being made a tool of reactionary and political movements.' Again the Committee denied the rumours concerning its intentions to interfere with religion: 'The religious beliefs and practices of our compatriots', read NUC proclamation no. 35, 'can be interfered with neither by law nor by force. With this aim, we would like to state categorically that statements, comments and propaganda emanating from certain organizations and individuals about the changing of the Qur'an and the *ezan* in Turkish, which might lead people to hold wrong views, cannot represent the views of the NUC.'[39]

Islam was to be given both a national and a progressive image in order to prevent its being used as an anti-reformist instrument. Cemal Gürsel set out on a provincial tour to carry this message to the people. In Malatya he asked his audience to make an effort to improve the economic situation and pointed out that 'Islam orders us to work and advance towards perfection'. In Erzurum he said: 'Those who blame religion for our backwardness are wrong. No, the cause of our backwardness is not our religion but those who have misrepresented our religion to us. Islam is the most sacred, most constructive, most dynamic and powerful religion in the world. It demands of those who believe in this faith always to achieve progress and higher wisdom. But for centuries Islam has been explained to us negatively and incorrectly. That is why we are lagging behind the nations of the world.'[40]

The retrogressive elements in 'Turkish Islam' had been imported from foreign parts. Gürsel told Iranian and Pakistani journalists that Islam had to be liberated from the slavery of the Arabic language.[41] The woman's dress with a veil (*çarşaf*) was certainly not Turkish. According to General Refik Tulga 'the wearing of the *çarşaf* is a habit inherited from the Christian Church and has no connection with Islam. In Italy I saw nuns wearing the same sort of *çarşaf*. The only association of *çarşaf* is reaction.' The Mufti of Istanbul, who knew his Islamic traditions better than the General, added: 'The word *çarşaf* is not even Turkish, it is of Persian origin.'[42]

On the whole, the approach of the NUC was far more sophisticated than the example of the *çarşaf* would suggest. The Committee, in spite of its deep-seated commitment to Kemalism, realized that Islam was a vital ingredient in the Turkish character. Since it was counter-productive and harmful to adopt a hostile attitude towards religion, it would be wiser for the state to retain control so that it could not be exploited by the narrow-minded and the reactionaries. At the same time the state could keep reforming Islam so as to make it serve social change in Turkey.

The NUC accepted the institutional changes of the fifties; for example, the *İmam-Hatip* schools and the Advanced Islamic Institute (*Yüksek İslâm Enstitüsü*) opened on 19 November 1959. Since these institutions were to train teachers it was decided to make their curricula more progressive and secular by introducing such subjects as economics, astronomy, civil law, and sociology. Minister of State Hayri Mumcuoğlu explained that the government intended to give better training to men of religion in order to combat superstition. The Directorate of Religious Affairs introduced the magazine *Hutbeler* (Sermons) designed to encourage the delivery of more enlightened Friday sermons. The mosques were to be repaired and restored by experts from the Academy of Fine Arts, since they were examples of Turkish architecture. The Qur'an was to be translated so that it could be read and understood by Turks. Finally, the government would hand over religious instructions to the men of religion but it would not permit them to be exploited for political purposes.[43] 'The path we are following', said Gürsel, 'is such that the day will come when, for the enlightenment of our people, the demand for the recitation in Turkish of the call for prayer and of the Qûr'an will come from below, from the people themselves. In our efforts we are following such a path. We are preparing the relevant organisations and training the necessary elements in such a way as to ensure that our people are trained and prepared in this way.'[44]

Had the NUC remained in power over a period of years, its religious policy may have borne fruit. But eighteen months were insufficient to have a lasting effect, especially with competitive politics restored at the end of this brief interregnum. As a feeble measure of precaution against the undoing of their work, the Commanders asked the parties to make a public declaration that they would not exploit Islam for political ends during and after the general election of 1961.[45]

The Ideological Dimension

In the 1960s Islam in Turkey acquired a new ideological dimension: the anti-liberal, anti-radical, anti-socialist dimension whose purpose was to combat those forces released by the 27 May revolution and the constitution of 1961. This dimension was new only because, under Menderes no radical or socialist activity was permitted; and one would be hard pressed to find even liberal activity. Nevertheless Islam was recognized as the 'antidote to communism' and it was natural for the Right to wield this weapon as soon as it felt threatened from the Left. In the context of Turkey in the sixties, 'the Left' embraced all those who wanted to implement the reforms initiated by the 1961 constitution and this category included the armed forces, the bulk of the intelligentsia, the RPP, and even major Turkish entrepreneurs like Vehbi Koç and Nejat Eczacıbaşı.

The sixties marked the beginning of a process of transformation from commercial to industrial capitalism. This process required major reforms such as reform of agriculture and taxation, which the landowners and the privileged classes naturally resisted. It also jeopardized the livelihood of the Anatolian artisans and merchants who could not compete with large-scale industry and enterprise. To make matters worse, this petty bourgeoisie felt equally threatened from below by the militancy and organization of the unions, especially after the formation of the WPT which carried the working-class cause into Anatolia. The relentless advance of capitalism brought it face to face with the possibility that it would be forced down the socio-economic ladder into the ranks of the working class, which it hated bitterly. Its reaction was to try to halt these advances on its two flanks, and the use of traditional symbols was one way to mobilize support against this onslaught.

In the fifties, when social tensions had not been so complex, the reformist opposition had been attacked as atheist (*dinsiz*) or infidel (*gâvur*). But in the sixties the terms that were used tended to be *Komünist* or *Moskof* for the radicals, liberals or socialists; and *Mason* or *Sionist* (Zionist) for those who favoured modern, monopoly capitalism. In all cases the connotation was primarily religious—and 'communists', 'freemasons', and 'Zionists' were all considered anti-Islam. At the same time there was a political dimension to these terms which had been lacking in 'atheist' and 'infidel'. This is what made it more difficult to combat this movement since its line of attack coincided with the anti-communist ideological commitment of the government. The liberals knew they were trapped and wrote numerous articles denying the existence of the communist threat in Turkey.[46]

Even the principal party of the Right, the JP, was no longer united, and was susceptible to attack from the Islamists. Süleyman Demirel, the technocrat, was suspected of 'progressive, freemason tendencies', and propaganda was carried out against him on these lines when he became a candidate for the party leadership. In order to appease the Islamists he had to deny that he was a mason and profess that he came from a religious background. This reassured the Islamist-traditionalist group (*mukaddesatçı*) for the time being and Demirel was elected. But they watched him closely, and finding some of his policies too 'liberal' denounced him for 'sliding to the left'.[47]

In spite of the experience of the fifties, electoral politics outside the big cities continued to be dominated by the religious factor. In the east, 'the electoral struggle is between the feudal landlords (*ağas*), *şeyhs* and *hacıs*', noted a reporter. The Republicans, trying to counteract the accusation of atheism, claimed that they were responsible for sending pilgrims to Mecca. Justice Party campaign ers were simply telling the people that those who voted for the RPP were communists.[48] As the parties prepared for the general election of October 1965 the slogans remained unchanged. The RPP, now in opposition, was still accused of being communist, while the Republicans accused the JP of being the party of masons.[49]

But in July 1965 the Justice Party decided to change its emblem. This was noteworthy because the party was abandoning an emblem—an open law book with the letters 'A.P.' on either side—which was said to carry great religious symbolism in the popular mind. The open book symbolized the Qur'an and although 'A.P.' in fact stood for Adalet Partisi—the name of the party—they had come to signify also *Allah* and *Peygamber* (the Prophet). In place of this, the JP adopted the white Horse, an obvious exploitation of the former DP symbol. The party leaders calculated that its connotation of the former Democrats would pay richer dividends than the religious symbol, and the election results seemed to justify their calculation.[50]

All parties, except perhaps the WPT, exploited Islam in the 1965 election. The RPP's adoption of the left-of-centre slogan left it open to the accusation of communism and the jingle '*Ortanın Solu Moskova Yolu*' (Left of centre is the road to Moscow). At the same time the JP adopted '*Ortanın Sağındayız, Allahın Yolundayız*' (We are right of centre and on the path to God). The Republicans, as usual ambivalent about exploiting Islam, used the old tactics of denouncing the JP as the party of masons and claimed to have proved that Demirel was a freemason. But this only brought the secular retort: 'We elected him as a political leader, not the *imam* of a mosque.'[51]

It is impossible to evaluate the influence of the religious factor on election results. Analysis of the elections of the fifties, especially that of 1957, suggests that this influence may have been only marginal. 'However ignorant the masses may be,' wrote Ecvet Güresin, 'the religious factor can only be effective for a certain time and in spite of everything economic problems retain their priority.'[52] İsmail Cem, voicing the sentiment of the Ecevit faction in the RPP, ridiculed as élitist the notion that people do not know what is in their interest when they vote for right-wing parties, seemingly on religious issues.[53] With this recognition the RPP began to disengage itself from the position of militant secularism in order to neutralize religion as a factor in politics.

Islam and the Petty Bourgeoisie

In the sixties Islam again began to play an open role in Turkish society. Even the Kemalist army which seized power in 1960 recognized the efficacy of Islam and made no attempt to undo the liberalization of the late forties and the fifties. The army's policy helped to normalize public attitudes to Islam, and even city dwellers began to feel comfortable with their religion. This openness towards Islam has been one of the healthiest social developments in Turkey in recent years. In the new atmosphere, the Director of Religious Affairs could issue a *fetva* giving religious sanction to birth control without an outcry from the opposition.[54] Later he even appealed for public support for the Campaign to Strengthen the Air Force, declaring that 'There is no need to explain that every contribution and service to this cause is a religious and national duty.'[55]

But parallel with this development was the growth of trade and artisan associations with a religious bias, as well as the Quranic schools (*Kuran Kursları*). These were set up in the developed areas while in the backward parts of the east the religious orders acquired greater influence. As noted earlier, it was the people in the east who were most threatened by the encroachments of an expanding modern capitalist economy, but their fears extended to all institutions which represented the modern sector. The modernist small-town and village school teacher therefore bore the brunt of their attacks, and, from the mid-sixties onwards, the press constantly reported on the violence against the teachers. Fakir

Baykurt, the noted writer and chairman of the Teachers' Union of Turkey, complained indignantly: 'Every day somewhere in Turkey a teacher is beaten up. The enemies of republican education have gone berserk. The responsible authorities do not even say anything about these incidents. The Government remains silent and this encourages ignorance.'[56]

One may well ask how such violent reactionary fanaticism could grow without the government's passivity and acquiescence, if not active connivance. It seems clear that the government viewed such fanaticism as a barrier against the Left and as a way to curb the radicalism of the 27 May movement. Turkey's foreign policy under the JP, which is discussed in the next chapter, was also marked by an improvement in relations with the conservative régimes of the Middle East and this also enhanced the role of Islam. Minister of State Refet Sezgin spoke of inviting religious men to a council, 'with the end in view of establishing the principles of the struggle by the Islamic world against extremist movements, especially communism'.[57] The government's attitude towards the Left, with constant appeals for the struggle against the enemies of capitalism, encouraged the forces of fanaticism to become aggressive and insolent.

These forces found expression in a movement known as Nurism (*Nurculuk*). Nurism is not a religious order (*tarikat*) as is sometimes thought, but a movement whose aim is to bring together all Turkish Muslims in opposition to the doctrine of secularism in order to restore the Islamic state. For this reason it opposed religious orders like the Ticanis, accusing them of being exclusive and dividing the community.

The Nurists were led by Saidi Nursî (1873-1960), who had been involved in reactionary activities as early as 1908-9. After the Democrats took office he emerged again and began to publish the *Risale-i Nur* (The Journal of Light) containing the interpretation of the Qur'an in the light of the twentieth century. The Menderes government went through the motions of suppressing the Nurists, but in fact the DP found it expedient to flirt with them for electoral reasons. The movement continued to grow in the fifties and by the early sixties it was organized throughout Turkey. It has even spread to Pakistan and Saudi Arabia, and in Europe it carries out propaganda among workers from the Islamic world, from its centre in Berlin. Its influence was not restricted to the illiterate and semi-literate masses and it enjoyed a following even in the universities and the bureaucracy. The bulk of its support came from the small towns of Anatolia. The Nurists may not have been a threat to the state but they were a divisive force in the country and they diverted attention away from the badly needed reforms.[58] Within six months of the JP's assumption of office in October 1965 there was the threat of reaction. İnönü warned the government that religious fanaticism was as dangerous for Turkey as communism: 'Give up your urge for fanaticism. Don't encourage it, don't see it as less dangerous than communism; whichever is more dangerous time will show.'[59] Some days later General Refet Ülgenalp, the Secretary-General of the National Security Council, told an audience of students: '... Bearded goats and goatee beards are gnawing away at this country: one at the forests, the other at the body of our society....'[60] Such was the growth of reactionary activity as manifested once more in attacks on Atatürk's statues, that even General Tural—a convinced supporter of the Right—was forced to denounce the activities of the Nurists.[61]

When İnönü issued his warning against reaction, Prime Minister Demirel agreed with İnönü's interpretation and promised that his party would not give ground to either kind of reaction, communism or fascism.[62] Demirel was probably sincere in making this promise but he was in no position to fulfil it, since he lacked full control of the party. At the party congress in November he was able to defeat the Islamist faction and hope was expressed that the party would now lose its 'religious, caliphatist' character. But that did not prove to be the case; the Right in the party had been weakened but not defeated.

From the moment Demirel became party leader he was the victim of a contradiction he found impossible to resolve. He was by education and inclination a technocrat—the former Director of Waterworks—whose ambition was to make his country modern and prosperous. Yet he led a party whose strength came from the traditional sectors of Turkish society, sectors which would have to be destroyed if Demirel was to fulfil his ambition. He tried to accomplish his aims by a liberal religious policy which he hoped would keep the traditionalists happy while he modernized the economic sector. The adverse impact of these economic policies was felt by the traditional sector and its representatives in the party; and the Islamist faction, led by Professor Osman Turan, denounced Demirel of going to the left and serving the masons.

The growth of the Islamist movement also served to control the expansion of the Left. The followers of the Nurists and the students of the İmam-Hatib schools attacked not only teachers but also the members and the meetings of the Workers' Party. Thanks to the government's liberal attitude towards the İmam-Hatib schools and the Qur'an courses, the country was no longer safe for any radicals. The government promised that graduates of the *İmam-Hatib* schools would be able to go on to university,[63] and the Minister of Education, İlhami Ertem, told the Assembly that his party's aim was to open an *İmam-Hatib* school in every province.[64] The aim in setting up these institutions was to produce enlightened men of religion but this aim was not fulfilled. Ironically, the first students' boycott in Turkey took place at the Faculty of Divinity at Ankara University because a female student insisted on wearing a traditional headscarf (*başörtü*) in class in defiance of the authorities.[65]

The Foreign Connection

In the mid-sixties a new factor was introduced into the question of Islam and politics, namely the alleged involvement of the foreign oil companies as supporters of the Islamists. Kasım Gülek's *Yeni Tanin* of 12 April 1966 reported that the Risale-i Nur Institute in Berlin had intensified its activities among Turkish workers in western Europe. With German, Dutch, and American financial assistance, the Institute was also producing propaganda to be distributed in Turkey. 'The Dutch aid to the Institute is made through the Dutch oil companies, namely the Shell group.... It would be interesting to learn through which companies the German and American aid is extended to this Kurdish movement run from Berlin.'

Allegations of indirect foreign involvement coincided with the growing movement for a non-aligned Turkey which found expression in the demonstrations against the presence of the US Sixth Fleet in Turkish waters. Such demonstrations were not only dispersed violently by the riot police but were often attacked by well-organized mobs. The worst example of such violence took place on 16 February 1969. A meeting to protest against the Sixth Fleet was attacked in Taksim Square by a mob shouting 'Muslim Turkey' in opposition to the slogan 'Independent Turkey' (*Bağımsız Türkiye*). When the violence ended, two youths had been killed and more than 200 people had been wounded. The date 16 February 1969 had become Turkey's 'Bloody Sunday'.[66]

By the spring of 1969 the foreign connection with the Islamic reaction in Turkey had been extended to ARAMCO, the Arabian American Oil Company. This company was said to be behind the Pan-Islamic organization known as the Union of the World of Islam (*Rabitatül Alemül İslâm*). Turkey was said to be represented in this organization by Yaşar Tunagür, the Deputy Director of Religious Affairs, a confirmed reactionary, who was allegedly spreading the organization's influence into the upper levels of the government.[67]

It was not only radical journalists like İlhan Selçuk (*Cumhuriyet*) or İlhami Soysal (*Akşam*) who interpreted politics in this light. Ecevit, an active and responsible politician, drew similar conclusions:

The disputes and clashes within the Turkish nation have nothing to do with the question of being a faithful believer or being against religion.... A handful of people in Turkey—acting by themselves or hand in hand with foreigners—are exploiting and impoverishing large masses of people. They are trying to keep the people in the dark or to frighten them in order to continue their exploitation.... The exploiters and the vested interests which at first opposed Islam and those who now use devotion to religion as a blind in order to undermine the reforms beneficial to the people are one and the same.... They put on a show of being defenders of the Islamic faith. In fact they are the defenders of Aramco...[68]

By 1969 there was an extremely complex relationship between Islam and politics. Islam was no longer merely a force to be exploited before elections, as it had been in the fifties. It was still that, but it was now an instrument to be used against the radical Left and on behalf of the NATO alliance. It was a means of mobilizing and organizing all the elements in the country against the rapid socio-economic change sought by monopoly capitalism. In this last area, Demirel was beginning to lose control of the Islamist movement.

As we have seen in this chapter, as well as in chapter IX above, Demirel had had to deal with opposition from the right wing of his party ever since he became chairman. But in 1969 the challenge came from outside the party, from Necmettin Erbakan, who, having failed to obtain the JP nomination as candidate for Konya, decided to stand as an independent. Erbakan, like Demirel, was a technocrat; in fact he had been Demirel's contemporary at the Istanbul Technical University. But, unlike Demirel, he claimed to believe in national capitalist development, free from external ties and pressures, and he defended the interests of the Anatolian petty bourgeoisie. The line of propaganda he adopted was Islamic. Demirel's Justice Party was denounced as the property of freemasons and was accused of having increased the number of masons in the bureaucracy by a hundred per cent in four years.[69] Erbakan was opposed to Turkey's joining the Common Market:

Turkey ought not to be in the Common Market of the western states but in the Common Market of the eastern nations. Turkey is backward in relation to the westerners but advanced in relation to the easterners. If

Turkey enters the Common Market under today's conditions it will become a colony. Today the Common Market resembles a three-storey building. The American Jews live on the top floor, the European workers in the middle. Now they are looking for the lackey-janitor to live on the bottom floor. That is why they want to take Turkey into the Common Market.[70]

But for the anti-semitic touch, this could have been the radical interpretation; the anti-semitism was designed to appeal to the Islamists and the nationalists.

The electoral performance of the Independents, who in 1969 obtained 5·62 per cent of the votes and 13 seats and became the fourth group in the Assembly, encouraged Erbakan to found a new political party. The National Order Party (NOP) was founded on 26 January 1970. Its aim was to fill the void on the right wing and it 'adopted a spiritual goal together with a material one.'[71] Thereafter the NOP took up an extreme religious position which made it the laughing stock of newspaper columnists and cartoonists.

Erbakan's speeches seemed designed to attract the wrath of the public prosecutor, for he openly criticized the secular policies of the Republic and Atatürk's reforms. Furthermore, his pronouncements were not likely to attract too many votes, for he promised to close down cinemas, theatres, and ballet schools and to prohibit football matches if he came to power.[72] There were many who expressed the cynical view that the only function of Erbakan's party was to provide the public prosecutor with the excuse to close it down. Such action would enable the government to follow its 'even-handed' policy towards the extreme Right and the extreme Left' and close down the Workers' Party as well. That is precisely what happened in 1971, as we saw in chapter XI above. The NOP was closed down in May 1971 but Erbakan's new party, the National Salvation Party behaved very differently from its predecessor.

Demirel saw the control of the Islamist movement slipping out of his hands. This trend was accelerated after the founding of the NOP and the new DP. The Islamists began to abandon the JP and to join these two new, explicitly right-wing organizations. Demirel took defensive action against Islamist groups such as the Nurists, not so as to destroy them but to demonstrate that their continued existence depended on his goodwill. In such ways might Islamists be dissuaded from supporting the new parties. (At the same time, however, the work of the government was undone at the provincial level by the JP organization, whose lawyers defended the Islamists.) Demirel's measures against the Islamists also helped to

384   *The Turkish Experiment in Democracy*

silence his secularist accusers and appeased those in the armed forces who were alarmed by the growth of reactionary trends.[73]

It is impossible to evaluate how successful Demirel would have been in restoring his hold over the Islamist movement if there had been no military intervention on 12 March 1971 and he had remained in power. The struggle between the JP and its two rivals on the right—the NOP and the DP—became more equal, and by the time the general election was held in October 1973 both the new parties had made great inroads into the vote banks and the JP was defeated.

NOTES

1 Lewis, *Emergence*, 252 (quotations); Çetin Özek, *Türkiye'de Gerici Akımlar* (1968), 63.

2 The best discussion of this period is to be found in Lewis, *Emergence*, 234-74 and Niyazi Berkes, *The Development of Secularism in Turkey* (1964), 431-60.

3 See above ch. I and 28, n. 67. See also Karaosmanoğlu, *45 Yıl*, 178-82 and Lewis, *Emergence*, 411-18.

4 *Cumhuriyet*, 17 June 1950; T. Z. Tunaya, *İslâmcılık Cereyanı* (1962), 225-6.

5 Belen, *Demokrasi*, 60. Baban, *Politika*, 30 states that Celâl Bayar was opposed to the change but acquiesced in Menderes's decision. See also Bayar, *Başvekilim Menderes*, 110-12.

6 *Cumhuriyet*, 6 July, and 11 and 22 Oct. 1950; for a fuller discussion of these events see Lewis V. Thomas, 'Recent Developments in Turkish Islam', *MEJ* vi/1 (1952), 22-40.

7 Ahmed Hamdi Akseki's press conference, *Cumhuriyet*, 28 Aug. 1950.

8 *Cumhuriyet*, 28 Feb. and 3 Mar., and *Vatan*, 12 Mar. 1951.

9 Aydemir, *İkinci Adam*, iii, 109 ff.

10 See above, 260, especially n. 98.

11 Interview with Ali Naci Karacan, *Milliyet*, 17 Mar. 1951.

12 *Cumhuriyet*, 1 May 1951. Freemasons are the *bêtes noires* of the Islamists in Turkey and are always under attack in their journals.

13 *Cumhuriyet*, 29-30 Mar. 1951; Ahmet Yücekök, *Türkiye'de Din ve Siyaset* (1971), 90-1.

14 *Milliyet*, 24 Mar. 1951.

15 *Cumhuriyet*, 28 June 1951; Lewis, *Emergence*, 420 and *passim*; Tunaya, *İslâmcılık*, 220-3.

16 *Cumhuriyet*, 11 July 1951. Özek, *Türkiye'de Gerici Akımlar*, 177-8 and Abdülbâki Gölpınarlı, *Türkiye'de Mezhepler ve Tarikatlar* (1969), 224-5 give a brief account of the Ticanis and other religious groups of this period.

17 *Cumhuriyet*, 23 and 28 Feb. 1952.

18 *Milliyet*, 4 Mar. 1952 and Nadir Nadi, 'Bir Dertleşme', *Cumhuriyet*,

2 Mar. 1952. For the background of this party see Tunaya, *Partiler*, 708-9 and 742-4.

19 *Zafer*, 17 July 1952 quoted by Ankara Radio (Arabic service), 17 July, in *SWB*, iv/279/22-3.

20 Ankara Radio, 25 Nov. 1952, in *SWB*, iv/316/5. The attempt on Yalman's life was made allegedly because the reactionaries regarded him as a *dönme* (a member of 'a Judaeo-Islamic syncretist sect founded in the seventeenth century': see Lewis, *Emergence*, 212, n. 4) and a freemason. See Özek, *Türkiye'de Gerici Akımlar*, 179; Yalman's own account is given in his *Gördüklerim*, iv, 278-80.

21 See *Cumhuriyet*, 23 July 1952 (Ustaoğlu); 13 Dec. 1952 (Kısakürek); 24 Dec. (Nursi); 23 Jan. 1953 and Yalman, *Gördülerim*, iv, 302 (Nationalists' Association); and Eroğul, *Demokrat Parti*, 90-1, on the new law. See also Tunaya, *İslâmcılık*, 231 ff.

22 Menderes's Kayseri speech adapted from Ankara Radio, 21 Nov. 1952, in *SWB*, iv/315/16 and *Zafer*, 22 Nov. 1952. The DP's position on secularism is expounded by Ali Fuad Başgil, *Din ve Lâiklik* (1962; this work was first published in 1954).

23 *Zafer*, and Ankara Radio, 7 Dec. 1952, in *SWB*, iv/319/25.

24 Ankara Radio, 1 Mar. 1953, in *SWB*, iv/342/21-2. A few days later Menderes held the 'communists' responsible for the reactionary activities. 'When communist activity was paralysed... the Rightist elements started to act. It is interesting that both Rightists and Leftists came from one centre. ... Our observations have convinced us that the Rightist instigations are being carried out by Leftist agitators.' *Cumhuriyet*, 5 Mar. 1953.

25 See above, 47-8.

26 Necdet Evliyagil reporting on the by-election campaign in *Cumhuriyet*, 2 Sept. Kasım Gülek had begun to pray in public but he was attacked by his political opponents for doing so without the proper ablutions. Nadir Nadi observed that this controversy would never have arisen if Gülek had not gone out of his way to pray in public. *Cumhuriyet*, 6 Mar. 1954.

27 Nadir Nadi, 'İnsaf Üstad' [Hüseyin Cahit Yalçın], *Cumhuriyet*, 6 Mar. 1954.

28 Reed, 'Revival of Islam in Secular Turkey', *MEJ* viii/3 (1954), 281. However, Osman Bölükbaşı's popularity in Kırşehir must also be taken into account for the RNP's success.

29 This has been amply demonstrated by scholars like Ahmet Yücekök, Ergun Özbudun, and Michael Hyland and accepted by the Ecevit wing of the RPP. See Yücekök, *Din ve Siyaset*, 91-4; Michael Hyland, 'The Party of Atatürk:Tradition and Change', unpublished PhD thesis, Harvard Univ., 1969. Ergun Özbudun has written a study on socio-economic change and political participation in Turkey and he was kind enough to let me read it while it was in manuscript form. I am most grateful to him for sharing his research in this way.

30 See the Turkish press, 14, 15, and 19 Nov. 1955, and Eroğul, *Demokrat Parti*, 129.

31 See above, 56. The 'concessions' included *inter alia*: the legalization of religious instruction in secondary schools (*Resmi Gazete*, 13 Sept. 1956); Menderes's private gift of TL 100,000 for a mosque (*Cumhuriyet*, 15 Feb. 1957); the granting of official status to *İmam-Hatib* schools on 6 Mar. 1957. These schools were set up to train prayer leaders and preachers. (Robinson, *Republic*, 318); Kasım Küfrevi, the son of a *Şeyh* of a religious order in eastern Turkey, rejoined the DP (*Cumhuriyet*, 21 Sept. 1957); in Kayseri, Menderes claimed that during the seven years of DP rule, 1,500 mosques were built and 86, including the magnificent Süleymaniye of Istanbul, repaired (*Zafer*, 20 Oct. 1957). As Professor Tunaya remarked in a conversation with the author, 'Reaction benefited from the Democrats; the Democrats did not benefit from reaction.'

32 Toker, *İsmet Paşa*, ii, 56.

33 *Vatan*, 9 May 1958 quoted by Annemarie Schimmel, 'Islam in Turkey', in A. J. Arberry, ed., *Religion in the Middle East*, ii (1969), 89.

34 *Cumhuriyet*, 13 Mar. 1958; Toker, *İsmet Paşa*, ii, 158-61.

35 İnönü's press conference in *Ulus*, 21 Mar. 1959, and İnönü, *Muhalefet*, ii, 369-71.

36 *Ulus*, 29 Mar. 1959.

37 Ankara Radio, 2 June 1960, in *SWB*, iv/351/c/4.

38 Ankara Radio, 28 June 1960, in *SWB*, iv/372/c/1; İpekçi and Coşar, *İhtilâl*, 460-3.

39 *Milliyet*, 26 July 1960. At the Congress of the Turkish Language Society there was a request that the *ezan* in Arabic be made illegal, and that the Qur'an be translated into Turkish. (*Cumhuriyet*, 15 July 1960). This must have alarmed the Islamists since the Language Society is an influential organization.

40 *Cumhuriyet*, 25 Oct. 1960 (Malatya); Ankara Radio, 25 Oct. 1960, in *SWB*, iv/473/c/2. See also *MER 1960*, 447-8.

41 *Cumhuriyet*, 25 Aug. 1960.

42 *Cumhuriyet*, 27 and 28 Aug. 1960, and *MER 1960*, 448. Refik Tulga was governor of Istanbul. When this line of propaganda did not work, Tulga issued an order forbidding the wearing of the *çarşaf* in the 'touristic districts' of Istanbul (*Cumhuriyet*, 25 July 1961).

43 Ankara Radio, 17 Dec. 1960, in *SWB*, iv/519/c/1-2 and the press, 18 Dec. 1960; *MER 1960*, 447. The Turkish translation of the Qur'an was published in Nov. 1961. See *The Times*, 23 Nov. 1961 cited in *MER 1961*, 527.

44 Ankara Radio, 2 Mar. 1961, in *SWB*, iv/581/c/1.

45 See the Joint Declaration of 5 Sept. in *Milliyet*, 6 Sept. 1961.

46 See for example Turan Güneş, 'Komünizm Tehlikesi', *Milliyet*, 18 Feb. 1967. Güneş was Foreign Minister in the RPP-NSP coalition government in 1974. See also President Gürsel's statement to Ecvet Güresin that 'the danger from the extreme Left is artificial.' *Cumhuriyet*, 18 June 1965.

47 See above, 242, and *Cumhuriyet*, 28 Nov. 1968.

48 *Cumhuriyet*, 30 May 1964 (partial Senate elections).

49 *Cumhuriyet*, 29 June 1965.

50 See above, 237.

51 *Cumhuriyet*, 29 June 1965 (quotation) and 2 Oct. 1965 (jingles).

52 'Dinsizlik Kompleksi', *Cumhuriyet*, 10 Sept. 1963.

53 'AP, DP ve Geçici Refah', *Cumhuriyet*, 5 Nov. 1965.

54 *Milliyet*, 1 May 1964. İnönü was PM at the time.

55 *Cumhuriyet*, 4 July 1970, 5.

56 *Vatan*, 1 June 1966. Baykurt was himself attacked and wounded while giving a talk on 'Education and Teaching'. The crowd chanted: 'Damn Communism'. *Cumhuriyet*, 17 Oct. 1968. The most brutal case was the castration of the literature teacher Kemal Abbas Altınbaş by a reactionary student. See the Turkish press, 20 Jan. 1969 and Sadun Tanju's articles in *Cumhuriyet*, 12-15 Jan. 1970.

The most complete study on the religious organizations is Ahmet Yücekök, *Türkiye'de Örgütlenmiş Dinin Sosyo-Ekonomik Tabanı, 1946-1968* (1971). In a brief summary describing his work Yücekök wrote: 'In short, the Turkish Islamic crusaders of the 1970's are a section of the petty bourgeoisie, who are trying to freeze a swiftly changing society with a static religious ideology and in this sense it can be claimed that they are in full realization of their economic interests as the "frozen" society will only help to secure their benefits. As they are trying to change a society that has covered a lot of way in the capitalist frame of development, their political and economic aims in bringing back the Islamic order can only be labelled as to be *"Status-quo ante".*' See *SBFD*, xxvi/2 (1971), 306.

57 *Tercüman*, 12 Apr. 1966.

58 On Nurism see Çetin Özek, *Türkiye'de Gerici Akımlar ve Nurculuğun İçyüzü* (1964), 237-300; idem., *Türkiye'de Gerici Akımlar*, 180-97; Tunaya, *İslâmcılık, 232 ff.; and Schimmel, 'Islam in Turkey', in Arberry, ed., Religion in The Middle East*, ii, 89.

59 *Cumhuriyet*, 16 Apr. 1966.

60 *Milliyet*, 21 Apr. 1966 and Abdi İpekçi, 'Ülgenalp'ın Uyarmaları', *Milliyet*, 22 Apr. 1966.

61 *Akşam*, 12 June 1966.

62 *Cumhuriyet*, 17 Apr. 1966.

63 *Cumhuriyet*, 18 May 1966. The aim was to strengthen the conservative element in the universities in order to counteract the growing radicalism. In 1975 the parties of the Right began to campaign to have graduates of *İmam-Hatib* schools recruited into the armed forces directly as reserve officers. This was seen by their opponents as a way to infiltrate the armed forces with reactionaries.

64 Discussion of the budget on 21 February 1969. See *1969 VY*, 226. See also Fehmi Yavuz, *Din Eğitimi ve Toplumumuz* (1969), 58-72.

65 The Turkish press, 13-16 Apr. 1968.

66 The Turkish press, 17 Feb. 1969 and following. It is worth noting that the rising tide of 'Islamic reaction' did not prevent Demirel from classifying beer as a non-alcoholic beverage so that it could be sold in coffee houses and in the street. But this was done only after the state abandoned its monopoly and the beer industry was thrown open to private

enterprise, local and foreign. International concerns like Tuborg quickly moved in.

67 See the columns of Ümit Gürtuna, İlhan Selçuk, and Mehmet Barlas in *Cumhuriyet*, 1-3 May 1969.

68 Ankara Radio, 10 July 1969, in *SWB*, iv/3124/c/1 and *Milliyet*, 11 July 1969.

69 Ediboğlu and others, eds., *Salname 1390*, 45.

70 *Cumhuriyet*, 28 Apr. 1970.

71 The Turkish press, 27 Jan. 1970; *Cumhuriyet*, 9 Feb. 1970; Sencer, *Sosyal Temeller*, 364-72. The principal material goal was to establish a national economy in which there would be more equal distribution of wealth, and social welfare.

72 *1971 VY*, 265.

73 See İlhan Selçuk, 'Nurculuk Okulları neden Basılıyor?', *Cumhuriyet*, 4 Feb. 1971. The Turkish press had been reporting such activity against the Islamists since the summer of 1969.

CHAPTER XIV

FOREIGN POLICY

The Turkish diplomat resembles a sort of super real-estate salesman; he bids up the price of his 900×300 mile rectangle of territory without of course delivering it. Therefore Turkish leaders embrace the 'Truman Doctrine' not only because it satisfies their anti-Russian feeling but also because it has enabled them to exploit their geographical position more profitably than ever before.

Andrew Roth, the *Hindu* (Madras), 12 June 1950

Turkey believes that lasting peace in the world can only be achieved by the removal of the fundamental disputes between the free and democratic nations' front and the Soviet bloc.

... Turkey does not intend to follow a policy of balance between the blocs and of using the weight of her exceptional geopolitical position as a means of political blackmail against the two sides ...

Foreign Minister Fuad Köprülü, 30 March 1956

From Neutrality to NATO

WHEN Adnan Menderes formed his government in May 1950 the foundations of Turkey's new foreign policy had already been laid. The Soviet Union's refusal in 1945 to renew the 1925 Treaty of Friendship without substantial concessions from Turkey had destroyed that link with the USSR. The Turkish government had begun to seek closer ties with the United States and had succeeded in obtaining military and economic assistance under the Truman Doctrine and the Marshall Plan respectively. The price of this American connection was the government's willingness to open up the economy to the private sector, indigenous and foreign. It would be wrong to interpret this as a concession made under pressure, for the RPP had already decided to loosen the political and economic structure in order to accommodate internal social change. The reorientation in foreign policy was therefore a logical step arising out of domestic policy. If the Republicans failed to accomplish

anything it was their inability to secure for Turkey a place in
NATO. Had they had more time they would probably have
accomplished that also. As it was, they laid the solid foundations
of a foreign policy upon which future governments would continue
to build; in fact, so rigid were the foundations that it became
difficult to move outside them without endangering the entire
structure of foreign policy.

Despite the bitterness of inter-party relations, before 1950 a
consensus over foreign relations had been established by the
parties and the press, save for the socialists like Mehmet Ali Aybar
and Zekeriya and Sabiha Sertel. The ratification of the military aid
agreement by the Assembly on 1 September 1947 had been
unanimous.[1] There was some dissent over the terms Washington
sought before signing the aid agreement. Congress had insisted on
guarantees of free access to American journalists to observe the aid
programme, the right to supervise it, the right to restrict the use of
American assistance and 'to terminate the program if recipient
governments failed to carry out their assurances ...' As Harris has
noted: 'If there was one sensitive nerve in the Turkish body politic,
it was according privileges to foreigners. Supervision implied
control; this in turn implied abandoning sovereignty.'[2]

The request for such privileges was criticized by people as
diverse as Hüseyin Cahid Yalçın and Fuad Köprülü, the deputy
leader of the DP. As a result the language of the agreement was
softened while its substance was retained, and it was signed
without further dissent.[3] Under the Democrats even token dissent
was discouraged; the emphasis was on an 'unquestioning consensus'. There was perhaps a reason for this attitude. Menderes did
not consider Turkey's foreign policy to be an expression of the
ruling party but that of the entire nation.[4] Therefore opposition to
such a policy was considered opposition not to the party but to the
nation. This concept was also consistent with the DP's interpretation of the national will.

The Democrats did not intend to make any radical departures in
their external relations. 'In the light of the results of the last
elections,' declared Foreign Minister Köprülü, 'our foreign policy,
which has been oriented towards the West since the Second World
War, will take a more energetic form in this direction.'[5] The
opportunity to play an energetic and active role was provided
almost immediately by the outbreak of the Korean War in June.
On 27 June the UN Security Council adopted a resolution
recommending that member states furnish assistance to South
Korea 'to repel the armed attack and to restore international peace
and security in the area'.[6]

Ankara's response was immediate. Fuad Köprülü informed the Secretary-General that 'my government declares that it is ready to execute loyally and in complete conformity with the provisions of the Charter the undertakings which Turkey assumed as a member of the United Nations'.[7]

The Democrats' enthusiasm for America's cause in Korea has been generally interpreted as being motivated by their anxiety to enter NATO. Strong and unwavering support of the type that was not forthcoming from even the NATO allies would weaken resistance to Turkey's membership. What was needed was a quick and dramatic decision to send troops to fight in Korea. Such an undertaking ought to have had the sanction of the National Assembly. But the Assembly could raise embarrassing difficulties and slow down the process of decision making. Besides, it would be a decision made in the national cause and no one ought to object. So on 18 July a meeting was held at the resort town of Yalova under the chairmanship of President Bayar and with the Prime Minister, the Foreign Minister, the Defence Minister, the Chief of the General Staff, and the Commanders of the army, navy, and air force all present. This was where they decided to send troops to Korea. 'In order to obtain a formal sanction, the cabinet was convened three or four days later. This was achieved by having only the docile members participate. Myself and the Honourable Nihat Reşat Belger were not invited to this meeting.'[8]

The opposition criticized this decision more on the way it was made than for its content. Menderes had neither consulted the opposition nor the Assembly, where he enjoyed overwhelming support. But as Hikmet Bayur, the leader of the Nation Party, commented: 'If we are able to enter the pact [NATO] as the result of our sending troops to Korea, the sacrifice will be in order.'[9]

Menderes decided to strike while the iron was hot and on 1 August the American, British, and French ambassadors were presented with the request that Turkey be taken into NATO.[10] Ever since the formation of the alliance, its members had been divided over Turkey's membership. The Europeans were not keen to extend their commitment beyond the north Atlantic region. Britain wanted Turkey to stay out in order to be the cornerstone of an alliance of Middle Eastern states. The US was the most forthcoming of the members in supporting Turkey's application. For the Turkish government, only membership of NATO could provide guarantees of security as full and as firm as those enjoyed by the European members of the alliance. It was true that the major Western powers had guaranteed Turkey's security, but, outside NATO, Turkey would still be regarded as a secondary zone of defence. Moreover, ever since the establishment of the alliance in 1949 Turkey had been suffering from the 'Atlantic Pact complex'.[11]

Ankara did not see any conflict between her role in the Middle East and her potential role in NATO. She was willing to play the Middle Eastern role asked of her by the West as soon as she became a member of NATO. As early as 19 September 1950 Turkey had been invited by Washington to associate herself 'with the appropriate phase of the planning work of the North Atlantic Treaty Organization with regard to the defence of the Mediterranean'.[12] Turkey accepted this invitation and temporized. Slowly the tide began to turn in her favour, thanks to the diplomatic pressure she maintained on the Western powers. The Pentagon had begun to appreciate the strategic value of Turkey as well as the military contribution she could make to the alliance. On 15 May 1951 Washington proposed formally to Britain and France that Turkey and Greece be admitted to NATO. Only in July did Britain, the principal stumbling block to Turkey's entry, agree to support the membership of these two powers. Foreign Secretary Herbert Morrison admitted that 'the main difficulty has been to reconcile her [Turkey's] desire to join the North Atlantic Treaty with her position in relation to the general defence of the Middle East. Her Majesty's Government ... have come to the conclusion that Turkish and Greek membership ... is in fact the best solution. At the same time, they are most anxious that Turkey shall play her appropriate part in the defence of the Middle East.'[13] Turkey's membership was now a formality. On 21 September 1951 the NATO Council meeting recommended the inclusion of Turkey and Greece in the alliance, and Turkey officially became a member on 18 February 1952.

Turkey's admission to NATO gave a great boost to the prestige of the DP government and a sense of euphoria prevailed in the capital. But it also led to the deterioration of relations with the Soviet Union. Ever since November 1948, when Premier Hasan Saka had held discussions with the Soviet ambassador, there had been rumours that Soviet policy towards Turkey was undergoing a radical change. Moscow, realizing that her aggressive policy had been a fiasco, tried to prepare the ground for a new relationship.[14] In March 1949, when there was talk of Turkey participating in a Mediterranean pact, British diplomatic sources announced that Russia would be hostile to such a move but would propose a non-aggression pact to Ankara as an alternative.[15] Thereafter relations between Ankara and Moscow were normal and correct until the Soviet Note of 3 November 1951, protesting against

Turkey's participation in NATO. The Note observed that, 'Under these conditions it is quite obvious that the invitation to Turkey, a country which has no connection whatever with the Atlantic, to join the Atlantic bloc can signify nothing but an aspiration on the part of the imperialist states to utilize Turkish territory for the establishment on the USSR frontiers of military bases for aggressive purposes.'[16]

Ankara rejected Soviet claims as baseless and declared that her membership of the Atlantic Pact was necessitated by a sense of insecurity, which she thought the Soviet Union ought to understand. 'If the Soviet Government were to carry out a sincere self-inspection, she would admit that there exist very genuine reasons for Turkey to feel anxiety about her own security. It should not be forgotten that Turkey has been confronted with demands which threaten her national independence and territorial integrity.'[17]

There was a further Soviet note on 30 November and threafter the matter was dropped. The Democrats were relieved that relations with their neighbour were cool, for this justified the extreme cold-war posture the government had adopted. Immediately after Stalin's death the USSR tried to mend its fences with Turkey. Its note of 30 May 1953 proposed renewal of the Treaty of Friendship it had denounced in 1945, and at the same time Moscow abandoned all claims to Kars and Ardahan, and relinquished claims to participate in the joint defence of the Straits. The Turkish reply of 18 July, writes Váli, was 'purposely delayed [and] was frosty, formal and laconic'.[18] There was no one in the Democrat or the Republican Party willing to take a step which might endanger Turkey's relations with America. Turkey had opted for the hard American position in the cold war and was reluctant to abandon it even after Washington had done so.

Turkey and the Middle East 1950–1960

The unofficial acceptance of Turkey by NATO in September 1951 marked the beginning of new initiatives to establish a Middle East Defence Organization (MEDO). The key to such an organization lay in Egypt and if Egypt could be persuaded to join, the other Arab governments were expected to fall in line. On 13 October the United States, Britain, France, and Turkey sent an identical note to Egypt, Syria, the Lebanon, Iraq, Saudi Arabia, Jordan, Yemen, and Israel proposing co-operation against external aggression. The Egyptians, whose principal concern was to have Britain evacuate the Suez Canal zone, turned down the proposal, claiming that they viewed it as 'the perpetuation of Egypt's occupation not only by Britain but also by other powers'.[19]

The inclusion of Turkey did not help. Some of the Arab states saw Turkey's role in MEDO as a cover for the designs of the Western powers in the region. This sparked off an anti-Turkish press campaigh in Cairo and one newspaper even published a cartoon showing the United States, Britain, and France with a dog (Celâl Bayar) on a leash.[20] Try as she might, Ankara could not convince the Arabs that there was no relation between Turkey's membership of the Atlantic alliance and MEDO. In January 1952 Churchill's proposal that Britain hand over the Suez Canal zone to American, French, and Turkish forces was rejected by all three states, in particularly clear terms by Turkey. But the proposal seemed to confirm Arab fears.[21] Turkey's leadership of a Middle East pact was not acceptable to the Arab states for another reason: Ankara's friendly relations with Israel. For the Arabs, Israel was enemy number one and pleas by Foreign Minister Köprülü on 'the need to thwart any threat by the enemy' (referring to communism) had no sense of urgency.[22]

Egypt's resistance to MEDO was seen only as a temporary setback and John Foster Dulles, the American Secretary of State, encouraged the creation of another anti-Soviet alliance based on the 'northern tier' states of Turkey, Iran and Pakistan, an alliance that would be open to the Arab states as well. Turkey already had a Treaty of Friendship (26 July 1951) and a Cultural Agreement (28 June 1953) with Pakistan. After President Eisenhower's approval of military aid for Pakistan (25 February 1954), Turkey and Pakistan signed a treaty of Mutual Defence on 2 April 1954. Turkey had become the link between NATO and any future defence pact farther east.[23] On 24 February 1955 Turkey and Iraq signed a regional defence pact in Baghdad which was joined by Pakistan on 17 September and by Iran on 23 October. Britain had already joined the pact on 25 March, raising a clamour among the Arab nationalists that she was retaining her dominant position in Iraq by indirect means.[24] Menderes and Dulles saw the Baghdad Pact as a device to draw the reluctant Syrians and Egyptians into MEDO. But Western policies had the reverse effect, and the attempt to cajole Egypt and Syria forced them to turn to the Soviet Union for arms, giving her an entry into the Middle East.[25]

Despite the unforeseen consequences, the Baghdad Pact was regarded as a break-through by Menderes. Not only had they succeeded in bringing together the 'northern tier' states but the alliance even included the Arab state of Iraq. Menderes had not expected Nasser's reaction to the signing of the Turkish-Iraqi Pact to be so harsh after the friendly exchanges that had taken place between Turkey and Egypt in December 1954. On 1 December Ankara Radio quoted Nasser:

Whatever the nature of past events, the Turks and the Egyptians are today, as in the past, brothers again. The generations have remained closely linked with each other throughout history and for centuries have fought side by side for the same cherished ideals. As in the past, the Turks and the Egyptians belong to the same family and although certain conditions may have separated them temporarily, they continue to be the owners of the same valuable heritage. The Mediterranean is the common sea of the Egyptians and the Turks and in the Mediterranean the Turks and Egyptians have friends and enemies. Like the two countries, the Mediterranean is an inseparable part of the Middle East. If Turkey is secure then the Egyptians will be secure. If we are both strong, with our alliance we can create a huge force ...[26]

The Turkish press, and especially the semi-official *Zafer*, reciprocated with articles friendly to Nasser and Egypt. Rıfkı Zorlu, the brother of Fatin Rüştü Zorlu—a member of Menderes's inner circle—was sent as ambassador to Cairo, presenting his credentials on 3 January 1955.[27] But the news of the pact altered everything, and Menderes, who was visiting the Arab capitals to persuade other states to join, was forced to abandon his plan to visit Cairo.[28]

Menderes had misjudged the temper of Arab nationalism and had no understanding of the position of non-aligned states like India. He continued to believe in the polarization of the world into two irreconcilable camps and was convinced that Turkey's interests were best served by following to the letter the policy dictated by Washington. Turkey seemed to have no foreign policy goals independent of those of America. During the ten years when the Democrats ruled Turkey there was hardly an occasion when there was a serious difference of view on foreign policy between Ankara and Washington. In fact the only time Ankara showed alarm was when Washington seemed to be heading for a limited détente with Moscow. If anything, Menderes's foreign policy was based on the assumption of a long-term cold war. 'The Russian calls for peace would not fool the Turkish nation,' Menderes told an audience in Dallas, Texas, in 1959.[29]

Throughout the fifties Ankara pursued the foreign policy objectives set in Washington or London with conviction and without complaint. Both the Democrats and the Republicans agreed on this policy except for rare differences over nuance. Turkey's role in the Middle East increased traditional Arab suspicion of the Turks and at the same time embittered Ankara's relations with the Soviet Union. Soon after the signing of the Baghdad Pact, in April 1955, the Turkish delegation at the Conference of Afro-Asian Nations at Bandung led the counter-attack on behalf of John Foster Dulles against the policy of non-alignment: 'There can be little doubt', writes David Kimche, 'that these [Turkey and Iraq] and other non-Western nations in Asia and Africa were urged by the United States to attend the Bandung Conference in order to defend Western positions and prevent the conference from being a spring-board for the communists or even the neutrals....'[30] The Turkish delegation and its partners did their job well and one result was to widen the rift between these pro-Western states and the non-aligned. For Turkey, as we shall see, this meant isolation and humiliation at the United Nations.

In the crisis over the nationalization of the Suez Canal by Nasser in July 1956, Turkey followed the American rather than the Anglo-French lead. After the Anglo-French-Israeli attack on Egypt, Turkey voted for the US motion calling for a cease-fire. But it took the lead in the Baghdad Pact meeting in Tehran on 8 November in proposing that Britain should not be expelled from the Pact.[31]

From the Turkish press of the time one senses that the Turks welcomed the embarrassment of the United Kingdom in the Suez affair, for it marked the end of British hegemony in the region. The Turks hoped that they would be able to replace the British, perhaps not directly, but as the delegates of America and the Western powers. This feeling had been there ever since the UK had shown that it wanted to organize MEDO under British leadership in the early fifties and Ankara had resented becoming a British satellite state.[32] Now, in 1956–7, Menderes believed that Turkey would be able to play a dominant role under the aegis of the Eisenhower Doctrine, which was widely welcomed in the Turkish press:

We note that this doctrine, like the Monroe Doctrine, is clear and simple. The principle it seeks to promote is that the Middle East is for the people of the Middle East. The guarantee it provides is US military strength and the good it promises is to provide assistance for the Middle East in the economic sphere through vast financial assistance....

... History will judge the soundness or the unsoundness of the Eisenhower Doctrine ... by the position and importance to be given by America to Turkey in this plan and its calculations.[33]

The days of 'political vacuums' in the Middle East were long over and it was out of the question for Turkey to take over from

Britain. Nevertheless, Turkish policy became more aggressively active, especially towards neighbouring Syria which had moved closer to the Soviet Union since 1955. The expulsion of the US officials from Syria 'on charges of plotting with Turkey and Iraq to overthrow the Syrian régime' and the visit to Turkey of Deputy Under-Secretary of State Loy Henderson in August 1957, increased tension between Ankara and Damascus.[34] With a general election approaching, it is probable that the Democrats exploited the situation for internal political reasons. The army was mobilized on the Syrian border, and that led to Soviet mobilization on the Turkish border in the Caucasus.

The Turkish government continued to give unquestioning support to US policy. After the revolution in Iraq on 14 July 1958, Ankara approved the landing of US Marines in the Lebanon, permitting the US forces to use bases in Turkey for a purpose which could not be justified by Turkey's commitment to NATO. Even before the landing, Turkey is said to have offered troops to the Lebanese government.[35] The revolution in Iraq was a blow to American policy in the Middle East and it also left the Turkish government more isolated than ever.

By the middle of 1958 Menderes, who had considered the United States the first amongst equals in the alliance, found that Turkey was becoming a dependant. The decline of her position had much to do with the internal set-backs suffered by the DP, such as the poor showing in the 1957 election and the emergence of a confident and aggressive opposition party. It is alleged that after the arrest of the nine officers in December 1957 and the overthrow of King Feisal in July 1958, Menderes began to appeal to the US to promise help if Turkey was threatened by the 'communists' internally.[36] One immediate outcome of this was the signing of a Bilateral Agreement between the US and Turkey. The United States agreed, in case of 'internal aggression' against Turkey, 'to take such appropriate action, including the use of armed force, as may be mutually agreed upon ... in order to assist the Government of Turkey at its request'.[37]

In February 1959 Admiral Charles Brown of NATO Southern Command told a press conference that rocket bases would soon be built in Turkey, and in October the government officially announced the existence of bases with Jupiter missiles.[38] The Turks had accepted what their neighbour Greece had refused: that was the extent of Menderes's commitment to the US alliance. Menderes continued to retain the cold-war posture of the early fifties, even while the United States was working towards a détente. When Moscow proposed an atom-free zone in the Balkans, Ankara rejected it, claiming that it would leave her open to the threat of aggression.[39] The Russians, however, persisted in their 'peace offensive' and even Washington was anxious that Ankara improve its relations with its giant neighbour. In April 1959 Khrushchev invited Menderes to Moscow, a visit intended to mark the opening of a new page in Turco-Soviet relations. The visit was to take place in July but Menderes's fall on 27 May 1960 ended the possibility of an early thaw in relations. However, before examining Turkey's foreign policy in the sixties let us examine the motives for her foreign policy of the fifties.

Recapitulation

Turkey's post-war foreign policy was an extension of her internal policy, whose aim was to transform Turkey from an underdeveloped and poor country to a developed and a prosperous one. In short, the political leadership wanted to make Turkey a 'little America' or the America of the Middle East, just as today the Shah of Iran often talks of making his country as prosperous as Germany. How was this to be accomplished?

The simplest way to achieve this goal seemed to be through large doses of American funds, private and public. Therefore the Republicans sought military aid under the Truman Doctrine and economic aid from the Marshall Plan. At the same time they passed legislation to attract foreign investment into Turkey. But from the very beginning the Turks were disappointed by the amount of aid coming from America. Cyrus Sulzberger who spoke to President İnönü on 1 July 1948, reported: 'He likes Americans although he complains that Turkey is getting a very stingy allotment under the Marshall Plan. He would very much like an alliance with the United States and is afraid that American interest in Turkey is not a permanent factor. That he cannot say publicly though for the fear of disturbing people.'[40]

These two factors—complaints about insufficient aid and the fear of America's interest in Turkey declining—remained major preoccupations of Ankara's foreign policy. The two were intimately linked in Ankara's planning: the greater Turkey's role in the foreign policy calculations of the West, the greater the size of aid to Turkey. The Turkish press never tired of emphasizing the importance of Turkey to the West and complaining, at the same time, that this was not appreciated by the Western allies. Official circles felt no sense of inferiority in this relationship, which they considered mutually beneficial; and the Democrats, whose commitment to the West was total, expected, rather naïvely, that the US would automatically reciprocate. Throughout their ten years in power the Democrats were disappointed by the US response and this was especially true in the mid-fifties, when the Turkish economy had become torpid and in dire need of support. The Democrats learned that their relationship was not a partnership after all, and that instead of interdependence it was they who were dependent on Washington.

As early as October 1954 Menderes had begun to seek aid in Europe, and Bonn seemed to hold forth the best hope. It was in this connection that Menderes visited Germany in October 1954 after America had refused to meet Turkey's financial needs.[41] President Theodor Heuss's visit to Turkey in May 1957 marked Turkey's increasing reliance on German economic aid.[42] Washington encouraged this trend, hoping that her European allies would share the burden of Turkey's economic needs. This was reflected in the $359 million loan of August 1958, made jointly by the US and the OEEC countries. The following year, Turkey's application for membership of the Common Market symbolized the Democrats' recognition that the future of the country was bound to that of Europe rather than America. The 'special relationship' that they had worked for so diligently had not materialized.

The Promise of Change 1960

In May 1960 there was no evidence that the US would acquiesce passively in the overthrow of the Democrats, for they had been a reliable ally. The military conspirators, many with intelligence backgrounds, feared American intervention; there were even rumours that Menderes had plans to call in American troops under the Bilateral Agreement of 1959.[43] After the *coup* of 27 May the soldiers took care to emphasize, in their first communiqué, that their régime would honour Turkey's foreign policy commitments.

We address ourselves to our allies, friends, neighbours and the entire world. Our aim is to remain completely loyal to the United Nations' Charter and to the principles of human rights. The principle of 'peace at home, peace in the world,' set by the great Atatürk, is our flag. We are loyal to our alliances and undertakings. We believe in NATO and CENTO and are loyal to them. We repeat: our ideal is 'peace at home, peace in the world'.[44]

There was further promise of continuity when Selim Sarper, a professional diplomat who had interpreted Turkey's foreign policy at the UN and NATO, was appointed Minister of Foreign Affairs in the new government. And he confirmed this in his first press conference on 1 June 1960. Within a few weeks it became clear that the US had no hesitation in supporting the new régime, which was badly in need of immediate financial aid. Washington announced that it would open a $400 million credit and *Cumhuriyet* of 5 July 1960 reported that 'an enquiry made on this subject [aid] by our government, in times blacker than we have ever witnessed before, was answered by the American government within 24 hours.... Yesterday an agreement related to this matter was signed in Ankara.'[45]

In spite of the continuity there was a feeling that the NUC would introduce changes in foreign policy just as it was expected to introduce them in all other walks of life. There was a need to broaden the base of Turkey's foreign relations and make them more independent, and the attempt to do this was reflected in the government's programme announced to the public on 11 July. The section on foreign policy emphasized the need to improve relations with the Arab countries, especially the United Arab Republic and Iraq. The new feature in Turkey's foreign policy was the question of support for the peaceful attainment of independence by those countries struggling for that goal.[46] The Middle East News Agency, citing the Ankara weekly *Kim*, stated that in this connection Cemal Gürsel had promised the ambassadors of the Arab states that Turkey would support the Algerian cause and back it in the international sphere.[47]

The Committee was divided on this issue. The radicals in the NUC, supported by the intelligentsia, wanted to adopt a more uncompromising position. They wished the NUC to make it a principle to support peoples struggling for independence, as the Turks had once struggled themselves.

Yet, by turning our backs on all these fine developments, we were denying both Atatürk and our historic task and mission. We almost shed tears when the Egyptian nationalists expelled King Faruq. A shameless Foreign Minister [Fatin Rüştü Zorlu] boasted that he had knocked Nehru down at the Bandung Conference. We almost sent troops to Baghdad to take revenge for Nuri as-Said and Abd al-Ilah, who were torn to pieces by nationalist Iraqis.... We denied the heroic struggle of Algeria....

... In short, as far as our foreign policy was concerned we were in a state of unawareness, denying ourselves both our leadership and our own selves. For this reason we greet the new basic idea brought to our foreign policy by the National Unity Committee as a restoration of our pride and personality and as a turning-point in our history....[48]

The expression of these sentiments reflected the new atmosphere of freedom which prevailed after 27 May more than a new orientation in foreign policy. Under Menderes, public discussion of foreign policy, and indeed all other issues, had been tightly controlled. Not even the opposition in the Assembly was given much freedom to debate such issues and any suggestion that there should be radical changes in foreign policy was likely to be denounced as treason. All this changed after May 1960, creating the illusion that a new foreign policy would follow in its wake. Throughout the sixties there was an ambiguity between the foreign policy aspirations of the vocal and articulate intelligentsia and the 'pragmatic' policies of the various governments. The intelligentsia was able to inhibit the activities of the government by constant criticism but it was never able to force the government to reformulate the policy.

Moscow launched a new peace offensive soon after Menderes's fall, undoubtedly encouraged by the trends her diplomats reported from Turkey. Khrushchev's goal was to persuade Ankara to become neutral and convince her to stop spending huge sums on armaments and devote them to development. But such arguments had no effect on Ankara. Although Gürsel welcomed the idea of improved relations he dismissed the other proposals firmly but politely.[49] Moscow nevertheless persisted with its offensive, interspersed with notes complaining of Turkish and US activities in the Black Sea. Finally in January 1962 Premier İnönü stated Turkey's position in unambivalent terms, declaring that Turkey was committed to a system and it was therefore impossible for her to become an ally of the USSR or even neutral. This was the only framework within which he could hold discussions with Moscow.[50]

Ironically, the post-27 May régime became more dependent on the United States and NATO than the Democrats had been. For one thing, military expenditure rose sharply under the military-dominated governments. This was only natural, since one of the complaints of the armed forces, especially of the junior officers, was that their salaries had become totally inadequate as a result of the inflation of the fifties. The law increasing officers' salaries was passed on 23 February 1961 and Defence Minister General Muzaffer Alankuş stated that military allocations constituted 26·5 per cent of the entire budget. When 'supplementary allied aid in arms, vehicles and funds is needed, the financial strength behind the armed forces amounts to nearly 50 per cent of the budget'.[51] The following year İlhami Sancar, the Defence Minister in the First Coalition, explained that

Our national budgets are incapable of providing all the necessary funds which our armed forces need. Nor can they provide the necessary funds needed to fully equip our forces with weapons and vehicles. Because of this a great part of the weapons, vehicles and facilities needed by our Army is being supplied by our great friend and ally, the US Government, under the current military aid programme. The budget now before you contains only the expenditure for the personnel and the upkeep of the Army.[52]

The Democrats had always complained to their allies that Turkey's military expenditure was far beyond her means. This rose even higher in the sixties, and the US Congress found that, on defence, Turkey was spending 27·2 per cent of its budget and 6·2 per cent of its GNP, one of the highest figures in comparison with the defence expenditure of her allies, and especially in relation to her wealth.[53] NATO's decision to provide large sums of money to meet Turkey's defence needs caused great satisfaction in Turkey.[54] However, the Western allies would not have to pay such a high price to subsidize the Turkish armed forces much longer, for already technological advances in rocketry were making the nuclear rocket bases in Turkey obsolete, thereby reducing her bargaining power for aid, both military and economic.

In July 1962 the Turkish press began to report that the Jupiter missile bases in Turkey would soon be dismantled and the rocket-carrying Polaris submarine would be introduced as a substitute. From the point of view of American and NATO strategy this was an advance, but it deflated the Turkish view of their importance in the alliance.[55] The Cuban missile crisis, which exploded in October, made the Turkish missile bases a matter of diplomatic bargaining, and Khrushchev asked that they be dismantled at the same time as those in Cuba. The Turks did not accept the analogy between Turkey and Cuba, and expected their allies to stand firm. But for the US it was a bargain, especially as these bases were to be dismantled in a short time anyway. President Kennedy publicly denied that the bases in Turkey (and Italy) had been bargained away. But the Turkish public was entirely convinced to the contrary, and the idea that Turkey's interests were negotiable became widely prevalent among the intelligentsia.[56]

The crisis had placed Turkey in the very centre of the stage, with the possibility that, in case of conflict, she would be the Soviet Union's primary target. 'It was a complete reversal of the long-held view that increased military force meant increased security.'[57] Yet the country was not prepared to retreat into neutrality. The East-West détente always worried Ankara, for the foreign policy specialists argued that Turkey's geographical position was too delicate to enable any government to pursue neutrality. Turkish commitment to the Western allies had to be absolute because even a show of lukewarmness might lead them to bargain away Turkey.[58] In 1963, therefore, Ankara knew that its role and status in NATO would be revised and that the country's influence would decline accordingly. This highlighted socio-economic problems, since aid would be more difficult to come by. Under these conditions Turkey moved cautiously so as to improve her relations with the Soviet Union. But the resurgence of the Cyprus question in the same year had a drastic effect on Ankara's foreign relations and forced the government and the intelligentsia to re-evaluate the country's position in the world.

Turkey and Cyprus 1954-1964

Turkey's policy towards Cyprus was perhaps the best example of her disinterest on behalf of her allies and the alliance. In 1954, when the Greek Cypriot movement began to demand independence from British rule and union (*enosis*) with Greece, Turkey's reaction had been most tempered. At first, Menderes had refused to comment, stating that his government was following the situation closely and that he wanted to maintain good relations with Turkey's ally Greece.[59] Later the government forbad the celebration of İzmir Liberation Day on 9 September, knowing that it would take an anti-Greek turn as a reaction to the *enosis* demonstrations in Athens. Menderes declared: 'I am of the opinion that to allow the sacred meaning of 9 September to be exploited through any form of political crisis would trouble our national conscience.'[60] A few days later, *Zafer* announced that: 'Turkey will not take the slightest action which may cause even a small crisis in the tripartite alliance.'[61]

If Turkey finally decided to play an active role in the Cyprus question it was probably on British urging. As early as December 1951 the government had made it clear that Turkey did not want the status of the island changed. The island had never belonged to Greece; Turkey had conquered it from Venice in 1570-1. It was 'loaned' to Britain in 1878 and became a British colony in 1914 when Turkey entered the war on the German side. But the island was considered vital for the defence of Anatolia, and Turkey would not permit it to fall into hands which could become hostile.[62] These arguments suited the British government, for they made the Cyprus question a tripartite issue instead of one to be resolved by London and Athens. Even before Ankara had made a formal commitment, Foreign Secretary Anthony Eden stated that 'the Turkish government has made it known on several occasions that it is positively opposed to any change being made in the status of Cyprus'.[63]

By the beginning of 1955 Turkey was deeply embroiled in the Cyprus question, which had become an explosive factor in internal politics. Yet the government had no clearly defined policy. Initially Ankara argued that it could not permit any change in the status of Cyprus and that if Britain vacated the island it must revert back to Turkey. '... Turkey is steadfast, as she has always been, in her opinion that the island can only be annexed to Turkey in the event of British sovereignty over it ceasing to exist,' wrote *Zafer* of 9 June 1956. But as British policy changed and veered towards autonomy for Cyprus, Ankara, at first bewildered and angered by Britain's vacillation, moved to accommodate. By May 1957 Menderes had abandoned the slogan 'Cyprus is Turkish' for 'Partition or Death'.[64] Turkey's primary concern was to find a compromise solution that would not damage her relations with Britain and Greece. Even partition was not a firm commitment and was used as a threat against the Greek insistence on *enosis*. In the end Athens abandoned *enosis* and Turkey quietly shelved partition. In February 1959 both parties agreed to the establishment of the Republic of Cyprus in which the rights of the Turkish minority would be safeguarded and guaranteed jointly by the United Kingdom, Greece and Turkey, and the agreement was signed in London on 19 February 1959.[65]

Such was the background of Turkey's Cyprus policy. All the parties had supported this policy and the day after the military takeover of 27 May 1960, the NUC went on record in support of the Zürich and London agreements.[66] Cyprus was proclaimed a republic on 15 August 1960 and Archbishop Makarios was elected President, and Dr Fazıl Küçük, the leader of the Turkish Cypriot community, Vice-President. The principal weakness of these agreements was that they had been made by the three powers with the local parties—the Greek and Turkish Cypriots—in the subordinate role. The Greek Cypriots, in particular, did not believe that the constitution of the new republic, which gave substantial rights to the Turkish minority, was workable.

President Makarios spoke of amending the constitution and in August 1963 the Turkish government gave what was perhaps the first formal warning against such action. The Foreign Ministry's statement protested at the 'completely irresponsible statements of the Greek leaders against the established constitutional regime in Cyprus', which could not be amended unilaterally. 'It is legally insupportable and impossible to argue that such an attempt is an internal affair, for the Cyprus Constitution was established in accordance with an international agreement, and the provisions of this Constitution were guaranteed by the treaty of guarantees to which Turkey is a party.' The statement ended: 'A Government that can abandon some 100,000 dear members of our race to the arbitrary administration of foreigners will never come to power in Turkey.'[67]

There was no question of the fragile coalition governments of the early sixties daring to negotiate even a compromise. Makarios, however, refused to recognize Turkey's rights under the agreements and on 30 November 1963 he proposed amending the basic articles of the constitution. This led to communal violence in Cyprus, anti-Makarios (not anti-Greek) demonstrations in Turkey, and Ankara's declaration that the Cyprus constitution was dead and therefore the island had to be partitioned. On Christmas Day Turkish jets buzzed the island and İnönü told the National Assembly that Turkey would use its rights and intervene. He said that the fleet was ready and he had proposed to the British and Greek governments that there should be joint intervention. Next day Britain and Greece accepted the principle of joint intervention, thus making it unnecessary for Turkey to act unilaterally.[68]

Cyprus had become a problem which Turkey was forced to discuss in different forums: with the other guarantor powers, Greece and Britain; at NATO, where the US had the dominant voice; and at the UN, where the non-aligned countries had the monopoly of votes. For Ankara, NATO was the most likely to produce a just solution, the conviction being that since the Turkish cause was a just one, Washington could make Athens and Nicosia see reason. Makarios refused to accept a 'NATO solution' and took his case to the United Nations where a resolution was passed unanimously to send an international peacekeeping force to Cyprus. Turkey had been totally isolated, for hardly anyone, not even her NATO and CENTO allies, supported her thesis or condemned the Makarios government.[69]

Ankara was disappointed but not demoralized, for it still believed that it had the right to intervene and any number of UN resolutions could not take away this right. On 13 March 1964 Makarios was told that Turkey would intervene unilaterally unless there was an immediate cessation of all actions against the Turkish Cypriot community, an immediate cease-fire, a 'green line' zone agreement in Nicosia, the lifting of the siege from Turkish districts, freedom of communications, and the return of Turkish hostages.[70]

President Makarios rejected this note, which was little short of an ultimatum, and in Turkey there were demonstrations demanding the invasion and partition of Cyprus. Premier İnönü convened an extraordinary session of the Grand National Assembly on 16 March and his government was given the authority to employ troops in Cyprus: 489 votes were cast in favour and there were only four abstentions. On the same day the Foreign Ministry announced that the 1930 agreement with Greece, which gave certain privileges to Greeks residing in Istanbul, would not be renewed when it expired after six months.[71] Ankara had been forced to abandon amicable relations with Athens, one of the pillars of its foreign policy.

Far more significant was the government's criticism of NATO and the United States. The press had made such criticisms even earlier, though official circles had shown greater restraint. However, on 16 April President Gürsel took NATO to task for not supporting 'our national and just cause' and concluded that 'Turkish-Greek friendship is dead'.[72] Such was the mood of the country that the press interpreted İnönü's cryptic statement to *Time* magazine—'I had faith in the leadership of America which has responsibility within the alliance; now I am paying the penalty'—to mean that US policy might force Turkey to seek new options in foreign policy.[73] İnönü was quick to deny this interpretation and stated categorically in the Assembly that he did not envisage any change in foreign policy.[74] The gates of discussion had been thrown wide open only to reveal the division between educated opinion and the government.

The turning-point in this debate was President Lyndon Johnson's letter of 5 June 1964 to Premier İnönü. The letter came at a time when Turkish forces were said to be preparing to land troops in Cyprus because UN forces were not providing adequate protection for the Turkish community on the island. Johnson warned that the NATO alliance would not come to Turkey's aid 'against the Soviet Union if Turkey takes a step which results in Soviet intervention without the full consent and understanding of its NATO allies'. İnönü was also reminded that 'Under Article IV of the Agreement with Turkey of July 1947, your government is required to obtain United States' consent for the use of military assistance for purposes other than those for which such assistance was furnished.... I must tell you in all candor that the United States cannot agree to the use of any United States supplied military equipment for Turkish intervention in Cyprus under present circumstances.'[75]

Although the texts of the letters were not made public for the next eighteen months, the contents were partially known to the press and confirmed what the radical intelligentsia had been saying about the United States and NATO, namely that Turkey could not rely on its allies unconditionally. 'From that time forth', notes Harris, 'all Turkish governments would be on the defensive in regard to the American connection, and the memories of the Johnson letter would color popular impressions of the United States for many years to come.'[76]

The impact of the Jonhson letter on Turkey's foreign policy has been greatly exaggerated. It generated a great deal of noise and emotion but little action. There was never any question that a government of one of the major parties would consider severing the American connection. Once the Justice Party came to power the connection became stronger than before. Even İnönü, who had been dealt the rebuff, did not question the NATO alliance, for to do so would have meant questioning the very foundations on which the Turkish régime rested.

Reappraisal and Diversification

The Johnson letter did, however, accelerate a trend that had been in evidence since the late fifties—the Turkish government's desire to diversify its foreign policy. It is quite probable that Washington encouraged this trend in order to be relieved of some of its obligations. The fashionable view of the mid-sixties regarding Turkey's foreign relations was that Turkey must remain within her alliances but that she ought to review her policy. The need for a re-examination was brought about by a rapidly changing world and Cyprus proved to be the catalyst which forced Turkey in this direction. America and the Soviet Union were no longer the enemies they were when Turkey joined NATO, and Moscow had become conciliatory now that it was threatened by the growing power of the People's Republic of China. There was also a strong possibility that the European Community would emerge as a rival bloc, and in a world dominated by four blocs—the United States, the Soviet Union, China, and Europe—it was likely that the US and the USSR would collaborate. Once again the neutral states would suffer and that is why Turkey had to remain inside NATO.[77]

The proposals of Hamit Batu, the Director-General of the Fourth Department of the Foreign Ministry, went a step further. He agreed that Turkey must remain in NATO yet readjust her foreign relations in conformity with changing conditions, which called for a fresh analysis of international relations. Batu proposed a stronger orientation towards Europe and presumably away from the US, though this was not stated explicitly. Such a course, he argued, was prompted by Turkey's historical evolution; moreover, a Europe moving towards integration had to be an important

element in Turkey's foreign policy. If Turkey remained outside
Europe and Europe became the 'third force' then Turkey's position
in international affairs would be considerably weakened. Therefore
Turkey had to work to secure a sound place within an integrated
Europe.

Turkey, Batu pointed out, was destined to be the odd-man-out
in the European community. She was included for geopolitical and
strategic reasons but could not be considered a part of Europe
culturally, nor because she had a developed economy (like
Japan's). Therefore Turkey's role in Europe would depend on her
credit and prestige in the Afro-Asian countries, and if that was
strong Turkey could become the bridge between East and West.
Thus her relations with the Afro-Asian bloc must be established on
a sound basis.

Turkey, he continued, had long been alienated from the
Afro-Asian bloc and this had to be repaired immediately. Historically, Turkey had played a prominent role in Asia and Africa and
her experience could prove useful now. But, declared Batu, Turkey
must remain outside the neutral bloc, otherwise there would be
damage to her relations with the West, of which her Afro-Asian
policy was only a part. In the past Turkey's membership of NATO
had caused friction with Afro-Asian nations, especially in the
Middle East. But other members of the Atlantic alliance had
overcome this obstacle and there was no reason why Turkey
should not do the same. She could improve these relations by
supporting the Arabs at the UN; however, her policy towards the
Arabs ought to be one of 'political non-intervention' and neutral
friendship. Turkey must not interfere in internal affairs or appear
to be running errands for others; she must not place herself in a
position where she answered criticisms or unjustified attacks. She
had to make her presence felt in the region and also act with
personality within NATO.[78]

These loose and ill-defined guidelines were used to shift
Turkey's foreign policy from total to limited reliance on the United
States. Ankara's first task was to improve relations with Moscow.
On the very day İnönü received President Johnson's letter he took
a step in this direction, and a radio broadcast appealed to Moscow
for more fluid relations. He seemed to place only one condition on
the establishment of good relations between the two countries,
namely understanding for Turkey's position on Cyprus. 'But, there
is something we ask of them: they must acknowledge our need for
security in causes we are pursuing. Under these conditions [that
Russia appreciate Turkey's need for defence and accept her
membership of NATO] we have always supported a policy of good

and straightforward relations with our neighbours.' He concluded
that, 'Compared with conditions prevailing 20 years ago, the
supporters of two contrasting political and social trends have, in a
discernible and understandable way, directed the world on to the
path of peace. We deem it our duty to serve this happy development.'[79]

The Soviet Union, which had been trying to woo Ankara since
the death of Stalin, reacted vigorously. By October there was talk
of improved economic relations to follow the visit to Moscow of
Foreign Minister Erkin on 30 October. The rumour that Moscow
might finance the Keban dam in eastern Anatolia suggested to *The
Economist* (24 October 1964) the dramatic possibility of an
'Aswan on the Euphrates'. But there was no danger of that and
Ankara was always cautious in her relations with Moscow. Erkin's
visit was followed by the visits to Ankara of Nikolai Podgorny in
January and Foreign Minister Gromyko in May 1965. Prime
Minister Ürgüplü travelled to Moscow in August 1965 and Premier
Alexei Kosygin returned the visit in December 1966.[80] Ironically it
was Prime Minister Süleyman Demirel's visit to the Soviet Union
in September 1967 which symbolized the establishment of a
working relationship between the two countries. Demirel, whose
policies were said to be closely identified with US interests, and
whose first name cartoonists spelled with the $ sign, was able to
declare:

I think we have entered a new era in our dealings with the Russians. As is
known, there had been great strain between our countries over the years,
and in the period after World War II we had no relations at all. Now that
gap has been bridged; I am not suggesting that all doubts are gone, but I
think the hostility is gone.[81]

If Ankara had any apprehensions that its changing relations
with the Soviet Union and Eastern Europe could jeopardize its
position within NATO, this must have been dispelled by the
Harmel Report entitled 'The Future Tasks of the Alliance', drawn
up by the Belgian Foreign Minister. The report stated that since
they are 'sovereign states, the allies are not obliged to subordinate
their policies to collective decision ... [and] each ally can decide its
policy in the light of close knowledge of the problems and
objectives of the other.... Each ally should play its full part in
promoting an improvement in relations with the Soviet Union and
the countries of Eastern Europe, bearing in mind that the pursuit
of détente must not be allowed to split the Alliance ...'[82]

According to Fahir Armaoğlu, the Harmel Report 'has been
applied in a most advantageous manner by Turkey. A sudden

development in Turkey's relations with socialist countries has been noticeable, especially since 1967. They have experienced significant progress and expansion, particularly in the field of trade, tourism and cultural exchanges. Increasing commercial and economic relations with these countries have not only been useful in securing the machinery, the equipment and materials needed for Turkey's economic growth from these sources, but have also contributed to our export potential.'[83]

Another feature manifesting the diversification of Turkey's foreign policy was the creation of RCD or Regional Co-operation for Development. This idea originated with Pakistan and was introduced by Ayub Khan in July 1964 during his visit to Ankara.[84] Later in the month, Ayub Khan, the Shah of Iran, and President Gürsel met in Istanbul and proposed the formation of the RCD in a joint communiqué. The proposal was for the realization of joint projects, the establishment of closer trade relations, the formation of a joint RCD chamber of trade and industry, and closer co-operation in the fields of communications, tourism, technical research, and cultural exchanges.[85]

Initially, Ankara did not show much enthusiasm for this scheme, and 'The Turks', commented The Economist (15 August 1964), 'stand in relation to the new community rather like the British in Europe. For forty years they have been westwards away from Asia. The more ardent heirs of Kemal Atatürk have no wish to see Turkey turn, or as they would say, turn back, towards Asia on the basis of Islam.' But Ayub Khan's proposal was timely and caught the Turks in the moment of their political isolation. Sosyal Adalet even suggested that the Istanbul meeting was anti-British and anti-American and inspired by General de Gaulle.[86] Even a year later Ankara showed little enthusiasm, and Ayub Khan, sensing their reluctance, told the Turkish delegation that 'however much they wanted to be a part of Europe they would never be accepted as equals by Europeans, while the new organisation offered them a chance to be "first-class Moslems and first-class Turks".'[87] Hamit Batu's proposals, which were also written at about this time, suggest that the Turkish foreign ministry had reached a similar conclusion that Turkey's position in Europe would depend on her prestige and credit in Asia. RCD could serve as the first step in this direction.

In 1964 Turkey's credit with the Afro-Asian bloc was bankrupt. At the Cairo Conference of Non-Aligned Nations (5-11 October 1964), Ankara had sent her ambassadors, Vahit Halefoğlu (Lebanon) and Semih Güven (Algeria), as observers and in order to counteract Makarios's campaign against Turkey. They had failed to make any impact: the conference had supported Makarios's thesis and the communiqué had called for the right of self-determination in Cyprus and the withdrawal of foreign troops from the island.[88]

Ankara was determined to put on a better show at Algiers, where the next Afro-Asian conference was scheduled to meet. In order to prepare the ground, Turkish diplomats attempted to improve relations with countries such as India which exercised influence in this bloc. The conference would provide Turkey with the first opportunity to practise her new orientation towards the Third World, and the government and the press were taking the occasion most seriously. There were now twice as many independent Afro-Asian states as there had been in 1955, ten years earlier, and it was worth gaining their support. To do that, Turkey would have to avoid giving the impression—as she had done at Bandung—that she was running errands for the West. Initially Prime Minister Ürgüplü was to lead the Turkish delegation and his inability to do so, because of internal politics, was seen as a set-back.[89] The overthrow and arrest of the President of Algeria, Ahmad Ben-Bella, by Houari Boumedienne led to the postponement of the conference until November. It therefore followed the Turkish general election of 10 October, which left the country virtually without a government; when the meeting of foreign ministers opened on 28 October, Turkey was represented by her new ambassador to Algiers, İsmail Soysal.

The Pressure of Public Opinion

The UN's acceptance of Makarios's thesis on 17 December 1965 once again exposed Turkey's isolation. Forty-seven members of the United Nations—mainly from the Afro-Asian bloc—voted against Turkey; only five (the US, Albania, Pakistan, Iran, and Libya) voted in her favour; and 51, including the Soviet bloc, abstained.[90] 'If the shock created by the UN resolution will awaken us to the fact that our foreign policy is leading us to becoming a satellite, we may find consolation in this unfavourable decision ...' declared Ahmet Şükrü Esmer. While Turkey acted as a 'satellite'—her vote against China at the UN was the latest example of this—the neutral powers could never be won over. The neutrals voted against Turkey's position on Cyprus because she guaranteed British bases on the island from which Egypt had been attacked in 1956. Turkey had to realize that their attitude towards Cyprus was guided by this consideration and Turkey's position in the alliances rather than by an abstract anti-Turkish policy.[91]

This was indeed the dilemma of Turkey's attempt to revise her foreign policy. All the political parties, except the Workers' Party, and most of the foreign-policy pundits of the establishment wanted Turkey to retain the NATO alliance as the keystone of her external relations. All those who wished the country to remain in NATO also wished Turkey's relationship with it to be revised in order to guarantee her freedom of action and her independence. They did not see the contradiction between these two aims, especially for an underdeveloped country like Turkey, which had come to depend—and they liked to think in terms of interdependence—on the developed West ever since the end of World War II.

Turkey's dependence on the West, especially the United States, had increased with the East-West détente as well as with the revolution in arms technology which made Anatolia relatively less important for Western military strategists. It was because of such innovations as the missile-firing Polaris submarine that NATO was able to adopt the strategy of 'flexible response' which 'raised the specter for Turkish military planners—and for their civilian colleagues as well—that their partners in the alliance might not consider a localized attack from the Soviet forces on Turkey as necessitating military response'.[92] Put more bluntly, this meant that the allies could conceivably sacrifice Turkey in order to win an advantage somewhere else.

. Had it not been for the freedoms granted under the 1961 constitution this dilemma of Turkey's foreign-policy planners would not have aroused such a hostile response from the intelligentsia. It was no longer possible to crush or ignore dissenting views and the only way to silence them was by changing the character of the democratic régime. Under the influence of socialist ideas, which were widely prevalent, especially after the founding of the WPT, the radical critics made the issue of NATO not merely one of foreign policy but of the internal régime as well. They viewed their struggle in Turkey as one against the domination of Western capitalism and its indigenous allies, and the US and NATO were described as the representatives of this capitalism. The first step was to disengage Turkey from the alliance and only then could the struggle against capitalism be joined.[93]

What was perhaps most damaging to the establishment's cause was the parallel the radicals and socialists sought to draw between the current situation and the situation in the early twenties, when Mustafa Kemal Atatürk had led the struggle against Western imperialism. It is worth quoting Mehmet Ali Aybar, the leader of the Workers' Party, who was one of the most articulate spokesmen for this thesis:

Brothers, our fathers and grandfathers forty-three years ago succeeded in concluding our war of independence in victory. Today, forty-three years later ... we, all of us, as a nation, as individuals and as working people are obliged to win our independence and freedom once again.

Brothers, since 1947 the United States of America has penetrated our country.... Today 35 million square metres of this soil of our fatherland is under American occupation....

... It is not over our political life alone that America has established pressure. America has at the same time brought our economic life under its domination. Our economic life, which since 1947 has been revolving around an axis of foreign indebtedness and aid, is faltering in a progressively deteriorating imbalance. This economic course has put Turkey in a more dependent position. In addition our ruling circles—that is, the large landowners and the capitalist circles acting as intermediaries for foreigners—have increased their power and influence, thanks to this foreign aid....

Brothers, your first duty in the face of this situation lies in restoring independence.... We, as the Workers' Party of Turkey, shall abrogate ... all treaties, all agreements that have reduced us to a status of dependence....

My worker brothers, everything depends on our being independent.... being dependent means being deprived of the power to carry out these tasks that are meant to benefit the nation.[94]

It was under the constant pressure of this thesis, which soon caught the imagination of Turkey's youth, especially in the universities, that the government was forced to reconsider its relations with the US. By the middle sixties there was a vast gap between the Justice Party government and the intelligentsia. There was little Demirel could do to bridge this gap, for the intelligentsia was demanding that Demirel take a position *vis-à-vis* America resembling that of General de Gaulle. Such a position was out of the question, for Turkey was not France and Demirel was no de Gaulle.

The Cyprus Crisis of 1967

When the Cyprus crisis erupted in November 1967 the political climate in Turkey was very different from what it had been in the fifties and the early sixties. The government had become more receptive to an urban public opinion, better educated by a larger and freer press. Demirel was forced to pay lip service to the demand for independence and freedom of action, and, under constant pressure from opposition both inside and outside the National Assembly, he announced that Turkey's Bilateral Agreements with the United States would be discussed and revised.[95] The opposition parties, especially the Workers' Party, raised the question of US bases in Turkey—Aybar's 35 million square metres under occupation—and made Demirel juggle with words: he denied that there were any bases (*üs*) but admitted that there were installations (*tesis*), without ever explaining the difference between the two.[96] Just prior to the outbreak of the Arab-Israeli War on 5 June 1967 the press reported, citing *al-Ahram* (Cairo), that Egypt had been told that NATO bases would not be used against the Arab states.[97] The war radicalized opinion in Turkey and accelerated the pro-Arab trend which had begun about 1965. There was a sharp increase in anti-American sentiment—Israel being seen merely as a pawn—and the government refused to look after American interests in Baghdad when Iraq broke off diplomatic relations with the United States.[98]

Throughout the rest of the year Demirel's government was forced onto the defensive by its critics at home. It responded by acting more energetically on the Middle East question, where it refused to countenance Israeli territorial gains made with the use of force, and in Cyprus, where the position of the Turkish minority was constantly worsening. Demirel invited the Greek Premier Collias to discuss the situation and the two met on 9 and 10 September 1967 at Keşan and Alexandroupolis, two small towns on the Thracian border. The government of the Greek colonels, in power since the *coup d'état* of 21 April, needed a diplomatic success in Cyprus in order to win popularity at home. The Greek delegation demanded *enosis*, and then proposed partition, but Demirel rejected both schemes. He insisted on the validity of the 1960 agreements, which, he said, could be amended only by joint action of all the interested parties, and which ensured a balance of power in the eastern Mediterranean.[99]

What the Greek junta could not obtain by diplomacy, it tried to seize by force. On 15 November the Cypriot National Guard, led principally by Greek officers from the mainland under the supreme command of General Grivas, attacked Turkish Cypriot positions. 'The attacks brought not only strong protests from the United Nations Secretary-General and force commander, but also a new threat of invasion by Turkey ...'[100] In Turkey, there were nation-wide demonstrations and a public clamour for immediate intervention. On 16 and 17 November the National Assembly and Senate met in joint session and voted the government authority to use the Turkish armed forces abroad if circumstances required it.[101] The forces had already been mobilized and the air force was carrying out reconnaissance flights over Cyprus; an invasion seemed imminent. Cemal Tural, who was Chief of the General Staff, wrote later:

> In the 1967 crisis the cabinet took the decision to intervene in Cyprus. But in the four hours that followed I do not know what happened; the cabinet decided to postpone the action. There was not a thing left for us to say. I obtained the decision to postpone the action in writing ...[102]

The decision not to intervene militarily was probably a wise one, for its outcome could have been partition of the island by Turkey and Greece. Strategically, this was never seen as being in the interest of Turkey, for 'double *enosis*' would permit a Greek military presence only forty miles from the coast of southern Anatolia, and could prove most dangerous in an armed conflict. It was in Turkey's interest to maintain an independent Cyprus, provided that the security and rights of the Turkish minority were guaranteed. It seemed possible that Demirel would accomplish that aim through diplomacy. Already on 20 November the junta in Athens showed signs of retreat when it appointed Panayiotis Pipinelis Minister of Foreign Affairs. He 'was considered to favor a solution for Cyprus that would be satisfactory to the Turks', and most likely to accept Cağlayangil's 'strong demand for action on the Greek side to ensure security for Turkish Cypriots', made on the same day as Pipinelis's appointment.[103] On 23 November President Johnson's emissary Cyrus Vance arrived in Ankara— because of the anti-American demonstrations at Esenboğa, his aircraft was forced to land at the military airport—and Turks were immediately reminded of President Johnson's letter of 1964. The Turkish government was told that arms supplied to Turkey under the terms of the NATO alliance ought not to be used in Cyprus, a statement that served only to increase anti-American feeling amongst the public.[104]

Despite the war scare which gripped Turkey in the last days of November, there was no invasion. The Greek junta continued to make concessions: General Grivas was recalled to Athens, and Greek troops stationed in Cyprus since 1964 were withdrawn. For the time being *enosis* was dead. However, the Turkish demand for implementation of the 1960 agreements, which would remove pressure from the Turkish minority and guarantee it freedom of movement and equal rights, depended on the goodwill of President Makarios and the Greek majority. It was a difficult demand to enforce, even though there were formal commitments. Diplomatically, the 1967 crisis ended successfully for Demirel though it did not resolve the inter-communal problems; politically it was a failure.

Demirel was criticized by all the opposition parties for having missed the opportunity to intervene and settle the Cyprus crisis once and for all. The parties of the extreme Right—Türkeş's RPNP and Feyzioğlu's RP—were the most vocal in condemning the government for not invading and partitioning the island. Demirel had been as weak as İnönü; nor had he been prevented by American pressure, which had become the stereotyped excuse, said the RPNP communiqué of 29 November. The Workers' Party criticized Demirel for accepting a compromise which guaranteed neither the security of Turkey nor that of the Turkish Cypriots. Senator Kadri Kaplan, speaking for the National Unity Group, made the charge that by accepting and returning to the 1960 formula Demirel had closed the road to a Cyprus federation based on physical separation between the two communities. This was perhaps the only valid and serious criticism of Demirel's policy, though it is doubtful whether federation could have been achieved without armed invasion. The problem, said Kaplan, had been settled to the advantage of the great powers, but against the long-term interests of Turkey. Only the Republicans—remembering their own discomfiture in 1964—were surprisingly moderate and sympathetic to the government.[105]

However, Turkish public opinion was convinced that, in calling off the invasion of Cyprus, the politicians had once again bowed to US pressure. After the 1967 crisis anti-Americanism became virulent, and in the years 1968 to 1971 it grew from demonstrations against the Sixth Fleet to the kidnapping of US military personnel. During these years the Americans tried to make their presence in Turkey less visible, and for this reason Sixth Fleet visits were reduced, and even temporarily stopped. When in 1969 Athens began to be used as the 'home' port for US ships, Turkish official circles feared that the United States commitment to Turkey might be reduced as a result, and along with it military and economic aid. So intimately was Demirel identified with the US that he no longer had the prestige to heal wounds at home. He was unable to establish a new consensus on foreign policy or to curb the increasing anti-Americanism, except by coercion. In the end the armed forces intervened on 12 March 1971 to cope with a situation Demirel had found impossible to resolve.

The Opium Controversy

One immediate consequence of military intervention was that foreign policy was rescued from the obstructionism of the political parties, especially that of the Workers' Party, and the radical and revolutionary youth movement. As was the case with domestic policy, foreign policy also became 'above party', free of the restraints of 'narrow interests and party politics'. The Foreign Minister in Erim's cabinet was Osman Olcay, a career diplomat of the new generation—he was born in 1924—who was brought from the NATO General Secretariat, after a successful term as ambassador to India.

The foreign policy section of Erim's programme did not suggest any departure from the programmes of earlier governments, though the stress on its 'Kemalist foundations' was greater:

The basis of foreign policy will be the facts outlined by Atatürk. A policy based on rational and scientific principles will be implemented. Our national interests will be borne in mind in our international relations. Our relations will be expanded with such international organisations as the UN, the Council of Europe, and the European Economic Community. NATO is a defence organisation that constitutes the soundest external guarantee of our security.

... We are bound to the United States by ties of close friendship and alliance based on mutual respect and understanding. The fact that from time to time we view certain problems from different points must be regarded as a natural expression of friendship based on a reciprocal understanding and frankness between our countries. This is the proof of the soundness of this friendship, and a requirement of the political philosophy of the Western world, to which both Turkey and the United States belong. In line with our traditional policy we can see the possibility of further development along a course of confidence in our relations with our great northern neighbour, the USSR, in accordance with neighbourliness and the spirit of the 1921 Moscow agreement, and based on the principles of independence, territorial integrity and non-interference in each other's internal affairs.[106]

A novel feature of the programme—though few people paid any attention to it at the time—was the government's promise to pay 'serious attention' to the problem of narcotics. In this connection Erim stated:

... Believing that contraband trade in opium—which has assumed the aspect of an overwhelming blight for the youth of the whole world—is offensive on humanitarian grounds in the first place, the Government will pay serious attention to this problem. Turkish opium growers will be shown a way to earn a better living ...[107]

The implementation of this promise became a most controversial issue. As yet the drug problem hardly touched or affected Turkish youth, though it was known to be a grave problem in the United States, and to a less extent in Europe. But it was seen as an 'American problem' to be solved in America, not in Turkey.

The Turkish Experiment in Democracy

American ambassadors to Turkey began to take up the opium question with the government in the mid-1960s. Prime Minister Ürgüplü, 'as nonpartisan head of a transition government, was reluctant to initiate any far-reaching moves.... [Demirel] showed greater willingness to assist in stamping out the illegal opium trade.... There were press reports that at one point Demirel had even committed Turkey to eradicate all opium production by 1971.'[108]

By the beginning of 1970, after the defections from the JP and the formation of the Democratic Party, Demirel was no longer strong enough in the Assembly to initiate measures totally eliminating opium cultivation, though he had already restricted it to certain provinces.[109] Moreover, constant US pressure, as well as the threats of sanctions against Turkey, and a reduction of aid if Ankara did not comply with American wishes, made the issue public and therefore increased Demirel's difficulties in handling the question of concessions.

The Erim government faced neither the problem of a majority in the Assembly—at least not on an issue such as opium cultivation— nor public opinion. Thus in July 1971, Nihat Erim agreed to prohibit the cultivation of the opium poppy after the 1972 crop was harvested. In return the 'United States undertook to provide $35 million over a three-year period: $15 million to compensate the poppy growers ... and $20 million for investments to orient poppy farmers to other crops.'[110]

Erim's 'bargain' was an economic disaster for the cultivators, for as Harris has written, 'Poppy planters earned far more from this crop—even selling it legally to the state—than they could expect from other produce grown on their land; hence to restrict or abolish the crop would be an economic blow to the traditional producers.'[111] Public reaction was one of shame and dismay: the government, most people believed, had succumbed to US pressure and 'bribery'; for that is how they understood the $35 million agreement. Thus in the country as a whole Erim's decision was very unpopular, one which all parties promised to overturn if they were elected to power in the 1973 general election. It was a decision only a government unconcerned about popular support or popular discontent could pass.

The period between 12 March 1971 and September 1973 was devoid of public debate on foreign policy. The governments of this period did not attempt anything controversial, except Erim's ban on poppy cultivation, and perhaps the recognition of the People's Republic of China.[112] For the rest, Prime Ministers Erim, Melen, and Talu engaged in day-to-day diplomacy, Undisturbed by party politics in the Assembly and criticism in the press. But the situation changed in September 1973 when the political parties began the campaign for the general election of 12 October. 'It now seems certain', wrote the *Guardian Weekly* 'that any Government likely to emerge from Sunday's general election will cancel the ban on the growing of opium poppies.... Mr. Suleyman Demirel's Justice Party, which may well head the next Government, has promised to allow farmers to grow poppies again, though under state control. The Social Democrats [a reference to Ecevit's RPP] have promised simply to abolish the ban...'[113] The question was viewed not merely as a matter of restoring the cultivator's right to grow opium poppies but of regaining Turkey's right to exercise autonomy. The parties promised to rectify this situation and restore the independence, dignity, and prestige of Turkey.

Bülent Ecevit won the 1973 election, and from his earlier pronouncements it was clear that his government would attempt to be more independent in its relations with the outside world, especially the United States. There was no question of Turkey abandoning its alliances (such as NATO or CENTO) and retreating into non-aligned isolation. But within the alliances Turkey would pursue a policy designed to serve her 'national interests' and not those of others. That, according to Ecevit, was to be the difference between his foreign policy and that of his predecessors, though his predecessors were quick to deny that they had ever sacrificed Turkey's national interests or her independence. In fact they were most indignant that Ecevit should take it upon himself to become the guardian of Turkey's independence (*bağımsızlık*).

The coalition that Ecevit formed with the NSP in January 1974 expressed what were essentially the RPP views on foreign policy. In the government's programme, presented in the Grand National Assembly on 1 February, the opening statement declared: 'The aim of our foreign policy—founded on principles established by Atatürk—is to pursue a course of action which is peaceloving, respectful of the principles of international law, and watchful of Turkey's independence.'[114] Initially there were no outstanding questions of foreign policy to be resolved and the new government's concern was primarily with internal affairs. But on 15 July the *coup d'état* against President Makarios of Cyprus, supported by the military junta in Athens, confronted Ecevit with a crisis both military and diplomatic. In chapter 12 above we saw how he handled a most delicate situation with calm confidence, and how his initial success established his reputation as the 'second Atatürk'. Ecevit's response was in marked contrast to the way in which İnönü and Demirel had responded to the two earlier crises of 1964 and 1967. The situation was very different in 1974: this time it was not possible to argue that the *coup* was an internal affair in which the guarantor powers—Britain, Turkey, and Greece—had no legal right to intervene. Ecevit was able to claim that he was intervening to defend the Republic of Cyprus whose president had been overthrown. And once the Turkish position had been firmly established on the island, he was able to pursue the goal of a federal republic with autonomy for the two communities, as outlined in the government's programme.[115]

Ecevit resigned on 18 September at the height of his popularity. He had succeeded in inculcating a widespread belief in the country that only he was capable of taking it from success to success. Perhaps he resigned in the hope that the needs of the Cyprus negotiations would restore him to power after an early general election. But that was not to be. Turkey experienced another long ministerial crisis during which its foreign policy was in limbo. Finally on 31 March 1975 Demirel announced his four-party Nationalist Front government. Meanwhile, on 5 February, during the transitional government of Senator Sadi Irmak, the US Congress imposed an arms embargo on Turkey, which was to continue until 'the President could certify to Congress that "substantial" progress had been made in the negotiations for a Cyprus settlement or that Turkey was removing her American-supplied military equipment from the island'.[116]

This action aroused great indignation throughout Turkey but the Irmak government was in no position to take counter-measures. The embargo, declared Irmak, 'would compel Turkey to review her ties with the North Atlantic Treaty Organization', and there were reports that Ankara would inform NATO that she could no longer protect the alliance's flank without US aid. This was all the more important as Greece had withdrawn from NATO's military command after the Turkish invasion of Cyprus.[117] On 10 February the *New York Times* reported that 'Turkey will probably order the closing of some United States military installations here if Congress does not restore military aid to Ankara soon ...' But neither Irmak nor Demirel, who took over the government on 31 March, was able to have the embargo lifted and the flow of aid restored.

As the partial Senate elections approached, the Front government adopted a more nationalist posture *vis-à-vis* the United States. At the end of July Demirel's government stopped operational activities on all but one of the twenty-seven US bases in Turkey, the exception being İncirlik in the southeast, reportedly the most important US and NATO base in the country.[118] This was Turkey's first 'reprisal' against the arms embargo. Demirel refused to hold discussions on any future co-operation with the United States while the embargo continued, and he proposed 30 September as the deadline, after which the evacuation of the bases would begin.[119] The embargo had become an issue in the election campaign. Demirel, with his superb sense of political timing, had arranged things so that he would benefit, no matter what the outcome: if the embargo continued after 30 September, he would immediately issue orders to begin dismantling the bases; if Washington lifted the embargo, he would take the credit. Either way, his strategy promised to increase his popularity at the polls. On 2 October the US Congress voted to lift the embargo partially, agreeing to supply Turkey with arms worth $185 million which she had already paid for. Few people found this gesture from Congress satisfactory, but it was sufficient to enable Demirel to retreat from his 'ultimatum', return to the path of negotiation, and begin the process of salvaging Turkish–American relations.[120]

New Orientations

In the mid-seventies Turkish foreign policy changed its structure but not its foundations. We have seen how Ankara's relations with Moscow were modified, in keeping with guidelines established by NATO. Turkey was less successful in improving her relations with countries of the Afro-Asian bloc because of their suspicions concerning ties with the West. New links were forged with the Arab world, especially with conservative countries like Saudi Arabia, and with the 'radical-Islamist' Libya, in which Turkish nationals began to seek work. Since the Islamic factor was useful in cultivating these relations it received some emphasis. But there were other, more pragmatic reasons for establishing closer relations with the Arab world; perhaps the most important, the need to find markets for Turkish consumer goods—which the oil-rich conservative states are better placed to buy than the radical states. This orientation seems destined to continue and it may be that Turkey will become the bridge between the Middle East and the West.

The emergence of Bülent Ecevit has been marked by a trend which stresses the pursuit of Turkey's national interest in her foreign relations, and greater independence in decision making. This trend is directly related to Ecevit's aspiration to create a 'national capitalism' based on a 'national bourgeoisie' within a social democratic political framework. He was in power only briefly—and then as the leader of a precarious coalition government. But even during his short term of office it is possible to see him resisting the pressure of the foreign oil companies and the pharmaceutical industry, as well as the pressure of the United States on the opium question. We may perhaps gain a better understanding of his own policy—which never had time to mature—by looking at his criticisms of the policies and practices of the Nationalist Front government.

Addressing the convention of the Chambers of Turkish Engineers and Architects on 23 May 1975, Ecevit criticized the 'secret conventional diplomacy' of the Front in contrast to his open diplomacy:

> ... we believe that secrecy in foreign politics, and secret diplomacy can only bring weakness to contemporary governments and never bring strength. For we know that a government which aimed at protecting the rights and liberty of its people could achieve this aim only by the mandate of the people. For we believed that the fundamental condition to receive the mandate of the people was openness.
>
> Yet today we observe that the *present government believes ... in the ways of secret conventional diplomacy....*[121]

This criticism was in keeping with Ecevit's populism, and populism in foreign relations was translated into 'openness'. He also criticized the leaders of the Right for their failure to protect Turkey's 'national interests', especially in the realm of the economy:

> ... one of the first deeds of the present-day government has been to accept the unfair demands of the foreign oil companies.
>
> Another policy of appeasement by this government has been to allow the exportation of raw mineral ores, and thus to make multinational companies richer at the cost of reducing Turkey's foreign currency reserves.... The very same government which closes the way to increase Turkey's foreign currency reserves through her own resource is at the same time trying to obtain foreign loans and credits with very inconvenient terms.
>
> Another example of the foreign economic policies of the present-day government can be given with respect to [the pharmaceutical industry]. According to the laws involved, [the] Social Security Institution should undertake the production of medicine. But this does not go well with the foreign firms. We then learn that in the short time the government has been in power, they have begun undermining the enterprises of the Social Security Institution.[122]

As we saw earlier, in the sixties Turkish governments began to turn more strongly towards Europe in order to avoid being left out if Europe developed as the 'third force'. This orientation had become markedly stronger by the mid-seventies, especially after the US arms embargo. Ankara had already considered Germany as an alternative to the United States, and that was again emphasized by Ecevit in June 1975. He told the *Frankfurter Allgemeine Zeitung* that it was necessary for Turkey to co-operate with Germany over the economy and defence, now that her relations with America had unexpectedly cooled, to Turkey's disappointment. Then he added: 'If Turkey gets separated from the West, after being separated from America, there will be only one alternative left, as you all know and the whole world knows, and one which no one wants. We should not be dragged to this.'

He hinted that 'Germany's aid could prevent that alternative which no one in Turkey wants', and expressed regret and sorrow that the ties between Ankara and Washington had weakened so drastically. He declared: 'If I had been in power we would not have come to this state. It is vital for our external security to work together with a super-power and a friend of the West like America.'[123]

Turkey, however, found it frustratingly difficult to achieve its goal of being accepted in Europe as an equal partner. She soon learned that Europe was segregated into two groups: on the one hand the Nine who were full members of the Common Market, and on the other the economically under-developed associate members such as Turkey and Greece. Turkish policy makers found that the Nine had become an institution. 'Their ministers or prime ministers meet officially not only to discuss economic matters but also to resolve political and military problems and to determine a joint basis for discussion with the United States on political and military matters.'[124] Countries such as Turkey were left out of such deliberations and faced only with the final decision. Such a state of affairs was obviously most unsatisfactory. But how was Turkey to overcome her subordination to Western Europe? Muharrem Nuri Birgi's answer was that Turkey must reach the same level of economic development as the developed members of the Atlantic community. Then she would be accepted. But this was easier said than done.

Another response to the realization that Turkey was being treated as a second-class nation was to turn to the oil-rich states of the Middle East and North Africa. This time the aim was not to find markets, but to reach agreements for collaboration in development: Turkey providing the know-how, and Iran, Libya, and Saudi Arabia the petro-dollars. The Turkish business community placed great hope in such schemes. But it was doubtful whether Turkish entrepreneurs and technologists would be able to compete in this area with their Western European, American, and Japanese counterparts.

One last trend worth mentioning is Ecevit's attempt to build bridges between Turkey and the social democratic régimes of Scandinavia and Western Europe, as well as the more independent countries of the Soviet bloc, especially Romania. This presents the possibility of an alignment which could stand up to the United States, the Nine, or the USSR, and is reminiscent of the non-aligned bloc of the fifties. But the development of this trend depends almost entirely on whether Ecevit can come to power at the next general election in 1977 and stay in power for some years.

NOTES

1 *Ayın Tarihi*, Sept. 1947, 19-21. For a comprehensive discussion of Turkey's post-war policy see Suat Bilge and others, *Olaylarla Türk Dış Politikası (1919-1965)* (1969), 205-37.

2 Harris, *Alliance*, 27.

3 Ibid., 27-8.

4 See the government's programme of 1950 in Öztürk, *Hükümetler*, 363.

5 *Cumhuriyet*, 1 June 1950.

6 Mehmet Gönlübol and Türkkaya Ataöv, *Turkey in the United Nations* (1960), 27; and IIR, *Turkey and the United Nations* (1961), 160-5.

7 Ibid. See also *The Times*, 29 June 1950.

8 General Fahri Belen, quoted in Mümtaz Soysal, *Dış Politika ve Parlamento* (1964), 201-2; Türkkaya Ataöv, *N.A.T.O. and Turkey* (1970), 109. Bayar gives his account in *Başvekilim Menderes*, 118-19.

9 Quoted in Yalman, *Gördüklerim*, iv, 228. This seems to have been the prevailing attitude.

10 Bilge, *Olaylar*, 245; Harris, *Alliance*, 40.

11 See Nadir Nadi, 'Açıkça', *Cumhuriyet*, 9 June 1951.

12 Ataöv, *N.A.T.O.*, 110.

13 Ibid., 113. For British policy see Elizabeth Monroe, *Britain's Moment in the Middle East 1914-1956* (paperback ed., London, 1965), 170 ff.

14 *Cumhuriyet*, 23 and 24 Nov. 1948.

15 *Cumhuriyet*, 9 and 12 Mar. 1949.

16 The Turkish press, 4 Nov. 1951 and the text monitored by the BBC from Radio Moscow, in *SWB*, iv/206/6-7. The note is published in RIIA, *Documents on International Affairs 1951* (London, 1954), 68-9. See also Ataöv, *N.A.T.O.*, 114-15.

17 *Cumhuriyet*, 13 Nov. 1951; Ankara Radio, 12 Nov. 1951, in *SWB*, iv/209/5.

18 Váli, *Bridge*, 77-8.

19 *Egypt News,* Oct.-Nov. 1951, 3 quoted in Ataöv, *N.A.T.O.,* 130.
20 *Cumhuriyet,* 20 Oct. 1951.
21 The Turkish press, 19-22 Jan. 1952, especially Bülent Daver's article 'Churchill'in Son Teklifi', *Cumhuriyet,* 21 Jan. 1952.
22 Köprülü's statement to *al-Misri* (Cairo) in *Cumhuriyet,* 11 Dec. 1952. See also, Eren, *Turkey Today—and Tomorrow,* 238-40.
23 Ataöv, *N.A.T.O.,* 131; Bilge, *Olaylar,* 269 ff.
24 *Ayın Tarihi,* Feb. 1955, 165-94; Ataöv, *N.A.T.O.,* 132-3.
25 Harris, *Alliance,* 63. On 9 Aug. 1954 Turkey signed the Balkan Pact with Greece and communist Yugoslavia. The significance of this pact for Turkey's foreign relations was limited both by the Soviet Union's rapprochement with Yugoslavia, and by the deterioration of Turco-Greek relations over Cyprus. For the diplomacy of the Balkan Pact see Bilge, *Olaylar,* 225-68; Ataöv, *N.A.T.O.,* 116-25.
26 *SWB,* iv/524/14.
27 Ankara Radio, 4 Jan. 1955, in *SWB,* iv/533/19. F. R. Zorlu was Deputy Prime Minister, Minister of State, and virtually acting Foreign Minister. Moreover, he was very close to Menderes.
28 *Cumhuriyet,* 21 Jan. 1955.
29 *Cumhuriyet,* 13 Oct. 1959. Three years earlier Foreign Minister Köprülü had also stated that Turkey would not be deceived by Russia's peace offensive. See the second quotation at the head of this chapter.
30 *The Afro-Asian Movement* (Jerusalem, 1973), 63-4; Bilge, *Olaylar,* 240-3.
31 Ataöv, *N.A.T.O.,* 134.
32 Aptülahat Akşin, *Türkiye'nin 1945 den Sonraki Dış Politika Gelişmeleri: Orta Doğu Meseleleri (1959), 31.*
33 *Zafer* and Ankara Radio, 4 Jan. 1957, in *SWB,* iv/139/11-12. The Eisenhower Doctrine pledged 'to defend Middle Eastern countries threatened by indirect aggression from international communism'. See Harris, *Alliance,* 64; Váli, *Bridge,* 283-5; and Ataöv, *N.A.T.O.,* 135-6.
34 Harris, *Alliance,* 64.
35 *Kim,* 4 July 1958, 9. The troops were offered through Suat Hayri Ürgüplü, ambassador in Washington; *MEJ* xii/4 (1958), 444.
36 Toker, *İsmet Paşa,* ii, 39.
37 This agreement was signed on 5 Mar. 1959. The text is given in *Cumhuriyet,* 6 Mar. 1959 and Harris, *Alliance,* 221-3.
38 *Vatan Yıllığı 1960,* 7 (11 Feb. 1959) and *Cumhuriyet,* 13 Feb. 1959; Eroğul, *Demokrat Parti,* 169.
39 *Cumhuriyet,* 15 July 1959.
40 Cyrus Sulzberger, *A Long Row of Candles* (New York, 1969), 396.
41 Yalman, *Gördüklerim,* iv, 319. Yalman was a member of the corps of journalists who accompanied Menderes to Germany.
42 The Turkish press, 5-14 May 1957.
43 See the NUC press conference of 22 June, *Cumhuriyet,* 23 June 1960; Seyhan, *Gölgedeki Adam,* 73; the conspirators arranged to have Seyhan sent to Washington in Jan. 1960 in order to explain the nature of

the *coup* and to argue against US intervention if it was requested. See also *MER 1960*, 430.

44 Erdemir, ed., *Milli Birlik*, 293 and *MER 1960*, 433. The Baghdad Pact was renamed the Central Treaty Organization (CENTO) after Iraq withdrew from the pact in 1959.

45 See also Harris, *Alliance*, 86–7 and *Cumhuriyet*, 22 June 1960. The Soviet Union offered to provide economic aid but the Turkish government gave an evasive answer, claiming that it was not in a position to say 'yes' or 'no' until the Planning Bureau had studied the needs of the country (*Cumhuriyet, 24 June 1960*).

46 Öztürk, *Hükümetler*, 469–73; *MER 1960*, 440–1.

47 MENA, 9 Aug. 1960, in *SWB*, iv/407/A/5. In August Seyfullah Esin, one of Turkey's most experienced diplomats, was sent as ambassador to Cairo with the specific task of improving relations with Egypt. Conversation with Ambassador Esin.

48 *Telgraf* (Ankara), 16 Sept. 1960 quoted by Ankara Radio, 16 Sept. 1960, in *SWB*, iv/440/c/1.

49 Messages between Khrushchev and Gürsel were reported in the Turkish press, 1 Sept. 1960. As part of the diplomatic offensive, the USSR published Ambassador S. I. Aralov's memoirs entitled 'In the Turkey of Atatürk: Reminiscences of an Ambassador', *International Affairs* (Moscow), Aug.–Nov. 1960. They were not published in Turkey until Feb. 1967, when they were serialized in *Cumhuriyet*, 17–25 Feb. 1967, and as *Bir Sovyet Diplomatının Türkiye Hatıraları* (İstanbul, 1967).

50 *Ulus*, 10 Jan. 1962.

51 *Cumhuriyet*, 24 Feb. 1961; Ankara Radio, 23 Feb. 1961, in *SWB*, iv/W98/3; *MER 1961*, 522–3.

52 Ankara Radio, 7 Feb. 1962, in *SWB*, iv/866/c/4.

53 *Cumhuriyet*, 3 Apr. 1962. Basing its report on statistics published by the NATO Secretariat, *Akşam* (26 Nov. 1965) wrote that Turkey, the poorest country in NATO, furnished the third largest contingent (480,000 men), allocated to NATO purposes the largest percentage of her budget after the US, Britain, and Germany who were all rich and developed, and came second in keeping men of working age under arms. Although Turkey bore the heaviest burden, concluded *Akşam*, she received the least aid.

54 See the Turkish press, 5–7 May 1962, reporting on the NATO Ministers' Meeting in Athens.

55 *Cumhuriyet*, 29 and 30 July 1962.

56 On the question of the Jupiter missiles and the Cuban crisis see Bilge, *Olaylar*, 349–50; Toker, *İsmet Paşa*, iv, 99–104; Váli, *Bridge*, 128–9; Harris, *Alliance*, 92–4.

57 Harris, *Alliance*, 94.

58 See the Assembly debate on foreign policy reported in the Turkish press, 10 and 11 Jan. 1963.

59 *Zafer*, 22 Aug. 1954.

60 Ankara Radio, 9 Sept. 1954, in *SWB*, iv/501/21–2.

61 15 Sept. 1954. The tripartite alliance referred to the Balkan Pact between Turkey, Greece, and Yugoslavia.

62 Abidin Daver, 'Kıbrıs Yunanistan'a Verilemez', *Cumhuriyet*, 21 Dec. 1951. The best account of the Turkish position is A. Suat Bilge, *Le conflit de Chypre et les Cypriotes turcs* (1961).

63 Quoted in *Cumhuriyet*, 26 Oct. 1954.

64 See Menderes's Bursa speech in *Zafer*, 4 May 1957; Toker, İsmet *Paşa*, i, 196; and Fahir Armaoğlu, 'Le conflit de Chypre et l'attitude du gouvernement turc en 1957', IIR, *The Turkish Yearbook of International Relations: 1961* (1963), 40-61.

65 Váli, *Bridge*, 228-59; Bilge, *Olaylar*, 361-99.

66 Ankara Radio, 28 May 1960, in *SWB*, iv/347/c/3.

67 Ankara Radio, 13 Aug. 1963, in *SWB*, iv/1327/c/1.

68 The Turkish press, 26 and 27 Dec. 1963; Toker, İsmet *Paşa*, iv, 105-10.

69 The Turkish press, 5 Mar. 1964 and following; Váli, *Bridge*, 253-4.

70 *Cumhuriyet*, 14 Mar. 1964.

71 Ibid., 17 Mar. 1964.

72 Ibid., 17 Apr. 1964.

73 The Turkish press, 17 Apr. and Hilmi Yavuz, 'İnönü'nün Demeci ve Dış Politikamız', *Cumhuriyet*, 18 Apr. 1964, 3.

74 *Cumhuriyet*, 6 May 1964.

75 Johnson's letter and İnönü's reply were kept secret until 13 Jan. 1966 when they were published, against the wishes of the Demirel government, by the Istanbul daily *Hürriyet*. They caused great embarrassment to both the Turkish and the American governments, which then decided to publish the official texts. See *MEJ* xx/3 (1966), 386-93 and IIR, *The Turkish Yearbook of International Relations: 1966* (Ankara, 1969), 139-41 for the text of the letters. See also Harris, *Alliance*, 114-16 and Váli, *Bridge*, 130-2. Needless to say, there was no Turkish landing in Cyprus.

76 Harris, *Alliance*, 116.

77 F. Armaoğlu, 'Batı İttifakından Ayrılamayız', *Cumhuriyet*, 29 Apr. 1964.

78 Adapted from Hamit Batu's article in the *Foreign Ministry Monthly*, Mar. 1965 and translated and excerpted in *Pulse* (Ankara), no. 528, 25 Aug. 1965. See also the Ürgüplü government's programme presented in the Assembly on 26 Feb. 1965, in Öztürk, *Hükümetler*, 600-5.

79 Ankara Radio, 5 June 1964, in *SWB*, iv/1573/c/1-2.

80 Váli, *Bridge*, 177-8. For the Turkish-Soviet Joint Communiqué of 27 Dec. 1966 see IIR, *The Turkish Yearbook of International Relations: 1966*, 172-5.

81 *Milliyet*, 14 Oct. 1967, quoted in Váli, *Bridge*, 179.

82 Quoted in F. Armaoğlu, 'The European Security Conference and Mutual and Balanced Force Reductions', *FP* ii/4 (1972), 109-10. The Harmel Report was issued in late 1967.

83 F. Armaoğlu, 'Recent Developments in Turkish Foreign Policy', *FP* i/1 (1971), 89. It is important to note that cutbacks in US credits and Turkey's growing economic needs played a role in the development of these relations.

428   *The Turkish Experiment in Democracy*

84 *Cumhuriyet*, 4-6 July 1964 and Kayhan Sağlamer, 'Eyüb Hanın Birlik Teklifi', *Cumhuriyet*, 6 July 1964.

85 *Cumhuriyet*, 23 July 1964, and Selçuk Karaçam, 'A Report on RCD—Regional Co-operation for Development', *FP* i/1 (1971), 156-9. RCD was an economic and cultural extension of CENTO.

86 Aug. 1964, 41-2.

87 *The Economist*, 23 Mar. 1965.

88 *Cumhuriyet*, 4, 5, 6, 10, and 12 Oct. 1964; Arslan Başer Kafaoğlu, 'Tarafsızların Toplantısı', *Sosyal Adalet*, Nov. 1964, 37-40.

89 Kayhan Sağlamer, 'Asya-Afrika Konferansının Önemi', and 'Cezair Konferansında Türkiye', *Cumhuriyet*, 29 May and 19 June 1965 respectively.

90 *Cumhuriyet*, 18 Dec. 1965.

91 *Ulus*, 21 Dec. 1965 (quotation).

92 Harris, *Alliance*, 150.

93 Mehmet Gönlübol, 'Turkish-American Relations: a General Appraisal', *FP* i/4 (1971), 73.

94 Adapted from Aybar's radio broadcast as published in the Turkish press, 26 Sept. 1965, and reported in *SWB*, iv/1971/c/1-2.

95 *Milliyet*, 1 Apr. 1966. See also Demirel's statement broadcast over Ankara Radio, 5 Apr. 1966, in *SWB*, iv/2132/c/1.

96 *Milliyet*, 5 Apr. 1966.

97 *Cumhuriyet*, 1 and 2 June 1967. Demirel refused to confirm or deny these reports. For a discussion of Turkey's changing attitude towards the Arab states after 1965 see Ömer Kürkçüoğlu, *Türkiye'nin Arap Orta Doğusu'na Karşı Politikası (1945-1970)* (Ankara, 1972), 137-82.

98 *Cumhuriyet*, 13 June 1967.

99 The Turkish press, 9-10 Sept. 1967, and A. G. Xydis, 'The Military Régime's Foreign Policy', in Richard Clogg and George Yannopoulos, eds., *Greece under Military Rule* (New York, 1972), 201-2. See also Andreas Papandreou, *Democracy at Gunpoint* (New York, 1970), 240-1.

100 Thomas Erlich, *Cyprus 1958-1967 (New York, 1974)*, 90-116, gives an excellent account of the 1967 crisis.

101 *Cumhuriyet*, 16-18 Nov. 1967.

102 *Yeni Ortam*, 12 May 1975. In the same statement Tural said that there were those in the government who even wanted to send troops to Vietnam. But he opposed this just as he had opposed sending Turkish troops to Korea in 1950.

103 Papandreou, as cited in n. 99 above, 242-3.

104 The Turkish press, 24 and 25 Nov. 1967.

105 See the Turkish press, 27 Nov.-6 Dec. 1967; *MER 1967*, 527; and Ankara Radio, 26 Nov. 1967, in *SWB*, iv/2632/c/3-4; 29 Nov. 1967, in *SWB*, iv/2635/c/3; 30 Nov. 1967, in *SWB*, iv/2636/c/3; and 4 Dec. 1967, in *SWB*, iv/2640/4-6.

106 Excerpts from report, including passages read by Nihat Erim and broadcast by Ankara Radio, 2 Apr. 1971, in *SWB*, iv/3653/c/3. For the full text of the programme see Ulus, 3 Apr. 1971. See also Osman Olcay, 'Turkey's Foreign Policy', *FP*, i/2 (June 1973), 79-84.

107 Ankara Radio, as in preceding note.

108 Harris, *Alliance*, 192–3. Numerous Turkish and English language sources are given in Harris.

109 Ibid., 193–5.

110 Ibid., 197.

111 Ibid., 192. See also, Henry Kamm, 'Turkish Farmers See Poverty in Ban on the Poppy', *New York Times*, 3 Oct. 1972.

112 This was another decision which a party government dependent on votes in the Assembly would have found difficult to take. There was talk of recognizing the People's Republic of China after the revolution of 27 May 1960 but no action was taken throughout the decade. Then, rather suddenly, the Erim government recognized the People's Republic on 5 Aug. 1971. It was widely noted that the timing coincided with the thaw in Sino-American relations, especially after Secretary of State Henry Kissinger's visit to Peking, and there was speculation as to whether there had been US influence or pressure on Turkey's decision. But Deputy Premier Koçaş denied any external influence. See the Turkish press, 5–7 Aug. 1971 and Fahir H. Armaoğlu, 'Turkey and the People's Republic of China', *FP*, 1/iii (Sept. 1971), 109–27, where the question is discussed in some detail.

113 *Guardian Weekly*, 109/5, 13 Oct. 1973, 12. In fact the Republicans also promised to remove the ban and permit cultivation under an effective control system: 'The RPP government', stated the 1973 election manifesto, 'will reorganize the cultivation of opium under an effective system of controls which will overcome international anxieties ...' See Cumhuriyet Halk Partisi, *Ak Günlere* (Ankara, 1973), 51.

114 *Milliyet*, 2 Feb. 1974, 7; and *Ak Günlere*, 217–27.

115 *Milliyet*, 2 Feb. 1974, 7.

116 *New York Times*, 5 Feb. 1975; the Turkish press, 5 Feb. 1975 and following. *Yankı*, 204, 10 Feb. 1975, 4–10, which gives interviews with Ecevit, Foreign Minister Melih Esenbel, and Hasan Işık, Minister of Defence in the Ecevit government.

117 *New York Times*, 5 Feb. 1975.

118 Metin Ormancıoğlu, 'Turkey Sets Deadline for US to Leave', *The Guardian*, 7 Aug. 1975. On the importance of İncirlik to US regional strategy see İlhan Selçuk, 'İncirlik'teki Amerika', *Cumhuriyet*, 29 July 1975. See also 'The Vendetta's Victim is Cyprus', *The Economist*, 9 Aug. 1975.

119 *Cumhuriyet*, 3 and 9 Aug. 1975.

120 See the Turkish press, 3 Oct. 1975 and following, and *Yankı*, 239, 13 Oct. 1975, 7–8.

121 CHP Genel Merkez Basın Bürosu, 'Ecevit on the State of Affairs Inside and Outside Turkey' (Ankara, 23 May 1975), 2, italic as in the original. This brochure was published in English.

122 Ibid., 4. Ecevit also revealed that the leaders of the Front opposed his decision to allow the cultivation of the opium poppy: 'We allowed the cultivation of the poppy in the face of a variety of foreign pressures, and we made the world accept our decision. Yet certain party leaders who

monopolized verbal Nationalism in Turkey opposed us then. They said "You cannot allow poppy cultivation without the consent of and without negotiating with this or that state." ' (p. 6.)

123 'Ecevit: Germany Must Take USA's Place', reported in *Milliyet*, 27 June 1975 by its correspondent in Cologne.

124 Muharrem Nuri Birgi, 'Developments Within The Atlantic Community and Turkey', *FP*, iii/4 (1973), 73–4. Birgi had been Turkish ambassador to NATO. Perhaps European attitudes such as those he describes help to explain the report in *The Economist*, 9 Aug. 1975, concerning Ecevit's statements: 'In the past week Mr Ecevit has come close to advocating a neutralist policy ... and he argued that Turkey should not look to western Europe ("because it would not follow a course much different from the Americans") but should follow a new concept of national security and defence, whatever that means....' We must remember that Ecevit was speaking with an eye to elections, and in an attempt to outbid Demirel during the controversy over the embargo.

GENERAL ABBREVIATIONS AND GLOSSARY

AFU   Armed Forces Union (*Silahlı Kuvvetler Birliği*), founded in 1961 as an informal organization whose aim was to represent all shades of opinion in the armed forces and thus to prevent factionalism and the threat of *coups*. It was successful in defusing military conspiracies in the early sixties; it then lost its *raison d'être* and ceased to function.

AID   Agency for International Development (USAID), founded in 1961 to administer aid provided under the US Foreign Assistance Act of 1961.

AP   *See* the entry JP below.

CENTO   Central Treaty Organization, the name adopted for the mutual defence pact between Great Britain, Turkey, Iran, and Pakistan in 1959 when Iraq withdrew from the Baghdad Pact after the revolution of July 1958.

CHP   *See* the entry RPP below.

COGS   Chief of the General Staff.

DİSK   *Devrimci İşçi Sendikaları Konfederasyonu* (The Confederation of Revolutionary Workers' Unions), founded in 1967 by a splinter group from *Türk-İş*. It believed that the 'above-party' and moderate policies of *Türk-İş* served the interests of the employers and not the workers. DİSK attracted a large following, especially in the private sector, and by 1970 it threatened to become the principal confederation of unions. Its growth was halted by the semi-military régime established on 12 March 1971.

DP   Democrat Party (*Demokrat Parti*), founded in 1946, won the general elections of 1950, 1954 and 1957, and was in power until the military *coup* of 27 May 1960, after which it was dissolved by court order.

Also Democratic Party (*Demokratik Parti*), founded in January 1970 by a splinter group from the Justice Party which was opposed to Demirel's policies and which wanted to appear as the successor of the dissolved Democrat Party. The DP became the fourth party after the 1973 election, but the Senate elections of 1975 suggest that it may be declining very rapidly.

FP   Freedom Party (*Hürriyet Partisi*), founded in December 1955 by the liberal wing of the Democrat Party. After losing the 1957 general election very badly, the leaders dissolved the party and many of them joined the Republican People's Party.

GNP   Gross National Product.

IBRD   International Bank for Reconstruction and Development (or World Bank), conceived at the Bretton Woods Conference in July 1944, and began operations in June 1946. Its purpose is to provide and facilitate international investment.

JP   Justice Party (*Adalet Partisi*), founded in February 1961 and soon became the principal successor to the Democrat Party. It won the elections of 1965 and 1969 but was removed from power by the military intervention of 12 March 1971. Weakened by factionalism, its vote was shared with four other parties of the Right in the 1973 election. Since 1973 it has been recovering some of its old strength.

MEDO Middle East Defence Organization (1951), was intended to replace the United Kingdom's Middle East Command; in the absence of Egyptian membership, proved abortive.

MİT *Milli İstihbarat Teşkilâtı* (National Intelligence Organization), the name adopted by the Turkish intelligence service when it was modernized in 1963. MİT has played an important role in disrupting the Turkish Left by Infiltrating *agents provocateurs* into various organizations and parties. It has also been active in ferreting out conspiracies in the armed forces.

NAP Nationalist Action Party (*Milliyetçi Hareket Partisi*), the name adopted by the Republican Peasants' Nation Party in February 1969. The new name symbolized the more militant character of the party which manifested itself in the organization of a youth commando wing and street violence.

NATO North Atlantic Treaty Organization, founded in April 1949 by Belgium, Canada, Denmark, France, Iceland, Italy, Luxembourg, the Netherlands, Norway, Portugal, the United Kingdom, and the United States. Greece and Turkey were admitted in 1952 and West Germany in 1955.

NOP National Order Party (*Milli Nizam Partisi*), founded in January 1970 to represent the interests of the petty bourgeoisie of Anatolia under pressure from the expanding modern capitalist sector of the economy. It was dissolved by the Constitutional Court in May 1971 for exploiting religion for political ends. The NOP reappeared in October 1972 in the guise of the National Salvation Party.

NP Nation Party (*Millet Partisi*), founded in July 1948 by a right-wing faction of the Democrat Party. It was closed down by the government in July 1953 for engaging in subversive activities under a religious cloak. Dissolved by court order in January 1954, it reappeared in February as the Republican Nation Party, absorbing the Peasants Party of Turkey (*Türkiye Köylü Partisi*, founded in May 1952) after the 1957 election, and became the Republican Peasants' Nation Party. In June 1962 a faction left the RPNP and again formed the NP. The NP continues to exist but has no national significance. See also the entry RPNP below.

NRP National Reliance Party (*Milli Güven Partisi*), *see* the entry RP below.

NSC National Security Council (*Milli Güvenlik Kurulu*), an institution created according to Article III of the 1961 constitution. It is presided over by the President of the Republic, and includes the Prime Minister, the Chief of the General Staff, the commanders of the armed forces, and cabinet ministers. It is the most important consultative body in the country, and through it the service chiefs are able to exert great influence on the government.

NSP National Salvation Party (*Milli Selamet Partisi*), founded in October 1972 by former members of the dissolved National Order Party. It did very well in the 1973 election, becoming the third party and a partner in both coalitions.

NTP   New Turkey Party (*Yeni Türkiye Partisi*), founded in February 1961 as one of the successors to the dissolved Democrat Party. Unable to compete successfully with the Justice Party and other parties of the Right, it merged with the JP in March 1973.

NUC   National Unity Committee (*Milli Birlik Komitesi*), the committee of 38 former officers created after the *coup* of 27 May 1960 to govern the country. Fourteen 'radical' members were removed in November 1960; the NUC continued to function until political power was restored to the politicians after the general election of 1961.

NUG   National Unity Group (*Milli Birlik Grubu*), a group in the Senate composed of former members of the NUC who became Life Senators after the NUC was dissolved in October 1961.

OYAK   *Ordu Yardımlaşma Kurumu* (Army Mutual Assistance Association), founded in 1961 and soon developed into one of Turkey's most powerful and prosperous corporations.

RCD   Regional Co-operation for Development, the economic and cultural extension of CENTO, founded in 1964 and still active—especially in the cultural field.

RNP   Republican Nation Party (*Cumhuriyetçi Millet Partisi*), see the entry NP above.

RP   Reliance Party (*Güven Partisi*), founded in May 1967 by a right-wing faction in the Republican People's Party opposed to the party's adoption of the left-of-centre platform. Its name was later changed to the National Reliance Party, and finally in March 1973 to the Republican Reliance Party, when the Republican Party (*Cumhuriyetçi Parti*, founded in September 1972) merged with it.

RPNP   Republican Peasants' Nation Party (*Cumhuriyetçi Köylü Millet Partisi*), see the entry NP above. In 1966 the party leadership was taken over by Alparslan Türkeş and many of its old members returned to the Nation Party. In 1969 the RPNP became the Nationalist Action Party.

RPP   Republican People's Party (*Cumhuriyet Halk Partisi*), founded in 1923 and ruled Turkey until 1950, when it was defeated by the Democrat Party. It was led by Kemal Atatürk until 1938, and by İsmet İnönü until 1972. In 1972 Bülent Ecevit became its chairman and began to give it a social democratic character. In 1973 the RPP won the general election and led the coalition government with the National Salvation Party.

RRP   Republican Reliance Party (*Cumhuriyetçi Güven Partisi*), see the entry RP above.

SPO   State Planning Organization (*Devlet Plânlama Teşkilâtı*), created in September 1960 by the military régime to advise the government on economic matters.

Türk-İş   *Türkiye İşçi Sendikaları Konfederasyonu* (The Confederation of Workers' Unions of Turkey), officially founded in July 1952 but remained ineffective until 1963, when the right to strike was granted. Because of its moderate policies and its failure to make substantial gains for its members, it lost support to DİSK.

TRT   *Türkiye Radyo ve Televizyonu* (Turkish Radio and Television).

UP   Unity Party (*Birlik Partisi*), founded in October 1966 as a progressive, Kemalist, and reformist party said to represent the prosperous members of the Shia minority. It never became a party of any consequence.

UPT   Unity Party of Turkey (*Türkiye Birlik Partisi*), the name adopted by the Unity Party in November 1971.

WPT   Workers' Party of Turkey (*Türkiye İşçi Partisi*), founded by trade unionists in February 1961, it began to play a political role totally out of proportion to its strength in the Assembly. It was dissolved by court order in July 1971.

BIBLIOGRAPHICAL ABBREVIATIONS

Ağaoğlu, *İki Parti* — Samet Ağaoğlu, *İki Parti Arasındaki Farklar* (1947)

Aksoy, *Toprak* — Suat Aksoy, *Türkiye'de Toprak Meselesi* (1970)

Aktan, 'Land Reform' — Reşat Aktan, 'Problems of Land Reform in Turkey', in ESSCB, *Agricultural Aspects of Economic Development* (1965)

Altuğ, *Erim Olayı* — Kurtul Altuğ, *12 Mart ve Nihat Erim Olayı* (1973)

Aren, *Ekonomi* — Sadun Aren, *Ekonomi El Kitabı: Türkiye Ekonomisinden Örneklerle* 3rd edn (1972)

Ataöv, *N.A.T.O.* — Türkkaya Ataöv, *N.A.T.O. and Turkey* (1970)

Aybar, *12 Mart* — M. A. Aybar, *12 Mart'tan Sonra Meclis Konuşmaları* 2nd edn (1973)

Baban, *Politika* — Cihad Baban, *Politika Galerisi* (1970)

Başgil, *27 Mayıs* — A. F. Başgil, *27 Mayıs İhtilâli ve Sebepleri* (1966)

Bayar, *Başvekilim Menderes* — Celâl Bayar, *Başvekilim Adnan Menderes* (n.d. [1970])

Belen, *Demokrasi* — Fahri Belen, *Demokrasiden Diktatörlüğe* (1960)

Bilge and others, *Olaylar* — Suat Bilge and others, *Olaylarla Türk Dış Politikası (1919-1965)* (1969)

Boratav, *Gelir* — Korkut Boratav, *Gelir Dağılımı* (1969)

Bulutoğlu, *Yabancı Sermaye* — Kenan Bulutoğlu, *Türkiye'de Yabancı Sermaye* (1970)

Cumhuriyet Halk Partisi, *Seçim Neticeleri* — Cumhuriyet Halk Partisi, *Seçim Neticeleri Üzerinde bir İnceleme* (1959)

Demokratik Parti, *72'ler Hareketi* — Demokratik Parti, *72'ler Hareketi ve Demokratik Parti* (1971)

Dereli, *Turkish Trade Unionism* — Toker Dereli, *The Development of Turkish Trade Unionism* (1968)

EI² — *Encyclopaedia of Islam*, 2nd edn

ESSCB — Economic and Social Studies Conference Board (Istanbul)

ESSCB, *Social Aspects* — ESSCB, *Social Aspects of Economic Development* (1964)

—— *Agricultural Aspects* — ESSCB, *Agricultural Aspects of Economic Development* (1965)

ESEKH	Ekonomik ve Sosyal Etüdler Konferans Heyeti
Erdemir, ed., *Milli Birlik*	Sabahat Erdemir, ed., *Milli Birliğe Doğru*, i (1961)
Erer, *On Yıl*	Tekin Erer, *On Yılın Mücadelesi* (n.d. [1963?])
Erkanlı, *Anılar*	Orhan Erkanlı, *Anılar ... Sorunlar ... Sorumlular* (1972)
Esirci, *Menderes*	Sükrü Esirci, *Menderes Diyorki!* i (1967)
FA	*Foreign Affairs* (New York)
FP	*Foreign Poliicy* (Ankara), the English language version of *Dış Politika*
Faik, *Gazeteci*	Bediî Faik, *İhtilâlciler Arasında bir Gazeteci* (1967)
Genç, *12 Mart*	Süleyman Genç, *12 Mart'a Nasıl Gelindi* (1971)
Gevgilili, *1971 Rejimi*	Ali Gevgilili, *Türkiye'de 1971 Rejimi* (1973)
Giritlioğlu, *Halk Partisi*	Fahir Giritlioğlu, *Türk Siyasi Tarihinde Cumhuriyet Halk Partisinin Mevkii*, i, ii (1965)
Harris, *Alliance*	George Harris, *Troubled Alliance* (1972)
Hershlag, *Turkey*	Z. Y. Hershlag, *Turkey: the Challenge of Growth* (1968)
IA	*International Affairs* (London)
IIR	Institute of International Relations, Faculty of Political Science, Ankara
İlkin and İnanç, eds., *Planning*	S. İlkin and E. İnanç, eds., *Planning in Turkey* (1967)
İnönü, *Muhalefet*	İsmet İnönü, *Muhalefet'de İsmet İnönü* ed. Sabahat Erdemir, i, ii, iii (1956–62)
İpekçi & Coşar, *İhtilâl*	Abdi İpekçi ve Sami Coşar, *İhtilâlin İçyüzü* (1965)
JCH	*Journal of Contemporary History*
Karaosmanoğlu, *45 Yıl*	Y. K. Karaosmanoğlu, *Politikada 45 Yıl* (1968)
Karpat, *Politics*	Kemal Karpat, *Turkey's Politics* (1959)
Karpat, *Social Thought*	Kemal Karpat, ed., *Political and Social Thought in the Contemporary Middle East* (1968)
Kışlalı, *Forces Politique*	A. T. Kışlalı, *Forces Politiques dans la Turquie Moderne* (n.d. [1970])
Kuran, *İktidar*	Alp Kuran, *Kapalı İktidar* (1962)
Kuruç, *İktisat*	Bilsay Kuruç, *İktisat Politikasının Resmi Belgeleri* (1963)
Lewis, *Emergence*	Bernard Lewis, *The Emergence of Modern Turkey*, 2na edn (1968)
MEA	*Middle Eastern Affairs*

MEJ   *Middle East Journal*

MER   *Middle East Record*

Menderes, *Konuşmalar*   Adnan Menderes, *Adnan Menders'in Konuşmaları*, ed. Mustafa Doğan, i, ii (1957)

Öztürk, Hükümetler   Kâzım Öztürk, *Türkiye Cumhuriyeti Hükümetleri ve Programları* (1968)

RIIA   Royal Institute of International Affairs

Robinson, *Republic*   R. D. Robinson, *The First Turkish Republic* (1963)

SBFD   *Siyasal Bilgiler Falkültesi Dergisi*

SWB   *Summary of World Broadcasts*, British Broadcasting Corporation, Reading (1950-71)

Sencer, *Türkiye'de Köylülük*   Muzaffer Sencer, *Türkiye'de Köylülüğün Maddi Temelleri* (1971)

Sencer, *Sosyal Temeller*   Muzaffer Sencer, *Türkiye'de Siyasal Partilerin Sosyal Temelleri* (1971)

Sönmez, 'The Re-emergence of Planning'   A. Sönmez, 'The Re-emergence of the Idea of Planning and the Scope and Targets of the 1963-1967 Plan', in S. İlkin and E. İnanç, eds., *Planning in Turkey* (1967)

TY   *Türkiye Yıllığı*

Toker, *İsmet Paşa*   Metin Toker, *İsmet Paşayla 10 Yıl (1954-1964)*, i, ii, iii, iv (1965-9)

Toker, *Tek Parti*   Metin Toker, *Tek Partiden Çok Partiye* (1970)

Tökin, *Türk Tarihi*   F. H. Tökin, *Türk Tarihinde Siyasi Partiler ve Siyasi Düşüncenin Gelişmesi 1839-1965* (1965)

Tunaya, *İslâmcılık*   T. Z. Tunaya, *İslâmcılık Cereyanı* (1962)

Tunaya, *Partiler*   T. Z. Tunaya, *Türkiye'de Siyasi Partiler, 1859-1952* (1952)

Türkeş, *Milliyetçilik*   Alparslan Türkeş, *1944 Milliyetçilik Olayı* (1968)

Ulay, *Harbiye*   Sıtkı Ulay, *Harbiye Silâh Başına: 27 Mayıs 1960* (1968)

Üstünel, *Kalkınma*   Besim Üstünel, *Kalkınmanın Neresindeyiz* (1966)

VY   *Varlık Yıllığı*

Váli, *Bridge*   Ferenc A. Váli, *Bridge Across the Bosporus* (1971)

WP   *World Politics*

Weiker, *Revolution*   Walter F. Weiker, *The Turkish Revolution 1960-1961* (1963)

Yalman, *Gördüklerim*, iv   A. E. Yalman, *Gördüklerim ve Geçirdiklerim*, iv (1971)

Yücekök, *Din ve Siyaset*   Ahmet Yücekök, Türkiye'de Din ve Siyaset (1971)

SELECT BIBLIOGRAPHY

1. Works in Turkish

Abadan, Nermin. *1965 Seçimlerinin Tahlili.* Ank., 1966.
Abadan, Yavuz. *Türkiye'de Siyasi Partiler ve Tazyik Grupları in SBF'nin Yüzüncü Yıl Armağanı.* Ank., 1959.
Adalet Partisi. *Milli Hakimiyet Mücadelesinde AP.* Ank., 1963.
—— *Adalet Partisi İkinci Büyük Kongresinde Genel Başkan Adaylarının Konuşmaları.* Ank., n.d. [1964].
—— *Hükümet Buhranı-Hükümet Teşkili-Hükümet Programı-Kıbrıs Olayları Karşısında Adalet Partisi.* Ank., n.d. [1964].
—— *Tüzük ve Program.* Ank., 1964.
—— *Seçim Beyannamesi.* Ank., 1965.
—— *Adalet Partisi Üçüncü Büyük Kongresi: Raporlar.* Ank., 1966.
—— *Adalet Partisi IV Büyük Kongresi, 29 Kasim 1968: Raporlar.* Ank., 1968.
—— *Tüzük ve Program.* Ank., 1969.
—— *AP Politikasında Genel Görüşler.* Ank., 1969.
—— *Seçim Beyannamesi 1969.* Ank., 1969.
—— *Yeni Bir Türkiye.* Ank., 1970.
—— *Oniki Mart ve Sonrası.* 2 vols. Ank., 1971 and 1972.
Ağaoğlu, Samet. *İki Parti Arasındaki Farklar.* Ank., 1947.
—— *Arkadaşım Menderes.* Ist., 1967.
—— *Marmara'da bir Ada.* Ist., 1972.
—— *Demokrat Partinin Doğuş ve Yükseliş Sebepleri: Bir Soru.* Ist., 1972.
Ağralı, Sedat. *Türk Sendikacılığı.* Ist., 1967.
Aksal, İsmail Rüştü. *İstikrar Politikası: CHPnin 1959 Bütçe Tenkidi.* Ank., 1959.
Aksoy, Muammer. *Partizan Radyo.* Ank., 1960.
—— *Sanayi Bakanı Çelikbaş'ın Rejime, Hukuka ve Memleket Menfaatlerine Aykırı Tutumu.* Ank., 1963.
Aksoy, Suat. *Türkiye'de Toprak Meselesi.* Ist., 1970.
Akşin, Aptülahat. *Türkiye'nin 1945 den Sonraki Dış Politika Gelişmeleri: Orta Doğu Meseleleri.* Ist., 1959.
Aktan, Reşat. *Zirai İstihsalde Makinalaşma Hadisesinin Ekonomik Analizi. SBFD,* ix/1 (1954).
Altan, Çetin. *Taş.* Ist., 1964.
—— *Onlar Uyanırken.* Ist., 1967.
—— *Suçlanan Yazılar.* Ist., n.d. [1969].
—— *Ben Milletvekili İken.* Ank., 1971.
Altuğ, Kurtul. *12 Mart ve Nihat Erim Olayı.* Ank., 1973.

440 Select Bibliography

Ankara Üniversitesi Hukuk Fakültesi. *Türkiye'de Toprak Reformu Semineri.* Ank., 1968.
Ankara Üniversitesi Siyasal Bilgiler Fakültesi. *Profesor Dr. Yavuz Abadan'a Armağan.* Ank., 1969.
Arar, İsmail. *Hükümet Programları 1920-1965.* Ist., 1968.
Aras, Tevfik Rüştü. *Görüşlerim,* ii. Ist., 1968.
Aren, Sadun. *Ekonomi El Kitabı: Türkiye Ekonomisinden Örneklerle.* 3rd edn. Ist., 1972.
Aslan, İffet. *İktidar Adayları.* Ank., 1965.
Asya Uluslar Enstitüsü. 'Ruslara Göre 27 Mayıs ve Sonrası', in *Amerikalı, Fransız, Rus Gözüyle 1960 Türk İhtilâli.* Ist., 1967.
Avcıoğlu, Doğan. *Türkiye'nin Düzeni.* 2 vols. Ank., 1969.
— *Devrim Üzerine.* Ank., 1971.
Aybar, Mehmet Ali. *Mehmet Ali Aybar Dış Politikamızı Anlatıyor.* This pamphlet was distributed with *Sosyal Adalet,* Oct. 1964.
— *Bağımsızlık Demokrasi Sosyalizm, Seçmeler 1945-1967.* Ist., 1968.
— *12 Mart'tan Sonra Meclis Konuşmaları.* 2nd edn. Ist., 1973.
Aydemir, Şevket Süreyya. *İkinci Adam,* iii (1950-64). Ank., 1968.
— *Menderes'in Dramı.* Ist., 1969.
Aydemir, Talât. *Ve Talât Aydemir Konuşuyor.* Ist., 1966.
Aytekin, M. Emin. *İhtilâl Çıkmazı.* Ist., 1967.
Aytur, Memduh. *Kalkınma Yarışı ve Türkiye.* Ank., 1970.
Baban, Cihad. *Politika Galerisi.* Ist., 1970.
Bahadırlı, Yusuf Ziya. *Türkiye'de Eğitim Sorunu ve Sosyalizm.* Ank., 1968.
Balkır, S. Edip. Dipten Gelen Ses: Arifiye Köy Enstitüsü. *Cumhuriyet* (1 Feb. 1971) and following.
Barlas, Cemil Sait. *Sosyalistlik Yolları ve Türkiye Gerçekleri.* Ist., 1962.
— ed. *Devrilen Diktatörler.* Ist., 1960.
Barlas, Mehmet. *Türkiye Üzerinde Pazarlıklar.* Ist., 1970.
Başar, Ahmed Hamdi. *Demokrasi Buhranları.* Ist., 1956.
— *Demokrasi Yolunda Nereye Gidiyoruz?* Ist., 1959.
— *Yaşadığımız Devrin İçyüzü.* Ank., 1960.
Başgil, Ali Fuad. *İlmin Işığında Günün Meseleleri.* Ist., 1960.
— *Demokrasi Yolunda.* Ist., 1961.
— *Din ve Lâiklik.* Ist., 1962. (This work was first published in 1954.)
— *27 Mayıs İhtilâli ve Sebepleri.* Ist., 1966. (For the original French edition see Part 2 below.)
Bayar, Celâl. *Celâl Bayar Diyorki, 1920-1950.* Ist., 1951.
— *Türkiye Reisicumhuru Celâl Bayar'ın Söylev ve Demeçleri, 1945-56.* Ed. Özel Şahingiray. Ank., 1956.
— *Başvekilim Adnan Menderes.* Ist., n.d. [1970].
Bekata, Hıfzı Oğuz. *Birinci Cumhuriyet Biterken.* Ank., 1960.
— *Türkiye'nin Bugünkü Görünüşü.* Ank., 1969.
Belen, Fahri. *Demokrasimiz Nereye Gidiyor.* Ist., 1959.
— *Demokrasiden Diktatörlüğe.* Ist., 1960.
Belli, Mihri. *Savcı Konuştu Söz Sanığındır.* Ank., 1967.
— *Yazılar 1965-1970.* Ank., 1970.

Berkes, Niyazi. *200 Yıldır Neden Bocalıyoruz*. Ist., 1965.
— *Batıcılık, Ulusçuluk ve Toplumsal Devrimler*. Ist., 1965.
Besin-İş (and eleven other trade unions). *Sosyal Demokrat Düzen*. Ank., 1971.
Beşikçi, İsmail. *Doğu'da Değişim ve Yapısal Sorunlar*. Ank., 1969.
— *Doğu Anadolunun Düzeni*. Ist., 1969.
Bilge, Suat and others. *Olaylarla Türk Dış Politikası (1919-1965)*. Ank., 1969.
Bilginer, Recep and Mehmet Ali Yalçın, eds. *Türkiye Reisicumhuru Celâl Bayar'ın Amerika Seyahatleri (27 Ocak-27 Şubat 1954)*. n.p., n.d. [1954].
Boran, Behice. *Türkiye ve Sosyalizm Sorunları*. Ist., 1968.
Boratav, Korkut. *Türkiye'de Devletçilik (1923-1950)*. Ank., 1962.
— *Gelir Dağılımı*. Ist., 1969.
Bozkurt, Celâl. *Siyaset Tarihimizde Cumhuriyet Halk Partisi*. n.p., n.d. [1968?].
Bozbeyli, Ferruh, ed. *Kalkınma ve Plânlama; Türkiye'de siyasi partilerin ekonomik ve sosyal görüşleri—Belgeler*, ii, pt. 1 [AP] (1969); ii, pt. 2 [CHP] (1969); ii, pt. 3 [GP-MP-MHP-TİP-YTP] (1970). Ist., 1970.
— ed. *Parti Programları; Türkiye'de siyasi partilerin ekonomik ve sosyal görüşleri—Belgeler*, i, pt. 1. İst., 1970.
Bulutoğlu, Kenan. *Türkiye'de Yabancı Sermaye*. Ist., 1970.
Cem, İsmail. *Türkiye Üzerine*. Ist., 1970.
— *Türkiye'de Geri Kalmışlığın Tarihi*. Ist., 1970.
Cumhuriyet Halk Partisi. *Muhalefet Yok Edilmek İsteniyor, Bu Gaye ile B.M.M.'e Getirilen Kanun Teklifi Karşısında CHP'nin Görüşü*. Ank., 1952.
— *İktisadi Kalkınma*. Ank., 1958.
— *İçtimai Meseleler*. Ank., 1958.
— *İnönü'ye Atılan Taş ve Akisleri*. Ank., 1959.
— *Seçim Neticeleri Üzerinde bir İnceleme*. Ank., 1959.
— *Halkevleri*. Ist., 1963.
— *CHP Halk Hizmetinde Neler Yaptı*. Ank., 1965.
— *CHP'nin İktisadi Görüşleri*. n.p., 1966.
— *İkinci Beş Yıllık Plân ve CHP*. Ank., 1967.
— *CHP XIX Kurultayı: Parti Meclisi Raporu*. Ank., 1968.
— *Halktan Yetki İstiyoruz*. Ank., 1969.
— *CHP XX Kurultayı: Parti Meclisi Raporu*. Ank., 1970.
Çamlı, İbrahim. *Dünya, Amerika, Türkiye*. Ist., 1966.
Çavdar, Tevfik. *Türkiye 1968*. Ist., 1969.
Çeçen, Anıl. *Türkiye'de Sendikacılık*. Ank., 1973.
Demirel, Süleyman. *Adalet Partisi Genel Başkanlığına Adaylığımı Neden Koyuyorum?* Ank., 1964.
— *Yazdıkları ve Söyledikleri*. Ank., 1965.
— *Seçim Konuşmaları*. Ank., 1966.
— *Kongre Konuşmaları*. Ank., 1967.
— *1967 Bütçesi Münasebetiyle Bütçe ve Plân Komisyonu, Cumhuriyet Senatosu ve Millet Meclisindeki Konuşmaları*. Ank., 1967.

442   *Select Bibliography*

— *1969 Bütçesi Münasebetiyle Cumhuriyet Senatosu ve Millet Meclisindeki Konuşmaları.* Ank., 1969.
— *Süleyman Demirel' in 5 Büyük Kongreyi Açış Konuşması.* Ank., 1970.
Demokrat Parti. *26 Mayıs Seçimleri.* İst., 1946.
— *Yeni İktidarın Çalışmaları, 25.5.1950-22.5.1952.* İst., 1952.
— *Genç Demokratlar Teşkilâtı ve Esasları: Gençlik ve Siyasi Eğitim.* Ank., 1954. (DP Neşriyati 5.)
— *Kalkınan Türkiye.* Ank., 1954.
— *Demokrat Parti Tüzüğü.* Ank., 1957.
— *Üç Devir.* İst., 1957.
Demokratik Parti. *Tüzük ve Program.* Ank., 1970.
— *72'ler Hareketi ve Demokratik Parti.* Ank., 1971.
Dijon Üniversitesindeki Açık Orturum. 'Türkiye'de Ordu'nun Rolü', in *Amerikalı, Fransız, Rus Güzüyle 1960 Türk İhtilâli.* İst., 1967.
Dilligil, Turhan. *Bayar-İnönü Yakınlaşması.* Ank., 1969.
Ecevit, Bülent. *Ortanın Solu.* İst., 1966.
— *Bu Düzen Değişmelidir.* Ank., 1968.
— *Atatürk ve Devrimcilik.* İst., n.d. [1970].
— *Perdeyi Kaldırıyorum.* Ank., n.d. [April 1972].
Ediboğlu, Servet and others, eds. *Salname 1390/1970 Yıllığı.* İst., 1970.
Ekonomik ve Sosyal Etüdler Konferans Heyeti. *Türk Vergi Sisteminin Ekonomik Gelişme üzerindeki Etkileri.* İst., 1970.
Elevli, Avni. *Hürriyet İçin.* Ank., 1960.
— *1960-1965 Olayları ve Batırılamiyan Gemi 'Türkiye'.* Ank., 1967.
Erdemir, Sabahat, ed. *Milli Birliğe Doğru,* i. Ank., 1961.
Erdost, Muzaffer. *'Türkiye Sosyalizmi' ve Sosyalizm.* Ank., 1969.
Erden, Ali Fuad. *İsmet İnönü.* İst., 1952.
Erer, Tekin. *On Yılın Mücadelesi.* İst., n.d. [1963?].
— *Yassıada ve Sonrası.* İst., 1965.
Erginsoy, Halûk Faruk. *Türk İşçi Hareketi Üzerine bir Deneme.* İst., 1968.
Erkanlı, Orhan. *Anılar ... Sorunlar ... Sorumlular.* İst., 1972.
Eroğul, Cem. *Demokrat Parti.* Ank., 1970.
Ertuğ, H. R. and others. *Yeni Türkiye.* İst., 1959.
Esirci, Şükrü, *Menderes Diyorki!* i. İst., n.d. [1967].
Faik, Bedii. *İhtilâlciler Arasında bir Gazeteci.* İst., 1967.
Fersoy, Orhan Cemal. *Adnan Menderes.* İst., 1971.
Feyzioğlu, Turhan. *Demokrasiye ve Diktatörlüğe Dair.* İst., 1957.
— *Büyük Tehlike Komünizm.* Ank., 1969.
Fişek, Kurthan. *Devlete Karşı Grevlerin Kritik Tahlili.* Ank., 1969.
— *Türkiye'de Kapitalizmin Gelişmesi ve İşçi Sınıfı.* Ank., 1969.
Genç, Süleyman. *12 Mart'a Nasıl Gelindi.* Ank., 1971.
Gevgilili, Ali. *Türkiye'de 1971 Rejimi.* İst., 1973.
Giritlioğlu, Fahir. *Türk Siyasi Tarihinde Cumhuriyet Halk Partisinin Mevkii.* 2 vols. Ank., 1965.
Gölpınarlı, Abdülbâki. *Türkiye'de Mezhepler ve Tarikatler.* İst., 1969.
Güresin, Ecvet. *1950 ve 1954 Seçimlerini Tetkik Ederek Vardığımız Neticeler ve İllerin Durumu. Cumhuriyet* 25-28 Sept. 1957.

Select Bibliography 443

Güven Partisi. *Güven Partisi Programı.* Ank., 1967.
— *Seçim Beyannamesi.* Ank., 1969.
Hürriyet Partisi Meclis Grubu. *Görüşümuz 1957.* Ank., 1957.
İnönü, İsmet. *Muhalefet'de İsmet İnönü,* ed. Sabahat Erdemir: i (1950-6);
ii (1956-9); iii (1959-60). Ist., 1956; 1959; 1962.
— *1958 de İnönü.* Ank., 1959.
— *İhtilâlden Sonra İsmet İnönü: 27 Mayıs 1960-10 Kasım 1961,* ed.
Sabahat Toktamış. Ist., 1962.
— and Bülent Ecevit. *İç Barış ve Demokrasi Mücadelesi.* Ank., 1969.
İpekçi, Abdi. *Liderler Diyorki.* Ist., 1969.
— and Ömer Sami Coşar. *İhtilâlin İçyüzü.* Ist., 1965.
İsen, Can Kaya. *Geliyorum diyen İhtilâl.* Ist., 1964.
Jäschke, Gotthard. *Yeni Türkiye'de İslâmlık.* Ank., 1972.
Kafesoğlu, İbrahim. *Türk Milliyetçiliğinin Meseleleri.* Ist., 1970.
Karaibrahimoğlu, Sacit. *Türkiye Büyük Millet Meclisi.* Ank., 1968.
Karaosmanoğlu, Yakup Kadri. *Politika da 45 Yıl.* Ist., 1968.
Kazgan, Gülten. *Ortak Pazar ve Türkiye.* Ist., 1970.
Keleş, Ruşen. *Türkiye'de Şehirleşme, Konut ve Gecekondu.* Ist., 1972.
Kemal, Mehmed. *Acılı Kuşak.* Ank., 1967.
Kemal, Yaşar. *Bu Diyar Baştan Başa.* Ist., 1971.
Ketenci, Tayfur. *Türk Silâhlı Kuvvetleri ve Aşırı Sol.* Ank., n.d. [1971].
Kirişçioğlu, Nusret. *Yassıada Kumandanına Cevap.* Ist., 1971.
— *12 Mart, İnönü-Ecevit ve Tahkikat Encümeni Raporum.* Ist., 1973.
Kıvılcımlı, Hikmet. *Kuvayimilliyeciliğimiz ve İkinci Kuvayimilliyeciliği-
miz.* Ist., 1965.
— *27 Mayıs ve Yön Hareketinin Sınıfsal Eleştirisi.* Ist., 1970.
Köprülü, Fuad. *Demokrasi Yolunda.* The Hague, 1964.
Köseoğlu, Talât. *Demokraside Davalarımız.* Ist., 1962.
Küçük, Yalçın. *Plânlama, Kalkınma ve Türkiye.* Ist., 1971.
Küçükömer, İdris. *Düzenin Yabancılaşması: Batılaşma.* Ist., 1969.
Külçe, Süleyman. *Mareşal Fevzi Çakmak, askeri, siyasi, hususi hayatı.*
İzmir, 1946.
Kuran, Alp. *Kapalı İktidar.* Ist., 1962.
'Kurtuluş'. *1965-1971 Türkiye'de Devrimci Mücadele ve Dev-Genç.* Ank.,
1971.
Kuruç, Bilsay. *İktisat Politikasının Resmi Belgeleri.* Ank., 1963.
Lefranc, George and Kemal Sülker. *Dünyada ve Bizde Sendikacılık.* Ist.,
1966.
Madanoğlu, Cemal. *Cemal Madanoğlu İnkilabi Anlatıyor,* ed. Cevat
Oktay. Ank., n.d. [1960].
Madanoğlu Dosyası. Töre—Devlet Yayınları. Ank., 1973.
Makal, Mahmut. *Yer Altında bir Anadolu.* Ist., 1968.
Menderes, Adnan. *Adnan Menderes'in Konuşmaları,* ed. Mustafa Doğan.
2 vols. Ist., 1957.
— *Adnan Menderes'in 1957 Seçim Nutukları ile Paris Nato
Koferansındaki Tarihi Hitabesi,* comps. Ayetullah Kocamemi and
Vahdettin Ayberk. Ank., 1958.
Milliyet 1970, 1971, 1972, 1973, 1974 (yearbooks). Ist., 1971-5.

Mülâyim, Ziya Gökalp. *Tarımda Düzen Değişikliği.* Ank., 1970.
Naci, Fethi, *Kompradorsuz Türkiye.* Ist., 1967.
Nadi, Nadir. *Atatürk İlkeleri Işığında Uyarmalar: bir iflâsın kronolojisi.* Ist., 1961.
— *Perde Aralığından.* Ist., 1965.
— *27 Mayıs'tan 12 Mart'a.* Ist., 1971.
Otyam, Fikret. *Gide Gide: Doğudan Gezi Notları.* Ank., 1959.
— *Uy Babo.* Ank., 1962.
— *Topraksızlar.* Ist., 1963.
— *Gide Gide 6: 'hû dost.* Ank., 1964.
— *Budur Ol Hikâyet Ol Kara Sevda.* Cumhuriyet, 18-28 March 1971.
Ozankaya, Özer. *Köyde Toplumsal Yapı ve Siyasal Kültür.* Ank., 1971.
Örtülü, Erdoğan. *Üç İhtilâlin Hikâyesi.* Ank., 1966.
Özbey, Cemal. *Demokrat Partiyi Nasıl Kapattırdım.* Ank., 1961.
Özbudun, Ergun. *Batı Demokrasilerinde ve Türkiye'de Parti Disiplini.* Ank., 1968.
Özden, Ekrem. *Demokrasi Yolunda Mücadele.* Ist., 1970.
Özek, Çetin. *Türkiye'de Lâiklik.* Ist., 1962.
— *Türkiye'de Gerici Akımlar ve Nurculuğun İçyüzü.* Ist., 1964.
— *Türkiye'de Gerici Akımlar.* Ist., 1968.
— *141-142.* Ist., 1968.
Özgür, Özlem. *Türkiye'de Kapitalizmin Gelişmesi.* Ist., 1972.
Özkol, Sedat. *Geri Bıraktırılmış Türkiye.* Ist., 1969.
Öztürk, Kâzım. *Türkiye Cumhuriyeti Hükümetleri ve Programları.* Ist., 1968.
— *Cumhurbaşkanlarının T. Büyük Millet Meclisini Açış Nutukları.* Ist., 1969.
— *Gerekçeli Anayasa.* Ank., 1971.
Pekin, Orhan. *Türkiye'yi Ekonomik Buhrandan Kurtaralım.* Ist., n.d. [1968].
Sarç, Ömer Celâl. *Gelir Dağılımı: Dışarda ve Türkiye'de.* Ist., 1970.
Sarıca, Murat. *Toplumcu Açıdan Halkçılık-Milliyetçilik-Devrimcilik.* Ist., 1966.
— *Anayasayı Niçin Savunmalıyız.* Ist., 1969.
Satır, Kemal. *CHP'de Bunalım.* Ank., April 1972.
Savcı, Bahri. *İhtilâlin Liberal-Burjuva Yönünden Sosyal Muhalefet Akımının Gelişme Çizgisi. SBFD* xx/2 (1965).
— *1965 Milletvekilleri Seçimi Üzerinde bir Analiz. SBFD* xx/4 (1965).
— *1966 Kısmi Senato Seçimleri Tahlili. SBFD* xxi/3 (1966).
— *İktidarın ve Ana Muhalefetin Rejim ve Uygulamalar Üzerine Bazı Görüşleri. SBFD* xxi/3 (1966).
— *Hürriyetler Üzerine Düşünceler.* Ank., 1968.
Sayılgan, Aclan. *Solun 94 Yılı (1871-1965).* Ank., 1968.
Selik, Mehmet. *Türkiye'de Yabancı Özel Sermaye 1923-1960.* Ank., 1961.
Sencer, Muzaffer. *Türkiye'de Köylülüğün Maddi Temelleri.* Ist., 1971.
— *Türkiye'de Siyasal Partilerin Sosyal Temelleri.* Ist., 1971.
Sencer, Oya. *Türk Toplumunun Tarihsel Evrimi.* Ist., 1969.
Sertel, Sabiha. *Roman Gibi.* Ist., 1969.

Sertel, Yıldız. *Türkiye'de İlerici Akımlar ve Kalkınma Davamız.* Ist., 1969.
Seyhan, Dündar. *Gölgedeki Adam.* Ist., 1966.
Soysal, İlhami. *Sıfıra Sıfır Elde Sıfır.* Ist., 1969.
Soysal, Mümtaz. *Demokratik İktisadi Plânlama için Siyasi Mekanizma.* Ank., 1958.
— *Dış Politika ve Parlamento.* Ank., 1964.
— *Dinamik Anayasa Anlayışı.* Ank., 1969.
— *Anayasanın Anlamı.* Ist., 1969.
Sülker, Kemal. *Türkiye'de Sendikacılık.* Ist., 1955.
— *Türkiye'de İşçi Hareketleri.* Ist., 1968.
Şahoğlu, Fikret. *AP'nin İçyüzü.* Ist., 1965.
Şeref, Muvaffak. *Türkiye ve Sosyalizm.* Ist., 1968.
Şnurov, A. and Y. Rozaliyev. *Türkiye'de Kapitalistleşme ve Sınıf Kavgaları,* trans. G. Bozkaya and M. Anibal. Ist., 1970.
Tanör, Bülent. *Siyasi Düşünce Hürriyeti ve 1961 Türk Anayasası.* Ist., 1969.
Tansel, Selâhattin. *27 Mayıs İnkilâbını Hazırlayan Sebepler.* Ist., 1960.
Tansu, Ziya. *AP'deki Kırmızı Oyların Nedenleri.* Ank., 1970.
Tayanç, Tunç. *Sanayileşme Sürecinde 50 Yıl.* Ist., 1973.
Tevetoğlu, Fethi. *Türkiye'de Sosyalist ve Komünist Faaliyetler (1910-1960).* Ank., 1967.
Timur, Taner. *Türk Devrimi ve Sonrası, 1919-1946.* Ank., 1971.
Toker, Metin. *İsmet Paşayla 10 Yıl (1954-1964).* 4 vols. Ank., 1965, 1966, 1967; Ist., 1969.
— *Tek Partiden Çok Partiye.* Ist., 1970.
— *Solda ve Sağda Vuruşanlar.* Ank., 1971.
Tökin, F. Hüsrev. *Türk Tarihinde Siyasi Partiler ve Siyasi Düşüncenin Gelişmesi, 1839-1965.* Ist., 1965.
Tunaya, Tarık Zafer. *Türkiye'de Siyasi Partiler, 1859-1952.* Ist., 1952.
— *Türkiye'nin Siyasi Hayatında Batılılaşma Hareketleri.* Ist., 1960.
— *İslâmcılık Cereyanı.* Ist., 1962.
— *Siyasi Müesseseler ve Anayasa Hukuku.* Ist., 1969.
Tunçkanat, Haydar. *İkili Anlaşmaların İçyüzü.* Ank., 1970.
Turhan, Mümtaz. *Toprak Reformu ve Köy Kalkınması.* Ist., 1964.
Türk, İbrahim. *Türk Toplumunda Sosyal Sınıflar.* Ist., 1970.
Türkeş, Alparslan. *1944 Milliyetçilik Olayı.* Ist., 1968.
— *Türkiye'nin Meseleleri.* Ist., 1969.
Türkiye Cumhuriyeti, Başbakanlık Basın-Yayın Genel Müdürlüğü. *Erim Hükümetlerinin 1 Yılı (7.4.1971-7.4.1972).* Ank., 1972.
— *Türkiye Yıllığı 1973.* Ank., 1973.
— Başbakanlık Devlet Basımevi. *Ak Devrim.* Ank., 1960.
— Basın-Yayın ve Turizm Vekâleti. *27 Mayıs: 1960 Türk İnkilâbı.* Ank., 1960.
— Dışişleri Bakanlığı. *Dışişleri Bakanlığı Belleteni.* Ank. (July 1964) no. 1.
Türkiye İşçi Partisi. *Türkiye İşçi Partisi Programı.* Ist., 1964.
Türkiye Milli Gençlik Teşkilâti. *Gençlik Partilere Soruyor.* Ist., 1965.

Türkiye Yıllığı 1947; 1948; 1962; 1963; 1964; 1965. Ist., 1947; 1948; 1962; 1963; 1964; 1965, respectively.
Tütengil, Cavit Orhan. *Ağrı Dağındaki Horoz.* Ist., 1968.
—— *Türkiye'de Köy Sorunu.* Ist., 1969.
—— *Az Gelişmenin Sosyolojisi.* Ist., 1970.
Ufuk Ajansı Yayınları, *12 Mart'a Nasıl Getirildik.* Ank., 1971.
Ulay, Sıtkı. *Harbiye Silâh Başına: 27 Mayıs 1960.* Ist., 1968.
Uran, Hilmi. *Hatıralarım.* Ank., 1959.
Uraz, Abdullah. *1970 Siyasi Buhranı ve İçyüzü.* Ist., 1970.
Ünen, Nurettin. *CHP Neden Çöktü?* Ist., 1950.
Ünsal, Engin. *İşçiler Uyanıyor.* Ist., 1963.
Üstün, Nevzat. *Türkiye'deki Amerika.* Ist., 1969.
Üstünel, Besim. *Kalkınmanın Neresindeyiz.* Ank., 1966.
Varlık Yıllığı 1962-1975. Ist., 1962-75, respectively.
Vatan 1960 Yıllığı. Ist., 1960.
Velidedeoğlu, Hıfzı Veldet. *Türkiye'de Üç Devir,* vol. i. Ist., 1972.
Weiker, Walter F. *1960 Türk İhtilâli in Amerikalı, Fransız, Rus Gözüyle 1960 Türk İhtilâli,* trans. Mete Ergin. Ist., 1967.
Yalçın, Aydın. *Demokrasi, Sosyalizm ve Gençlik.* Ist., 1969.
—— *İktisadi Politika Üzerinde Düşünceler.* Ist., 1969.
Yalman, Ahmed Emin. *Gördülerim ve Geçirdiklerim,* iv (1945-71). Ist., 1971.
Yapı ve Kredi Bankası. *1939-1963: Önemli İç ve Dış Olaylar Kronolojisi.* Ist., 1964.
Yasa, İbrahim. *Türkiye'nin Toplumsal Yapısı ve Temel Sorunları.* Ank., 1970.
Yavuz, Fehmi. *Din Eğitimi ve Toplumumuz.* Ank., 1969.
Yetkin, Çetin. *Siyasal İktidar Sanata Karşı.* Ank., 1970.
—— *Türkiye'de Soldaki Bölünmeler, 1960-1970.* Ist., 1970.
Yücekök, Ahmet. *Türkiye'de Örgütlenmiş Dinin Sosyo-Ekonomik Tabanı, 1946-1968.* Ank., 1971.
—— *Türkiye'de Din ve Siyaset.* Ist., 1971.

2. Works in Other Languages

Abadan, Nermin. Turkish Election of 1965. *Government and Opposition,* i/3 (1966).
Ahmad, Feroz. The Turkish Guerrillas: Symptoms of a Deeper Malaise. *NME,* 55 (1973).
Aktan, Reşat. 'Problems of Land Reform in Turkey', in ESSCB, *Agricultural Aspects of Economic Development.* Ist., 1965.
Alexander, A. P. Industrial Entrepreneurship in Turkey: Origins and Growth. *Economic Development and Cultural Change,* July 1960.
—— 'Turkey', in Adamantis Pepelasis and others, *Economic Development: Analysis and Case Studies.* New York, 1961.
Armaoğlu, Fahir. 'Le conflit de Chypre et l'attitude du gouvernement turc en 1957', in IIR, *The Turkish Yearbook of International Relations: 1961.* Ank., 1963.

— Recent Developments in Turkish Foreign Policy. *FP* i/1 (1971).
— The European Security Conference and Mutual and Balanced Force Reduction. *FP* ii/4 (1972).
Ataöv, Türkkaya. 'The 27th of May Revolution and its Aftermath', in IIR, *The Turkish Yearbook of International Relations: 1960.* Ank., 1961.
— *N.A.T.O. and Turkey.* Ank., 1970.
Başgil, Ali Fuad. *La Révolution Militaire de 1960 en Turquie.* Geneva, 1963. (For the Turkish translation *27 Mayıs İhtilâli ve Sebepleri* see Part 1 above.)
Bayülken, Halûk. Turkey's Foreign Policy. *FP*, iii/1 (1973).
Bener, Erhan. 'Foreign Trade Régime of Turkey', in ESSCB, *Foreign Trade and Economic Development.* Ist., 1968.
Berkes, Niyazi. *The Development of Secularism in Turkey.* Montreal, 1964.
Bilge, A. Suat. *Le conflit de Chypre et les Cypriotes turcs.* Ank., 1961.
Bisbee, Eleanor. Test of Democracy in Turkey. *MEJ*, iv/2 (1950).
— *The New Turks.* Philadelphia, 1961.
Carey, J. P. C. and A. G. Carey. Turkish Industry and the Five Year Plans. *MEJ*, xxv/3 (1971).
Carlson, Sevinç. Turkey: Is Democracy in Danger? *NME*, 44 (May 1972).
Chenery, H. and others. *Turkish Investment and Economic Development.* Ank., 1953.
Dalmış, Doğan. *Turkish Government, Organisation Manual 1959.* Ank., 1959.
Denktaş, Rauf. The Cyprus Problem. *FP*, i/1 (1971).
— Cyprus: On the Threshold of New Talks. *FP*, ii/2 (1972).
Dereli, Toker. *The Development of Turkish Trade Unionism: a Study of Legislative and Socio-political Dimensions.* Ist., 1968.
Devereux, Robert. Society and Culture in the Second Republic. *MEA*, xii (1961).
Dodd, C. H. *Politics and Government in Turkey.* Manchester, 1969.
Dollot, Louis. *La Turquie Vivante.* Paris, 1957.
Eastham, J. K. The Turkish Development Plan: the First Five Years. *Economic Journal*, lxxxiv (Mar. 1964).
Eberhard, Wolfram. Change in Leading Families in Southern Turkey. *Anthropos*, 49 (1954); also published in L. E. Sweet, ed., *Peoples and Cultures of the Middle East*, ii. New York, 1970.
Economic and Social Studies Conference Board. *Capital Formation and Investment in Industry.* Ist., 1963.
— *Social Aspects of Economic Development.* Ist., 1964.
— *Agricultural Aspects of Economic Development.* Ist., 1965.
— *Planning and Growth under a Mixed Economy.* Ist., 1966.
— *Education as a Factor of Accelerated Economic Development.* Ist., 1967.
— *State Economic Enterprises.* Ist., 1969.
— *Foreign Trade and Economic Development.* Ist., 1970.
Eczacıbaşı, Nejat. Turkey Rediscovers a Satisfying Blend. *Columbia Journal of World Business*, i/2 (1966).

448   *Select Bibliography*

Eldem, Vedat. Turkey's Transportation. *MEA*, iv/10 (1953).
Eren, Nuri. Turkey: Problems, Policies, Parties. *FA*, xxxx/1 (1961).
— Turkey Today—and Tomorrow. New York, 1963.
— 'The Foreign Policy of Turkey', in Joseph E. Black and Kenneth W. Thompson, eds., *Foreign Policies in a Changing World*. New York, 1963.
— Financial Aspects of Turkish Planning. *MEJ*, xx/2 (1966).
Erim, Nihat. The Turkish Experience in the Light of Recent Developments. *MEJ*, xxvi/3 (1972).
Eroğlu, Hamza. 'La constitution turque de 1961 et les relations internationales', in IIR, *The Turkish Yearbook of International Relations: 1961*. Ank., 1963.
Esmer, Ahmet Şükrü. 'Cyprus, Past and Present', in IIR, *The Turkish Yearbook of International Relations: 1962*. Ank., 1964.
Ete, Muhlis. *A Short Survey of the Turkish Economy*. Ank., 1951.
— State Exploitation in Turkey. Ank., 1951.
Fernau, F. W. Le neo-kémalisme du Comité d'Unité Nationale. *Orient* xvi/4 (1960).
— Courants sociaux dans la deuxième republique turque. *Orient*, vi/23 (1962).
— Les partis politiques de la deuxième republique turque. *Orient*, x/39 (1966).
— Die Entwicklung der Mehrparteidemokratie in der Türkei. *Europa-Archiv*, xxi/9 (1966).
Feyzioğlu, Turhan. Les partis politiques en Turquie: Du parti unique à la démocratie. *Revue Française de Science Politique*, iv/1 (1954).
Frey, F. W. 'Political Development, Power and Communications in Turkey', in Lucian Pye, ed., *Communications and Political Development*. Princeton, 1963.
— The Turkish Political Elite. Cambridge, Mass., 1965.
Gilead, Baruch. Turkish-Egyptian Relations 1952-1957. *MEA*, x/2 (1959).
Giraud, R. La vie politique en Turquie après le 27 Mai 1960. *Orient*, vi/21 (1962).
Giritli, İsmet. Some Aspects of the New Turkish Constitution. *MEJ*, xvi/1 (1962).
— Turkey since the 1965 Election. *MEJ*, xxiii/3 (1969).
Gökmen, Oğuz. Turkish-German Relations. *FP*, i/1 (1971).
Gönlübol, Mehmet. Turkish-American Relations: General Appraisal. *FP*, i/4 (1971).
— and Türkkaya Ataöv. *Turkey in the United Nations*. Ank., 1960.
Goodman, S. S. Turkey's Trade Prospects in the Common Market: an Exploratory Study. *Journal of Common Market Studies*, June 1969.
Gülek, Kasım. Democracy Takes Root in Turkey. *FA*, xxx/1 (1951).
Hadley, Guy. *Cento, the Forgotten Alliance*. Brighton, Sussex, 1971.
Hamitoğulları, M. Beşir. *La Planification du Développement Économique en Turquie*. Ank., 1968.
Hanson, A. H. Turkey Today. *Political Quarterly*, xxvi/4 (1955).

— Democracy Transplanted: Reflections on a Turkish Election. *Parliamentary Affairs*, ix/1 (1955/6).

Harris, G. S. The Role of the Military in Turkish Politics, i, ii. *MEJ*, xix/1 and 2 (1965).

— The Causes of the 1960 Revolution in Turkey. *MEJ*, xxiv/4 (1970).

— *Troubled Alliance: Turkish-American Problems in Historical Perspective, 1945-1971.* Washington, DC, 1972.

Hart, P. T. Northern Tier: i. The Vital Importance of the Northern Tier; ii. The Go-Between: a Role the US Can No Longer Play. *NME*, 49 and 50 (1972).

Hershlag, Z. Y. *Turkey: the Challenge of Growth.* Leiden, 1968.

— *Economic Planning in Turkey.* Ist., 1968.

Heyd, U. Islam in Modern Turkey. *Journal of the Royal Asiatic Society*, xxxiv (1947).

Hirsch, Eva and Abraham Hirsch. Changes in the Terms of Trade of Farmers and their Effect on Real Income per capita of Rural Population in Turkey, 1927-1960. *Economic Development and Cultural Change*, xiv/4 (1966).

Hurewitz, J. C. *Middle East Politics: the Military Dimension.* New York, 1969.

Hyland, Michael. 'The Party of Atatürk: Tradition and Change.' Unpublished PhD thesis, Harvard University, Cambridge, Mass., 1969.

— Crisis at the Polls: Turkey's 1969 Elections. *MEJ*, xxiv/1 (1970).

İlkin, S. and E. İnanç, eds. *Planning in Turkey.* Ank., 1967.

International Bank for Reconstruction and Development. *The Economy of Turkey.* Baltimore, Md, 1951.

Institute for International Relations. *Turkey and the United Nations.* New York, 1961.

Jäschke, Gotthard. *Die Türkei in der Jahren 1942-1951.* Weisbaden, 1955.

— *Die Türkei in der Jahren 1952-1961.* Weisbaden, 1965.

Kapani, Münci. Outlines of the New Turkish Constitution, *Parliamentary Affairs*, xv (1961/2).

Karaçam, Selçuk. A Report on RCD—Regional Corporation for Development. (A Step towards Economic Integration). *FP* i/1 (1971).

Karpat, K. H. *Turkey's Politics: the Transition to a Multi-party System.* Princeton, NJ, 1959.

— Social Effects of Farm Mechanization in Turkish Villages. *Social Research*, xxvii (Spring 1960).

— Contemporary Turkish Literature. *Literary Review*, issue on Turkey, Winter 1960.

— 'Economic, Social Change and Politics in Turkey', in IIR, *The Turkish Yearbook of International Relations: 1960.* Ank., 1961.

— The Turkish Elections of 1957. *Western Political Quarterly*, xiv/2 (1961).

— Recent Political Developments in Turkey and their Social Background. *IA*, xxxviii (July 1962).

450 *Select Bibliography*

— Society, Economics and Politics in Contemporary Turkey. *WP*, xvii/1 (1964).
— Réflexions sur l'arrière-plan social de la révolution turque de 1960. *Orient*, 37 (1966).
— The Turkish Left. *JCH*, i/2 (1966).
— Socialism and the Labour Party of Turkey. *MEJ*, xxi/2 (1967).
— The Military and Politics in Turkey, 1960-64. *American Historical Review*, lxxv/6 (1970).
— Political Development in Turkey, 1950-70. *MES*, viii/3 (1972).
— ed. *Political and Social Thought in the Contemporary Middle East.* New York, 1968.
Kayran, D. 'The Plan and the Agricultural Sector', in S. İlkin and E. İnanc, eds., *Planning in Turkey.* Ank., 1967.
Kazgan, Gülten. 'Structural Changes in Turkish National Income, 1950:60', in Taufiq M. Khan, ed., *Middle Eastern Studies in Income and Wealth.* Lond., 1965.
Kazamias, Andreas M. *Education and the Quest for Modernity in Turkey.* Chicago, 1966.
Kerwin, R. W. Private Enterprise in Turkish Industrial Development. *MEJ*, v/1 (1951).
— 'Étatism and the Industrialization of Turkey'. Unpublished PhD thesis, Johns Hopkins University, Baltimore, Md, 1956.
Key, K. K. Comment on the Constitution of 1961. *MEJ*, xvi/1 (1962).
Kili, Suna. *Kemalism.* Ist., 1969.
Kılıç, Altemur. A Visit and its Implications: Professor Erim's Visit to the U.S. *FP* ii/1 (1972).
Kışlalı, Ahmet Taner. *Forces Politiques dans la Turquie Moderne.* Ank., n.d. [1970].
Kocatopçu, Şahap. 'The Role of Management in the Development of Turkish Industry', in ESSCB, *Capital Formation and Investment in Industry.* Ist., 1963.
— 'Formation and Growth of Employers' Associations in Turkey', in ESSCB, *Social Aspects of Economic Development.* Ist., 1964.
Kostanick, H. L. Turkish Resettlement of Refugees from Bulgaria 1950-1953. *MEJ*, ix/1 (1955).
Kruguer, Anne O. Some Economic Costs of Exchange Control: the Turkish Case. *Journal of Political Economy*, lxxiv/5 (1966).
Kurdaş, Kemal. 'Basic Factors Impending a Rapid Growth of the Turkish Economy', in ESSCB, *Capital Formation and Investment in Industry.* Ist., 1963.
Kürkçüoğlu, Ömer. Recent Developments in Turkey's Middle East Policy. *FP*, i/2 (1971).
Lenczowski, George *Soviet Advances in the Middle East.* Washington, DC, 1971.
Lerner, Daniel. *The Passing of Traditional Society.* New York, 1964.
— and R. Robinson. Swords into Plowshares: the Turkish Army as a Modernizing Force. *WP*, xiii/1 (1960).
Lewis, Bernard. Recent Developments in Turkey. *IA*, xxvii (1951).

— Islamic Revival in Turkey. *IA*, xxviii/1 (1952).
— History-writing and National Revival in Turkey. *MEA*, iv/6-7 (1953).
— Democracy in Turkey. *MEA*, x/2 (1959).
— 'Dustūr: Turkey', in *EI²*, 2nd edn. Leiden, 1966.
— *The Emergence of Modern Turkey*. 2nd edn. London, 1968.
Lewis, Geoffrey. 'Modern Turkish Attitudes to Europe', in Raghavan Iyer, ed., *The Glass Curtain between Asia and Europe*. Oxford, 1965.
— *Turkey*. 3rd edn. London, 1966.
Loğoğlu, Osman Faruk. 'İsmet İnönü and the Political Modernization of Turkey 1945-1965'. Unpublished PhD thesis, Princeton University, 1970.
Magnarella, Paul. From Villager to Townsman in Turkey. *MEJ*, xxiv/2 (1970).
Malik, Abdul. 'Inflation and Monetary Policy in Turkey: 1950-1961'. Unpublished PhD thesis, American University, Washington, DC, 1964.
— Inflation in Turkey 1950-61. *Economia Internazionale* xix/1 (1966).
Mango, Andrew. *Turkey*. London, 1968.
Mardin, Şerif. Opposition and Control in Turkey. *Government and Opposition*, i/3 (1966).
Meyer, A. J. *Middle Eastern Capitalism*. Cambridge, Mass., 1959.
Michaelis, Alfred. The Economy of Turkey, *MEA*, iv/8-9 (1953).
Middle East Record. 1960, London, n.d. [1962]; *1961*, Tel Aviv, 1966; *1967*, Jerusalem, 1971.
Millen, Bruce. Factions in the Turkish Labour Movement. *Monthly Labor Review*, June 1969.
Mitchell, William. Turkish Villages in Interior Anatolia and von Thunen's 'Isolated State': a Comparative Analysis. *MEJ*, xxv/3 (1971).
Nicholls, W. H. Domestic Trade in an Underdeveloped Country—Turkey. *Journal of Political Economy*, lix/6 (1951).
— Investment in Agriculture in Underdeveloped Countries. *American Economic Review (May 1955)*.
Okyar, Osman. Industrialization in Turkey. *MEA*, iv/6-7 (1953).
— Economic Framework for Industrialization: Turkish Experience in Retrospect. *MEA*, ix (1958).
— The Turkish Stabilization Experiment—Before and After. *MEA*, xi/8 (1960).
— 'Inflation in a Mixed Economy', in ESSCB, *Capital Formation and Investment in Industry*. Ist., 1963.
— 'Agricultural Price Policy: the Turkish Experience', in ESSCB, *Agricultural Aspects of Economic Development*. Ist., 1965.
— The Concept of Étatism. *The Economic Journal*, lxxv (Mar. 1965).
— Universities in Turkey. *Minerva*, vi/2 (1968).
Olcay, Osman. Turkey's Foreign Policy. *FP*, i/2 (1971).
Öngüt, İbrahim. 'The Development of a Capital Market in Turkey', in ESSCB, *Capital Formation and Investment in Industry*. Ist., 1963.

Özbudun, Ergun. *The Role of the Military in Recent Turkish Politics.* Cambridge, Mass., 1966.

Özelli, M. T. The Estimates of Private Internal Rates of Return on Educational Investment in the First Turkish Republic, 1923-1960. *IJMES,* i/2 (1970).

Pine, W. H. Some Land Problems in Turkey. *Journal of Farm Economics,* May 1952.

Poroy, İbrahim. 'Planning for Development: an Input-Output Model for Turkey'. Unpublished PhD thesis, University of California, 1965.

— Planning with a Large Public Sector: Turkey (1963-1967). *IJMES,* iii/3 (1972).

Reed, Howard A. A New Force at Work in Democratic Turkey. *MEJ,* vii/1 (1953).

— Revival of Islam in Secular Turkey. *MEJ,* viii/3 (1954).

— Turkey's New İmam-Hatib Schools. *Welt des Islam,* n.s., iv (1955).

— The Faculty of Divinity in Ankara. *Muslim World,* x/6 (1956) and x/7 (1957).

— 'The Religious Life of Modern Turkish Muslims', in R.N. Frye, ed., *Islam and the West.* The Hague, 1957.

Rivkin, M. D. *Area Development for National Growth: the Turkish Precedent.* New York, 1965.

Robinson, Richard D. The Lesson of Turkey. *MEJ,* v/4 (1951).

— Tractors in the Village—a Study in Turkey. *Journal of Farm Economics,* Nov. 1952.

— *The First Turkish Republic: a Case Study in National Development.* Cambridge, Mass., 1963.

— *High-Level Manpower in Economic Development: the Turkish Case.* Cambridge, Mass., 1967.

Roos, L. L. and N. P. Roos. *Managers of Modernization: Organizations and Elites in Turkey (1950-1969).* Cambridge, Mass., 1971.

— and Gary R. Field. Students and Politics in Turkey. *Daedalus,* 97/i (1968).

Rosen, S. M. 'Turkey', in Walter Galenson, ed., *Labor in Developing Countries.* Berkeley, 1962.

Rustow, D. A. *Politics and Westernization in the Near East.* Princeton, 1956.

— 'Politics and Islam in Turkey', in R. N. Frye, ed., *Islam and the West,* The Hague, 1957.

— 'Foreign Policy of the Turkish Republic', in R. C. Macridis, ed., *Foreign Policy in World Politics,* Englewood Cliffs, N.J., 1958.

— The Army and the Founding of The Turkish Republic. *WP,* xi/4 (1959).

— Turkey's Second Try at Democracy. *Yale Review,* lii/4 (1963).

— 'Turkey: the Modernity of Tradition', in L. W. Pye and S. Verba, eds., *Political Culture and Political Development,* Princeton, 1965.

— 'The Development of Parties in Turkey', in J. La Palombura and M. Weiner, eds., *Political Parties and Political Development,* Princeton, 1966.

Sadak, Necmeddin. Turkey Faces the Soviets. *FA*, xxvii/3 (1949).

Sanjian, A. K. The Sanjak of Alexandretta (Hatay): Its Impact on Turkish-Syrian Relations (1939-1956). *MEJ*, x/4 (1956).

Sarç Ömer Celâl. Economic Policy of the New Turkey. *MEJ*, ii/4 (1948).

— International Bank Report on Turkey. *MEJ*, vi/3 (1952).

Saymen, Ferit Hakkı. 'The Role of Labor Legislation in Turkey', in ESSCB, *Social Aspects of Economic Development*. Ist., 1964.

Schimmel, Annemarie. 'Islam in Turkey', in A. J. Arberry, ed., *Religion in the Middle East*, ii. London, 1969.

Sherwood, W. B. The Rise of the Justice Party in Turkey. *WP*, xx/1 (1967).

Shorter, F. C., ed. *Four Studies on the Economic Development of Turkey*. London, 1967.

Simpson, D. Development as a Process: the Menderes Phase. *MEJ*, xix/2 (1965).

Snyder, W. W. Turkish Economic Development: the First Five Year Plan, 1963-67. *Journal of Development Studies*, vi/1 (1969).

Sönmez, A. 'The Re-emergence of the Idea of Planning and the Scope and Targets of the 1963-1967 Plan', in S. İlkin and E. İnanç, eds., *Planning in Turkey*. Ank., 1967.

Soysal, Mümtaz. The Policy of Mixed Industrial Enterprises in Turkey and its Socio-political Consequences. *Development and Change*, i/2 (1969-70).

Stirling, Paul. Religious Change in Republican Turkey. *MEJ*, xii/4 (1958).

— *Turkish Village*. London, 1965.

Szyliowicz, Joseph. The 1961 Constitution—an Analysis. *Islamic Studies*, ii/3 (1963).

— *Political Change in Rural Turkey—Erdemli*. The Hague, 1966.

— The Turkish Elections: 1965. *MEJ*, xx/4 (1966).

— The Political Dynamics of Rural Turkey. *MEJ*, xxvi/4 (1969).

— Student and Politics in Turkey. *MES*, vi/2 (1970).

Tachau, Frank. The Face of Turkish Nationalism. *MEJ*, xiii/3 (1959).

— and A. H. Ülman. 'Dilemmas of Turkish Politics', in IIR, *The Turkish Yearbook of International Relations: 1962*. Ank., 1964.

— Turkish Politics: the Attempt to Reconcile Rapid Modernization with Democracy. *MEJ*, xix/2 (1965).

Tamkoç, Metin. *A Bibliography on the Foreign Relations of the Republic of Turkey 1919-1967*. Ank., 1968.

Taşhan, Seyfi. Foreign Policy Issues in the 1973 General Election. *FP*, iii/3 (1973).

Thomas, L. V. Recent Developments in Turkish Islam. *MEJ*, vi/1 (1952).

— and R. N. Frye. *The United States and Turkey and Iran*. Cambridge, Mass., 1951.

Thornburg, M. W. and others. *Turkey: an Economic Appraisal*. New York, 1949.

Tibawi, A. L. Islam and Secularism in Turkey Today. *Quarterly Review (London)*, 1956.

Tuna, Orhan. 'Growth and Functions of Turkish Trade Unions', in ESSCB, *Social Aspects of Economic Development.* Ist., 1964.
— Trade Unions in Turkey. *International Labor Review,* Nov. 1964.
Turkish State Information Organization. *The Turkish Constitution (As Amended).* Ank., 1972.
Türkkan, R. Oğuz. The Turkish Press. *MEA,* i (1950).
Ülgener, Sabri. 'Value Patterns of Traditional Societies: the Turkish Experience', in ESSCB, *Social Aspects of Economic Development.* Ist., 1964.
Váli, F. A. *Bridge Across the Bosporus.* Baltimore, Md, 1971.
— *The Turkish Straits and Nato.* Stanford, Calif., 1972.
Vernier, B. *Armée et Politique au Moyen-Orient.* Paris, 1966.
Ward, R. E. and D. A. Rustow. *Political Modernization in Japan and Turkey.* Princeton, 1964.
Weiker, W. F. Academic Freedom and Problems of Higher Education in Turkey. *MEJ,* xxvi/3 (1962).
— *The Turkish Revolution 1960-1961.* Washington, DC, 1963.
— The Aydemir Case and Turkey's Political Dilemma. *MEA,* xiv/9 (1963).
Windsor, P. *N.A.T.O. and the Cyprus Crisis.* London, 1964. (Adelphi Papers, No. 14.)
Yalçın, Aydın. Turkey: Emerging Democracy. *FA,* vl/4 (1967).
Yalman, Ahmed Emin. *Turkey in My Time.* Norman, Oklahoma, 1956.
Yalman, Nur. 'Intervention and Extrication: the Officer Corps in the Turkish Crisis', in Henry Bienen, ed., *The Military Intervenes: Case Studies in Political Development.* New York, 1968.
— 'On Land Disputes in Eastern Turkey', in Girdharilal Tikku, ed., *Islam and Its Cultural Divergence: Studies in Honour of Gustave E. von Grunebaum.* Urbana, Illinois, 1971.
Yaşa, Memduh. 'Marshalling of Capital by the State and Direct Investment in Industry: the Turkish Experience', in ESSCB, *Capital Formation and Investment in Industry.* Ist., 1963.
— 'The Development of the Turkish Economy and Foreign Trade', in ESSCB, *Foreign Trade and Economic Development.* Ist., 1970.
Yavuz, Fehmi. 'Planning the Development of Villages and Cities', in ESSCB, *Social Aspect of Economic Development.* Ist., 1964.
Yücekök, Ahmet Naki. 'The Process of Political Development in Turkey'. Reprint from IIR, *The Turkish Yearbook of International Relations: 1968.*

3. Other Sources

Akşam (Istanbul, daily)
Ant (Istanbul, weekly: 1968-71)
Aydınlık (Ankara, monthly: 1968-71)
Ayın Tarihi (Ankara, monthly: last published, 1963)
Cumhuriyet (Istanbul, daily)
Devrim (Ankara, weekly: 1969-71)

Emek (Ankara, fortnightly, later monthly: 1969-71)
Kim (Ankara, weekly: 1958-65)
Milliyet (Istanbul, daily)
Ortam (Istanbul, weekly: 1971)
Özgür İnsan (Ankara, irregularly)
Proleter Devrimci Aydınlık (Ankara, monthly, later weekly: 1970-1)
Sosyal Adalet (Ankara, monthly: 1963-4)
Toplum (Ankara, irregularly)
Yankı (Ankara, weekly)
[Yedi] *7 Gün* (Ankara, weekly)
Yeni Ortam (Istanbul, daily)
Yön (Ankara, weekly: 1961-7)
Zafer (Ankara, daily: 1946-60)
Summary of World Broadcasts, Part IV (British Broadcasting
    Corporation, Reading)

INDEX